975.791503 D457p

Designs against Charleston

DATE DUE

APR 2 0 2000			
	261-2500		Printed in USA

Designs against Charleston

Designs against Charleston

The Trial Record of the Denmark Vesey

Slave Conspiracy of 1822

Edited and with an introduction

by Edward A. Pearson

The
University of
North Carolina
Press
Chapel Hill
and London

© 1999 The University of North Carolina Press
All rights reserved
Manufactured in the United States of America
The paper in this book meets the guidelines for permanence
and durability of the Committee on Production Guidelines
for Book Longevity of the Council on Library Resources.
Library of Congress Cataloging-in-Publication Data
Designs against Charleston: the trial record of the Denmark
Vesey slave conspiracy of 1822 / edited and with an introduction
by Edward A. Pearson.
    p.   cm.
Includes bibliographical references (p.   ) and index.
ISBN 0-8078-2446-1
1. Charleston (S.C.)—History—Slave Insurrection, 1822.
2. Vesey, Denmark, 1767 (ca.)–1822. 3. Slavery—South Carolina—
Charleston—Insurrections—History—19th century.
4. Afro-Americans—South Carolina— Charleston—Social
conditions. 5. Vesey, Denmark, 1767 (ca.)–1822—Trials,
litigation, etc. I. Pearson, Edward A.
F279.C49N418   1999
975.7′91503—dc21   98-5871
                CIP

03 02 01 00 99   5 4 3 2 1

975.791503 D457p

Designs against Charleston

To my parents

Ronald Joseph Pearson

Deborah Sheila Pearson

and to

Kathleen Brown

CONTENTS

Acknowledgments *xi*

Abbreviations *xv*

Editorial Note *xvii*

Introduction. Culture and Conspiracy in Denmark Vesey's Charleston *1*

Transcript of the Denmark Vesey Conspiracy Trial *165*

Appendix 1. A Conspiratorial Chronology *283*

Appendix 2. The Conspirators and Witnesses *297*

Appendix 3. Additional Documents *314*

Bibliography *357*

Index *379*

MAPS

The City of Charleston, ca. 1822 2

The Caribbean Basin at the End of the Eighteenth Century 21

The Eighteenth-Century Atlantic World 36

Charleston and the South Carolina Lowcountry, ca. 1822 58

ACKNOWLEDGMENTS

This project has taken me from Wisconsin to the Carolinas and Georgia as well as to Pennsylvania and Massachusetts. I now want to thank those people and institutions that have made this journey memorable. At the University of Wisconsin, I was very fortunate to work with Charles L. Cohen who, in his capacity as my dissertation adviser, went to extraordinary lengths to read, edit, and critique my work during my years in Madison. Chuck has read several incarnations of the introductory essay, drawn from that larger project, offering useful advice about its organization. Fellow South Carolina scholar Leslie Schwalm has generously taken time away from her own important work to comment on the essay. The staff of the State Historical Society of Wisconsin also provided much help and assistance over the years.

In Columbia and Charleston, I received help and encouragement from archivists and librarians that greatly facilitated this project. At the South Caroliniana Library at the University of South Carolina, Allen Stokes and his staff provided a very congenial atmosphere in which to work. Likewise, the librarians at the South Carolina Department of Archives and History (SCDAH) made several important suggestions. I am especially indebted to Alexia J. Helsley of the SCDAH, who granted permission for the publication of the Denmark Vesey trial transcript. In Charleston, Alexander Moore and his staff at the South Carolina Historical Society shared their extensive knowledge of Charleston's history as well as the library's wonderful holdings. I am grateful to the SCHS for allowing me to publish selections from their archives. The staffs of the Charleston Library Society, the Robert Smalls Library of the College of Charleston, and the City of Charleston Archives also assisted me in the research for this project.

The staffs at the libraries of the University of North Carolina at Chapel Hill and Duke University in Durham also played an important role in my research. Richard Shrader at the Southern Historical Collection in Chapel Hill and William Erwin at Duke's Perkins Library along with their respective staffs suggested additional sources and allowed me to reprint materials from their collections in this volume. The Museum of Early Southern Decorative Arts in Winston-Salem funded my research there and allowed me to range through their collections on the artisans and craft workers of Charleston. I am grateful to Sally Gant for facilitating my visit. I also wish to thank librarians at the Bermuda Historical Society (Hamilton), the Georgia Historical Society (Savannah), the Southern Baptist Historical Collection (Nashville, Tennessee), the Historical Society of Pennsylvania, and the Library Company of Philadelphia for their assistance. A research associateship at the American Antiquarian Society enabled me to put the finishing touches on this project.

Panelists and audiences at several conferences, including meetings of the Society for Historians of the Early Republic and American Historical Association, have offered useful suggestions and advice. Material from the essay has been presented at seminars at the Newberry Library (Chicago), the Commonwealth Center (Williamsburg), the Institute for U.S. Studies at University College (London), the University of Delaware (Newark), the Museum of Early Southern Decorative Arts (Winston-Salem), and the Johns Hopkins University (Baltimore). Comments and words of encouragement from Ira Berlin, Philip Curtin, David Brion Davis, Graham Hodges, Charles Joyner, George Rogers, and Al Young all proved useful. I also want to thank a number of friends and colleagues for their support and encouragement: Mark Bond-Webster, Saul Cornell, Colin Gordon, Rick Halpern, Roger Horowitz, Simon Newman, Leslie Reagan, Tom Ryan, Beverly Sensbach, Jon Sensbach, Darren Staloff, Peter Thompson, Tracey Weis, Michael Wilson, and Joel Wolfe.

At the University of North Carolina Press, Lew Bateman has faithfully championed this project, and I want to thank him for his guidance. I also want to thank Pam Upton and Suzanne Comer Bell for guiding me through the editing and production stages with great patience. Paul Finkelman has read this manuscript probably more times than he would have liked, but his care and attention have improved it immeasurably. I also want to thank the anonymous reader for the press for comments. In addition, I wish to thank Doug Egerton, who took time from his own work on Vesey to read the essay, and Bernie Herman at the University of Delaware, who also provided a series of thoughtful and provocative comments.

At Franklin and Marshall College, I have benefited not only from research monies from the Dean's Fund, but also from input from colleagues and students. David Schuyler (American Studies) offered advice on editing the transcript while Stephen Cooper (Religious Studies) provided information on the Book of Tobit. Conversations with Joel Martin (Religious Studies) on Vesey and matters related to black religion have proven invaluable. In addition, I want to thank members of the History Club and students in several courses who have been regaled with this story on many occasions for their patience and understanding. Mary Shelly in the Interlibrary Loan Office handled requests as well as overdue books with good humor.

My parents have remained interested in my research on South Carolina and supportive of this project. Little did they know when they encouraged my childhood interest in history that it would take me across the Atlantic. Throughout this process, Kathy Brown, my co-conspirator in all things, has offered astute criticism and emergency computer assistance at several crucial moments. Above all, she has encouraged me to see this project through to completion. As much as she was interested in Vesey's world, she will be glad to see me return to the one we share together with our new son, William.

ABBREVIATIONS

CCA
: City of Charleston Archives, Charleston, South Carolina

CLS
: Charleston Library Society, Charleston, South Carolina

DTT
: documentary trial transcript

MESDA
: Museum of Early Southern Decorative Arts, Winston-Salem, North Carolina

PRO
: Public Record Office, London

SBHC
: Southern Baptist Historical Collection, Nashville, Tennessee

SCHS
: South Carolina Historical Society, Charleston, South Carolina

SCDAH
: South Carolina Department of Archives and History, Columbia, South Carolina

SCL
: South Caroliniana Library, University of South Carolina, Columbia

SHC
: Southern Historical Collection, Wilson Library, University of North Carolina, Chapel Hill

WPL
: William Perkins Library, Duke University, Durham, North Carolina

EDITORIAL NOTE

The documentary trial transcript is contained in the Records of the General Assembly, Governors' Messages, in the South Carolina Department of Archives and History. Governor Thomas Bennett submitted two copies of the transcript to the South Carolina Assembly in late 1822. Document A, Copy One, starts with the first trials on 19 July 1822 and closes with the proceedings of 26 July. Document B, Copy Two, replicates the first document but contains testimony from the proceedings of early August. In the transcription of the trial document, I have used both Documents A and B, remaining faithful to the transcript as it appeared in the original.

Writing to South Carolina's House of Representatives and Senate, Bennett informed the members that "[A] brief narrative of the principal circumstances which developed, and attended the investigation of a Plot, lately formed within the Parishes of Saint Philip and Saint Michael, by a number of evil disposed negroes will be found in the accompanying document marked A. The proceedings of the Court and the testimony received and the trials of those charged as principals and accomplices are also transmitted and marked B" (Governor's Message #1328, 28 November 1822, Governors' Messages, SCDAH).

Lionel Kennedy and Thomas Parker published a version of the trial in late 1822, entitled *An Official Report of the Trials of Sundry Negroes Charged with an Attempt to Raise an Insurrection in the State of South Carolina*. Although it purports to be the full record, this volume, as noted elsewhere, contains many omissions and offers synopses of testimony rather than the complete account. It does, however, contain information that does not appear in the trial transcript, which sheds further light on the trial. The use of ⟨⟨ ... ⟩⟩ enables me to show information from the Kennedy/Parker edition in my presentation of the trial transcript. Published by James B. Schenck of Broad Street in Charleston in late 1822, its cover price was $1.75. In adding material from this source to the transcript, I have used the volume once owned by Thomas Wentworth Higginson and given to him as a gift by Harriet Beecher Stowe. It is currently held in the Houghton Library of Harvard University.

Designs against Charleston

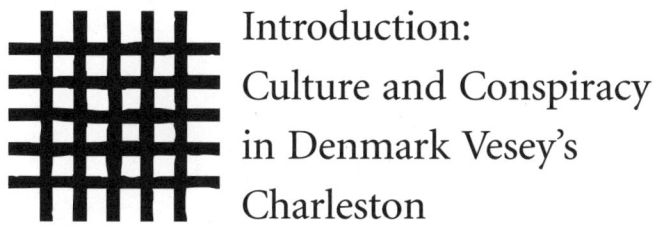
Introduction: Culture and Conspiracy in Denmark Vesey's Charleston

With his arms folded and his eyes fixed on the floor of Charleston's workhouse, Denmark Vesey stood before a court made up of five freeholders and two magistrates. Charged as "the author and original instigator . . . [of a] diabolical plot" that sought to bring "blood, outrage, rapine and conflagration, and to introduce anarchy and confusion in their most horrid forms" to South Carolina's leading port city in the summer of 1822, this middle-aged free black carpenter listened as Judge Lionel Kennedy sentenced him to death on Friday, 28 June. "'Your lamp of life is nearly extinguished,'" the judge announced, "your race is run, and you must shortly pass from 'time to eternity.'" Just two days before white Charlestonians would mark the nation's birthday with patriotic sermons and speeches that celebrated the "liberty, peace, and independence" they enjoyed as citizens of the republic, constables transported Vesey and five other rebels to the gallows at Blake's Fields on the city's northern outskirts.

Only moments before his death, Peter Poyas, a leading conspirator, entreated those prisoners still awaiting trial "not to open your lips! [D]ie silent, as you shall see me do." But the rebels involved in this plot did not remain silent. Between the first arrest on Friday, 31 May, until the end of the trials on Saturday, 3 August, the authorities arrested 117 enslaved and 11 free black men, charging them with "attempting to raise an Insurrection." By the time Judges Lionel Kennedy and Thomas Parker adjourned, another 29 enslaved men had made the journey from their cells to gallows erected on the Lines—an earthen defensive line built during the War of 1812 that stretched from Meeting Street to Line Street. Of the remaining 93 prisoners found guilty, the court either ordered or recommended that 40 black Charlestonians (37 slaves and 3 free blacks) be banished "beyond the limits of the United States," acquitted and discharged 15 suspects (10 slaves and 5 free blacks),

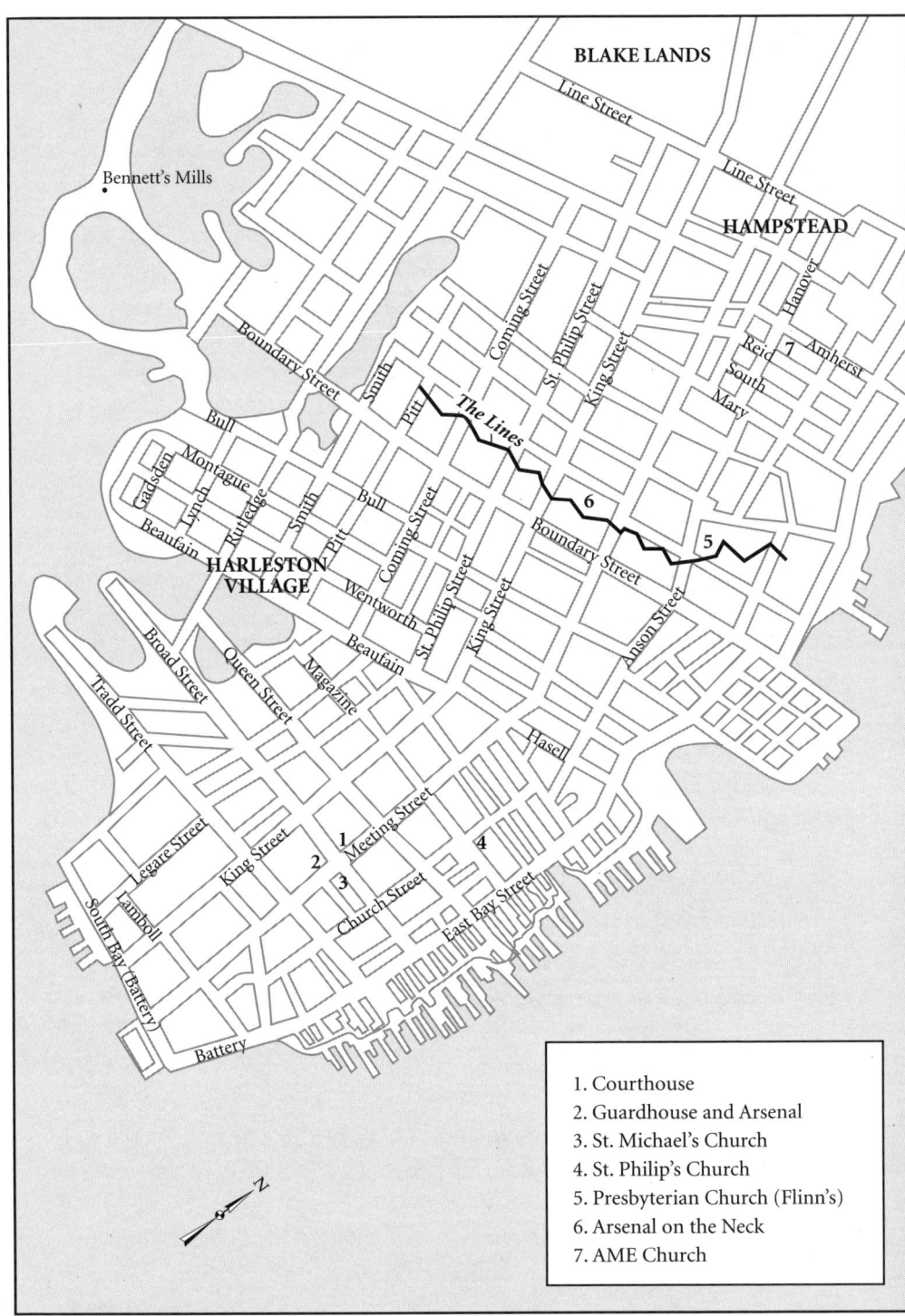

The City of Charleston, ca. 1822

and released the remaining 38 prisoners (36 slaves and 2 free blacks) before their trials.[1]

That several free black men and a greater number of enslaved Charlestonians planned to destroy the city came as a profound shock to its white population. In addition to entertaining the idea that their slaves were content with their lot, many urban slaveholders believed that they had forged emotional bonds with the enslaved men and women with whom they lived and worked. Sentencing ten rebels to death, Kennedy observed how Vesey's accomplices had "displayed the vilest ingratitude" toward their owners as they schemed "to destroy the bosom [that] had sheltered and protected" them. Rather than reinforcing the belief that slaves and masters lived in a climate of familial harmony, the trials clearly revealed that these slaves had spurned "the hand of kindness" offered by owners who had "assumed many of the duties of a parent." Enslaved coachman John Horry revealed the animus harbored by many insurgent slaves, providing a full-throated expression of rage that had doubtless been suppressed during his years of servitude. Angrily turning to Elias Horry, who believed his slave to be innocent, John Horry told his owner that had the plot succeeded the coachman had intended "to kill you, to rip open your belly, and throw the guts in your face." Clearly, such hostile sentiments and explicit statements of revenge sent powerful shockwaves through the ideological bedrock on which the social order of Charleston and the South Carolina lowcountry rested.[2]

The trials also revealed the intellectual sophistication, organizational skills, and tactical abilities that Vesey and his closest associates brought to this project. Displaying a real understanding of urban guerrilla warfare, the ringleaders decided to divide their forces into several smaller bands, enabling them to capture the arsenal, with its vital supplies of arms and ammunition, and other key buildings simultaneously. The rebels, now well armed, would then neutralize the militia before they set fire to the city and

---

1. The freeholders were William Drayton, Nathan Heyward, James Pringle, James Legare, and Robert Turnbull, while Lionel Kennedy and Thomas Parker served as justices. See Kennedy and Parker, *Official Report*, 31, 135–36, 140–46; and Furman, *America's Deliverance and Duty*, 20. In percentage terms, 27 percent of the conspirators died, 33 percent were banished, and 40 percent were acquitted. Biographical information on those arrested is contained in Appendix 2 of this volume. For a standard narrative of the plot, see Lofton, *Insurrection in South Carolina* (reprinted as *Denmark Vesey's Revolt*); Carroll, *Slave Insurrections in the United States*, 83–117; and Aptheker, *American Negro Slave Revolts*. See also Douglas Egerton's forthcoming book, *"He Shall Go Free": The Lives of Denmark Vesey*.

2. Kennedy and Parker, *Official Report*, 139; M[artha] Richardson to Dr. James Screven, 7 August 1822, Arnold-Screven Papers, SHC.

made their escape via ship to the island of Haiti. Commenting how the "plan of insurrection [was] organized with an address and cunning as would much surprise the community," local banker John Potter later concluded that "had [its] execution been as well supplanted, many of us this day would not have been left to tell the tale." The young niece of Governor Thomas Bennett and daughter of U.S. Supreme Court justice William Johnson, Anna Johnson put matters more succinctly, telling her cousin in Pennsylvania that she had never heard about "more deeply laid plots or plots more likely to succeed" than "the excellent plot" orchestrated by Denmark Vesey against Charleston's white inhabitants.[3]

Following the executions of the conspirators, circumspection replaced outright fear among white Charlestonians. One shopkeeper noted in mid-July that "the alarm has subsided. . . . I think there is no danger to be apprehended from the slaves." Leading lowcountry politician Joel Poinsett concurred, informing President James Monroe a few weeks later that Charleston "is again restored to order and tranquility." By August, the city's leaders appear to have regained their confidence. Devoting that month's meeting to a postmortem discussion of the plot, the council commended city intendant James Hamilton's "unremitting attention to the public interest . . . [during] a season of extraordinary commotion and alarm" as well as the civic-mindedness of the men who had spent long hours in a small courtroom prosecuting the rebels in the oppressive heat of a lowcountry summer. Only when "a most furious hurricane" slammed into the city and surrounding countryside on 27 September did the region's free and enslaved populations turn their attention to other matters, burying several hundred dead, repairing damaged plantations, and salvaging the rice and cotton harvest. A year that had begun, perhaps prophetically, with an exhibition of Rembrandt Peale's painting entitled *The Court of Death*—an allegorical work designed "to show the universal subjection of man to 'the king of terrors'"—at the South Carolina Academy of Arts on Broad Street came to a violent close with a natural disaster. "Our city has been most severely scourged this last eight months," noted one resident, "what with Insurrection and then Storm."[4]

---

3. John Potter to Langdon Cheves, 29 June 1822, and 16 July 1822, Langdon Cheves Papers, SCHS; Anna Johnson to Elizabeth Haywood, 18 July 1822, Ernest Haywood Papers, SHC. Although a leading figure among Charleston's social and political elite, Cheves was living in Philadelphia during the Vesey crisis, serving as president of the Bank of the United States. See Huff, *Langdon Cheves of South Carolina*.

4. Zalmon Wildman to E. M. Starrs, 19 July 1822, Zalmon Wildman Papers, SCL; Joel Poinsett to James Monroe, 13 August 1822, in Starobin, *Denmark Vesey*, 84; City of Charleston Council Minutes, 17 August 1822, in James Hamilton Jr. Papers, SHC; *Charleston*

No sooner had the trials and executions ended in August than debate over the summer's events began. A number of pamphlets, written by leading members of the lowcountry's political and legal community, discussed the conspiracy, slavery, and some practical measures that might prevent the recurrence of such an alarming event. Some writers, including former governor Thomas Pinckney and lawyer Henry DeSaussure, used this opportunity to air their views about the economic and political benefits of slavery and the impracticality of emancipation, adding their voices to the small but growing number of white southerners who were starting to formulate arguments in defense of the institution. Many white inhabitants agreed with Edwin C. Holland, editor of the *Charleston Times*, who proclaimed Vesey and his followers to be "misguided and deluded incendiaries." The few northern newspapers that carried the story argued that such dramatic acts of resistance would inevitably happen in a slave society. In Boston, the *Evening Gazette* commented that "nobody can blame the servile part of the population (the blacks) for attempting to escape from bondage," while New York's *Daily Advertiser* noted that "white men, too, would engender plots and escape from their imprisonment were they situated as are these miserable children of Africa."[5]

As the movement against slavery gathered momentum north of the Mason-Dixon line in the 1830s and 1840s, Vesey emerged as a powerful symbol of resistance for militant black abolitionists. Henry Highland Garnet, a northern free black and a formidable opponent of slavery, declared Vesey to be an exemplar of black political activism, telling one audience in Buffalo, New York, in 1843, that he had formulated "a tremendous plan . . . and died a martyr to freedom." In a pioneering work of African American history published in 1855, *Colored Patriots of the American Revolution*, black abolition leader William Nell concluded that "History . . . will engrave the name of denmark veazie on the same monument with Moses, . . . Toussaint [L'Ouverture], Lafayette, and Washington."[6]

Mercury, 30 September 1822; J. W. Wright to Elizabeth Yates, 12 November 1822, M. Mitchell to Elizabeth Yates, 26 October 1822, Elizabeth Yates Papers, SCHS. On Peale's painting, see *Charleston Mercury*, 25 January 1822.

5. For newspaper reports on the plot, see Starobin, *Denmark Vesey*, 86–91; Holland, *Refutation of the Calumnies*, 78; *Evening Gazette* (Boston) quoted in *Charleston Mercury*, 26 August 1822; and *Daily Advertiser* (New York), 31 July 1822, in Starobin, *Denmark Vesey*, 87, 89.

6. Henry Highland Garnet, "Address to the Slaves of the United States of America" [1843], in Ripley et al., *Witness for Freedom*, 168; Nell, *Colored Patriots of the American Revolution*, 255. For an analysis of Garnet's thought, see Stuckey, *Slave Culture*, 138–92. For

During the Civil War, Vesey's reputation continued to grow. On the day that Union commander Major Robert Anderson surrendered at Fort Sumter in Charleston harbor on 13 April 1861, the New York–based *Weekly Anglo-African* called for immediate action led by "men determined to do or die," demanding "Nat Turner—not speeches; Denmark Vesey—not resolutions; John Brown—not meetings." Calling on northern blacks to enlist in the Union army two years later, Frederick Douglass also invoked the names of Vesey, Turner, and the ex-slaves who joined in John Brown's ill-fated raid against Harpers Ferry in October 1859. Thomas Wentworth Higginson, a militant white abolitionist and member of the Secret Six, the small band of radicals who financed Brown's attack, and who went on to serve as colonel of the First South Carolina Volunteers, an all-black regiment who fought in the South Carolina lowcountry during the Civil War, published a short essay in the *Atlantic Monthly* in 1861 in which he discussed the plot. Drawing information from printed accounts, including a copy of Judges Kennedy and Parker's *Official Report of the Trials of Sundry Negroes* given to him by Harriet Beecher Stowe, as well as from conversations with a free black Charlestonian who had left the city for the north, Higginson applauded the plot's "boldness of conception and thoroughness of organization," concluding that it was "the most elaborate insurrectionary project ever formed by American slaves, and came the nearest to a terrible success."[7]

The plot resonated as part of the collective memory of African America long after the end of slavery. Nearly eighty years after Vesey's execution, Archibald Grimké, who later became a prominent figure in the National Association for the Advancement of Colored People, concluded that "it was

---

another thumbnail sketch of Vesey by a prominent black abolitionist and author, see William Wells Brown, *The Black Man*, 142–48.

7. *Weekly Anglo-African*, 13 April 1861, in Ripley et al., *Witness for Freedom*, 210; Frederick Douglass, "Men of Color, To Arms!" [2 March 1863], in Grant, *Black Protest*, 114; see also McFeely, *Frederick Douglass*, 226–27; and Higginson, "Denmark Vesey," 730. Higginson's essay, originally published in the *Atlantic Monthly*, is reprinted in his book *Black Rebellion*, 215–75. Douglass hoped that his audience would join the Fifty-fourth Massachusetts, the African American regiment that mounted an unsuccessful attack against Charleston's Fort Wagner in 1863 and was memorialized in the motion picture *Glory*. On Higginson's activities in the lowcountry during the war, see Rose, *Rehearsal for Reconstruction*, 193–95; McPherson, *Battle Cry of Freedom*, 564–65; and Higginson, *Army Life in a Black Regiment*. Higginson is probably best known for bringing Emily Dickinson's poetry to a wider audience. His copy of Kennedy and Parker's *Official Report*, from which he drew information for his essay about Vesey, is now held by the Houghton Library at Harvard University, and is inscribed "Mr. [Thomas W.] Higginson from H[.] B[.] Stowe."

no light thing for the Negroes of the United States to have produced such a man, such a hero and martyr." Calling for equal opportunity and social justice in 1935, the National Negro Congress reminded its members that "the unconquerable spirits of Nat Turner and Denmark Vesey . . . symbolize a spirit no less alive today." That determination persisted during the 1960s when civil rights workers invoked Vesey as a founding figure in the struggle for black freedom. In 1966, as the battle for racial justice grew increasingly turbulent, historian and activist Sterling Stuckey wrote that Vesey "stands today, as he did 143 summers ago . . . an awesome projection of the possibilities for militant action on the part of a people who have—for centuries—been made to bow down in fear."[8]

The conspiracy and its leader have also inspired artists, including several musicians, who have memorialized the events of 1822. Composer and author Paul Bowles, best known for his novel *The Sheltering Sky*, wrote an opera based on the plot in 1937. Fifty years later, Charleston native Thomas Cabaniss followed in Bowles's footsteps, writing an opera called *Denmark Vesey*. The plot also attracted the attention of one of the nation's greatest songwriters and composers. George Gershwin, who drew heavily on the folktales and language of lowcountry blacks for *Porgy and Bess*, began work on a libretto with collaborator DuBose Heyward for a musical drama about Vesey. After Gershwin's death in 1937 and Heyward's three years later, Dorothy Heyward eventually completed the work as a play called *Set My People Free*, which opened on Broadway in 1948. More recently, Australian composer Vincent Plush premiered a piece entitled *Denmark Vesey Takes the Stand* that drew on the trial record as well as Heyward's play, using voices, instruments, and theatrical devices to recreate the last days of Vesey and his fellow insurgents.[9]

Perhaps the controversy that arose over a painting that depicted Vesey preaching to a small gathering of black Charlestonians best exemplifies the hold that this event still appears to have over the lowcountry's collective memory. Within a month of its dedication in early August 1976, the painting

---

8. Grimké, "*Right on the Scaffold*," 24. In one of history's odder coincidences, Vesey Street in New York City was the location of offices for both the American Freedman's Union Commission and the NAACP in its early days. See Grant, *Black Protest*, 212. See also National Negro Congress, "A New Crisis Confronts the Negro People (1935)," in ibid., 241; Stuckey, "Remembering Denmark Vesey," 41.

9. For information on musical adaptations of the Vesey plot, see *Charleston Post and Courier*, 29 September 1996, and 30 September 1996; and Vincent Plush, *Denmark Vesey Takes the Stand* (score and libretto in author's possession). On the work of Plush, see ibid.; *Pittsburgh Post-Gazette*, 20 January 1997, and 27 January 1997. I am indebted to Vincent Plush for alerting me to these works.

was stolen from the city's Galliard Municipal Auditorium. Although it was soon recovered, the incident provoked a storm of protest in the columns of the local papers where Vesey "was variously denounced as akin to Judas, Hitler, Attila the Hun, Idi Amin . . . and Herod, the murderer of babies." Twenty years after this incident, a group of Charlestonians announced plans to build a statue to commemorate the free black carpenter, establishing the Denmark Vesey Spirit of Freedom Monument Committee to raise money for a memorial to be erected in the city. "Charleston history," as committee head Henry Darby has rightly noted, "isn't complete without him."[10]

Vesey's plot constituted the last major challenge that enslaved South Carolinians mounted against slavery and one of the only slave conspiracies in North America to leave such a rich trail of documents revealing the ideas and intentions of the insurgents. Of the many plots uncovered by southern slaveholders, very few exhibited the tactical and ideological complexity displayed by Vesey. One notable exception was the conspiracy organized by Gabriel, an enslaved blacksmith owned by Thomas Prosser, against Richmond, Virginia, in the summer of 1800. Bearing some similar political and military hallmarks to the conspiracy that Vesey orchestrated twenty-two years later, Gabriel's cause drew skilled and semiskilled slave artisans and found political inspiration in the Haitian Revolution of the early 1790s.[11] The rebellions planned by these two men constituted the leading threats against southern towns from the beginning of the nineteenth century to the Civil War.

In contrast to these two urban plots, a majority of conspiracies originated in rural districts among enslaved farm and plantation laborers. The rebellion planned by slaves who worked in the countryside surrounding the small town of Camden in the South Carolina upcountry in July 1816 and the insurrectionary schemes of several enslaved men from the cotton estates of

---

10. On the incident at the Gaillard Auditorium, see *Charleston Post and Courier*, 9 August 1976, and 30 September 1996. For other representations of Vesey, see the following: in print, Killens, *Great Gittin' Up in the Morning*, and Edward, *Denmark Vesey*; on sound recording, Kramer, "Denmark Vesey," in Kramer, *"On Freedom's Side,"* and his *Denmark Vesey and Other Poems*; on video, *The Gift of Black Folk*, and Morse, *Brother Future*; on radio, McDonald, *"Denmark Vesey: Dark Explorers"*; CBS Radio Workshop, *Sweet Cherries in Charleston* and *The Heart of a Man*; and *Destination Freedom: Denmark Vesey*. In addition, there has been a PBS television drama, called *Denmark Vesey's Rebellion*, with Yaphet Kotto in the leading role. On this program, see Freehling, "History and Television." Vesey's house on Bull Street is on the National Historic Landmark register.

11. For a comprehensive and illuminating discussion of this plot, see Egerton, *Gabriel's Rebellion*; see also Gerald W. Mullin, *Flight and Rebellion*, 140–63, and Sidbury, *Ploughshares into Swords*.

Adams County in southwestern Mississippi in May 1861 appear typical of the size and scope of most antebellum conspiracies.[12] Although rural plots such as these appear to have been modest affairs, involving just a handful of slaves, they should not be dismissed as trivial. That these enslaved agricultural laborers in Camden, Adams County, and elsewhere in the antebellum South even contemplated plotting against their masters highlights the contested social relationships that existed between slaves and slaveholders.

The rural South also provided the setting for three of the largest slave insurrections in North America, although it should be noted that even these revolts were modest in scale compared with those elsewhere in the New World. Involving nearly one hundred enslaved men who worked on farms and plantations in Saint Paul's Parish just south of Charleston, the Stono rebellion of September 1739, the insurrection of more than five hundred slaves in parishes along the Mississippi River outside New Orleans in January 1811, and Nat Turner's uprising against the white inhabitants of the rural Virginia backwater of Southampton County in August 1831 constitute the most important rural revolts in the South.[13] Invariably, these rebels quickly found themselves facing insurmountable odds in the form of well-armed militias and local planters. Although these uprisings enjoyed success at first, taking their neighborhoods by surprise, they rarely lasted longer than twenty-four hours before the overwhelming firepower of the authorities suppressed them.

Although the towns and cities of North America experienced fewer slave rebellions, enslaved city dwellers proved no more placid than their rural counterparts. In April 1712, a group of enslaved Africans in New York destroyed several buildings, killing nine and injuring a number of other white

---

12. On the Camden conspiracy, see Johnson and Roark, *Black Masters*, 23, 352 (n. 61); and Kirkland and Kennedy, *Historic Camden*, 2: 187–91. On the Adams County conspiracy in southwestern Mississippi, see Jordan, *Tumult and Silence at Second Creek*.

13. The literature on slave revolts is extensive, but the following works offer useful points of entry: Aptheker, *American Negro Slave Revolts*; Frey, *Water from the Rock*; Genovese, *Roll, Jordan, Roll*, 587–98, and *From Rebellion to Revolution*; Harding, *There Is a River*; and Michael Mullin, *Africa in America*. On the Stono rebellion, see, for example, Wood, *Black Majority*, 308–30; Pearson, "'A Countryside Full of Flames,'" 22–50; Thornton, "African Dimensions of the Stono Rebellion," 1101–13; and Wax, "'The Great Risque We Run,'" 136–47. For work on slave resistance in revolutionary and early-nineteenth-century South Carolina, see Michael Johnson, "Runaway Slaves and Slave Communities in South Carolina," 418–41; Norrece Jones, *Born a Child of Freedom, Yet a Slave*; Wood, "Taking Care of Business," 268–94, "'Liberty Is Sweet,'" 149–85, and "'The Dream Deferred,'" 166–87. On the 1811 Louisiana rebellion, see Taylor, *Negro Slavery in Louisiana*. On Nat Turner, see Oates, *The Fires of Jubilee*; Greenberg, *Confessions of Nat Turner*; and Tragle, *Southampton Slave Revolt*.

people before making their escape. Arresting around seventy slaves, the authorities hanged thirteen, burned three at the stake, and broke another on the wheel. Twenty-nine years later in the same city, a multiracial group of free and servile men, including Africans, African Americans, and English and Irish, plotted "to burn the town and kill as many white people as they could" until patrols stopped them after they had set fire to some buildings. By the end of this incident, more than thirty slaves and four white men had lost their lives. On the eve of the war between American colonists and the British in 1775, free black boatman Thomas Jeremiah (known locally as Jerry) was arrested for plotting an insurrection of lowcountry slaves against Charleston. After a contentious trial that pitted the colony's radical leadership against the royal governor, who believed Jerry to be innocent, the court found him guilty, hanging him and then burning his body in late August. Between the end of War of Independence and 1822, as we will see, a handful of enslaved Charlestonians conspired on one more occasion. Thus, Vesey's designs against Charleston stand as part of a long tradition of collective resistance by urban slaves.[14]

The rich archive generated during this moment of crisis has enabled historians to investigate many aspects of urban slave life. These documents shed light on the intellectual world that the insurgents inhabited, illuminating the lives of people who ordinarily leave little or no trace in the historical record. The otherwise hidden life of the street, the workshop, the tavern, and the meeting house come alive through such materials. These moments of dramatic confrontation between the powerful and the weak prove invaluable for understanding the past lives of "the so-called inarticulate" who speak and make themselves heard only during times of disorder and disruption. Moreover, as historian Emilia Viotti da Costa has noted, only in such moments of great upheaval do the conflicts and tensions that "in daily life are buried beneath the rules and routines of social protocol" burst into the open, exposing the inner workings of the social order to public scrutiny. Such events reveal the social organization of power and subordination in addition to disclosing the texture of everyday life that is so often absent from the historical record. The transcript of the Vesey trial uncovers the ways in

---

14. On the events of 1712 in New York, see Aptheker, *American Negro Slave Revolts*, 172; and Kenneth Scott, "Slave Insurrection in New York in 1712," 43–74. On the conspiracy of 1741, see Thomas J. Davis, *Rumor of Revolt*; Nash, *The Urban Crucible*, 108; and Pierson, *From Africa to America*, 129. For a fine discussion that places these events in an Atlantic context, see Linebaugh and Rediker, "Many-Headed Hydra," 225–26. On Jerry's plot, see Frey, *Water from the Rock*, 57–58; and Weir, *Colonial South Carolina*, 201–3.

which slaves fashioned their own lives as well as the ways in which they tested the authority of their owners.[15]

These records thus permit the partial excavation of the subterranean history of black Charleston during the early nineteenth century, enabling the social, political, and cultural contexts that gave rise to the conspiracy to be unearthed. From the day that Vesey considered rebelling against slavery until his arrest, he sought to recast the language of revolution and reconfigure the religious practices of Afro-Carolinians to forge a powerful critique of prevailing social and economic arrangements. This critique ultimately found a receptive audience among a small group of enslaved artisans and laborers in Charleston and some rural slaves. Of course, this discourse of insurgency did not emerge in a vacuum. The material circumstances in which the rebels lived and labored provided the context for their bold endeavor. Just as Vesey shaped a message that resonated with the thoughts and experiences of these slaves, he also built a new community of men who became highly politicized as they engaged in conspiracy. Conversing with enslaved artisans beyond the gaze of their owners in tippling houses or in workshops, Vesey fashioned a "hidden transcript"—a term used by anthropologist James Scott to describe the backstage discourse and subversive practices formulated by subordinate groups to critique and undermine the power of dominant groups. Ranging from minor infractions of the law to petty insubordination to open rebellion, Vesey's "hidden transcript" provided his followers with a new way of understanding the world in which they lived. The decision of enslaved Charlestonians to risk all by joining Vesey and becoming rebels was, as Scott has written, one of "those rare moments of political electricity when, often for the first time in memory, the hidden transcript [was] spoken directly and

---

15. Natalie Zemon Davis, "The Reasons of Misrule," 122; da Costa, *Crowns of Glory, Tears of Blood*, xiii. For further discussions on this topic, see Hobsbawm, "From Social History to the History of Society," 1–22; Haynes and Prakesh, "The Entanglement of Power and Resistance," 1–22; James C. Scott, *Domination and the Arts of Resistance* and *Weapons of the Weak*; Muir and Ruggiero, "The Crime of History," vii–xviii; and Trouillot, *Silencing the Past*, 1–31.

Slaves resisted in various ways, ranging from petty insubordination and vandalism to escape to full-scale rebellion. In some cases, resistance took unusual forms. Adam Ferguson, a minor figure in the conspiracy who worked as the enslaved domestic of Ann Ferguson, protested against slavery in a rather novel fashion. Unhappy with the uniform that his owner forced him to wear as he performed his daily chores about the house, Adam devoted his spare time to disassembling these clothes, that functioned as a sign of servitude, stitch by stitch, button by button, "until all signs of livery had gone." In addition, Adam regularly failed to deliver verbal messages entrusted to him correctly, garbling their contents. See Samuel Wragg, "Memoirs," typescript, WPL.

publicly in the teeth of power." That such events ever take place also serves as a reminder that, as Michel Foucault once observed, "no matter how terrifying a given system may be, there always remain the possibilities of resistance, disobedience, and oppositional groupings."[16]

The published accounts of the plot and the trials also expose the attitudes of the people who wrote them. The slim volume compiled by Lionel Kennedy and Thomas Parker, entitled *An Official Report of the Trials of Sundry Negroes Charged with an Attempt to Raise an Insurrection*, which provided a synopsis of the trials as well as various pamphlets, editorials, and personal letters penned by white Charlestonians, may be read as a bundle of narratives about this event. Just a few days after Vesey's hanging on 2 July, Mary Beach told a friend how "the events of this week were calculated to excite *much* painful & *bitter* reflection." The white men and women who recorded their emotions and experiences during this crisis sought to arrange the events of the summer into a coherent story, shaping what they knew or thought they knew into an orderly narrative that gave form to a disorderly and contingent existence. Both their world and our world, as literary critic Hayden White has rightly noted, does not "present itself to perception in the form of well-made stories, with central subjects, proper beginnings, middles and ends, and a coherence that permits us to see 'the end' in every beginning." Sitting at their writing desks with pens in hand and paper before them, a number of white Charlestonians dedicated hours to crafting "well-made stories," constructing their own history of the plot as they tried to explain the summer's dramatic events to friends, families, and strangers.[17]

The textual variations between the verbatim trial record (which follows this introduction) and the version published by Kennedy and Parker for public consumption just months after the court adjourned vividly show how the authorities sought to understand and manage the plot. Most nota-

---

16. James C. Scott, *Domination and the Arts of Resistance*, xiii; Foucault, "Space, Knowledge, and Power," 245. Borrowing from Haynes and Prakesh, I define resistance "as those behaviors and cultural practices by subordinate groups that contest hegemonic social formations, [and] that threaten to unravel the strategies of domination." See Haynes and Prakesh, "The Entanglement of Power and Resistance," 3.

17. Mary Beach to Elizabeth Gilchrist, 5 July 1822, Mary Lamboll Beach Papers, SCHS; Hayden White, *Content of the Form*, 24; see also Natalie Zemon Davis, *Fiction in the Archives*, 1–6. Both letters and pamphlets appear to have circulated fairly widely throughout the nation. In early 1823, Jane Jones, a resident of East Hartford, Connecticut, acknowledged the receipt of "pamphlets relating to the intended insurrection" from a family member in Orangeburgh, South Carolina. Jane Jones to Samuel Jones, 22 January 1823, Jane Bruce Jones Papers, SCL. Hamilton's pamphlet on the plot was published in Boston as well as in Charleston.

bly, the judges excised Harry Haig's testimony about rebel plans to poison Charleston's water pumps and wells in their own volume. Commenting on this deliberate omission to Langdon Cheves, John Potter noted how any information about poisoning the water supply remained "all private."[18] The judges also censored testimony about "Gullah" Jack Pritchard's plan to organize an attack on the workhouse to free imprisoned rebels. By collapsing repetitive statements into one or two sentences, and rearranging the chronological sequence in which slaves testified, the judge composed a more linear and coherent narrative. Through their particular editing style, the two judges reshaped the narrative of the conspiracy for their own purposes. Published in October 1822 by local printer James B. Schenck, Kennedy and Parker's account of the trial, along with their short commentary on the plot, enabled the justices to use the authority derived from print to reassert their power over events that they initially had been unable to control. In short, they authored the conspiracy for a public audience, even titling their volume *An Official Report*.

Although the insurgents had no control over the composition of these texts, many seized the opportunity to speak in court. They told magistrates not just about their lives as slaves, but also about their violent desires to destroy Charleston and seek retribution against its slaveholders. During his confession, Smart Anderson spoke about a gathering at Monday Gell's house at which Vesey announced that the rebels should kill both men and women. "[W]hat was the use of killing the louse," Vesey proclaimed, "and leaving the nit." John Horry, as already noted, openly stated his murderous intentions, planning to disembowel his owner and throw the viscera in his face. Such defiant declarations spoke volumes about the attitudes of slaves toward owners who often represented relationships with their slaves in the language of family and kinship. Even the less forceful statements made by slaves demonstrated that they had fashioned an alternative vision of the future in which slavery did not exist.[19]

Although rich with information, the trial transcript unfortunately remains silent on several topics concerning Vesey, the conspiracy, and the men who joined his insurrection. It offers little or no biographical information about several key conspirators, including Monday Gell, Peter Poyas, "Gul-

---

18. John Potter to Langdon Cheves, ca. July 1822, Langdon Cheves Papers, SCHS.

19. Confession of Smart Anderson, 16 July 1822, DTT; M[artha] Richardson to Dr. James Screven, 7 August 1822, Arnold-Screven Papers, SHC. For a discussion on reading documents produced by those in power against the grain, see Dirks et al., Introduction to *Culture/Power/History*, 17–22; Guha, "The Prose of Counter-Insurgency," 336–71; and da Costa, *Crowns of Glory, Tears of Blood*, xv.

lah" Jack Pritchard, or Vesey. Although Vesey addressed the court during his trial, his words have not survived. Perhaps fearing that the rebel leader's words might inspire slaves to follow in his footsteps, Kennedy and Parker did not include any of his statements in the verbatim trial record or in their published account. Moreover, the testimonials that masters offered the court about the character of slaves accused of conspiracy reveal very little additional information about the conditions in which their slaves lived or even personal details about the slave in question. Most slaveholders simply claimed, as did William Harth, that "Robert is of good character, his general conduct is good ... I would place my life in his hands."[20] The court disagreed with Harth's assessment of his slave's character in this case, however, sentencing Robert to transportation. Despite such problems, the trial transcript remains an extremely valuable source for telling the story of Vesey and his confederates.

Historians have used the trial materials to examine various dimensions of antebellum southern history. For those scholars concerned with the intellectual world of urban slaves, the transcript and other documents reveal how Vesey effectively combined the ethnic customs of western Africa, the radical ideas of the age of revolution, and Old Testament texts to create a politics of black liberation. Broadening the geographical reach of their inquiries to include the Atlantic basin, several historians have examined the cultural and political networks established by black mariners as they manned the ships that transported African slaves and New World plantation commodities. Vesey belonged to an admittedly tiny group of self-taught black intellectuals, including African-born mariner Olaudah Equiano, Afro-Jamaican antislavery radical Robert Wedderburn, and Quobna Ottobah Cugoano, author of *Thoughts and Sentiments on the Evil and Wicked Traffic of the Slavery and Commerce of the Human Species* (1787), who drew on both their own experiences and the democratically inspired rhetoric that circulated throughout the Atlantic basin at the end of the eighteenth century. Although these men never met, they each tried to nurture an alternative political tradition in the midst of unfettered capitalism and plantation slavery.[21]

20. Trial of Peter Poyas, 21 June 1822, DTT. As noted elsewhere, two copies of the transcript were deposited with the legislature, labeled A and B.

21. For a discussion that places Vesey within the broad context of African and African American thought and action, see Genovese, *From Rebellion to Revolution* and *Roll, Jordan, Roll*, 593–94; and Stuckey, *Slave Culture*, 43–53. On Vesey and other radicals of African descent in the eighteenth- and early-nineteenth-century Atlantic world, see Gilroy, *Black Atlantic*, 1–40; Bolster, *Black Jacks*; Julius S. Scott, "Common Wind"; McCalman, *The Horrors of Slavery*; and Potkay and Burr, *Black Atlantic Writers of the Eighteenth Century*. For a

For scholars exploring the political path down which antebellum white southerners traveled, the plot serves as a useful benchmark from which to chart the growth of southern radicalism. In his study of the Nullification Crisis of the early 1830s, William Freehling has observed that the conspiracy resulted in lowcountry politicians taking measures "to check abolitionist propaganda and to stop congressional slavery debates." Regaining their equilibrium in late 1822, lowcountry planters acknowledged that their social order had barely "escaped the reality of slave revolution." The conspiracy haunted them, ensuring that they would "never again forget the possibility" of servile insurrection. Writing about the panic that gripped South Carolina when Abraham Lincoln won the election of 1860, thirty-eight years after Vesey's plot, Steven Channing noted how the constant fear of rebellion shaped the attitudes of white South Carolinians as they debated secession during that tumultuous year.[22]

Not all scholars have accepted the existence of Vesey's plot, however. Writing in 1964, Richard Wade dismissed the conspiracy as nothing more "than loose talk by aggrieved and bitter men" that nervous authorities quickly translated into rebellion. Conjuring up conspiracies from idle remarks made by slaves, he argued, a handful of white people invented a plot where none existed, plunging the city into turmoil. Offering a detailed critique of this argument in an article entitled "Denmark Vesey's Peculiar Reality," William Freehling has rightly concluded that Wade missed "a pivotal document" about rebel intentions to poison the city's water supply that confirmed the plot's existence. Wade also failed to appreciate how subtle differences between the texts of the verbatim trial record and Lionel Kennedy and Thomas Parker's *Official Report* led to his erroneous conclusions. By closely examining the archival record, Freehling has demonstrated that the plot was not, as Wade argued, "a vague and unformulated plan in the minds or on the tongues of a few colored townspeople," but a real threat to slavery in the lowcountry.[23]

---

broad survey of the early modern Atlantic world, see Curtin, *Rise and Fall of the Plantation Complex*; Meinig, *Shaping of America*, esp. 55–65, 144–201, 280–84; and Thornton, *Africa and Africans in the Making of the Atlantic World*.

22. Freehling, *Prelude to Civil War*, 53–64; Channing, *Crisis of Fear*.

23. Wade, "The Vesey Plot," 160; see also Wade, *Slavery in the Cities*, 228–41. The date of Wade's article, which was published in 1964, is worth comment. That year witnessed the inauguration of "the JFK industry" as many Americans began concocting various theories, ranging from the plausible to the outlandish, about the assassination in Dallas. Wade's findings are challenged in Freehling, "Denmark Vesey's Peculiar Reality," 25–47 (reprinted

Examining social relations between masters and slaves in Vesey's Charleston, Freehling posited an alternative interpretation of the plot. Underpinning these relationships, he argued, was a particularly permissive form of "domestic patriarchy" that fostered rising expectations among certain slaves, creating a situation in which "[t]oo many privileges left the semiprivileged too often desiring full privilege."[24] Enslaved Charlestonians well knew that, even though their masters might occasionally display affection and leniency, they still remained slaves, a species of property, and subject to the economic needs of their owner. Vesey's plot, according to Freehling, stripped the white population of its most cherished beliefs, undermining the myth of paternal benevolence and stewardship that slaveholders had so assiduously cultivated and reminding white Charlestonians that behind the seemingly benign countenance of every slave lay a potential rebel. That a conspiracy could be organized under the noses of slaveholders not only suggests how little these people knew about the men and women that they held in bondage, but also demonstrates the ability of slaves to keep their personal lives hidden from the sight of their owners. When asked by an agent of the Freedman's Inquiry Commission in 1863 whether "masters know anything of the secret life of the colored people," Robert Smalls, a slave who escaped from Charleston in the previous year, replied "[N]o sir; one life they show their masters and another life they don't show." By directly striking slaveholders' perceptions of their relationships with their slaves, the conspiracy shook their convictions about their ability to govern them. "All confidence in them [slaves] now," reflected Mary Beach as she considered the consequences of the plot, "is forever at an end after the treachery of several in this business."[25]

Having examined the documentation and scholarship devoted to the Vesey plot, this introductory essay opens with a discussion of Vesey's early

---

as "Denmark Vesey's Antipaternalistic Reality" in Freehling, *Reintegration of American History*, 34–58). Likewise, Starobin has questioned Wade's findings; see his "Denmark Vesey's Slave Conspiracy of 1822," 142–57. On urban slavery, see, for example, Goldfield, "Black Life in Old South Cities," 123–54; Goldin, *Urban Slavery in the American South*; and Parrish, "The Edges of Slavery in the Old South," 106–25. On Charleston, see Koger, *Black Slaveholders*; and Powers, *Black Charlestonians*.

24. Freehling, "Denmark Vesey's Peculiar Reality," 28. For further discussions on this subject, see Rose, "The Domestication of Domestic Slavery," 18–36; and Michael Johnson, "Planters and Patriarchy," 45–72.

25. "American Freedman's Inquiry Commission Interviews, 1863," 377. Smalls, using his skills as a boatman, made a dramatic escape from Charleston in May 1862 when he piloted the Confederate steamer *Planter* from the harbor to Union naval forces stationed nearby. Mary L. Beach to Elizabeth L. Gilchrist, 5 July 1822, Beach Papers, SCHS.

years from the 1760s until his manumission in late 1799. I then shift to examine the social and cultural life of early-nineteenth-century Charleston where Vesey spent the last twenty-two years of his life. The next section explores the world of work that enslaved Charlestonians inhabited before it turns to look at the political and religious ideas that played so formative a role in the plot's conception. The conspiracy itself forms the heart of the narrative, which comprises the next two sections. The essay closes by looking at the consequences of Vesey's conspiracy for both free black and enslaved Afro-Carolinians. Our story begins, however, with the man who concluded that freedom for the enslaved would be realized only through armed insurrection.

FROM SLAVERY TO FREEDOM: TELEMAQUE'S EARLY YEARS

Perhaps in chains he left his native shore
Perhaps he left a hapless offspring there,
Perhaps a wife, that he must see no more,
Perhaps a father, who his love did share.
—Philip Freneau, "The Beauties of Santa Cruz (1776)"

About the man who masterminded this "enterprise so wild and visionary," we know very little. Although eyewitnesses report that Vesey questioned prisoners and addressed the court "at considerable length" during the trial, his words never appear in the court record. The following biographical sketch thus derives from a scattering of other materials as well as from the broad context of the times in which he lived. From these sources, a portrait of a man who possessed formidable oratorical skills and impressive powers of persuasion emerges. In one case at least, he used these traits to convince an enslaved man, Bacchus Hammet, to become a conspirator. Accepting Vesey's point that God had made him as well as his owner, the slave had to acknowledge the rebel leader's contention that "if God made him and you . . . you are as free as your master." Faced with this argument, Hammet joined the plotters. Employing his considerable intellectual gifts, Vesey articulated the aspirations of a group of enslaved Charlestonians who, as Peter Poyas told Robert Harth, stood determined "to break the yoke" that bound them.[26]

With a voracious appetite for the printed word, Vesey read Old Testament

26. Trial of Peter Poyas, 21 June 1822, DTT; Confession of Bacchus Hammet, Hammet Papers, WPL.

texts, works about slavery, and the handful of antislavery tracts then in circulation, the latter possibly obtained from a free black sailor aboard the New York–based *Minerva* who smuggled "several hundred pamphlets of an insurrectionary character" into Charleston in 1809.[27] Apparently devoting much time to reading and analyzing these texts, he often brought an aggressive originality to these materials as he sought confirmation for his ideas. The encounter between the printed page and the circumstances of black life in Charleston created an incendiary mix in Vesey's head. In addition, he appears to have had a capacious memory, which allowed him to quote large portions of antislavery speeches and writings to his followers.[28] How Vesey reported these speeches and told biblical tales is lost to history, but he may have turned storytelling into a performance, conveying their meaning as much through gesture as through language and further adding to his reputation as a man of words. During his years at sea, Vesey perhaps learned how to spin a good yarn, possibly using these skills later in Charleston to create compelling stories that may have highlighted the injustice of slavery even as they entertained his audience.[29]

Borrowing from Italian Marxist Antonio Gramsci's formulation, we might categorize Vesey as an "organic intellectual," a man who emerges from the ranks of ordinary workers to gain a position of leadership through his own skill and ability while still retaining close links to those people. From his early life as an enslaved mariner and carpenter as well as during his later years as a free black artisan and leading member of the city's African Methodist Episcopal (AME) church, Vesey attempted to fashion "new modes of thought" through reading and his own experiences as he sought to overturn prevailing social relations.[30] Moreover, his understanding of the world resonated with the views of a number of black Charlestonians, enabling him to articulate their consciousness and organize a rebellion. At some point, he decided to share his thoughts with others, openly declaring his intention to foment a rebellion, gaining a positive response from people who recognized that Vesey spoke directly to their concerns.

27. Kennedy and Parker, *Official Report*, 159; Confession of Monday Gell, 13 July 1822, DTT.

28. Trial of Peter Poyas, 21 June 1822, DTT. For a brilliant discussion on how texts take on a life of their own in the hands of a self-taught laboring man in early modern Europe, see Ginzburg, *The Cheese and the Worms*.

29. Bolster, *Black Jacks*, 41.

30. Gramsci, *Selections from the Prison Notebooks*, 9; see also Joll, *Gramsci*, 91; Simon, *Gramsci's Political Thought*, 93–99; Said, *Representations of the Intellectual*, 5–13; and Feierman, *Peasant Intellectuals*, 3–45.

But, as one prisoner confessed, Vesey was not just "a man of great capacity," but also a man believed to have "a bloody disposition." Both his deep engagement with particularly militant Old Testament texts as well as his desire to replicate the violence and destructiveness that Saint Domingue's rebellious slaves had inflicted on their owners and plantations in the 1790s may partially explain his uncompromising and fiery approach toward revolt. Clearly, organizing a slave rebellion in the face of tremendous obstacles, including the danger of discovery or betrayal, required extraordinary commitment in addition to a considerable degree of ruthlessness and subterfuge. He had no qualms about telling his followers to kill white women and children as well as men. Vesey was equally unflinching when confronting his own followers, threatening that any slave who did not join the cause would be treated as "an enemy, and put to death."[31] In the words of accused rebel Pompey Bryan, "the blacks stood in fear of him" when he made such menacing promises. Although ideas would come to play a large part in the conspiracy, it is important to remember that Vesey's ultimate goal was the destruction of Charleston and its slaveholders. Had his plans succeeded, Charleston, as Kennedy and Parker noted, "would probably have been wrapped in flames —many valuable lives sacrificed—and an immense loss of property sustained by the citizens . . . while the plantations in the lower country would have been disorganized, and the agricultural interests have sustained an enormous loss."[32] Rebellions entail violence and bloodshed, and Vesey appears to have embraced that underlying reality, as he was willing to kill both whites and uncooperative blacks to achieve his goal.

Beyond the particular conditions that prevailed in Charleston, Vesey also appears to have immersed himself in the radical political culture of the period. He undoubtedly drew on the revolutionary discourses that swirled around the Atlantic world at the end of the eighteenth century as well as from the rhetoric of antislavery that circulated throughout the American republic in the early nineteenth century. The discourse that he shaped integrated the radical language of the black Atlantic with that drawn from the oratory and writings of Americans who opposed slavery. Newspapers, antislavery pamphlets, and other tracts along with firsthand accounts of political unrest or social conflict all constituted the raw materials from which the Atlantic world's laboring people sought, often against formidable odds, to forge alternative political traditions. Besides these sources, Vesey also drew on the cultural practices of urban and plantation slaves, recognizing the

---

31. Confession of Bacchus Hammet, Benjamin Hammet Papers, WPL.
32. Kennedy and Parker, *Official Report*, 40.

importance of both Old Testament texts and African traditions as he created his insurrectionary philosophy.[33] This fusion would draw cosmopolitan urban slaves as well as rural slaves to his ranks.

The massive slave rebellions that broke out in the French West Indian colony of Saint Domingue in the 1790s, culminating in the destruction of slavery on the island and the establishment of Haiti, the New World's first black republic in 1804, became a vital touchstone in the formation of Vesey's political thought.[34] This revolution symbolized the possibility of liberation for enslaved peoples throughout the Americas even as it alerted slaveholders to the terrifying violence and destructive power that slaves could unleash against their oppressors. Besides the extraordinary political upheavals that characterized the late-eighteenth-century Atlantic world, including revolutions in British North America as well as in France and on its island colony of Saint Domingue, Vesey's world was further informed by the work culture that developed among black Charlestonians as they labored on its wharves, in its warehouses, and streets, and the sense of community that developed in its tippling houses and places of worship. Within these settings, Vesey and his companions could discuss and perhaps embrace the enormous changes occurring in the political culture of the Atlantic basin.

Although neither the place nor date of his birth is known precisely, some evidence suggests that he was born around 1767 in western Africa or on Saint Thomas, a small mountainous island that was part of Denmark's West Indian empire that included the neighboring islands of Saint John and Saint Croix, located at the western end of the Leeward Islands. Part of the New World plantation complex producing staple crops, including sugar, for the European market, these islands were home to about 26,000 of the 2.5 million enslaved people of African descent who lived in the western hemisphere in the last quarter of the eighteenth century. Only when Captain Joseph Vesey,

---

33. See Blackburn, *Overthrow of Colonial Slavery*, 213–64; Curtin, *Rise and Fall of the Plantation Complex*, 144–69; and Frey, *Water from the Rock*. For a theoretical discussion on the creation of political discourse by nontraditional intellectuals, see Feierman, *Peasant Intellectuals*, 3–45.

34. A note on the terminology used to describe the island on which present-day Haiti and the Dominican Republic are located is in order. Its aboriginal inhabitants—the Arawak Indians—called the island Quisqueya or Hayti ("The Land of the Mountains"). Between 1492 and 1697, when the Spanish governed the entire island, it was known as Hispaniola. From 1697 until 1804, the French ruled the island's western half, naming this territory Saint Domingue, while the Spanish retained control of the eastern districts, known as Santo Domingo. In 1804, following the expulsion of white settlers and soldiers from Saint Domingue, Jean-Jacques Dessalines proclaimed the independent republic of Haiti.

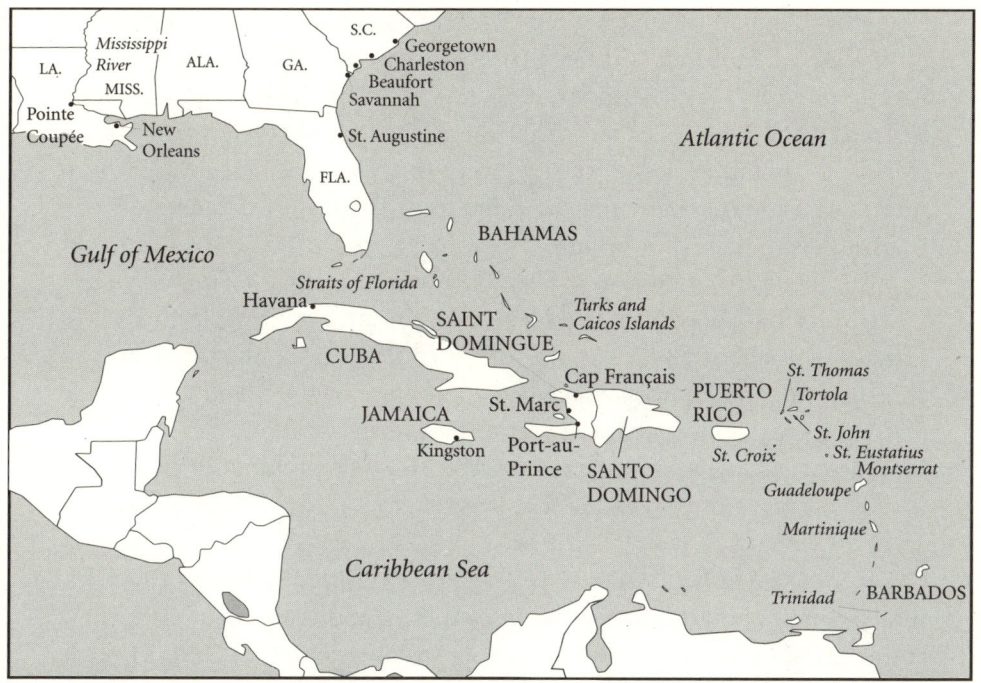

The Caribbean Basin at the End of the Eighteenth Century

a Charleston-based slave trader and mariner, purchased him in the market in the island's port town of Charlotte Amalie in 1781 does Denmark Vesey first emerge in the historical record.

If Vesey had been born in Africa, Royal Danish African Company merchants who traded along the Gold Coast from the forts of Christianborg and Frederiksborg may have bought him from Akan or Asante traders before transporting him to the Danish West Indies. Although a majority of enslaved Africans purchased by Danish slaveholders came from these trading posts on the Gulf of Guinea, others originated from elsewhere in Atlantic Africa, resulting in a rich ethnic mix on Saint Thomas and the neighboring islands. Moravian missionary Christian Georg Oldendorp, who arrived on Saint Thomas in 1761, noted that many slaves came from the hinterlands around Loango, a port from which traders often shipped enslaved Africans from the Kingdom of the Kongo to the New World.[35] Oldendorp also identified sev-

---

35. On the Danish trade, see Paiewonsky, *Eyewitness Accounts of Slavery*, 65; Winsnes, *Letters on West Africa and the Slave Trade*; and Gobel, "Danish Shipping to the Caribbean and Guinea," 103–31. On Saint Thomas, see Neville A. T. Hall, *Slave Society in the Danish West Indies* and "Slavery in Three West Indian Towns," 17–38; and Rogozinski, *Brief History of the Caribbean*, 80–81.

eral other ethnic groups on Saint Thomas, including Fulani, Mandingo, Amina, Akim, Igbo, and Yoruba, that had been drawn from the vast region stretching from the Senegal River to the Bight of Benin. The arrival of enslaved Africans from other Caribbean islands to Saint Thomas only increased the island's ethnic diversity. Accordingly, even if Vesey was born in Africa, we cannot assume that he came from the main catchment area of Danish slave traders on the Gulf of Guinea.[36]

Vesey alternatively may have been born a slave on Saint Thomas or another West Indian island. The local trade in enslaved people thrived in Charlotte Amalie as its merchants purchased slaves from one island only to sell them to another, occasionally keeping some for the island's own labor force. Knowing so little about Vesey's origins raises yet another problem. We should not assume that he was of purely African descent; although rather unlikely, it is remotely possible that he was the son of a white man and an enslaved woman. Whether born in Guinea, Angola, or in the Caribbean, however, he spent his formative years among enslaved workers whose cultural resources came directly from the traditions and practices of the various ethnic groups of Atlantic Africa. As the slave population of Saint Thomas easily outnumbered its white community—about four thousand enslaved Africans lived among just four hundred Europeans in the mid-1760s—ethnic African customs largely retained their integrity.[37]

When Joseph Vesey dropped anchor in Charlotte Amalie's harbor in 1781 to purchase slaves, the island's population had grown slightly, but the ratio between free and enslaved people remained about the same. Although most slaves worked on the island's seventy or so sugar and coffee plantations, nearly 40 percent of them lived in the port town, working on its waterfront as stevedores, cart drivers, and ship workers. Like the population of the countryside, a majority of the port's inhabitants was enslaved. As a young boy, Vesey may have been a field hand, becoming familiar with the disciplined order of plantation agriculture, or he may have lived in town, working as either a domestic servant or an apprentice to a trade.[38]

With its excellent harbor and strategic location in the Anegada Passage, a major trade route between the Atlantic Ocean and the Caribbean archipelago, Charlotte Amalie soon emerged as a leading port for merchants

36. Neville A. T. Hall, *Slave Society in the Danish West Indies*, 71–72.
37. See Highfield, "Danish Atlantic and West Indian Slave Trade," 11–32.
38. On the population of Saint Thomas, see Johansen, "Demographic Arguments to Abolish the Danish Slave Trade," 221–30; Green-Pederson, "Slave Demography in the Danish West Indies," 231–57; Neville A. T. Hall, *Slave Society in the Danish West Indies*, 5. See also Tyson and Highfield, eds., *The Kamina Folk*.

transporting slaves, sugar, and other commodities throughout the region. Declared a free port for vessels from all nations by Danish monarch Frederik V in 1764, the town became a place where "people of every colour speaking in almost every language" gathered to buy and sell, gossip and socialize. Drawn to the port's commercial opportunities, Joseph Vesey sailed from the small port of Suffolk on the Massachusetts coast, purchasing some 390 slaves that he intended to sell in Cap Français (located on Saint Domingue's north coast and known colloquially as Le Cap and later as Cap Haïtien), where he hoped to take advantage of the high prices that slaves fetched in its markets. Among the enslaved men and women Captain Vesey bought and put aboard the *Prospect* was a young boy about fifteen years old who unknowingly had just encountered the man who would soon become his master.[39]

Apparently struck by the young boy's "beauty, alertness and intelligence," the crew called him "by way of distinction *Telemaque*," gave him decent clothing, and allowed him to move freely around the ship as it made the short passage to the Caribbean's most prosperous plantation colony. Unlike the other slaves aboard, Telemaque apparently did not have to suffer in shackles in the hold. Remaining on deck, he perhaps assisted the sixty-man crew in the hard work of sailing the two-masted brigantine *Prospect*. Although called Telemaque on this voyage and during his years as a slave in Charleston, he eventually became known as "*Denmark*, or sometimes *Telmak*." How the crew stumbled on the name "Telemaque" remains another mystery of his early life. Like many owners who named their slaves after figures from ancient history and classical literature, Captain Vesey or his crew may have been inspired by *The Iliad*, an archetypal story about seafaring in which Odysseus and Penelope's son is named Telemachus. Alternatively, they may have taken the name from eighteenth-century English novelist Tobias Smollett's *The Adventures of Telemachus, the Son of Ulysses*, a translation of a popular French rendition of the classical tale. That he later called himself "Denmark" may reflect his acknowledgment of his purchase in a Danish colony or, as Kennedy and Parker suggest, the evolution of his name "by gradual corruption, among the Negroes" to either Denmark or

---

39. Paiewonsky, *Eyewitness Accounts of Slavery*, 66. According to Charleston intendant James Hamilton, Vesey was born around 1767; see Hamilton, *Account of the Late Intended Insurrection*, 17. On slave life on Saint Thomas, see Neville A. T. Hall, "Slaves Use of Their 'Free Time,'" 335–44, and "Maritime Maroons," 387–400. The port of Charlotte Amalie was a major hub of the northeastern Caribbean. About 39 percent of the island's slave population lived in the city, and more than 70 percent of its population was enslaved. See Olwig, *Cultural Adaptation and Resistance on St. John*. On slave prices in Saint Domingue, see Rotberg, *Haiti*, 40.

Telmak. Named after a hero from a mythic tale of adventure and daring, the young boy commenced his own odyssey through the plantation societies of the Atlantic world.[40]

Sailing along Saint Domingue's northern coast toward Le Cap, Telemaque perhaps watched the fires and smoke rise from the boiling houses of the Plaine du Nord's sugar plantations as he stood on the *Prospect*'s deck. Dominating the landscape, these estates with their armies of "Africans working in cadence" in the cane fields had turned this region into the island's most profitable land, generating substantial profits for their owners.[41] By the 1780s, the planters of Saint Domingue were widely regarded as the most efficient and, in some circles, the most ruthless in the Caribbean, producing about two-fifths of the world's sugar and half the world's coffee. The majority of the island's population was enslaved: by 1789, its 465,000 slaves easily outnumbered the 30,000 whites and 27,500 free people of color. Making landfall at Le Cap—a city of about 50,000 people—Captain Vesey sold his cargo of slaves and bade farewell to Telemaque amid its crowded wharves. While his crew enjoyed the diversions of the city, including taverns, billiard halls, and brothels, as well as markets selling everything from pots and pans to parakeets and monkeys, the captain reprovisioned his ship, preparing to set sail again.[42]

After entering the island's labor force of nearly half a million slaves, Telemaque again vanishes from the record.[43] As the vast majority of the forty thousand slaves who were imported annually cultivated or processed cane, Telemaque was probably purchased for field labor, although the name of his new owner and his new work assignment remain unknown. Some circumstantial evidence, as we shall see later, suggests that he may have become

---

40. Hamilton, *Account of the Late Intended Insurrection*, 17. In 1787, a black man named Telemaque was arrested along with his associate Jerome for holding large, nighttime meetings with plantation slaves in Saint Domingue's northern provinces at which they distributed magical objects and demanded independence. See Fick, *Making of Haiti*, 74–75. Carrying a cargo of slaves, a ship called *The Telemachus* dropped anchor in Charleston harbor in early 1748. See Henry Laurens to James Pardoe, 21 February 1748, in Hamer et al., *Papers of Henry Laurens*, 1:213; see also *Charleston Gazette*, 6 August 1750; and Kennedy and Parker, *Official Report*, 160.

41. Saint-Méry cited in Stoddard, *French Revolution in San Domingo*, 50; Parham, *My Odyssey*, 23.

42. Herbert Klein, *African Slavery in Latin American*, 188. On Le Cap, see Saint-Méry, *A Civilization That Perished*, 93–106; Perkins, *Reminiscences of the Insurrection in St. Domingo*, 61, cited in Ott, *Haitian Revolution*, 6. After the Haitian Revolution, Cap Français or Le Cap became known as Cap Haïtien.

43. See Rogozinski, *Brief History of the Caribbean*, 163; see also Geggus, "Sugar and Coffee Cultivation," 73–100.

a house slave, working among "the crowds" of enslaved men and women who served in the households of the island's planters, attending to their every need.

The thousands of enslaved Africans who grew cane and turned it into sugar endured the harsh discipline of planters and overseers. Toiling at the backbreaking tasks of planting and cutting cane, and risking serious injuries from working in the mill and boiling house, enslaved field hands labored long hours under "the merciless eye of the plantation steward." Demanding a punishing pace, these men delivered "harsh blows to those who seemed too weary to sustain the pace. . . . [N]one escaped the crack of the whip if they could not keep up."[44] Even if Telemaque did not work in the fields, he would soon have become familiar with the brutal and unyielding work routine that turned Saint Domingue, known by planters and merchants as "the Pearl of the Antilles," into the most dynamic plantation economy in the French Caribbean.

Telemaque may possibly have been introduced to voodoo here. A syncretic form of religion, the voodoo that developed on Saint Domingue emerged as the linguistic, religious, pharmacological, and performative traditions of slaves, drawn primarily from Dahomey, Yoruba, and the Kongo, became increasingly intertwined, creating new beliefs and practices in the process. More precisely, *rada* rituals, which sought to effect reconciliation, originated with the peoples of Lower Guinea while *petro* practices, associated with healing and attacking evil, arrived with Kongo slaves, who constituted the bulk of the Plaine du Nord's plantation workers. These traditions formed the panoply of religious and magical beliefs for the island's slaves, becoming a vital and creative expression of autonomy for enslaved Africans and offering psychological liberation from the terrors of the plantation order.[45]

The central place of voodoo in the lives of these slaves in addition to the enormous influence wielded by *hougans*, the voodoo priests who, wrote French official Médéric Louis Elie Moreau de Saint-Méry in the late 1780s, "know all and can do anything," quickly led to its suppression by planters in the early 1700s. Forced to worship secretly, slaves regularly gathered in the cane breaks, woods and creeks far from the plantation houses and the routes of the slave patrols. Hidden away among the trees, the assembly would begin a series of tightly choreographed dances designed to unite people from different ethnicities. Moving to the sound of drums and other percussive

44. Girod-Chantrans, *Voyage d'un Suisse*, cited in Fick, *Making of Haiti*, 28.
45. For a discussion of voodoo, see Metraux, *Voodoo in Haiti*, 25–57; Fick, *Making of Haiti*, 40–55; Robert Farris Thompson, *Flash of the Spirit*, 164–65; and James, *The Black Jacobins*.

instruments fashioned from gourds and hollowed logs, participants, aided by a potent cane-based drink known as *tafia*, soon entered an altered state. In their "transports of frenzy," noted Saint-Méry, who claimed to have witnessed these events unobserved, the dancers "spin around ceaselessly . . . and utter shouts," calling on their gods for protection, cures from sickness, and revenge against their owners.[46]

These ceremonies came to a dramatic climax when the *hougans* and their entourage slaughtered a goat or fowl, consuming its blood in an act of communion. Besides inaugurating new members into voodoo, such rituals were also designed to "bind the lips of the observers, who promised to suffer death rather than divulge anything." At other celebrations, participants called for a violent end to slavery, promising "to destroy the whites and all that they possess; let us die rather than fail to keep this vow."[47] Not until August 1791, however, did large numbers of slaves on the Plaine du Nord begin to act on that vow, rebelling in large numbers, burning plantations, destroying crops, and killing their masters. Even though no direct evidence links Telemaque to voodoo ceremonies during his sojourn on Saint Domingue, he possibly recognized the importance of supernatural forces and ritual for forging a sense of collectivity, enjoining people to silence, and sustaining an identity independent of slavery rooted in African tradition.

Voodoo was not the only vehicle that enabled slaves on Saint Domingue to maintain an identity independent of their bound condition. Like virtually every Caribbean slave society, the slaves of Saint Domingue established maroon communities, a form of resistance whereby enslaved men and women absented themselves from their owners' control, escaping from the discipline of the plantation to pursue lives as they wished. These communities usually consisted of small villages located in sparsely populated forest regions or inaccessible hill regions in the interior. To supplement their subsistence economy, maroons invaded "the plains from time to time," mounting raids from their secluded settlements to take supplies and slaves and "spreading alarm and causing great danger to the inhabitants" as they swept down from their redoubts. As the thunderclouds of political unrest gathered over Saint Domingue in 1789, generated by the outbreak of revolution in France that same year and by constant squabbles among the island's *petit blancs* (a broad social group that embraced tradesmen, artisans, and overseers, as well as "the dregs of waterfront life" who made up the middling and lower orders), *grands blancs* (the ruling class comprising large planters, merchants, and top colonial administrators), and *gens de coleur* (free people

---

46. Saint-Méry, *A Civilization That Perished*, 6–7.
47. Ibid., 4; James, *Black Jacobins*, 18.

of color), maroon villages emerged as sites of revolutionary activity. Not surprisingly, the massive slave rebellions that exploded across the Plaine du Nord in August 1791 largely originated in these communities.[48]

Although these camps played an important role in the island's history, only a handful of slaves escaped from their estates to become members of maroon bands. The vast majority of field workers remained enslaved on their plantations, choosing to struggle against the repression and terror of the plantation order through prosaic forms of resistance, ranging from the theft of food or destruction of property to the murder of an owner or overseer. These everyday forms of resistance along with the powerful oppositional currents of voodoo and marronage, prompted French radical Honoré-Gabriel Mirabeau to observe dryly how the island's slaveholders slept "*au pied du Vésuve* (at the foot of Vesuvius)." The attempt by maroon leader François Makandal to poison every white person on the island in 1757 confirmed that planters daily walked "on powder kegs."[49] Although Telemaque did not witness the massive rebellions of 1791 that heralded the protracted struggle involving planters, free people of color, slaves, and several European armies, he doubtless saw and perhaps even participated in the various forms of resistance in which his fellow workers engaged.

Shortly after Telemaque's sale in Le Cap's slave markets in 1781, his new owner diagnosed him as "unsound, and subject to epileptic fits." That his owner even sought out medical advice suggests that the young slave may have been a household worker rather than a field hand, who probably would have been left to suffer. Although a physician diagnosed Telemaque as an epileptic, no direct evidence exists to show that he suffered from this affliction. Like many slaves who affected sickness to avoid work, Telemaque very probably feigned fits. He alternatively may have suffered from seizures as a consequence of participating in voodoo ceremonies. In Jamaica, a planter encountered a slave with similar symptoms. Although a white doctor believed that poison caused these fits, the slave remained firmly convinced that he had been "struck down by the duppy [ghost] of a white person not long deceased, whom he had offended, and that these repeated fainting-fits were

---

48. Derived from the French word *marron*, the term *marronage* refers to escaped slaves who, in many instances in Latin America and the Caribbean, established their own communities which ranged in number from several dozen to several thousand. See Fick, *Making of Haiti*, 49–57, 275; Price, *Maroon Societies*, 1–30. For their importance on Saint Domingue, see Geggus, "On the Eve of the Haitian Revolution," 112–28, and *Slavery, War, and Revolution*, 9.

49. Geggus, *Slavery, War, and Revolution*, 1; Coulon, *Rapport sur les Troubles de Santo Domingo*, cited in Stoddard, *French Revolution in San Domingo*, 150; de Vaissière, *St. Domingue*, cited in Fick, *Making of Haiti*, 74.

the consequence of that ghostly blow."[50] Whatever may have caused these fits in Telemaque, no reports indicate that he ever suffered any more attacks.

Returning to Saint Domingue at some point in 1781 or 1782, Joseph Vesey found himself in the possession of Telemaque again. Rather than sell a slave regarded as damaged goods to another customer, the captain incorporated the youth into his own crew. Now back among the men with whom he had previously struck up a friendship, Telemaque became a cabin boy aboard Captain Vesey's ship. How many voyages Telemaque made alongside his owner remains an open question. As Captain Vesey did not end his sailing career for another eight or nine years, Telemaque probably spent a significant time at sea. Instead of facing a short and brutal life as a plantation hand, he now entered the world of deep-water mariners, learning their craft and adapting to their customs as he sailed to the port towns of the Atlantic world. Departing Le Cap aboard the *Prospect*, Telemaque left an island that a decade later would erupt in violence as the shock waves of revolution in France hit Saint Domingue's deeply divided social and racial order.[51]

Telemaque now followed in the footsteps of thousands of men of African descent, both free and enslaved, who worked as sailors in the eighteenth-century Atlantic. "Black sailors," as historian W. Jeffrey Bolster has noted, "established themselves as a visible presence in every North Atlantic seaport and plantation roadstead between 1740 and 1865." Visiting the lowcountry in the 1790s, the French aristocrat Duc de La Rochefoucauld-Liancourt tried to assess the number of black mariners who sailed in and out of Charleston as he watched the daily activity on the wharves along the Cooper River. He claimed that local slaves often comprised a majority of the crews on "coasters and such ships as trade within the district of Charleston," while free blacks from northern ports often constituted at least a third of the crews on larger, oceangoing vessels, with American or European sailors making up the remainder. The Frenchman's estimate about the number of free black sailors from northern towns appears to have been fairly accurate. Bolster has concluded that these men "signed aboard ship in disproportionately large numbers," calculating that "Afro-American men filled between seventeen

---

50. Hamilton, *Account of the Late Intended Insurrection*, 17; Lewis, "Journal of a West Indian Proprietor," 143. During her travels though the English Caribbean, Janet Schaw also commented on slaves who were "very nervous and subject to fits of madness," noting how these people regarded themselves victims of witchcraft. See Schaw, *Journal of a Lady of Quality*, 128.

51. There is little information on the length of time spent at sea by Telemaque, but Douglas Egerton suggests that it may have been as little as nine months. Personal correspondence with author.

percent and twenty two percent of Philadelphia's seafaring jobs between 1800 and 1820." Although La Rochefoucauld did not include those enslaved men owned by captains of blue-water ships in his calculations, a number of slaves, including Telemaque himself, would have worked on these vessels. Unfortunately, we do not know how many enslaved Charlestonians worked as deep-sea sailors in the 1780s and 1790s. Many ships sailing out of Charleston would have also been manned by sailors recruited from a number of Atlantic ports, resulting in ships' companies that were interracial, international, and cross-cultural in character.[52]

The autobiography of Olaudah Equiano, an Igbo man originally from the villages around the Niger Delta at the eastern end of the Gulf of Guinea, provides a lively and vivid account of the experiences of such workers. Enslaved in the late 1750s when he was about ten years old, Equiano spent several decades as a sailor before he purchased his freedom and settled in England. During his years at sea, he sailed to nearly every corner of the Atlantic world as well as into the Mediterranean, leading a life of great drama that included nearly drowning in the surf off the Caribbean island of Montserrat, encountering Indians along Central America's Mosquito coast, and watching fireworks burst over Charleston as its residents celebrated the repeal of the Stamp Act in 1766. Equiano also survived the considerable dangers of maritime life, including violent seas, shipwreck, disease, and unscrupulous masters. His travels and experiences endowed him with a sense of worldliness, giving him practical knowledge as well as the confidence to speak publicly against the slave trade and to write his autobiography.

Working aboard Captain Vesey's ship may have fostered the development of similar qualities in Telemaque. Apart from his duties as a cabin boy, Telemaque doubtless spent many hours on deck or aloft, repairing rigging, furling, reefing, and setting sails, and keeping watch as his master's ship traversed the oceans. At some point during these years, he gained an education, learning how to read and write English, possibly acquiring "a smattering of arithmetic, as far as the rule of three," as did Equiano. As he became schooled in the art of seamanship, Telemaque would have picked up the distinctive argot of sailors and other European languages commonly spoken in the Atlantic basin. Fluent in French, a skill that later enabled him to talk with refugee slaves from Saint Domingue who landed in Charleston in the early 1790s, he also spoke English and likely knew some Danish from his years on Saint Thomas. He also picked up Gullah, the distinctive language spoken by slaves in lowcountry South Carolina, and he may have known the

---

52. Bolster, *Black Jacks*, 4, and " 'To Feel Like a Man,' " 1174; La Rochefoucauld-Liancourt, *Travels through the United States*, 1:630.

creole spoken on Saint Thomas that drew its vocabulary and syntax from Dutch, German, and African sources.[53]

These seafaring years probably shaped Telemaque's political consciousness. Working with sailors from every corner of the Atlantic during the last decades of the eighteenth century, he would have received an education in the politics of radicalism and revolution. The Caribbean during these times of great upheaval was, as historian Julius Scott has observed, "a landscape of imperial soldiers and warships, plantations and sugar mills, masters and slaves." To this list, we might add those men who forged a critique of this particular political and economic order, creating an alternative tradition in the process. Sailors, as historian Marcus Rediker has persuasively shown, constituted a militant vanguard among working people, challenging arbitrary authority, exchanging news, imparting opinions, and formulating ideas as they worked on deck or gathered in waterfront taverns. Mariners from northern European ports labored alongside men from coastal towns and villages throughout the Americas as well as drinking and socializing with them in grogshops. Besides transporting sugar, slaves, and other tropical commodities around the Atlantic, these ships also constituted "an extraordinary forcing house for internationalism [as] African, Briton, quashee, American, not to mention Portuguese, Lascar, and Spanish would have cooperated, for their lives depended on it, in the rigging and the decks."[54]

The ethnic diversity of crews and the collaborative nature of shipboard work likely influenced Telemaque's politics in several ways. Manned by sailors from many countries, these ships were, as cultural critic Paul Gilroy has noted, "micro-systems of linguistic and political hybridity" in which the politics of rebellion, revolution, and emancipation traveled. In some cases, these ships literally carried the news, taking newspapers, letters, and journals from one port to another, spreading word of dramatic events in the process. Had Telemaque acquired newspapers printed in Caribbean port towns, he could have read about "the convulsions in France" in late 1789 as well as the unrest that these events had inspired among slaves in the French Caribbean. He could also have learned about the crew of the *Bounty* who had mutinied in the Pacific Ocean or about debates in the English parliament on the

---

53. Equiano, *Narrative of the Life of Olaudah Equiano*, 83. On Equiano, see Potkay and Burr, *Black Atlantic Writers*; Philip D. Morgan, "British Encounters with Africans and African-Americans," 157–59. For details on creole in the Danish West Indies, see Oldendorp, *History of the Mission of the Evangelical Brethren*, 154.

54. Julius S. Scott, "Common Wind," 5; Rediker, *Between the Devil and the Deep Blue Sea* and "'A Motley Crew of Rebels,'" 155–98; Linebaugh, "All the Atlantic Mountains Shook," 209.

abolition of the slave trade. For Telemaque and his shipmates, news picked up in portside taverns or from newspapers provided them with food for thought and conversation in the fo'c'sle.[55]

The organization of work and authority on board ship gave the Atlantic world's radical political ideologies added resonance. The safe passage of any vessel invariably depended on the performance of arduous and dangerous tasks in a disciplined and collective manner. In teams of four or five, ordinary seamen worked with considerable energy as they climbed rigging, set sails, raised and lowered anchors, and tied down cargo in the holds. The collective character of this work in addition to its attendant risks helped to foster a sense of solidarity among deck hands. As they labored at these tasks, many tars fell from the rigging to their deaths, were swept overboard or suffered severe injuries as unsecured tackle and ropes fell on them. Mariners also faced the perils of turbulent seas and violent storms during which, as veteran Charleston mariner Thomas Jervey recalled, "the wind and the sea roar'd dreadfully" and a ship might easily be "turn'd over like a top." Equiano, too, found himself fighting for his life when his master's ship ran aground on the Bahama Bank, nearly drowning in the towering waves that crashed "with unremiting fury" against the rocks. Of the thousands of men who went out to sea in ships, a large number never returned.[56]

Sailors who worked aboard slave ships faced the additional threat by the men and women who lay shackled below deck. While at sea, Equiano witnessed "cruelties of every kind . . . exercised on my unhappy fellow slaves," including rape and whippings, inflicted by fellow crew members. As a mariner on a ship that transported slaves as well as other goods, Telemaque possibly heard stories about enslaved Africans who rebelled as their homeland disappeared over the horizon, trying to overpower their European captors and return to the shore. In one episode in 1787, a cargo of slaves sailing from the Danish trading fort of Christianborg to Saint Croix attacked the ship's company with any weapon that came readily to hand, including shackles and chains that they had "hammered off" their legs. After a pitched battle that lasted over two hours, the crew finally regained control of the ship, but not before thirty-four slaves "sprang overboard into the sea." Investigating this revolt, the captain discovered that an Afro-Caribbean sailor, deeply in debt, had told the slaves if they "should beat the Whites to death,"

---

55. Gilroy, *Black Atlantic*, 12; *Bermuda Gazette*, 10 October 1789 and 6 November 1790.

56. For a technical discussion on the operation of sailing ships, see Harland, *Seamanship in the Age of Sail*; Louis P. Jervey, "Thomas Hall Jervey," 140–41; and Equiano, *Narrative of the Life of Olaudah Equiano*, 127. For a riveting account of life and death at sea, see Sebastian Junger, *The Perfect Storm*.

he would then sail the ship back to Africa for a fee. Although no evidence exists to indicate that slaves carried aboard the *Prospect* ever rebelled, Telemaque, like Equiano, doubtless questioned the morality of this dreadful commercial enterprise.[57]

This shipboard culture also fostered an environment in which sailors of African descent experienced a degree of equality with fellow mariners that they rarely encountered on land. Equiano believed his "condition much mended" when he became a sailor, noting that he "had sails to lie on . . . plenty of good victuals to eat" as he lived and worked among men who "used me very kindly, quite to the contrary to what I had seen of any white people before." Even on land, mariners appeared to adopt the same attitude toward enslaved people. James Kelly, an Irish wharf owner in Jamaica, commented on the ease with which visiting sailors traded with local slaves, exchanging food, news, and stories "on the most amicable terms." Characterized by "mutual confidences and familiarity," these interactions contrasted sharply with dealings between "slave and resident white." In the presence of sailors, Kelly concluded, "the Negro feels like a man." In addition, slave mariners also agreed that, as black seaman George Teamoh noted in his autobiography, "to be carried on the 'high seas' was also tantamount to giving the slave his freedom." The ship, as one historian has noted, provided the black man with "a unique workplace where his color might be less a determinant of his daily life and duties than elsewhere."[58]

Seafaring slaves were the most cosmopolitan and autonomous of bound laborers in the New World. Sailing around the Atlantic basin, they not only gained a sophisticated sense of worldliness, but they also drew from their experiences to fashion distinct occupational identities. Isolated from the bulk of other laboring people by their travels, mariners spoke a language rooted in nautical terms, decorated their bodies with tattoos, and wore distinctive clothes, creating a unique seafaring culture. The sense of pride and independence that derived from his years at sea may have imparted a sense of self-confidence and powerful affect that Telemaque was described as

---

57. Equiano, *Narrative of the Life of Olaudah Equiano*, 93; Winsnes, *Letters on West Africa and the Slave Trade*, 178–80. For a compelling fictional account of a slave uprising aboard ship, see Barry Unsworth's Booker Prize–winning novel, *Sacred Hunger*. The most famous rebellion of this type, and now the subject of a film directed by Steven Spielberg, remains the uprising by enslaved men aboard the *Amistad* in 1839. See Howard Jones, *Mutiny on the Amistad*.

58. Equiano, *Narrative of the Life of Olaudah Equiano*, 6; Kelly, *Voyage to Jamaica*, cited in Brathwaite, *Development of Creole Society in Jamaica*, 30; Boney et al., *Autobiography of George Teamoh*, 96; Bolster, *Black Jacks*, 75.

radiating later in his life. Moreover, he could draw from his experiences of strange and exotic places as well as his seafaring adventures to assume a knowing and worldly wise persona, enabling him to speak authoritatively on various topics. Again, the parallel with Equiano's years before the mast are instructive. A capable mariner and a man whom his owner could rely on at the dockside to receive and deliver cargo and to purchase stores, he also acquired enough confidence to address a Quaker meeting in Philadelphia in 1785 and to petition England's Queen Charlotte on behalf of "the wretched Africans" brutalized by the slave trade three years later.[59]

The self-contained wooden worlds in which Telemaque and Equiano sailed were the exclusive province of men who found themselves bound together not just by the demands of seafaring, but also by their gender. Sailing "made men" just as much as these men made maritime culture. During his time aboard the *Industrious Bee*, Equiano struck up a close friendship with a young American sailor named Richard Baker, who became his "constant companion and instructor." Not only did these men depend on each other during storms and other moments of danger at sea, but they probably spent time together in taverns, billiard halls, and other places of recreation. Toughness and bold exploits all contributed to a reputation for manliness that African American sailors sought. The masculine cast of shipboard life possibly influenced Telemaque's decision later in life to recruit only men to his cause.[60]

Sailing throughout the Caribbean, black mariners also became familiar with the lives led by free black and enslaved men and women in port towns such as Bridgetown, Havana, Le Cap, and Kingston. On one Sunday afternoon in Kingston, for example, Equiano looked on as "each different nation of Africa" gathered on the outskirts of town "to meet and dance after the manner of their own country." Witnessing a funeral, the slave sailor watched as mourners placed food and tobacco in the grave "in the same manner as in Africa." Atlantic ports and their taverns provided ideal settings where free and enslaved mariners might earn money by selling "trifling perquisites" acquired during their voyages. On one voyage, Equiano parlayed his "very small capital" of a half a bit into a dollar, trading some glass tumblers purchased in Saint Eustatius for a jug of Geneva gin that he sold in Monserrat for a tidy profit. From these types of transactions, Equiano became "the master of a few pounds," eventually accumulating enough cash to purchase

---

59. Equiano, *Narrative of the Life of Olaudah Equiano*, 92, 186, 192.

60. Creighton, "American Mariners and the Rites of Manhood," 145, and "Women and Men in American Whaling," 195–218; Gorn, "Seafaring Engendered," 219–25; Equiano, *Narrative of the Life of Olaudah Equiano*, 61.

his freedom, which he did in July 1766. Although Telemaque would gain his freedom in a rather different way, he likely engaged in similar pursuits, perhaps using his earnings to follow his fellow crew members to the taverns and other places of entertainment that they patronized in port.[61]

These coastal towns probably played as important a role in Telemaque's life as did his experiences at sea. Like the vessels that dropped anchor in their harbors, these towns were also crucibles of interethnic and racial contact. Commenting on the men and women who inhabited the waterfront in Kingston, Jamaica, Lord Balcarres, an imperial official, saw them as dangerous criminals and radicals. "Turbulent people of all nations," he observed, "engaged in Illicit Trade" and embraced "the general leveling spirit" that prevailed among the city's "lower orders." Although Balcarres found these rowdy and disorderly places rather alarming, Telemaque would likely have felt more at home in the Atlantic basin's "radical underworld," brushing shoulders with the sailors, pirates, and escaped slaves who nourished traditions of popular politics and dissent in the face of the plantation order.[62]

These seaports also enjoyed a reputation among black mariners as "asylums for runaway negroes." In 1796, for example, three enslaved mariners who hailed from various Atlantic ports decided to desert the *Friendship* as it lay in Charleston harbor, taking "the canoe that crosses the River Ashley" and heading for Savannah. Losing himself in the bustle and clamor of waterfront districts, an enslaved sailor determined to jump ship could claim to be a free man, establishing himself among the port's free black community. Alternatively, he could obtain passage on a ship departing for another port city, such as Boston or Philadelphia, where he might easily pass as free. Still other enslaved people who sought their freedom became, in the historian Neville Hall's words, "maritime maroons," seeking refuge in small settlements in inaccessible coastal regions or sailing in stolen or hand-built boats between the islands. Drawing on the radical ideas that circulated around coastal towns and villages, several "maritime maroons," including former slave Boukman Dutty, would later play leading roles in Caribbean uprisings. Dutty became a key figure in the 1791 slave rebellion on Saint Domingue after he had made his escape from Jamaica.[63]

We know as little about Telemaque's owner as we do about the cabin boy

61. Equiano, *Narrative of the Life of Olaudah Equiano*, 85, 102, 105, 145.

62. Lord Balcarres, cited in Julius S. Scott, "Common Wind," 33. The term "radical underworld" is from McCalman; see his *Radical Underworld*, 2. See also C. L. R. James, *Mariners, Renegades, and Castaways*.

63. Carrion, *Puerto Rico and the Non-Hispanic Caribbean*, 81; Bolster, *Black Jacks*, 23; Neville A. T. Hall, "Maritime Maroons," 387–400; Julius S. Scott, "Common Wind," 81.

himself. Born in 1747 into a seafaring family from Warwick, a parish located in the southwestern corner of the island of Bermuda, Joseph Vesey spent about thirty of his eighty-eight years at sea. Growing up on an island where seven thousand Europeans lived among five thousand enslaved African men and women, who worked primarily in maritime trades or as fishermen, Vesey would have been acquainted with the cultural practices of enslaved Afro-Caribbean men and women. Spending his early days at sea aboard the *Molly*, a vessel captained by family member Abraham Vesey that sailed throughout the Caribbean and along the North American seaboard, Joseph often visited Charleston, trading in slaves and other commodities with low-country merchants.[64]

With the outbreak of war between Britain and the American colonies, Joseph Vesey took up arms for the revolutionary cause. Sailing from Charleston to Philadelphia in early 1776, he helped to recruit men for the small naval force that the Continental Congress was struggling to assemble. Returning to South Carolina, Vesey's ship ran aground after a British frigate pursued him along the North Carolina coast. This was the first of his many naval adventures. Successfully evading capture, he spent the next two years in the Continental navy, participating in several engagements as he pursued Royal Naval frigates stationed off the eastern seaboard under the command of John Paul Jones. After obtaining a letter of marque from the Continental Congress that entitled him to plunder British ships in the name of the United States, Vesey became part-owner and master of the *Adriana*, a sloop armed with fifteen guns and manned by forty-seven sailors between 1778 and 1781.[65]

Taking command of the *Prospect* in early 1781, Joseph Vesey sailed from the small Massachusetts port town of Suffolk for Saint Thomas, where he purchased Telemaque and other slaves. Making Charleston his home port in the 1780s, Captain Vesey bought property in the city, married, and raised a family. With his business partners, he leased his vessel as well as his expertise as a mariner to city merchants, advertising that he would sail "to any West Indian island" in pursuit of commercial opportunity. For the next decade,

---

64. Henry Laurens to Martin & Stephens, 11 February 1764, in Hamer et al., *Papers of Henry Laurens*, 4:167–71.

65. Issued by the government, these letters served as commissions that enabled captains of privately owned ships to engage and capture enemy vessels and their cargoes during wartime. These ships, known as privateers, played a critical role during the imperial wars of the eighteenth and nineteenth centuries, supplementing naval operations as well as disrupting commercial shipping. See Minchinton and Starkey, "Privateers Operating from the British Isles," 252–54; Middlekauf, *Glorious Cause*, 529–30; and Lofton, *Insurrection in South Carolina*, xiv.

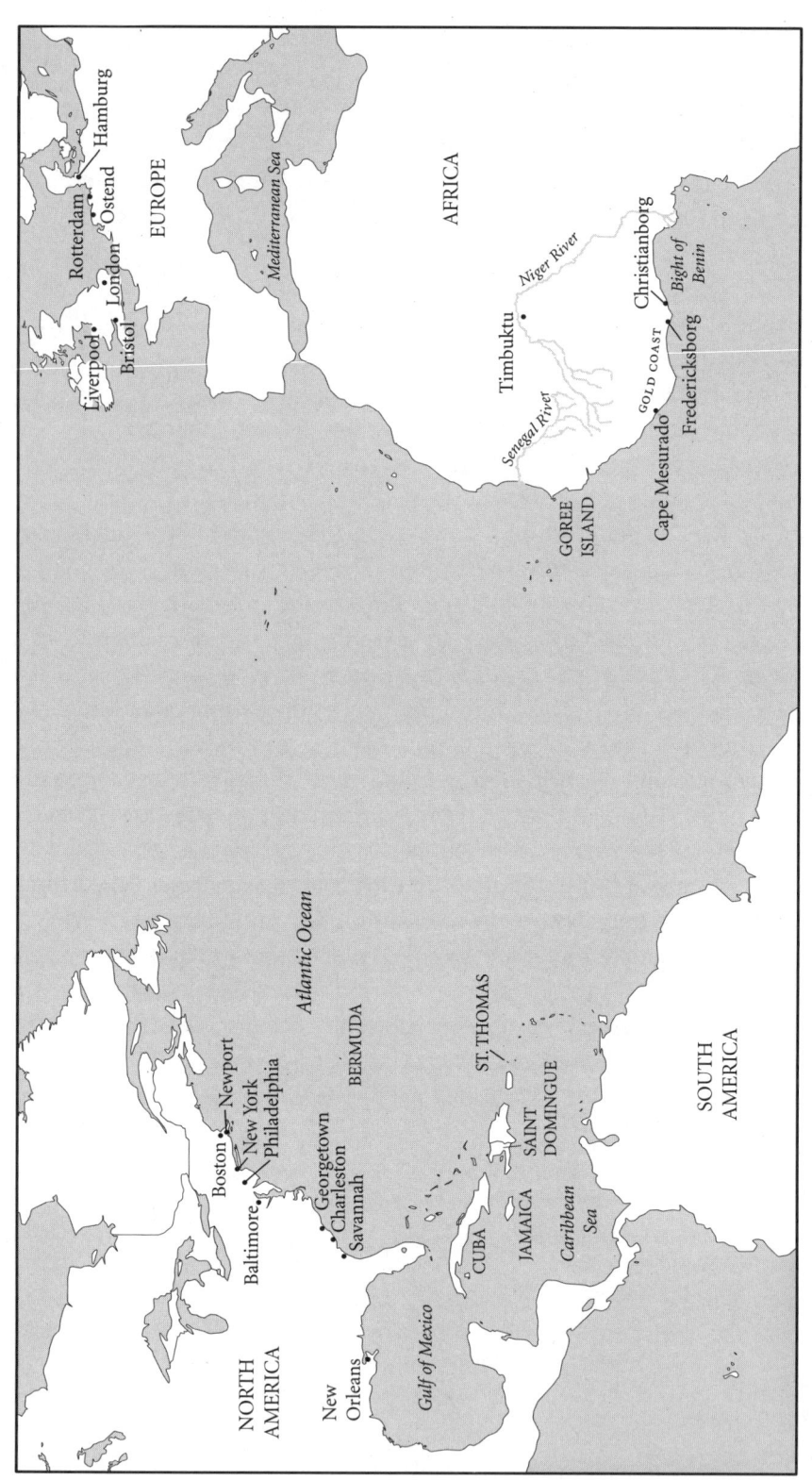

The Eighteenth-Century Atlantic World

Vesey sailed with Telemaque and the rest of his crew throughout the region, trading in a range of commodities, including salt from the Turks and Caicos Islands as well as slaves and other goods from the Caribbean and wider Atlantic world. In February 1789, Vesey sailed to several major European port cities, including London, Ostend, Rotterdam, and Hamburg. Telemaque possibly accompanied his master aboard the *Joseph and Mary* on one of the captain's last Atlantic voyages. A year later, Captain Vesey decided to leave the sea, concentrating his energies on his shore-based enterprises. The captain also threw himself into civic life, serving as president of the Charleston Marine Society and as treasurer for a committee that raised more than $12,000 to provide relief for "the unhappy sufferers from Saint Domingue," who had arrived in the city in the wake of the slave rebellions on the island.[66]

Like many men who captained their own ships, Joseph Vesey had acquired the considerable skills needed to command an oceangoing vessel from years of practical experience before the mast. Besides his knowledge of sailing and navigation, Vesey would also have established commercial relationships with merchants and traders throughout the Atlantic world. This expertise clearly paid dividends. Not only did Vesey elude capture by the Royal Navy during the War of Independence, but he also managed to survive nearly three decades at sea during a period in which ships sank with great regularity. He also appears to have been a successful trader, accumulating enough capital to invest in a ropewalk and ships' chandlery in Charleston, where he sold canvas, ropes, and other maritime equipment.

The authority that Vesey derived from his nautical skills apparently made him a competent captain and master. That Telemaque did not jump ship during his years at sea as did many free and enslaved mariners offers some slight evidence that Captain Vesey may have conducted himself in a fair manner, a speculation that his behavior on land tends to confirm. Asked by one free Afro-Bermudian, a man called John Bean, to bear witness to his status in 1794, Vesey willingly testified that the man was not a slave. Although Joseph Vesey clearly did not oppose slavery—he owned several and made his living buying and selling them—his action in this case suggests that he

---

66. On Joseph Vesey's career, see Stephen Crane to John Lofton, 27 January 1983, Denmark Vesey File, SCHS; *Charleston Evening Gazette*, 29 September 1795; and Lofton, "Denmark Vesey's Call to Arms," 397–98. Captain Vesey acted as the factor in the sale of about 100 slaves in September 1783 (see *City Gazette*, 24 September 1783); on his involvement in the Bahamian salt trade, see *Bermuda Gazette*, several issues ca. 1770–85, and *Columbian Herald*, 26 February 1789. On the trade itself, see Craton and Saunders, *Islanders in the Stream*, 1:285–88. On slavery on Bermuda, see Packwood, *Chained on the Rock*. On Captain Vesey's post-seafaring activities, see *Columbian Herald*, 16 September 1790.

opposed enslaving free blacks.⁶⁷ Still a Charleston resident in 1822, the captain, now in his mid-seventies, does not appear to have played any role in the trial of his former slave.

After establishing himself in Charleston, Joseph Vesey ran a chandlery store on East Bay Street. With his partner, he also owned and operated a ropewalk in Hampstead, a neighborhood on Charleston Neck, offering "the highest prices for clean hemp" to local farmers to supply his yard with the raw material necessary to manufacture rope. In addition, he continued to trade in various tropical commodities, including sugar, coffee, and, on one occasion, a cargo of "prize indigo" imported from the port of Saint Marc on the west coast of Saint Domingue. Although Telemaque probably spent some time working for his owner in the chandlery store or at the Hampstead ropewalk, he appears to have primarily hired out his labor as a carpenter, gaining a reputation as a man of "great strength and activity." At some point in the 1790s, Captain Vesey transferred ownership of Telemaque to Mary Clodner Vesey (also known as May Vesey), who was, according to historian John Lofton, a free woman of color who lived in the family's King Street house. That Joseph Vesey administered her estate, which included property outside Charleston, after her death at the turn of the century perhaps suggests a close relationship between the two, possibly as common-law husband and wife.⁶⁸

During the 1790s, Telemaque's earnings, often totaling $1.50 a day, supplemented the income of a household in which seven other slaves as well as a white servant and several family members lived. Experiencing a modest degree of independence as a hired artisan, he would have been able to travel widely in the city and surrounding countryside, perhaps visiting May Vesey's property. Telemaque clearly had enough money to purchase a $6 ticket in the East Bay lottery in late 1799. On November 9, the lottery's commissioners drew ticket number 1884, enriching the slave by the astounding sum of $1,500. Twenty-three years later, according to enslaved stonecutter George Evans, Vesey again purchased several lottery tickets, possibly in the "Grand Lottery for the Benefit of the South Carolina Academy of Arts" with a first

67. Petition of John Bean, 13 September 1794, General Assembly Petitions, SCDAH; see also Miscellaneous Records, 13 September 1794, vol. CCC, p. 537, ibid. See also Lofton, *Insurrection in South Carolina*, 77–78.

68. *Columbian Herald*, 21 December 1793, 1 January 1794; Hamilton, *Account of the Late Intended Insurrection*, 17. On Mary Clodner Vesey, see Lofton, *Insurrection in South Carolina*, 77; Letters of Administration, 1797–1803, Miscellaneous Records, vol. RR, p. 360, SCDAH. I am indebted to Douglas Egerton for the suggestion that May Vesey was perhaps Joseph Vesey's common-law wife.

prize of $20,000, perhaps hoping to bankroll the insurrection with any winnings. But his luck in picking winning lottery numbers had run out by 1822.[69]

Telemaque decided to use his windfall to purchase his freedom. Until the passage of a new law in 1800 that tightened up regulations governing manumission requirements, the procedure by which a slaveholder freed a slave simply required the owner to draw up a contract stating the terms under which freedom had been granted. Apart from recording the deed of manumission, the state played no role in this transaction. Accordingly, Telemaque struck his own deal for his freedom with May Vesey in private. After paying her $600 of his winnings—a sum that Kennedy and Parker claimed was "much less than his real value"—May Vesey along with Joseph Vesey, who served as a witness, signed and dated the deed that freed "from the Yoke of Servitude . . . a certain Negro man named Telemaque." On the last day of 1799, a local official recorded the manumission in his ledger, formally granting freedom to the former cabin boy, enabling him to join the nearly one thousand men and women who made up the city's community of free people of color.[70]

"AN EMPORIUM OF TRADE":
CHARLESTON AT THE TURN OF THE CENTURY

Places, Preferments bought and sold;
Houses to purchase, new and old;
Ships, shops of every shape and form,
Carriages, horses, negroes swarm.
No matter good or bad,
We'll tell you where they may be had.
—Charleston Evening Gazette, *20 August 1785*

The city through which Denmark Vesey strolled as a free man in the first weeks of January 1800 had been prospering for nearly a decade. Resulting in large measure from war in Europe and the substantial growth in cotton exports from the backcountry, the city's economy had expanded in the

---

69. On the lottery, see *City Gazette and Daily Advertiser*, 10 July 1799, 1 October 1799, 8 October 1799, 9 November 1799, 9 December 1799, and 11 December 1799; Hamilton, *Account of the Late Intended Insurrection*, 17; Testimony of George Evans, DTT, SCDAH; *Charleston Mercury*, 21 February 1822, 8 April 1822.

70. Manumission of Telemaque, 31 December 1799, Miscellaneous Records, vol. KKK, p. 427, SCDAH; Philip D. Morgan, "Black Life in Eighteenth-Century Charleston," 188.

1790s. The construction of several elegant new public buildings, including a new courthouse, the opening of the Santee Canal that linked the interior's cotton farms and plantations to the coast, and the establishment of a branch of the First Bank of the United States all testified to this affluence. Reaping the benefits of this postwar boom, Charleston's "leading citizens," noted Luigi Castiglioni at the end of the 1780s, "surpass in luxury . . . those of the other capitals in the United States." Their "manner of life, dress, equipages, [and] furniture," noted another European traveler, "denotes a higher degree of taste and love of show" than any other place that he had visited in the new republic. The quality of daily life had also improved. Charleston, noted Governor John Drayton in 1802, was "like [the] polished cities of other countries," providing its citizens with a range of amenities, including fresh water piped in from nearby Goose Creek, a pleasure garden in which patrons could listen to music or take refreshments, and a theater that offered its audiences a range of plays and other entertainments.[71]

These visible signs of prosperity masked a number of severe problems that city officials faced. Despite municipal codes that tried to limit the consumption of "strong liquor" by visiting sailors, the waterfront's taverns and alleys regularly became home to disorderly mariners, who constantly threatened public order not just by fighting and carousing, but also by providing slaves with drink. In addition to breaking up the drunken brawls of rowdy tars, city authorities had to manage a population of enslaved men and women who had little regard for the voluminous ordinances designed to regulate their behavior. In the early 1790s, the arrival of a large number of free blacks, enslaved Africans, and their owners who had fled Saint Domingue only compounded the difficulty of maintaining law and order. Beyond these concerns, city leaders also had to contend with the problems of managing a large port town in which fire and the outbreak of epidemic disease were frequent occurrences.

Of greater significance to municipal authorities was the presence of a black majority whose numbers showed no signs of falling. Charleston, observed German traveler and scientist Johann David Schoepf in 1784, "swarms with blacks, mulattoes, and mestizoes." In 1800, the combined total of free people of color (1,024 or 5 percent) and enslaved men and women (9,819 or 48 percent) slightly outnumbered the white population (9,626 or 47 percent). Between 1790 and 1810, the free black population grew dramatically, rising from 586 to 1,472 people (an increase of 151 percent), easily outstripping the increase in enslaved and white populations (52 percent and 43

---

71. Castiglioni, *Luigi Castiglioni's Viaggio*, 163; Schoepf, *Travels in the Confederation*, 2:168; Drayton, *View of South Carolina*, 224.

percent respectively) during the same period. As slaveholders manumitted only a modest number of slaves in the 1790s, both natural increase within the free black community and the arrival of hundreds of free people of color from Saint Domingue in 1793 and 1794 may account for the sharp rise in their numbers. By 1820, nearly three thousand free people of color and more than nineteen thousand slaves lived in the city and its immediate environs.[72]

To survey the topography of the city and the surrounding countryside, travelers regularly made for Saint Michael's Church. Perched high above the junction of Meeting and Broad Streets in the gallery of the 180-foot steeple, visitors could look over Charleston laid out before them, as indefatigable antebellum tourist Harriet Martineau later noted, "as a living map." Below lay a complex collection of residential neighborhoods containing modest wooden houses and elegant brick dwellings, as well as workshops and wharves, warehouses and markets, retail establishments and taverns, churches and commercial buildings. In this varied urban landscape, enslaved and free, male and female, rich and poor, native and immigrant brought the city to life, interacting on the streets, in alleyways, in the marketplace, or along the waterfront. Within these public spaces, enslaved men and women, who owned virtually nothing, daily encountered their owners and other white Charlestonians, who were not only free but invariably enjoyed greater material prosperity.[73]

The men and women of Charleston lived and labored in a cosmopolitan city that drew sailors, traders, and travelers from virtually every corner of the Atlantic world. Among other southern cities, perhaps only New Orleans could compete with Charleston for ethnic and racial diversity in this period. Just days before the authorities uncovered Vesey's plot, the *Charleston Mercury* observed how the city streets provided a stage on which "the sounds of many languages meet your ears" and where "you may see in miniature all the nations of the world." Even the money that changed hands in taverns and stores, including Spanish doubloons, English guineas, Portuguese moidores, German johannes, and Bengal rupees, attested to the city's international character.[74]

---

72. Schoepf, *Travels in the Confederation*, 221; Philip D. Morgan, "Black Life in Eighteenth-Century Charleston," 188; Berlin, *Slaves without Masters*, 36, 55.

73. Martineau, *Retrospect of Western Travel*, 1:228. For other contemporary descriptions of the city, see Martin, "Ebenezer Kellogg's Visit to Charleston," 1–14; Moffatt and Carrière, "A Frenchman Visits Charleston," 131–54; Moore, "Abiel Abbott Journals," 51–73; Mohl, "'The Grand Fabric of Republicanism,'" 170–88; Severens, *Charleston*, 7–12; and Mills, *Statistics of South Carolina*, 406.

74. *Charleston Mercury*, 23 May 1822; *Charleston Evening Gazette*, 10 November 1822.

Many of the city's neighborhoods reflected this racial and ethnic diversity. With their small stores, houses, and workshops, these neighborhoods became the focal point of daily life for both free and enslaved people. Ties of friendship, kinship, and employment resulted in the creation of dense social networks that residential patterns further reinforced. As historian Ira Berlin has noted, class rather than race or ethnicity tended to determine where people lived, with individual blocks rather than entire neighborhoods separating people of different ethnic backgrounds. Many of the city's wealthiest families lived alongside the enslaved men and women who ran their households, while less prosperous white families also shared their quarters with their slaves. Such living arrangements enabled many slaveholders to control and observe the activities of their slaves. Not all enslaved men and women lived with their owners, however. Obtaining their owners' permission and using their own money, a number of slaves established their own households, renting rooms elsewhere in the city, especially on Charleston Neck where accommodations were cheap. Perhaps motivated by a desire to remove himself from owner John Gell's surveillance, Monday Gell followed this course of action, living with his wife several blocks from his owner's livery stable.[75]

Owned by elite planters and merchants, the large houses that stood in these neighborhoods often bore the spatial hallmarks of plantation design. Concealed from the street by brick walls or wooden fences, these houses usually had retinues of slaves, ranging from kitchen staff to coach drivers. Behind the main house lay a yard in which several small outbuildings stood, including the stable block and kitchen where these enslaved household workers lived and worked. Here, slaves would launder clothes, prepare and cook food, groom horses, and maintain the household's chair or carriage. These yards also served as gathering places for slaves to meet and socialize and, in a few cases, swap secret, conspiratorial gossip. Rolla Bennett, an enslaved domestic belonging to Governor Thomas Bennett, regularly visited his wife Amaretta as well as his friend Joe La Roche, both of whom lived in La Roche's mistress's yard.[76]

The heart of the city's commercial district lay between the waterfront and Meeting Street on which Saint Michael's stood. Looking from this vantage point, travelers would have seen the jumbled forest of masts and rigging of ships moored alongside the series of wharves that extended into the Cooper

---

75. Berlin, *Slaves without Masters*, 254–55; Radford, "Race, Residence, and Ideology," 329–46.

76. Wade, *Slavery in the Cities*, 60; Examination of Rolla Bennett, 20 June 1822, DTT.

River. A well-sheltered harbor lying at the confluence of the Ashley and the Cooper, Charleston was regarded as the premier "Emporium of trade for an extensive and valuable Part of the Southern Continent of North America" in the early nineteenth century, ranking as the nation's sixth city in 1820. Picking his way along the waterfront piled high with "great bales of cotton, boxes of fruit, barrels of flour," as well as "bananas, plucked from the trees only four or five days earlier in the Island of Cuba," English traveler and artist Basil Hall also would have seen dozens of slaves carting the agricultural staples on which South Carolina had built its prosperity from the rows of warehouses that lined the quay to the holds of the waiting ships. Had Hall witnessed the arrival of the ship loaded with fruit from Cuba, he might have seen weary sailors heading for the nearest grogshop, perhaps greeting waterfront workers as they made their way to a favorite watering hole or boardinghouse along East Bay Street.[77]

This quarter also served as home to the city's merchants, factors, and ship chandlers, including Joseph Vesey. Armed with the latest shipping news and commodity prices, traders would gather in establishments like Sampson Clarke's Exchange Coffee House to buy and sell "vessels, lands, and negroes," as well as rice and cotton, meeting with captains and negotiating cargo rates. Between March and May 1822, for example, ships carrying cargoes from Port-au-Prince (Haiti), Trinidad, Havana, and Rio de Janeiro, and from London, Bristol, and Liverpool, all dropped anchor in Charleston harbor. In addition to the deep-sea vessels bringing goods into the city, a large number of smaller ships involved in the coastal trade between Savannah, Beaufort, and Georgetown, as well as vessels from northern ports including Boston, New York, and Philadelphia, also tied up alongside the Cooper River's wharves. In the alleys and streets surrounding the waterfront, ships' masters from these places outfitted and provisioned their vessels while crews rubbed shoulders with fellow sailors from around the Atlantic, exchanging stories, gaming in billiard rooms, and drinking in local taverns as they waited to ship out.

Charleston's harbor was a magnet for slaves determined to leave the South. With warehouses and sheds in which to hide and the lure of ships heading for distant destinations, escaped slaves headed to the waterfront, waiting to enlist on or stow away aboard a vessel about to depart to Europe or the northern states. Slaveholders often acknowledged this strategy when they posted notices in the newspapers describing the escaped slave, reminding "Masters of Vessels" that the law forbade them from taking him "out of

---

77. Letter #25, Letters of an American Traveller, 1810, SCHS; Basil Hall, "An Illustrator's View," 123.

the state." Harry, the slave of G. Morrell, was just one of many fugitives who tried to "pass himself off as a free man" and head to port towns north of the Mason-Dixon line. In some cases, slaves relied on free black mariners to assist them in their flight. Even though Joseph Lawrence, a free black sailor from New York, managed to hide a slave belonging to Major James Dunwoody aboard the *Fair Play*, bound for his home port in July 1822, the authorities, who had become increasingly vigilant in the wake of Vesey's plot, soon uncovered this escape attempt, imprisoning and later selling Lawrence into slavery and returning the unlucky stowaway to Dunwoody. The port, as we have already seen in the case of the enslaved mariners who deserted from the *Friendship*, also provided opportunities to jump ship.[78]

In this quarter, a multicultural cosmopolitanism prevailed that was not as apparent elsewhere in the city. In its streets and on its wharves, "dark African faces mingled with pale Irish ones to mark an ethnic spectrum that embraced French Huguenots, North and South Germans, Sephardic Jews, and Creole emigres from Saint Domingue." The alleys that ran between warehouses and wharves, the corners of streets, and the doorways to tippling houses all provided settings in which working people, both free and enslaved, might strike up conversations or trade gossip. In the closing years of the eighteenth century, sailors disembarking from long ocean voyages, their pockets laden with their wages, would head to nearby taverns and boardinghouses, carrying news about political upheaval and revolutionary change from distant corners of the Atlantic world. Besides talking and recounting adventures on the high seas in taverns, an evening's entertainment might also include singing, gambling, drinking, and having sex. Thus, grogshops, billiard rooms, and brothels all served as points connecting the wide Atlantic world to the streets of Charleston.[79]

The city's waterfront was home to a number of enslaved maritime workers who would eventually join Vesey's insurgency. Of the thirty-five men hanged in the summer of 1822, over half worked in trades directly associated with the port's economic life. Jack Pritchard, known locally as "Gullah" Jack, worked as a carpenter and joiner at his owner's shipyard near Gadsden's Wharf on East Bay Street. Polydore Faber also worked on Gadsden's Wharf,

---

78. *Charleston Courier*, 21 August 1807; *Charleston Evening Gazette*, 20 August 1785; *City Gazette and Commercial Daily Advertiser*, 17 February 1816; *Charleston Patriot and Commercial Advertiser*, 9 August 1817; *Charleston Courier*, 1 July 1822.

79. Pease and Pease, *Web of Progress*, 7–8. On the interracial character of the Atlantic world, see, for example, Philip D. Morgan, "British Encounters with Africans and African-Americans"; Bolster, *Black Jacks*; Rediker, *Between the Devil and the Deep Blue Sea*; and Gilroy, *Black Atlantic*.

cutting lumber and making rope. Regarded as "a first-rate ship carpenter," Peter Poyas likewise spent his working days in the city's boatyards. On Craft's Wharf, three slaves (Adam, John, and Robert) who made rope and rigging at Robertson's ropewalk became conspirators. Several slaves were involved in the production of barrels, including Thomas Forrest, who worked in a cooper's shop on Chisholm's Wharf, and Bellisle, Adam, and Naphur Yates, who labored in an establishment on East Bay Street. In addition, there were a number of conspirators who worked in trades that regularly brought them to this part of town or who performed unskilled labor in warehouses or on the wharves. Working as cart drivers, Smart Anderson and Caesar Smith often transported goods to and from the port while Dick Simms packed and baled cotton in a nearby warehouse (see Appendix 2).[80]

Perhaps one reason for Vesey's success in recruiting waterfront workers, besides his own history as a mariner, was the visibility of the slave trade; the wharves and yards in this part of town also served as the center for the commerce in both imported and local slaves. From the early eighteenth century until the ban on the transatlantic slave trade came into effect in January 1808, Charleston was the leading North American harbor for the import of enslaved men and women from Africa and the Caribbean. In the century between the English settlement of South Carolina in 1670 and the start of the American Revolution, more than ninety thousand enslaved Africans entered the city. Making the long and brutal voyage from the slave forts on the coasts of western Africa to the poorly constructed quarantine sheds that stood in the harbor on Sullivan's Island, a place that historian Peter Wood has rightly dubbed "the Ellis Island of black Americans," these people ended their terrifying Atlantic journey at the auction blocks in Charleston's slave markets. When farmers in the backcountry began to produce cotton commercially at the end of the 1790s, they called for the reopening of the Atlantic trade to satisfy their demand for labor. In December 1803, the South Carolina Assembly granted their request, enabling merchants to outfit ships "in numbers for Africa." The market in slaves accordingly flourished as merchants imported more than 39,000 slaves into Charleston between early 1804 and January 1808.[81]

---

80. Kennedy and Parker, *Official Report*, 29.

81. Wood, *Black Majority*, xiv. Wood estimates that more than 40 percent of the slaves brought to British North America between 1700 and 1775 landed first in Charleston. See Walter J. Fraser, *Charleston! Charleston!*, 188; *Charleston Courier*, 1 January 1808. On the slave trade to Charleston, see Brady, "Slave Trade and Sectionalism," 615; Higgins, "Charleston," 114–31; Holloway, "Origins of African-American Culture," 7; and Littlefield,

Even after the Atlantic trade closed, the city still played a role in the South's domestic slave trade. In his narrative, former slave Charles Ball recalled overhearing a conversation at the turn of the century in which one trader informed another how, by going to Charleston, he could "buy as many Guinea negroes as I please for two hundred dollars each." Nearly twenty years later, Scottish traveler Peter Neilson watched as prospective purchasers quizzed slaves about their medical history, previous owners, and work skills before the bidding began. As they went about their daily business, both black and white Charlestonians would have witnessed slaves "with most melancholy and disconsolate faces, and . . . an air of vacancy and apathy" undergoing examination from prospective buyers, and being sold on the auction block.[82] Not until 1856 did the city pass an ordinance that banned the public sale of slaves, resulting in the establishment of private auction rooms along State and Chalmers Streets.

Between Meeting Street to the east, the Ashley River to the west, and Boundary Street to the north lay several neighborhoods, including Harleston and Mazyck Lands, in which private dwellings stood alongside workshops, boarding houses, and retail stores. Meeting Street was a major commercial boulevard that ran from the heart of the lowcountry south to the Battery, the sea wall at the tip of the peninsula that Charleston architect Robert Mills regarded as "the most beautiful and agreeable promenade" with its panoramic view of the busy harbor. Boundary Street ran from east to west, dividing Charleston from Charleston Neck. Along the Ashley's banks stood rice and saw mills that used the hydraulic action of the tide to power the machinery that slaves operated to grind rice into flour and cut lumber. Located between Boundary Street in the north and Beaufain Street to the south lay Harleston. An early suburb of Charleston, this neighbor-

---

"Slave Trade to Colonial South Carolina," 68–98, and *Rice and Slaves*, 33–55. To understand the daily operations of a Charleston slave trader, see the correspondence of Henry Laurens, one of the city's premier merchants, in Hamer et al., *Papers of Henry Laurens*. A discrepancy exists in the figures offered by Holloway and Brady for the number of slaves imported between 1803 and 1807. Using figures from an unpublished essay, entitled "A Reconsideration of the Sources of the Slave Trade to Charleston, S.C." by William S. Pollitzer, Holloway calculates that 29,029 enslaved Africans were imported into the city, while Brady cites the figure of 39,075 and quotes Senator William Smith in *Annals of Congress*, 16th Cong., 2d sess., 8 December 1820, p. 77.

82. Ball, *Slavery in the United States*, 102; Hodgson, *Letters from North America*, 1:56. The letter describing the slave auction is dated 26 February 1820. For additional information on the slave market in Charleston, see Neilson, *Six Years' Residence in America*, 284–89. See also Tadman, *Speculators and Slaves*; and *City Gazette and Commercial Daily Advertiser*, 4 December 1820.

hood lay about a dozen blocks from the city's commercial epicenter along East Bay Street. In addition to the small community of free blacks who lived in this district, including AME minister Morris Brown and Vesey himself, a number of leading enslaved conspirators resided in this part of town, including Batteau, Ned, and Rolla who worked in Governor Thomas Bennett's house on Lynch Street.[83]

The neighborhoods south of Boundary Street constituted the incorporated city of 12,625 slaves (50 percent), 11,300 whites (44 percent) and 1,475 free blacks (6 percent) in 1820. To the north of this thoroughfare lay Charleston Neck, an unincorporated collection of neighborhoods where, according to the census of 1820, 6,700 slaves (53 percent), 4,442 whites (35 percent), and 1,587 free blacks (12 percent) lived. In total, 19,352 slaves (51 percent), 15,742 whites (41 percent) and 3,062 free blacks (8 percent) resided on the thin spit of land that lay between the Cooper and Ashley Rivers. With the exception of its free black population, which was proportionately greater than that of the state, Charleston's racial demographics resembled those of South Carolina.[84]

Presided over by an intendant, a council consisting of thirteen wardens governed the city. Elected as city intendant in 1821, James Hamilton Jr. had served as an officer during the War of 1812 before purchasing several cotton plantations on the Sea Islands. He entered national politics in the wake of the Vesey trials, completing the term of lowcountry politician William Lowndes in the U.S. House of Representatives, and becoming governor of the state in 1830. Besides his administrative duties, Hamilton was also responsible for municipal safety. Commanded by several officers, a small force of about one hundred men, aided by a number of constables from each ward, protected Charleston from public disorder. To maintain a constant presence throughout the city, the municipal authorities stationed men in the main guardhouse, located at the junction of Broad and Meeting Streets, as well as on Charleston Neck in a piquet guardhouse on the corner of Meeting and Tobacco Streets. They also dispatched patrols, comprised of a sergeant and four privates armed with muskets, bayonets, and rattles, at regular intervals

---

83. Mills, *Statistics of South Carolina*, 425; Lander, "Charleston," 330–51; see also Lander, "Ante-Bellum Milling in South Carolina," 125–32. For a general survey on this subject, see Starobin, *Industrial Slavery*; and Wade, *Slavery in the Cities*.

84. Boundary Street is now known as Calhoun Street; Shecut, *Medical and Philosophical Essays*, 7; Federal Population Census, Charleston District, South Carolina, 1820, SCDAH. Of the 19,352 slaves in Charleston, 10,443 (54 percent) were female and 8,909 (46 percent) were male; of its 3,063 free people of color, 1,316 (43 percent) were men and 1,746 (57 percent) were women. The number of enslaved people in South Carolina in 1820 tallied to 258,475 (51 percent), while there were 237,440 white people (48 percent) and 6,826 free people of color (1 percent).

during the night to enforce slave and free black curfews. The city also maintained thirteen fire companies to extinguish the large number of "premeditated or accidental conflagrations" that frequently broke out. By using patrols on the streets and watchmen posted in several prominent church steeples, including Saint Michael's, the authorities maintained law and order through constant surveillance. And when disorder threatened, swift and decisive displays of power, including deployment of the militia, served to reestablish the authority and mastery of the city's rulers.[85]

Although wealthy planters and merchants had initially envisioned the Charleston Neck neighborhoods of Mazyckborough and Wraggborough as a residential area distant from the clamor of the waterfront, its streets were no longer exclusive or tranquil by the early nineteenth century. Charleston Neck had instead become home to trades and manufacturing shops banned from operating within the city itself. Adjacent to residential streets stood livery stables, slaughter houses, tanning yards, and other enterprises vital to the city's economic life. This district also served as the commercial crossroads between the port and the backcountry. Along King Street stood the offices of factors and merchants as well as the yards where backcountry wagon drivers unloaded bales of cotton for export and other agricultural goods for local consumption.[86]

With its opportunities for employment and low rents, this part of the city attracted both free and enslaved workers.[87] Owing in part to these economic advantages, the Neck quickly emerged as the most important residential enclave for slaves and free blacks. Away from the watchful gaze of the city guard and technically outside the jurisdiction of onerous municipal ordinances, they could pursue their own cultural and social activities with some degree of freedom. Although grand jurors often complained about unlicensed shopkeepers on the Neck selling "spirituous liquors" to slaves with impunity, little was done to remedy the situation. Not only did this quarter gain a reputation of being "a place of refuge for run away negroes," but it also became home to clubs and associations organized by free blacks. In the aftermath of the Vesey trials, however, the assembly passed legislation de-

---

85. On Hamilton's political career, see Freehling, *Prelude to Civil War*, 149–52; and Bailey and Edgar, *Biographical Directory*, 5:643. On the city guard, see Mills, *Statistics of South Carolina*, 396. On patrols, see *Alphabetical Digest of Ordinances*, 110–12. On fire companies, see Hodgson, *Letters from North America*, 134–35; Charleston Fire Masters Book, SHC.

86. Charles Fraser, *Reminiscences of Charleston*. Charles Fraser attended the College of Charleston during the 1790s, witnessing the city's embrace of the French Revolution.

87. *City Gazette and Commercial Daily Advertiser*, 12 June 1817; Charles Fraser, *Reminiscences of Charleston*, 15. On Charleston Neck, see Grimes et al., *Between the Tracks*.

signed "to control and keep in order the numerous black population" of the Neck, by increasing the number of patrols that policed its neighborhoods.[88]

Charleston Neck's African Methodist Episcopal Church, established in 1816, rapidly became the most important institution for many black Charlestonians. Standing on the corner of Reid and Hanover Streets in the Hampstead neighborhood, this church soon attracted many "noisy frantic worshipers" who prayed and sang there every evening.[89] Before the founding of the AME church, Charleston's five thousand Afro-Methodists had enjoyed considerable independence in church governance. They remained formally affiliated with the city's white Methodists, however, who nominally oversaw their affairs, including the collection and disbursement of funds. Anxious to bring its black members under closer supervision, in 1815 the parent church revoked these privileges after Anthony Senter, a newly arrived white minister, accused them of "much corruption," claiming that they had used funds to purchase the freedom of enslaved members. In addition to this accusation, the planned construction of a house by the church's white trustees on the hallowed turf of a black burial ground further deepened the rift between black and white Methodists.[90]

Determined to worship on their own terms, more than four thousand black Methodists voted with their feet, leaving their congregations in order to establish a new church free from white governance. Led by free black shoemaker Morris Brown, who had received religious instruction from AME founding father Richard Allen in Philadelphia and who became a deacon in the church in 1817, this newly constituted congregation petitioned the legislature to conduct services from dawn until dusk. To ensure that the assembly would grant their request, the petitioners collected signatures from several white pastors, offered to keep church doors open at all times, and agreed to let other ministers attend their services. The galleries of many churches that had been "hitherto crowded" with black worshipers now became "almost

88. Grand Jury Presentments of the Charleston District, January 1818, and Grand Jury Petitions, SCDAH; *City Gazette and Commercial Daily Advertiser*, 29 January 1818; Charleston *City Gazette*, 13 June 1788; "An Act to Regulate the Performance of Patrol Duty on Charleston Neck, 20 December 1823," in Elliott and Stroebel, *Militia System of South Carolina*, 45.

89. *Charleston Times*, 12 August 1816; Gravely, "Rise of African Churches in America," 59–73. On the number of black congregants (both free and enslaved) at other city churches, see Shecut, *Medical and Philosophical Essays*, 34–37. For example, the Roman Catholic Church had 150 black members, the Congregationalists boasted more than 300, and the Lutherans had some 50 congregants.

90. Mood, *Methodism in Charleston*, 132; *Southern Patriot*, 19 September 1835, cited in Henry, *Police Control of the Slave*, 144.

completely deserted," as several thousand black men and women began holding services at their own church. By the end of the decade, the AME had established meeting places in several houses in the city in addition to the countryside, organizing congregations on James Island, at Team Boat Ferry on the Ashley River, and at several sites along Goose Creek.[91]

The church drew considerable fire from several civic leaders who denounced its establishment as "unnecessary and impolitick." Directly attacking the activities of Brown and his assistants, Edwin Holland and his allies roundly condemned the practice of allowing ministers ordained in "Eastern States" (particularly Pennsylvania, widely regarded as a leading center of antislavery sentiment due to its Quaker connections and the presence of the Pennsylvania Society for Promoting the Abolition of Slavery in Philadelphia) to preach in Charleston. That Brown, along with deacons Marcus Brown, Charles Carr, Amos Cruckshank, and Henry Drayton, had openly and publicly established the church in the face of these protests and had traveled to AME meetings in Philadelphia and Baltimore only angered their white adversaries more. In addition, Holland not surprisingly objected to the church's firm antislavery stance, while several white religious figures questioned the theological qualifications of its leaders. A few clerics, including the city's leading Protestant Episcopal minister, Theodore Dehon, believed black preachers to be "worse than ignorant . . . indolent, deceitful, and sometimes grossly immoral."[92] Despite these and other attacks, the church persisted, weathering several storms as Brown and his fellow deacons forcefully asserted the right of the congregation to worship independently.

Holland, however, had assessed the situation correctly. The church did become a center of opposition to slavery, presenting a challenge to public order and to the social order through its connections to Vesey's conspiracy. In June 1818, constables arrested more than four hundred free black and enslaved worshipers for participating in "a large and unlawful assemblage" that resulted in Brown's imprisonment for a month. The court ordered that other church leaders be fined $5 or receive ten lashes, although what punishment they received went unrecorded. Holland's *Charleston Times* thundered

---

91. Free Persons of Colour to Members of the House of Representatives, 1817, General Assembly Petitions, SCDAH. On the AME church, see Raboteau, *Slave Religion*, 204–5; Donald Mathews, *Religion in the Old South*, 203–7; Mood, *Methodism in Charleston*, 129–33; and Clarke, *Wrestlin' Jacob*, 129.

92. Petition to the House of Representatives, 16 October 1820, General Assembly Petitions, SCDAH; see also Payne, *History of the African Methodist Episcopal Church*, 26–27, 31–45; Nash, *Forging Freedom*, 109–33; Edward D. Smith, *Climbing Jacob's Ladder*; Clarke, *Wrestlin' Jacob*; and Gadsden, *Life of the Right Reverend Theodore Dehon*, 200.

against the "religious convocation[s]" that took place every evening. Rather than benefit the community, the editor concluded, such gatherings only spread "many evils" among church members. Moreover, these late-night assemblies directly defied an 1800 law that banned worship by black men and women "either before the rising of the sun, or after the going down of the same." As the authorities unraveled Vesey's plot, many white people became firmly convinced of the church's central place in the conspiracy, an opinion confirmed by a number of accused slaves, who testified that several members had played leading roles in the plot.[93]

Between its founding and late 1822, the faithful congregants of the AME church met these challenges to their independent worship. As a visiting teacher from New England noted in 1817, they maintained "the fight of faith under many difficulties and discouragements." Their struggle, however, came to an end in the wake of the trials when the city demolished the church, forcing its members to seek alternative congregations. Benjamin Hammet, owner of conspirator Bacchus Hammet, summed up white attitudes to the church's members when he remarked that "they were great rascals." Although no evidence directly implicated Brown, Carr, Cruckshanks, or Drayton in the plot, they nonetheless chose to leave Charleston, escaping to Philadelphia in late August 1822, never to return. Brown later succeeded Richard Allen as bishop in 1829, becoming national leader of the church. After the authorities tore down the AME church in Hampstead, its members either joined the Scotch Presbyterians or returned to their former Methodist congregations. Twenty-seven years later, black Charlestonians established another independent church, opening the Calvary Protestant Episcopal Church on Beaufain Street in 1849.[94]

The AME church was not the only institution where black Charlestonians might gather away from the gaze of the white population. Determined to set up their own institutions, the city's free people of color established several benevolent societies. After being denied permission to purchase burial plots in the whites-only graveyard of Saint Philip's Protestant Episcopal Church where some of them worshiped, five "free brown men" organized the Brown Fellowship Society (BFS) in late 1790, dedicated, as its motto proclaimed, to

---

93. *Charleston Patriot*, 9 June 1818, 10 June 1818; *Charleston Times*, 17 July 1818; Brevard, *Digest of the Public Statute Law*, 2:254–55. On the church's role in the plot, see, for example, testimony from William Paul, DTT.

94. Martin, "Ebenezer Kellogg's Visit to Charleston," 11; Confession of Bacchus Hammet, Benjamin Hammet Papers, WPL; Edward D. Smith, *History of the African Methodist Episcopal Church*, 14; Berlin, *Slaves without Masters*, 296; Walter J. Fraser, *Charleston! Charleston!*, 228; Durden, "Establishment of the Calvary Protestant Episcopal Church," 63–84.

"Charity and Benevolence." Limiting its membership to just fifty men who had to pay the considerable fee of $50 to join, this society became, as historians Michael Johnson and James Roark have noted, "an exclusive, color-conscious enclave whose members sought to separate themselves from blacks, whether slave or free," filling its membership rolls with the city's most prosperous free mulattoes. Several free brown slaveowners counted themselves as members of the BFS, including former slave-trader Samuel Holman, who had once worked along the Pongo River on the Senegambian coast and who now owned a plantation with more than forty slaves in the parish of Saint James Santee. Besides providing a range of welfare services, including benefits to aid families of sick and injured members, small loans to establish businesses, and cemetery plots, the BFS also ran a modest program to educate a few "poor colored orphans." A year after its founding, the BFS decided to limit membership to men of mixed parentage only, leading other free men of African descent to establish the Society of Free Dark Men of Color in 1791. Although less prestigious than the BFS, this new association admitted only "respectable" men to its ranks.[95]

The establishment of the racially exclusive Brown Fellowship Society and its rule to exclude black-skinned men from membership points to divisions among the free people of African descent in Charleston. Constituting a very small percentage of that population, the elite members of this society distinguished themselves not just by the light tone of their complexion but also by the ownership of slaves and real estate and their occupations as highly skilled craftsmen or small business owners. Linked together through intermarriage, these people forged a distinct identity that set them apart from enslaved Charlestonians as well as other free blacks. This small free brown elite also forged links with prosperous white men, cultivating personal ties with prominent planters, merchants, and bankers. Unable to join the exclusive ranks of the city's free brown elite due primarily to skin color and modest economic circumstances, the rest of the city's free blacks appear not to have affiliated themselves closely with Charleston's enslaved population, instead maintaining some distance from that community. Thus, caste consciousness played a critical role not only in dividing the city's small free brown and free

---

95. On the Brown Fellowship Society, see Johnson and Roark, "'Middle Ground,'" 247, and *Black Masters*, 107–8, 212–17; Berlin, *Slaves without Masters*, 73–76; Koger, *Black Slaveowners*, 98–99, 167–68; Wikramanayake, *A World in Shadow*, 81–85; Browning, "Beginnings of Insurance Enterprise among Negroes," 417–32; and Harris, "Charleston's Free Afro-American Elite," 289–310. The Robert Scott Smalls Library at the College of Charleston holds the organization's records, including a copy of *Rules and Regulations of the Brown Fellowship Society* (Charleston, 1844).

black populations into separate communities, but also in segregating free people of color from enslaved Charlestonians.

These divisions appear to have affected Vesey. Although a free man after 1799, Vesey appears to have remained on the margins of the city's free black population, associating himself more closely with enslaved people, whose ranks included members of his own family. That some free people of color owned slaves might also explain his distance from this sector of black Charleston. As we will see, he drew very few free blacks into the ranks of his conspiracy. In addition, he does not appear to have joined any free black society, an affiliation that would have enlarged his circle of acquaintances. For many Afro-Charlestonians, the only institution that cut across class and caste lines was the AME church, which brought free brown, free black, and enslaved people together under one roof.

Grogshops and tippling houses emerged as important alternative venues for black Charlestonians, providing informal settings in which they might gather to gossip, game, argue, and fight. Offering customers a congenial atmosphere in which to drink and socialize, these places enabled their clients to plan their activities, praise and condemn fellow tavern habitués, analyze their present circumstances, and perhaps curse their owners. Free and enslaved patrons might engage in illegal activities like playing EO table (a betting game similar to roulette, so called because the betting layout was marked E or O) or hazard (also known as rolly polly or *rolae polae*), a dice game widely regarded by the authorities as "exceedingly dangerous, and tending in so a degree to promote a spirit of gambling and idleness that it is requisite . . . [it] should be prohibited." In fact, municipal codes demanded that "each and every such [EO] table . . . be publicly broken to pieces and destroyed by the head Constable." Participants in these and other games spun the wheel of fortune in the hope of accumulating some cash from these pastimes. Away from the gaze of city constables, they could dance and drink, smoke and swear, and wager their meager fortunes on games of chance, forging new friendships and renewing old ones in the process.[96]

Such places became important institutions for the political culture and popular traditions of the radical underworld of the Atlantic basin. Offering alternative public space for the production of an oppositional discourse,

---

96. On the role of conversation in these types of informal settings, see Lindstrom, *Knowledge and Power in a South Pacific Society*, 28–29, 52–66. On gaming restrictions, see *Alphabetical Digest of Ordinances*, 97–98; see also *Collection of the Ordinances of the City Council*, 12. Numerous grand juries complained about drunkenness in the African American community; see Grand Jury Presentments, SCDAH.

these grogshops and tippling houses proved popular with all manner of subversives. Enabling their patrons to drop the mask of subservience that they wore during their interactions with white people, these places provided a setting in which a dissenting political culture might flourish. Their appeal, as James Scott has noted, rested in the fact that they were "places of subversion [in which] subordinate classes met offstage and off-duty in an atmosphere of freedom encouraged by alcohol." Familiar with these places from his own days at sea, Vesey appears to have found such ramshackle establishments an ideal setting in which to talk politics, to make "some bold remark on slavery," and to establish his persona as a profound critic of the institution.[97]

Cramped and dingy, frequented by sailors and slaves alike, and located in the neighborhoods of the city's poorest residents, grogshops were invariably associated with "robbery, poverty, destitution and crime." City fathers regarded these "receptacles of iniquity" as a menace to public order, declaring on numerous occasions that too many black Charlestonians passed too much time within their walls. Complaining about these "retail liquor shops with which our city and neighbourhood is so much infested," the *Charleston Courier* railed against the free black and enslaved men who stumbled out of their doors, "surcharged with fumes of whiskey and segars in their mouths, staggering on their way, brawling and rioting totally regardless of decorum or decency." Demands by the grand jury to control these "temptation[s] to our Domestics" had no impact. In addition to providing the resources to escape temporarily from the daily grind and indignities of enslavement, these places enabled Afro-Charlestonians to articulate their own ethnic practices. Talking in Gullah, the lowcountry creole, playing games like EO table or mankala (a popular African and Afro-Caribbean board game in which two players vie to capture their opponents' pieces), enslaved men, and to a lesser extent women, saw taverns as places in which they could carve out their own cultural space and express themselves with a greater degree of freedom.[98]

---

97. James C. Scott, *Domination and the Arts of Resistance*, 122–23. For further discussion about taverns as places for the generation of subversive discourse, see also Stallybrass and White, *Politics and Poetics of Transgression*, 80; Brennan, *Public Drinking and Popular Culture*; Clark, *English Alehouse*, 145–65; and Kennedy and Parker, *Official Report*, 12. On slaves' drinking habits, see Genovese, *Roll, Jordan, Roll*, 641–48.

98. Warden of Charleston to House of Representatives, 1816, General Assembly Petitions, SCDAH; *Charleston Courier*, 25 April 1834, cited in Henry, *Police Control of the Slave*, 51; Grand Jury Presentments for District of Charleston, October 1820, SCDAH. On mankala (or mancala), see Bell, *Board and Table Games*, 111–19; Iliffe, *Africans*, 96; and Zaslavsky, *Africa Counts*, 118–31.

Black Charlestonians also gathered and socialized in streets and alleyways outside taverns and tippling houses. The Battery—the sea wall at the tip of the peninsula—became so popular among slaves and free blacks as a place to meet and fish that authorities restricted access to it in 1818. Several travel accounts suggest that the city's dusty streets became vital public spaces where Afro-Carolinians interacted. Going to work, running errands, buying and selling goods on the street or passing the time of day with friends and acquaintances, slaves crowded the city's waterfront and streets. On a few occasions, the street corner also became a place of conspiracy. Testifying before the court, Robert Harth recalled how Peter Poyas told him about the plot as the two men conversed on the corner of Legare and Lambol Streets. During a later encounter on the same corner, Harth confirmed his allegiance to the conspiracy to Ned Bennett. In a city where, as more than one traveler observed, slaves "thronged the streets at every hand ... busy in grog shops or standing at the doors of them," such meetings would have passed unnoticed. Blending in with their surroundings, these conspirators, hidden in plain sight, could move through Charleston inconspicuously, organizing rebellion virtually unseen.[99]

Charleston's streets also gave slaves a stage on which to lampoon their owners. Walking around the city, Neilson watched slaves engage in "much ceremony" as they greeted one another, "bowing and curtseying to the ground, and expressing every mark of politeness."[100] Satirizing their owners' gestures, these slaves provided their own commentary on a lowcountry elite obsessed with refined behavior and genteel conduct. Through these subtle means, enslaved men and women expressed their opposition to slavery. Rather less subtly, enslaved cart and coach drivers racing through the streets took great delight in splashing white pedestrians with mud and water, violating ordinances that required carts and wagons be driven "no faster than a walk, moderate trot, or pace." Breaking these rules of the road might result in the slave cart driver receiving "no less than twelve or more than twenty

---

99. *Charleston Courier*, 12 September 1818; Trial of Peter Poyas, 21 June 1822, DTT; Neilson, *Life and Adventures of Zamba*, 109. An interesting attempt to fashion a narrative about the lives of free blacks and enslaved people in antebellum Charleston, this book purports to tell the story of Zamba, described in the book's subtitle as "An African Negro King," and his experiences as a slave in South Carolina. Neilson, who lived in Charleston in the early 1820s and who later wrote *Recollections of Six Years' Residence* based on his sojourn in the city, drew on his experiences to impart a sense of verisimilitude to his novel. That slaves could gather on street corners to plan rebellion prefigures the key advantage enjoyed by guerrilla fighters—an ability to move, as Mao Tse-Tung commented, like fish through water.

100. Neilson, *Six Years' Residence*, 264.

lashes upon his bare back at the public market place." White Charlestonians who chose to travel about the city in a chair or carriage may have been responding in part to the presence of large numbers of black pedestrians. "Ladies," noted French aristocrat La Rochefoucauld, "are never seen to walk on foot."[101]

Charleston's thoroughfares also served as workplaces for many enslaved men and women. Dominating the haulage trade as carters and draymen, enslaved men and free blacks spent their days transporting goods throughout the city. Others worked as hired hands for the city on the streets themselves. Equipped with wheelbarrows and shovels, these enslaved laborers (known as city scavengers) leveled and raked the streets, removed horse dung, and kept drains "free from sand, filth, and other obstructions" for a set rate.[102] Combining conviviality and commerce, the market stalls that lined East Bay often proved to be the liveliest part of this rich street culture. Here, rural slave women sold goods from plantation provision grounds to urban slaves, either for their own domestic use or for their owners' households. Female slaves "traded from morn till night . . . buy[ing] and sell[ing] on their own Accounts what they please." Market stalls became the location for "one hundred and one personal transactions . . . where news was passed, rumor and gossip flew around [and] politics [was] discussed."[103] In using city streets and markets as places in which to gather, work, trade, game, dance, and converse, Charleston's enslaved population effectively claimed its own public space in the city.

Through a series of ineffective municipal codes, city leaders attempted to regulate black Charlestonians' economic and social behavior. Several ordinances governed how slaves who hired themselves out were to obtain the licenses and badges required for this type of work. Slaves who worked as porters or day laborers, meanwhile, remained subject to an equally complicated set of wage rates and work rules. Although these regulations appeared in newspapers and in each volume of the city's ordinances, grand jurors often complained that both slaves and slaveholders frequently ignored these rules, conducting business as they pleased.[104] Unsurprisingly, these arrangements stood at odds with public order. Both slaves and slaveholders regularly bypassed statutes governing hiring procedures, rarely honoring the

101. *Alphabetical Digest of Ordinances*, 37, 40; La Rochefoucauld-Liancourt, *Travels through the United States*, 557.

102. *Alphabetical Digest of Ordinances*, 223.

103. *South Carolina Gazette*, 17 September 1772; E. P. Thompson, "Moral Economy of the English Crowd," 135.

104. See, for example, *South Carolina Gazette and General Advertiser*, 25 November 1783.

rules that occasionally appeared in the paper. In addition, grand jurors' repeated calls for more effective policing of hiring procedures largely went unheeded. The system remained virtually ungovernable.

The city also tried to control black sociability, imposing curfews that limited "the hours of mirth" to ten o'clock during the summer and nine o'clock in winter. Both slaves and free blacks who ignored "the thundering drum" that signaled curfew risked imprisonment in the workhouse and a whipping. Clad in their blue uniforms, wearing cocked hats decorated with feathers, and armed with muskets and rattles, the patrol, wrote English traveler William Faux, would clear the streets "of all men, women, or children stained with negro blood." Local ordinances also restricted other forms of social activity, including smoking "a pipe or segar" in "any street, lane, alley or open place in Charleston" and prohibited public dancing or "other meriment" unless a warden granted permission. Slaves and free blacks might also be punished for "whooping or hallooing any where in the city, or of making a clamorous noise or of singing aloud any indecent song." Besides these measures, the grand jury tried to regulate clothing, the most individual form of expression, through the imposition of sumptuary regulations. "The expensive dress worn by many of them," they concluded, "is highly destructive to their Honesty and Industry and subversive of that subordination which policy requires to be enforced." They should be clad, argued these Charlestonians, not in "silks, satins, crapes, lace [and] muslins," but in "coarse woolens or worsted stuffs for winter—and coarse cotton stuffs for summer."[105]

In stark contrast to the noise and bustle of the city's streets and markets, the rhythm of rice and cotton cultivation dominated the lives of the thousands of enslaved plantation workers who lived in the rural lowlands beyond the Ashley and Cooper Rivers. "The whole face of the countryside," noted Samuel Sitgreaves, who hailed from the rolling hills of eastern Pennsylvania, "is covered with woods, except the plantations, which are like islands in a sea of forest . . . [that is] elevated but three or four feet above the water of the

---

105. Faux, *Memorable Days in America*, 12:103; see also Mills, *Statistics of South Carolina*, 396; *Alphabetical Digest of Ordinances*, 110. Curfew regulations were passed in 1788 and the ban on smoking in 1806; see *Alphabetical Digest of Ordinances*, 181; *Charleston Courier*, 4 February 1819. Sumptuary laws to regulate the type of clothing that slaves might wear were passed in the early eighteenth century. The violation of that law frequently appeared in grand jury presentments; see, for example, *South Carolina Gazette*, 5 November 1774; *Charleston City Gazette & Daily Advertiser*, 19 July 1797. The quote is from the Grand Jury Presentments of the District of Charleston, October 1822, SCDAH; see also "Memorial of the Citizens of Charleston," 2:113.

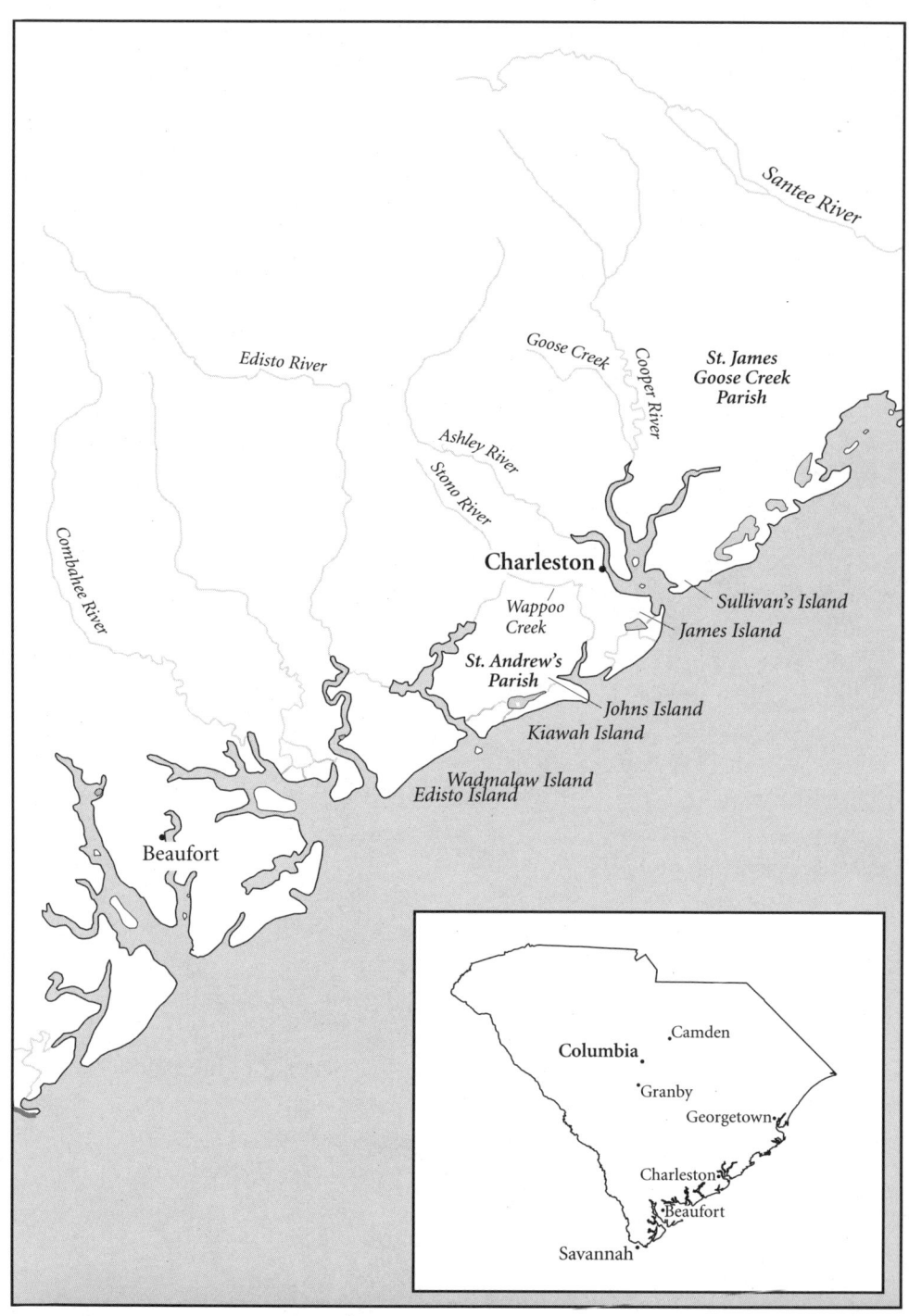

Charleston and the South Carolina Lowcountry, ca. 1822

swamp." Unlike the makeup of Charleston, in which an approximate demographic equilibrium prevailed between black and white populations, the vast majority of the people who lived in these rural districts were enslaved people of African descent. To the north of the city lay Saint James Goose Creek, where 4,192 slaves (75 percent) and 86 free blacks (2 percent) lived among just 1,271 white people (23 percent) in 1820. Across the Ashley River in Saint Andrew's Parish, where just 389 whites (12 percent) resided among 2,710 slaves (87 percent) and 29 free blacks (1 percent), the imbalance between slave and free was even more marked.[106]

As early as the third decade of the eighteenth century, when Swiss immigrant Samuel Dyssli described the coastal lowlands as "more like a negro country than like a country settled by white people," the region's enslaved plantation workers had fashioned a distinctive rural culture by adapting the various ethnic practices of peoples brought from Atlantic Africa to meet the conditions of the lowcountry's rice economy.[107] Drawn primarily from the many societies along the Upper Guinea coast as well as from Kongo-Angola, enslaved men and women who had been transported to this corner of the New World created a culture firmly anchored in African customs. Even though these slaves lived within the broad framework of the lowcountry's plantation order, their religious and social lives remained more African than Anglo-American in form and content.

Laboring in the lowcountry's fields, legions of enslaved men and women cultivated a wide range of agricultural products for both the domestic and international marketplace. Rice and long-staple cotton from the coastal islands constituted the major crops produced for export to the kitchens and textile mills of Europe and New England. The task system, an arrangement whereby slaves performed a preassigned job such as hoeing a certain acreage, clearing a set length of ditch or cutting a certain number of cords of wood, structured plantation work. After completing that day's particular task, slaves then pursued their own economic or social activities. Working on their own time, rural slaves grew vegetables in kitchen gardens, tended poultry, or went hunting or fishing. A vital supplement to the dreary subsistence slave diet, this produce also provided city dwellers with additional supplies of meat and vegetables. By selling goods from plantation provision grounds to Charleston's inhabitants in city markets, enslaved women from

---

106. Staudenraus, "Letters from South Carolina," 210; Federal Population Census for 1820, Charleston District.
107. Letter from Samuel Dyssli, 3 December 1737, in Kelsey, "Swiss Settlers in South Carolina," 90.

the countryside accumulated some cash, enabling them to engage in modest consumption.[108]

The concentration of slaves in the rural lowcountry and their pursuit of their own economic activities had several consequences for Vesey's organization of the rebellion. First, the volume of slaves traveling between the town and the countryside, transporting crops for export or goods for market, facilitated the transmission of information. News gathered by slaves, observed a lowcountry resident on the eve of the Revolutionary War, often traveled "severall hundreds of Miles in a Week or a Fortnight." Returning from the city, plantation slaves could pass information and contraband to their fellow workers and serve as guides for the rebels. Kennedy and Parker well understood the importance of these connections for the rebellion, noting how "the immense numbers of canoes of various sizes (many of which could transport upwards of 100 men) employed in bringing to the Charleston market, vegetables ... and the staple of the country, would have afforded conveyance for thousands."[109]

In addition, "abroad" marriages, an arrangement whereby the couple either lived on different plantations or where one partner lived in the town and the other in the country, also enabled slaves to pass news from one part of the lowcountry to another. Several slaves involved in the plot regularly visited enslaved family members who worked in rural districts. Testifying before the court, Joe La Roche noted these connections, telling his interrogators how "Sambo, the brother of Rolla's [Bennett] wife and who stays at the plantation (on Johns Island), sent word down by his Sister to Rolla, that he would be in town on Sunday night last." The informal networks generated by conversation, trade, and family ties supplemented the lines of communication that Vesey and his associates established throughout the region.[110]

In both the countryside and city, the ethnic practices of western and west-central Africa remained a central part of daily life for black Carolinians.

---

108. For a broad survey of social and economic conditions in the plantation lowcountry on the eve of the Vesey plot, see Freehling, *Prelude to Civil War*, 7–17, 27–48. For a detailed analysis of the region's economy, see Coclanis, *Shadow of a Dream*, 111–58. On lowcountry slave life and the organization of work, see Creel, *"A Peculiar People"*; Joyner, *Down by the Riverside*; Philip D. Morgan, "Work and Culture," 563–99, and "Task and Gang Systems," 189–220; Pearson, "From Stono to Vesey," 143–223; and Smith, *Slavery and Rice Culture*. On the activities of rural slave women in the city's markets, see Olwell, "Slave Women in the Eighteenth-Century Charleston Marketplace," 97–110.

109. Butterfield, ed., *Diary and Autobiography of John Adams*, 2:183; Kennedy and Parker, *Official Report*, 27.

110. Testimony of Joe La Roche, 20 June 1822, DTT, SCDAH.

African folkways persisted to a greater degree among the lowcountry's plantation slaves, however, than among the city's enslaved workers, although they still retained their power among some urban slaves. The arrival of nearly forty thousand enslaved Africans between 1803 and 1807 rejuvenated ethnic traditions among the people of African descent who lived in the region. Although planters from the backcountry and elsewhere in the South purchased a majority of these imports, a significant number became slaves to lowcountry owners, working either in the Charleston or rural coastal districts. As the plot took shape in early 1822, practices rooted in both African religious traditions and ethnic origin came to play a major role in its planning. "Gullah" Jack's rituals to inaugurate slaves into the circle of conspiracy, as well as Vesey's decision to place several African-born slaves in command of slaves from their particular ethnic group, highlight the persistence of African customs among the conspirators.[111]

Several leading conspirators, including Perault (or Peirault) Strohecker, Monday Gell, and "Gullah" Jack Pritchard, had been brought to Charleston from Africa between 1804 and 1807. A blacksmith owned by John Strohecker, Perault had been born in the late eighteenth century to one of the ethnic groups that constituted the Songhay Empire in the western Sudan. His master claimed that Perault's home was the town of Jumba, a town in the interior that was about a week's journey from Goree Island, a trading station that lay off Cape Vert Peninsula on the Senegambian coast. Perault had apparently accompanied his father, a man named Mamadu who owned at least "60 working hands," on several long-distance expeditions deep into Hausa territory, as well as to places like Timbuktu and western Morocco, to trade tobacco and salt before the Dar'a captured him during a war, selling him into slavery. The Igbo Monday Gell likewise originated from western Africa. Before his capture by Atlantic slave traders sometime in the early 1800s, Monday had lived in the kingdom of Benin. One of the three thousand slaves imported from the Gold Coast between 1803 and 1807, Monday was purchased by livery stable owner John Gell, becoming a skilled harness maker and enjoying considerable latitude in his working life.[112] The most

---

111. On early-nineteenth-century slave culture in the plantation lowcountry, see Creel, *"A Peculiar People"*; and Joyner, *Down by the Riverside*. For broader discussions on rural slave culture and community, see, for example, Blassingame, *Slave Community*; Genovese, *Roll, Jordan, Roll*; Kolchin, *American Slavery*, 133–68; and Rawick, *From Sundown to Sunup*. For additional studies, see Levine, *Black Culture and Black Consciousness*; Mintz and Price, *The Birth of African-American Culture*; and Robert Farris Thompson, *Flash of the Spirit*.

112. Kennedy and Parker, *Official Report*, 29, 163. On the volume of slave imports from Africa to South Carolina between 1803 and 1807, see Holloway, "Origins of African-Ameri-

important African-born rebel, however, was "Gullah" Jack Pritchard, who, as we shall discuss later, brought native magical practices to the conspiracy.

Testifying at Pompey Lord's trial in August, Perault alluded briefly to the appearance of a book at one meeting that apparently "came from Africa." Neither Gell nor Strohecker disclosed the title or contents of this volume, but it may possibly have been a copy of the Koran. In his narrative, former slave Charles Ball recalled several enslaved Africans in the city who "must have been, from what I have since learned, Mohamedans." At least one enslaved Muslim left a very brief account of his short time in Charleston. Landing in 1807 after his capture from his village in Futa Toro (now present-day Senegal), a Fula man named Omar ibn Said spent several years working for "a weak and wicked man called Johnson, a complete infidel," before escaping to Fayetteville in North Carolina. Apparently an Islamic scholar who could read the Koran, ibn Said may possibly have known Perault, who had spent some time in Timbuktu, a center of Islamic learning in the interior of western Africa. Although the presence of Muslims may have encouraged a few slaves to become interested in Islam, this religion does not appear to have influenced Vesey's own thought.[113]

For many enslaved people in Charleston, ethnicity became a cornerstone for cultural identity and group affiliation. Several rebels provided evidence about its role in the conspiracy's overall organization. Recalling a conversation with Monday, one witness said that he believed the harness maker "to be at the head of the Ebo Company. . . . he was the Captain of his Countryman's Company." Vesey perhaps recognized that Monday's ethnicity would not only bring other slaves with Igbo roots to the plot, but would also foster a sense of ethnic loyalty among his band, ensuring secrecy and making threats of punishment more effective. At his trial, William Paul testified how Mingo Harth had told him about "a Gullah Society going on once a month" and that "Gullah" Jack had emerged as a leading figure among this group. Such secret societies appear to have been an integral part of black life in Charleston. In 1863, Robert Smalls told his interviewer that he "belonged to seven societies" at which members discussed religion, freedom, and other topics. Other rebels described how Vesey appointed Pritchard to command a company of Gullah rebels. These informal alliances not only revitalized

---

can Culture," 7; on the politics of this question, see Brady, "Slave Trade and Sectionalism," 601–20.

113. Trial of Pompey Lord, 6 August 1822, DTT; Ball, *Slavery in the United States*, 164–65. See also Joyner, " 'If You Ain't Got No Education,' " 278; Jameson, "Autobiography of Omar Ibn Said," 787–95; and Austin, *African Muslims in Antebellum America*, 133–35.

ethnic identity among participants, but also provided Vesey with a useful way to organize the insurgents.[114]

The clandestine fraternal orders of conspirators may have had an African antecedent in the *poro* (a term derived from Mende, meaning "the great secret society of men"). A universal feature of life across Upper Guinea, the *poro* comprised a council that adjudicated village disputes, tried and condemned criminals, and set collective goals. The *poro*, moreover, served as the vehicle in which young boys, after undergoing training and initiation rites, made the journey from childhood to adulthood. These secret societies, as historian Margaret Washington Creel has observed, functioned "as the primary psychological and physical coercive agent for the common good." By the 1770s, similar clandestine institutions appear to have existed in South Carolina, as an anonymous visitor to the lowcountry reported. Hiding behind an unused plantation hut, the "Stranger" witnessed a small group of slaves engaged "in a secret council [that] had much the appearance of Doctors, in deep and solemn consultation upon life or *death*."[115] If institutions like the AME church brought Afro-Charlestonians together under one roof to celebrate their common experiences, then these smaller assemblies allowed people of African descent to express their ethnic differences.

By the early nineteenth century, Charleston had developed into a socially complex and multifaceted town where friends and neighbors, clients and patrons, and the free and enslaved interacted with one another in public and private places. Moreover, it was a city in which western African as well as Anglo-American practices collided to create new cultural forms. Although slavery provided the foundation on which the city's social and economic order stood, Charleston nonetheless found itself immersed in the politics of revolution and liberation. The town in which Vesey lived remained a crucible of change as the new century dawned. Charleston was not just a place in which people talked politics, however; it was also a working city that relied on its enslaved population to create the goods and provide the services that made it the leading commercial center of the southeastern states in the early nineteenth century.

---

114. Littlefield, "'Abundance of Negroes of That Nation,'" 19–38; Creel, *"A Peculiar People,"* 150–66; Testimony of Y (Yorrick Cross, the slave of Colonel George Cross), Testimony of William Paul, and Testimony of Charles Drayton, DTT; "American Freedmen's Inquiry Commission Interviews," 377. In Latin America, *confradia*, or mutual-aid societies, served as centers of worship for enslaved people where cultural and ethnic traditions could be maintained. See Hünefeldt, *Paying the Price of Freedom*, 100.

115. Creel, "Gullah Attitudes toward Life and Death," 78; *South Carolina Gazette*, 17 September 1772.

LABORING LIVES:
WORK AND SLAVERY IN CHARLESTON

Whereas it appears, many persons of late,
Have neglected the Badges for Negroes to take;
And numbers of slaves, with owners consent,
Without a licence to work have been sent

. . . .

That no negroes in future shall dare to appear,
Without our badge of permission they wear;
And this shall be visible and open to view,
And for which they shall pay us a crown sterling too.
—Verse by "Clio" in Charleston Evening Gazette, 30 August 1786

Whether they lived in the town or the countryside, work constituted the central experience for New World slaves. The discipline of the plantation, workshop, or household structured the daily lives of enslaved men and women while the laws and practices that constituted the institution of slavery acted as the instruments of their oppression. In the workplace, enslaved people might test the authority of their owners, fashion a culture rooted in the shared experience of labor, or, on occasion, resist the regimen of the field or workshop. Slaves might feign illness—as perhaps Vesey had done, leading to his diagnosis as an epileptic—remove items from their owners' houses, engage in a work slow-down, or commit acts of petty vandalism. Every work arrangement under slavery generated its own particular brand of quiet resistance or "counter-appropriation." The continual struggles over work, as historians Ira Berlin and Philip Morgan have noted, "informed all other conflicts between master and slave, and understanding that contest opens the way to a full comprehension of slave society."[116]

Like millions of slaves throughout the Americas, the specific environment and the particular arrangement under which enslaved laborers performed their tasks played a central role in shaping the daily character of work. Laboring amid work benches, tool racks, and the raw materials and finished products of their craft, the city's male slaves acquired the skills demanded by their particular trade. Following in the footsteps of skilled practitioners, they learned the common wisdom, customs, and jargon that defined the culture of their craft, attaining the "property of skill" that distinguished them as men with the ability to make barrels, forge iron, or carve stone. The work-

---

116. James C. Scott, *Weapons of the Weak*, 34, 188; Berlin and Morgan, "Labor and the Shaping of Slave Life," 2.

shop, as Johnson and Roark have noted, was "a world of tangible objects and physical process . . . [and] a place of creative thought" that united "intellectual power" with "manual prowess."[117]

But these small workshops also acted as social centers. Artisans, both free and enslaved, used them as places at which to hear news, swap gossip, or just pass the time of day. The workplace also became a place of exchange and interaction. In addition, the workshop was also an enclave of masculinity, where men might display their skill and strength as they went about their daily work. In Charleston in 1822, however, a handful of workshops took on a more overtly political purpose, becoming the setting in which a number of enslaved craftsmen gathered to discuss politics and plan armed rebellion.

When assigning work to their slaves, owners invariably followed prevailing gender arrangements. For enslaved women, urban labor consisted primarily of domestic tasks, including washing and ironing clothes, processing and cooking food, cleaning houses and raising children. In the eyes of slaveholders, most slave women performed work defined as menial and unskilled. Enslaved men, on the other hand, worked at tasks that ranged from the unskilled, including street cleaning and well digging, to highly skilled tasks, such as cabinet making and forging iron tracery for gates and fence railings. Conspirator and enslaved carpenter Scipio Sims, for example, could frame a three-story house "in the completest manner" as well as build "as good a saw gin or roller gin as any man in the State."[118] With greater opportunity to acquire skills recognized by their owners, enslaved men frequently enjoyed greater control over the labor process than did their female counterparts.

The routines of daily work gave male slaves an opportunity to shape their own habits of industry, fashioning an urban work culture in warehouses, workshops, and yards. Inside and outside the workplace, a substantial number of slave artisans enjoyed broad discretionary powers over the work they performed and the money they spent. Several slaves, including Monday Gell, earned enough money to live in rented property at some distance from their owners' houses. How slave artisans viewed themselves within the occupational structure of the city's work force, however, is difficult to gauge. Able to effect some degree of control over their working lives and to enjoy an element of economic and geographic mobility, these slaves perhaps saw themselves as distinct from the men who cleaned the streets or dug ditches and

---

117. E. P. Thompson, "Custom and Culture," 7–8; Rule, "Property of Skill," 104; Johnson and Roark, *Black Masters*, 12.

118. General Assembly Petitions, 1822, SCDAH.

wells. Their place in the work force may have fostered a limited sense of power and self-worth among this class of enslaved workers.

Deploying their skills as designers and decorative artists, enslaved artisans could stamp their own individual imprint on their work. Contracted to cast door hinges and other ironwork for the city's Congregational Church, master John Strohecker relied on the skills of his enslaved blacksmiths. These workers, who included the enslaved ironworker Perault, likely left their own distinctive signatures, decorating the door hinges, fence railings and gates that adorned the churchyard. Other slave artisans often added touches to their work by carving ornamentation on furniture, casting tracery on iron gates, or etching patterns on stone. In his work on African American material culture and the people who created it, historian John Michael Vlach has noted how craft workers used local materials, genres, and technologies while drawing inspiration for decoration and design from African artistic traditions. The hybrid objects produced, Vlach has commented, "tell the tale of survival in a creole culture."[119] Their ability to produce objects on which they left their own mark perhaps restored some dignity to their lives, enabling them to gain a sense of pride as they completed work on a piece of furniture or cast-iron tracery.

In contrast to the laboring lives of skilled slave artisans, waterfront workers performed strenuous unskilled work. Using ropes and pulleys, these men hauled bales of cotton weighing about five hundred pounds each and equally weighty barrels of rice into the holds of Atlantic merchant ships. They then secured the cargo to prevent it from shifting in transit. These muscle-wrenching tasks required that dockers work in concert, using songs and chants to coordinate the movement of the unwieldy cargo.[120] As quayside workers hoisted cotton or rice aboard, the crew readied themselves and their ship for its transatlantic voyage, buying provisions, repairing rigging, and doing other essential tasks for the upcoming journey between visits to favorite dockside taverns.

The work required to build and repair oceangoing ships also demonstrates the collective nature of maritime work. Although only a minor shipbuilding center, Charleston nonetheless boasted several shipyards and rope walks that serviced the transatlantic ships anchored in the harbor. Counting the number of craft workers in Charleston in 1826, Robert Mills estimated the city had at least 120 shipwrights, 16 boatbuilders, 32 sailmakers, and 20

---

119. See Accounts of the Independent Congregational Church, Charleston, 1807–22, SCHS; Vlach, *By the Work of Their Own Hands*, 48. On the material culture of slave life, see Singleton, "Archaeology of Slave Life," 155–75; Robert Farris Thompson, *Flash of the Spirit*.
120. Rediker, *Between the Devil and the Deep Blue Sea*, 90.

riggers. These figures do not take into account those workers indirectly associated with the maritime trades, such as coopers, pumpmakers, and iron founders. At the north end of Gadsden's wharf stood Paul Pritchard's yard in which a number of white craftsmen and about twenty slaves, including "Gullah" Jack, worked in its shops, milling lumber, rigging sails, and performing the variety of other tasks associated with ship construction, maintenance, and repair. After sawyers cut timber into keels, transoms, and decking, shipwrights then fashioned these roughly hewn pieces into a hull. Using pitch and tar, caulkers sealed the hull, making the vessel watertight—the job that Frederick Douglass performed in Baltimore's yards. In the last stage, carpenters finished the fo'c'sle, rigged the mast, and installed running gear and other superstructural equipment.[121] Like most labor associated with the maritime world, these jobs required considerable skill and cooperative work practices.

The everyday organization of slave work encompassed a broad spectrum of arrangements. Living and laboring in their owner's house or workshop, many enslaved men and women spent the bulk of their lives close to their owners. Harry and Nero Haig, for example, passed their working days in a Meeting Street cooper's shop, making buckets and barrels for owner David Haig. Likewise, Governor Bennett's domestic slaves (Batteau, Ned, and Rolla) did their daily duties in his Lynch Street house, doubtless picking up much information about state politics as they attended their owner and his family. In addition to these three men, Bennett's residence required another seventeen enslaved domestics to ensure that the household ran smoothly. Although a powerful political figure, the governor apparently inspired neither loyalty nor fear among the enslaved people with whom he and his family shared his house. Despite the physical proximity to their owners, these slaves did not hesitate to plot against them and the social order over which they presided.[122]

Some masters hired out the services of their slaves on a daily basis. Working various jobs that included digging wells, cleaning streets, or working on the waterfront, slaves earned cash for their owners at rates authorized by the council and published in the city's ordinances and, on occasion, in news-

---

121. Clowse, "Shipowning and Shipbuilding in Colonial South Carolina," 221–44; Mills, *Statistics of South Carolina*, 423. On shipyard owner Paul Pritchard, see *South Carolina Gazette and General Advertiser*, 17 April 1784; *Charleston Times*, 7 May 1806; and Will of Paul Pritchard Sr., 7 April 1814, Charleston County Wills, 1807–18, 32:817, MESDA. On ship construction, see Linebaugh, *The London Hanged*, 382–88; Bridenbaugh, *Colonial Craftsman*, 92–94.

122. Anna Johnson to Elizabeth Haywood, 18 July 1822, Haywood Papers, SHC.

papers. Required to stand at assigned positions on central streets, these enslaved day laborers would wait until "engaged to work." Leaving "his stand to such place, as shall be ordered by the person engaging him," the slave would then go to work. A full day's labor lasted "from sun-rise till twilight in the evening" with only a short break for a meal, for which exertions hired-out slaves returned to their owners with eighty-one and a quarter cents. Slaves collected modest remuneration from their masters, who would give them only a portion of the cash they had earned in the course of the day.[123]

The city's thirteen fire companies also provided enslaved men with an opportunity to supplement their incomes, earning twenty-five cents for every hour they worked on the pumps at a blaze. Although commanded by white men, these companies appear to have been manned almost exclusively by enslaved or free black men. Both the frequency of fires and time taken to extinguish them enabled slaves to earn modest amounts of cash for their efforts. Fighting a huge blaze on Gadsden's Wharf in 1821, nearly four hundred black Charlestonians struggled for five hours before dousing the flames, collecting $1.25 each for their labor. These incidents not only resulted in slaves from across the city assembling in one place, but also enabled them to engage in friendly competition. In July 1821, several white residents complained about slave firemen "whooping, yelling & running races" as they made their way to and from fires, resulting in "citizens unnecessarily alarm'd."[124] Although slaves often set fires, no direct evidence suggests that these enslaved firemen deliberately set blazes in order to put them out and collect money.

Self-hire, or "hiring out their own time," constituted an alternative permutation of work arrangements for urban slaves. In this case, the onus of securing labor and paying the owner a portion of the cash earned rested with the individual slave. Charles Ball, passing through the port town of Savannah in the early 1800s, recalled how slaves who hired out their labor "acted as freemen in so far as they went out to work, where and with whom they pleased, received their own wages, and provided their own subsistence."[125] Sometimes, slaves would receive their earnings directly from their hirer, who would then charge them with the responsibility of returning a prearranged share to their owners. Alternatively, slaves might give the lump sum to their owners at the end of the week, leaving it to their masters to distribute a share of the earnings. In other cases, slaves might never actually see the money they had earned until they received compensation from their owner. An

---

123. Bolster, *Black Jacks*, 41.
124. Minutes, 13 July 1821, Charleston Fire Masters Record Book, SHC; for rules governing fire companies, see *Alphabetical Digest of Ordinances*, 82–96.
125. Ball, *Slavery in the United States*, 368.

element of ambiguity seems to have characterized each transaction under this arrangement.

Hiring proved ideal for slaveholders wishing to supplement their incomes, enabling them to extract additional value from their slaves. Many people, observed one traveler, "obtain a handsome living by letting out their slaves for $6 to $10 per month." Some slaves earned money by driving their masters' horse and cart, moving people and goods around the city, paying their owners "so many dollars per month" from their takings. "The negro," wrote Joseph Ingraham as he traveled extensively throughout the South, "is a third arm to every working man," providing labor and generating income. As Johann David Schoepf commented during his visit to Charleston, slaveholders who had invested "their capital in negroes" could live "carelessly on the bitter sweat of the hired."[126]

The petitions for compensation that several female slaveholders sent to the legislature after the Vesey trials suggests that money brought into their households by their slaves provided an important source of income and, in some cases, their only means of support. Requesting compensation after the execution of her slave Polydore, Catherine Faber informed the assembly that his earnings had provided her household on Montague Street with its only income ever since her husband deserted her family. Earning $12 a month as an "excellent sawyer of lumber [and] a ropemaker," Polydore had kept Faber and her five children from utter destitution. As Polydore was only thirty years old when he was hanged and regarded as "hearty, sound, [and] strong," his owner doubtless expected that he would provide support for herself and children for many years to come.[127] Reimbursed $122.44 by the legislature a year after Polydore's death for the loss of her only means of support, Faber and her family somehow managed to stay off the poor rolls.

Several other single women and their households also faced impoverishment after the execution of their slaves, upon whom they relied almost exclusively for money. Destitute after the hanging of Pharaoh, Jane Thompson petitioned for compensation, claiming that her slave had been "the victim of a wicked combination among his accusers." Likewise, Naomi Smith faced reduced circumstances after the execution of her slave Caesar. Though she owned two other slaves—aged four and fourteen—they were unable to provide enough money to sustain her family, forcing her "to look to her friends

---

126. Lambert, *Travels through Lower Canada and the United States*, 2:163; Neilson, *Six Years' Residence*, 290; Ingraham, *South-West by a Yankee*, 2:249; Schoepf, *Travels in the Confederation*, 2:201.

127. Petition of Catherine Faber to the General Assembly, November 1822, General Assembly Petitions, SCDAH.

for support." Just twenty-two of the hundred-plus slaves arrested were owned by women of which the court sentenced seven to death, banished six, and acquitted the remaining nine. In contrast, while twenty-one male slaveowners had their slaves executed, fewer appear to have petitioned for compensation. Governor Bennett, who lost three slaves to the hangman, apparently did not seek compensation. For sixty-year-old William Sims, however, the execution of Dick and the banishment of Scipio apparently resulted in a steep reduction in his income. Sims requested compensation, wondering who would support him during "the evening of my life."[128]

Hiring out extended the benefits of slave ownership to nonslaveholders who could ill afford it otherwise. The person who hired a slave had only to purchase the enslaved person's labor temporarily rather than invest the substantial capital necessary for long-term ownership. In addition, hiring also enabled slaveholders and nonslaveholders alike to hire enslaved workers skilled in a particular trade for a specific period. In the years before Vesey's plot, enslaved laborers were very expensive to purchase outright. In 1819, for example, a Mr. McGillivray put a "prime and young" carpenter up for sale at $1,050, while a prime field hand cost about $850 that same year. In her petition for compensation for her executed slave, Martha Garner claimed that she had been offered $1,500 for William Garner, her cart driver. Had someone wished to hire William, he or she would have paid a fraction of that amount. According to rates published by city officials in 1818, a porter could be hired for 12.5 cents an hour. By the mid-1820s, a slave worker could be hired for between $10 and $12 a month. Although Mary Beach believed incorrectly that the plot led to a steep decline in the price of slaves, noting that they "could not bring $150" at auction, field hands sold for an average of $650 in 1822 and $600 the following year in the Charleston marketplace.[129]

Even though hiring gave slaves a modest degree of control over their working lives, it also enabled slaveholders to ignore their responsibilities as masters. Hiring out his own time in Baltimore's shipyards in the late 1830s, Frederick Douglass understood the advantages of this form of work for

---

128. Petition of Jane Thompson to the General Assembly, 22 November 1822, Petition of Naomi Smith to the General Assembly, 16 November 1822, Petition of William Sims to the General Assembly, ca. November 1822, and Petition of Martha Garner, November 1822, all in General Assembly Petitions, SCDAH. On the role of charitable societies in Charleston, see Bellows, *Benevolence among Slaveholders*, 38–39.

129. *City Gazette and Commercial Daily Advertiser*, 12 February 1819; *Alphabetical Digest of Ordinances*, 189; Petition of Martha Garner to the General Assembly, November 1822, General Assembly Petitions, SCDAH; Mills, *Statistics of South Carolina*, 423; Mary Beach to Elizabeth Gilchrist, 23 July 1822, Mary Lamboll Thomas Beach Papers, SCHS. See also Phillips, "Slave Labor Problem," 25. The drop in slave prices represents a decline of 8 percent.

owner Hugh Auld. Douglass observed that such transactions "relieved him [Auld] of all anxiety concerning me. His money was sure . . . he derived all the benefits of slave holding by the arrangement, without its evils."[130]

However advantageous slave hiring proved to individuals, it created its own set of problems for city authorities eager to monitor the activities of slave workers. Demanding that the assembly impose stricter hiring regulations in December 1822, several white Charlestonians observed how these slaves "assemble together whenever they wish . . . [and] can originate, prepare, and mature their own plans for insurrection." The case of Jesse Blackwood illustrates the failure of the authorities to regulate slaves who hired out their own time. Spending almost as much time traveling around Charleston and its hinterlands recruiting for the rebellion as he did working for his owner, Jesse found himself needing money in order to fulfill his obligations to Thomas Blackwood. To ensure that his clandestine activities would not lead to the plot's discovery, Vesey requested that several rebels contribute money to Blackwood so that he could, as Bacchus Hammet testified, "pay wages to his master."[131] That Jesse could follow this course without his owner's knowledge highlights the lax supervision of some slaves who hired themselves out. The flexibility demanded by this arrangement, the mobility and cash earnings enjoyed by slaves, and the sensations of freedom that ensued all affected the control that the urban slaveholder enjoyed over the slave's working life.

Douglass's arrangements to hire out his services as a caulker in Baltimore, which paralleled the experiences of enslaved artisans in Charleston, suggest that the burden of finding employment lay primarily with the slave. Auld insisted that his slave find work and negotiate both contract and wages. In return, Douglass "was required or obliged, to pay three dollars at the end of each week, and to board and clothe myself, and to buy my own caulking tools." Contemplating the inequity of this arrangement, Douglass noted how he "endured all the evils of being a slave, and yet suffered all the care and anxiety of a responsible freeman."[132]

By juxtaposing the words "slave" and "freeman," Douglass directly addressed the social and economic position occupied by this type of enslaved worker within the structure of the institution. Slaves who hired out lived

---

130. Douglass, *My Bondage and My Freedom*, 199. For a discussion of Douglass's life in Baltimore, see McFeely, *Frederick Douglass*; Preston, *Young Frederick Douglass*.

131. "Memorial of the Citizens of Charleston," 2:111; Confession of Bacchus Hammet, DTT.

132. Douglass, *My Bondage and My Freedom*, 199.

outside the web of social relations that informed the organization of plantation slavery, but did not enjoy the liberties and privileges, albeit limited, of the free black community or share in the wider economic freedoms and political rights of free white working men. Slave artisans thus inhabited a shadowy realm between freedom and bondage. By retaining part of their slaves' earnings, slaveholders accentuated the dichotomy between their slaves' legally defined position as property and their status as people able to obtain work and earn money as free wage laborers.

The use of money rather than other media of exchange further masked the ties that bound owner and slave together. Money itself erodes bonds of personal dependency, replacing them with abstract and impersonal relations structured by market prices and commodity transactions. After pocketing their portion of their earnings, these slaves enjoyed relative liberty in its disposal. Within limits, this cash gave slaves access to the marketplace, enabling them to consume goods and services that other forms of compensation did not allow. Yet just as money could be an instrument of opportunity, enabling enslaved artisans to enter the marketplace, it could also be used as a mechanism of control. Slaveholders could ration the amount of cash that they distributed to their slaves and, during times of economic crisis, the shortage of money further thwarted black expectations.[133]

The organization of hiring highlighted the problem of slaves working, in effect, as free wage laborers. While working on hire, a slave might distinguish between the time required to earn the money that the slaveholder would collect and the hours required to accrue the portion retained by the slave.[134] Accordingly, these slaves may have experienced directly the dichotomy between their legally defined status as property owned by another person and their ability to procure work, earn money, and interact in the marketplace in a fashion similar to their free counterparts.[135] While white and free black workers pocketed all their earnings, enslaved artisans took home only an arbitrary portion.

This aspect of hiring, as historian João José Reis has noted in his study of

---

133. On the use of money in an urban setting, see Harvey, *Consciousness and the Urban Experience*, 1–6; Douglas, *In the Active Voice*, 58. See also McDonnell, "Money Knows No Master," 31–44.

134. The time required to earn the money that the government takes from workers for tax purposes and the time taken to earn money that remains in workers' pockets serves as a modern analogy to the division of time taken to earn "master's money" and "slave's money."

135. On slave hiring, see Schweninger, *Black Property Owners in the South*, 36–44; Starobin, *Industrial Slavery in the Old South*, 128–37; and Philip D. Morgan, "Black Life in Eighteenth-Century Charleston," 187–232.

urban slaves in the Brazilian city of Salvador, was "the weak link in the political economy of slavery and a point of great stress." Douglass also recognized that the organization of hiring exposed the contradictions of slavery, noting how "the practice, from week to week, of openly robbing me of all my earnings, kept the nature and character of slavery constantly before me." Collecting the weekly wage, Douglass's owner would then "dole out . . . a sixpence or a shilling, with a view, perhaps, of kindling up my gratitude; but his practice had the opposite effect—it was admission of *my right to the whole sum.*"[136]

South Carolina politician and planter James Henry Hammond acknowledged the consequences that such arrangements had for white society, arguing that the modest economic power and mobility enjoyed by slave artisans made them among the most dangerous members of the servile population. Standing before the South Carolina Institute in 1849, he told his listeners that "[W]henever a slave is made a mechanic, he is more than half freed and soon becomes . . . the most corrupt and turbulent of his class." Douglass's escape from slavery and subsequent career as an abolitionist bore out the truth of the latter half of Hammond's observation. After attaining the requisite skills as a caulker, Douglass concluded that he was "in all respects, equal to them [white artisans] by nature and by attainments." The future leader of African Americans then asked himself: "*Why should I be a slave?*" Following some reflection, he finally "bade farewell to the city of Baltimore, and to that slavery which had been my abhorrence from childhood," making his escape to the whaling port of New Bedford, Massachusetts, where he joined the ranks of free laborers in early September 1838.[137]

Neither owners nor municipal officials could effectively monitor the enslaved bricklayers, carpenters, painters, and other craft workers who traveled freely around the city and surrounding countryside between jobs. Commenting on the activities of slaves who hired out their time in Savannah, Charles Colcock Jones commented that they "go about from house to house—some carpenters, some house servants, etc.—who never see their masters except at pay day . . . [and] hire themselves without written permission." From the late seventeenth century until the Civil War, a series of provincial and municipal laws unsuccessfully sought to regulate these workers. These local ordinances required that all slaves who worked out on hire

---

136. Reis, *Slave Rebellion in Brazil*, 173; Douglass, *My Bondage and My Freedom*, 197.

137. James Henry Hammond, "Progress of Southern Industry," 518. On this nonpareil of South Carolina's planter class, see Faust, *James Henry Hammond and the Old South*, 275; Douglass, *My Bondage and My Freedom*, 193, 202.

register every year, appear before a municipal court with their owner to be licensed, and wear a small copper badge issued by the city treasurer "on some visible part of his or her dress" that indicated their trade and status.[138]

Apart from these mandatory arrangements that appear to have been more honored in the breach, owners might informally supervise their slaves' activities. Casual conversations with hirers enabled masters to learn about their slaves' diligence and skill. Masters could also monitor the work and behavior of their slaves as they collected and distributed earnings. How many slaveholders followed these informal measures remains unknown. Although hiring did not alleviate shortages of labor that occurred periodically, it did provide the city with a substantial work force of skilled and semiskilled slaves who could move between jobs with some ease.

However much hiring troubled city authorities, slaves able to work out such arrangements with their owners appear to have eagerly embraced it. William Garner, who worked on hire as a cart driver, alluded to these attitudes as he attempted to convince the court of his innocence at this trial, asking his inquisitors why a man like him, who was "master of his own time, as good as free (and as he emphatically expressed it), 'as happy as the day is long,' would have any motive to engage in such a scheme." Beyond the degree of social and economic independence that hiring offered them, many slaves also saved money to purchase freedom for either themselves or their families. Besides Vesey, who had acquired the money needed to buy his freedom through his good fortune in a lottery, Philander Michau, following an opportunity to gain his freedom in England which he declined, had returned to Charleston and "*purchased* his freedom."[139]

---

138. Charles Colcock Jones, cited in Schweninger, "Free Blacks," 267; *Alphabetical Digest of Ordinances*, 186. See also Singleton, "Badges of Urban Slavery," 4–5; Schweninger, "Slave Independence and Enterprise in South Carolina," 101–25. Hiring laws periodically appeared in newspapers; see, for example, *South Carolina Gazette and General Advertiser*, 25 November 1783.

139. Trial of William Garner, trial of Philander Michau, DTT. That enslaved men and women in South Carolina might use their earnings to purchase freedom for themselves or others was settled in the case of *The Guardian of Sally, a Negro, against Beaty*. Heard in 1792, the court ruled that if a slaveholder allowed a slave to work on his or her own and paid that slave a specified sum from the money earned, then any extra cash that remained in the slave's pocket could be spent however he or she pleased. Accordingly, many slaves who worked on hire, noted Peter Neilson, decided to "lay up" their earnings, hoping to "procure their freedom" after years of diligent saving. On this case, see Bay, *Reports of the Cases*, 258–61; and Morris, *Southern Slavery and the Law*, 381; on manumission in South Carolina, see Senese, "The Free Negro," 140–53; Wikramanayake, *World in Shadow*; and Berlin, *Slaves without Masters*. Neilson, *Six Years' Residence*, 290.

That enslaved Afro-Charlestonians might earn enough money to save and buy their freedom depended in large measure on the health of the region's economy. In the 1790s, for example, a building revival provided work for enslaved artisans and craftsmen in the building trades. Bricklayers, plasterers, stonemasons, and carpenters worked on a new customshouse, rebuilt the statehouse, and constructed a large number of private houses. Fires and other calamities that periodically leveled sections of the city, such as the blaze in October 1812 that destroyed more than two hundred buildings and a devastating hurricane a year later, also kept slaves involved in the construction trades hard at work. The rising number of enslaved men and women who were able to buy their freedom from their owners in the last years of the century suggests that they reaped some modest benefits from this prosperity.[140] It should be noted, however, that slaves trying to purchase freedom in the early nineteenth century faced new legal obstacles following the passage of laws in 1800 and 1820 that made manumission progressively more difficult to obtain.

Regarding slaves as competitors in the labor market, white workers frequently demanded tighter controls over their enslaved counterparts. While many slaves did jobs that no white man would contemplate performing, such as road maintenance or well digging, many skilled slaves, claimed white artisans, endangered the integrity of "the mechanic part of the community" by undercutting their prices or by failing to complete lengthy apprenticeships. As the city felt the economic impact of the Panic of 1819, white artisans again petitioned for relief, concluding that any white person who intended on becoming a tradesman was about to sentence himself to "a life full of gloom and almost one of Despair." A survey taken by Robert Mills for his *Statistics of South Carolina* in 1825 bore out the truth of this observation, with the author concluding that "the wages of white workmen is 2 dollars per day . . . Black, or colored, 1 dollar." Moreover, white artisans blamed "the city's most Opulent Inhabitants" for their economic distress. Often leaving arrangements for house repairs with their enslaved domestics, who promptly hired "Men of their own colour and condition" to perform the work, wealthy Charlestonians inadvertently allowed slave artisans to dominate the trade in fixing and maintaining their residences.[141]

---

140. Walter J. Fraser, *Charleston! Charleston!*, 102. In the 1780s, for example, owners manumitted 118 slaves in Charleston as opposed to just 61 in the previous decade. See Philip D. Morgan, "Black Society in the Low Country," 116.

141. Petition of the Society of Master Coopers to the House of Representatives, 3 December 1793, and petition of Sundry Mechanics of Charleston to the General Assembly, 1822,

The material well-being of enslaved artisans also depended on economic forces beyond their control. Relying on strong and stable prices for rice and cotton in the European marketplace, the region's economic fortunes proved as changeable as the winds that carried ships in and out of Charleston's harbor. After weathering the end of the slave trade in 1808, the embargo on international trade in the years before the War of 1812 and the conflict itself, city merchants enjoyed only a brief postwar boom before they found themselves virtually ruined by the Panic of 1819, which plunged the nation into the most severe economic crisis since its founding.

With the expansion of the cotton kingdom into Alabama and Mississippi, the world market for the fiber soon became glutted, resulting in a sharp drop in its price. A severe recession in Britain caused additional problems, leading textile factories in northern England to reduce their orders for raw cotton. Writing from the English port city of Liverpool, Alexander McGregor, an agent for the Charleston-based merchant house of Napier, Rapelye, and Bennett, noted that there was "little hope of prices improving much," concluding that demand for the South's leading agricultural product continued "to drag along heavily." Jacob Rapelye concurred, informing his brother that "cotton . . . is a great drug on the market." As the price of cotton steadily dropped from thirty cents per pound in 1818 to just thirteen cents by the summer of 1822, Rapelye summed up the lowcountry's troubled economic situation, commenting that "we have had a Miserable Season of business." Rice, a leading export stable from the lowcountry, fared no better, dropping in price from $6.38 to $2.91 per hundredweight over the same period.[142]

Usually a time of great activity on the waterfront as dockers loaded ships and shipwrights refitted them, the autumn instead brought severe unemployment and underemployment. "Where once reigned wealth and happiness," observed one newspaper five years into the crisis in 1824, "nothing is now to be found but indolence, apathy, poverty and misery." Because wages fell while the price of consumer goods remained stable, many people suffered material and psychological hardships. Workers, both free and enslaved, felt the absence of hard cash, with local lawyer Robert Hayne complaining

---

General Assembly Petitions, SCDAH; Mills, *Statistics of South Carolina*, 427–28. Computing the average wages of both black and white artisans, Mills determined that it cost 82 cents a day to hire a black artisan, while an equivalent white worker cost $1.37 to employ.

142. Alexander MacGregor to Paul Rapelye, 16 July 1822, and Jacob Rapelye to Paul Rapelye, 5 August 1822, in Napier, Rapelye, and Bennett Papers, SCL. On the value of cotton and rice exports, see Cole, *Wholesale Commodity Prices in the United States*.

how the amount of specie circulating in the city had "greatly diminished," leaving the city's inhabitants "suffering most severely."[143]

Both rising poverty among many working Charlestonians as well as the arrival of growing numbers of impoverished white people from the countryside seeking work placed a considerable strain on meager municipal resources. An increase in petty crime led Charleston's grand jurors to demand the construction of a new workhouse and an increase in the poor rate.[144] Although Vesey never directly discussed how the city's failing economic fortunes frustrated the expectations of his friends and followers, they undoubtedly suffered hardships as a result of the depression and the consequent loss of income.

SALVATION AND SUBVERSION:
THE MAKING OF AN INSURGENT

Let your motto be RESISTANCE! RESISTANCE! RESISTANCE! *No oppressed people have ever secured their Liberty without resistance.*
—Henry Highland Garnet, "Address to the Slaves of the United States of America," delivered in Buffalo, New York, 1843

The workplace, the tavern, and the meetinghouse constituted the public world inhabited by Vesey in the first two decades of the nineteenth century. We know little about his private life during this period. Between his manumission in the last days of 1799 and his execution twenty-two years later, he virtually disappears from the record. Appearing only intermittently in city directories, he is listed in the *Charleston Directory and Strangers' Guide* for 1822 as "Vesey Denmark, carpenter, 20 Bull," a street in the Harleston neighborhood where he rented a one-story, single house from Dr. Alexander Trezevant.[145]

Continuing to work as a carpenter, Vesey must have enjoyed considerable success in this trade. After his death, a local newspaper reported that he had

---

143. *City Gazette and Commercial Daily Advertiser*, 20 September 1824; Robert Hayne to Langdon Cheves, 22 February 1822, cited in Theodore Jervey, *Robert Y. Hayne and His Times*, 85–86.

144. *Charleston Mercury*, 15 September 1819; Grand Jury Presentments for the District of Charleston, October 1821, Grand Jury Presentments, SCDAH. See also Klebaner, "Public Poor Relief in Charleston," 210–20. Appropriations for the city's transient poor rose from $4,280 in 1818 to $8,000 in 1819, and to $12,000 in 1820. See Cooper and McCord, *Statutes at Large*, 6:111, 135, 153.

145. *Directory and Stranger's Guide to Charleston*, 109.

accumulated an estate of several thousand dollars. On the eve of his insurrection, therefore, Vesey had acquired the financial resources to free enslaved family members. That he did not purchase their freedom is puzzling. While no definitive answer exists, there are several plausible explanations. Vesey may have made informal inquiries into purchasing enslaved family members, only to be rebuffed by slaveholders unwilling to manumit them. These owners, including John Schnell, a grocer who owned his son Sandy Vesey, perhaps needed their slaves more than they needed the cash generated by their sale. A law passed in 1820 stating that slaves could be manumitted only by a special act of the legislature may also have deterred Vesey. Alternatively, had he freed his family, it might possibly have weakened his links to the city's slave community, thus damaging his credibility as an outspoken critic of slavery. That he intended to destroy the institution which enslaved members of his family, freeing them in the process, perhaps heightened the necessity of rebellion in his eyes.

Vesey joined the AME church very soon after it opened its doors, taking responsibility for leading a small number of members in worship and discussion as a class leader. Close in age to Morris Brown, Vesey probably struck up a friendship with the church's leader. In his study of David Walker, historian Peter Hinks suggests that this militant free black pamphleteer, author of *An Appeal to the Colored Citizens of the World* (1829), might have known Vesey during his brief sojourn in Charleston in the early 1820s, noting the "remarkable similarity between the rhetoric and ideas expressed by Walker in his *Appeal* and those expressed by Vesey in the trial transcripts pertaining to him." Moreover, it is also likely that Walker attended the AME church where Vesey and a number of his accomplices worshiped.[146]

Vesey also established relationships with several female slaves. When he was arrested, he had recently parted from an enslaved woman named Beck, who appears to have worked as a laundress. Although we do not know whether Vesey fathered Beck's daughter, Sarah, he had at least two other children, Polydore and Sandy. The slave of dry-goods store owner John Paul, who also owned conspirator William Paul, Sarah appears to have worked as a laundress or dressmaker. Although the authorities did not implicate Beck, Sarah, or Polydore, they did arrest Sandy, sentencing him to exile. Apart from Sandy, Vesey apparently fathered another son named Robert who, according to historian Leon Litwack, was the architect for a new AME church that broke ground in Charleston in 1865. The shape of his family tree is further complicated by Monday Gell's brief reference to "Vesey's mulatto

---

146. Hinks, *To Awaken My Afflicted Brethren*, 30–31.

boy" whom he met one evening, as he testified, "at my house." Given his outspoken dislike of white people, however, it seems rather implausible that he had had sexual relations with a white woman. Alternatively, he may have fathered the child with a light-complected woman of African descent. Although virtually nothing else is known about Vesey's family, Hamilton had no hesitation portraying him as a man whose "passions were ungovernable and savage" and who treated his "numerous wives and children" with the "haughty and capricious cruelty of an Eastern Bashaw" (or Turkish military commander).[147]

During these years, Vesey must have spent considerable time studying and reflecting upon the institution of slavery and the oppression of Africans and African Americans. To this end, he apparently read works devoted to the origins of Africans as well as classical mythology and the Old Testament, a text that played a central role in his radicalism. Enslaved cooper John Enslow recalled how Vesey, in talking about a book on the differences between African and European skin color, concluded that black people "were not inferior to Whites on that account." In his small clandestine library of antislavery works, Vesey may have owned a copy of an essay written by "Humanitas" that appeared in February 1822 in Benjamin Lundy's newspaper, *Genius of Universal Emancipation*, which drew similar conclusions, arguing that "the African race notwithstanding their differences in shape and hue . . . are descended from the same original stock."[148]

Perhaps spurred by his naming aboard the *Prospect* and the classical roots of his name, Vesey also appears to have read some mythological stories of Greek heroes. In one case, he used the figure of Hercules to make a point about black liberation and slavery. Questioning Joe La Roche on whether he found his "present situation" to be satisfactory on one occasion, Vesey told him a story from classical literature designed to convince the slave that rebellion was the right course of action. The tale began with Hercules encountering a wagoner standing helplessly on the road after his wagon had become stranded in a ditch. After Hercules learned that the driver was unable to remedy the situation, the great man then used his immense strength to haul the cart back onto the road. Using this story as a parable, Vesey emphasized the need for slaves to take matters into their own hands and

---

147. *City Gazette and Commercial Daily Advertiser*, 21 August 1822; Litwack, *Been in the Storm So Long*, 467; Hamilton, *Account of the Late Intended Insurrection*, 17.

148. Confession of John Enslow, Henry Ravenel Papers, SCHS; *Genius of Universal Emancipation*, February 1822. On this subject, see, among other works, Frederickson, *Black Image in the White Mind*; Jordan, *White Over Black*; and Stanton, *The Leopard's Spots*.

determine their own destiny, unlike the wagoner who had failed to put "his shoulder to the wheel" with sufficient energy. "If we did not put our hand to the work and deliver ourselves," Vesey told La Roche, "we should never come out of slavery."[149] That this story bears only a passing resemblance to any of the tales of Hercules's twelve labors suggests Vesey's ability to bend and embroider well-known stories to his own purpose.

In the decades before he joined the AME church, however, little is known about his religious education. At some point, he joined one of Charleston's Presbyterian congregations. He possibly acquired some scriptural knowledge during his early years on Saint Thomas. Establishing congregations on several plantations, Moravian missionaries encouraged enslaved field workers to read scripture and eventually published a hymn book written in the local creole. And, as noted above, he may have been exposed to voodoo during his brief sojourn on Saint Domingue. Vesey may have also spent time reading the Bible during his seafaring years. Although a "notoriously irreligious" group of people, as Marcus Rediker has noted, sailors did not totally forgo religion, often combining folk traditions with Christian practices to form their own set of beliefs. Huge seas and violent storms, South Carolina mariner Theodore Jervey remembered, concentrated the mind wonderfully on survival as well as salvation. As sails and masts collapsed around him during one gale, he recalled how every deck hand "breathed out different prayers [to] save us from the Watery Grave then Yawning before us."[150]

For Vesey, texts from the Old rather than New Testament became central to his ideology of rebellion. Like many antebellum black leaders, Vesey drew inspiration from the Book of Exodus. As historian Albert Raboteau has observed, this book served as an archetypal myth for enslaved people, predicting a future radically different for the conditions they daily endured, providing "meaning and purpose to lives threatened by senseless and demeaning brutality." With its narrative of deliverance from bondage, it held out revolutionary promise for enslaved men and women willing to imagine their own liberation. Exodus, in short, proved that slavery was not part of God's grand design, promising instead that the captivity they endured would one day come to an end. But Vesey used scripture not just to "prove that slavery was contrary to the laws of God," but also as a call to action, claiming,

---

149. Kennedy and Parker, *Official Report*, 43. Vesey's entreaty to Joe La Roche to act prefigured Douglass's observation of 1855 "THAT OUR ELEVATION AS A RACE, IS ALMOST DEPENDANT UPON OUR OWN EXERTIONS" (*Frederick Douglass' Paper*, 13 April 1855, in Foner, *Life and Writings of Frederick Douglass*, 2:360). See also trial of Rolla Bennett, 20 June 1822, DTT.

150. Oldendorp, *History of the Mission of the Evangelical Brethren*, 573; Rediker, *Between the Devil and the Deep Blue Sea*, 169; Louis P. Jervey, "Thomas Hall Jervey," 140.

as Kennedy and Parker correctly concluded in their account, that "slaves were bound to attempt their emancipation . . . and that such efforts would not only be pleasing to the Almighty, but were absolutely enjoined, and their success predicted in the Scriptures."[151]

Rolla Bennett recalled how Vesey used these stories to inspire his followers. Drawing parallels between the experiences of the slaves and the Hebrews, Vesey concluded "that we ought to rise up and fight against the whites for our liberties." At the same meeting, he took Exodus 21:16 ("And he that stealeth a man, and selleth him, or if he be found in his hand, he shall surely be put to death") as a compelling justification for violence, demanding that the rebels "be ready with axes, knives, and clubs, to kill every man." Vesey used other militant biblical texts to inspire and outline his plan of action, drawing on the story of Jericho's destruction from the Book of Joshua to inspire his followers to destroy "all that was in the city, both men and women, both young and old, and ox, and sheep, and ass, with the edge of the sword."[152]

William Paul remembered how a group of conspirators had read chapters from Tobit (a book considered apocryphal by Protestants) at one gathering. Recounting the suffering and healing of a poor Israelite and his family, this book chronicles the trials of diasporic Jews struggling to maintain cultural integrity in captivity in Assyria, emphasizing the importance of maintaining traditions and calling on exiles to remain true to their faith. Tobit, moreover, does not deserve the privations and sickness that he experiences during his captivity. Through the stories of the families of Tobit and Raguel, this book anticipates an end to the Diaspora, and the restoration of the Jewish community to Israel. The story closes with Tobit lying on his deathbed, prophesying the destruction of the Assyrian capital of Nineveh and an end to exile.[153]

Vesey might have used this text along with Exodus to conclude that the conditions of the ancient Jews and of Afro-Carolinians in the early nineteenth century bore great similarities. If so, he may have sought to inculcate a greater sense of group affinity among the conspirators. Only by investing them with a sense of self-worth could Vesey hope to bring his enterprise to a successful conclusion. He thus may have used these texts as more than a call to arms; he may have employed them as a means of instilling a deeper sense of black identity among the rebels. Just as slaveholders employed biblical

---

151. Raboteau, *Slave Religion*, 311; Gilroy, *Black Atlantic*, 206–7; Walzer, *Exodus and Revolution*; Kennedy and Parker, *Official Report*, 11.

152. Testimony of Rolla Bennett, DTT; Joshua 6:21.

153. On Tobit, see Mays, *Harper's Bible Commentary*, 791–803; Moore, *Tobit*.

arguments to justify slavery, so Vesey would use Old Testament texts to help bring about the destruction of the institution. "Slavery and bondage," as Vesey told William Paul on one occasion, "is against the Bible."[154]

Vesey also looked to contemporary political events as he shaped his ideology. Having spent many years at sea, encountering other sailors and their politics, he probably understood the dynamics behind the series of revolutions that broke out around the Atlantic basin better than most working people at the time.[155] Had Vesey ever encountered Jacques, the enslaved domestic of Saint Domingue refugee Etienne Delavincendiere, during his forays around Charleston, he would have had the chance to hear a remarkable story about war and revolution in the eighteenth-century Atlantic. Born a free black in South Carolina in the late 1740s, Jacques found himself imprisoned by the French during the Seven Years' War and then enslaved on Martinique. He was then sold to Saint Domingue on the eve of the French Revolution, working in Cap Français and Saint Marc for a few years until his owner fled to Charleston in 1793. Conversations with people like Jacques would have honed Vesey's political awareness, which was drawn largely from his own experiences.[156]

Though Vesey did not witness the American Revolution in South Carolina, its legacy remained very much part of daily life. Veterans from the war still walked Charleston's streets, former Continental army officers dominated its politics, local author and physician David Ramsey had published the first comprehensive history on the subject in 1789, and its citizens staged lavish celebrations every fourth of July. Even the tea cups and dinner plates that enslaved domestics handled daily memorialized the revolution, with platters decorated with Washington's crossing of the Delaware and dishes depicting Cornwallis's defeat at Yorktown adorning the dining tables of the wealthy. As the revolution unfolded, a few enslaved Charlestonians appeared to have grasped its political implications. During the Stamp Act crisis of 1765, merchant and planter Henry Laurens witnessed a band of slaves running through the streets, "crying out 'Liberty'" just as the Sons of Liberty had done in protest against British policy some weeks earlier. Several months later, Equiano witnessed the celebrations greeting the repeal of the

---

154. Trial of William Paul, 19 June 1822, DTT.

155. See Palmer, *The Age of Democratic Revolutions*; David Brion Davis, *Problem of Slavery in the Age of Revolution*; Curtin, *Rise and Fall of the Plantation Complex*, 144–72; Frey, *Water from the Rock*; and Langley, *The Americas in the Age of Revolution*.

156. Petition of Etienne Delavincendiere, 3 May 1797, vol. JJJ, p. 220, Miscellaneous Records, SCDAH.

Stamp Act, watching bonfires and fireworks from his ship anchored in Charleston harbor.[157]

Just weeks after British soldiers and colonists clashed at Lexington and Concord in April 1775, the authorities uncovered a plan for a slave rebellion led by a free black fisherman named Thomas Jeremiah (known locally as Jerry), who announced that the "great war coming" would be a struggle "to help the poor Negroes." By August, Jerry had been tried and executed, but this plot heralded a period of restiveness among enslaved plantation laborers in the lowcountry who grew increasingly truculent, engaging in "impertinent Behavior" as war became "common talk throughout the Province" and rumors about emancipation began to circulate in the summer of 1775. A few months later, John Murray, the earl of Dunmore and last royal governor of Virginia, issued a proclamation that granted freedom to any slave who left his owner for the royal standard and joined the Ethiopian regiment, whose bandoliers were emblazoned with the words "Liberty to Slaves." Jerry's plot as well as the growing intransigence among some lowcountry slaves suggests that they may have recognized the possibilities presented by the deepening crisis between England and the colonies.[158]

The outbreak of revolution in France in 1789 led many Charlestonians to demonstrate enthusiastic support for another experiment in republican government. The "tri-coloured cockade of France was the great badge of honour," recalled Charles Fraser, a student at the College of Charleston in

---

157. Ravenel, *Charleston*, 364; Henry Laurens to John Lewis Gervais, 29 January 1766, in Hamer et al., *Papers of Henry Laurens*, 5:54; on this and other similar events, see Rediker, "'A Motley Crew of Rebels,'" 155–56. For studies on enslaved Africans during this and other events prior to 1776 in the lowcountry, see Frey, *Water from the Rock*, 45–80; Maier, "Charleston Mob and the Evolution of Popular Politics," 173–96; Olwell, "'Domestick Enemies,'" 21–48; Wood, "Taking Care of Business," 268–93, and "'The Dream Deferred,'" 166–87. On the war in the lowcountry itself, see Frey, *Water from the Rock*, 108–42; Philip D. Morgan, "Black Society in the Low Country"; Nadelhaft, *Disorders of War*; and Pancake, "This Destructive War." For broader discussions of African American involvement in the conflict, see Kaplan and Kaplan, *Black Presence in the Era of the American Revolution*; Quarles, *Negro in the American Revolution*. Reaction among some lowcountry slaves to the coming of war is discussed by plantation manager Josiah Smith in letters to his employer. See Smith to George Austin, 14 June 1775, and Smith to George Appleby, 16 June 1775, Josiah Smith Letterbook, SHC.

158. On Jerry, see George Milligan, "Narrative by George Milligan of His Experiences in South Carolina," in K. G. Davis, *Documents of the American Revolution*, 11:109; Governor Lord William Campbell to the Earl of Dartmouth, 31 August 1775, in ibid., 11:95; Correspondence of the Secretary of State, 15 September 1775, CO5/396, Public Record Office, London; Weir, *Colonial South Carolina*, 201–3; Walter J. Fraser, *Charleston! Charleston!*, 144–45.

the early 1790s, "and *Ca'ira* and the Marseillaise hymn the most popular airs—and 'Vive la république Français' the universal shout." An elaborate parade in January 1791 followed by church services and a grand fête, as well as the establishment of several political clubs including the Democratic-Republican Society and the French Patriotic Society, further marked the city's embrace of the French Revolution. Walking along East Bay at night, Telemaque perhaps heard members of the Société Patriotique Française, who addressed each other with "the cogomen of *citoyen*," burst into "La Marseillaise" during their weekly meeting at Thomas Harris's waterfront establishment.[159]

This enthusiasm for France as well as the presence of a French Huguenot community in Charleston may have prompted Edmond Genêt, minister plenipotentiary of the French Republic to the United States, to start his sojourn in the United States in Charleston, spending ten days in the city before leaving for Philadelphia. Fireworks and cannonades greeted his arrival in April 1793, a fanfare that city residents repeated a few months later when they celebrated Bastille Day on 14 July. Participants wore cockades and attended banquets where they made toasts to "the Rights of Man," "July 14, 1789," and those who "love liberty and equality."[160] A few months after Genêt left the city, another group of Charleston's Francophiles founded La Société Républicaine de la Caroline du Sud, in which tradesmen, artisans such as shipwrights, and ships' masters joined in large numbers to support the revolution in France.[161]

With Genêt's departure, French consul Michel Ange Bernard de Mangourit now carried the torch for the revolutionary cause in Charleston, but as dispossessed planters began arriving from Saint Domingue in growing numbers, he quickly discovered that not all Frenchmen shared his enthusiasm. "We have here," he informed his superiors in Paris, "a great number of aristocrats *under the skin*," who were opposed to the actions of the revolutionary government in France. Trying to recruit men for an expedition to seize Florida and Louisiana from the Spanish, the young revolutionary discovered that fewer than a dozen of the six hundred or so Frenchmen in Charleston were ready to "shed blood" for the republic. The "most obstinate enemy against the Republic in the United States," he complained, "are the

---

159. See David Brion Davis, *Revolutions*, esp. 29–54; Charles Fraser, *Reminiscences of Charleston*, 35, 39–40; Kennedy, "French Jacobin Club in Charleston," 4–21; Link, *Democratic-Republican Societies*; George C. Rogers Jr., *Evolution of a Federalist*, 245–47; Hazen, *Contemporary American Opinion of the French Revolution*, 171–75.

160. Kennedy, "French Jacobin Club in Charleston," 18, 21.

161. George C. Rogers Jr., *Evolution of a Federalist*, 256.

French," who blamed "the terrible anarchy" that had befallen their plantations on the actions of the revolutionaries.[162]

Living and working in Charleston during these years, Vesey appears to have absorbed some ideas from the revolutions in France and in its Caribbean possessions into his own thinking. No doubt aware that 14 July commemorated the day on which the Parisian crowd attacked the Bastille, the event that heralded the start of the revolution, Vesey initially selected that date to launch his own attack on slavery, exclusion, and inequality. This particular day in 1822 also gave the rebels some tactical advantage. Although the city no longer celebrated Bastille Day, Vesey may have discovered from an almanac that the night of Sunday, 14 July, fell between the moon's last quarter and the rising of a new one, enabling the insurgents to move into position under the cover of complete darkness. Moreover, thanks to the summer exodus of planters, merchants, and their families to the countryside, "the numbers of white inhabitants would be much diminished" in the city, further helping the rebels to launch their attack.[163]

The revolution on Saint Domingue, however, proved to be the most dramatic political and social event in an era notable for political and social upheaval.[164] For Vesey, this protracted, complicated, and bloody struggle between armies of revolutionary slaves, property-owning free people of color, plantation owners, and legions of European troops provided indisputable proof that the dispossessed could overthrow the tyranny of slavery. A former Saint Domingue slave himself, Vesey likely followed the course of this conflict and the establishment of the black republic of Haiti with some interest. Slaves who worked in the offices of Charleston's *City Gazette* regularly stole copies when "interesting extracts" about this revolution appeared in its pages, presumably distributing them among friends in taverns and other places.[165] When French planters and their enslaved retinues arrived in Charleston, Vesey had the opportunity to acquaint himself further with events on Saint Domingue, conversing with newly arrived slaves about the latest events on the island.

As he plotted the insurrection, Vesey appeared determined to emulate the

---

162. Citizen Michel de Mangourit to Citizen Gaspard Monge, 29 May 1793, in Murdoch, "Correspondence of French Consuls in Charleston," 10, 15–16. For a provocative analysis of the national political and intellectual implications of this revolution, see Zuckerman, "Power of Blackness," 175–218, and Alfred N. Hunt, *Haiti's Influence on Antebellum America*.

163. Kennedy and Parker, *Official Report*, 24.

164. See Jordan, *White Over Black*, 375–402.

165. *City Gazette and Daily Advertiser*, 12 February 1791, cited in Julius S. Scott, "Afro-American Sailors and the International Communication Network," 41.

violence of Saint Domingue's black Jacobins, perhaps seeing himself as another Toussaint L'Ouverture, the former enslaved coachman who became the revolution's leading general and who contributed enormously to the eventual destruction of the island's French ruling planter class. Only when armies of former slaves obliterated the European presence on the island did they establish freedom on their own terms, founding the Haitian republic in 1804. Several leading conspirators in 1822 recognized the close relationship between the two events, confessing that the Saint Domingue uprisings had served as a model for their rebellion. Besides exhorting his followers "not to spare one white skin alive, as this was the plan they pursued in Santo Domingo," Vesey also persuaded them that military aid would be forthcoming from the island and that they would seek refuge there after they had destroyed Charleston.[166]

French refugees brought the rebellion home to Charleston when they fled there by the hundreds in 1793 and 1794. The fires that destroyed large portions of the port city of Le Cap in June 1793 served, as one French official alarmingly noted, "as the harbingers of black supremacy." The intense ferocity of these attacks foreshadowed the extraordinary violence that would characterize the struggle for power on the island. Marching down from the mountains armed with torches and knives, "immense hordes of Africans" stormed into the city. So intense were the fires these men set that "the flames," wrote one French planter, "were lifted as in a whirlwind and spread everywhere," reducing Le Cap to ashes. Slaves also devastated the Plaine du Nord's sugar plantations, destroying crops, burning property, and killing plantation owners. Anxious to escape this destruction, planters and their personal retinues of slaves as well as free people of color all headed to Le Cap's harbor, "over which black ashes still hovered," setting sail in a small armada of ships for the security of other Caribbean islands and the North American mainland. In June and July 1793, several hundred refugees, both free and enslaved, landed in Charleston. As they clambered ashore, seeking food and shelter, "daily life," as local scientist Alexander Garden noted, subsequently "became more precarious."[167]

The unpredictable course of events in the Caribbean unnerved national as well as local political leaders. Fearing that growing violence and political

---

166. Kennedy and Parker, *Official Report*, 59.

167. Parham, *My Odyssey*, 91, 94. See also Terry, "Impact of the French Revolution"; Carteau, *Soirées Bermudiennes*, cited in Stoddard, *French Revolution in San Domingo*, 224; "Rusticus" [Alexander Garden] to Gentlemen, 20 June 1794, Alexander Garden Papers, SCHS.

instability would soon lead to "a total expulsion of the whites sooner or later" from "the West India Islands," Thomas Jefferson grimly warned fellow Virginian James Monroe in July 1793 that "we should forsee the bloody scenes which our children certainly, and possibly ourselves (south of [the] Potomac) [will] have to wade through & try to avert them." Accordingly, when Jefferson learned from a French informant in Philadelphia that two refugees from Saint Domingue—a man called Castaing who was "a small dark mulatto" and "a Quateron of a tall fine figure" named La Chaise—had apparently left that city bound for Charleston, harboring "a design to excite an insurrection among the negroes," he immediately alerted Governor John Drayton, urging swift action.[168] Neither La Chaise nor Castaing, however, succeeded in his purported scheme to foster rebellion in the lowcountry.

Beside these immediate concerns, lowcountry planters clearly recognized that the social and demographic conditions that prevailed on their own estates bore a striking resemblance to Saint Domingue's plantation regime, now rapidly collapsing beneath the onslaught of rebellious slaves. Governor Charles Pinckney even shared such thoughts with beleaguered members of Saint Domingue's Colonial Assembly, observing in a letter "how nearly similar situation of the Southern States and St. Domingo are in the profusion of slaves—that a day may arrive when they may be exposed to the same insurrections—we cannot but sensibly feel for your situation." By the end of the struggle in 1804, at least twenty thousand of the island's thirty thousand whites had died or emigrated, more than one-third of its half million slaves were no longer alive, and ten thousand out of forty thousand mulattos and free blacks had vanished. To prevent such bloodshed in the lowcountry, Colonel Vanderhorst ordered militia commanders to break up "large meetings of Negroes," observing that "the peace of our country and the lives of our fellow citizens are depending on our punctual and vigilant conduct." Fears about slave insurrection only increased when the National Assembly in Paris abolished slavery, extending the rights of citizenship to all men regardless of color throughout the French empire in early 1794. In the wake of this proclamation, Garden averred that French slaves would reject "the authority of their masters" and insist on their rights as free men.[169]

---

168. Thomas Jefferson to James Monroe, 14 July 1793, cited in Aptheker, *American Negro Slave Revolts*, 42; Thomas Jefferson to Governor John Drayton, 23 December 1793, in Washington, *Writings of Thomas Jefferson*, 4:97–98. See also Sharp, *American Politics in the Early Republic*, 241.

169. Governor Charles Pinckney, cited in Ott, *Haitian Revolution*, 53. On the demographic consequences of the Haitian Revolution, see Rotberg, *Haiti*, 48; Dillon, *Slavery*

Few slave societies appeared immune from the contagion of liberty as revolution in metropolitan France spread across the Atlantic to the New World. On Martinique, between three and four hundred slaves set out to burn the town of Saint Pierre in August 1789 until planters halted their slaves' "most diabolical designs." Within weeks, another conspiracy came to light in Demerara, resulting in public executions of "the infatuated Wretches." The following year, slaves on Cuba, Guadeloupe, Tortola, and again on Martinique all mounted concerted challenges against their enslavement. These incidents, however, were minor brush fires when compared to the conflagration that broke out on Saint Domingue where rebellion had become, as lowcountry planter and politician Charles Pinckney fearfully noted, "a flame which will extend to all the islands, and may eventually prove not a very pleasing or agreeable example to the Southern States."[170]

White Charlestonians greeted all these events with some concern. A group of English sailors who, following a "drunken orgy" to celebrate Saint George's Day (23 April) in 1793, proceeded to attack and insult any French pedestrian they could find and "lay their daring hands on their tricolours," further alerted the city's residents to the potential for domestic unrest and disorder caused by this revolution. Two years later, a party of French émigrés gained revenge when, after celebrating Bastille Day, they first walked on "the British flag" before burning "said degraded flag." Those who exhibited even the slightest support for the rebellion on Saint Domingue quickly found themselves excoriated by white residents as "Madmen, Robbers of their Neighbors Property and enemies to the Peace of Society." To demonstrate their support for the counterrevolutionaries that Mangourit had found so troubling, city leaders organized a series of events designed to raise money for "the Benefit of the Distressed Inhabitants of St. Domingo," providing these newly impoverished émigrés with "money, linens and lodging." No

---

Attacked, 46; Colonel Vanderhorst to Captain McKelvey, 26 August 1793, South Carolina Militia Book, 1793–1814, SCHS; "Rusticus" [Alexander Garden] to Gentlemen, 7 August 1794, Alexander Garden Papers, SCHS.

170. Moitt, "Slave Resistance in Guadeloupe and Martinique," 136–59; Geggus, "Slavery, War, and Revolution," 1–50, and "The Enigma of Jamaica in the 1790s," 274–99; Michael Mullin, "British Caribbean and North American Slaves," 235–68. For broader surveys on this topic, see, for example, Blackburn, *Overthrow of Colonial Slavery*; Curtin, *Rise and Fall of the Plantation Complex*; Langley, *The Americas in the Age of Revolution*; Michael Mullin, *Africa in America*; and Rogozinski, *Brief History of the Caribbean*. *Bermuda Gazette*, 21 November 1789, 26 December 1789. On the symbolic importance of the revolution on Saint Domingue, see Sundquist, *To Wake the Nations*, 31; Alfred N. Hunt, *Haiti's Influence on Antebellum America*.

doubt anxious to exhibit their cultivation and refinement to French planters and their families, the lowcountry gentry held several concerts and staged a special performance of Henry Brooke's *The Tragedy of the Earl of Essex* in the city's theater. Accompanied by friends and family members, Joseph Vesey no doubt attended several of these events in his capacity as treasurer of the Benevolent Committee that raised $12,000 for the cause.[171]

Besides organizing these fund-raising events, several local citizens took practical steps to prevent the outbreak of disorder as ships packed with refugees from Saint Domingue dropped anchor in the harbor. So that Charleston would not become a crucible of black rebellion, these men, including Joseph Vesey, drew up a series of resolutions at a town meeting held in early October 1793 to demand that "negroes and people of colour be on no account suffered to land in any part of the state." Governor William Moultrie responded quickly to this committee, ordering that "all free negroes and persons of colour, who have arrived within twelve months from any other place, to depart . . . within TEN DAYS." While a few slaveholders ignored this executive order and some refugee planters from Saint Domingue managed to land their slaves, petitions from the city council to the legislature, requesting that it pay for the cost of "confining French negroes" as well as their passage from South Carolina between 1793 and 1796, suggest that this measure had some teeth. For the next several years, city fathers appear to have enforced this resolution informally. Taking this injunction seriously, city merchant Christopher Fitzsimmons instructed a captain of his vessel preparing to sail for Saint Domingue in 1799 to "take no person's property aboard . . . [and] you are not to take any passengers going or coming here." In 1803, the same year that South Carolina reopened the Atlantic slave trade, a new law prohibited the import of any slave from the West Indies and South America, and closed the door on any black person who had resided in any French possession in the Caribbean.[172]

Yet some slaves from Saint Domingue remained undeterred by these attempts to maintain order. In the same month that Joseph Vesey and his

---

171. *Charleston Courier*, 28 February 1793; William Read to Jacob Read, 21 July 1795, Jacob Read Papers, WPL; Charles Nisbet to Reverend William Rogers, 17 August 1792, cited in Matthewson, "American Reaction to the Haitian Revolution," 149; La Rochefoucauld-Liancourt, *Travels through the United States*, 1:557; Rogers, *Charleston in the Age of the Pinckneys*, 110.

172. Nathaniel Russell to Ralph Izard, 6 June 1794, cited in Phillips, "South Carolina Federalists," 735; Terry, "Negro Seaman Acts," 78–93; Christopher Fitzsimmons to John Hathaway, 18 July 1799, Christopher Fitzsimmons Letterbook, SCL; Brevard, *Digest of the Public Statute Law*, 2:261.

fellow committee members called for the immediate expulsion of refugee slaves and free blacks from Charleston, a visitor from New York reported that "St. Domingue negroes have sown the seed of revolt and that a magazine has been attempted to be broken open."[173] Four years later in November 1797, constables arrested a number of Saint Domingue slaves, who had apparently organized into companies by their leaders and were preparing to rebel and destroy the city. As French émigrés often earned their livelihoods "by letting negroes," these slaves probably enjoyed some degree of mobility, enabling them to organize their plot. Planning to capture weapons from the city arsenal before beginning their "bloody work," these slaves intended "to massacre and slaughter" white worshipers as they headed home from church on Christmas Day. They then planned to "fire the city and act here as they had formerly in St. Domingo." Betrayed by one of their own number, these rebels were quickly hanged after their arrest, although such speedy justice did not allay the fears of local residents who, reported one Charlestonian, suffered from an "Agitation of the Spirits" in the wake of this episode.[174]

Concerned about this conspiracy and fearful of further unrest, city authorities tried yet again to tighten security, strictly enforcing patrol and pass laws, and censoring inflammatory literature. Perhaps choosing the date purposefully, constables arrested Swiss immigrant printer Jean Negrin on 4 July 1804 for printing and selling copies of *The Declaration of Independence of the French Colony of Santo Domingo*, written by Jean-Jacques Dessalines, the former field hand who had risen to political and military power to lead Haiti to independence. Just a few weeks after Dessalines proclaimed Haitian independence, he had ordered the massacre of more than three thousand French planters and their families. Such actions doubtless added to concerns about the presence of Saint Domingue slaves and heightened fears that the circulation of such provocative material might fall into the wrong hands.[175] Finding Negrin guilty of "seditious and traitorous intentions against the peace and welfare of this country," the court imprisoned him for several months. That a Monsieur Herbemont, a French teacher who lived on nearby Sullivan's Island, had translated a biography of Toussaint L'Ouverture two years earlier published by local printer T. Bowen and that several other works on the

---

173. *New York Journal and Patriotic Register*, 11 October 1793, cited in Jackson, *Privateers in Charleston*, 93.

174. *Worcester Gazette*, 20 December 1797; La Rochefoucauld Liancourt, *Travels through the United States*, 584; *South Carolina Weekly Museum*, 25 November 1797; Jacob Alison to Jacob Read, 5 December 1797, Jacob Read Papers, WPL.

175. Petition of Jean Negrin to Senate, ca. 1805, General Assembly Petitions, SCDAH; Dayan, *Haiti, History, and the Gods*, 143–86.

struggle on Saint Domingue sat on the shelves of city bookstores did not deter the authorities from prosecution.[176]

The document that led to Negrin's arrest began with a rhetorical flourish that Vesey would have likely admired, clearly stating the intentions of the newly established Haitian republic: "Restored to our primitive dignity, we have asserted our rights, we swear never to yield them to any power on earth, the frightful veil of prejudice is torn to pieces, be it so forever."[177] Although slaves were not supposed to read about events on Haiti by the late 1790s and early 1800s, a significant amount of material about the revolution was readily available. Apart from conversing with sailors recently arrived from the island, slaves might also gain information from the several journals and newspapers that often printed reports on the conflict. Writing under the pseudonym "Rusticus," Alexander Garden complained bitterly that Charleston's *Columbian Herald* had published glowing accounts by General Etienne Laveaux, who partly attributed his success over a Spanish force on Saint Domingue to the beneficial effect of the National Assembly's emancipation proclamation on his black troops. Lavishing such "a tribute of praise . . . upon a race of men who by their example and success hold up every inducement to our domestics to resist our authority" might only encourage local slaves to "rise up in arms against us," Garden observed.[178] "They are told," he continued, "that actuated by the spirit of Liberty their Brethren have become heroes." Seeking to prevent the circulation of similar materials among the black population, state legislators strengthened the law under which Negrin had been charged, making the writing and publication of "any inflammatory discourse, tending to alienate or seduce the fidelity of any slave . . . [a] high misdemeanor." Regardless of such statutes, city slaves still had access to several publications regarded as provocative, possibly including copies of the December 1791 edition of the Boston *Argus* in which Yale graduate Abraham Bishop argued that Saint Domingue's slaves were "fighting in a just cause . . . and are now sealing with their blood, *the rights of man*."[179]

Even as the legislature sought to ban books that contained "inflammatory

---

176. Petition of Jean Negrin. Six years later, Negrin had left Charleston, establishing himself in the more congenial political climate of Philadelphia, publishing a literary and political journal entitled *L'Hemisphere*. Herbemont, *Life of Toussaint Louverture*. Louis Dubroca was the original author of this volume, which Herbemont translated into English.

177. Rainsford, *Historical Account of Black Hayti*, 439.

178. "Rusticus" [Alexander Garden] to Gentlemen, 20 June 1794, Garden Papers, SCHS; see also Jackson, *Privateers in Charleston*, 94.

179. Brevard, *Digest of the Public Statute Law*, 2:202; Abraham Bishop, "The Rights of Black Men," *The Argus* (Boston), 6 December 1791, cited in Matthewson, "American Reaction to the Haitian Revolution," 153. See also Curtin, "Declaration of the Rights of Man," 157–75.

discourse," the Charleston Library Society ensured that its shelves remained stocked with several volumes that openly explored the politics of slavery, abolition, and revolution. During the first decades of the nineteenth century, the library acquired a number of texts that were at odds with the cherished ideas of many white Charlestonians. Copies of Thomas Clarkson's two-volume *History of the Rise, Progress, and Accomplishment of the Abolition of the African Slave Trade by the British Parliament* (1808) stood alongside a translation of *The Life of Toussaint Louverture* (1802) and *A Vindication of the Rights of Woman* (1792), written by Mary Wollstonecraft. Library members could also check out John Stedman's *Narrative of an Expedition against the Revolted Negroes of Surinam* (1796) in addition to several works devoted to the course of the French Revolution. For those patrons interested in other genres, the library also held a large collection of fiction, including William Cowper's translation of *The Iliad* and *The Odyssey*, as well as *The Adventures of Telemachus*, by French author François Fenelon.[180]

As the eighteenth century waned, so did popular support for the French Revolution in South Carolina. Even though newspapers still carried reports about events in France and the approach of war in Europe, the passion that many Charlestonians had once shown for the cause had evaporated. Writing under the pseudonym "A South Carolina Federalist" in 1797, Henry DeSaussure reflected on this decline, observing how "the sad conviction that the conductors of the revolution . . . were ruining the cause of genuine republican liberty" had "extinguished the generous enthusiasm" that once greeted news from France. Several years earlier, the *State Gazette of South Carolina* had branded Mangourit as "an intriguant and a promoter of discord." In other cases, the rhetoric was considerably more hostile as open criticism replaced the genuine excitement that had once awaited word from Paris. Summarizing this antagonistic attitude toward France's experiment with republicanism, the *Charleston Courier* fulminated against "the jacobins [who] are equally enemies to all morality and moral and civil order." In their eyes, the revolutions in France and on Saint Domingue were primarily responsible for "the deplorable state to which the world has been reduced."[181]

On the American mainland, slaves in several places emulated the rebellious activities of Caribbean slaves, launching revolts against their masters. In 1795, French officials in Louisiana uncovered a plot involving slaves from the French Caribbean. Sixteen years later, several hundred slaves, led by

180. Charleston Library Society, *Catalogue of Books*.
181. South Carolina Federalist, *Answer to a Dialogue*, 9; *State Gazette of South Carolina*, 3 December 1793, cited in Jackson, *Privateers in Charleston*, 37; *Charleston Courier*, 20 April 1803, 4 February 1803.

a free black man from Saint Domingue, marched on New Orleans, cutting a swath of destruction along the Mississippi until they were stopped after several skirmishes. Farther south, in the Brazilian city of Rio de Janeiro, slaves wore necklaces bearing the image of Dessalines just after he had declared his nation's independence in 1804. These and many other slaves living and laboring in the vast New World plantation complex wanted, in the words of a small band of rebel slaves captured on the Plaine du Nord in 1791, "to enjoy their liberty they are entitled to by the Rights of Man."[182]

In the new republic of the United States, the most prominent episode of organized black resistance inspired by Saint Domingue took place in Richmond, the capital of Virginia. During the summer months of 1800, black and white Charlestonians heard news about a complicated plot that involved slaves from three other towns in the state. Led by an enslaved blacksmith named Gabriel, this conspiracy, as historian Douglas Egerton has observed in his comprehensive study, aimed to bring together " 'the most redoubtable democrats in the state' to destroy the economic hegemony of the 'merchants,' the only whites he ever identified as his enemies." Although Gabriel's scheme never endangered the lowcountry, John Drayton, the governor of South Carolina, nonetheless ordered the strict enforcement of all patrol laws, instructing the militia to "search all Negro houses for arms and ammunition."[183] The source of Gabriel's political inspiration proved more disturbing for white Virginians than the plot's scale. Gabriel, Egerton has concluded, was "no apolitical servant but a literate artisan whose breadth of vision was truly international." Assessing the impact of Saint Domingue on the plot, James Monroe, the governor of Virginia, concluded that: "the scenes which are acted in St. Domingo must produce an effect on all the people of colour in this and the States south of us. . . . [I]t is our duty to be on our guard to prevent any mischief resulting from it."[184]

In the wake of these Atlantic revolutions at the end of the eighteenth century, other liberation struggles coursed through the region. Just a few months before Vesey's arrest, Charleston's newspapers reported on the

---

182. On the 1795 conspiracy at Pointe Coupée, see Gwendolyn Midlo Hall, *Africans in Colonial Louisiana*, 343–74. On the 1811 rebellion, see Julius S. Scott, "Common Wind," 274; Reis, *Slave Rebellion in Brazil*, 48; and *General Advertiser* (Philadelphia), 10 October 1791.

183. Egerton, *Gabriel's Rebellion*, x; Governor John Drayton to Governor James Monroe, 27 September 1800, General Orders, 27 September 1800, Executive Letterbooks, Governor John Drayton to South Carolina Senate, 25 November 1800, and Governor's Message #768, all in Governors' Messages, SCDAH.

184. James Monroe to Brigadier General Mathews, 17 March 1802, cited in Egerton, *Gabriel's Rebellion*, 47; see also Gerald W. Mullin, *Flight and Rebellion*, 140–63.

growing popularity of independence movements in Spanish America as figures like Simón Bolívar and José de San Martin began to emerge. These papers also gave readers several accounts of Haitian leader Jean-Pierre Boyer's successful campaign against the island's Spanish provinces in early 1822, resulting in the abolition of slavery in Santo Domingo (the modern-day Dominican Republic). The "spirit of the age," noted the *Carolina Gazette*, "is everywhere felt in countries oppressed by despotism in regions benighted with bigotry."[185] Vesey, who may have been unaware of the ideologies that informed these Latin American movements, would have agreed wholeheartedly with such sentiments.

Public rhetoric celebrating American independence and the new nation inadvertently echoed the stirring language used by slavery's Atlantic world opponents. The fanfare that marked every fourth of July both recalled the nation's revolutionary beginnings for free and enslaved Charlestonians alike, and highlighted the racial exclusivity of independence. From dawn to dusk, thanksgiving services, patriotic addresses, picnics, and other events publicly exposed the gulf between the reality and the rhetoric of the revolution's ideology. In sermons, ministers preached about how God's providence had delivered America from Britain's "oppressive designs," enabling the republic's citizenry to enjoy "possession of liberty, peace and independence." To reinforce these patriotic messages, congregations punctuated their celebratory services with song, singing hymns that employed images of the slave trade to celebrate freedom, including one that opened with the following verse:

> Oppression shook his iron rod,
> And slav'ry clank'd her galling chain;
> We sought protection from our God,
> And he did freedom's cause maintain.[186]

On several occasions, this holiday provided slaves an opportunity to protest their circumstances. In 1814, a band of enslaved musicians in Savannah decided to withdraw their services "from the procession formed in honor and celebration of that day." Not all enslaved people protested the national birthday in so peaceful a fashion. Two years later, a group of slaves from Camden, a small town in the South Carolina upcountry, earmarked this day to revolt against their owners, taking advantage of holiday diversions to press home their attack. Led by enslaved men who "occupied a respectable stand in one of the churches," noted the *Camden Gazette*, these rebels in-

---

185. Logan, *Haiti and the Dominican Republic*, 32; *Carolina Gazette*, 16 February 1822, 23 March 1822.

186. Furman, *America's Deliverance and Duty*, 20.

tended "to set fire to one part of the town" and capture the arsenal and its weapons before proceeding "to murder the men." The discovery of this plot led to the execution of six slave men. Virginia slave Nat Turner initially chose 4 July as the day on which to attack Southampton County's slaveholders in 1831, although this rebellion did not take place until August as Turner fell ill in early July.[187]

For enslaved ship carpenter and leading conspirator Peter Poyas, however, 4 July apparently bore sinister overtones. Answering Robert Harth's remark about benevolent city leaders who had advertised their plans "to build a Missionary House for the blacks" in local newspapers, Poyas shot back by dismissing such reports, telling his fellow rebel that white people planned to massacre black people on 4 July. Afraid that knowledge about the rebellion had leaked out, Poyas claimed that "the Whites are going to create a false alarm of fire and every black that comes out will be killed to thin them."[188]

That white Charlestonians celebrated this holiday with the usual gusto in 1822 should come as little surprise. The execution of Vesey and several other rebels two days earlier, the speed with which Hamilton and his men had uncovered the plot, and the relentless pace of the trials all served as reason enough to enjoy the day. John Legare's address to an audience in Saint Michael's Church on the morning of 4 July, in which he spoke about a future in which "the Nations of the Earth shall unite in one great and successful effort for the overthrow of tyranny and the establishment of UNIVERSAL FREEDOM," probably had greater resonance among white men and women at a time when threats to their own freedom and liberty had been successfully defused.[189] How black Charlestonians marked this particular day remains unrecorded, but Douglass's comments on Independence Day in an address given in Rochester in July 1852 possibly captured their own feelings. Stripping away the layers of nationalistic rhetoric that surrounded this holiday, he provided his audience with a devastating critique about the day on which slaveowners commemorated their declaration of independence from oppressive imperial rule, observing how such celebrations constituted "fraud, deception, impiety and hypocrisy." Those slaves who accompanied their

---

187. *Columbian Museum and Savannah Advertiser*, 11 July 1814; *Camden Gazette*, 4 July 1816, 11 July 1816. See also *New York Evening Post*, 18 July 1816; Johnson and Roark, *Black Masters*, 23, 352 (n. 61); Kirkland and Kennedy, *Historic Camden*, 2:187–91; Kershaw County Papers, SCL; and Aptheker, *American Negro Slave Revolts*, 297. On Turner, see Greenberg, *Confessions of Nat Turner*. Turner fell ill on 4 July, causing him to postpone his revolt until 21 August.

188. Examination of Robert Harth, 21 June 1822, DTT.

189. Legare, *Oration on 4th. July 1822*, n.p.

owners to listen to orators such as John Legare perhaps recognized their "denunciation of tyrants" as "brass-fronted impudence" and "shouts of liberty and equality" as "hollow mockery."[190]

For enslaved people, the message of liberation incorporated in the language of the American Revolution found expression through the writings and activities of the few antislavery advocates who struggled to oppose the institution in the early republic. By the end of 1784, every northern state, with the notable exceptions of New York and New Jersey, had passed laws allowing for the gradual emancipation of its slaves; by 1804, these two mid-Atlantic states had enacted similar legislation. The burst of idealism that had brought about the end of slavery in states north of the Mason-Dixon line during and just after the American Revolution, however, had virtually no supporters in South Carolina. The dislocation of the local economy, the destruction of a number of rice plantations, and the death or flight of several thousand lowcountry slaves caused by the Revolutionary War generated some debate about the future of the slave trade during which planters expressed concerns that new imports might be agents of rebellion, but the future of the institution itself was never questioned. The intellectual legacy left by the revolution's radical tendencies, however, may have led to an increase in manumissions during the 1780s, when Charleston's slaveholders freed more slaves (118) in that decade than they had in the previous thirty years (from the 1750s to the end of the 1770s).[191]

In the early 1800s, Alexander Garden concluded his essay "On the Evils of Slavery" with a call to his fellow countrymen to "relinquish a practice so destructive to your happiness," hoping that they would turn "toward the path of justice" that would lead to "happy days when the groans of slavery shall no longer be heard."[192] Manumitting his slave in 1781, John Peronneau embraced similar sentiments, noting on the petition that he had freed Romeo because of "his aversion to and abhorrence of Slavery which natural Religion and common sense do equally condemn."[193] Most notable of those

---

190. Frederick Douglass, "The Meaning of July Fourth for the Negro" [5 July 1852], in Foner, *Life and Writings of Frederick Douglass*, 2:192. For further discussion of this and other holidays, see Huff, "Eagle and the Vulture," 10–22; Travers, *Celebrating the Fourth*; and Newman, *Parades and the Politics of the Street*.

191. Stewart, *Holy Warriors*, 23; Philip D. Morgan, "Black Society in the Lowcountry," 116. See also Zilversmit, *The First Emancipation*.

192. Alexander Garden, "An Essay on the Evils of Slavery," Alexander Garden Papers, SCHS.

193. Miscellaneous Records, vol. TT, p. 36, SCDAH, cited in Philip D. Morgan, "Black Society in the Lowcountry," 115.

people in Charleston who embraced antislavery views were Sarah and Angelina Grimké. The daughters of Judge John Grimké, they left the city and the South in the 1820s, escaping "the sound of the lash and the shrieks of tortured victims" for the North and lives dedicated to the causes of abolition and woman's rights, never to return.[194]

Likewise, the growing conviction among several evangelical churches that slavery was an immoral institution posed problems for the state's political leaders. Gathering in Charleston, a group of lowcountry Methodist ministers denounced slavery as "an evil" at a meeting in 1795. At their General Conference five years later, they decreed that ministers should emancipate their slaves and draw up petitions calling for eventual abolition of slavery.[195] Baptists and Presbyterians likewise questioned the institution's morality. Fearing that their evangelizing mission in the South would suffer by embracing such a controversial position, the Methodists decided to compromise in 1804, accepting different disciplines for the North and South. Other churches gradually retreated from this antislavery position, but both the Baptists and Methodists nonetheless enjoyed a reputation among enslaved people as more "friendly toward freedom" than others.[196]

These prominent discussions about the morality of slave holding among church members, noted Governor John Drayton in November 1800, were "highly incompatible with the rights of all Southern States."[197] Seeking to halt these contentious exchanges as well as the spread of antislavery materials, a group of white Charlestonians took matters into their own hands that same month. Angered by the presence of John Harper, an antislavery Methodist clergyman from England, the mob demanded that he destroy all his tracts advocating the emancipation of slaves. While Harper set fire to the offending material, his companion, a minister named George Dougherty, fared less well. The crowd dragged him from his lodgings to a pump, nearly drowning him until a bystander rescued him from the cascade of water being forced down his throat.[198] This violent reaction prompted local magis-

---

194. Sarah Grimké, "Narrative and Testimony" [1830], in Weld, *American Slavery as It Is*, 22. Sarah's sister, Angelina, married Weld; see Lerner, *The Grimké Sisters from South Carolina*.

195. Ford, *Origins of Southern Radicalism*, 22. See also Donald Mathews, *Religion in the Old South*, 67–76; David Brion Davis, *Problem of Slavery in the Age of Revolution*, 206; Frey, *Water from the Rock*, 255–56.

196. Raboteau, *Fire in the Bones*, 24.

197. Governor John Drayton to South Carolina Senate, 26 November 1800, Senate Journals, SCDAH.

198. Frey, *Water from the Rock*, 256; Donald Mathews, *Religion in the Old South*, 75, and *Slavery and Methodism*, 21–22.

trates to inform ministers that there would be no "peace in the State, unless [the Methodists] objured [their] principles respecting slavery."[199]

The renaissance of lowcountry plantation agriculture and the rise of cotton cultivation in the interior in the late 1790s strangled the weak voice of antislavery as calls to reopen the slave trade grew ever louder. Addressing the state's representatives in Charleston as they discussed whether to hold a convention to ratify the Federal Constitution in early 1788, Charles Cotesworth Pinckney, who had been a prominent member of the state's delegation to the Constitutional Convention in Philadelphia the previous year, summed up the prevailing attitudes of his fellow planters, arguing that enslaved Africans were absolutely essential while "one acre of swamp land" remained in the state. The "nature of our climate, and the flat, swampy situation of our country," he continued, "obliges us to cultivate our lands with negroes, and without them S. Carolina would soon be a desert waste." Lowcountry planter William Lowndes agreed wholeheartedly, remarking that "without slavery, this state would degenerate into one of the most contemptible in the Union."[200] On the national stage, lowcountry Federalist William Loughton Smith told the first Congress that slavery was so deeply embedded in the southern social order that it "could not be eradicated without tearing up by the roots, their happiness, tranquility, and prosperity." By the end of 1803, the growing political muscle of farmers in the South Carolina backcountry demanding new laborers to cultivate their cotton fields resulted in the reopening of the transatlantic slave trade in late 1803, reinvigorating slavery throughout the state and the lower South.[201]

The legislature tightened the rules governing manumission in 1800, bringing the state's judiciary into the process. Just a few months after Vesey gained his freedom by striking a contract privately with his owner, the assembly passed a law requiring that a magistrate and five freeholders examine the slave petitioning for freedom to assess that person's "ability to gain a liveli-

---

199. John Harper to [Ezekiel Cooper], [November] 1800, cited in Donald Mathews, *Slavery and Methodism*, 22.

200. Charles Cotesworth Pinckney, 17 January 1788, House Proceedings, South Carolina House and Senate Journals, 8 January 1788–29 February 1789, p. 20, South Carolina Files, Documentary History of the Ratification of the Constitution, Department of History, University of Wisconsin, Madison. See also Kaminski, *Necessary Evil?*, 169–70; and William Lowndes, in Jonathan Elliot, *Debates in State Conventions*, 4:272–73. For a discussion on this subject, see Finkelman, *Slavery and the Founders*, 1–33.

201. William Loughton Smith, 1st Cong., 2d sess., 1790, p. 1200. See also MacLeod, *Slavery, Race and the American Revolution*, 101; Zuckerman, "Thermidor in America," 354; and Brady, "Slave Trade and Sectionalism," 601–20.

hood in an honest way" and to ensure that the candidate was "not of bad character." If the slave provided "satisfactory proof" to the court about his or her abilities, then a certificate of manumission would be issued. As the law "always presumed, that every negro . . . is always a slave, unless the contrary can be made [to] appear," the recording and issuing of the deed were a critical part in the process of becoming free.[202] Twenty years later, the assembly placed further restrictions on manumission. Claiming that "migration and emancipation" had resulted in the "great and rapid increase of free negroes and mulattoes," lawmakers decided to remove the courts from all manumission proceedings, enacting legislation that granted freedom to individual slaves only "by act of Legislature." Slaveholders, as Berlin has noted, always found legislatures far less receptive to manumission petitions than local courts. By the 1850s, the number of manumissions granted by South Carolina's lawmakers had dropped to single figures.[203]

These statutes may have only deepened discontent among slave artisans, who harbored greater expectations of purchasing their freedom than did their plantation counterparts. The frustrations born from the growing distance between dreams of earning enough money to free either themselves or family members and the reality of these legal obstacles perhaps convinced some to join the conspiracy. An anonymous black pamphleteer in Philadelphia later attributed the plot to a sense of deprivation among slaves who had "toiled anxiously . . . to earn sufficient means to purchase freedom for themselves." He concluded that such dashed hopes had resulted in "disappointed slaves, justly incensed with the cruel passage of such uncivilized laws, which were a great and intolerable hinderance to their peace and happiness," who then "had conspired to free themselves from the yoke of the most unholy bondage ever invented by man in that liberty-loving country—to become owners of their own sacred persons, over the bodies of their masters."[204]

Even as slaves found freedom increasingly elusive, their owners recast their own attitudes toward their enslaved property, fashioning themselves as figures of paternal authority, trying to run their estates as they would their own families. Embracing the ideals of Christian stewardship, planters used the metaphor of "family" as a means to legitimate their behavior toward

202. Cooper and McCord, *Statutes at Large*, 7:398, 442; see also Hurd, *Law of Freedom and Bondage*, 2:97.

203. Berlin, *Slaves without Masters*, 140.

204. A Colored American, *Late Intended Insurrection in Charleston*, cited in Starobin, *Denmark Vesey*, 154–55. Starobin has suggested that this author was either fugitive slave Henry Bibb or black newspaper editor Thomas Hamilton.

their property, turning slavery into a "domestic institution."[205] Writing in the plot's aftermath, Baptist minister Richard Furman, who owned fourteen slaves in 1820, encapsulated this attitude when he observed that "a master may, in an important sense, be the guardian and even father of his slaves," concluding that "[t]hey become part of his family, (the whole forming under him a little community) and the care of ordering it, and of providing for its welfare, devolves on him. The children, the aged, the sick, the disabled, and the unruly, as well as those, who are capable of service and orderly, are the objects of his care." As the minister well knew, slaveholders were not just the legal owners of their slaves, but, in many cases, were also their biological fathers. That Furman chose the word "objects" to describe the people over whom he exercised his benevolence also speaks volumes about the ideology of slavery.[206]

Visiting the rural lowcountry in 1810, one English traveler noted how some wealthy planters had apparently tried to "lighten the toils of servitude and render the days of his slave as easy as possible" through the provision of decent clothes and housing. Writing about plantation work and "the Duties and Employments of the Carolina Farmer" in 1815, Judge William Johnson, a lowcountry native who later incurred the wrath of white Carolinians during the trials of the rebels seven years later, advocated that "independent, enlightened agriculturalist[s]" should conduct themselves as benevolent masters, embracing "humanity and encouraging benevolence." A regime that combined "reasonable and uniform, but firm discipline," he argued, would result in a work force "generally less restless and discontented" than one subject to harsh and brutal treatment. For Johnson, this arrangement took on the trappings of a contract between the enslaved and the enslaver in which the latter would provide the former with "every thing necessary to primary wants, and every comfort that his condition admits of," in return for "respect and faithful discharge of the duties assigned him."[207]

Zaphaniah Kingsley, a planter from Florida who claimed to have purchased "Gullah" Jack in the East African port town of Zanzibar, also elaborated on this topic. Slaveholders should, Kingsley argued, show "feelings of

---

205. Wallace, "Paternalism and Violence." On paternalism, perhaps the most controversial subject in slave historiography, see Genovese, *Roll, Jordan, Roll*, 3–70; and Philip D. Morgan, "Three Planters and Their Slaves," 37–79. For the case of post-revolutionary South Carolina, see Rachel N. Klein, *Unification of a Slave State*, 269–302.

206. Furman, "Exposition of the Views of the Baptists," in Rogers, *Richard Furman*, 279–80; see also Rose, "Domestication of Domestic Slavery," in Freehling, *Slavery and Freedom*, 18–36.

207. Letter #9, Letters of an American Traveller, 1810, SCHS; William Johnson, *Nugae Georgicae*, 105, 135.

affection . . . to every slave," regarding them "as members of his family, whose happiness and protection is identified with that of his own family, of which the slave constitutes a part." Such conduct, he concluded, would be "most beneficial . . . to both." The vast majority of enslaved people ridiculed such ideas, however, believing, as did escaped slave Charles Ball, that "there never can be any affinity of feeling between master and slave."[208]

Even though enslaved men and women appeared to live in "comfortable situations" and slaveholders believed themselves to be bathed in the benign light of paternalism, the violence and coercion inherent in slavery did not evaporate.[209] Corporal and other forms of punishment, including the separation of families through sale, remained integral to slave life in South Carolina until the destruction of slavery during the Civil War. Many travelers to the lowcountry included at least one anecdote in their recollections about slaves who, as Neilson wrote in his own memoirs, had "fallen victim to the rage of inhuman masters," including accounts of whippings, the removal of teeth and other forms of physical violence and discipline in their narratives. Planters, to a large extent, cared for their slaves only insofar as they served their economic interests, thus practicing paternalism as a way to mask their own needs.

As masters began to embrace this new self-perception, they also began recasting their own history as slaveholders. Writing in *Niles Register* in 1822, Charles Pinckney argued that the "mildness of treatment" that planters demonstrated toward their slaves during the American Revolution had resulted in "a remarkable attachment" between enslaved and enslaver, helping to avert the outbreak of massive rebellions and widespread flight as warring armies clashed in the lowcountry in the early 1780s. In fact, Pinckney's account of the revolution in the lowcountry was not quite accurate. Although no insurrections broke out, plantation slaves were not models of obedience and subservience. Many headed toward the royal standard and the promise of freedom offered by the British, while others abandoned their plantations, seeking refuge in Charleston or establishing maroon encampments in the lowcountry's woods and forests. Furthermore, the exodus of several thousand lowcountry slaves with the British fleet as it evacuated Charleston in late 1782 suggests that ties between slaves and slaveholders might not have been as close as Pinckney wanted to believe.[210]

---

208. Kingsley, *Treatise*, 3; Ball, *Slavery in the United States*, 298–99.

209. Letter #9, Letters of an American Traveller, 1810, SCHS; Neilson, *Six Years' Residence*, 290.

210. *Niles Register*, 15 July 1822; Philip D. Morgan, "Black Society in the Lowcountry,"

Underlying this attitude lay the persistent—and, in some cases, fully justified—belief that slaves presented a real danger to the future of the plantation regime. By the 1820s, many white southerners had become convinced that the slave population had become increasingly restive and disorderly, feeding fears about maintaining control over the region's enslaved population. The contentious debates in Washington over the expansion of slavery into the Missouri Territory in 1819 and 1820, and the growth of antislavery sentiment in the North, further deepened concern among southern leaders about the institution's future.[211]

The public outcry that greeted the publication of a letter in the *Charleston Courier* in June 1819 illustrates how white Carolinians, sensitive to bad publicity, met any criticism of their cherished institution. Written by English traveler William Faux, this letter recounted his journey from Columbia to Charleston during which he stumbled upon the exhumation of an enslaved man who had been "wantonly whipped" until "*its bowels gushed out*, and it expired." Condemning such barbaric behavior by slaveholders, Faux then proceeded to comment on the "Monstrous anomaly!" that existed in a nation that ostensibly served as "an asylum for the distressed and oppressed of all other lands," but that tolerated an institution that "offended humanity" with "a spectacle so genuinely hellish, or so purely demonical!" as he had witnessed. Within hours of its publication, several people beat a path to Faux's door at the Planter's Hotel, claiming that this account would be "greedily copied and extensively read to our injury, in the northern and eastern states, and all over Europe," thus besmirching "the character of South Carolina." Over the next few days, enraged Charlestonians wrote angry letters to the newspapers while Faux's few remaining friends advised him to remain indoors at night unless he wanted to be attacked. Unlike Faux, many white southerners saw themselves not as murderers but as the protectors of their enslaved property who presided over a benevolent institution.[212]

Despite efforts to fashion themselves as paternalists by deploying the language of family and household, slaveholders ensured that the subordination that sustained the institution remained firmly in place. Sentencing several conspirators, Kennedy and Parker expressed anger and dismay at their skill in dismantling this rhetorical mask, concluding that these men had been "[R]eared by the hand of kindness, and fostered by a master who

---

111. Morgan estimates that some 25,000 slaves were lost either through flight or death as a result of the war in the lowcountry.
211. Dillon, *Slavery Attacked*, 130–38.
212. Faux, *Memorable Days in America*, 12:91–96.

assumed many of the duties of a parent." Rather than embrace their owners' benevolence, these insurgents, the justices concluded, had "realized the fable of the Frozen Serpent, and attempted to destroy the bosom that sheltered and protected you."[213]

The slaveholders of the lowcountry had failed to build an order in which affective familial ties were universal; rather, they had fashioned a society in which "the confidential house servant" was as likely to "plunge a dagger into his affectionate owner's heart" as to perform his daily tasks in an obedient and dutiful manner. Through their conspiratorial deeds, Vesey and his confederates had managed to expose the ethos of paternalism as hollow rhetoric. Rather than accept the identity foisted upon them by their owners, these slaves recognized themselves as self-conscious agents of rebellion.[214]

The political ideas that drove the Atlantic revolutions profoundly influenced Vesey, who reformulated a common phrase of the period, "all men had equal rights," by adding the words "blacks as well as whites" to it. On another occasion, he told Rolla Bennett that "we are made free, but the white people here won't let us be so." By drawing on his own experiences as an enslaved mariner and carpenter in addition to his life in Charleston as a free black man in a slave society, Vesey incorporated his radical interpretation of liberty and equality, explicit in the content of revolutionary discourse, with militant Old Testament texts to forge an insurgent ideology. As he approached his late fifties, Vesey decided to move beyond theory and prepared to act upon the ideas he had formulated.[215]

THE BEST-LAID PLANS:
THE MAKING AND UNMAKING OF CONSPIRACY

De most of dis time he [Vesey] was sowin' de seeds of discontent 'mong Charleston Negroes and in de districts round it. But he was so sly 'bout it, de white folks do not 'spicion him.
—Israel Nesbitt, WPA *interview, ca. 1938*

Let us turn to the events of the summer of 1822. The afternoon of Saturday 25 May found William Paul, the enslaved laborer of local grocer John Paul, walking by the wharves along the Cooper River. Here he fell into conversation with Peter Desverneys, a slave owned by John Prioleau, and

---

213. Kennedy and Parker, *Official Report*, 139.
214. *Charleston Mercury*, 26 August 1822.
215. Kennedy and Parker, *Official Report*, 64; Examination of Rolla Bennett, 25 June 1822, DTT.

began to talk about a particular vessel, possibly either the *Sally* or the aptly named *Liberty* recently arrived from Haiti, anchored in the harbor. Perhaps believing that this ship carried the supplies and troops from Haiti that Vesey had promised his followers, Paul decided to confide in his companion, informing Desverneys that he along with several other slaves were "determined to shake off our bondage," adding that "for this purpose we stand on a good foundation." He then told Desverneys that "many have joined, and if you go with me, I will show you a man, who has the list of names who will take yours down." Perhaps stunned by this dramatic invitation to join a rebellion, Desverneys could only reply that he was "satisfied . . . [and] wished no change in his condition," claiming to be "grateful to my master for his kindness."[216]

Leaving Paul by the harbor, Desverneys now found himself troubled by "the burden of such a secret." Seeking advice, he turned to free black tinplate worker William Penceel, who advised him "with great earnestness to communicate what had passed" to his owner. Unable to tell John Prioleau as he was out of town for a few days, Desverneys related his meeting to his owner's wife. Not until Friday, 31 May, did Prioleau learn about his slave's remarkable conversation and the impending rebellion. In turn, Prioleau informed Intendant James Hamilton who, after convening the council to listen to Desverneys's story, ordered Paul's immediate arrest and interrogation. Quizzed by the council about his conversation with Desverneys, William initially stalled, but "[a]fter a vast deal of equivocation" provided his inquisitors with some information about the events of that Saturday afternoon. The next day Hamilton put Paul in "solitary confinement in the black hole of the Work House," hoping that this experience would loosen his tongue. During the night, he relented, providing a full account of his conversation and the names of two conspirators to his jailers.[217]

As a result of this confession, the guard arrested Mingo Harth (an enslaved domestic belonging to William Harth), as well as Peter Poyas, confiscating trunks in their possession in which they believed "the muster-roll of insurgents" might have been hidden. The authorities not only failed to discover any list, but Harth and Poyas displayed such "composure and coolness" during their interrogation that the intendant discharged them on 31 May. As a precaution, however, he decided to have them watched, hiring "spies . . . of their own colour for this purpose, in such a manner as to give

---

216. Hamilton, *Account of the Late Intended Insurrection*, 4. For reports on the arrival of the *Liberty* on 16 May and the *Sally* a week later, see *Charleston Mercury*, 17 May 1822, 23 May 1822.

217. Kennedy and Parker, *Official Report*, 34–35.

advices of all their movements." Nearly a week elapsed before Paul, now fearing "that he would soon be led forth to the scaffold," told a prison warder that a large number of slaves had planned "the indiscriminate massacre of the whites" on the second Sunday in June.[218]

During his trial, however, Paul sought to turn the tables on Desverneys, casting him in the role of the rebel who had spread reports about "a disturbance and interruption between blacks and Whites." Recalling his encounter with Desverneys on that Saturday, Paul told the court how "he did not understand such talk, and stopped the conversation." This attempt to establish his innocence by throwing doubt on Desverneys's statement ultimately failed. Not only had Kennedy and Parker learned about Paul's interrogation during which he named several key rebels, but their examination also revealed that he had attended a few conspiratorial gatherings. As the court probed further, it discovered that of the handful of meetings in which Paul had participated, he had discovered the numbers of rebels who had joined the plot from Mingo Harth. In addition, Vesey had spoken to Paul about slavery, telling him that "he had a great hatred for the Whites and that if they were all like him, they would resist the whites." Weighing the evidence, the court concluded that Paul had played only a minor role in the plot, sentencing him to confinement in the workhouse until his owner could arrange for his exile, which took place some five months later.[219]

Peter Desverneys was not the only slave who collaborated with Intendant Hamilton, however. As rumors began to circulate about an intended rising, Major John Wilson persuaded George Wilson, his enslaved blacksmith, and a man described by his owner as "distinguished for his uncommon intelligence and integrity," to unearth further information. Using his position as a class leader in the AME church, George, "a dark mulatto man of large frame," learned that the rebels had set the night of Sunday, 16 June, for their attack, having changed the date of the rebellion from 14 July when they feared that their plans might be uncovered. Like 14 July, however, 16 June also fell on a night after the moon's last quarter, providing the rebels with a moonless night on which to attack. Giving evidence, Wilson told the court

---

218. Hamilton, *Account of the Late Intended Insurrection*, 6–7; Kennedy and Parker, *Official Report*, 35. Paul, in fact, was wrong about the date. Vesey planned the rebellion for Sunday, 16 June (the third Sunday of the month), not the second Sunday (which was 9 June). John Wilson, the owner of George, would succeed Thomas Bennett as governor in late 1822.

219. Trial of William Paul, 19 June 1822, DTT; On the length of time endured in prison by the accused, see "A List of Negroes Committed by the Council for an Attempt to Raise an Insurrection," General Assembly Petitions, n.d. 1822, SCDAH.

that he had met Rolla Bennett (an enslaved domestic of Governor Bennett), who informed him that the plot was "gone too far now to be stopped." Bennett apparently further warned the blacksmith to leave town on Sunday if he wished to avoid the violence. Wilson also learned something about the rebels' tactics, discovering that some four thousand men led by Peter Poyas planned to cross from James Island and land at South Bay. From there, they would attack the guardhouse and arsenal by Saint Michael's Church, killing its sentries and capturing fresh arms and ammunition before moving through other city neighborhoods, "not permitting a single white soul to escape" as they burned houses and attacked their inhabitants. Without Wilson's information, John Potter, a local banker, believed that had "their well-laid plans" come to fruition then "a dreadful time of carnage" would have followed as the city's "unprepared . . . sleeping people" would have been murdered in their beds.[220] The rebels, as we shall see, also planned to attack the city from other directions, including assaults launched from Charleston Neck, Gadsden's Wharf, and Bennett's Mills on the banks of the Ashley.

Receiving this additional information on Friday, 14 June, Hamilton hurriedly mobilized the militia and constabulary, doubling the guard and ordering them to prepare three hundred muskets and twenty thousand cartridges to stop the rebels. By Sunday, 16 June, several units, including Captain William Catell's Corps of Hussars, Captain James Martindale's Charleston Neck Rangers, and the Charleston Riflemen, stood mustered and ready to meet any challenge. To ensure that his men were ready to fight, Martindale personally "assumed the responsibility of arming his own corps at his own expense," purchasing more than a hundred muskets and bayonets. As night fell, Colonel Robert Hayne deployed his men throughout Charleston. Rather than find the streets empty as the curfew sounded, Vesey and his men saw "the whole town encompassed at 10 o'clock by the most vigilant patrols." Throughout the night, soldiers both on horse and foot mounted numerous patrols while other militiamen set up posts on the main roads into the city. For the next seven or so days, Hamilton and his assistants were "unceasingly occupied both night & day," organizing and dispatching guards as well as conducting their investigations.[221]

On that Sunday evening, one white woman recalled, "no one, not even

220. Hasell Wilson Memoirs, Robert Wilson Papers, CLS. Mrs Wilson's grandfather owned enslaved blacksmith George Wilson. Examination of George Wilson, DTT; John Potter to Langdon Cheves, 15 July 1822, SCHS.

221. Hamilton, *Account of the Late Intended Insurrection*, 10; James Hamilton to William Lowndes, 16 June 1822, James Hamilton Papers, SHC; petition of Louisa Martindale, 1823, General Assembly Petitions, SCDAH. See also Charles Graves Militia Book, SCHS.

children ventured to retire." The "passing of every patrol and every slight noise excited attention" as tired and fearful white Charlestonians anxiously waited for the dawn. By the next morning, "a general feeling of relief" swept the town and people began to go about their daily business. Mary Jones, who had survived an earthquake, told her friend Mary Beach that she "never went through such a Night of Terror." Even after the threat had passed, one young man, who was so alarmed by the prospect of insurrection that he slept with a pair of loaded pistols under his pillow, met his death when one accidentally "went off and blew out his brains." This accidental death and the demise of another man, who died while attending the hangings on Friday, 26 July, were the only white fatalities during the crisis.[222]

During these tense hours, Hamilton also mobilized the city's legal machinery. The council held an emergency meeting, assigning Justices Lionel Kennedy and Thomas Parker to convene a court of five freeholders to prosecute those rebels already imprisoned, charging them with *"attempting to raise an Insurrection among the Blacks against the Whites."* At the same time, Hamilton set up a Committee of Vigilance and Safety to coordinate security efforts, although he did not call for Federal troops. Only several weeks later did Governor Bennett contact Secretary of War and native South Carolinian John Calhoun, who subsequently ordered fresh troops to march from Saint Augustine to Charleston in order "to remove the uneasiness in the publick mind" fostered by the crisis. Calhoun then dispatched orders to Lieutenant Colonel Abram Eustis to take "one effective Company of Artillery . . . [and] proceed to Charleston." The intendant, moreover, did not forget the man who had furnished him with information about the plot, requesting that the city council appropriate $200 for "the secret services" rendered by Desverneys.[223]

The presence of heavily armed troops patrolling the streets on that Sunday forced Vesey to reconsider his plans. That the authorities were well prepared for insurrection was confirmed when Jesse Blackwood (who hired out and was owned by Thomas Blackwood, president of the Planters and Mechanics Bank) breathlessly arrived at Vesey's Bull Street house with the news that the militia had posted guards at major river crossings and road junctions on the outskirts of the city. Charged with leading rebels from local

---

222. Hasell Wilson Memoirs, Robert Wilson Papers, CLS; Mary Beach to Elizabeth Gilchrist, 5 July 1822, Mary Lamboll Thomas Beach Papers, SCHS; Anna Johnson to Elizabeth Haywood, 24 July 1822, Haywood Papers, SHC.

223. Hamilton, *Account of the Late Intended Insurrection*, 12; John Calhoun to Thomas Bennett, 22 July 1822; Calhoun to Eustis, 22 July 1822 in Hemphill, *Papers of John C. Calhoun*, 7:220; "Statement of Money," Minutes of July 1822, City Council of Charleston, CCA.

plantations into Charleston just hours before the rebellion, Blackwood had discovered roads swarming with patrols. Although he successfully evaded two patrols, a third one stopped him and escorted him back to Charleston. Unable to complete his mission, Blackwood managed to reach Vesey, telling him that "the guard is too strong tonight." Faced with city streets filled with soldiers as well as with an arsenal secured by guards, and lacking support from the countryside, Vesey had no choice but to accept that his plans had been discovered. Talking with his closest confederates, Vesey decided to abandon the rebellion. Rather than ignite a revolt to overthrow the institution that had so long oppressed them, Vesey's men instead made hasty plans to flee for their lives.

The sheer numbers of soldiers both in Charleston and in the surrounding countryside made escape virtually impossible. The court record indicates that only two rebels—Lot Forrester and William Garner—managed to evade patrols and leave the city, eluding capture for a short time until they joined their fellow rebels behind bars. Rather than escape, Vesey appears to have remained in town, burning incriminating letters and other papers, perhaps including his small library of materials about slavery, with Monday Gell's assistance. Although Mary Beach stated that the authorities uncovered "voluminous papers" in which the rebels discussed "their cause . . . [and] their deliverance," the court saw only one piece of written evidence, suggesting that her claims may have been rather overstated. Over the next few days, constables arrested several slaves named by Paul, including members of Governor Bennett's household (Batteau, Ned, Mathias, and Rolla), as well as Peter Poyas. On Saturday, 22 June, as a violent storm lashed Charleston, the hunt for Vesey ended when Captain William Dove, the commanding officer of the city guard, found and arrested the rebel leader at the house of his former partner, Beck.[224]

It had taken Hamilton and his colleagues several weeks to unravel the plot, arrest its participants, and organize trials; the rebels, by contrast, had been hard at work for many months, planning tactics, recruiting men, collecting weapons, and attending meetings in secret. Although neither the trial record nor other related documents reveal its exact origin, there are several possible moments when Vesey might have decided to put aside his outspoken comments about slavery in favor of a full-scale rebellion against the institution. Three events—the War of 1812, the series of clashes between the city and worshipers at the AME church in 1817 and 1818, and an offer to leave

---

224. Mary Beach to Elizabeth Gilchrist, 5 July 1822, Mary Lamboll Thomas Beach Papers, SCHS; Kennedy and Parker, *Official Report*, 17; Hamilton, *Account of the Late Intended Insurrection*, 17.

Charleston and sail to Africa under the auspices of the American Colonization Society—all emerge as plausible catalysts for his decision to plan a revolt.

Perhaps seizing on the first of these possible provocations in conversation with her uncle Thomas Bennett, Anna Johnson indicated in one letter that Vesey "had been nine years in devising to effect the diabolical scheme." Although no direct evidence supports this claim, Vesey perhaps recognized that disruptions caused by the War of 1812 might present an opportunity to launch a rebellion. Unlike the circumstances that prevailed in the lowcountry during the revolutionary war, when the presence of British troops regularly prompted small parties of plantation slaves to head for their lines, the presence of several Royal Navy frigates blockading the South Carolina coast did not prompt widespread restiveness among enslaved plantation workers between 1813 and 1815. Although British raiding parties occasionally seized a few slaves from isolated farms and plantations close to the shore, enslaved people did not seem to regard these scattered raids as harbingers of invasion and possible liberation. Even the attack that the British mounted against an artillery battery on Simons Island in early 1815 and the capture of about seven hundred field hands did not cause disturbances among the region's slaves. Rather than bring chaos, the war resulted in increased demands for food and additional work for Charleston's laboring population as its free and enslaved shipbuilders, including those who worked in Paul Pritchard's yard, constructed several barges for the United States Navy, while other slaves constructed a defensive barrier, known as the Lines, across Charleston Neck to protect the city from attack from the north. This site later served as a place of execution for the rebels.[225]

The protracted battle between city leaders and the AME church probably played a more crucial role in turning Vesey from a severe critic of slavery into its potential destroyer. He was, noted Mary Beach, "considered the Champion in the African Church business. . . . [I]t is the generally received opinion that *this* church commenced this awful business." On several occasions, constables imprisoned members for gathering illegally and holding "a species of worship that the neighborhood found a nuisance." In his confession, Bacchus Hammet commented on the connection between these episodes and the plot's genesis, remarking that "the time we had the uproar about the African Church we been after the same thing, but had to put it off,

---

225. Anna Johnson to Elizabeth Haywood, 18 July 1822, Ernest Haywood Papers, SHC; Captain John Dent to Secretary of the Navy, 18 August 1813, in Dudley, *Naval War of 1812*, 3:212–13; *Charleston Courier*, 26 January 1815, 24 February 1815; Dent to Secretary of the Navy, 17 July 1812, in Dudley, *Naval War of 1812*, 1:194.

that now they begin to raise all about it." Hamilton concurred with these assessments, writing that Vesey "had spoken of it for upwards of four years." The number of slaves connected to the plot as well as the AME church makes the mass arrest of members as well as general harassment of the congregation more likely catalysts for Vesey's insurgency.[226]

In his testimony, Frank Ferguson recalled another episode that may have led Vesey down the path to rebellion. In 1821, George Creighton, a prosperous free black slaveholder who ran a barber's shop on East Bay Street, apparently invited Vesey to sail with him to the settlement founded by the American Colonization Society (ACS) on Cape Mesurado in Liberia. Rather than end his days among other free people of color from the United States who had decided to carve out a living on the Upper Guinea coast, Vesey declined this offer, choosing to remain in Charleston and "see what he could do for his fellow creatures." Creighton extended his invitation to other free blacks as well as to his own slaves. Although several free black families seized this opportunity to leave the city, only one slave from Creighton's household "could be prevailed upon to proceed with him." As Creighton sailed for his new home in western Africa, Vesey turned to forge his future among Charleston's enslaved people.[227]

Considering the spirited debate that colonization schemes generated among free blacks throughout the nation, Vesey's decision to remain in Charleston is not particularly surprising. As city papers often carried reports on the ACS's efforts to establish a settlement on the coast of western Africa for free blacks, Vesey likely knew of its goal of removing them from the United States. The free blacks in Charleston also received entreaties from this organization. In 1819, Episcopal minister and ACS official William Meade visited the city, "commending the cause of colonization" to several prominent lowcountry political figures, including Joel Poinsett and Charles Pinckney, as well as to an audience of free blacks that possibly included George Creighton. Vesey possibly discussed this subject with Morris Brown who, as an associate of AME founding father Richard Allen, probably knew about the stormy meeting held in Philadelphia's AME church in early 1817 when that city's free blacks rejected colonization as nothing more than "a circuitous route back to bondage." Perhaps agreeing with the black antislavery leader

---

226. Mary Beach to Elizabeth Gilchrist, 25 July 1822, Mary Lamboll Thomas Beach Papers, SCHS; *City Gazette*, 4 December 1817; *Charleston Patriot*, 10 June 1818; see also Wikramanayake, *World in Shadow*, 126–27; Confession of Bacchus Hammet, DTT; Hamilton, *Account of the Late Intended Insurrection*, 16.

227. Examination of Frank Ferguson, 27 June 1822, DTT; *Pendleton Messenger*, 8 December 1820.

and former mariner James Forten, who believed that the project of the ACS would hamper "the cause of the entire abolition of slavery in the United States, and . . . may defeat it altogether," Vesey elected to stay in Charleston and take another, more direct, approach to the abolition of slavery.[228]

Although several of the conspiracy's ringleaders claimed to have been involved with the plot since 1818, the evidence suggests that Vesey did not start to formulate concrete plans for rebellion until late 1821. At some point, he concluded that fragmentary acts of defiance, including his own habit of denouncing slavery in public settings to friends and strangers alike, had to be translated into bold and decisive action. As he deliberated, Vesey may have also taken his age—he was in his mid-fifties in 1822—into consideration, perhaps believing that if he did not act soon it would be too late. Once determined to act, Vesey exchanged carpentry for conspiracy. Monday Gell recalled how "about three months prior to June 16 . . . [Vesey] ceased working at his trade and employed himself exclusively in enlisting men." At least one other rebel followed his example. Jesse Blackwood, as noted earlier, worked only intermittently for his owner, spending the rest of his time traveling around the countryside on conspiratorial business. That his activities would remain undetected, Vesey asked that other rebels "put in money to raise a sum to pay his master's wages while he is gone."[229]

During late 1821 and early 1822, a number of key conspirators appear to have joined Vesey's cause. Monday Gell, for example, claimed that "the first time I heard of the Insurrection was about last Christmas," while Perault Strohecker also enlisted around the same time. At first, Vesey and his closest associates appear to have been fairly selective in recruiting, trying to avoid slaves who might harbor friendly feelings toward their owners. Although several enslaved house servants, including members of Governor Bennett's household, did join the rebels' ranks, Peter Poyas believed that the presence of such people might endanger the conspiracy, telling Robert Harth that he should not divulge their plans to "those waiting men who receive presents of old coats etc. from their masters, or they will betray us." Reflecting on his involvement in the plot as he sat in his prison cell on the eve of his execution, enslaved domestic Rolla Bennett confessed that he would have been unable

---

228. Johns, *Life of the Right Reverend William Meade*, 120–22; Quarles, *Black Abolitionists*, 3–9; James Forten, *Resolutions and Remonstrances of the People of Color Against Colonization to the Coast of Africa* (Philadelphia, 1818), in Ripley et al., *Witness for Freedom*, 32. On the question of colonization, see Miller, *Search for Black Nationality*; Staudenraus, *African Colonization Movement*.

229. Confession of Monday Gell, DTT; Bacchus Hammet, Benjamin Hammet Papers, WPL.

to murder his owner at the appointed hour, claiming that "I cannot kill my master or mistress, for they use me, more like a son, than a slave," suggesting that Poyas's concerns were not misplaced.[230]

The sparse biographical information available suggests that at least eleven and probably more insurgents were African born. By and large, the rebels were fairly young men with an average age of thirty-one years, thus making them nearly twenty years younger than Vesey. At least nineteen were members of the AME church, while four served as class leaders. Although the ringleaders worked in a variety of skilled trades, including shipbuilding, cooperage, and metal working, Vesey drew the bulk of his foot soldiers from the ranks of the city's cart drivers, porters, sawyers, laborers, stevedores, and other unskilled and semiskilled workers who, as Kennedy and Parker noted, "had certain alloted hours at their own disposal." Moreover, many of these workers would have had occasion to visit the waterfront, its surrounding workshops, warehouses, and yards during the course of their working day, enabling them to pass on information or, in some cases, weapons or gunpowder. In contrast, we know nothing about the type of rural slave who might have been drawn to the plot, as no plantation hand was arrested.

Although the conspirators lived throughout the city, many dwelt on adjacent streets in the same neighborhood. Propinquity likely played a role in drawing people into the conspiracy. The streets surrounding Vesey's house on Bull Street proved to be a fertile ground for recruiting. In addition to Governor Bennett's enslaved domestics (Batteau, Ned, and Rolla), who lived and worked on nearby Lynch Street, Polydore Faber resided on Montague Street while enslaved drayman William Garner and George Evans, an enslaved stonecutter and marble polisher, lived on Wentworth Street, just a short walk from Bull Street.[231]

Throughout early 1822, Vesey and his closest confederates assembled a network of conspirators. Using these channels, they could pass on information about meetings and the progress of the plot to fellow insurgents. At several locations in the city, including Vesey's house on Bull Street, Gell's Meeting Street harness shop, and William Harth's lumberyard on Gibbes Street, the rebels would gather to talk and plan, turning their places of work into centers of conspiratorial activity.[232] Even though white tradesmen and clients visited these workplaces, the rebels presumably decided to take this risk, hoping that they would not be discovered.

---

230. Confession of Monday Gell, Trial of Peter Poyas, 21 June 1822, and Confession of Rolla Bennett, all in DTT.

231. Kennedy and Parker, *Official Report*, 17.

232. Examination of William Paul, 19 June 1822, DTT.

Of these places, Gell's shop appears to have been a leading center for conspiracy. The rebels, Gell told the court, "were in the habit of coming into my Shop to talk on this business." Regarded as a "most excellent harness maker," Monday enjoyed considerable latitude in his working life, keeping "a large portion of the profits of his labor" that enabled him to live away from his owner's house. Sitting around work benches amid the metal and leather of Gell's trade, rebels exchanged information, stored weapons, and laid plans. At one meeting, they contributed twelve cents each to hire "a man to make pikes" for the rising. Enslaved blacksmith Tom Russel, who worked nearby on East Bay Street, fashioned the blades while Polydore Faber made handles for them. On another occasion, Perault Strohecker and Bacchus Hammet hid a keg of powder at Gell's shop. While in jail, Gell would recall the names of forty-two rebels, who spent time in his shop "for the purpose of combining and confederating in the intended insurrection."[233]

This workshop also served as an important rendezvous for enslaved men simply wishing to pass the time of day and socialize with fellow workers. Enslaved stonecutter George Evans recalled meeting Vesey, deep in thought as he examined "the newspaper for Lottery Reports as he had tickets in one," during a visit to Gell's shop. William Colcock, an enslaved house painter, also saw Gell frequently, stopping by "to hear what was going on in Congress," to discuss the "Missouri question," and gossip with Monday and others gathered there.[234] Like the taverns that black Charlestonians frequented, these workshops became sites in which enslaved men might formulate their own critique of the society in which they lived.

The insurgents also gathered at Bulkley's farm, an isolated farmstead located several miles outside of town on the Meeting Street Road. Here, the rebels conducted ceremonies, held meetings, stored weapons, and made forays into the countryside. Accessible by water as well as by foot, this property, overseen by Billy Bulkley, an enslaved rope-walk worker who soon became involved in the conspiracy, proved to be a "Capital Place of Mutiny." On at least one occasion, more than thirty slaves assembled there to plot and pray. Its isolated stands of pine and oak provided "Gullah" Jack with an ideal setting in which to stage his "conferences of blood . . . prayer and psalm singing" with his band of Gullah rebels. Their active participation in these rituals helped to fashion an insurgent consciousness, creating and cement-

233. Trial of Naphur Yates, Trial of George Bampfield, DTT; Hamilton, *Account of the Late Intended Insurrection*, 21, 28; Examination of Perault Strohecker, Examination of Tom Russel, 16 July 1822, DTT.

234. Examination of George Evans, 6 August 1822, and Examination of William Colcock, 16 July 1822, DTT.

ing bonds of solidarity. Placing themselves temporarily outside the context of their enslavement, the rebels who passed time at this farm found a congenial setting in which to speak openly about the society in which they lived and to hide the weapons with which they planned to destroy it. At one meeting in April 1822, "Gullah" Jack presided over a ceremony at which Adam Robertson and Robert Robertson "roasted a fowl and ate it half raw as an evidence of union," a rite that, according to abolitionist Thomas Wentworth Higginson, symbolized "pulling Buckra to pieces." A few weeks later, several other slaves traveled to the farm, spending the night in prayer and song under the direction of Peter Poyas.[235]

Although Vesey regularly visited the farm, no evidence indicates that he participated in these rituals, although he doubtless knew that such ceremonies took place. As the conspiracy's leader, he may have been more concerned that the weapons stored there remained undiscovered. Searching the farm soon after the plot's discovery, a militia patrol discovered several pike handles, although they never found the blade heads that Tom Russel had apparently forged. In one minor incident, Vesey signaled his violent intentions when he killed a snake by the farm's gate, provoking another rebel to exclaim, "That's the way we would do them." For Vesey, the farm provided an ideal location to talk "about this rising" and for his followers to embark on journeys into rural districts where they intended "to get men."[236]

The rebels also assembled a small arsenal during these months. Bacchus Hammet, for example, obtained his owner's pistol by removing it "out of the closet one afternoon." Besides the motley collection of swords and pistols removed from their owners' houses, the insurgents planned to seize arms and ammunition from the storehouse of the Charleston Neck Militia on King Street as well as from Duquercron's store on nearby Tobacco Street as they stormed into the city. Weapons were also stored at two sites on Meeting Street and in Cannonsboro. Using Russel's blacksmithing skills, the rebels also fabricated their own weapons by turning tools from their workshops into lethal objects. Taking a scythe from his owner, Pharo Thompson hoped

---

235. John Potter to Langdon Cheves, 15 July 1822, Langdon Cheves Papers, SCHS; Testimony of Smart Anderson, 16 July 1822, and Testimony of Billy Bulkley, 13 July 1822, DTT; Higginson, "Denmark Vesey," 733. A Gullah word widely used by lowcountry slaves to describe slaveholders, "buckra" means "he who surrounds or governs, white man." It probably derives from "mbakara," a word used by the Efik (a people from the eastern end of the Gulf of Guinea). See Cassidy, *Dictionary of American Regional English*, 421.

236. Trial of George Evans, 6 August 1822, Trial of Jerry Cohen, 20 July 1822, Trial of Lot Forrester, 17 July 1822, Confession of William Colcock, 16 July 1822, and Confession of Monday Gell, all in DTT.

that Russel could fashion it into a sword. Russel also intended to use a mold designed for casting lead weights for fishing nets to make musket balls. Pompey Haig informed William Colcock that "some black Frenchmen very skilful in making swords, such as they use in Africa" had also been drawn into the scheme, suggesting perhaps that people familiar with events on Saint Domingue knew about the plot. They also stockpiled other essential equipment, acquiring lengths of slow match to use as a fuse to ignite a keg of gunpowder that Bacchus Hammet had obtained and hidden in Gell's shop, and contributing money to purchase lanterns. Just a few days before the rising was to take place, enslaved cooper John Enslow testified that his fellow insurgents had gathered "a quantity of arms of different kinds," including "about 150 to 200 pikes" that they had secretly stored at Bulkley's farm.[237]

Despite the rather questionable effectiveness of the old pistols, knives, scythes, and other instruments that the rebels had obtained, the arsenal they assembled may have fostered some degree of confidence among their ranks. That they had gathered these weapons with considerable stealth suggests that the rebels were serious about their enterprise. Their presence may have also encouraged some slaves to perceive themselves not just as enslaved people, but also as soldiers about to fight a significant battle. Testifying during Batteau Bennett's trial, Bram Lucas recalled Governor Bennett's slave talking about himself as "one of the army." In addition to adopting a martial posture, several rebels began to speak confidently about their skills with weapons and their readiness to kill. Peter Poyas exhibited this sense of bravado, telling Robert Harth that the guard posted at the arsenal would be "a gone man" on the night of the attack once he, Poyas, had got "a gripe at his throat" and then used his sword upon him. Although Peter, Batteau, and others may have seen themselves as soldiers, their skill at handling weapons appears to have been rather limited. Gathered at Bulkley's farm on one occasion, several slaves tested their skill with a stolen pistol that "everyone tried to fire." Only after considerable practice with the piece did one slave manage to discharge it successfully.[238]

Besides acquiring these weapons, the rebels apparently procured some disguises, intending to don them on the night of the rising. According to several white Charlestonians, they hired a local barber and hair dresser to fashion "a number of wigs and false whiskers of the hair of white persons" to camouflage their identities. By wearing these hair pieces and painting their

237. Confession of Bacchus Hammet and confession of John Enslow, Benjamin Hammet Papers, WPL; Trial of Pharo Thompson, 16 July 1822, Trial of George Evans, 6 August 1822, Trial of Jerry Cohen, 20 July 1822, and Trial of Lot Forrester, 17 July 1822, all in DTT.

238. Trial of Batteau Bennett, 20 June 1822, DTT.

faces white, the insurgents hoped that "in the darkness of the night and in the confusion," patrols would mistake them for white people, enabling them to surprise sentries stationed at strategic buildings, including the arsenal and guardhouse. Kennedy and Parker later reported how, on a visit to Vesey's cell, Intendant Hamilton dramatically "took out of his pocket the very wig made for Vesey himself," eliciting a cry of "Good God" from the rebel leader as well as an acknowledgment that he had ordered the wig and knew its maker.[239]

To forge links between the city and the countryside, the conspirators took advantage of the dense kinship networks that crisscrossed the lowcountry, stretching from its communities of enslaved plantation workers to city neighborhoods. Several slaves testified how they had visited friends and families on local plantations "to gather the people's mind on the subject." Whether traveling by foot, on horseback, or in a canoe, Vesey and his men assembled a significant force of foot soldiers during these forays into the countryside. Lydia, an enslaved woman owned by Edward Perry, testified how Agrippa, her son who worked as a wheelwright in Charleston, spent a night with her and other family members on their owner's plantation. Although Agrippa found no "prime men" to recruit here, he had probably set out on this journey with the goal of recruiting men to the rebels' ranks. Traveling to Perry's plantation presented Agrippa with no problems. Holding a "general Ticket" that enabled him to move freely so that he could "work out in Town or Country," he rented a horse from fellow rebel Scipio Sims for a nominal charge.[240]

As planters and farmers in rural districts learned about the plot in late summer, they speculated about whether they had met any conspirators earlier in the year. Lowcountry planter Stephen Elliott believed that he had encountered one rebel, who had been traveling through the countryside disguised in the "garb of the preacher." Demanding to know the nature of the man's errand, Elliott learned that this preacher told slaves "the pure and unsophisticated doctrines of the Gospel" at the gatherings over which he presided because "whites only garble it to suit their purposes." Given Vesey's penchant for telling people the unvarnished truth and the content of these comments, Elliott may have unwittingly encountered the rebel leader. Alternatively, Elliott may have stumbled upon a class leader or church steward travelling from Charleston to hold a meeting of black worshipers in the rural

239. Kennedy and Parker, *Official Report*, 27–28. See John Potter to Langdon Cheves, 5 July 1822, Langdon Cheves Papers, SCHS; Mary Beach to Elizabeth Gilchrist, 5 July 1822, Mary Lamboll Thomas Beach Papers, SCHS.

240. Examination of Charles Perry, 24 July 1822, Examination of Lydia Perry, 24 July 1822, Testimony of Mr. Perry, 23 July 1822, and Trial of Agrippa, 24 July 1822, all in DTT.

parishes of Saint Paul, Saint James Santee, or Saint John. Vesey thus may have used connections between the AME church in the city and its scattered rural satellites to further his cause. Whether disguised as itinerant ministers or clad in ordinary clothes, slaves used their knowledge of local roads, rivers, and creeks as well as the lax enforcement of pass laws to gather supporters and inform rural slaves about the plot.[241]

Since those insurgents charged with recruiting slaves in rural districts appear to have traveled through the countryside with comparative ease, calculating how many enslaved South Carolinians actively participated in or had casual knowledge of the plot is virtually impossible. Enslow claimed that the plotters had made connections with plantation workers along the Combahee River (about sixty miles west of Charleston) and slaves in the small coastal settlement of Georgetown (sixty miles to the northeast), where some rebels had apparently made plans to burn the town and kill its inhabitants. While Joe La Roche claimed that Mingo Harth had recruited four thousand slaves from James Island, Paul testified that Peter Poyas had a list "with 9,000 names on it." "Gullah" Jack also made similar claims, informing Frank Ferguson that he had spoken to more than six thousand slaves in and around the Goose Creek and Dorchester neighborhoods (about twenty miles north of the city) who had "agreed to join."[242] The sheer number of people that "Gullah" Jack and others claimed to have spoken with about the rebellion is worth considering. Exaggerating the number of men who had joined their cause may have convinced slaves ambivalent about the rebellion to throw in their lot with Vesey who, they may have been led to believe, had the strength of numbers on his side.

Vesey also tried to expand the scope of the plot beyond the confines of the lowcountry. With Haiti playing such a central symbolic role in his thinking, he tried to draw the island into his insurrectionary designs. He set about opening "a correspondence with Port au Prince," hoping that Haitian leader Jean-Pierre Boyer would offer assistance to the rebels. Perhaps Vesey remembered Dessalines' *Declaration of Independence of the French Colony of Santo Domingo*, in which the rebel general proclaimed that "the God of Free men bids us stretch out towards them [the enslaved] our conquering arms" as he composed his plea for help. Recruiting an enslaved cook named Williams about to ship out for Haiti, Vesey gave him a letter addressed to Boyer that

---

241. Stephen Elliott to William Elliott, 22 July 1822, Elliott and Gonzales Papers, SHC. On black congregations in Charleston's hinterlands, see Hinks, *To Awaken My Afflicted Brethren*, 25–29.

242. Confession of John Enslow, Benjamin Hammet Papers, WPL; Testimony of William Paul, 19 June 1822, and Examination of Frank Ferguson, 15 July 1822, DTT.

presumably requested some form of military assistance and discussed plans to use the island as a refuge after the rising. Although the fate of this message and its messenger is unknown, Vesey told several rebels that "St. Domingo... would come over and cut up the white people."²⁴³

Even if Boyer had received this communication, he would have been in no position to act. The protracted struggle to gain independence at the turn of the century had been followed by a period of considerable social and political turmoil, leaving Haiti economically devastated and isolated. Although Boyer successfully concluded a short war against the Spanish-governed eastern half of the island in 1822, bringing about the end of slavery in those provinces, he was not situated to engage in foreign adventurism. Moreover, transporting soldiers from Haiti to South Carolina would have been virtually impossible, as Boyer had no navy.²⁴⁴

That Vesey decided to sail to Haiti after the rebellion highlights his political thinking as well as his tactical practicality. For people of African descent, the island held out the promise of a future free from white domination. Writing in *Niles Register* in 1818, Haitian secretary general Joseph Inginac announced how "men of color who may desire to become Haytians" might pursue a variety of skilled trades, including carpentry, coopering, smithing, and ship building, in a country where "no white man ... shall ever set foot under the title of *master* or *planter*." Just months before Hamilton and his men uncovered the plot, the *Genius of Universal Emancipation* reported on the nineteenth anniversary of Haitian independence, describing celebrations during which several speakers proclaimed that "nothing is more formidable than a people oppressed and driven to despair." This same paper had published a poem two months earlier that virtually encapsulated Vesey's intended plans to escape to the island.

> To Hayti let us go, and then
> We may enjoy our natural rights,
> For negroes there are viewed as men
> And there thought as good as white.

As the rebels intended to capture several ships along with their captains during the rebellion, and as Vesey was a former mariner, this voyage would have presented few problems. Moreover, as the United States did not estab-

---

243. Confession of Monday Gell, 23 July 1822, DTT; Dessalines, "Proclamation," 74; Kennedy and Parker, *Official Report*, 28; Trial of Rolla Bennett, 20 June 1822, DTT.

244. See Blackburn, *Overthrow of Colonial Slavery*, 213–64; Baur, "Mulatto Machiavelli," 307–53.

lish diplomatic relations with Haiti until 1862, there was little chance that the rebels would have been returned to South Carolina.[245]

The conspirators also appear to have spent a good deal of time just talking. The future of the institution that bound them probably provoked many discussions. Newspaper reports and conversations with sailors, who may have passed on news about antislavery activities in the North and perhaps some pamphlets on the subject, doubtless furnished Vesey with evidence that slavery was emerging as the single most controversial item on the national political agenda. Peter Neilson, a Scot who spent several years in the lowcountry, witnessed slavery's corrosive effect on the new republic when his host in Charleston announced that northerners were no better than "a low, hypocritical pack of cheating scoundrels." Even as early as 1812, an officer in the U.S. Navy noted how white South Carolinians treated "National Councils with Contempt." Eight years later, in the wake of the Missouri Compromise, Judge Daniel Huger presciently told Pennsylvanian Samuel Sitgreaves at a dinner gathering that he fully expected the Union to dissolve "in the natural course of things, probably in the life time of my children." As the political distance between North and South widened after the Compromise of 1820, Vesey seems to have monitored debates about slavery with some care, studying speeches that addressed the issue.[246]

The importance that Vesey placed on the Missouri Compromise as he organized his rebellion suggests the importance of antislavery politics in the creation of an insurgent consciousness. Jack Purcell confessed that Vesey's considerable knowledge of these activities both inside and outside Congress proved to be an effective recruiting technique. Collecting "every pamphlet he could lay his hands on that had any connection with slavery," Vesey could readily quote from several speeches made by prominent figures in antislavery circles, further enhancing his status as outspoken critic of the institution. Unfortunately, no record exists of the materials that Vesey had in his library. As abolitionist literature did not appear in any appreciable volume until the 1830s, his collection probably consisted of a handful of pamphlets, some clippings from newspapers as well as a few books on race and slavery. He may have had a volume of *The Book and Slavery Irreconcilable* (1816) by George Bourne, a Presbyterian minister from Virginia's Shenandoah Valley, which called for the "immediate and total abolition" of slavery, or a copy of John Kendrick's *Horrors of Slavery* (1817), a powerful attack on the institu-

245. *Niles Register*, 17 October 1818; *Genius of Universal Emancipation*, January 1822, March 1822. On emigration to Haiti, see Miller, *Search for Black Nationality*, 75.
246. Neilson, *Six Years' Residence*, 234; Dent to Secretary of the Navy, 27 April 1812, in Dudley, *Naval War of 1812*, 1:102; Staudenraus, "Letters from South Carolina," 213–14.

tion that circulated as far west as Tennessee. He possibly saw a few copies of Benjamin Lundy's *Genius of Universal Emancipation*, a newspaper dedicated to "purging the land of the foul and corrupting principle of slavery" that began publication in January 1821. He had also doubtless read *Niles Register*, widely available in the South, which reprinted Senator Rufus King's speeches to Congress urging that slavery be excluded from Missouri.[247]

Just as Vesey refashioned the story of Hercules for his own purposes, he appears to have deliberately distorted the result of the Missouri debates for consumption by his followers, circulating rumors that the compromise promised them freedom. Rather than tell his followers that this legislation dealt with the question of slavery's expansion in the West, Vesey misled his followers, claiming that it promised imminent liberation for enslaved people. Rolla Bennett clearly accepted this reading, testifying that "Congress had set us free, and that our white people here would not let us be so." In their account, Kennedy and Parker reprinted a letter from James Ferguson in which the Saint John's Parish planter remarked "that reports of their [slaves'] emancipation had of late years been much in circulation." Until these slaves learned about the planned rebellion from Frank Ferguson, owned by Ann Ferguson, however, they "had no idea it was to be effected in the manner proposed by Denmark Vesey." By transforming the Missouri Compromise into an emancipation proclamation, Vesey may have tapped into a deeply held wish among slaves who believed that the long-awaited day of jubilee was on the horizon. As this promise remained unfulfilled, ringleaders could persuasively point to the injustice of slaveowners as they tried to convince other men to join the insurrection. By interpreting the compromise in this way, the rebel leader held out a promise of liberation that may have ameliorated the subordination of some slaves. Whatever his reasons, Vesey did mislead his followers in this case, perhaps deliberately as a means to further his cause.[248]

Vesey likely discussed the politics of liberation with AME church members. In addition to participating in regular services, the congregation divided itself into small groups known as classes, consisting of about twelve people each. Led by individual class leaders, which included rebel slaves such

247. Dillon, *Benjamin Lundy*, 15; *Genius of Universal Emancipation*, July 1821. King's speech during the debates over Missouri was reprinted in *Niles Register*, 4 December 1819. See also Ernst, *Rufus King*; and Glover Moore, *Missouri Compromise*.

248. Testimony of Rolla Bennett, 25 June 1822, DTT; Kennedy and Parker, *Official Report*, 21. Joel Poinsett informed President James Monroe in August 1822 that the Missouri Compromise "was considered by this unfortunate and half instructed people as one of emancipation." See Dillon, *Slavery Attacked*, 135–36.

as Ned Bennett, Charles Drayton, Jack Glen, and Peter Poyas, as well as Vesey himself, these gatherings would sing, pray, and discuss biblical texts and other theological issues. Church rules demanded that leaders attend to the spiritual welfare of their class members, requiring that they "advise, reprove, comfort or exhort, as occasion may require," and ensure that they "are indeed working out their own salvation." They also played minor administrative and pastoral roles, introducing new members to church life, arranging aid for the sick, and ensuring that "any who walk disorderly" be suitably punished as enslaved butcher George Bampfield discovered when the church expelled him "for keeping a girl."[249]

Drawn from church members who were usually literate, class leaders could exert some degree of influence over class members and the wider community. Not only had they read the Bible, enabling them to speak authoritatively on scripture as well as on other issues, but they had gained access to a new way of comprehending the world. The ability to read "transforms the consciousness of those who acquire it," as anthropologist Jean Comaroff has noted, generating "an awareness of the process of abstraction" among those able to understand the written word. But, as we have seen in the case of the Missouri Compromise, the ability to read also enabled literate conspirators to mislead nonliterate followers by shaping the news to their own ends.[250]

Literacy also blurred the sharply drawn lines of social and racial stratification imposed by slaveowners. Slaves able to read could bring their analytical skills to bear on the construction of slavery as an institution of subordination, enabling them to consider their current circumstances and possible alternatives. For Frederick Douglass, the acquisition of reading skills proved transformative. Ploughing through copies of *The Columbian Orator*, Douglass read several speeches and essays that offered "a bold and powerful denunciation of oppression, and a most brilliant vindication of the rights of man"; they enabled him to penetrate "the secret of all slavery and oppression." Literate insurgents played an important practical role in the plot. Not only could these rebels read articles and speeches on key political issues to their confederates, but Vesey and Gell also appear to have compiled lists of recruits and composed letters requesting help from Haiti.[251]

Although several rebels alluded to Vesey's library as well as to lists and

---

249. Allen, *Doctrines and Discipline*, 97–98. On classes, see Walker, *Rock in a Weary Land*; Trial of George Bampfield, 20 July 1822, DTT.

250. Clarke, *Wrestlin' Jacob*; George, *Segregated Sabbaths*, 109–10; Comaroff, *Body of Power, Spirit of Resistance*, 143; Darnton, "First Steps in the History of Reading," 154–90.

251. Douglass, *My Bondage and My Freedom*, 100.

other notes that he made during meetings, the evidence indicates that the court only saw one such piece of written evidence. Composed in a rather elliptical manner by accused slave Abraham Poyas, this letter was discovered by the authorities when they first arrested Peter Poyas. Drawing on the Book of Daniel, this communication from Abraham to Peter refers to an event that might be construed as an uprising, beginning with the words "I will endeavor to do it," and closing with "Fear not, the Lord God that delivered Daniel is able to deliver us." After much deliberation, the court accepted explanations from Abraham's owner (Dr. James Poyas) as well as from the accused Peter that the letter referred not to rebellion, but to Abraham's plans to leave one church and join another.[252]

As a class leader, Vesey enjoyed influence and standing among the larger congregation as well as a pulpit from which to address them. He articulated his message of liberation and insurrection through his own interpretations of biblical texts and perhaps through songs like the hymn that invoked "ye oppressed, ye Afric band," to "let *Independence* be your aim," urging slaves to "wrest the scourge from Buckra's hand" and to "drive each tyrant from the land." The African church also provided a forum in which slaves and free blacks could forge community through collective prayer and song, listen to provocative sermons on the need to redress the injustices under which they lived, and participate actively in services that combined spirituality with theatrical performance. Drawing on popular styles of oratory, African customs of call and response, and their own improvisational skills, black preachers and exhorters raised "the feelings of their audience" to what white observers viewed as "an extravagant and ridiculous pitch." They spoke to their congregations about their collective hopes for the future, in addition to depicting "hell's torments with all the logic they can muster." As the service closed with "prayers . . . intermingled with yelling and hooting," Neilson observed female worshipers "tearing off their caps . . . [and] beating their heads on posts" in a state of spiritual fervor. In short, the modest building that housed the AME church and its worshipers became a site in which a dissident subculture emerged and flourished.[253]

If the language of revolution and the radical messages taken from Old Testament texts provided one essential ingredient for armed insurrection, then the magical practices of "Gullah" Jack served an equally important

252. Trial of Abraham Poyas, 27 June 1822, DTT.

253. John Hammond Moore, "Hymn of Freedom," 50–53; Neilson, *Six Years' Residence in America*, 258; Joyner, " 'If You Ain't Got No Education,' " 255–78; Genovese, "Black Plantation Preachers," 204–29. For contemporary descriptions of black worship, see John Hammond Moore, "Abiel Abbott Journals," 70.

purpose in the conspiratorial equation. Little is known of Jack's early history. Although the term "Gullah" refers primarily to the linguistic and other cultural practices that the Gola as well as other groups from the Upper Guinea coast fashioned on lowcountry rice plantations during the eighteenth century, James Hamilton noted in his account that "this Necromancer" did not come from this part of Africa; rather, he was born "a conjuror and physician" in Angola, arriving in South Carolina sometime between 1804 and 1808.[254]

Perhaps apocryphal, another account lends further credence to this observation. Buried in a footnote in a tract entitled *A Treatise on the Patriarchal, or Co-Operative System of Society*, Zaphaniah Kingsley, a slave smuggler, planter, and proslavery pamphleteer from the Saint John's River in East Florida, claimed to have bought Jack when he was sold as "a prisoner of war in Zinguebar [the East African port town of Zanzibar]." According to Kingsley, this captive was a native of a country called "M'Choolay Morcema," where its inhabitants spoke "a dialect of the Angolan tongue." As they sailed from the island into the Indian Ocean, Kingsley noticed that his new slave had a set of "conjuring implements with him in a bag which he brought on board the ship and retained them." Called a *nkisi nkita nsumbu*, the bag that Jack carried was probably made from folded raffia cloth and contained his charms, including ritual stones, roots, and other objects associated with healing and magical practices.[255]

If Kingsley's account is trustworthy, then Jack probably came from the eastern margins of the Kingdom of the Kongo or the Luba kingdom, both of which had commercial connections to Zanzibari and Indian Ocean traders. After his capture, slave traders would have marched him across central Africa to Zanzibar Island, selling him in its markets before he was taken to the New World. Although more than 50 percent of the enslaved Africans who entered Charleston between early 1804 and late 1807 came from Angola, at least two ships from Mozambique or the island of Madagascar also arrived with cargoes of slaves. Jack possibly was one of the four hundred slaves taken from the east coast of Africa to South Carolina, sailing around the Cape of Good Hope and then across the Atlantic to the southern United States. Before arriving in Charleston, Jack may have worked among the one hundred or so enslaved workers on Kingsley's Saint John's River plantation. Among his slaves, Kingsley owned an African couple named Jack and Ta-

---

254. Hamilton, *Account of the Late Intended Insurrection*, 23–24.
255. Kingsley, *Treatise*, 13. On Kingsley, see Tise, *Proslavery*, 66–67; Schafer, "Shades of Freedom," 130–54. On *nkisi nkita nsumbu*, see Thompson, *Flash of the Spirit*, 118–19.

mana who had also come from "Zinguebar." Whether "Gullah" Jack and Tamana's partner were one and the same remains a mystery, but the presence of East African slaves on Kingsley's plantation further supports his story about the purchase of "Gullah" Jack in Zanzibar's slave market. By 1810, however, Jack was working alongside dozens of other enslaved laborers as a joiner and caulker in the yards of Paul Pritchard, a prominent Charleston shipbuilder.[256]

With the influx of enslaved Angolans between 1804 and 1807, Jack would have likely found himself among people who followed familiar folkways. Although many slaves from this region had some passing familiarity with the Catholic practices imparted by Capuchin missionaries in the sixteenth and seventeenth centuries, a syncretic Kongo-Christian cosmology had evolved in which the rituals of Rome had been filtered through the mesh of traditional religious rites and beliefs. The *nganga* (ritual expert) retained his hold over village inhabitants as did the *ndoki* (sorcerer). Within the rural societies from which Jack came, these men not only acted as healers, but they also guided the course of communal life through their guardianship over the metaphysical environment. As a figure who possessed these skills and advertised his command over the supernatural, Jack embodied these traditions for the large number of slaves in Charleston and its environs who still placed magic at the center of their world.[257]

Jack could reach out to those slaves for whom magic was the intellectual cornerstone of their lives. His claims that "he could not be killed nor could a white man take him" may have had a dramatic impact on the men who subscribed to his skills as a conjuror. Providing these people with a conceptual system that offered a coherent explanation for their afflictions and circumstances, Jack's mastery over the supernatural environment may have been more readily comprehensible to them than Vesey's hybrid message of militant Christianity and revolutionary ideas rooted in western political traditions. Jack further extended his influence over the rebels under his command by appointing Tom Russel as his right-hand man, training him as "a Doctor . . . [and] his Second." Moreover, Jack suggested that Tom, acting in the role of the sorcerer's apprentice, functioned as his double, informing

---

256. Schafer, "Shades of Freedom," 130–54. On the Indian Ocean trade, see Alpers, *Ivory and Slaves* and *Ivory and Slaves*; Sharif, *Slaves, Spices, and Ivory in Zanzibar*. On Paul Pritchard's property, see Land Records, Charleston County, 1 August 1810, vol. A8, pp. 408–10; MESDA.

257. Thornton, "Development of an African Catholic Church," 147–67; Thompson, *Flash of the Spirit*, 106–7.

Harry Haig that "when you do not see him [i.e., Jack], and you see Tom, you see him [i.e., Jack]."[258]

Moreover, he imparted an air of commanding authority, drawn from his ritualistic and conjurational abilities as well as his physical appearance. His "conjurations" gave Jack considerable power over rebels who joined the insurrection under his guidance. Not only did his initiation rites stamp these men as rebels, but the ceremonies also enabled them to take on new identities as insurgents. Once initiated into rebel ranks, these men had to behave accordingly, exchanging a demeanor of servility for a more militant and aggressive posture. In addition, Jack's dramatic appearance, which included a large black beard so central to his self-presentation that, as his owner deposed, "nothing could induce [him] to cut off," further added to the dramatic style of his public persona. No doubt exaggerating for his audience, Hamilton also commented on Jack's performance, noting that "his wildness and vehemence of gesture and the malignant glance with which he eyed the witnesses who appeared against him, all indicated the savage, who indeed had been *caught*, but not *tamed*." Before George Vanderhorst would take the stand against Jack, the court had to reassure the agitated slave "that he need no longer fear Jack's *conjurations* (as he called them)." A few days after Vesey abandoned the rebellion, however, Jack deemed it prudent to shave off his beard, leaving his owner mystified "at the cause of it, little dreaming that it was to prevent him [from] being apprehended."[259]

Enslaved cooper Harry Haig was among the slaves who fell under "Gullah" Jack's powerful influence, telling the court how he had "charmed Julius [Forrest] and myself ... and we consented to join." Jack had not merely asked Haig and his friend to join, but had "charmed" them into the conspiracy. Convinced that the spirit world orchestrated the patterns of daily life, Jack viewed his ability to manage the forces outside human control as essential to the conspiracy's ultimate success. The psychic comfort and confidence that Jack imparted via talismans, including the use of crab claws invested with mystical properties, and animal sacrifices that entailed the ritual slaughter of chickens, converted passive bystanders into active and engaged rebels.[260]

---

258. Myscofski, "Ritual Trance in Brazilian *Umbanda*," 88; Parrinder, *West African Religion*, 156–71; Mbiti, *African Religions and Philosophy*; Examination of Harry Haig, DTT.

259. Deposition of Mr. Paul Pritchard, 10 July 1822, DTT; Kennedy and Parker, *Official Report*, 163; Hamilton, *Account of the Late Intended Insurrection*, 24.

260. Testimony of Julius Forrest, Testimony of Harry Haig, DTT; Kennedy and Parker, *Official Report*, 79. For travelers' accounts of magic and witchcraft in eighteenth- and early-nineteenth-century Africa, see, for example, John Mathews, *Voyage to the River Sierra Leone*, 130–33; Meredith, *Account of the Gold Coast*, 30–35. For able discussions in its New World

Just days before the revolt, Jack presided over several meetings at which he promised invincibility to those who ate a special diet of smoked corn and groundnuts, and then placed crab claws in their mouths. Leaders of other slave rebellions had used this strategy, including a free black conjuror who guaranteed that his magic powder would make rebels involved in the insurrection in New York in 1712. The use of these claws bore a close resemblance to Bakongo *nkisi* charms, designed to protect people from illness. Another gathering saw Jack presiding over the ritual slaughter and consumption of a half-raw fowl. This ceremony also drew on native customs in which the slaughter of a chicken held malevolent spirits at bay. Perhaps the gastric consequences of consuming semicooked poultry, including fevers and vomiting, further enhanced Jack's reputation as a man of mystical power.[261] Jack, moreover, may have used plants with psychoactive properties to induce trancelike states among those slaves who participated in ceremonies held at Bulkley's farm.

Even though Jack cast a long shadow over the plot, he also claimed that his shamanistic powers "would not protect him against the treachery of his own colour." To ensure that the conspirators did not betray the plot, both Vesey and "Gullah" Jack went to great lengths to ensure secrecy. Swearing fidelity to the cause, a number of rebels including Smart Anderson, Rolla Bennett, Charles Drayton, Monday Gell, and Sandy Vesey all pledged to "not tell if taken by the whites, nor will we tell if we are to be put to death." Secrecy thus became part of the daily lives of Vesey and his accomplices, creating further bonds between rebels who had access to this exclusive knowledge. As he stood on the gallows awaiting the hangman's noose, Peter Poyas reminded his fellow conspirators not to break their oath, but to "die silent" as he was about to do. In his testimony, Joe La Roche recalled Rolla saying that if any black Charlestonian gave out any information or evidence, the rebels would "watch for them day and night and kill them."[262]

The collective participation in ritual forged bonds of solidarity among the rebels. Presiding over ceremonies that symbolically inaugurated slaves like

---

context, see, for example, Bastide, *African Civilizations in the New World*, 89–151; Thompson, *Flash of the Spirit*. For a discussion of these practices in a different cultural context, see Keith Thomas, *Religion and the Decline of Magic*, 774–75. On the lowcountry slaves, see Creel, *"A Peculiar People"*; Joyner, *Down by the Riverside*.

261. Kennedy and Parker, *Official Report*, 76, 130; Thompson, *Flash of the Spirit*, 117; Creel, *"A Peculiar People,"* 154–55; Genovese, *Roll, Jordan, Roll*, 209–323; Gorn, "Black Magic," 314.

262. Confession of Y[orrick] Cross, Confession of Bacchus Hammet, and Examination of Joe LaRoche, 20 July 1822, all in DTT.

Harry Haig and Julius Forrest into the community of insurgents, "Gullah" Jack sought to remove Haig and his companions from the reality of their daily lives as enslaved workers and transform their perceptions of the world. Shifting from an identity as slaves via these rituals to a liminal state—a condition defined by anthropologist Victor Turner as "being betwixt and between the positions assigned and arrayed by law, custom, convention and ceremonial"—these men would emerge from the ceremony as fully fledged rebels. The altered consciousness fostered by these rites distanced slaves from a world in which they were subordinate to their owners. Once removed from that set of social relationships, these men could more easily articulate anger and resentment against their owners. In short, "Gullah" Jack sought to fashion an alternative reality through ritual performance.[263]

Through these rites, the insurgents hoped to inoculate themselves from the militia's musket balls. Although the rebels would enjoy an element of surprise as they opened their attack, they would not possess as many weapons as their adversaries until they captured the arsenal and guardhouse. Accordingly, they hoped that Jack's talismans would neutralize the firepower of a militia that could, as Robert Harth noted, "fire three times to our once." To prevent their assault from collapsing in this hail of lead, Jack announced that crab claws placed in their mouths along with the consumption of some parched corn would shield them from white musket balls.[264]

"Gullah" Jack's command of these ritual practices and embodiment of magical customs sheds further light on the mental world of the conspirators. As they went about the business of conspiracy, the rebels immersed themselves not just in the politics of Atlantic radicalism but in the customs of their homeland. Just as Vesey may have used the Book of Tobit to argue that a people caught in a diaspora should endeavor to maintain their cultural integrity, "Gullah" Jack perhaps used religious initiations to reinvigorate components of African culture that had begun to disappear from the lives of urban-dwelling slaves. Although Jack drew the content for his rituals from the traditions of the Kongo, slaves from other parts of Africa would likely have understood their idiom.

Even the language used by Vesey to broadcast his message suggests that he sought to rejuvenate and restore a culture that had once been firmly anchored in African ways. Accordingly, language became an important me-

---

263. Victor Turner, *Ritual Process*, 95; Crapanzano, "Introduction," 9. For modern accounts of such ceremonies, see Plotkin, *Tales of a Shaman's Apprentice*, 101–3; Wade Davis, *Serpent and the Rainbow*, 114–16, and *One River*, 74–76, 173–75.

264. Trial of Peter Poyas, DTT. On the use of talismans in insurgent movements, see Adas, *Prophets of Rebellion*, 150–56.

dium to sustain these practices. James Mall, a young white artisan, testified how Monday and his companions frequently conversed in Gullah "so that I could not understand them." Using Gullah as a language of secret communication, slaves created a cultural space that excluded most white people from their conversation. As the collective property of every man and woman within this particular speech community, Gullah acted as the primary vehicle for expressing shared values and engaging in intellectual activity. The spoken word not only served as a device to generate distance between slaves and slaveholders, but also as an instrument of resistance and rebellion. For Vesey, Gullah provided the medium through which he articulated his ideology of the dispossessed and message of liberation.[265]

The use of Gullah, the ritual practices of "Gullah" Jack, and the reading of an obscure book from the Old Testament may be seen not just as the rebellion's intellectual underpinnings, but as the ingredients of a revitalization movement. The deliberate measures taken by the leader of an oppressed group and his followers to create satisfying cultural forms from which to mount challenges against their subordination, revitalization movements are often associated with periods of rapid and disruptive change during which certain groups improve their social and economic position while others experience a decline in their status. In times of accelerated social upheaval and disruption, historian Michael Adas has noted, charismatic figures occasionally surface, equipped with the intellectual ability and spiritual power to fashion new syntheses of values and meanings.[266]

Seen in this light and assisted in this project by "Gullah" Jack, Vesey emerges as an agent of cultural revitalization who forged a new political discourse of rebellion from ethnic African practices and customs, militant Old Testament Christianity, and the language of revolutionary emancipationism. By integrating these distinct discourses into a strident demand for black liberation through armed insurrection, Vesey found a receptive audience among a group of enslaved Charlestonians. Moreover, the conspiracy took root just as profound political and economic changes swept Charleston, South Carolina, and the nation. Tolling "like a firebell in the night," as Thomas Jefferson noted, the debates over Missouri forced the question of slavery onto the front page while the Panic of 1819 dealt a severe blow to the

265. Testimony of James Mall, DTT; Joyner, "'If You Ain't Got No Education,'" 265.
266. Adas, *Prophets of Rebellion*, xvii–xxvii. Most work on revitalization movements explores the subject from the perspective of indigenous peoples. See Anthony F. C. Wallace, "Revitalization Movements," 149–65, and *Death and Rebirth of the Seneca*; Dowd, *Spirited Resistance*, xix–xx.

economic fortunes of the South Carolina lowcountry. The passage of a bill that further tightened the regulations governing manumissions as well as staunch opposition to the AME church by Charleston's local government generated additional friction between slaves and masters.

Vesey's followers perhaps saw the carpenter not just as the mastermind of an armed insurrection, but also as a charismatic figure who genuinely embodied their aspirations and articulated their beliefs as people of African descent captive in the New World. Although he did not participate directly in the Atlantic revolutions, he had lived through that era of immense social and political change as an enslaved man. Unlike the majority of his followers who had been children during this period, Vesey could draw on his own fund of memories, recollections, and stories. Accordingly, he no doubt recognized that to challenge authority successfully, people must look at themselves and the world in which they live in new and critical ways. He also understood that violence was an integral part of any such movement. Vesey offered those willing to listen a way to remove themselves from the clutches of domination and to appraise the world in which they lived with a more penetrating eye.[267]

This message of subversion and salvation that Vesey spelled out and the rituals conducted by "Gullah" Jack, however, appear to have excluded enslaved women from participation. The conspiracy remained the province of male slaves and a handful of free black men. Even though William Paul stridently claimed to the court that "no woman knows anything about it," some evidence suggests that several female slaves inadvertently learned about the plot in the days before the arrests in May and June. An enslaved domestic of Alexander Howard, Sally overheard Jesse Blackwood and his brother talk about finding a horse "to go into the country to bring down men to fight the white people" in her owner's backyard. Another domestic, Prudence Bussaker, talked with Harry Haig, who was looking for his close friend Julius Forrest. As they spoke, Haig told about his journey to Johns Island, where he planned to meet a "black army that was coming to fight in town" on the eve of the rising. Aware of such activities, these women appear to have kept their silence, remaining faithful to the conspirators.[268]

The testimony of Sally and Prudence further revealed how the rebels used kin relationships for recruiting purposes. Sally's mother had married Jesse

---

267. Comaroff, *Body of Power, Spirit of Resistance*, 213.
268. Kennedy and Parker, *Official Report*, 86; Testimony of Sally Howard, Testimony of Prudence Bussaker, DTT. In his work on Gabriel's plot, Douglas Egerton notes that women did not participate (*Gabriel's Rebellion*, 53).

Blackwood's brother, while Prudence, although not Julius Forrest's biological parent, was "like a kind of mother to Julius—having raised or brought him up." Lydia Perry, the mother of Agrippa Perry, also testified that either biological or fictive kin on the plantation where she worked may have known about the conspirators' plans. Although Vesey was no longer Beck's partner, he continued to visit her home where, according to William Paul, he would "speak of the rising." We do not know whether they discussed the plot in great depth, but bonds of kinship likely strengthened the bonds of secrecy that held the conspiracy together, perhaps accounting for the silence that slave women kept as the plot unfolded. That Vesey was hiding in Beck's house when he was captured suggests that several slave women had more than a passing acquaintance with the conspiracy.[269]

During the trials, the accused often alluded to the shadowy presence of slave women. Familiar with daily household routines and traveling about the city on errands, enslaved domestics occupied an ideal position from which to discover information valuable to the conspirators. The mother of Sally Howard (the wife of Jesse Blackwood's brother) could have informed the rebels about the daily routine in the household of Thomas Blackwood, the president of the Planters and Mechanics Bank, located on East Bay Street. Such reports might have proved useful to rebels intent on emptying the city's banks before they escaped. The presence of rural slave women in Charleston's produce markets, moreover, offered the rebels with an ideal opportunity to forge additional links between the city and the countryside, enabling them to pass on news and, possibly, weapons.

That the city's female slaves do not appear to have played a more active role in the conspiracy may be explained in several ways. The organization of female slave life may have discouraged their full participation in the plot. Like Rosetta, an enslaved laundry woman from Angola who was "well known on the Neck," many slave women worked on their own, hiring out their services as domestics, spending their days laboring in the houses of a certain neighborhood, or as street vendors, selling food and other items. Their absence might have been noticed by mistresses anxious to maintain clean and well-run households. Even though some slave women worked for hire, they do not appear to have enjoyed the autonomy of a slave like Agrippa, who held a pass enabling him to travel throughout the city and countryside. Because slave women did not participate in skilled trades conducted in workshops, as men did, their work-place culture evolved in different ways. Besides their daily tasks, moreover, slave women also had to attend to their own house-

---

269. Testimony of Mr. Thomas Forrest and Examination of William Paul, DTT.

holds and children and may have been unwilling to involve themselves in a project that threatened the security of their families.²⁷⁰

It also seems likely that the bonds forged by Jack's rituals and by Vesey's own persuasive powers were based in part on the exclusion of women. During his years at sea, Vesey had lived and worked in the homosocial environment of ships and sailors in which men depended upon one another for their lives. The plot's masculine cast may have been a legacy of these years. Vesey, furthermore, may have regarded the destruction of Charleston and the killing of its white inhabitants as the ultimate test of black manhood. When questioned by Smart Anderson about the planned slaughter of women and children, the rebel leader chastised him, saying that "he did not have a man's heart . . . that he was a friend to Buckra." Alternatively, the persistence of western African practices, including the presence of the *poro* with its exclusive male cast, among enslaved men may have further discouraged the rebels from building networks that crossed gender boundaries. Moreover, no black women appear to have held the position of class leader in the AME church. In more practical terms, the conspirators also may have wished to protect their families from the dangers inherent in organizing an insurrection. In fashioning a masculine world of rebellion, Vesey and his followers drew on western African martial customs and a vital African American urban culture that centered on the male enclaves of workshop and tavern.²⁷¹

That Charleston's enslaved women did not take leading roles in the plot should not be interpreted to mean that slave women failed to resist slavery. Even though the few slave rebellions that broke out in North America were led and supported by men, female slaves persistently challenged the authority of their owners. Rather than resist collectively as did enslaved men, slave women struggled in other ways, administering poison, feigning illness, stealing, committing arson, and escaping from their owners. This repertoire of opposition was, as historian Elizabeth Fox-Genovese has observed, "woven into the fabric of slave women's lives and identities."²⁷²

Although enslaved women may have been deliberately excluded from the plot, the city's free black population chose to distance themselves from the

---

270. In his essay on the plot, Higginson noted that Vesey's followers "took no women into counsel—not from any distrust apparently, but in order that their children might not be left uncared for in case of defeat and destruction" (Higginson, "Denmark Vesey," 111). See also Fox-Genovese, *Within the Plantation Household*, 307.

271. Trial of Smart Anderson, 16 July 1822, DTT; Horton, "Freedom's Yoke," 98–121.

272. Fox-Genovese, *Within the Plantation Household*, 329. On enslaved women and resistance, see Deborah G. White, *Ar'n't I a Woman?*, 76–84; Terborg-Penn, "Black Women in Resistance," 188–209.

message of rebellion. Apart from Vesey and nine other free black men, every other conspirator was a slave. Although free for the twenty-two years before his death, Vesey clearly drew his support from slaves rather than his free peers. He apparently did not join either the Brown Fellowship Society or the Society of Free Dark Men after gaining his freedom, while his inability or unwillingness to purchase his own family perhaps drew him closer to the slave community. During the ten years he spent as a slave in Charleston, Vesey doubtless forged close ties with city slaves, working alongside them at Joseph Vesey's ropewalk, encountering them daily as he hired out his services as a carpenter, and forming romantic attachments to at least one enslaved woman. Although the story of antebellum black Charleston was largely the tale of two cities, one free and one enslaved, Vesey managed to retain his ties to the latter even though he claimed membership of the former.[273]

With the exception of Vesey, the lowcountry's free blacks—a majority of whom lived in Charleston—showed considerably more interest in maintaining their precarious economic and legal position within the established order than in its destruction. When approached by Monday Gell to join their ranks, free blacks Philander Michau encapsulated the attitudes of a majority of his peers when he informed him that he "would have no part in any such business as he was already free." Most free black people recognized that they enjoyed their limited freedoms on the sufferance of the white population. As Ira Berlin has observed, "freedom within the context of slavery gave free Negroes something to protect and transformed them into a conservative caste." That free black William Penceel advised the enslaved Peter Desverneys to divulge news of the conspiracy to his owner confirms Berlin's conclusions. But Vesey proved to be the exception to the rule, determined to chart his own radical course rather than embrace the conservatism prevailing among a majority of the city's free blacks.[274]

An unwillingness to jeopardize their vulnerable social and economic position may offer clues as to why several free blacks chose to collaborate with Hamilton. The divisions that existed between the city's enslaved and free black population may also explain the actions of William Penceel, a tinplate worker and member of the elite Brown Fellowship Society, and Isaac Scott. Penceel received a substantial reward for urging Desverneys to speak to his master, as did Scott for his services. By giving the authorities such

---

273. Harris, "Charleston's Free Afro-American Elite," 289–310; Koger, *Black Slaveholders*, 167.

274. Testimony of Philander Michau, 6 August 1822, DTT; Berlin, *Slaves without Masters*, 271. See also Curry, *Free Black in Urban America*; Wikramanayake, *World in Shadow*; Fitchett, "Traditions of the Free Negro," 139–52, and "Origins and Growth," 421–37.

information, these men further consolidated their relationship with the city's white leadership and further distanced themselves from slaves. A few other free blacks were less calculating. When approached by some rebels to join, free black Edward Johnson hedged his bets, announcing that "he would have nothing to do with slaves" before contradicting himself, claiming that he would join the rebels only on "the night they began." The first statement reflects the attitudes held by a majority of the city's free blacks.

The trials and executions may have been a catalyst for the small exodus of free black people that sailed for the ACS settlement on Cape Mesurado in mid-August. Besides several free black families who had no role in the plot, the *Dolphin* also carried Prince Graham, a free black implicated in the plot and sentenced to transportation. Certainly, the polemicists, who would later author tracts attacking the presence of free blacks in a society built on slavery, and politicians, who would pass several new laws further constraining free black life in late 1822, needed no reminders that the man behind the conspiracy had been free.[275]

At the heart of the conspiracy lay the planned attack against the city. For the vast majority of white inhabitants, this plan constituted "deeds of darkness and misery," but at least one complemented the rebels for their "fine Military *Tact*[ics] and admirable combination." The rebellion's timing as well as its strategic organization suggests that Vesey and his inner circle had carefully considered how best to deploy the men under their command and the most effective way of taking key points in the city. By attacking in midsummer, when many white residents had left for Sullivan's Island or had traveled to "the cliffs of the Hudson and the perfumed meadows and valleys of Long Island," the rebels and their black allies would enjoy a very slight numerical advantage. Moreover, if the rebellion began successfully and the insurgents seized enough weapons, Vesey could be fairly confident that other slaves would join his ranks, further swelling their numbers and presenting a real threat to the militia.[276]

The success of the rebel plan depended on several factors. Vesey's men needed to move with speed and stealth from their positions on the city's outskirts into the town itself. The insurgents then had to capture much-needed weapons from the arsenal and neutralize the guard. Should the rebels fail to complete these tasks, the militia would have an opportunity to muster,

---

275. Confession of Monday Gell, DTT; *Southern Patriot and Commercial Advertiser*, 18 August 1822.

276. M[artha] Richardson to James Screven, 6 July 1822, Arnold-Screven Papers, SHC; John Potter to Langdon Cheves, 29 June 1822, Langdon Cheves Papers, SCHS; *Charleston Mercury*, 24 May 1822.

mount a counterattack, and saturate the city with men. The key to rebel victory would lie in the ability of Vesey's lieutenants to command and control their men effectively and secure their positions quickly. Thus, victory or defeat would become apparent shortly after they crossed into the city. To increase the chances of success, the rebels decided to divide their forces and attack the city from two directions, creating additional problems for the militia.

Vesey accordingly entrusted his closest associates with the task of leading rural slaves into the city. Peter Poyas would guide some four thousand plantation slaves from James Island across the Ashley and land on the western side of the city, before leading them "to seize the Arsenal and Guard House opposite St. Michael's Church" (on Broad and Meeting Streets). Another group of slaves led by Ned Bennett would attack from the north, advancing down Charleston Neck and taking weapons from its arsenal before moving into the city "to destroy the inhabitants." Under Rolla Bennett's command, a third band of slaves would gather near Bennett's Mills. After murdering the governor and intendant, these men would cut off the neighborhood of Cannonsboro from the rest of the city. Other slaves would rendezvous at Gadsden's Wharf, at Bulkley's farm, and at Vesey's house, moving through the streets killing "every person they might meet, and prevent them from assembling, or extending the alarm." Moreover, as rural slaves often traveled into the city on Saturday afternoon, an increase in the traffic of enslaved men between the town and the countryside would have gone largely unnoticed by the authorities. Thus, under the cover of this movement, rebel slaves from the plantations could prepare themselves for the rising.[277]

Once the attack had been launched, the rebels would assault and capture several strategic buildings, simultaneously providing themselves with additional weapons and neutralizing the guard. As rebels on foot secured the arsenal, guardhouse, and any stores selling guns, a band of enslaved draymen and carters, organized by William Garner and Perault Strohecker into a small cavalry force, would use their speed and mobility to attack the patrols. Having taken Charleston's main buildings, the rebels then planned to obliterate the city and its white residents, using "fire and sword [so that] not a single white soul would survive." Under the cover of the resulting confusion and panic, they intended to loot the city's banks and houses before "hoisting sail to Santo Domingo" in ships captured by a band of slaves led by Peter

---

277. Examination of Joe La Roche, 20 June 1822, and Trial of Rolla Bennett, 20 June 1822, DTT.

Poyas. Doubtless savoring the destruction of the slaveholding South's premier intellectual and cultural center, they would then head out toward the open sea. The goal was simple and straightforward. "We shan't be slaves to these damn rascals any longer," Vesey bluntly told Bacchus Hammet on one occasion. "We must kill everyone that we can get hold and drive the rest from the City."[278]

The conspirators also laid plans in the event of failure. Should the militia beat back their assault, the rebels, according to enslaved cooper John Enslow, would retreat from the city and head for the Lines. Here, they intended to make a stand and "fight man for man." Having inflicted as much damage as possible, the remaining insurgents would disperse into the woods to "do all the harm they could" by mounting raids on local plantations until they could escape deep into the countryside.[279]

As a prelude to the insurrection, the rebels apparently planned to poison city wells a few days before the attack. According to Harry Haig, "Gullah" Jack intended to send Haig and several other trustworthy rebels to pour "a bottle of poison" into wells throughout the city, polluting its water supply and causing widespread sickness. Talking later with Intendant Hamilton, local banker John Potter discovered to his horror that "Gullah" Jack had instructed these men to contaminate as many cisterns and pumps as they possibly could, prompting him to note how this plan was "to have been General!!!" Clearly, Charleston's inhabitants were more vulnerable to the introduction of poison into their water supply, households, and bodies than to an uprising that the militia could beat back with their superior firepower. Although there is no information on how "Gullah" Jack obtained the poison, he perhaps used his extensive knowledge of toxic plants to create a poisonous liquid or powder. The case of Philip, an enslaved man owned by Daniel Cork, suggests that slaves in the city could obtain poison with little difficulty. Charged with "administering poison" in 1822, Philip was imprisoned and sentenced to death, although he hanged himself in his cell just a few hours before his execution.[280]

Rather than help the rebel cause, an outbreak of poisoning might have put city authorities on the alert, prompting them to increase the number of patrols and enforce the nightly curfew strictly, thus removing the element of surprise on which the rebellion's success hinged. Further, poisoning city wells posed a danger to black Charlestonians unaware of "Gullah" Jack's

---

278. Confession of John Enslow and Examination of Bacchus Hammet, DTT; Kennedy and Parker, *Official Report*, 47.

279. Confession of John Enslow, Benjamin Hammet Papers, WPL.

280. Committee Reports, 3 December 1822, General Assembly Petitions, SCDAH.

plan, although whether he considered the possibility of injuring these people is unknown. Perhaps believing that the rebels would be unable to effect complete surprise, "Gullah" Jack may have wanted to improve the odds by attacking a force disabled from the ill effects of poison. Only when the rebels had armed themselves with weapons captured from the arsenal could they meet their opposition on equal terms. Although he was instructed to execute this scheme, Harry Haig did not fully approve of the order to poison "as many pumps as he could about town." Apparently ready to accept the mayhem and carnage that would result from the uprising itself, Haig appeared reluctant to carry out this command, believing that such tactics constituted "murder" and were "not like fair fighting."[281]

Some indirect evidence suggests that the rebels intended to engage in sexual violence and kidnap some white women. During his trial, Joe La Roche testified that Rolla told him that "when we have done with the men, we know what to do with the wenches." Although this is the only allusion to rape in the transcript, the fact that the insurgents had even contemplated such action soon became known. La Roche's use of the term "wench" is worth comment. When used by white southerners in the early nineteenth century, it frequently referred to an enslaved woman. That La Roche here designated white females as "wenches" perhaps foreshadows rebel designs on them. Peter Neilson learned that the authorities had uncovered lists naming "the most accomplished young ladies in the city" who were to suffer "a fate ten thousand times more horrible than death in its worst form" at rebel hands. In her letters, Anna Johnson talked not of sexual coercion, but about her fears of kidnap and her own enslavement. Her cousin, she claimed, "was set apart for the wife or more properly the 'light of the Harem' for one of their chiefs." She noted elsewhere how Vesey aimed to "carry *us*... to St. D[omingo], there to be sold as slaves." This bore a striking similarity to the action of rebellious slaves on that island who, as they swept into Le Cap, took "some females of that complexion, whom they force[d] to do the duties of servants."[282]

---

281. John Potter to Langdon Cheves, ca. July 1822, Langdon Cheves Papers, SCHS; Confession of Harry Haig, DTT. On the role of poison rituals among free and enslaved Africans, see Fick, *Making of Haiti*, 66–67; Vansina, *Paths in the Rainforest*, 97; and Genovese, *Roll, Jordan, Roll*, 363, 633–34.

282. On the history of the term "wench," see Kathleen Brown, *Good Wives*, 368–69; see also the case of Sally, a Negro, against Beaty in which both Sally and her enslaved emancipator are referred to as "wenches." Examination of Joe La Roche, DTT; Neilson, *Six Years' Residence*, 295; Anna Johnson to Elizabeth Haywood, 28 June 1822, 18 July 1822, Ernest Haywood Papers, SHC; *Bermuda Gazette*, 29 October 1791.

As we know, however, these plans came to naught when an idle conversation between William Paul and Peter Desverneys on the Charleston waterfront ultimately led to the plot's exposure. After Paul's arrest and interrogation at the end of May and the subsequent questioning of Peter Poyas and Mingo Harth a few days later, about two weeks elapsed before the pace of arrests quickened. On Friday, 14 June, Major Wilson learned from his slave that the uprising's date had been moved from Sunday, 14 July, to Sunday, 16 June, prompting Hamilton to secure the city with patrols. On Monday, 17 June, and Tuesday, 18 June, constables imprisoned ten slaves, including those belonging to Governor Bennett (Batteau, Ned, Rolla, and Thomas) and Peter and Mungo Poyas, finally capturing Vesey a few days later on Saturday, 22 June. Over the next few days, the authorities managed to arrest several slaves who would have played an important role in the plot, including Monday Gell and Frank Ferguson on Thursday, 27 June, and "Gullah" Jack on Saturday, 6 July. Not until Wednesday, 10 July, did the case break wide open when, after the court sentenced "Gullah" Jack, John Horry, Charles Drayton, Monday Gell, and Harry Haig to death, the last three confessed, saving themselves from the gallows. A few days later, a new round of arrests began in which several conspirators, including Perault Strohecker, John Robertson's three slaves (Adam, John, and Robert), and Bacchus Hammet, were confined in the workhouse. The last arrest took place on Thursday, 8 August, when free blacks Philander Michau and Edward Johnson were imprisoned.

As the number of slaves arrested rose, those rebels who remained free reacted in very different ways to the collapse of the conspiracy. Some continued to go about their daily business, including Billy Palmer who, according to Mary Beach, was "constantly at [the Congregational] Church," performing his duties the evening before his arrest. At least two endeavored to escape. Lot Forrester headed toward Saint James Santee until "several gentlemen" captured him by Hibben's Ferry (about three miles outside town), while William Garner was somewhat more successful, traveling for more than one hundred miles undetected, reaching Granby on the outskirts of Columbia before he was taken. Several others simply lost heart. Julius Forrest, on learning that constables had "taken up" his close friend Harry Haig, became resigned to his fate, telling an acquaintance that "I suppose my time will come next." A few other rebels remained more sanguine, however, and, undeterred by the plot's discovery, argued that they should still launch the rebellion as planned. According to Bacchus Hammet, Perault Strohecker told those conspirators not yet arrested to keep themselves ready for action. In part, he recommended this course as several conspirators still at large thought that "those under sentence . . . would give up all the names." Accordingly, they hoped "to raise and make a rescue," trying to organize an attack on Tuesday, 2 July. As Hamilton had posted a large number of troops around the workhouse to prevent such an attempt, any rescue mission would have been suicidal. Like the larger plot, this plan came to nothing, and the court continued to try prisoners unhindered.[283]

As Vesey and his confederates contemplated the conspiracy's collapse on Sunday, 16 June, Hamilton and his officers moved swiftly to uncover and sever its roots and branches. With corroborating reports from William Paul and George Wilson in his hands, Hamilton assembled a court to try those slaves already imprisoned, using his powers as city intendant to take those steps as "shall appear most advisable for preventing or suppressing riot and tumult." Calling on Kennedy and Parker to serve as the presiding magistrates and on five prominent citizens, Hamilton convened the Court of Justices and Freeholders, which began its preliminary work on Tuesday, 18 June, questioning Governor Bennett's domestic slaves, Mungo Poyas, Peter Poyas, Amherst Lining, Stephen Smith, Richard Lucas, and John Lucas. From the next day, when Kennedy and Parker charged William Paul with "attempting to raise an Insurrection amongst the Blacks against the Whites," until Tuesday, 6 August, nearly 130 enslaved and free black Charlestonians stood before the court.[284]

Before opening the proceedings, the court considered how to conduct the trials. Neither law nor custom granted black southerners many procedural rights in court. In the majority of cases, they found themselves convicted with scant regard to the charges and suffered severe punishments for any minor transgression. Examining their law books, Kennedy and Parker would have instantly concluded that Vesey and his followers—men "that do confeder or bind themselves by oath, covenant, or other alliances . . . to maintain their malicious enterprizes"—fit the legal definition of conspirators. Moreover, eighteenth-century slave codes offered additional guidelines for court protocol. In cases of slave conspiracy, the law allowed "the confession of any slave accused, or the testimony of any other slave that the justices and freeholders shall have reason to believe to speak the truth," to be admitted, enabling the court to assess the scale of the threat. Although the court treated confessions from accused slaves with great caution, it allowed these

283. Mary Beach to Elizabeth Gilchrist, 23 July 1822, Mary Lamboll Thomas Beach Papers, SCHS; Testimony of Prudence Bussaker, 10 July 1822, Examination of Perault Strohecker, 3 August 1822, DTT. See also Confession of Bacchus Hammet, DTT; Benjamin Hammet Papers, WPL.

284. Brevard, *Digest of the Public Statute Law*, 3:38; Kennedy and Parker, *Official Report*, 41.

statements to be entered into evidence because they often exposed additional conspirators as well as serving as admissions of guilt. That several slaves did confess raises questions about the collection of such statements. Even though the bill that prison physician John Righton presented the assembly after the trials did not record treatment that might be construed as torture, Bennett revealingly stated some months after the trials that "no means which experience or ingenuity could devise were left unessayed to eviscerate the plot." Finally, as the same criminal statutes applied to both free blacks and slaves, the court made no special dispensations when Vesey and the other free people involved in the plot took the stand.[285]

Kennedy, drawing on these codes, compiled rules to guide the court in its deliberations. No slave would be tried unless either his owner or some legally appointed representative was present. The uncorroborated testimony of a single witness would not result in the death penalty. Witnesses had to confront the prisoners against whom they were testifying, and the accused would be represented by counsel whenever owners or free blacks requested it. The court also decided to allow any prisoner to examine any witness that he wished. Whatever restraint these protocols might have seemed to embody in theory, the court fell far short of this standard in practice; it persuaded several defendants to testify in secret, thus preventing them from confronting their accusers. The infrequent appearances made by the defense suggest that accused slaves had very little contact with the men appointed to represent them. Certainly no defense counsel appears to have mounted a vigorous defense on behalf of the accused. Several owners attended the trials of their own slaves, occasionally providing character references for the court. Such testimonials, however, carried little weight. For example, even though Joe Jore's owner and defense counsel told the court that his "general conduct was good," he was still sentenced to death. Finally, Hamilton did not convene a grand jury to consider the merits of each case, nor did he empanel a jury to reach the verdicts. The fate of the defendants invariably rested in the hands of the magistrates and the five white freeholders appointed to represent Charleston's citizenry.[286]

These arrangements deeply troubled both William Johnson, an associate justice on the U.S. Supreme Court and a native South Carolinian, and Governor Thomas Bennett, his brother-in-law, who questioned Hamilton's haste

---

285. Cooper and McCord, *Statutes at Large*, 2:423, 7:400; Thomas Bennett to Senate and House of Representatives, Governors' Messages, SCDAH. On slave law, see Morris, *Southern Slavery and Law*, 238–39; Senese, "The Free Negro," 140–53; and Hindus, *Prison and Plantation*.

286. Kennedy and Parker, *Official Report*, 3; Trial of Joe Jore, 15 July 1822, DTT.

in convening the court as well as the procedures that it chose to follow. Although both Johnson and Bennett accepted that the plot existed, they believed that hasty action served only, as Johnson noted, "to produce great excitement and alarm" among the city's inhabitants. Johnson later concluded that the conspiracy had been "infinitely exaggerated [by] a few timid and precipitate men." Voicing these concerns in a short essay, entitled "Melancholy Effects of Popular Excitement," which appeared in the *Charleston Courier,* Johnson warned against instigating a witch-hunt that might result in the death of innocent people and the perversion of justice. Although court members complained that they had been "injured and defamed" by such remarks, Johnson's broadside had little significant impact on the proceedings. The judge then partially retracted his earlier comments, claiming that he regretted casting "censure on respectable men." Nonetheless, he defended his views in *To the Public of Charleston*, a short pamphlet, in which he called upon the city's white inhabitants to withhold judgment until trials ended.[287]

Johnson, moreover, found Kennedy and Parker's cavalier attitude toward the rights of the accused equally worrying. Writing Thomas Jefferson some months later, Johnson complained that the court had abrogated the defendants' right to a fair trial. "I have lived to see what I never really believed possible," he informed the former president, "courts with closed doors, and men dying by scores who had never seen the faces nor heard the voices of their accusers." Although he dismissed Vesey and his followers as "a trifling cabal of a few ignorant, pennyless, unarmed, uncombined fanatics," Johnson had no desire to see the law so blatantly ignored. Already smarting from several poor reviews of his recent book on a leading figure of the American Revolution, entitled *Sketches of the Life and Correspondence of Nathanael Greene*, Johnson now found himself ostracized by white Charlestonians who "took up the cudgels... [and] thundered their anathema at him." Johnson, as we shall see, would obtain some modest revenge against his critics when he ruled the Negro Seaman Act, passed in the wake of the conspiracy in December 1822 by the state legislature, to be unconstitutional.[288]

Sharing Johnson's concerns, Bennett believed that "the scheme has not

287. William Johnson to John Quincy Adams, 3 July 1824, cited in Donald G. Morgan, *Justice William Johnson*, 131; Thomas Bennett, 10 August 1822, Governors' Messages, #1328, p. 51, SCDAH; *Niles Register*, 7 September 1822; Johnson, "Melancholy Effect of Popular Excitement," *Charleston Courier*, 21 June 1822; ibid., 29 June 1822; William Johnson, *To the Public of Charleston*.

288. William Johnson to Thomas Jefferson, 10 December 1822, cited in Donald G. Morgan, *Justice William Johnson*, 138; Anna Haywood to Elizabeth Haywood, 24 July 1822, Ernest Haywood Papers.

been general nor alarmingly extensive." Nonetheless he took no chances with the city's safety, informing Secretary of War John Calhoun about "the State of alarm" resulting from "the discovery of insurrectionary movements" among enslaved Charlestonians. The governor also demanded that the state's attorney general, Robert Hayne, investigate the propriety of the court's activities. Perhaps thinking about his candidacy in the forthcoming fall elections for the U.S. Congress, Hayne made some perfunctory inquiries, concluding that the court had been legally constituted. Bennett informed the legislature that he had received "an elaborate opinion in which the attorney general sought to remove the embarrassments to which the course of these proceedings had given birth." Only after the trials ended did Kennedy admit, in a moment of rare candor, that the court had departed "from the principles of common law and some of the settled rules of evidence." Despite such statements, however, Johnson and Bennett remained in a minority, offering unpopular opinions to citizens largely indifferent to the principles of jurisprudence and concerned more with swift justice.[289]

Unmoved by these criticisms, Kennedy and Parker transacted court business "with great energy," hearing a large number of cases each day. On Monday, 15 July, for example, six slaves (Monday Gell, Mingo Harth, Joe Jore, Jack Purcell, Lewis Remoussin, and Tom Russel) stood before the court on trial as well as dozens of people brought in to testify in these cases. Between eleven o'clock and the late afternoon, the court not only listened to numerous individual statements, but also scheduled the following day's trials, considered verdicts, and passed appropriate sentences. Rebels who had gathered at Bulkley's farm, Vesey's house, or Gell's shop, and the men who had relayed information, gathered weapons, and embraced "the spirit of insurrection" were sentenced to death. Slaves who "had merely consented to join the plot" and took no active part in its organization were to be banished from the United States. Those prisoners whom the court believed to be innocent were acquitted and discharged even though several spent a long time behind bars before they gained their freedom.[290]

The workhouse served as both prison and court room during the trials.

289. Thomas Bennett to House and Senate, 10 August 1822, and Thomas Bennett to House of Representatives and Senate, 22 November 1822, Governors' Messages, #1328, p. 52, SCDAH; Thomas Bennett to John Calhoun, 15 July 1822, in Hemphill, *Papers of John C. Calhoun*, 7:210. See also Calhoun to Major James Bankhead, 22 July 1822, in ibid., 7:219. Hayne later became a U.S. senator.

290. M[artha] Richardson to Dr. James Screven, 6 July 1822, Arnold-Screven Papers; Kennedy and Parker, *Official Report*, 4–5. See also "A List of Negroes Committed by the Council for an Attempt to Raise an Insurrection," ca. July 1822, General Assembly Petitions, SCDAH.

Standing on the corner of Meeting and Mazyck Streets, this forbidding building had become temporary home to "the destitute and deviant of all kinds," in addition to slaves incarcerated for a variety of offenses by 1822. As June proved to be "unusually severe in its heat," the prisoners sat in their shackles in unpleasantly hot and humid cells. The bill for more than three hundred dollars presented by John Righton to the city for treating sick slaves further suggests that conditions inside prison were barely tolerable. Apart from pulling numerous teeth, he administered a large number of powders and mixtures, opened abscesses on several slaves, bled others, and tried to care for those who succumbed to respiratory ailments. If Righton tended slaves who had been beaten or whipped by their captors, he did not record their treatment on his bill. Righton's ministrations proved insufficient to save the lives of some slaves. Escaping the gallows after their sentences were reduced to transportation, both Harry Haig and John Enslow, who had spent nearly three months in jail, died prisoners as they awaited their exile.[291]

The cramped accommodations provided for accused and convicted rebels further helped the authorities in making their case. To prevent prisoners from fabricating stories before they took the stand, the warden tried to keep them in solitary confinement. Limited jail space, however, forced the warden to put several rebels in one cell, enabling him to gather additional information through eavesdropping. In one incident, Hamilton intentionally placed two conspirators in one cell to collect further evidence. Charles Drayton, in "a state of the most lamentable depression and panic" over his impending execution, made "the most ample declarations" to his jailers so that he would not suffer in "the consequences of an *hereafter*." Hamilton then put Drayton in a cell with the condemned Monday Gell, whom he apparently convinced to reveal more details about the conspiracy. Gell confessed his part in the plot to the intendant in return for a commutation of the death sentence. Both prisoners were subsequently sentenced to transportation.[292]

About the dramatic events that unfolded in the court room, there is practically no information. The transcript yields only the statements of the accused while Kennedy and Parker's *Official Report* offers just a few cursory comments on the prisoners' demeanor. Vesey, according to the judges' account, listened attentively to testimony presented against him while Rolla

---

291. See McCandless, *Moonlight, Magnolias, and Madness*, 21–22; *Charleston Mercury*, 26 June 1822; Petitions of Dr. John Righton to the Assembly, 3 December 1822 and 10 December 1822, Joseph Enslow to Assembly, n.d., 1822, and David Haig to Assembly, n.d., 1822, all in General Assembly Petitions, SCDAH.

292. Hamilton, *Account of the Late Intended Insurrection*, 20–21; Mary Beach to Elizabeth Gilchrist, 15 July 1822, Beach Papers, SCHS.

Bennett sat through his trial with "great presence and composure." The judges doubtless exploited the theatricality inherent in the proceedings to assert their power and authority, effecting an air of intimidation as they presided over the trials. A virtually impenetrable veil of secrecy cloaked the courtroom. The city's papers, editorialized the Hartford *Courant* in mid-July, "have been silent on the subject of the insurrection." Writing to her nephew James Screven in Europe, Martha Richardson noted how she could not "give a correct account of the proceedings in Charleston [as] everything has been kept a profound secret." Not until the court passed its first sentence did city papers break their silence, and then only to announce the name and time of those prisoners to be executed. In the meantime, they filled their columns with news from Europe, advice on pruning fruit trees and breaking horses, and the usual notices advertising sales of land, slaves, and other forms of property. Only when the *Official Report* appeared at the end of the year could white Charlestonians read about the trials.[293]

The absence of any trial reports in the newspapers, however, did not prevent people from speculating about the plot. We might imagine the scene in Thomas Bennett's drawing room as the governor along with his brother-in-law William Johnson and his niece Anna Johnson discussed the fate of Batteau, Ned, and Rolla, who had all worked in his Lynch Street house. At the best dinner tables, people quizzed those involved in the trial as well as those who had visited the accused in the workhouse. From these conversations, several people, including Mary Beach, discovered details about the conspiracy and the conspirators that she later shared with her sister in a series of letters. From Thomas Legare, she learned that Vesey sat in his cell in "a very hardened state," claiming that "he had not had a *fair* trial" because he had been unable to face and challenge his accusers. By the eve of his death, however, his attitude appeared to have changed. He apparently spent his final hours praying and singing Psalms, traveling to the gallows with his spiritual house in order. According to Beach, Vesey claimed that "his *Spiritual* enjoyment never had been as great or greater than that night," believing that the cause for which he was about to die was "Glorious." Peter Poyas, who would die alongside Vesey, acted as a "hardened villain" toward other inmates and warders as he awaited his fate. For several others, the toll of the trial, imprisonment, and impending execution destroyed their defiance. Lutheran pastor John Backman found Bacchus Hammet to be "very dejected

---

293. *Hartford Courant*, 16 July 1822; M[artha] Richardson to Dr. James Screven, 7 August 1822, Arnold-Screven Papers, SHC. See also Kennedy and Parker, *Official Report*, 31. On the theatricality of court proceedings, see Hay, "Property, Authority, and the Criminal Law," 17–64. On slave trials, see Schwartz, *Twice Condemned*.

[and] in deep study" as he sat in his cell, and the condition of Rolla Bennett "evinced much feeling & penitence even to tears."[294]

Perhaps reluctant to have the leading conspirators remain in prison from which they could conceivably escape or be rescued, the court swiftly executed the thirty-five conspirators it had sentenced to death. The first executions took place at Blake Fields on Tuesday, 2 July, while the remaining four sets of hangings occurred by the Lines on Friday, 12 July; Friday, 26 July; Tuesday, 30 July; and Friday, 9 August.

Although Peter Poyas had used the scaffold as a platform from which to call upon his fellow rebels not to betray additional conspirators on 2 July, the most dramatic hangings took place on 26 July when, as Anna Johnson recounted, "22 unfortunate wretches were at one fatal moment sent to render up their dread account." To prevent any disorder on that day, Hamilton deployed cavalry patrols throughout the city. In the early morning, an "immense crowd . . . of white as well as black" watched the condemned leave the workhouse at dawn to make their way up Meeting Street to the gallows. Along this *via dolorosa* stood several children, including one young boy who would later recall "the ghastly procession . . . [with] each negro seated on a coffin" as an enslaved cart driver took them to their place of execution.[295]

The authorities constructed a gallows of such size, recalled Charles Fraser in his memoirs, that it would "strike terror into the heart of every slave" who might witness this scene. Designed to convey the state's awesome power, these spectacles of terror often included addresses from ministers as well as the final words of the condemned. In this case, however, we know little about the ceremonies that took place on the gallows. According to one witness, Vesey and the four other rebels hanged on 2 July apparently "met their fate with the heroic fortitude of Martyrs" after Peter Poyas had enjoined other insurgents to "die silent." Perhaps the sheer scale of the scaffold besides the sight of twenty-two rebels waiting to die on 26 July enabled the authorities to dispense with the rituals intended to reinforce their rule. The hangings did not lack for drama, however, provided by the defiant behavior of several condemned rebels and an incompetent performance by the executioner.[296]

---

294. Mary Beach to Elizabeth Gilchrist, 5 July 1822, Mary Lamboll Thomas Beach Papers, SCHS; Report of John Backman, ca. July 1822, Benjamin Hammet Papers, WPL.

295. Samuel Wragg Ferguson, "Memoirs of Samuel Wragg Ferguson," [1900], Samuel Wragg Ferguson Papers, WPL; Anna Johnson to Elizabeth Haywood, 27 July 1822, Ernest Haywood Papers, SHC.

296. Charles Fraser, *Reminiscences of Charleston*, 18; Adger, *My Life and Times*, 3. Adger was eleven years old when the executions took place. M[artha] Richardson to Dr. James Screven, 6 July 1822, Arnold-Screven Papers, SHC. On executions, see Masur, *Rites of*

Always a slow and painful way to kill people, the hangings that took place on this particular July morning proved to be more grisly than usual. Perhaps unwilling to play the role of the passive victim, Bacchus Hammet decided to die with much fanfare, inverting the somber ritual of execution into absurd theater. No longer depressed after his fourteen days in jail, Bacchus rode from jail to the Lines in a cart, "laughing and bidding his acquaintances in the streets 'goodbye'" as he traveled to a death that was to be equally eventful. On the gallows, Bacchus continue to laugh as the executioner placed the hood over his head and secured the rope around his neck. Then, in a dramatic gesture, Hammet took control over his own death as he "threw himself forward and as he swung back, he lifted his feet so that his knees might not touch the board" of the gallows.

The executioner had no better luck with several other prisoners at this hanging. By failing to adjust the ropes correctly so that they would "choke effectually the sufferers to death," the hangman found himself gazing at several hooded slaves gasping "in the agony of . . . strangulation" as they slowly twisted in the nooses and fought for air. Screaming "to be despatched," these victims of the hangman's error were shot dead by the guard captain. This macabre event finally came to a terrifying end when a horse, frightened by the gunfire, bolted and spread panic through the crowd, leading to the death of a white spectator and several injuries. "A deathlike silence," noted Beach, "reigned in the city" as these rebels died. That night the patrol reported "all quiet" as they inspected the workhouse and its surrounding neighborhoods.[297]

Even in death, the rebels found neither rest nor peace. The court instructed that the bodies be buried or delivered "to surgeons for dissection if required" after the hangings. Thrown into poorly dug graves, the corpses quickly attracted vermin, forcing Line Street residents to complain to the council about "the alarming nuisance occasioned by the offensive manner in which many of the culprits have been interred." Following these executions, several slaves appeared in the streets clad in sack cloth as a sign of mourn-

---

Execution; Williams, *Vogues in Villainy*, 100–103. On the spectacle of executions and their impact, both intended and unintended, on the public, see Foucault, *Discipline and Punish*, 32–69.

297. Anonymous note, Benjamin Hammet Papers, WPL; A Colored American, *Late Intended Insurrection in Charleston*, 6; Mary Beach to Elizabeth Gilchrist, 27 July 1822, 25 July 1822, Mary Lamboll Thomas Beach Papers; Charles Graves Militia Book, 26 July 1822, SCHS. The chains and padlocks used to shackle the prisoners cost $47, the hoods for the condemned came to $30, while the council paid Thomas McMillan $61 "for erecting a gallows." Council Minutes, August 1822, CCA.

ing, a gesture for which they were imprisoned and whipped. On Thursday, 9 August, following the hanging of William Garner, who had been captured just outside Columbia and brought back to Charleston to face the court, the executions as well as the trials came to an end.[298]

Those slaves sentenced to transportation awaited their exile in the workhouse. Their banishment presented a problem to the authorities as prominent Charlestonian and veteran diplomat Joel Poinsett discovered when he unsuccessfully tried to organize their sale to South American slaveholders. Unable to remove them from the United States, the city arranged to sell these slaves to planters in southern Georgia and Alabama. Exchanging the relative freedom of the city for the strict regime of plantation agriculture, men including Charles Drayton, Monday Gell, and William Paul found themselves transformed into rural slaves. They remained in the workhouse until their new owners took possession of them in late autumn. John Enslow and David Haig faced the expense of providing coffins for their slaves who died in prison, as well as the cost of their incarceration.[299]

Although city newspapers heralded a return to normal life and the state legislature formally thanked the court for its services in mid-August, there was an epilogue to the conspiracy trials two months later. On 7 October, four white men—William Allen and John Igneshias (both sailors), Jacob Danders (a peddler and "vagabond" of German extraction) and Andrew Rhodes (a store owner and accused counterfeiter)—faced charges of inciting slaves to rebel. Although the authorities believed that they were not part of Vesey's conspiracy, they suspected them of encouraging and taking advantage of the planned insurrection.

The trial record does not provide a coherent account of the activities of these men, but they appear to have contributed to the atmosphere of panic that prevailed in Charleston. Allen, having landed in Charleston in late May, befriended a free black man named Scott from whom he tried to discover more about the conspiracy. Soon after, Scott informed John Stoney, a prominent merchant, of Allen's inquiries. To discover Allen's intentions, Stoney suggested that Scott set up a meeting between people who pretended to be involved in the plot. Subsequently, Allen and Scott met in the house of a free black called Joe. As they talked, Joe and Scott quizzed Allen, who consumed large amounts of brandy, about his loyalty to slaves about to rebel. Eager to involve himself in the plot and now thoroughly intoxicated, Allen began declaring that "*there ought to be an indiscriminate destruction of all the*

---

298. Court Instructions, 22 July 1822, DTT; Council Minutes, 27 August 1822, CCA. The mourning rituals are noted in Higginson, "Denmark Vesey," 741.

299. Wikramanayake, *World in Shadow*, 134; *Charleston Mercury*, 25 December 1822.

whites, men, women and children." He further announced that even though he was a white man, "he was a negro at heart." Once arrested, however, the drunken sailor adopted a rather different position on slave insurrections, asserting to his captors that "the freedom of the blacks was an object of no importance to him."

Unlike Allen, who had unsuccessfully tried to inveigle his way into the conspiracy for his own gain, the other three men appear to have been guilty of nothing more than making comments regarded as incendiary by the authorities. When talking about the conspiracy with several free black men after the execution of "Gullah" Jack, Rhodes announced that "the Negroes ought to fight for their liberty." Likewise, Danders made similar observations while drinking in the company of slaves, arguing that the rebels already executed were innocent and urging his listeners to "rescue those who are still to be hanged." In a conversation with several slaves about the conditions under which they lived, Igneshias remarked that "how can you think the white people use you well by keeping you in slavery?" At the summation of their trials, Judge Elihu Bay concluded that "*plunder, and indemnity to their own persons* were the objects sought for by these offenders." He sentenced them to jail terms ranging from three months to one year and fined them from $100 to $1,000. These four men of "the lowest character" were the only white people ever implicated in the plot.[300]

POLITICS AND PAMPHLETS:
THE CONSEQUENCES OF THE CONSPIRACY

The press is free . . . use it freely; write, print, publish what you please; it is your constitutional privilege; but while you do so, remember that the whole South, with the Constitution of the Union spread out before it, as a broad banner, reads your writings . . . see to it, as you would when taking a solemn oath in a court of justice, that you utter, the truth, the whole truth, and nothing but the truth.
—Daniel R. Whittaker, *"The Necessity of a Southern Literature,"* 1842

The trials and executions did not end slave resistance in the lowcountry. Enslaved men and women persisted in challenging their subordination until slavery's destruction at the end of the Civil War. As the court concluded its business in mid-August, a band of escaped slaves attacked the mail coach that ran between Charleston and Savannah. Some weeks later, Martha Rich-

300. Kennedy and Parker, *Official Report*, 147–52.

ardson informed James Screven that several slaves had been tried "for attempting to poison their Master," while Governor Bennett had to order the militia to track down "a number of armed fugitive slaves" who had been "destroying cattle, breaking into, and robbing dwellings, and threatening the lives of faithful domestics" on Johns Island in December. On Christmas Eve in 1825, the first in a series of fires that continued throughout early 1826 broke out, resulting in the arrests and imprisonment of a number of slaves. In 1829, seven years after Vesey's plot, the slave patrol in Georgetown arrested a group of enslaved men who were planning to destroy the small coastal settlement. Yet 1822 proved to be a watershed, prompting state legislators to take several practical measures to isolate the province from the social and political currents that had inspired Vesey. Even though South Carolina's slaveowners would not have to deal with a conspiracy of such magnitude again, the threat of massive insurrection remained constant.[301]

The story of Vesey's defiance entered the oral traditions of black Carolinians. Interviewed in 1937 for the Works Project Administration, seventy-four-year-old Daniel Goddard recalled how "the Vesey conspiracy was discussed often in my presence, by my parents and friends." Israel Nesbitt, great-grandson of Robert Nesbitt, a free black man who was arrested for his purported involvement in the plot and subsequently acquitted by the court, heard " 'bout de Vesey uprisin' " from his father. Passed down through the generations, the account that Nesbitt provided WPA interviewer Stiles Scruggs offered a very brief, but remarkably faithful summary of some aspects of the plot. Not only did his account include an outline of Vesey's biography, but it also recounted the midnight meetings and the "tumult" that accompanied the arrests and hangings of the rebels. Claiming that he could neither read nor write, Nesbitt had clearly learned about the plot through oral traditions rather than from any printed materials.[302] As enslaved Carolinians folded the story of Vesey's plot into their own oral history, lowcountry politicians passed new laws to prevent the recurrence of such challenges to the cornerstone of southern society, and Charleston's small intellectual community put down their thoughts on the summer's events on paper.

Passed in December 1822, the Negro Seaman Act proved to be the most controversial piece of legislation enacted in the wake of the conspiracy.

---

301. Martha Richardson to James Screven, 16 September 1822, Arnold-Screven Papers, SHC; Thomas Bennett to Senate, 9 December 1822, Governors' Messages, #1325, SCDAH; *Charleston Mercury*, 13 August 1822; Walter J. Fraser, *Charleston! Charleston!*, 209. On the Georgetown plot, see Rogers, *History of Georgetown County*, 236–37.

302. Daniel Goddard, WPA interview, in Rawick, *South Carolina Narratives*, 151, and ibid., 261–63.

Designed primarily to prevent the circulation of subversive ideas or literature between free and enslaved people, this law required that all free blacks "from any other State of *foreign port* . . . [be] seized and confined in gaol until such vessel shall clear out and depart from this state." This statute further required that individual captains pay for the incarceration of any free black crew member. Should any captain fail to comply, they, too, would face imprisonment. Rather than frequent grogshops during their time in port, black sailors would now be placed behind bars or, as attorney Benjamin Hunt commented, "take up their abode in a very airy and healthy part of the city until their vessel [was] ready to depart." Despite the federal government's efforts to stop the state from enforcing this law, which threatened to damage interstate commerce and diplomatic relations with nations that used free black mariners, a group of prominent lowcountry leaders organized the South Carolina Association (SCA) to "aid in the enforcement of such of our laws as relate to the '*government* and *discipline* of our colored population.'" Just months after its passage, an incident in Charleston would result in a court case that would test its constitutionality, bringing the newly formed SCA into the spotlight and Justice William Johnson back on the front pages of the city's newspapers.[303]

Disembarking from the *Homer* in Charleston in midsummer 1823, Henry Elkison, a free Afro-Jamaican mariner who shipped out of Liverpool and held British citizenship, found himself in the city jail following his arrest by the SCA, who had acted on behalf of Charleston sheriff Francis G. Deliesseline. After an official protest by the British consul in Charleston failed to free Elkison, the unfortunate sailor applied to Johnson for a writ of *habeas corpus*, arguing that the law that had led to his arrest violated a longstanding agreement between Britain and the United States which gave inhabitants of both countries free access to their respective ports. As one clause of the Federal Constitution stipulated that "treaties made . . . under the authority of the United States, shall be the supreme law of the land," the Negro Seaman Act was clearly unconstitutional. Elkison's petition went before Johnson who, in his capacity as chief judge of the U.S. Circuit Court for the District of South Carolina, was currently presiding over cases in his home state.

A complex legal struggle then ensued in which Isaac Holmes and Benjamin Hunt, as attorneys for the SCA, argued that the state government

---

303. On the Negro Seamen Act, see Hamer, "Negro Seamen Acts," 6; Freehling, *Prelude to Civil War*, 111–15; *Charleston Mercury*, 3 August 1825, cited in Severens, *Charleston: Antebellum Architecture and Civic Destiny*, 64. The clauses relating to black mariners are contained in "An Act for the Better Regulation and Government of Free Negroes and Persons of Color," 21 December 1822, in Cooper and McCord, *Statutes at Large*, 7:462.

remained sovereign in this case, claiming that laws designed to prevent insurrections took precedence over any federal treaty. From "the moment he [Elkison] touches the soil of Carolina," wrote Holmes, "he is as much subject to our police regulations, and to all the disabilities of his race, as if he had been born in this city." They further argued that the Negro Seaman Act was no different from quarantine laws that sought to prevent the spread of epidemics. Using disease as a metaphor, Hunt concluded that white South Carolinians would "dread the moral pestilence which a free intercourse with foreign negroes will produce." For these men, the French Revolution, an event they compared to the eruption of a "volcano, which vomited from its crater, every doctrine which was calculated to overturn all governments, and to unsettle the principles of obedience," lay at the heart of the problem.[304]

Such arguments failed to sway Johnson. From the bench, he opened by criticizing the assembly who had passed this act "hastily and without due consideration." Questioning the legality of excluding the "coloured subjects" of Great Britain from the port, Johnson wondered whether mariners from elsewhere might also be banned from entering the state. "[I]f the colour of skin is to preclude the Lascar or the Sierra Leone seaman," he argued, "why not the colour of his eyes or his hair exclude from our ports the inhabitants of other territories." Under this act, he continued, a ship from Massachusetts with a crew of "Nantucket Indians . . . might all become slaves" when they landed in Charleston. Even as Johnson concluded his deliberations, black mariners continued to be arrested as soon as they landed in Charleston. Between late July and September 1823, more than 150 sailors of African descent from throughout the Atlantic basin languished in the city's jail.[305]

Finding the act "clearly unconstitutional" on several counts in early August 1823, Johnson argued that this law violated the constitution's commerce clause and interfered with the treaty-making powers of the federal government. Within days of his decision becoming public, letters and editorials in city newspapers denounced Johnson. No stranger to controversy, the judge again found himself reviled by his fellow South Carolinians. Publishing his decision in a pamphlet, entitled *The Opinion of the Hon. William Johnson . . . in the Case of the Arrest of the British Seaman*, he reminded his critics that the Negro Seaman Act was "altogether irreconcilable with the powers of the general government . . . [and] implies a direct attack upon the sovereignty of

---

304. Benjamin Faneuil Hunt, *The Argument of Benj. Faneuil Hunt, in the Case of the Arrest of the Person Claiming to Be a British Seaman* (Charleston, 1823), cited in Finkelman, *Slavery in the Courtroom*, 262. See also Caroliniensis, *Arrest of a British Seaman*, 45; Wiecek, *Sources of Antislavery Constitutionalism*, 128–35.

305. William Johnson, *Opinion*, 1:290; Bolster, *Black Jacks*, 196.

the United States." A strident voice of opposition, Hunt had little time for Johnson's nationalist sentiments, claiming in *The Argument of Benj. Faneuil Hunt in the Case . . . of the Person Claiming to be a British Seaman* that he would find the dissolution of the Union preferable to the state surrendering its power to the federal government. Despite the decision and the subsequent uproar, South Carolinians continued to imprison black mariners for another year until the legislature modified the law to exempt free blacks serving on naval vessels from arrest. As William Freehling has noted, however, this episode alerted lowcountry planters to the need for "adopting strict-construction principles if the federal government was to be prevented from touching the slavery issue."[306]

Wary lawmakers also moved to regulate the lives of enslaved and free black Carolinians as well as the domestic slave trade. To control the movement of slaves and the ability to acquire property, the assembly followed Charleston's grand jury call to restrict the number of slaves "working out and bringing wages to their owners" by imposing tighter controls over hiring procedures. Grand jurors further noted how such measures would prevent slaves who worked on hire from "act[ing] in concert and 'concert is the very life of conspiracy.'" Like virtually every regulation governing hiring, this new code was ineffective. Another law, also unenforceable, sought to curb the traffic in gossip and rumor, adjudging any slave who made even a passing remark about insurrection a felon and subject to execution.[307] New statutes also limited the few liberties enjoyed by free blacks, including laws that severely constrained their freedom of movement, prohibited any free black who traveled outside South Carolina from returning, increased their annual poll tax from $2 to a prohibitively high $50, and required them to obtain a white guardian to vouch for their conduct. The city council also imposed a tax on all free black tenants and landlords, and levied a $10 fee on free blacks who worked in any "Mechanick Trade" in order to defray the cost of improving the city guard.[308]

Legislators also sought to insulate the state from unwanted influences, curtailing the arrival of slaves from politically sensitive areas: masters could not bring in slaves "from any port or place in the West Indies, or Mexico, or any part of South America, or from Europe, or from any sister State . . . north of the river Potomac or the city of Washington." As Henry DeSaussure

306. Johnson, *Opinion*, 299; Freehling, *Prelude to Civil War*, 115.
307. *Carolina Gazette*, 19 October 1822; "Memorial of the Citizens of Charleston," 2:111.
308. "Memorial of the Citizens of Charleston," 2:108–9; *Charleston Courier*, 1 July 1822. The authorities imprisoned the free black and then sold him into slavery and returned the fugitive slave to his owner. See also Wikramanayake, *World in Shadow*, 67.

told Joel Poinsett at the height of the Vesey crisis, "those who have been engaged in scenes of blood in the West Indies . . . beguile our slaves into rebellion with false hope." In addition, Charleston officials also tried to halt the distribution of any "pamphlets of a very seditious & inflammatory character among the Slaves & persons of color," arresting a white sailor who brought copies of David Walker's *Appeal to the Coloured Citizens of the World*, first published in 1829, into the city in early 1830.[309]

In addition, the legislature allocated funds to improve Charleston's security. Using state funds along with the revenues newly collected from free blacks, the city established "a Competent Force to Act as a Municipal Guard for the City of Charleston and Its Vicinity" and financed the construction of a new guardhouse. Demolishing an old tobacco inspection warehouse on King Street, the city built a new fort in 1825 to house these men and their weapons. Visiting the city in the same year, Revolutionary War veteran and hero Marquis de Lafayette inspected this force, complimenting them on "the excellence of their discipline and the good taste of their uniforms." The general then listened to an address by their commanding officer that emphasized how the maintenance of public order stood among "the first duties of the citizen." Twenty-two years later, the state replaced this building with an imposing new structure (known as the Citadel) to house the South Carolina Military Academy, the institution that later became the training ground for many leading Confederate officers, on the junctions of Meeting, King, and Boundary Streets.[310]

Lawmakers were not alone in responding to Vesey's plot. The gravity of the crisis prompted lowcountry residents to organize vigilante groups to supplement ineffective slave patrols. A year after the trials, the Edisto Island Auxiliary and the Black Swamp Association petitioned to be incorporated as a volunteer militia force. Living among thousands of enslaved plantation workers and mindful of the slave rebellions on Saint Domingue as well as the Vesey conspiracy, these planters well knew the potential for revolt. Scattering references to "the midnight incendiary . . . the assassin with his schemes of horror" and attacking "the misguided philanthropy" of antislavery advo-

---

309. "An Act the More Effectually to Prohibit Free Negroes and Persons of Color from Entering into This State; And for other Purposes," in Cooper and McCord, *Statutes at Large*, 7:464; Henry DeSaussure to Joel Poinsett, 6 July 1822, cited in Freehling, *Prelude to Civil War*, 112; Pease and Pease, "Walker's *Appeal* Comes to Charleston," 288; Hinks, *To Awaken My Afflicted Brethren*, 145–46.

310. Walter J. Fraser, *Charleston! Charleston!*, 205; Bond, *Story of the Citadel*; John Thomas, *South Carolina Military Academy*. In 1922, the Citadel moved to Hampden Park on the outskirts of Charleston.

cates in the North in their petitions, these slaveowners articulated the deep-seated unease caused by the plot as well as the growing animus toward northern reformers. Established to halt "daily violations or evasions of the laws made to regulate the conduct of our colored population," the SCA proved to be among the most successful of these groups, serving as an effective guard against slave insurrection and as a congenial home for southern radicalism.[311]

The assembly also received appeals from slaveowners demanding compensation for slaves who had been executed or exiled. Rather than reimburse each owner for the specific value of the slave killed or banished, the assembly paid a flat rate of $122.44 for each slave. Not only did the state treasurer deny owners the market value of their deceased slaves, but he also proved rather dilatory in paying their compensation, finally distributing the money nearly a year after the trials. Other bills also came due. For their "services and faithful conduct," free black William Penceel pocketed $1,000, of which he used $700 to buy a slave woman named Sukey and her two children, perhaps his wife and daughters, while Isaac Scott collected $500. Both men were also exempt from the newly levied tax on free blacks. The two slaves, George Wilson and Peter Desverneys, who had provided Hamilton with vital information, gained their freedom besides an annuity of $50. In addition, Desverneys also collected an engraved silver pitcher. Paying the militia, holding the trials as well as housing, feeding and providing rudimentary medical care to the prisoners, and compensating owners for their losses cost the state at least $12,000.[312]

Writing to friends and family in their private correspondence, several white women considered the impact of the conspiracy on their own attitudes toward slaves and slavery. Discussing "the mournful state of things in our guilty city," Mary Beach recounted how one of her female companions believed that she would now be unable "to bear the sight of a Negroe again."

311. Petition of the Black Swamp Association, 9 December 1823, and Petition of the Edisto Island Auxiliary Association, 18 November 1823, General Assembly Petitions, SCDAH. See also Berlin, *Slaves without Masters*, 336–37; January, "South Carolina Association," 191–201; and Freehling, *Prelude to Civil War*, 112–13.

312. Journal C, October 1814–September 1824, Treasury Records, Ledgers and Journals, Account of the Contingent Expenses Incurred in the Late Insurrection, August and September 1822, Fees and Charges for the Detention of the Late Conspirators, and Petition of Dr. John Righton, December 1823, all in General Assembly Petitions, SCDAH; *Charleston Mercury*, 25 December 1822. Desverneys prospered as a free man, leaving several lots and two houses in his will. See Will of Peter Desverneys, Charleston County Wills, vol. 49, Book B, 1856–62, p. 866, cited in Wikramanayake, *World in Shadow*, 10, 139. Wilson fared less well, later committing suicide. I am indebted to Douglas Egerton for this information.

Refusing to "have *one* about me," this woman concluded that she would leave the South for the North. Anna Johnson harbored similar thoughts, telling her cousin that if she could only leave, she would "not stay in this city another day." Paralyzed by dread and anxiety, she further noted that "when I think what I have escaped & what yet I might suffer my blood curdles." No doubt aware that the authorities had arrested several of her uncle's domestic slaves for conspiracy, the young woman concluded that her "feelings have been so lacerated of late" that she was barely able to "think [or] speak."[313]

In these letters, several people tried to explain the summer's events not just to their readers but also to themselves. Using the metaphor of family as an explanatory device, Beach wondered how "these people[,] growing up like children as is the case of many of the *condemned* could be brought to such a fiend[-]like temper that they would imbrue their hands in the blood of their Masters & their little sons, who could never have shed theirs." Grappling with this problem, Beach tentatively blamed the French Revolution as well as "lust of dominion or want of revenge." John Potter likewise cited external influences, including the ideas and writings of antislavery advocates, as a leading cause for the conspiracy, informing Langdon Cheves, then living in Philadelphia, that "much of the poison that flows in this way comes from your city!!"[314]

Besides these private reflections, several leading political figures and white churchmen published their opinions in local newspapers or in pamphlets, often revealing as much about their own ideological inclinations as they did about the plot itself. In writing about the conspiracy and its broader ramifications, several essayists launched into spirited defenses of slavery. Taken together, these works constitute an early articulation of proslavery thought in the early republic. In addition to essays that provided thoughtful and reasoned arguments about the necessity of slavery and its place as the cornerstone of southern life, other writers simply trafficked in polemical and *ad hominem* attacks. Hamilton, for example, believed that Vesey's motives could be explained only by "a malignant hatred of whites, and [an] inordinate lust of power and booty," while Kennedy and Parker, as they sentenced several rebels to death, suggested that "depravity" combined with the absence of "settled principles, and . . . the virtues of civilized life" led to the plot.[315]

---

313. Mary Beach to Elizabeth Gilchrist, 5 July 1822, Mary Lamboll Thomas Beach Papers, SCHS; Anna Johnson to Elizabeth Haywood, 23 July 1822, Ernest Haywood Papers, SHC.

314. Mary Beach to Elizabeth Gilchrist, 23 July 1822, Mary Lamboll Thomas Beach Papers, SCHS; John Potter to Langdon Cheves, 24 June 1822, Langdon Cheves Papers, SCHS.

315. Hamilton, *Account of the Late Intended Insurrection*, 29; Kennedy and Parker, *Official*

Considering the plot and its implications, some pamphlet writers regarded free blacks as the most dangerous members of the population. Their presence, argued several Charleston citizens, "excites discontent among our slaves," resulting in enslaved people becoming "dissatisfied" and "pant[ing] after liberty." That a free black from New York attempted to smuggle an escaped slave aboard his ship bound for the North at the height of the crisis served only to confirm such conclusions. Even though the authorities imprisoned and then enslaved this free black mariner after he completed his prison sentence, both the conspiracy and this episode further fueled fears that the presence of free blacks threatened the security of slavery.

Although virtually no other writer embraced the position expressed in the Charleston-based *Southern Intelligencer*, which saw slavery as "a common evil" against which people should employ "any just and honourable means to free the country of so unwelcome a burden," many pamphleteers, as historian Larry Tise has noted, did not immediately leap to "the defense of slavery as a perpetual institution of southern society." Several writers considered what measures should be taken to prevent the recurrence of such conspiracies. Noting that "draymen, porters, fishermen, hucksters, butchers, barbers, &c." all played key roles in the plot, Thomas Pinckney, a former governor, advocated that the city "get rid of the blacks, who now occupy these employments," substituting them with white workers, who doubtless would have been delighted by prospect of the higher wages that such a measure would produce. This plan would require "the sale, hire, or other disposal out of town, of the coloured people." Never explicitly stating what he meant by "other disposal," Pinckney, who supported the efforts of the ACS, may have considered repatriation under their auspices to Liberia as one potential solution to the problem. By calling for a virtual abandonment of skilled slave labor in the city and making slavery an exclusively rural institution, Pinckney sailed against the currents of the time.[316]

Not all commentators suggested such radical solutions to the problem. Writing under the pen name "A Columbian," distinguished jurist Henry DeSaussure encapsulated the main themes of most pamphlets that poured from the presses by concentrating on the impracticality of dismantling slavery. Emancipation, he argued, would rob southern farmers of their labor force as well as deprive New England manufacturers and merchants of the

---

Report, 137–38. For a wide-ranging discussion on proslavery writings, see Faust, *Ideology of Slavery*; Greenberg, *Masters and Statesmen*, 85–103; and Tise, *Proslavery*.

316. *Southern Intelligencer*, 16 November 1822, cited in Tise, *Proslavery*, 59; Achates [Thomas Pinckney], *Reflections Occasioned by the Late Disturbances*, 14–15, 20.

raw materials that had made them wealthy as textile producers. Having analyzed the benefits that northern industrial and commercial interests gained from slavery, DeSaussure then launched into a discussion on "the practicality of and effect of emancipation." Dismissing the idea, he argued that economic ruin would result from the high costs of compensating owners for the loss of their property as well as from the anarchy that would ensue in the labor market as cotton and rice planters tried to hire the newly freed men and women to work in their estates. Moreover, he also noted that these freed people would prove incapable of fulfilling their civic duties as new citizens of the republic. "Are the blacks now prepared," DeSaussure inquired rhetorically, "or could their descendants be prepared for the enjoyment of liberty or political rights? The answer founded on experience must be in the negative." Issuing a standard diatribe against abolitionists who, declared DeSaussure, failed to understand the benign nature of southern slavery or the widespread economic and political disorder that would result from emancipation, the jurist concluded that slaves "must of necessity remain in their present condition, improved by humane regulation and wise provisions, adapted to their state."[317]

Revising an earlier essay written in response to the Compromise of 1820, newspaper editor Edwin Holland wrote perhaps the most popular and polemical article on the plot. Entitled *A Refutation of the Calumnies Circulated Against Southern States and Western States*, Holland obtained a copyright on this essay, making it, as Tise has noted, "the first autonomous proslavery treatise written and published by a native southerner." The editor first took direct aim at northerners, regarding them as "totally ignorant of the actual state and character of our Negro Population." He then attacked free blacks, characterizing them as "an idle, lazy, insolent set of vagabonds, who live by theft or gambling or other means equally vicious and demoralising." Launching into a diatribe about the intellectual abilities of both free black and enslaved people, he argued that their "general inferiority in the gifts of nature . . . forever baffle all prospects of successful rebellion." Not wishing to tempt fate, however, Holland advocated the expulsion of free blacks, asserting that their "*comparative* degree of *freedom*" prompted slaves to consider their own situation, resulting in deep dissatisfaction among slaves that led to " 'a black flood of long-retained spleen.' " Perhaps mindful of the role played by several people of mixed ancestry in uncovering the plot, including William Penceel, Holland exempted "free mulattoes" from his sustained attack. He viewed the latter as "industrious, sober, hardworking mechanics" who

---

317. A Columbian, *Numbers Addressed to the Public*.

would ally themselves with the white community rather than with either free blacks or slaves during a crisis.

For most white southerners, the editor's aim was true as he struck his targets with great rhetorical skill. Slaveholders, angered at northerners attacking them in newspapers, from pulpits and "in pamphlets and orations," had found a dedicated advocate for their cause in Holland. Scornfully dismissing the sentiments of northerners who demanded an end to slavery, he also defended the honor of southern slaveholders, emphasizing the benevolence of the social order over which they presided. Employing the language of scientific racism, he dismissed black Charlestonians as intellectually inferior and incapable of mounting a rebellion. To conclude his essay, the editor returned to his polemical tone, reminding readers that "our NEGROES are truely the *Jacobins* of the country; that they are the *anarchists* and the *domestic enemy*; the *common enemy of civilized society* and the barbarians who would, IF THEY COULD, become the DESTROYERS *of our race.*" Grand jurors in Charleston agreed with Holland's assessment, reminding lawmakers in Columbia that "we should always act as if we had an enemy in the very bosom of the State, prepared to rise upon and surprise the whites."[318]

Equating "slaves" with "Jacobins," Holland offered readers a compelling parallel between the fury and violence of the French Revolution, especially its incarnation on Saint Domingue, and the threat presented by Vesey. Intentionally or not, Holland's comparison of "our NEGROES" to "Jacobins" recast slaves and free blacks into people who possessed an ideology that drew its strength from the radical notions embedded in the emancipatory actions and language of Haitian slaves. Three years later, lowcountry planter and agricultural essayist Whitemarsh Seabrook, perhaps reflecting on the conspiracy, again invoked the Haitian Revolution in a proslavery treatise, observing that "God will raise up a Toussaint or a Spartacus against us."[319]

While these commentators reflected secular concerns, the city's religious leaders also drew important lessons from the conspiracy. In a public statement, Richard Furman called on Governor Bennett to hold "a Day of Humiliation and Thanksgiving" so that Charlestonians might praise "the Heavenly Majesty" whose "Divine Providence" had rescued them from "the

---

318. Holland, *Refutation of the Calumnies*, 14, 78, 83–84; "Memorial of the Citizens of Charleston," 114. In *Proslavery*, Tise has observed that Holland obtained a copyright on this essay, "making it the first autonomous proslavery treatise written and published by a native southerner" (p. 59); on Holland and his circle, see Moltke-Hansen, "Expansion of Intellectual Life," 30.

319. Seabrook, *Concise View*, 13; see also Hunt, *Haiti's Influence on Antebellum America*, 114–15.

horrors of the intended Insurrection [and] the ravages of a dreadful Hurricane." Privately, Furman was more outspoken, telling Bennett that only "God's superintending power" had saved the city from "the execution of a ferocious Diabolical Design . . . by Domestic barbarians." Proclaiming that "the right of holding slaves is clearly established in the Holy Scriptures," the Baptist minister then argued that only dedicated missionary work among lowcountry slaves and an "acquaintance with that Holy Book" would ensure "the internal and domestic peace of the state." He denounced the independence that black worshipers had enjoyed, noting that only when their congregations were again placed under white control would their "vices and transgressions" end. Episcopal minister Frederick Dalcho agreed wholeheartedly with such advice. To instill "the obedience . . . that is the fruit of the gospel" among enslaved men and women, Dalcho believed that effective religious training in addition to constant monitoring were necessary. He also remarked how the "ignorance and superstition" of the city's black church leaders only further excited "the malignant passions of their deluded hearers," presenting additional threats to peaceful coexistence between slaves and slaveholders.[320]

Order and discipline did not depend just on inculcating "obedience, submission, [and] subjection" among the city's slaves. Theodore Dehon took considerable pride in the fact that not one of the three hundred black members under his tutelage at Saint Michael's Episcopal Church fell under Vesey's spell, claiming that their "general character for orderly conduct . . . [should be] attributed to the excellent foundation which was laid for their moral and religious instruction." The real sin, proclaimed another minister from his pulpit, lay "in not spreading the Gospel . . . among our own heathen, the mass of which were as destitute of it as if they were in the 'heart of Africa.'" These preachers believed that slaveowners must also take their share of responsibility and embrace the values of Christian stewardship by treating their slaves in a humane manner and allowing them access to religious teachings. Only then could a society based on the institution of slavery free itself from the "Anarchy, Despoilation, Violence and Massacre" that Vesey had threatened.[321]

The literary production sparked by the plot served several purposes. In their responses, the lowcountry's white intelligentsia had introduced several

---

320. Richard Furman to Governor Thomas Bennett, September 1822, Richard Furman Correspondence, SBHC; Furman, "Exposition of the Views of the Baptists," 274–75, 277, 284; Donald Mathews, *Slavery and Methodism*, 40–43.

321. Gadsden, *Life of the Right Reverend Theodore Dehon*, 205; Richard Furman to Governor Thomas Bennett, September 1822, Richard Furman Correspondence, SBHC.

major themes that would pervade proslavery writing throughout the antebellum period. By mid-decade, local essayist Edward Brown confidently argued that "slavery has ever been the step ladder by which civilized countries passed from barbarism to civilization." Drawing on classical history as well as scripture and current anthropological theory, Brown's *Notes on the Origin and Necessity of Slavery* wove the main strands of proslavery discourse together. But the pamphlets and other literary materials also enabled civic leaders to offer their own analysis of the summer's events, serving as a literary pulpit from which they expounded on the question of slavery. By writing and selling their accounts for popular consumption, they helped to fix the meaning of the conspiracy in the public mind. Through the use of the printed word, the city's intellectual community attempted to regain their hold over a social order that was momentarily placed in jeopardy by Vesey's conspiratorial designs.[322]

The differences between the published version of the trial and the verbatim transcript also highlight how the authorities sought to reassert their control. Although Kennedy and Parker claimed in the introduction to their *Official Report* that "the evidence is in most cases preserved, as it was originally taken, without even changing the phraseology," they did in fact censor some testimony, rearrange the order of the trials, and collapse multiple statements by a single witness or defendant into brief synopses. The most striking difference between the two versions was the omission of testimony in which Harry Haig described how "Gullah" Jack planned to poison the city's water supply. Here, Kennedy and Parker tantalize the reader, introducing Haig's statement before inserting several rows of asterisks in place of text. Presumably the judges thought that this material might furnish future rebels with a blueprint for terrorism; alternatively, they might have believed that such information would incite an already nervous white citizenry to engage in gratuitous acts of revenge against slaves.

Like their fellow pamphleteers, Kennedy and Parker tried to shape the published narrative of events in ways that they were unable to do in the verbatim record. Thus, the *Official Report* and the other writings produced for public consumption enabled those men who presided over the trial and over the lowcountry's social order to regain their authority over events that had nearly slipped from their control. In short, these men used authorship to fashion the "authorized" account of the dramatic summer of 1822, using the medium of print to reassert their legitimacy.[323] But, even as these men

---

322. Edward Brown, *Origins and Necessity of Slavery*, 2; see also Tise, *Proslavery*, 65–66.
323. Kennedy and Parker, *Official Report*, 1; Testimony of Harry Haig, DTT.

WILLIAM, Mr. Paul's Slave, gave the following evidence :—Mingo Harth told me that he knows the little man who can't be shot, who told him that there was a Gullah Society going on which met once a month.

WITNESS, No. 5, testified that "the little man who can't be killed, shot or taken, is " named Jack, a Gullah Negro.

FRANK, Mrs. Ferguson's Slave testified as follows: The first time I spoke with Monday Gell 'twas one night at Denmark Vesey's house, where I heard Vesey tell Monday that he must *send one into the country to bring the people down*—Monday said *he had sent up Jack* and told him *to tell the people to come down and join in the fight* against the whites, and also to ascertain and inform him how many people he could get—A few days after I met Vesey, Monday and Jack in the street, under Mr. Duncan's trees, at night, where *Jack stated he had been into the country round by Goose Creek and Dorchester*, and that he had spoken to 6,600 persons who had agreed to join.

THE COURT *unanimously* found Gullah Jack GUILTY, and passed upon him the sentence of DEATH.

Subsequently to his conviction, HARRY HAIG, who received sentence of death at the same time that he did, made the following CONFESSION :

" Julius Forrest and myself always worked together—Gullah Jack calls himself a Doctor Negro—he induced Julius and myself to join at last, but at first we refused—before the 16th of June, Jack appointed to meet us at Bulkley's farm—when we got there Jack was not there, but Peter Poyas came—we broke up at day light. Not quite a month before the 16th of June, Jack met us and talked about war—I asked Jack how he would do for arms—bye and bye,

(as he called them.) It was in the course of this witness' evidence that Jack laid aside the character of the fool he was counterfeiting, and shewed his real character.

said Jack, we will have arms—he said he would have some arms made at the blacksmith's—Jack was going to give me * * * * *
* * * * * * *
 * * * * * *
* * * * * * *

I refused to do this as I considered it murder, and that God would never pardon me for it; 'twas not like fair fighting. Until Jack was taken up and condemned to death, I felt as if I was bound up, and had not the power to speak one word about it—Jack charmed Julius and myself at last, and we then consented to join—Tom Russel the Blacksmith and Jack are partners, (in conjuring) Jack learnt him to be a Doctor. Tom talked to Jack about the fighting and agreed to join, and those two brought Julius and myself to agree to it. Jack said Tom was his second and " when you don't see me, and see Tom, you see me." Jack said Tom was making arms for the black people—Jack said he could not be killed, nor could a white man take him."

THE TRIAL of HARRY, a Negro Man belonging to Mr David Haig.—James Haig, Esq. attending as Counsel for his owner.

EVIDENCE.

WITNESS No. 10, testified as follows :—After Peter Poyas had twice called on me about this business, he and Harry Haig called on me. I was not at home, but the next morning I met Harry who asked me for my name—I refused it—he said I would be killed if I did not join—I said I would join when they came out, if they were stronger than the whites—Harry called on me again, and asked me if I was willing, that the thing would break out soon—I asked him where he would begin—he said in Boundary-street—at what hour—he said at 12 o'clock at night or early

sought to demonstrate their mastery through the printed word, they revealed fissures in their ideological armor, seeking to defend an institution that had been profoundly threatened by those it pretended to protect while demonstrating that slavery was, in fact, vulnerable to attack by those determined to challenge it. Visiting South Carolina in 1841, a friend of Thomas Higginson discovered that slaveowners were uneasy with such material in their houses. After asking his hostess if he could see her edition of the *Official Report*, he learned that the only copy in the house had been "carefully kept for years under lock and key, had been burned . . . lest it should reach the dangerous eyes of the slaves." Many other families followed suit, turning a publication designed for a large audience into "the rarest of American historical documents."[324]

CONCLUSION

Incendiaries! Come ye, firebrands, to light the flame of revolt? Know ye not that here are many serfs who, incited to obtain their liberty, might wreak some dreadful vengeance.
—Herman Melville, Mardi and a Voyage Thither, 1849

The intellectual world that Denmark Vesey and his fellow insurgents inhabited may be defined as a hybrid form of "artisan republicanism" that, as Sean Wilentz has argued, constituted the distinct political culture of craft workers in northeastern cities. The ideology to which these men subscribed derived in part from the democratically inclined rhetoric of the American Revolution as well as from the independence and individual mastery gained from the acquisition of a particular skill. Mastering the skills of a craft and learning its "mystery," such as its distinctive argot and rituals, provided workers with the credentials to establish their own shops and an entrance into the fraternity of its practitioners. Both Charleston's slaves and New York's mechanics, for example, worked in a predominantly male environment and followed similar work routines, experiencing cycles of intense activity and slack times during certain months. The regimen in the small shops, wharves, and yards that lined the Hudson and East Rivers bore hallmarks similar to the daily organization of work along the Cooper River.[325]

Yet these similarities should not be drawn too tightly. Clearly, race and

324. Higginson, *Black Rebellion*, 274. According to Higginson, Kennedy and Parker's volume went through four printings within a month of its publication in October 1822.
325. Wilentz, *Chants Democratic*, 61–63. See also Rorabaugh, *Craft Apprentice*; Rule, "Property of Skill," 99–118.

legal status fundamentally divided the free from the enslaved, regardless of the organization of work. In addition, the competition between black and white workers for jobs only deepened divisions between these groups in the North. Even though the revolutionary politics that transformed the late-eighteenth-century Atlantic world influenced white artisans as well as Vesey, the revolutionary violence on Saint Domingue likely had a far greater impact on the latter. In fact, the prospect of black rebellion spreading from the Caribbean to the mainland not only worried Jefferson and other political leaders, but it profoundly alarmed ordinary white people.

Combining the rhetoric of the Haitian Revolution, militant texts from the Old Testament, and with African religious practices, Vesey and his closest associates endeavored to forge an ideology of rebellion. Living at the end of an era of revolution, Vesey reworked Jefferson's well-known phrase from the Declaration of Independence, proclaiming that "all men had equal rights, blacks as well as whites," highlighting for his followers the contradiction between the institution of slavery and the ideas of liberty and equality. But the aspirations encapsulated in this sentiment tell only part of the story. Vesey's goal was, like the black Jacobins on Saint Domingue, the destruction of Charleston and its ruling class.

United by a common identity as skilled men able to earn money, slave artisans also found themselves bound together by the organization of work on the wharves, surrounding warehouses, and shops. Several additional factors reinforced this communal ethos: the gendered workplace, the complex fusion of white evangelicalism and African beliefs, and the language of Gullah. From these experiences, the city's slaves generated a collective identity through the secular and religious institutions they had struggled to establish and sustain. Embedded in these networks of community, more than a hundred slaves found the messages of armed insurrection, revolutionary emancipation, and cultural rejuvenation highly appealing and they elected to join Vesey's project to seek their own liberation.

The charismatic personalities of Denmark Vesey and "Gullah" Jack, the decline in economic opportunities, the tightening of manumission laws, and the continued efforts of white officials to limit black autonomy transformed a small band of skilled urban slave men into armed insurgents, imbued with revolutionary zeal. Frequently denouncing the institution, Vesey offered a sophisticated critique of slavery drawn from his wide reading as well as from his own experiences as a slave. While Vesey combined the messages of the Old Testament, the Declaration of Independence, and the Haitian Revolution, "Gullah" Jack embodied the magical practices of Atlantic Africa.

Trapped by an oppressive institution that continually denied enslaved people their aspirations, Vesey championed its destruction and planned accordingly with his confederates. Regarding political arrangements on Haiti as a genuinely alternative form of social organization, these slaves recognized that they could remedy their intolerable and deep-seated grievances. Vesey drew upon their recognition that this problem was not an intractable one, and he recruited slaves who accepted this view. The workplace, the tavern, and the meeting house provided Vesey with an environment in which to articulate his vision of the world. An active cultural creator, he and his followers collectively fashioned a new discourse into a compelling ideology of rebellion that promised to take a politically engaged band of slave artisans, to borrow a phrase from Frederick Douglass, from "the tomb of slavery" to "the heaven of freedom."[326]

326. Douglass, *Life of Frederick Douglass*, 79.

Transcript of the Denmark Vesey Conspiracy Trial

《THE TRIALS, &C.

THE COURT organized for the trial of sundry Negroes apprehended and charged *"with attempting to raise an Insurrection amongst the Blacks against the Whites,"* and of such others as might be brought before them on the same charge, met on Wednesday, the 19th June, 1822, and consisted of the following Gentlemen, viz.:

LIONEL H. KENNEDY, Q.U.	*Magistrates*
THOMAS PARKER, J.P.	

WILLIAM DRAYTON	
NATHAN HEYWARD	
JAMES LEGARE	*Freeholders*
JAMES R. PRINGLE	
JAMES LEGARE	
ROBERT J. TURNBULL 》[1]	

19 JUNE 1822

Examination of Mr. John Paul's negro man WILLIAM made by the Court of Justice and Freeholders on Wednesday 19 June, 1822—He stated as follows (vizt.)

I have heard something about an insurrection of the blacks—but was not concerned in it—Mr. Harth's negro man Mingo told me about it and referred

---

1. These men constituted both judge and jury at the trial. Both Kennedy and Parker were members of the Charleston Bar. Colonel William Drayton (a planter) served as court recorder. The remaining men all held important positions within the lowcountry's social and economic order. Nathaniel Heyward was a leading planter and merchant, J. R. Pringle worked as a customs collector, and R. J. Turnbull was a lawyer and planter, as was James Legare.

me to Peter Poyas for further information who he said had a list with 9,000 names upon it, and that he was still taking down names—On the week I was to see Peter, I was apprehended—Mingo said that 600 men on the bay, was already down on the list in Peter's possession. Mingo would not before the Wardens own what he had told me—I never had any conversation with Peter—Mingo said his name was not yet down, and he would not put it down, until he knew all that was to be done, that Ned Bennett knew all about it, and told it to all Mr. Bennett's people—and that letters were now passing between those concerned—I can read and count printed characters, but not written—One Saturday afternoon as I was going to market, I met a brown man belonging to Colonel Prioleau in Meeting Street named, I believe Peter, and walked with him down to the market Wharf, where he called my attention to a pendant on a vessel's mast, and said it was numbered 95, to which I said 'twas not, 'tis numbered 76.[2] He then showed me a small privateer in the stream and told me of the distress in which she had arrived here—I asked him for news, and if he had heard anything strange—when he replied he had heard that there would be a disturbance and interruption shortly between the blacks and White—I told him I did not understand such talk, and stopped the conversation—I did not endeavor to get Colonel Prioleau's man to join the rising of the blacks—On Saturday night Mingo told me as we were going towards his Wife's house, that every day at 2 O'Clock, Peter went to Mr. Harth's lumber yard and talked to the other men about this matter, to make them sensible of the plan—At Mingo's house I took up the Bible and read two Chapters from the prophet Tobit.[3] Mingo said that all those belonging to the African church are engaged in the insurrection from the Country to the town[4]—that there is a

---

2. The boat may have been either the *Liberty* or the *Sally*. Both vessels originated from Cap Haïtien, with the former dropping anchor in Charleston on 16 May 1822 and the latter a week later. Its arrival in port perhaps prompted William Paul to tell Peter Prioleau about the planned rising which, as Vesey had told his followers, would involve some support from Haiti. See *Charleston Mercury*, 17 May and 23 May 1822. Whether the number on the flag held any significance is not known.

3. An Old Testament book contained in the Apocrypha, Tobit describes the trials and tribulations of life during the Diaspora of Jewish people after their escape from Egypt. The book counseled them that God would protect and heal those who were pious and compassionate. Set in the eighth century B.C., the story revolves around two families (Tobit's family and that of his cousin, Raguel) and their attempts to preserve Jewish identity in the Diaspora. It also anticipates an end to their exile and the restoration of the full Israelite community in Jerusalem. In addition, the book emphasizes that Jewish people should not be tempted by the ways of the Gentiles. Vesey perhaps recognized the parallels between this story and the situation of slaves in Charleston. See Cary A. Moore, *Tobit*.

4. Established in 1816 after a large number of the city's slaves and free blacks broke away

little man amongst them who can't be killed, shot or caught, who was to be their General and who would provide them with arms—that some arms were provided, but did not tell me where they were, and that Ned Bennett and Charles Shubrick are Officers—Peter, Ned and Charles are Class Leaders in the African Church—the African Association have also a church in Anson Street near Boundary Street and one in Cow Alley, where they have service[5]— I first spoke to Mr. Prioleau's man Peter about the rising—I believe that Mingo was endeavoring to get me to join them in the rising, and from his conversation I have no doubt, but that he was engaged in the conspiracy—and that all he said to me was to get me to join them—It was also told to me that our colour from the North to the South had combined together to fight against New Orleans—Mingo was no doubt satisfied that I would join—I never had any conversation with anyone about the rising, but with Mingo and Colonel Prioleau's man—Mingo said that Peter Poyas would tell me when the rising would take place—that Mr. Bennett's Ned was one of them, that Denmark Vesey was the Chiefest Man and more concerned than any one else—Denmark Vesey is an old man, in whose yard my master's negro woman Sarah cooks—he was her father in law, having married her mother, Beck[6]— they have been parted some time, but he visited her at her house near the Intendant Major Hamilton's, where I have often heard him speak of the rising[7]—He said he would not like to have a white man in his presence, that he

---

from white Methodist congregations, the African Methodist Episcopal Church (or the African Church) provided the city's black population with an institution in which they could worship and socialize. The first AME church was built in Cow Alley (now Philadelphia Street) on the corner of Hanover and Reid Streets in the predominantly black neighborhood of Hampstead. By the time the authorities closed down the AME in 1822, some 5,000 slaves and free blacks counted themselves as members of this church. Running at right angles to Boundary Street (now Calhoun Street), Anson Street lies close to Charleston's wharf district along the Cooper River. On the AME church, see, for example, Mood, *Methodism in Charleston*; Payne, *History of the African Methodist Episcopal Church*, 31–45; and George, *Segregated Sabbaths*, 109.

5. These constitute the various branches of the AME church in Charleston. Class leaders were responsible for the spiritual welfare and material health of their class, which comprised of small groups of the congregation. Several class leaders were prominent figures in the conspiracy, perhaps using their position within the AME church to draw recruits to the cause.

6. Paul's testimony provides some evidence about Vesey's family. Evidence suggests that Beck worked as laundress.

7. James Hamilton Jr. held the post of city intendant during the Vesey crisis. See Hamilton, *Account of the Late Intended Insurrection*. For further biographical details on Hamilton, see Freehling, *Prelude to Civil War*, 149–52; Bailey and Edgar, *Biographical Directory*, 5:643.

had a great hatred for the whites, and that if all were like him they would resist the whites. He studies all he can to put it into the heads of the blacks to have a rising against the Whites, and tried to induce me to join—he tries to induce all his acquaintances—This has been his chief study and delight for a considerable time—My last conversation with him was in April—he studies the Bible a great deal and tries to prove from it that Slavery and bondage is against the Bible. I beg you won't take up Sarah, for no woman knows any thing about it—Mingo said that letters were passing between Peter Poyas and Ned Bennett and Charles Shubrick[8]—I am persuaded that Denmark Vesey was chiefly concerned in this business—Mingo said that the country places were engaged in the plot, and also the Islands—that he knows the little man who can't be shot, who told him there was a Gullah Society going on which met once a month—that all the orders he got, he got from Peter, Mingo always denied that he was engaged, but yet always talked to me as if he wanted me to join.

20 JUNE 1822

《 The Trial of ROLLA, a negro man, the slave of His Excellency, Governor Bennett—Jacob Axson, Esq.,[9] attending as Counsel for his owner. 》

Examination of JOE, a negro man belonging to Mr. La Roche.
《 WITNESS No. 1. This witness came forth voluntarily, and gave information of the intended Insurrection, and of the places and those concerned, as far as his information extended, *previously* to the appointed day, and only asked that his name would not be divulged, which the Court pledged themselves to conceal as far as it depended on them. His name is therefore suppressed—He is in no way *inculpated.* 》
I know Rolla belonging to Mr. Thomas Bennett, we are intimate friends and eat our meals together[10]—All I knew of the intended rising I got from

---

8. As only one letter—a short note between Abraham Poyas and Peter Poyas—was entered into evidence, the communications to which Mingo Harth refers were probably destroyed once the plot was discovered.

9. Jacob Axson was a well-known city attorney who resided at 70 King Street.

10. Owner of several slaves accused, Thomas Bennett was a leading political and business figure in South Carolina. Elected to the governorship in 1820, Bennett began his political career in 1804 when he was elected to serve as representative for Charleston. During his term of governor between 1820 and 1822, he lived in the city's Harleston neighborhood at 19 Lynch Street. As a Democratic-Republican, Bennett opposed the slave trade and advocated greater leniency in the criminal and slave codes. This belief was reflected by his concern over the ways in which city authorities handled the conspiracy trials. In addition to his political

him—He asked me about three months ago to join with him in slaying the whites—I asked him to give me time to consider of it—a week after he put the same question to me on that subject and at the end of another week, he again came to me on that subject I told him take care, God says we must not kill, you are a coward he said, and laughed at me—he said he would tell me how it was to be done—there are white men who have come from afar and who say that St. Domingo and Africa will assist us to get our liberty, if we will only make the motion first[11]—I advised him to let it alone, and told him I would oppose them if they came to kill my mistress, and he again laughed at me as a coward. He summoned me to go to their meetings where said he, you will hear what is going on, and be better informed—I told him yes, I would go—Friday about three weeks ago he appointed to take me to this meeting—at that night he came to me and again called me to go—I went away from him—the next day he came to me and said the meeting had been expecting me, and I must send my name to be put down as one of the band—This thing has been going on for 4 months—he told me that at the meetings 'twas said that some white men said, our Legislature had set them free and our people here would not let us be so[12]—that St. Domingo and Africa would come over and cut up the white people, if we only made the motion

---

career, Bennett ran lumber and rice mills in the city. With his business partner, Daniel Cannon, he operated several mills on the eastern banks of the Ashley River that were powered by the ebb and flow of tides. Bennett also built a complex of mills (known as Bennett's Mills) on the banks of the Cooper River. With his second marriage in 1840, Bennett entered the ranks of the state's planter class, obtaining three plantations in the parishes of Saint John's Berkeley and Saint Philip's and Saint Michael's. The 1820 census records that he owned 51 slaves; by 1850, he had 260 slaves. See Bailey and Edgar, *Biographical Directory*, 5:54–56; Freehling, *Prelude to Civil War*, 59–60.

11. This reference to "white men" may be an allusion to the only four white people—William Allen, John Igneshias, Jacob Danders, and Andrew Rhodes—who had some vague knowledge of the plot. Tried, convicted of a misdemeanor for inciting slaves to rebel in October 1822, and imprisoned briefly, these men apparently told some enslaved men, in the words of Allen, "*that there ought to be an indiscriminate destruction of all the whites, men, women, and children.*" In his defense, Allen claimed that both drunkenness and a desire to obtain a reward for uncovering a conspiracy had led to his actions as "the freedom of the blacks was an object of little importance to him." Judge Elihu Bay believed that they played no part in the plot; rather, these "desperate men, [and] outcasts" hoped to profit from any uprising. See Kennedy and Parker, *Official Report*, 147–49.

12. This is a reference to the rebels' interpretation of the Missouri Compromise, fostered initially by Vesey's false claims about its meaning. Placing their own spin on this legislation, they believed it to be a proclamation of emancipation rather than a measure to address the question of slavery in the territories.

here first[13]—that last Saturday night might be the last he had to live, as they were determined to break open the thing on Sunday night[14]—I told him it could not be done, it could not succeed, that our parents for generations back had been slaves, and we had better be contented. He desired me to tell George Wilson on Sunday last (his and my Class Leader) to come up to him, that he wished to see him—George went up after Church in the evening—Rolla told George in my presence what he was going to do—George told him let it alone, he could not succeed and wept—Rolla replied 'tis now gone too far to stop it. He told George to go out of town on Sunday night, as he did not wish him to be hurt—I told George to sound the alarm, and if he did not, I would—I asked Rolla what was to be done with the women and Children—he said "when we have done with the fellows, we know what to do with the wenches"—There are a great many involved in it in the Country—that Mingo from James Island was to come over to Charleston with 4,000 men, land on South Bay, march up and seize the Arsenal by the Guard House and kill all the City guard—that another body was to seize upon the powder magazine and another body to seize the Arsenal on the neck, then march to town and destroy the inhabitants who could only escape by jumping into the river[15]—My Army, he said, will first fix my old Buck, and then the Intendant—I asked if he could bind his master or kill him[16]—he laughed at me again—I then told him I would have nothing to do with him—He begged me to lend him my boat to go into the Country and hasten down the country negroes as he feared they would not come—I lent it to him, but again charged him to let it alone—He was going to Johns Island, where he wanted me to enlist people as I knew the country—he went to Johns Island at

---

13. Comments made by Vesey and his closest lieutenants about military assistance from Haiti and Africa surface on several occasions in the transcript. Vesey perhaps hoped to convince the rebels that their enterprise stood a good chance of success by indicating to them that reinforcements would land in Charleston as the rebellion began. Moreover, the idea that soldiers from these places would join their uprising gave the rebels additional evidence that the struggle against slavery was not just local, but broad based and international in character.

14. Saturday, 15 June, and Sunday, 16 June.

15. The arsenal on the Neck was located in the Citadel that stood on the northern edge of Marion Square on Boundary Street. The state arsenal and the guardhouse were located on the corner of Broad and Meeting Streets in the heart of the city's business quarter. One of the numerous barrier islands that surrounded the peninsula on which Charleston stands, James Island lies to the south of the city. See Mills, *Statistics of South Carolina*, 420–21; Walter J. Fraser, *Charleston! Charleston!*

16. The use of the word "army" suggests that some rebels saw themselves more as soldiers and less as slaves.

Christmas, but then this business was not in train, he only went to get acquainted with the people[17]—I felt that it was a bad thing to disclose what a bosom friend had confided, that it was wicked to betray him—but when I thought on the other hand that by doing so, I would save so many lives, and prevent the horrible acts in contemplation, that 'twas over balanced, and my duty was to inform—I refused to go to the meetings as Rolla wished, as I feared if I opposed them there, they might make away with me to prevent me from betraying them—I don't know where the meetings were held but I believe it was in Bull Street in which street Denmark Vesey lives[18]—Rolla said that Ned and Mathias were concerned I am well acquainted with Stephen Smith. I believe him to be a worthy good man, and in a conversation with him on this subject he agreed with me that this was an abominable plot—I have not seen him for the last 4 weeks—I know Denmark Vesey—I was one day on horseback when I met him on foot, he asked me if I was satisfied in my present situation—if I remembered the Fable of Hercules' Waggon that was stalled, when he began to pray and that God said you fool, put your Shoulder to the Wheel, whip up the horses, and your Waggon will be pulled out, that if we did not put our hand to the work and deliver ourselves, we would never come out of Slavery[19]—that the Legislature had made us free—I know that he is intimately acquainted with Rolla—Rolla said that there had been a sort of disagreement and confusion at their place of meeting, and that they meant to meet at Vesey's—Vesey told me that a large army from St. Domingo and Africa were coming to help us, and that we must not stand with our hands in the pocket—He was bitter toward the whites—Rolla has a wife in my mistress' yard—Sambo, the brother of Rolla's wife and who stays

---

17. Johns Island was another of the islands that stood to the south of the city. The Stono River and the Wappoo Creek cut this island from the mainland.

18. The 1822 City Directory records Denmark Vesey as living at 20 Bull Street in the city's Harleston District. Now numbered 56 Bull Street, this one-story, three-roomed, Greek Revival–style house is now listed as a National Historic Landmark. Vesey rented this house from Dr. Peter Trezevant. Bull Street, moreover, was home to Thomas Bennett from the early 1800s until he moved to nearby Lynch Street in 1820. It is probable that Vesey became acquainted with Bennett's house slaves (Batteau, Mathias, Ned, and Rolla) during these years when they were neighbors. On Vesey's house, see *Charleston News and Courier*, 23 August 1976; Hudgins et al., *Vernacular Architecture of Charleston*, 219.

19. Although this particular task was not included among the mythical twelve labors that Hercules (Herakles) had to perform, it does bear some of the hallmarks of those endeavors. Why Vesey drew upon classical sources remains a mystery, but perhaps being given the name Telemaque (a hero in *The Iliad*) led him to read stories of classical literature. Vesey used his knowledge of such material to fashion a parable that ably demonstrated the need for self-determination among enslaved people.

at the plantation,[20] sent word down by his Sister to Rolla, that he would be in town on Sunday night last—Rolla said that they would have a countersign to be known to their friends, and in the action, those blacks who could not give it, would be killed—that they would fire the town—Rolla's threats are, that if any black person is found out giving information or evidence against them, they will watch for them night and day and kill them certainly—that even now the friends of these in prison are trying about the streets to find who has given information—If my name was known, I would certainly be killed—I advised Rolla to let it alone, but told him that if they persevered and commenced it, I had no arms, but that they passed by my house, I would fall in behind with my line and grains which was all that I had.

Examination of BRAM, a negro belonging to Jon. Lucas
《WITNESS No. 3. Against this witness there was no charge in relation to the Insurrection—secrecy as to his name was pledged to him.》
《A Negro, about 18 years of age testified as follows.》
I know Batteau, he belongs to Mr. Thomas Bennett—Sunday before last, he met me and stopped me and told me something very grievous—he asked if I would go as one of the army—I told him I could not as I was so bound to my father that I could not go out without his leave—nothing more then took place as I immediately left him—I have not seen him since—

Cross examined. He told me that this army was to raise the blacks against the Whites—he said the army was to act last Sunday night—before he commenced speaking to me, he took me to one side & then spoke low to me—my brother Richard and myself afterwards spoke together on this business, who said Batteau had likewise spoken to him about it.

Examination of RICHARD, a negro belonging to Jon. Lucas.
《WITNESS No. 4. This witness is in the precise situation, and had the same pledge given him as No. 3.》
I know Batteau, belonging to Mr. Bennett—He said once to me that he wanted me to agree to join them with as many blacks as I could get to kill the Whites. This was last Sunday week in the evening after Church—I said I could not attempt such a thing—He tried to persuade me to join, but I refused—he said he could raise armies directly—that he was one at the head—that they would put one force at the bridge and another in the town, he expected some aid from the Country—the last time I saw Bram was last

---

20. This plantation was located on Johns Island.

Saturday night when he was taken up by the patrol—Batteau said the rising would be on Sunday night.

Cross examined. On Saturday evening as I was going home, I saw Batteau near the Rev. Mr. Bachman's near Cannons Bridge talking with a woman;[21] he called to me and took me to one side, and began the conversation, speaking low so that no one could hear him—he said that if I could raise men enough 'twixt Saturday and Sunday to meet him to kill the White people, he said that they could get arms enough—he is called Batteau and Botteau. My brother Bram and myself afterwards spoke together on the matter and he said Batteau had spoken to him too.

Examination of MR. JOHN STROHECKER[22]—one of the Wardens.
The testimony which Bram and Richard have just given is precisely what they some days ago gave before me.

Examination of GEORGE—a negro belonging to Major Wilson.[23]
《WITNESS No. 2. This witness regards the concealment of his name, stands precisely in the same situation as No. 1.》
The first I heard was from Joe[24]—he told me that such was the idea of the col-

---

21. A Lutheran clergyman, the Reverend John Bachman arrived in South Carolina in 1815 to begin a ministry in Saint John's Lutheran Church at the corner of Clifford and Archdale Streets. In the following year, Bachman reported that "several persons of colour" wished to receive instruction in "the doctrines of the Christian Church." Out of a congregation of nearly three hundred, some fifty were either slaves or free blacks. Among their number was Denbow Martin, who left the AME church to join the Lutherans. Bachman subsequently instructed these members of Charleston's black community, reserving the church's north gallery for them. By 1822, Bachman was pastor of the German Church on Pinckney Street and a member of the Committee of Charity of the German Friendly Society.

Cannon's Bridge joined the Cannonsborough district that lay north of Boundary Street in Charleston Neck to the Harleston neighborhood. An area that comprised creeks, ponds, and some settlement on its western margins, Cannonsborough eventually provided important sites for rice and lumber mills. Harleston, although home to some commercial concerns, was primarily a residential district. See Neuffer, *Christopher Happoldt Journal*; and Moltke-Hansen, "Expansion of Intellectual Life," 3–44.

22. John Strohecker, who ran a construction business, owned Perault, who was arrested on July 10. Perault was one of several rebels born in Africa.

23. George Wilson, a class leader in the AME church, served as a spy for city intendant James Hamilton, unearthing information about the plot from his friends, including Rolla Bennett. He later committed suicide.

24. Wilson is referring here to Joe La Roche.

ored people—that he was asked to join, but that he asked time to consider—that he was told to tell me to come out of town, that at 12 o'clock on Sunday night the rising would take place. I told him I would tell my master, and he said he would do the same—On Friday myself and Joe told my master every thing—I saw Rolla who complained of his hard living—I found he was at something wrong and my heart got so full that I wept—Rolla never told me in express words, that he was intending to join in a rising to kill the whites—Joe was present when Rolla and myself where speaking and heard most of what passed—Rolla's last words were 'tis gone too far now to be stopped. Though Rolla said nothing expressly to me about insurrection, yet we seemed to understand each other, and that such was in contemplation—Rolla told me that on Sunday evening I must go out of town, as he did not wish me to be hurt; he said words to the effect that he was going to join in the rising—he said that on Sunday night at 12 O'Clock such and such a thing would take place—Joe said that Rolla told him they were to join and take the powder magazine and the Arsenal on the neck, and that an Army of 4,000 men from James Island would land at South Bay, march up and take the Laboratory in town and kill all the City Guard and then they would kill all the whites etc. Joe is truly a good man and Stephen too—[25]

Examination of MAJOR JOHN WILSON—What George has just said is substantially what he told me some days ago—He is of the best character, & every word he says may be relied upon, I never heard a complaint against him from white or black.

[Trail of Rolla Bennett continued on 25 June.]

《The trial of AMHERST, a Negro man belonging to Mrs. Lining was next tried. The strongest part of the testimony against him was, his requesting his class leader on Sunday, the 16th June to pray for him, as it might be the last day he had to live. Amherst admitted that he said so, and that he alluded to the intended insurrection, which he had that day heard of; but denied that he was in any manner engaged in it, and only asked for the prayers of his class leader, as in the confusion, he would be in danger of losing his life whether he was engaged or not.

The Court *unanimously* found him NOT GUILTY and discharged him.》

25. Stephen Smith.

21 JUNE 1822

《The trial of PETER, a Negro man, the property of Mr. James Poyas—Mr. Poyas with Robert Bentham, Esq., as his counsel attending.》

Examination of Y**, belonging to Colonel George W. Cross.[26]
(Before the name of this witness was given to the Court, his Master required of the Court a Solemn pledge that his name, should never be revealed, under which pledge this witness now produced and testified).
Peter Poyas first spoke to me and asked me to join—I asked to join what—the Church—he said no, have you not heard that the blacks are going to try to take the Country from the Whites—I asked him if he thought he had force enough to do it. He said yes aplenty that he could get aplenty of men and the Society will contribute, with which a white man would purchase Guns and powder for them—he said he would call back and I must consider if I would join them—He called back and asked if I was willing now. Why Peter says I, you have not got force enough—He said if I would not join he would turn all my Country people against me—said I, if so, I'll join you when you come out if I find you strong enough, but I will not put my name down. Well, said he, if you don't join you'll be killed. Peter and Harry Haig called on me afterwards, but I was not at home; the next morning I met Harry who asked me to put my name down, I refused—he said I would be killed if I did not join, I told him I would join when they came out, if they were stronger than the Whites—he called on me again and asked me if I was willing—that the thing would break out soon—I asked him where they would begin—he said in Boundary Street[27]—at what hour, at 12 o'clock at night, or early in the morning, as soon as the patrols were discharged. Jack Pritchard called on me—he is sometimes called Gullah Jack, sometimes Cooter Jack—he gave me some dry food, consisting of parched corn and ground nuts, and said eat nothing but this on the morning it breaks out, and when you join us, as we pass, put in your mouth this crab claw, and you can't be wounded and he said I give the same to all the rest of my Troops—if said he you drop the large crab claw out of your mouth, then put in the small one—I asked when he intended to break out, and have you got arms—he said aplenty, but they are over Boundary Street, and they could not get them now—but as soon as the

---

26. The evidence suggests that this witness was Yorrick Cross. This material is contained in Document B of the trial record.
27. Boundary Street served to divide the incorporated city of Charleston from the unincorporated Charleston Neck. This street is now called Calhoun Street.

Patrols were slack, they could get them—this was previous to the 16th. June, on which day he said they were to break out—On that day he came to me and said, they would break out that night—as the Patrols was too strong—that Sunday fortnight he came to me and said I must lay by still, that they would not break out then, as he had been round to all his company—and found them cowards—I said thank God then—he said give me back my corn and Cullah (meaning his crab claw) I refused and upbraided him for having deluded so many—He said all the Country born promised him because he was a Doctor—he said that Whites were looking for him and he was afraid of being taken—that two men came to his master's Wharf and asked him if he knew Gullah Jack, and that he told them no—he said that his charms would not protect him against the treachery of his own colour—He went away and I have not seen him since—Harry Haig has since seen me several times, and told me to hold myself ready—I said I'm ready when called on—He said that all the Dray men came to him at his master's Cooper yard, and said they were ready—but he told them they were only waiting for Gullah Jack—He said he would tell me when they were ready, they were now only waiting for the head man, who was a white man, but he would not tell me what was the white man's name, or where the powder and arms were—this was last Tuesday the very day the 6 men were hanged about 6 o'clock (a.m.) this was the last time we met though I have seen him since—I have seen Charles Drayton before 16th. June at Monday Gell's—I was going to market and Charles called to me—as I was crossing the street, a young man named Joe, formerly belonging to my master asked me if I did not know that Monday Gell is at the head of the Ebo company, who are going to fight the White people—Monday is an Ebo.[28] I asked Joe if he was one of that company, he said yes, he was—I asked him what he could do as he was an invalid, he said he would take Capt. Remoussin's Sword and Gun (at whose house his wife lived) and tell him to lay down in his bed and be quiet. Previous to 16th. June, Monday Gell asked me to go into his shop, I went in—I told him I heard he was the Captain of his Country man's Company, the Ebos, he said he was a sort of one—I bid him good morning—he said when you want to hear the news, come here—I never saw him afterwards—I met Charles Drayton on 1st. July in the street when he said to me, now get ready, we must break out at once, for we will not let 6

---

28. Like Oluadah Equiano, Monday Gell was a member of the Ebo people (also known as the Ibo or Igbo) who lived in the inland regions to the northwest of the Niger Delta at the southern end of the Gulf of Guinea. This region now corresponds to eastern and southeastern Nigeria.

lives be taken—I asked him where they would begin, he said at Boundary Street, directly as the Patrols and Light horse turned in, I said had you not better wait 'till after the 4th. July[29]—he said no, because in the meantime people will be hanged, he said they had force enough—we then parted—I met him in the market 'twixt 8 and 9 o'clock on the 2 July & said to him, now the people are hanged, I suppose you are sorry you joined in the business—he said yes and we parted—Peter Poyas told me also that they had force enough—that some would come from the Islands of James and John and some from Christ Church Parish where he generally went over to a meeting to have a talk, & that he had some about & about in town, the number of which he could show me from the Society's books if I would only come to the Society[30]—he said they were to fight the Whites and keep on fighting until the English came to help them—Harry told me they were to fight the Whites & in short told me the same as Peter—Jack being the head man, I asked him about the plan he said the same thing—that the English were to come and help them—that the Americans could do nothing against the English, & the English would carry them off to St. Domingo[31]—Monday and Charles were very great together—John, Mr. Elias Horry's coachman, came to me one day and asked me what I thought—are you ready, every one is ready, said John to fight the Whites—& he said "I am ready"—This took place some time before the 16th June & every day he asked the same questions—about this time George Vanderhorst who is with Mr. Crawford came to me & said they were going to take the City and he had joined—that he was ready whenever the blacks broke out—he requested me to let him sleep at my Wife's house in King Street near Boundary Street—I saw him almost everyday after 16th. June, and he always said he was ready whenever the troops were prepared.

29. Making it a "red letter" day in the social calendar, white Charlestonians celebrated the Fourth of July with a wide range of public events, including speeches, church services, parades, and banquets. In his sermon before the '76 Association in Saint Michael's Church, John Berwick Legare concluded his address by stating that he eagerly anticipated the moment "when the power and the glory of God shall be displayed . . . for the overthrow of tyranny and the establishment of universal freedom" (*An Oration on 4th. July 1822*, 6). See also *Southern Patriot and Commercial Gazette*, 5 July 1822; Huff, "Eagle and the Vulture," 10–22.

30. The "Society" might refer either to one of the clandestine ethnic clubs, such as the Gullah Society, that appear to have existed in Charleston, or to the AME church.

31. An obscure reference, this comment might allude to the activities of English abolitionists. During the late 1810s and 1820s, the British government was engaged in discussions with various European powers to end the international slave trade and create a maritime police to enforce such laws. British abolitionists, moreover, were calling for the abolition of slavery in the English Caribbean.

Jack also asked me to let 12 men sleep at my Wife's house on the 16 June, as they meant to break out on that night—on being refused he departed in anger and reproached me—George called on me yesterday morning & asked if I knew that Charles Drayton was taken up—He said he was afraid that Charles would name him but he was not on his list, but had joined Jack's company—On Monday the 1st. July, Charles Drayton told me that there would be a rising on 6th. July early in the morning as soon as the Guards turned in & were dismissed—He also said that he commanded the Country born company—Jack told me on the same day the same thing, & also that they were to rush with the Guns and Swords etc. they had got on the City Guard and take all the arms in the Arsenal—He also said there were some arms in King Street beyond Boundary Street in the possession of a white man that they intended to take[32]—George said he was afraid that Charles Drayton would name him because he had not met him at Jack's, but not because he belonged to Charles' company as he did not, and that when at Jack's house they were consulting on this subject—he said if he could hear that Charles had named him, he would run off—Charles Drayton said that he had prepared for himself a gun and a sword—John Horry came to me very often and once said to me, that he had a sword, & that as soon as it broke out, he would run up stairs & kill his master & family—on 17 June, John on his carriage box expressed himself to the same effect as before the 16th.[33]—I have known Gullah Jack a considerable time, he asked me to go into a house back in the yard by a mahogany shop—This house is about six steps from Monday Gell's—They would have risen on the night of the 16th. June if the guards had not been out so strong—this I know from Harry Haig & Jack, that if the Guards were not too strong, they would get the arms near the lines, but if the guards were out, they could not get them to break out with.

Colonel George Cross, the owner of Y, being present during the above examination, stated to the Court that this information just given by Y coincided with that which he had before given to him—that Y has been twice to the North with him, where he had many reasons to believe that attempts were made to induce not to return—he is a negro in whose honesty & veracity he

---

32. King Street ran along a north-south axis; Boundary Street (now Calhoun Street) ran east-west and marked the boundary between the incorporated city and the unincorporated Neck. The arsenal to which the testimony refers is the building in which the Charleston Neck Company, commanded by Captain James Martindale, stored their weapons.

33. A large wooden box located on the front of a carriage or cart, it holds either feed for the horse or bridles, harnesses, and other equipment.

would confide—that he has owned him since 1806 or 1807 when he bought him out of an African Ship, during which time he has behaved himself well.[34]

Examination of ROBERT, a negro belonging to Mr. Wm. Harth.

《WITNESS No. 5. Against this witness the Court had not a tittle of testimony—he consented without hesitation to become a witness, and to give all the information he possessed, a pledge having been previously given him by the Court that he should not be prosecuted or his name revealed.》 I know Peter Poyas—in May last Peter and myself met in Legare Street, at the corner of Lambol Street when the following conversation took place.[35] He asked me the news, I replied, none that I know of—he said, by George, we can't live so, I replied how well we do—he said we can do very well, if you can find any one to assist us, will you join—I asked how do you mean—he said why to break the yoke—I replied I don't know—he asked suppose you were to hear that the whites were going to kill you, would you defend yourself—I replied I'd try to escape—he asked have you lately seen Denmark Vesey, and has he spoken to you particularly; I said no—Well then, said he, that's all now, but call at the shop tomorrow after knocking off work and I will tell you more—We then parted—I met him the next day, according to appointment, when he said to me, we intend to see if we can't do something for ourselves, we can't live so—I asked him where we could get men—he said we'll find them fast enough, we have got enough—we expect men from Country and town—But how said I will you manage it—why, we will, said he, and they will march down and camp around the City—what will they do for arms; he answered they will find arms enough—they will bring down their hoes and axes etc. I said that won't do to fight with hoes—he said stop, let us get candidates from town, with arms and we will then take the guard house and arsenal in town, the arsenal on the Neck and the upper Guard House, and supply the Country people with arms—How, said I, will you approach these Arsenals etc. for they are guarded—Yes, said he I know that, but what are those guards, one man here and one man there, we won't let a man pass before us—Well, said I, will the black people from the Country and those from the Islands, know when you are to begin or how will you get the town people together,

---

34. Between December 1803 and January 1808, South Carolina resumed its engagement in the Atlantic slave trade, during which nearly 40,000 Africans were brought into the state. A number of conspirators of African descent arrived in the city at this time.

35. Located a block from the Battery and the waterfront, Legare and Lambol Streets lie in the residential heart of the eighteenth-century part of the city.

why said he, we will have settings up, that is night meetings for prayer, and there notify them when to start and as the Clock strikes 12 all must move—but, said I, the whites in the back Country, Virginia etc. when they have the news will turn to and kill you all and besides you may be betrayed—he said, well what of that—if one gets hanged we will rise at that minute—We then left his Shop and walked towards Broad Street, when, he said, I want you to take notice of all the stores with arms in them, take down their numbers and give them to me—I said I will see to it, and then we parted—About 1st June I saw in the public papers a statement that the white people were going to build a Missionary house for the blacks, which I carried and showed to Peter and said to him, you see the good they are going to do for us, when he said what of that, have you not heard that on the 4th. July, the Whites are going to create a false alarm of fire and every black that comes out will be killed in order to thin them[36]—Do you think they would be so barbarous, said I—yes, said he, I do—I fear they have some knowledge of an army from St. Domingo and they would be right to do it, to prevent us from joining that army, if it should march towards this land—I was then very much alarmed. We then parted & I saw no more of him 'till the guards were very strict about a fortnight ago, as I stepped out of Mr. Perroneau's gate, Peter and Ned Bennett, Isaac talking together at the corner of Lambol & Legare Streets—They crossed over and met me by Mr. Myles[37] & Ned Bennett said to me, did you hear what those boys were taken up for the other day, I replied No, but some say 'twas for stealing—Ned asked me if I was sure, I had never said anything to the Whites about what Peter Poyas had spoken to me about—I replied no—says Peter, you never did—no, I answered. Says Ned to me, how do you stand—at which I struck the tree box with my knuckles, and said as firm as this box—I'll never say a word against you—Ned then smiled and nodded his head and said that will do, when we all separated—Last Tuesday or Wednesday week, Peter said to me, you see my lad how the white people have got to the windward of us—You won't, said I, be able to do anything—O yes, he said, he will, by george, we are obliged to—He said all down this way ought to meet and have a collection to purchase powder—what said I, is the use of powder, the whites can fire three times to our once—he said but 'twill be such a dead time of the night, they won't know what is the matter and our horse companies will go about the streets and prevent the whites from assembling.

36. Benevolent treatment of the poor and indigent played an important part of civic life in Charleston. In the 1820s, there were a number of charitable societies aimed at helping these people. See Bellows, *Benevolence among Slaveholders*.

37. Myles operated a grocery store on Meeting Street.

I asked him where will you get horses—Why, said he, there are many Butcher Boys with horses, and there are public Stables where we have several candidates and the waiting men belonging to the White people of the horse companies will be told to take away their masters' horses—He asked me if my master was not a horseman—I said yes—has he not got arms in his house—I answered yes—can't they be got at—I said yes—then said he 'tis good to have them. I asked him what was the plan—Why he said after was have taken the Arsenal and guard houses, then we will set the town on fire in different places and as the whites come out we will slay them; if we were to set fire to the town first, the man in the steeple would give the alarm too soon.[38] I am the Captain, said he, to take the lower guard House and the Arsenal—but, I replied, when you are coming up the centinel will give the alarm—He said he would advance a little distance ahead and if he could only get a gripe at his throat, he was a gone man for his sword was very sharp; he had sharpened it, and had made it so sharp that it had cut his finger which he shewed me—as to the Arsenal on the neck, he said that is gone as sure as fate—Ned Bennett would manage that with the people from the Country and the people between Hibbens Ferry and Santee would land and take the Upper Guard House[39]—I then said, then this thing seems true—My man, said he, God has a hand in it, we have been meeting for four years and are not yet betrayed[40]—I told him I was afraid after all of the white people from the back Country, Virginia etc.—he said the blacks would collect so numerous from the Country we need not fear the Whites from other parts, for when we have once got the City, we can keep them all out—He asked if I had told my boys—I said no—then he said, you should do it for Ned Bennett has his people pretty well ranged—but said he take care and don't mention it to those waiting men who receive presents of old Coats etc. from their master, or they will betray us; I will speak to them.[41] We then parted and I have not conversed with him—He said the rising was to take place last Sunday night—that any of the coloured people who said a word about this matter would be killed by the others—The

---

38. Sentries manned guard posts in Saint Michael's Church steeple.

39. Situated on the road between Charleston and the Santee River in the heart of Saint Thomas's Parish lay the Club and Muster House. See Mills, *Atlas of South Carolina*.

40. This suggests that Vesey conceived the plot in 1818, the year in which Charleston authorities arrested about 140 free blacks and slaves for "holding an unlawful meeting in the form of a distinct congregation" at the AME church in Hampstead on Charleston Neck.

41. Although several enslaved domestics, including several house slaves owned by Governor Thomas Bennett, played a role in the plot, the leading conspirators tended not to recruit domestics, believing that they might choose to side with their owner rather than their potential liberators.

little man who cannot be killed &c. and is named Jack, a Gullah negro—Peter said he was to see Monday Gell about expediting the rising—I know that Mingo went often to Mr. Paul's to see Edwin, but don't know if he spoke with William—Peter said there was a french company in town of 300 men fully armed—that he had a sword and I ought to get one—he said he had got a letter from the country, I think from St. Thomas' from a negro man who belonged to the Captain of a Militia Company, who said he could easily get the key of the house when the company's arms were put after muster and take them all out, and help in that way—This business originates altogether with the African Congregation, in which Peter is a leader, when Bennett's Ned asked about those taken up, he alluded particularly to Mr. Paul's William and asked me if I had said anything to him about it.

Mr. William Harth. Robert is a good character, his general conduct is good, he was raised up in the family—I would place my life in his hands.

Mr. Paul's negro man, William.
Edwin is my fellow servant, he brought the first news of the rising into our yard—he has a wife at Mr. Parker's near the Lines.[42] One Monday morning when he came from his wife's he told me that there would be something shortly 'twixt the blacks and Whites, that he knew the parties and that the thing was going on, and all the African Congregation were engaged in it—and Peter Poyas and Ned Bennett—he told me generally about the matter—every Monday morning when he came home, he told us (vizt. Joe Jore and myself) what was going on—that Peter knew all and that all who wants to know goes to see him—that Harth's Mingo knew all and when I saw Mingo, he told me as much as Edwin—Edwin said that Mingo was as much engaged as Peter—Mingo said he was concerned with Peter, but denied having signed his name to the list—Edwin said Harth's Robert was engaged in it, and all his other negroes except Boston, who was doubting—Edwin and Mingo said Denmark Vesey was concerned—Mingo said they would get horses, which have been engaged at 1, 2, or 3 Livery Stables from the Stable boys; two stables he named in particular—viz. Mr. Billings[43] and the one behind the old Church—Mingo said a brown man, the Steward of the Cutter had stolen some of her arms & that Jim, a blacksmith of Mr. Bennett's, made arms.

42. A line of fortifications built to protect Charleston from a land-side invasion by the British during the War of 1812, the Lines stretched from the Ashley to Cooper Rivers. The Lines also served as a site of execution.

43. John Billings ran a public stable on Church Street.

22 JUNE 1822

Examination of PETER, a negro belonging to Thomas Bennett—a Witness for and in behalf of Rolla.
I know Joe La Roche—Rolla took away Joe's wife from him about 3 years ago—Rolla and his wife quarrelled last summer, but have made it up since—They all 3 live in the same yard—I have never seen Joe or Rolla quarrel—

Examination of MARCH, a negro belonging to Thomas Bennett—a witness for and behalf of Rolla.
I know Joe La Roche—I have never heard Joe and Rolla quarrel. Rolla still goes to Mr. La Roche's yard.

Examination of SAMPSON, a negro belonging to Thomas Bennett—a Witness for and in behalf of Rolla.
I know Joe La Roche, Rolla's wife was once Joe's—I never heard Joe and Rolla quarrel.

Examination of MR. LA ROCHE—a witness for and in behalf of Rolla.
Rolla's wife was once Joe's, by whom he had two children some years ago—Rolla and Joe had a quarrel some time ago, but have since made it up, and latterly live like brothers: Since Joe gave information against Rolla, he has been disheartened—this is the first day he seems composed—he thought and said he had acted like a traitor—there is not the slightest enmity existing between Joe and Rolla—Joe is not jealous on account of Rolla now having his former wife, for he was very glad to get rid of her—Rolla's wife Amaretta will do anything to injure Joe—she is a very blood thirsty character.

JOE, belonging to Mr. La Roche was called up and cross examined by Mr. Axson for Rolla—
Rolla and myself are very great friends—Rolla did not tell George Wilson all the particulars, but told him of the intended rising and the time—Rolla and myself are like brothers.

Examination of ISAAC, belonging to Mr. La Roche—a witness for and behalf of Rolla—
Rolla and Joe are not enemies, but good friends, they eat and drink together.

Examination of POLYDORE, belonging to Mr. Bennett.
Rolla proposed to me to join with the blacks to rise against the Whites—'twas last Saturday—he asked me to join him to raise an army against the Whites—I refused and went away—he said I was a fool.

Cross examined by Mr. Axson—When this was proposed August was near me and I told him what Rolla had said.

24 JUNE 1822

Examination of SAMBO, a negro the property of Mr. La Roche.
I reside on my mistress' plantation on Johns Island—about a month after Rolla advised me to join the blacks against the Whites—I told him it was in vain—he told me to come to town on Saturday week last—his wife is my sister—he said he would let me know what day to be down, and sent me word last Friday week not to come down on the Saturday, as the thing had been found out—He said the plan was to take the Guard House and the Magazine and then get ammunition and arms—that a great many were concerned, but no one was named to me—I mentioned it to no one on the Island—

《The Trial of SAMUEL GUIFFORD, a free Negroe, and ROBERT HADDEN, a free Mulattoe; both of them boys.》

Examination of JOHN WOODWORTH (on oath), a white boy.
I am 14 years old—about a week ago (subsequent to the 16th. June) I heard Robert Haddon say to Sam Guifford, he was going to join to set fire to the town, take the magazine and kill every white man who did not give up the Country—I do not think he meant me to hear him—Robert Herron, Jefferson Campbell and Henry Campbell also present.

Examination of ROBERT HERRON (on oath), a white boy.
I am 12 years old—I heard Robert Haddon say that on the night they raised, they would kill the Governor, fire the magazine and kill every damn white man who would not give up the Country to the blacks—he spoke moderately loud and did not seem to care who heard him—Sam Guifford afterwards repeated to me what Hadden had said—

《The Court were satisfied that the expressions charged had been used by the prisoners, but from their youth and other circumstances, they considered them rather as the effect of puerile boasting, than as evidencing a conspiracy on their part. The prisoners were therefore *unanimously found* NOT GUILTY, *but ordered* to be retained in custody *charged with a minor offence*. They were afterwards whipped in the Work House and discharged. MATHIAS, the Slave of Governor Bennett; MUNGO, the Slave of Mr. James Poyas; RICHARD and JOHN, the Slaves of Mr. I. Lucas; and

SANDY, belonging to Mr. Holmes, were discharged by the Court as not Guilty. JIM, belonging to Mr. Ancrum, and FRIDAY, the property of Mr. Rout, were found NOT GUILTY and discharged. Against them there was little or no testimony.⟩⟩

25 JUNE 1822

Examination of ROLLA, belonging to Thomas Bennett.
I know Denmark Vesey—on one occasion he asked me what news—I told him none—He replied we are made free, but the white people here won't let us be so—and the only way is to raise up and fight the whites—I went to his house one night to learn where the meetings were held—I never conversed on this subject with Batteau or Ned—Vesey told me he was the leader in this plot—I never conversed with Peter or Mingo—Vesey induced me to join—when I went to Vesey's house there was a meeting there, the room was full of people but none of them white—That night at Vesey's we determined to have arms made and each man put in 12½ cents for that purpose—though Vesey's room was full, I did not know one individual there—At this meeting Vesey said, we were to take the Guard House and the Magazine to get arms—that we ought to rise up and fight for our liberties against the whites—he was the first to rise up & speak & he read to us from the Bible, how the children of Israel were delivered out of Egypt from bondage[44]—he said the rising would take place last Sunday night week and that Peter Poyas was one—

Examination of SALLY, a negro woman belonging to Mr Alex. Howard.
I know Jesse and heard him speak several times in our yard about it. One day in particular he was anxious to see his brother who has my mother for a wife, and waited until he came, when they conversed together—Jesse said he had to get a horse to go into the country to bring down men to fight the white people, that he was allowed to pass by two parties of the patrol on the road, but that a third party had brought him back and that if there were but 5 men like him they would destroy the City—This was on last Sunday week—he said that before 3 O'Clock on that Night all the White people would be

---

44. With its account of the flight of the Jews from their bondage in Egypt and their long journey to the Promised Land under the leadership of Moses, this story was among the most important biblical texts for North American slaves. With its promise of deliverance, Exodus, as Albert J. Raboteau notes, provided slaves with "a way of articulating their sense of historical identity as a people.... In identifying with the Exodus story, they created meaning and purpose out of the chaotic and senseless experience of slavery" (*Slave Religion*, 311). See also Levine, *Black Culture and Black Consciousness*, 50–51.

killed—that if any black person informed or would not join in the fight, such a person would be killed or poisoned—he frequently came into the yard to see his brother, and I threatened to inform if he came there again and spoke in that way to get us all in trouble—We never had any quarrel—

《On BEHALF OF ROLLA, five Witnesses were introduced and examined prior to his confession to the Court, with a view to impeach the credibility of witness No. 1, but they rather strengthened it. The owner of that witness, (No. 1), who was introduced as a witness on behalf of Rolla, amongst other things creditable to that witness, stated, that since he had given information against Rolla, he had been distracted, that being the first day he seemed composed; that he thought and said he had acted like a traitor to his friend.
THE COURT *unanimously* found Rolla guilty. After sentence of death had been passed upon him, he made a CONFESSION in prison *to the Rev. Dr. Hall,* who furnished the Court with it in writing, and in the following words:[45]
"I was invited by Denmark Vesey to his house, where I found Ned Bennett, Peter Poyas, and others, some were strangers to me, *they said they were from the country*. Denmark told us, it was high time we had our liberty, and he could shew us how we might obtain it. He said, we must unite together as the St. Domingo people did, never to betray one another; and to die before we would tell upon one another. He also said, he expected the St. Domingo people would send some troops to help us—The best way, said he, for us to conquer the whites, is to set the town on fire in several places, at the Governor's Mills,[46] and near the Docks, and for every servant in the yards to be ready with axes, knives, and clubs, to kill every man, as he came out when the bells began to ring. *He then read in the Bible where God commanded, that all should be cut off, both men, women, and children, and said, he believed, it was no sin for us to do so, for the lord had commanded us to do it.*[47] But if I had read these Psalms, Doctor, which I have read, since I have been in this prison, they would never have got me to join them. At another meeting, some of the company were opposed to killing the Ministers, and the women and chil-

---

45. In their *Official Report*, Kennedy and Parker noted that "[T]he mode of execution ordered in this and subsequent cases where the convicts were sentenced to death, was the Gallows." Those executed were hanged either at Blake's Fields or on the Lines.
46. This refers to Bennett's Mills, which were located on the Ashley River in the Harleston neighborhood.
47. Rolla is referring to Exodus 21:16, which states that "he that stealeth a man, and selleth him, or if he be found in his hand, he shall surely be put to death."

dren, but Denmark said, it was not safe to keep one alive, but to destroy them totally, for you see, said he, the Lord has commanded it. When I heard this, master Hall, my heart pained me within, and I said to myself, I cannot kill my master and mistress, for they use me, more like a son, than a slave—I then concluded in my mind, that I would go into the country, on Saturday evening, before they were to commence on Sunday, that I might not see it—Some of the company asked, if they were to stay in Charleston; he said no, as soon as they could get the money from the Banks, and the goods from the stores, they should hoist sail for Saint Domingo, for he expected some armed vessels would meet them to conduct and protect them."

Rolla on his arraignment and throughout his trial, until after the evidence closed denied his guilt, and pretended ignorance of the intended insurrection.

[Note. Every possible care was taken by the Court throughout the trials, to prevent collusion between the witnesses, or either of them knowing what the others had testified to. Those in prison were confined in different rooms, or when, from their being wanted in Court it was necessary to bring them in the room adjoining that in which the Court was sitting, they were put together in one room, a confidential non-commissioned officer of the City Guard was placed in the room with them to prevent their communicating together. They were brought in and examined separately, none of them knowing against whom they were called, until they entered the Court Room; and the evidence given in the one room could not be heard in the next. Those who were not arrested, as they could not know who were to be the witnesses against a particular individual, or what individual was to be tried, could not well collude together.]》

《 The Trial of JESSE, a Negro Man, the slave of Mr. Thomas Blackwood—His owner attending. 》

Examination of LOT, a negro belonging to Mr. Forrester.
I know Jesse, he met me last Sunday week[48] at the corner of Boundary Street as I was coming into town—He said he was going to get a horse to go into the Country to bring down some geese—From what my master told me the Thursday before, I distrusted his errand and gave him something of a caution—when as I was going down into town towards Mr. Hibben's Ferry slip and conversing with him, he said "You shall see tonight when I come down

---

48. Sunday, 16 June.

what I am going up for, and if my own father does not assist, I will cut off his head"—he said he was going as far as Goose Creek bridge, and would get a horse if it cost him $9.[49] The church bells were then ringing and at ½ past 11 O'Clock of the same day I saw him at Mr. Howard's, and afterwards understood from Sally that he had set off for the country, and had been brought down by the patrol—

Examination of Mr. Waring's negro man, SYKE.
Jesse asked me on Sunday week last before breakfast where he could get a horse to go a little way in the Country with—I told him I did not know—he then went away and did not return before 9 O'Clock that night—he had a wife at Mr. Warings—

26 JUNE 1822

Batteau was brought before the court at the request of his Master— Bram and Richard being also present, when they again repeated that he was the individual who had spoken to them as they testified on the 20th. inst. and that they had been acquainted with him for some time—

William and Joe were again examined against Denmark Vesey and cross examined by Mr. Cross—their testimony was nearly the same as before— Rolla was also re-examined and cross examined by Mr. Cross and testified much as before.

《FRANK, Mrs. Ferguson's slave, testified as follows: On the 15th of June, Vesey gave to Jesse $2 to hire a horse *to go into the country to my Mistress' plantation in St. John's, to inform the people to be down* on the night of the 16th. Myself and Adam put in 25 cents each for it. Vesey told Jesse, if he could not go, he must send someone else.》

[Jesse offered the following confession on 27 June.]
《The voluntary CONFESSION OF JESSE *to the Court*, made after all the evidence had been heard, but before his conviction.》

---

49. Named after a small tributary of the Cooper River that lay about ten miles from Charleston, Goose Creek provided an ideal location for plantation agriculture. Part of the parish of Saint James Goose Creek, some 4,192 slaves (75 percent), 86 free blacks (2 percent) and 1,271 whites (23 percent) lived here in 1820. See Federal Population Census of 1820, Charleston District, SCDAH.

Jesse Blackwood being brought before him, he said that is the man who was to go into the Country.

Jesse requested to be heard and said—I have had several conversations with Denmark Vesey—the first about four weeks ago—he asked me if I had heard about the rising, and did I know that the coloured people were going to try and get their liberty—I then could stop no longer, and he asked me to call and see him, I afterwards met him on the Wednesday before the Sunday that the rising was to take place, we walked up at St. Phillips Street and were joined by Frank Ferguson opposite Liberty Street, and we all three went to Vesey's house—Says Frank, I am just from the Country—well, says Vesey, and what success—says Frank, I have got two fine men for our purpose on my mistress' plantation, who must be sent up to and informed when the people are wanted in town—Vesey asked me if I would be the man to go—I said yes, but I don't know the way—says Vesey, Frank will tell you—Frank then told me how to go to Mrs. Ferguson's plantation and that I must ask for John O and Pompey—and gave me other directions—Vesey then gave me $2 to hire a horse and Frank and Adam threw down on the table 25 cents each—this was about 1 O'Clock (P.M.) on Saturday before last—I promised to go that night—On Sunday I met Lot, who betrayed me—that day I told Vesey I had started, but that the patrol turned me back—In fact, I had not started and told him so to deceive him—The same day I met Charles Drayton at Vesey's who said that the business was postponed, Vesey asked Charles how he knew the business was postponed—Charles said Ned Bennett and Monday Gell told him so— But, said Vesey, how could they know it was postponed, as they have not seen me—says Charles that said they have seen you and you had told them so—as far as I know I believe Vesey and Monday Gell were the Chief men.

《THE COURT *unanimously* found JESSE GUILTY, and passed upon him the sentence of DEATH.

Subsequently to his conviction, he made the following CONFESSION in prison *to the Rev. Dr. Hall—*

I was invited to Denmark Vesey's house, and when I went, I found several men together, among whom was Ned Bennett, Peter Poyas, and others, whom I did not know. Denmark opened the meeting by saying, he had an important secret to communicate to us, which we must not disclose to any one, and if we did, we should be put to instant death. He said we were deprived of our rights and privileges by the white people, and that our Church was shut up, so that we could not use it, and that it was high time for us to seek for our rights, and that we were fully able to conquer the whites, if we were only unanimous and courageous, as the St. Domingo people were— He then proceeded to explain his plan, by saying that they intended to make the attack by setting the Governor's Mills[50] on fire, and also some houses near the water, and as soon as the bells began to ring for fire, that they should kill every man as he came out of his door, and that the servants in the yard should do it, and that it should be done with axes and clubs, and afterwards they should murder the women and children, for he said, God had so commanded it in the scriptures—At another meeting at Denmark's, Ned Bennett, Peter Poyas, and several others were present, in conversation, some said they thought it was cruel to kill the ministers, and the women and children, but Denmark Vesey said, *he thought it was for our safety not to spare one white skin alive, for this was the plan they pursued in St. Domingo*—He then said to me, Jesse, I want you to go into the country to enlist as many of the country Negroes as possible, to be in readiness to come down to assist us—I told him I had no horse and no money to hire one; he then took out two dollars, and gave them to me to hire a horse, and told me to enlist as many as possible. I got the horse the next Sabbath, and started, but the guard was so strict, I could not pass them without being taken up; so I returned and told Denmark, at which he expressed his sorrow, and said the business was urgent, for they wanted the country people to be armed, that they might attack the Forts, at the same time, and also to take every ship and vessel in the harbor, and to put every man to death except the Captains. For said he, it will not be safe to stay in Charleston, for as soon as they had all the money out of the Banks, and the goods out of the stores on board, they intended to sail for Saint Domingo, for he had a promise that they would receive and protect them. This Jesse asserted to me, was the truth, whilst the tears were running down his cheeks, and he appeared truly penitent, and I have reason to hope, that he obtained pardon from God, through the merits of Christ, and was prepared to meet his fate with confidence and that he was accepted of God. At 4 o'clock, on the morning of the execution, I visited all the prisoners condemned, and found Jesse at prayers—he told me, his mind was placid and calm; he then assured me, that what he had told me was the truth, and that he was prepared to meet his God.

The Court considered Jesse's confession good evidence, because it was voluntarily made under the conviction of approaching death, and because the court did not think the principle of common law relative to the testimony of a convicted prisoner to be applicable to an individual in the situation of this witness. Moreover, the confession of Jesse and Rolla to the Court were made before conviction.⟫

---

50. These mills, located on the eastern banks of the Ashley River, were built on land owned by the Bennett family.

《The trial of DENMARK VESEY, a free black man—Col. G. W. Cross, attending as his counsel.》

Examination of Benjamin Ford, a white lad about 15 or 16 years of age, being first sworn.
He stated that Denmark Vesey frequently came into our Shop, which is near our house, and always complained of the hardships of the blacks—he said the Laws were very rigid and strict, and that the blacks had not their rights, that every one had his time and that his would come round too—his general conversation was about religion, which he would apply to slavery—as for instance, he would speak of the creation of the world, in which he would say, all men had equal rights, blacks as well as whites etc. all his religious remarks were mingled with slavery—[51]

27 JUNE 1822

Examination of FRANK, a negro man belonging to Mrs. Ferguson.
I know Denmark Vesey, and have been to his house, I have heard him say that the negroes situation was so bad that he did not know how they could endure it—and was astonished that they did not rise and fend for themselves—and advised me to join and rise—he said he was going about to see different people and mentioned the names of Ned Bennett and Peter Poyas as concerned with him; that he had spoken to Ned and Peter on this subject, and that they were to go about and tell the blacks that they were free, and must rise and fight for themselves—that they would take the Magazines and Guard houses and the City and be free—that he was going to send into the Country to inform the people there too—he said he wanted to join them. I said I could not answer—he said if I would not go into the Country for him he could get others—he said himself, Ned Bennett, Peter Poyas and Monday Gell were the principal men, and himself the head man. He said they were the principal men to go about and inform the people and fix them &c. that one party would land on South Bay, one about Wappoo and about the farms[52]—that the party which was to land on South Bay was to take the Guard House and get arms—and then they would be able to go on—that the attack was to commence about 12 O'Clock at night—that great numbers would come from all about and it must succeed as so many were engaged in it—that they would kill all the whites—that they would leave their masters

---

51. Finding its way into many political tracts during this age of revolution, this popular phrase—"all men had equal rights"—was used by Vesey for his own ends.
52. Wappo Creek flows between the Stono and Ashley Rivers, cutting James Island off from the mainland.

houses and assemble together near the lines, march down and meet the party which would land on South Bay—that he was going to send a man into the Country on a horse to bring down the Country people, and that he would pay for a horse—he gave $2 to Jesse to get the horse on Saturday week last about 1 O'clock in the day and myself and Adam also put in 25 cents apiece, and he told Jesse if he could not go, he must send some one else—I have seen Ned Bennett at Vesey's—I one night met at Vesey's a great number of men, and as they came in, each handed some money to him—Vesey said there was a little man named Jack who could not be killed, and who would furnish them with arms—he had a charm and would lead them—that Charles Drayton had promised to be engaged with them—Vesey said the negroes were leading such an abominable life they ought to rise—I said I was living well—he said tho' I was, others were not, and that 'twas such fools as I, that were in their way, and would not help them—and that after all things were well, he would mark me—he said he did not go with Creighton to Africa, because he had not a will[53]—he wanted to stay, and see what he could do for his fellow creatures—I met Ned, Monday Gell and others at Denmark Vesey's when they were talking about this business—

Examination of ADAM, a negro belonging to Mr. Ferguson.
Denmark Vesey one day at his house asked me for 25 cents to hire a horse to send up into the Country—I afterwards met the man who was to go into the Country, who told me he had set off and had been brought back by the Patrol—that he was going to bring down the black people to take the Country from the whites—Vesey said the 25 cents would be for my benefit—I have been at Vesey's house and there saw the man who was to go into the Country—he was a yellowish man.

Examination of POMPEY, a negro man belonging to Mr. Bryant.
Denmark Vesey had often spoken to me about the insurrection and endeavored to persuade me to join them, he enquired of me if my master had not any arms in his house and tried to persuade me to get them for him—the blacks stood in great fear of him, and so much so that I always endeavored to avoid him—

Examination of EDWIN, a negro belonging to Mr. Paul—
Charles belonged to Judge Drayton—he told me that Monday Gell and Denmark Vesey knew about the insurrection of the blacks—he said that

---

53. A prominent free black in Charleston, George Creighton left Charleston from the settlement established by the American Colonization Society at Cape Mesurado in Liberia. He had invited Vesey, who declined, to accompany him on this journey.

William Paul in consequence of his having given testimony would run a great risk of his life if he went out—I heard every body, even the women say when several were apprehended that they wondered that Monday Gell and Denmark Vesey were not taken.

Jesse Blackwood being brought before him, he said that is the man who was to go into the country.

Jesse requested to be heard. [See Jesse Blackwood's confession, above.]

⟪The Court *unanimously* found Denmark Vesey GUILTY, and passed upon him the sentence of DEATH. After his conviction, a good deal of testimony was given against him during succeeding trials.⟫

⟪The trial of ABRAHAM, a Negro Man, the Slave of Dr. Poyas—His owner attending.⟫

Peter Poyas was brought before the Court and shewn the letters of Abraham, he admitted that he had received them from him and that every word now in them were there when he received the letter—he explained one of them to allude to the negroes in the neighborhood, who had all agreed that Abraham should be admitted to change his Church and join them, whose Church was of a different persuasion from Abraham's.

Doctor Poyas also stated that subsequent to Abraham's trial, Abraham admitted to him that he had written the words which he previously had denied and gave an explanation similar to the one given by Peter—

⟪The following LETTER, found in the trunk of Peter Poyas, was acknowledged by Abram, to have been written by himself:

Dear Sir: With pleasure I give you an answer. I will endeavor to do it. Hoping that God will be in the midst to help his own. Be particular and make a sure remark. Fear not, the Lord God that delivered Daniel is able to deliver us. All that I inform agreed. I am gone up to Beach Hill.

(Signed) ABRAHAM POYAS[54]

Abraham for several days denied that the following words in that letter, viz.: *fear not . . . all that I inform agreed*—were written by him, saying, that they must have been added by some one. This, however, was evidently false, as he himself in a day or two afterwards admitted, but not before Peter Poyas had stated to the Court that every word in the letter was there when he received it. On Peter's being asked to explain the meaning of the letter, he said, it alluded to the Negroes in Abraham's neighborhood, who had all agreed that Abraham should be permitted to change his Church and join theirs—Abra-

---

54. The evidence suggests that this letter was the only item of written evidence presented to the court.

ham, however, gave a different meaning to it, and said, it related to his having two wives. Dr. Poyas, however, stated to the Court, that Abraham had subsequently given to him the same explanation of the letter that Peter had done. Although this letter taken in connection with his conduct was extremely suspicious, yet there being no other testimony against Abraham, he was found NOT GUILTY.》

1 JULY 1822

《On the first day of July, the following letter was received from His Excellency Governor Bennett:

Charleston, July 1st, 1822

L. H. Kennedy, Esq. Q. U.
Thos. Parker, J. P.

Presiding Magistrates of the Court of Justices and Freeholders organized for the trial of slaves charged with attempting to raise an insurrection.
Gentlemen:

After a very attentive consideration of the evidence yesterday presented, permit me to request that the case of Batteau may be reviewed with a view to the mitigation of his punishment; such a power is vested in the Court by the provisions of the act for the better ordering and governing of slaves.

If guilty of an attempt to raise an insurrection, it does not appear from the evidence to extend beyond an invitation to two boys to join in the project: from no part of the evidence does it appear that he is further implicated.

It is known that one of the boys referred to, was charged with using improper threats, and therefore supposed to be involved in the general plot, for which he was arrested. As he states that he had subsequently a communication with his brother, and they both testify to a simple isolated fact, collusion may be inferred. And even admitting the truth of their evidence, it would not appear that he is equally guilty with the others. If so the benignant provisions of that act would sanction the request made.

I ask this Gentlemen, as an individual incurring a severe and distressing loss.

I am very respectfully,
  Your obedient serv't,
    Thomas Bennett

THE COURT agreeable to the request contained in the above letter, reviewed their decision, but after having sent for and again interrogated witness Nos. 3 and 4,[55] came unanimously to the conclusion they had at first

---

55. These witnesses were Bram Lucas and his brother, Richard Lucas.

done. After his execution it was incidentally proved, in the course of the subsequent trials, that he attended the meetings of the conspirators at Vesey's.⟫

⟪THE TRIAL of CHARLES, a Negro Man, belonging to the Honorable John Drayton—His owner attending.⟫

Examination of PATRICK, belonging to Miss Datty
I know Charles Drayton—about 5 months ago he met me in the street, when he stopped me and asked me to join with him—I asked him in what—he said he want to make up a Company—I said what for, he said for some respectable brown man coming here from abroad—I said I did not want death to take me yet and I quit him.
⟪The Court *unanimously* found Charles GUILTY, and passed upon him the sentence of DEATH

WEDNESDAY, 10 JULY 1822, 12 O'CLOCK

Present the same court
⟪The Trial of JULIUS, a Negro man belonging to Mr. T. H. Forrest—his owner attending.⟫
Julius Forrest on his Trial began on 8th. instant.

Prudence belonging to Mr. Bussaker Examined—
I know Julius Forrest I conversed with him first before the execution of the 6 'twas of a Sunday night two Sundays ago that he called at my house—he said he had just come from the Island—he was looking for Harry, but could not find him—that he and Harry were to go up the road on Sunday the 16th June to meet the black army that was coming to fight in Town—but the white people having got wind of it and turned out too strong, they were now obliged to go away—I saw him again last Saturday night, he came to my house and said Harry Haig was taken up for the same thing he was talking to me about that Sunday night—he asked me if I had said any thing to any person about what he had been talking to me that Sunday night—as they have taken Harry up, says he, I suppose my time will come next—if Harry don't call my name I shall be safe—this was our last conversation.

Mr. Forrest states that he has no questions to ask the witness that she is like a kind of mother to Julius—having raised or brought him up—that Harry Haig and Julius & very intimate and together at his shop every night—

Harry Haig Statement—I know Julius Forrest, we always worked together—Gullah Jack calls himself a Dr. negro—He induced me and Julius to join at last—but at first we refused—before the 16th. June, Jack appointed me to meet Julius and myself at Bulkley's Farm when we got there Jack was not there, but Peter Poyas came and asked for Jack—Jack did not come and Peter took out his book and we all prayed all night and broke up at day light, not a month before the 16th. Jack met me, and talked to him about war—I asked Jack how he'd do for arms—by and by, said Jack, we will have arms—he said, he would have some arms made at the Blacksmith's—Jack was going to give me a bottle with poison to put into my Master's pump, and into as many pumps as he could about town, and he said he wanted to give the other bottles to those he could trust to[56]—Until Jack was taken I felt as if I was bound up and had not the power to speak one word about it—I refused to poison as I considered that murder and God would not pardon me 'twas not like fair fighting—Jack charmed Julius and myself at last and we then consented to join—Tom Russel the Blacksmith and Jack are partners—Jack learned him to be a Doctor—Tom talked to Jack about the fighting and agreed to join, and those two brought Julius and myself to agree to it—Jack said Tom was his second, and when you did not see him, and see Tom, you see him—Jack said Tom was making arms for black people—Jack said he could not be killed nor could a white man take him—

   Adjourned to 12 o'clock tomorrow

THURSDAY, 11 JULY 1822

《The trial of GULLAH JACK, a Negro Man, belonging to Mr. Pritchard—His owner attending.》
The Same Court present
Billy—belonging to Mr. Bulkley—The first time I heard it was when I was working at the Rope Walk, about the middle of March from Gullah Jack[57]—

---

56. This testimony—regarding the intention to poison the city's water supply—was expunged from Kennedy and Parker's *Official Report*. This portion of the *Official Report* reads as follows: "Jack was going to give me *********** I refused to do this as I considered that murder."

57. Ropewalks comprise of long, open yards in which workers used hand-cranked jacks to twist lengths of hemp yarn together to make rope for rigging and other purposes. At least three slave rope makers (Adam Robertson, John Robertson, and Robert Robertson) were accused in the plot. Their owner, John Robertson, operated ropewalks along Meeting Street close to the Lines on Charleston Neck. These ropewalks comprise just one aspect of the city's trade in ship building and repairing in which sail makers, riggers, caulkers, carpenters,

Robert told me that Jack was coming to list hands—there were 5 or 6 people he saw going to Mr. Thayer's farm—he asked them what they were going to do—they said they were going to get hands—I asked them for what purpose—they said to fight the whites as the poor negroes suffer dreadful slavery—I refused to join and they told me all who did not join would be put to death—Jack was one of the five or six and Robert Robertson, Adam Robertson and John Robertson.

It was with great difficulty that the above witness could be understood, as he spoke english very badly[58]—The Court therefore postponed a further examination of him until the agent of his owner Mr. Bulkley could be present as he understood him with more facility.

《GULLAH JACK when apprehended denied to the Court that he ever wore whiskers, although the map of a large pair of them was plainly discernable on his face, and continued to deny it stoutly until confronted with his owner—he also positively denied that he ever pretended to be a Doctor or Conjurer.

MR. PAUL PRITCHARD deposed as follows: My Slave Jack always wore a very large pair of whiskers which he prized very much, and which nothing could induce him to cut off, and which I often threatened to shave off as a punishment when he misbehaved—These whiskers I found that he had cut off to my great surprise about three days ago, and wondered at the cause of it, little dreaming that it was to prevent him being apprehended by a description of him—I did hear some years ago that Jack was a Doctor or Conjurer—he is called Gullah Jack or Cooter Jack.》

Examination of GEORGE, belonging to Mr. Vanderhorst.

《When this witness was about to be examined in the presence of Gullah Jack, it was not without considerable difficulty that the Court satisfied him that he need no longer fear Jacks *conjurations* (as he called them). It was in the course of this witness' evidence that Jack laid aside the character of the fool he was counterfeiting, and shewed his real character.》

Gullah Jack is an enemy against the Whites—Charles Drayton told me that he would die with Gullah Jack, this he told me about the time of the execu-

---

and shipwrights worked. Captain Joseph Vesey owned a ropewalk in Charleston at the end of the eighteenth century where Vesey, then a slave, probably worked at some point.

58. This slave may have spoken nothing but Gullah, the creole language of lowcountry Africans and African Americans. Gullah, as noted elsewhere, was an important and private means by which the conspirators could communicate without revealing too much to their owners.

tion—I was in the company of Y. he asked me to join & carried me to Jack's house, where they met, Jack's house is next to Monday Gell's—Y. said he was ready to join & asked me to join, at Gullah Jack's house I met him, Y, John Horry, Harry Haig, Julius Forrest, Charlie Drayton & more whose names I don't recollect or know—this was long after Mr. Paul's man was taken up, & 'twas after the 16th. June—It was said there, they would come against the White people—Jack stood at the front of all, that is he was the head man— We all agreed to come against the whites—I said I would join with them—I was begged to do so first by Y, he introduced me to the meeting, he was the first person who told me so far about it, as to ask me to join—Jack was my leader—he is the head of the Gullah Company—I heard that amongst them, they have charms & from Y. I heard that they had also parched corn & ground nuts—Jack is a little man with large black whiskers—I did say after Charles Drayton was taken up, I was afraid he would name me, Jack said if any man betrayed them they would injure him, and I was afraid to inform— Peter Poyas asked me long back to join the Band—John Horry & myself have conversed on this business, he said he would be ready with these men, whenever they were ready—he spoke much against the Whites, & said that he would slaughter them & what & what he would have done—I have conversed with Harry Haig, who said he was ready and he would die with them—All the men at Jack's agreed to die together—I said to Julius Forrest once that I did not think we could get over the Whites, when he said he would die with his men. I have heard it said all about the streets generally. I cant name any one particularly, that whoever is the white man's friend, God help them, by which I understood that they would be killed.

《If I am accepted as a witness and my life spared, I must beg the Court to send me away from this place, *as I consider my life in great danger from having given testimony.*》

《The Court *unanimously* found Gullah Jack GUILTY, and passed upon him the sentence of DEATH.》

FRIDAY, 12 JULY 1822

Present the same court which met at 10 O'Clock (A.M.) according to adjournment—
The court for want of the presence of witnesses could proceed on no trial today—and adjourned to 10 O'clock tomorrow—the 13th. Instant—
《Mr. Hammet, while he was not desirous that Bacchus should escape punishment, yet was anxious to save his life, and previously to his trial handed to the Court in writing a confession which Bacchus had made to

him, and stated, that he came forward with this candid confession of Bacchus, in hopes of saving his life thereby; but that if the Court thought his case did not admit of a less punishment than death, he then requested that his confession should not be used against him. The Court after consultation determined to proceed to his trial. The following confession, though not used against Bacchus, is now given to the public:⟫

Confession of Mr. Hammet's Bacchus on 12 July 1822 to his master.
Perault, when hauling cotton from my store, told Bacchus in the yard secretly, that he wanted him to go to Society with him—asked Bacchus, what Society—he, Perault, told him that never mind what Society, and told Bacchus he would call for him that night—he did call and Bacchus went with him—That Perault carried him to Denmark Vesey's house by Bennetts Mills[59]—there he met about 12 men, among whom was Monday Gell and Smart Anderson, after he got in, they fastened the gate—it was before 9 O'Clock—Denmark and Perault took him to one side, and Perault told him they were going to tell him something—this was in another room, not before the gang—Denmark and Perault said that they were going to turn to and fight the white people, and take the Country—and that New Orleans was taken[60]—That Bacchus considered a long while, and they found him considering, and that at last Bacchus said to Perault, he was sorry he brought him there—he did not wish to belong to such a Society—That Denmark Vesey said to him before Perault, that the one that did not wish to join the Society

59. The lumber and rice mills erected by Thomas Bennett along the Ashley River.
60. This comment about New Orleans is somewhat mysterious. It may well refer to the rebellion in the Pointe Coupée district of Louisiana of January 1811, during which several hundred African slaves from local sugar plantations organized themselves, collected weapons, and headed toward New Orleans. A combined force of Federal troops, local planters and the militia quickly put down the rising, killing scores of rebels in the process. Prior to this rebellion, a number of slaves from this locale were arrested in April 1795 for plotting to kill their masters. Like the Vesey conspiracy, this plot drew much of its inspiration from the revolution in Saint Domingue. On Pointe Coupée, see Harding, *There Is a River*; on the 1795 conspiracy, see Gwendolyn Midlo Hall, *Africans in Colonial Louisiana*, 344–74.
It may also refer to the unsuccessful attack launched by British troops against New Orleans during the War of 1812, in which they were soundly defeated by Andrew Jackson. On the eve of the battle, Jackson addressed the black troops under his command, urging them "to share in the perils and to divide the glory of your white countrymen. Alternatively, it may possibly refer to *The Triumph of Liberty, or Louisiana Preserved*, a play written by long-time Charleston resident John Blake White in 1819 that was both published and performed locally. In addition to offering audiences a dramatic account of the Battle of New Orleans on stage, White also painted a canvas depicting this event. See Remini, *Andrew Jackson and the Course of American Empire*, 259; Hickey, *The War of 1812*, 206–14.

must be put to death as an enemy—that he told all the gang so after he went back with Bacchus into the room—That Denmark told the gang, that they must meet at his house that night next week—That Perault told him Bacchus to try to get powder—that the gang would throw in and make it up to Bacchus; that they all threw in the night of the meeting 12½ cents each and he Bacchus did also—that this money was thrown in to give a man to go into the Country, and bring down the Country Negroes, when they were all ready—That Bacchus asked about arms—whose they were—he Denmark Vesey recommended them to look through town for the stores that had the most guns—That Perault then jumped up and said Bacchus don't you know where Captain Martindale's arms is—says Bacchus, yes my man, but you can't get them—and you had better drop the thing altogether—about two or three weeks after the last affair—Perault came to Bacchus and told him that they had caught Denmark—That Perault came to him and carried him down to Monday Gell's—that Monday and Perault told him that Denmark said that if they caught him, he would tell nobody's name—and that he, Bacchus, must not tell his Perault's name nor Monday's—That Perault told Bacchus he must not mention his name, nor would he mention yours—That he Bacchus took the keg of powder out of the back store of his master and carried it in a bag to Denmark with a man belonging to Mr. Bennett which he believes is a blacksmith—that he, Bennett's man, met Bacchus at his master's gate—that he supposes Pritchard's Gullah Jack and Perault carried the powder to Monday from Denmark's house—That in company with Denmark Vesey and Perault that Denmark told him Bacchus to get what arms he could—that he said he could get on horseman's sword in a scabbard, which he took to Denmark's house—that he said also he Bacchus could get a pistol, but was afraid his master would miss it—That Perault told him, never mind, he could make him easy about it—that he did take the pistol to Denmark's house with the sword, that on Sunday night the 16th. June Denmark had told him Bacchus previously that he must not go home—This Denmark told me at the meeting previous—and said they were to go up the road and meet the Country negroes—that last night he Bacchus when he was put in the room in the work house with Perault, that Perault told him Gullah Jack had buried the powder and he thinks Purcell knows where it is—That all the negroes engaged in the plot were ordered by Denmark to leave their masters and go up the road—That the night they carried him to Denmark that he was so frightened that he was obliged to say yes—for they threatened to kill every man who did not wish to join—that a large book like the Bible was open before them at Denmark's house—that he does not know whether it was to sign names in or what purpose—At the first meeting at Denmark's, they asked him his name, that Perault answered your name is Bacchus belonging to Mr. Hammet—Denmark asked which Hammet—Bacchus said Benjamin Hammet, the gentleman who sued Lorenzo Dow[61]—That the week after Denmark was dead, Perault told him to mind and keep himself ready that they intended to come up at the corner where the arms of the Neck Company is kept—and he, Bacchus, said very well—that they were to take the arms, and that he, Bacchus, was to assist them, that they were to break open the door, that Monday Gell can tell who is at the heart of this last arrangement that he Bacchus believes Perault knows all about it, that Gullah Jack was to distribute the powder amongst them—that Perault told him Bacchus, that they had a blacksmith to make daggers for this party—that they had made some, that Perault told him on Sunday 16th. June that they had three or four hundred daggers, that he told Bacchus on the 11th July the night he was committed that he must not tell his name or anything about it—That this was the reason he was afraid to tell or make a confession to his master Mr. Hammet on this morning the 12th. July—That Perault is the fellow that had brought him this scrape—that a fellow about his (Bacchus') size, a dark black skin negro who he believes is called Charles took him Bacchus up the road just before you come to the fork of the road on the Meeting Street road to a farm; that the house on the farm had a piazza on the top—that Charles told this negro man on the farm—mind next Sunday the business is to be done, meaning to kill the white people and that the negroes from the Country were to stop at this farm—that Denmark Vesey and his party from town was to go there to the farm to meet the negroes from the Country—that he Bacchus solemnly declared as to his being brought into this scrape, and that Perault is the one who enticed him into it—that at the first meeting at Denmark Vesey's house, on the breaking up of the meeting Denmark said "friends you all throw in seven pence a piece, those who have got it, to make up for a friend to pay his wages to his master" before he went into the Country to bring the people down.

61. A prominent, if somewhat controversial, preacher in the Methodist Church, Lorenzo Dow was accused by Benjamin Hammet of "most scandalously" libeling his late father, Methodist minister William Hammet. Dow claimed that the late Hammet was "a person of vicious and depraved principles . . . that his actions were wicked and his motives impure [and] that he was so given to habits of intoxication that he died drunk." Tried in May 1821 by William Johnson, a justice who sat on the U.S. Supreme Court and who attained notoriety during the Vesey trials and the debates surrounding the Negro Seaman Act, Dow was found guilty, fined one dollar, and imprisoned for twenty-four hours. See Dow, *Stranger in Charleston!* On Dow, see Hatch, *Democratization of American Christianity*, 130–35.

We whose names are herewith affixed declare that this confession was in our presence and hearing this 12th. day of July 1822

Signed { B. Hammet (owner)
J. Tho Robinson
Duke Goodman[62]

13 JULY 1822

—Present the same court
The Court found Julius Forrest Guilty to be hung on the 26th. inst.
Mr. James Legare, one of the freeholders composing the court, stated that he was too much indisposed to continue to serve and withdrew—Whereupon a warrant was instantly issued by the presiding Magistrates to summon Mr. Henry Deas[63] in his stead—who soon appeared and was sworn as one of the court according to Law—

Confession of Monday Gell
I come out as a man who knows he is about to die—Some time after Christmas—Vesey passed my door and called in and said to me that he was trying to gather the blacks to try and see if any thing could be done to overcome the whites—he asked me to join—I asked him his plans and his numbers—he said he had Peter Poyas, Ned Bennett and Jack Purcell—he asked me to join and I said no—he left me and I saw him not for some time. About 4 or 5 weeks ago as I went up Wentworth Street, Frank Ferguson met me and said he had 4 Plantations of People who he was to go for on Saturday 15 June—how, said I, will you bring them down—he said through the woods—he asked me if I was going toward Vesey's to ask Vesey to be at home that evening and he would be there to tell him his success—I asked Jack Purcell to carry this message, he said he would—that same evening at my house I met Vesey's mulatto boy[64]—he told me Vesey wished to see me—I went with him—When I went into Vesey's I met Ned Bennett, Peter Poyas, and Frank Ferguson and Adam and Gullah Jack—they were consulting about the plan—Frank told Vesey on Saturday 15th. he would go and bring down the people,

62. Benjamin Hammet was a merchant, Thomas Robinson ran a baker's shop on Bedon's Alley, and Duke Goodman worked as a factor on Edmonston's Wharf.
63. Henry Deas was a local planter.
64. This reference to Vesey's "mulatto boy" provides additional information on the rebel leader's family. Since Vesey held white people in considerable contempt for much of his life, it seems unlikely that he would have fathered a child with a white woman, but may have done so with a light-complected woman of African descent.

and lodge them near town in the woods—the plan was to arm themselves by breaking open the stores with arms—I then told Vesey that I would join them—After some time, I told them I had some business of my own and asked them to excuse me—I went away and only then was I ever there—One evening Perault Strohecker and Bacchus Hammet brought to my shop a keg, and asked me to let it stay there 'till they sent for it—I said yes, but did not know the contents—the next evening Gullah Jack came and took away the keg, this was before the 16th. June—Since I have been in prison I learned that the keg contained powder—Pharo Thompson is concerned and he told me a day or two after Ned and Peter were taken up if he could get a $50 bill he would run away—about two Sundays before I was brought here, he asked me in Archdale Street when shall we be like these white people in the Church, I said when it pleased God—Sunday before I was taken up, he met me as I came out of Archdale Church and took me into a stable in said street, and told me he had told his master who had asked him, that he had nothing to do with this affair; which was a lie—William Colcock came to my Shop once and said a Brother told him that 500 men were making up for the same purpose—Frank said he was to send to Hell-Hole swamp to get men—Perault Strohecker is engaged—he used to go of a Sunday on horse up the road to a man he knows on the same errand—One Sunday he asked me to go with him, and I went and Smart Anderson—we went to a small house a little way from the road after you turn into the Ship yard road on its left hand—they two went into the Stable with an old man that lived there—I remained in the yard they remained in the stable about half an hour—as soon as they came out, I and Perault started to town to go to Church and left Smart there—I was told by Denbow Martin who has a wife in Mr. Smith's house that Stephen Smith belonged to some of the gangs—Saby Gailliard is concerned—he met me on the Bay before the 16th. June and gave me a piece of paper from his pocket—This paper was about the battles that Boyer had in St. Domingo in a day or two he called on me and asked if I had read it and said if he had many men he could do the same too, as he could whip 10 white men himself[65]—he frequently came to me to speak about this matter—and at last I had to insult him out of the Shop—He and Paris Ball was often together—a week before I was taken up Paris told me that my name was called—Bill Palmer and Vesey were constantly together—there was once in my Shop a long talk between

---

65. Capturing the Spanish-held territories on the island of Hispaniola, Haitian leader Jean-Pierre Boyer ended slavery in Santo Domingo (now the modern-day Dominican Republic). News of Boyer's victory over the Spanish reached Charleston just a short time before Vesey planned to launch his rebellion. See Logan, *Haiti and the Dominican Republic*, 32.

them on this same matter—I begged them to stop it—Vesey told him to try and to get as many as he could, and he said he would—

John Vincent told me that Ed Johnson, a free man, had said as he was a free man he would have nothing to do with Slaves, but the night they began he would join them—I told Charles Drayton what uproar there was about this business—and since we have been here we have talked together—Albert Inglis came to me and asked if I knew anything about it, I said yes—He asked me if I had joined, I said yes—he said he was one also—he said Adam, a free man, wanted to see me—I went with him one night—Adam asked me how many men had joined, I told him what Frank Ferguson had said—he asked me if I belonged—I said yes—he said if he could only find men behind him he would go before—Previous to the 10th., Albert said to me he would quit this business, I told him I was too far into it, so I must stick to it—I never wrote to St. Domingo or anywhere else on this subject, nor kept a list or books, nor saw any such things, but heard that Paul's William had a list; nor did I hear anything about arms being in possession of the blacks—I don't know that Tom Russell made pikes, nor that Gullah Jack had any of them— Louis Remoussin called at my shop, and asked me to call at his house, he had something to tell me—but I did not go—Jack Glen told me he was engaged— I met Scipio Sims one Sunday coming from the country who said he had been near the Savannah to Mr. Middleton's place[66]—I heard afterwards that his errand was on this business—I know John the Cooper who said he was engaged too in this business—William Garner said he was engaged in it and had got 12 or 13 draymen to join—Sandy Vesey told me he belonged in it too—at Vesey's house Frank told Gullah Jack to put one ball and 3 buck shot on each cartridge—Mingo Harth acknowledged to me that he had joined and Peter Poyas told me so too—he, Mingo, told me so several times, Mingo said he was to have his master's horse on the night of the 16th. Lot Forrester told me frequently that he was one of a company and I know that he had joined me in the business myself—Isaac Harth told me that he had joined, he knew I was in the business—Maurice Brown knew nothing of it and we agreed not to let him, Henry Drayton or Charles Corr know anything about it[67]—Yorrick Cross told me in my store that he was to get some powder for his master and give it to Peter Poyas—he seemed to have been a long time engaged in it and to know a great deal—Joe Jore acknowledged to me once or

---

66. The plantation owned by the Middleton family, Middleton Place lay on the Ashley River Road, about fourteen miles from the city.

67. Henry Drayton and Charles Corr were deacons at the AME church. There is no evidence to indicate that they were involved in the plot.

twice that he had joined—he said he knew some of the Frenchmen concerned, he knew I was in it.

Charles Drayton examined and said—I have seen Perault Strohecker talking with Monday Gell in his Shop. Jack Purcell said to me just before I was taken up that he had gone into the Country to gather the people's mind on the subject, but the overseer was so watchful that he had no chance to speak to the people—
《Subsequently to this confession [given on 13 July], Monday was examined as a witness in a number of cases, during, which he stated many things he had not mentioned in his confession. The Court conceiving it all important to obtain from Monday, all the information he possessed (believing him to possess more information on this subject than any man alive) offered to recommend him to the Governor for a conditional pardon, or commutation of his punishment to banishment, if he would reveal all he knew in relation to the plot. He promised to do so, and made this second CONFESSION.》
[See Gell's second confession given on 23 July]

Further confession of Bacchus made on the 13 July 1822—
At the meeting at Denmark Vesey's, the first time he saw a fat black fellow whom he thinks was Denmark's son, as he looked very much like Denmark[68]—had a full face, that he could read as he showed Monday Gell a large book on the table—that he said to Monday shewing him some of the leaves of the book on the table "see here they are making a real game at we"—and Monday looked at the book and said nothing—that Denmark took him Bacchus one side and said "we shan't be slaves to these damn rascals any longer. We must kill everyone that we can get hold and drive the rest out of the City"—that no one was with him (Bacchus) when he was requested by Charles (whom he calls Charles Drayton now) to go to the farm at the fork of the road, that when Charles set out to go there, he came from Monday Gell's house—that he Bacchus and Charles and he carried him to Monday's—that Monday was to go with Charles to the farm, but put it off on account of having a hog to kill, and said to Charles let this friend go with you, and that he and Charles went to the farm—when they went to the farm, Charles asked a negro woman on the farm if the old daddy was at home and she called him—that this old daddy is an African marked on both sides of his face or on his face[69]—that

68. This person was presumably Sandy Vesey.
69. A reference to ritual scarification, which was an integral part of African body decoration.

Charles took him in the stable and also Bacchus and told him about the Country negroes coming there etc. that the fellow who helped him to carry the powder belonged to Bennett, he thinks, because he saw this man at Bennett's blacksmith shop at the Mill years before this—that Perault told him that had two or three hundred Bayonets made already, and that Perault is a blacksmith—that he believes Monday knows as well as Perault where the arms or bayonets are—Monday said they were to have mounted horsemen that many draymen belonged to it, who had horses, that at Denmark's house they all rose up and swore, lifting up the right hand saying "we will not tell if we are found out, or if they kill us we will not tell any one"—That Denmark said that all must say so, and that they did say so—that Denmark told Bacchus that he gave the sword to Perault and Perault gave it to a man named Caesar—that he knows no other person Caesar but a drayman named Caesar Smith, a tall negro, an African who is an intimate acquaintance of Perault, who is often at the stable where Perault keeps his horses—that Perault told him, that french negroes were among them[70]—that Denmark said Country born, Africans and all kind joined—that Monday and Perault appeared to be intimate friends of Denmark, that he thought a heap of them—that Denmark took the pistol to himself, it was given to him in his own house—that their meetings were held at Denmark's house where he had a black wife—that two or three women are at his house ironing—

[See Bacchus Hammet's trial on 18 July]

Evidence of BILLY, belonging to Mr. Bulkley (taken three days after his arrest on July 10).
The first meeting was at Mr. Thayer's farm, one Sunday morning he joined them there, but did not hear what was done there, and he left them—after that came to Mr. Bulkley's farm, this was in April[71]—at that meeting there were Adam Robertson, Robert Robertson, and John Robertson, Dick Sims, Polydore Faber. At that meeting, they were considering about the means of rising against the whites—Gullah Jack was present, he came in company with Adam and Robert—they roasted a fowl and ate it half raw as an evidence of union[72]—Robert and Gullah Jack were the principal men—One day I met Adam and on my return from market, and he requested me to hide a

---

70. The presence of "french negroes" among the ranks of the rebels suggests that some slaves from Saint Domingue had some involvement in the plot.

71. Bulkley's Farm lay a few miles outside Charleston on the Meeting Street road.

72. Part of the rituals at which "Gullah" Jack Pritchard presided. The consumption of half-cooked fowl may have produced unforeseen consequences for those who ate it, further reinforcing Jack's reputation as a conjure man.

jug of powder and I refused to do so—at another meeting before the 16th. June at which the following persons were present (vizt.) Adam, Robert, Polydore, John Robertson, Dick Sims, and Gullah Jack—a pistol was exhibited and everyone tried to fire it, but no one could discharge it but Dick Sims—those in whose hands it could not go off, were considered as safe—Charles Drayton told me that the place of meeting for the draymen was to be the farm of Mr. Payne, and Charles also informed me that they wished to put their horses in my master's farm which I refused—Charles afterwards told me that the plot was discovered and that the blacks must remain quiet until the whites were off their guard—Robert called and gave me the same caution that Charles had done—Peter Poyas and four others whom I know not came to the farm on the night of the 27 April about 3 O'Clock (p.m.) and sung and prayed until day light—before this time, I asked Robert who was the principal man—he said Gullah Jack—I then asked him if there were others—he said that Gullah Jack had gone to father Morris (Morris Brown) to ask him whether he would sanction the insurrection and Morris Brown replied if you can get men, go on, but don't mention my name—I am going shortly to the north and shall hear there what you are about[73]—Will Bee told Peter Ward, who mentioned it to me, that all the Draymen without exception would be light horse men—Polydore, belonging to Mr. Faber, had more than twenty poles about 10 feet long on Mr. Bulkley's farm under the house—Polydore said that Robert would come and I supposed that he would fix something at the ends of the poles as Polydore had said, that something would be fixed on the end—Robert was coming—Robert came in the afternoon, and said it was useless that the business had been discovered.

Adjourned to 15th at 11 O'Clock

Trial of the following slaves vizt. Tom Russell, Louis Remoussin, Charles Drayton, Perault Strohecker, Monday Gell, Joe Jore, Saby Gaillard, Jack Purcell, and Mingo Harth.

Notice to the owners to be given, the Trial Monday 11 O'Clock.

MONDAY, 15 JULY 1822

Present the same Court as on Saturday met at 11 O'Clock

| Tom Russell | arraigned | plea not guilty |
| Louis Cromwell | ditto | ditto |

---

73. Morris Brown was minister at the city's African Methodist Episcopal Church. He escaped to Philadelphia after the trials, later becoming the church's national leader. No evidence has ever been uncovered to indicate that Brown played any role in the plot.

Mingo Harth	arraigned	plea not guilty
Saby Gaillard, a free man	ditto	ditto
Joe Jore	ditto	ditto
Jack Purcell	ditto	ditto

《THE TRIAL OF TOM, a Negro man, the slave of Mrs. Russel—James Gray, Esq., attending for his owner.》

Perault Strohecker examined—Tom Russell told me that he had joined a Gullah Band. I know that he belongs to this band, which was Jack's—and I belonged to Monday Gell's—this he told me at his Shop—this band was to rise against the whites—and he told me himself that he was with them to rise against the whites—I saw 6 pike heads at Monday Gell's Shop—3 of them were Spears of this shape (△) and 3 bayonets of this Shape (⌿) with holes to put poles in—I met the prisoner at Denmark's house when it was agreed that the 16th. was the day for the rising at which place Gullah Jack was also—Monday had a list of with 42 names on it, mine was one—he burnt the list when Peter Poyas was taken up—[74]

Mr. Grey attended as Counsel for Tom and cross examined the witnesses—The first time I ever met Tom at Vesey's was on 16th. June, when I went into Vesey's I met Tom there—I knew him long before, Tom was willing to agree to all that was adopted there, but did not talk himself—I met at Tom's shop Charles Drayton—Smart Anderson was present when the Spears were brought into Monday's shop—

Re-examined—I saw Gullah Jack carry those spears to Monday Gell's—

Charles Drayton examined—Tom told me himself in Monday Gell's shop that he was making the pikes for Gullah Jack, which pikes were to be used for fighting according as I suppose—

Cross examined—I did not meet Perault at Tom's shop, but at Monday Gell's—I never was in company with Tom and Purcell together on this business.

Monday Gell—Examined—Tom Russell and Charles Drayton talked together once in my shop, but I did not hear what they said—I had frequent conversations with Perault, but not with Tom—

---

74. Stored at Bulkley's farm, these spear handles, or lengths of wood that could have been used for such a purpose, were apparently found by the militia.

Mrs. Mark Marks testified—Mrs. Russel, the prisoner's owner, told me that Gullah Jack was constantly with Tom at breakfast, dinner and supper and that she cautioned Tom, not to have so much to do with Jack, or he would be taken up—

⟪[NOTE: Mr. Gray consented to this testimony being received instead of sending for Mrs. Russel.]⟫

James Mall, a white man sworn for the prisoner—⟪about 16 or 17 years of age.⟫

I was working with Tom from February to the last of March in his Shop—I then went into the Country, and received a message to come down to work with him again—and I came down in the last of May when he refused to employ me—one day I went to his shop, I saw him making a knife about a foot long, out of a file, which he had not finished, he is an edged tool maker—

Cross examined—When I was working with Tom, I did not eat any meals at the shop, but at home—Gullah Jack was frequently at his shop—and they frequently talked together in Gullah so that I should not understand them—he said after the people were taken up, that he would not as some had done tell upon one another for money.

⟪The Court *unanimously* found TOM GUILTY, and passed upon him the sentence of DEATH.⟫

⟪THE TRIAL of LOUIS REMOUSSIN, a Negro Man, the Slave of Mr. Cromwell—His owner attending.⟫

Perault examined and said—I know Louis—Louis and Joe and myself met in the Street—and Joe said to me, that Louis was one to join against the Whites—Louis did not deny it—this was on the 15th. Louis said he was ready to rise against the white people—Joe said the french band had been ready long time—this is all I know against Louis—the conversation was in creole french—I understand it (the Court required Louis and Perault to speak together in French which they did, and Perault evidently understood that language)[75]

Cross examined by Mr. Cromwell—nothing material

Charles Drayton examined and said—Louis met me one day as he came out of the work house and said to me, that he had not much to do with the

---

75. Evidence suggests that Louis Remoussin had arrived along with several hundred other refugee slaves from Saint Domingue in the early 1790s. Although Perault had been born in Africa, his knowledge of French suggests that he either spent some time in the French Caribbean before arriving in Charleston or that he picked up the language in the course of daily life in the city.

business, but that on the night the attack commenced against the Whites he would be ready—and he told me to get ready—I understood from his conversation plain enough that he was one of them—

Cross examined by Mr. Cromwell—this was the Saturday before the thing was to break out—I met him at his own house—he told me at Monday Gell's to come to his house to talk about this business—I have seen him often at Monday's.

Monday Gell—Louis came to my shop and told me to go to his house that night, that he wanted to see me about something particular—I did not go tho'—

《The Court *unanimously* found Louis Remoussin GUILTY, and passed upon him the sentence of DEATH, *but recommended* to the Governor to pardon him *upon condition* that he be transported out of the limits of the United States.》

《The trial of MONDAY GELL, a Negro Man, the Slave of Mr. John Gell—Col. Wm. Rouse as his friend, and Jacob Axson, Esq., Counsel for his owner attending.》

Examination of Frank, a negro man belonging to Mr. Ferguson.
The first time I spoke with Monday Gell 'twas one night at Vesey's house—where I heard Vesey tell Monday that he must send some one round into the country to bring the people down. Monday replied, that he had directed Jack to go up & told him to tell the people to come down and join in the fight against the whites—and to ascertain and inform him how many people he could get to agree. A few days after I met Vesey, Monday, & Jack in the street under Mr. Duncan's trees at night, where Jack stated that he had been in the country around Goose Creek & Dorchester and that he had spoken to 6,600 persons who had agreed to join.[76] At Vesey's the first time I spoke to Monday, he was going away early and Vesey asked him to stay; when Monday said he expected that night a meeting at his house to fix upon and mature the plan and he could not stay.[77] I afterwards conversed with Monday in his

---

76. A small rural settlement in the parish of Saint James Goose Creek, Dorchester, lay about twenty miles to the northwest of Charleston.

77. This meeting possibly took place on Bull Street, the street on which Vesey lived, outside the house of John Duncan, a merchant who lived at number 31. Two other men with the surname Duncan also lived in Charleston. Alexander Duncan, a blacksmith, resided at

shop,[78] where he asked me if I had heard that Bennetts' & Poyas' people were taken up, that 'twas a great pity—he said he had joined in the business—I told him to take care that he was not taken up—whenever I talked with Vesey, he always spoke of Monday as being his principal and active man in this business. I heard Jack say, he would pay no more wages, he was too busy in seeing about this Insurrection, besides what would the Whites want with wages—they would soon be no more—Monday Gell said to Vesey, that if Jack had so many men, they had better wait no longer, but begin the business at once and others would join.

Examination of PHARO, belonging to Mr. Thompson.
One evening I overheard two men in the street say that Hales Berry[79] and Denmark Vesey were two principal men—Perault belonging to Mr. Strohecker said to me last Tuesday that the black people were not worth any thing, but that there was a French Band, which if they could get only 100 men to join with them would attack the work house and take their friends out—I once went to Monday Gell, who told me he wanted to see me—this was before Mr. Paul's William was taken up, I there met Charles Drayton and Mr. Ferguson's Frank who frequents Monday's house—Monday said that he wanted to say something particular to one, and Charles winked at him, when Monday stopped short—Charles asked me on Friday 14th June in the streets to lend him a horse next Sunday evening—I said I could not.

Mr. James Ferguson who was present at Franks examination stated to the Court that the testimony of Frank was in substance what he had before told him.

William Palmer—I heard say in Monday Gell's shop that he was one—I met Pharo Thompson at Monday Gell's—he said what he would do when they commenced, that he had no sword, but that he had a part of a saw, which he would have ground into a sword, that he was one—he bragged of what he would do with his sword—Mingo Harth came once to Monday Gell's, when I was there—and he then spoke to the effect that he was one of them, but I cannot recollect his words—his brother also told me that Mingo had

---

25 Pinckney Street while a Patrick Duncan, who ran a candle and soapmaking business, lived on the Cannonsbridge Road.

78. Working for his owner, John Gell, who ran a livery stable, Monday Gell's harness shop was located on Meeting Street.

79. Owned by Alexander Berry, who worked as a clerk on D'Oyley's Wharf, Hales Berry worked in a tailor's shop on Boundary Street. He was never arrested or examined.

joined—Lewis the Mattress maker, said to me one day that he had something particular to say to me, of what was going to happen here, but that as he was a country born, they did not choose him—I took his meaning—Lewis Remoussin told me one day that when it broke out, he would be one—and that in the mean time he would be leagued in it—this was before 16th. June—Sandy Vesey, said he knew as much about this business as any one—and was engaged in it—this was after Jesse was taken up—Miss Datty's cook, a frenchman, said to me as I was Country born I should not know anything of what was going on 'till the horn blew and it broke out—I heard Tom Russell say in Monday Gell's shop that he was to make pikes—Monday, at the time, was working and may not have heard him.

《THE TRIAL of JOE, a Negro Man belonging to Mr. Jore—His owner attending.》

Perault examined and said I met Joe at corner of Boundary and Wall Street, he said to me how does this business stand now—this affair—I don't want to go home before I see this business (meaning the rising against the whites) terminates—he was then a runaway, and belonged to the man who keeps a shoe shop in King Street by Mr. Harts[80]—We parted—the next time we met was at Monday Gell's when the spears were on the Table—Joe said to Monday Gell in my presence that the french people would be ready when they were ready, and that he was one of them—the 3 times I met Joe was when we met Louis—after Louis parted Joe said that his master's store in King Street was not yet open, and that there were plenty of arms at Mr. Duquercron's Store near the Inspection, even to Bayonets[81]—he said that when we raised we must all run in there, break the door open and get arms—

Cross examined by Mr. Jore—he told me that he had run away, but I did not know it myself—this was about 1st. June—the 2 times was before any one was taken up on this business the 3rd. time I met him was on 15th. June—Our meetings were accidental.

Charles Drayton examined and said—I met Joe 3 or 4 times at Monday's—he generally speaks like a parable, that is gives hints and so forth—he said the french band was armed through out, and were ready, and he was ready, but

---

80. Nathan Hart ran a dry goods store at 139 King Street.
81. A merchant, Francis Duquercron ran his business from a store on the King Street Road that sold, among other goods, arms and ammunition.

he did not know how to trust country born—this he said in Monday's presence.

Monday Gell examined and said—Joe has been often at my shop, and I and he talking of this concern—he said he knew the french who were to join, but as they did not speak to him, he did not speak to them—that he was one of them who had joined—this was better than a month ago

Cross examined—he comes to my shop as a friend, and to get me to do work for him—he insinuated that he would be an active man.

《Mr. JORE and Col. CROSS testified that Joe's general conduct was good.
The Court *unanimously* found JOE GUILTY, and passed upon him the sentence of DEATH.》

《The trial of MINGO, a Negro Man, the property of Mr. William Harth—His owner attending.》
Monday examined and said he told me in my shop that Peter Poyas had told him of this business—and that he was to take his master's horse and act as a horseman in the fight—

Cross examined by Mr. Harth—this was before Peter was taken up on the 2nd. June—he was often at my Shop, and knows me well—he asked me if I know Peter—I said yes, and that he had spoken to me, he said so too—I some times visit the Society he belongs to—George Wilson is his Class leader—

Charles Drayton examined and said—I have seen Mingo Harth at Monday Gell's—he was talking about the rising—he said expressly he was one.

Cross examined—this was after William and Edwin were first taken up—
[Harth's trial continued on 16 July]

《The trial of JACK, a Mulatto Man, belonging to Mrs. Purcell—Mr. Thomas Smith, the brother of his owner, attending.》
Monday Gell says—I have seen him and Vesey talking together before my door—he told me that he was one of those to raise against the Whites—and Vesey told me so before—the message that Frank gave me to give to Vesey I got Jack to carry to Vesey for me—the message was that he had just come from the country—that he had there got 4 plantations of men to join and to

go to Vesey's and ask him to be at home at night as he would call on him—I know he carried it, because Vesey told me so that night—he came to my Shop afterwards, and said to me he was looking for Vesey and be sure that I called no name

Cross examined by W. Smith—not material

Frank Ferguson examined and said—I know Jack Purcell, but not that he is concerned in this business—I did give to Monday Gell a message for Vesey.

Charles Drayton examined and said—Jack told me that he had been at his Master's plantation and tried to get people to join in this business—but he could not go again—he said he had joined, and asked me where Lot lived that he was the proper person to go in the country to bring the people down—

Cross examined by the prisoner who stated that a meeting was called by Lot on Stono, but that Lot did not come.

《THE PRISONER asked permission to cross-examine Charles, which was granted; but his questions were such, that no one could well answer them but himself. In the course of this examination he admitted, that a large meeting had been called on Stono[82] by Lot, and that considerable preparations were made to receive him, but that Lot did not attend, and he was requested to reprove him for not doing so.
THE COURT *unanimously* found Jack GUILTY, and passed upon him the sentence of DEATH. A few moments preceding his execution, he made the following CONFESSION to the Intendant of Charleston:
If it had not been for the cunning of that old villain Vesey, I should not now be in my present situation. He employed every stratagem to induce me to join him. He was in the habit of reading to me all the Passages in the newspapers that related to St. Domingo, and apparently every pamphlet he could lay his hands on, that had any connection with slavery. He one day brought me a speech which he told me had been delivered in Congress by a

---

82. The largest slave rebellion in South Carolina's history took place along the Stono River in September 1739, when a band of enslaved Angolan plantation workers rose. In the attempt to reach Saint Augustine in Spanish Florida, the rebellious slaves destroyed a number of plantations and killed a number of planters and their families. The militia, however, quickly crushed the rebellion. See Wood, *Black Majority*, 308–30; Pearson "'A Countryside Full of Flames,'" 22–50.

Mr. King on the subject of slavery;[83] he told me this Mr. King was the black man's friend, that he Mr. King had declared he would continue to speak, write and publish pamphlets against slavery as long as he lived, until the Southern States consented to emancipate their slaves, for that slavery was a disgrace to the country.》

Adjourned to 11 O'Clock

Give notice of the following trials for tomorrow at 5 O'clock (p.m.)

Smart	Robert Anderson
William	Mrs. Colcock
Saby Gaillard	A free man
Jack	Estate Taylor
Pharo	Thompson
Lewis	Chappeau
Sandy Vesey	J. J. Schnell
Paris	Mrs. Ball

TUESDAY, 16 JULY 1822

Present the same Court

Frank Ferguson examined and said—I know Jack Purcell, but not that he is concerned in this business—I did give Monday Gell a message for Vesey—

Mingo Harth's Defence—

George Wilson examined and said—I never saw Monday Gell at my Society—he would not have been admitted as he was a member of the African Society.

Cross examined—he might have been there and I not have known it—there are some times 60 or 100 persons present.

Peter Parler, a free black man—I have never seen Monday Gell at my Society.

Cross examined I am generally at meetings unless sick.

《The Court *unanimously* found Mingo GUILTY, and passed upon him the sentence of DEATH.》

---

83. Rufus King, a U.S. senator from New York, often spoke out against slavery during the debates over Missouri. His most notable speech on the issue was printed in *Niles Register*, 4 December 1819.

《The trial of SMART, a Negro Man, the Slave of Mr. Robert Anderson—his owner and M. King, Esq., his Counsel attending.》 Arraigned and plea not guilty—confessions handed to the court.

Frank Ferguson Examined and said—I have seen the prisoner at Vesey's—he told me in the presence of Vesey he had joined and would be ready whenever called on—Vesey sent him one evening to call on me.

Cross examined—I think at Vesey's there were present Monday and Charles and others—

Monday Gell examined and said—I saw him (Smart) at Vesey's in the day—Perault and Peter Cooper were also there—I have often conversed with him on this business & he seemed to be as much in it as possible—I never asked this man to join—Vesey brought all of us into it—he belongs to the same gang that I did—

Cross examined—I was not the first man who spoke to him—I first saw him at Vesey's—he was as much attached to me and called me Pa and my wife Ma—I don't know that he ever got any one to join, and think he would have told me if he had—he was just such another as myself. I had a list with about 40 on it—but tore it up on the first discovery—he belongs to the African Church.

Perault examined and said—He (Smart) is a drayman and engaged in this business, and in the same company and confessed the same to me—I have met him at Veseys and at Bulkley's farm—at Vesey's on Sunday in the day, and there was Monday Gell also— where we talked about this rising 2 times at Bulkleys farm where were 13 in all—Smart and I have often spoken and promised to fight by one another against the White people. On Saturday the 15th. Smart got 2 muskets from Mr. Fordham's shop[84] to carry up to Gadsden's Wharf—they were shortly after taken away from Smart's dray, on which he was carrying them and he, Smart, made off with himself—I was present, one was for me, one for Smart. We borrowed the muskets from my Brother—

Cross examined—I met twice at Vesey's—he told me first and got me to join.

《The Court *unanimously* found Smart GUILTY, and passed upon him the sentence of DEATH.

84. This shop stood on Gillon Street.

When Smart was arraigned he pleaded Guilty to the charge, and his Counsel handed to the Court his confession in writing; but the Court advising that the plea of guilty should be withdrawn, his Counsel did so and pleaded Not Guilty. The CONFESSION handed to the Court was not used against him, but is now given to the public.》

Smart Anderson's Confession delivered to the Court by Mr. King, his Counsel, his master also being present.

Smart says that Monday Gell invited him to go up the road to Mr. Bulkley's Farm on Sunday about three months ago when there were upwards of thirty persons present—among them Bulkley's man Billy—Smart said he would not trust Country men—believes Denmark Vesey was there—did not see him—About four months ago, or going on 4 months say, William Garner drayman he told him to expect people from St. Domingo—white people would like to kill as many as they could—I call Monday Gell and his wife May about three weeks before going up to the farm—Monday Gell asked him to join him by telling him they were in servitude, licked and cuffed and abused &c—he spoke to Smart about St. Domingo people—turn and fight the white people, Smart said we can't do that, but Gell said we would make a contrivance to do it—Monday Gell told Smart that Gullah wanted to begin when the negroes of the African Church was taken up in 1818[85]—if Smart told any thing they would kill him, and made him hold up his hand and swear not to tell anything—Smart asked when they intended to raise—on Saturday night previous to the death of Dr. McCall—Monday told him, the old man said, we must begin tonight about 10 o'clock—Smart says to Monday he must stop it that Monday must send word to the old man to stop it, that it was a great sin—Smart met at Monday Gell's a black man named Jack Glen, a painter—when at the farm of Mr. Bulkley's met a snake at the gate which the old man (meaning Vesey) killed and one of them says that's the way we would do them—saw Monday and he says, they had better begin about 8 o'clock before the guard meet and if they don't do that, meet away on the green some where by the lines, march down through the streets, come down to the Guard house—Monday told him there were three or four gangs—asked him some questions about the mode of attack which he consented to—Monday told him that they would have a meeting or setting up at night and begin then—Smart says he did not agree to have a fire in the city—At a meeting at Monday Gell's house, Denmark Vesey present—Smart asked him if you were going to kill the women and children—Denmark answered what was the use

---

85. A reference to the disturbances outside the AME church when a large number of black worshipers, including minister Morris Brown, were arrested.

of killing the louse and leaving the nit—Smart said, my God, what a sin—Vesey told Smart he had not a man's heart, told Smart that he was a friend to Buckra—Monday told Smart that they sent to several places in the Country—Jack Glen, a black man, wanted to borrow Smart's horse to go up the Country—Smart said he had not one to lend—said must go to the country that day Sunday to Goose Creek[86]—the time he was at the farm, they told Smart, they had long things like his arm to put handles—that they would make contrivance—Vesey told him one day after they had taken the place, they would take the money, and he would go in a vessel and put as many as he could, and go back to his own Country. Vesey told Smart that all the powder was at the Magazine about three miles out of town, and they must take it, could easily get it—said they knew about a place in Queen Street opposite Planters Hotel, where there was arms &c.[87] the old man (meaning D. Vesey) said that they were to attack the guard house, in three of four ways—and they would get all the arms—Smart said he never heard about sending the two persons to St. Domingo—Monday told Smart that were about to engage some draymen in it—but he did not know how to trust them—Monday told him that they met every other night, and he would tell him more about it when he saw him again—The old man (meaning Vesey) told him to get some draymen who had horses, if you hear of a good ride, make him Captain of Troop—When they met they did not pray at the meeting in the kitchen—Smart says he was only there about an hour at the neck meeting—Peter Poyas was not at that meeting—Smart told Monday not to put his name on the list they had—Peter was not at the meeting, but was to go with us—Monday said that he expected Peter there—Smart denies any knowledge (after being repeatedly asked) of any deposit of arms, ammunition or that he promised to do any particular act in the business, or that he knows of any other person engaged in this business, than those he has already mentioned, and also that he never asked any other person to join in this affair.

《THE TRIAL of PHARO, a Mulatto Man, the property of John N. Thompson—His owner and David Ramsey, Esq., his counsel attending.》 Arraigned plea not guilty and put on trial.

Charles Drayton examined and said—Pharo told me himself in Monday's shop that he was engaged in the conspiracy. I met him one day with a Scythe

86. A small settlement located on a tributary of the Cooper River, Goose Creek was several miles outside Charleston.

87. Located at 60 East Bay Street in the city's port quarter, the Planters Hotel was an important meeting place for the city's commercial leaders.

in his cart which he told me he was carrying to a blacksmith's to have made into a Sword—about a week after and previous to the 16th. he said he was going to meet some young men who could tell him all about it—I have met him several times at Monday's.

Cross examined by Mr. Ramsey, his counsel—He bragged of what he could and would do with the white people—I did not hear Pharo tell a man to make a candlestick for him—

Monday Gell examined and said—I know from our talk about it together that he was one—he said he was making ready for the rising—2 days after Peter was taken, he told me, that if he could get a Ticket and a $50 bill, he would take his horse and run away—before he would be taken—On Sunday, about 2 weeks after Peter was taken up the 1st. time, he pointed to the Archdale Church where the white people were and said, when shall we be like them—I said, when God pleased—Sunday before I was brought here, he carried me to his Stable and said he had told his master, he had nothing to do in this business which was a lie.

Cross examined—Charles told me that Pharo had a Scythe which he was going to make into a Sword—

Perault Examined and Said—I know that he is one—one day in the street we met and conversed on this business when he told me, that he had carried something to a blacksmith to have a sword made for himself—I know he was just as willing as myself to join—

Cross examined I met him in Jim Yeadon's yard.
《The Court *unanimously* found Pharo GUILTY, and passed upon him the sentence of DEATH.》

《The trial of SANDY VESEY, a Negro Man, the property of J. J. Schnell—His owner attending.》 Arraigned plea not guilty and put on trial.
Charles Drayton Examined & Said—He (Sandy) had a hand in the rising—He told me that a gentleman had taken him up and asked him if he knew any thing about Jesse—that he said no—as there was no occasion to inform that the men knew how to make cartridges and would make some—he told me in Monday's Shop that he was one of those who had joined & was ready.

Cross examined—he did not tell me to what company he belonged he never gave his name to be put on a list that I know of.

Monday Gell examined and said—He (Sandy) has been in my Shop and he told me that he had joined—He said on Sunday 16th. in Archdale Street that he was waiting for Jesse who had gone to get a horse to go into the Country—he was frequently in my Shop, but only once spoke about this business—he appeared to be anxious and zealous about it—he belongs to the African Church.

Cross examined—nothing material

Mr. E. P. Simons—Sworn—The day after Jesse was taken up, I examined the fellow who stated that Jesse had told him "Vesey, the guard is too strong tonight"—Sandy is a peaceable character—Jesse and himself married sisters—

⟪The Court *unanimously* found Sandy Vesey GUILTY, and passed upon him sentence of DEATH; but recommended to the Governor to pardon him *upon condition that he be transported out the limits of the United States.*⟫

⟪The trial of PARIS, a negro man belonging to Miss Ball—Mr. Minot as the friend of his owner attending.⟫ Arraigned, plea not guilty upon his trial.

Monday—Examined and said—He (Paris) and Saby Gaillard were frequently in my Shop—the week after Peter was taken he came to me and said your name is called, be on your guard—He acknowledged he had joined and frequently came to me to know how the thing was going on—he belongs to the African Church.

Perault examined and said—I knew that he knew of this business—I saw him at Monday's and heard him speaking of this business—he was as much in it as I am.

⟪The Court *unanimously* found Paris GUILTY, and passed upon him the sentence of DEATH, but recommended to the Governor to pardon him *upon condition that he be transported out of the limits of the United States.*⟫

⟪The TRIAL OF SABY GAILLARD, a free black man—Mr. Wesner attending on his behalf as his friend.⟫

Monday examined and said—Saby frequently came to my Shop and talked on this business—he and Denmark Vesey in my shop talked on this business—he took out one day out of his pocket on the bay a piece of newspaper, and asked me to read it—I did so at my Shop, and afterwards he asked me if I had read it—I said yes—'twas about Boyer's battles in St. Domingo against the Spaniards—and he said to me afterwards, if he had men he could do the same as Boyer—and that he could whip 10 men himself[88]—

Cross examined he agreed with Vesey's discourse which was to kill the whites.

Perault examined and said—Saby said to me one day after Peter was taken up—I advise you to have nothing to do with this affair—let the Lord finish it and leave it to those who began it—Monday told me before this that Saby was concerned, and had given him a piece of paper to read.

⟪THE COURT found Saby Gaillard GUILTY, and passed upon him the sentence of DEATH, but recommended to the Governor to pardon him *upon condition that he be transported out of the limits of the United States.*⟫

⟪The trial of WILLIAM, a Negro Man, the Slave of Mrs. Colcock—Mr. D. D. Bacot[89] attending as the friend of his owner.⟫ Arraigned plea not guilty on his trial.
Monday Gell examined and said—William has often been at my Shop, and asked me what was going on—I did not tell him any thing—one the day he said to me a brother told him 500 men were making up for this purpose, he did not say that he was one.

Charles—I met him 2 or 3 times at Mondays.

Perault—I met him at Mondays several times.

William—The prisoner states that when he went so often to Mondays, it was to hear what was going on in Congress, as the blacks expected that Congress was going to set us free—and what was going on was printed in all the papers, so that every body, black as well as white might read it (he alluded to the Missouri question see his confession to Capt. Jervey).[90]

William Colcock's Confession to Thomas H. Jervey[91]—
Pompey Bryan told me that Mr. Bryan's Coachman held a Commission or was one of the Officers of Denmark Vesey—that some hundred draymen

---

88. Another reference to Haitian president Boyer's recent military success against the Spanish in Santo Domingo.
89. A bookkeeper employed by the South Carolina Bank, Daniel Bacot lived at 94 Church Street.
90. This refers to the Missouri Compromise of 1820.
91. Thomas Jervey was Inspector of Customs.

(Horsemen) of this City were engaged—this was a month ago (this was early June)—he also told me that Denmark Vesey had ordered them all out, so as to strike the first blow—on Saturday night 15th. June—I told him then that I should have nothing to do with it and would go home quietly to my bed—he said the same and we parted—One of Colonel Cross' wenches about house (of a yellow complexion having a small boy about 4 or 5 years old) told me that Joseph (Joe Jore), the former cook of Col. Cross, said that Morris Brown (the Bishop of the African Church) swore this on the Bible never to divulge the secret, even if they suffered death—Pompey Haig told me that there were some black frenchmen very skilful in making swords and spears, such as they used in Africa—this was about a month ago—he told me also that these were some frenchmen determined if those men were hung, they were ready to rise and defend them and he heard that there was a regular army ready in the woods to defend them—upon the separation of the Africans from the Methodist church—Henry Drayton (alias Harry Bull, one of the Bishops or Ministers in the African Church) in crossing the Mall in front of Flinn's Church told me on a Sunday afternoon that the Whites wanted nothing but a good spanking with a sword.[92]

The prisoner was liberated for want of testimony

《THE COURT *unanimously* found William NOT GUILTY, and discharged him.》

Robert Bounaparte	J. Mulligan
Adam (Mr. Robertson)	Sandy—J. Curtis
John (Mr. Robertson)	Butcher—J. Gibbes
Polydore—Mr. Faber	Isaac—P. Trapier
Cuffy—Charles Graves	

Arraigned—plea not guilty and all put upon their trial

《The trial of POLYDORE, a Negro Man, the property of Mrs. Faber—Mr. C. H. Faber, his brother's owner attending.》

Billy Bulkley examined and said—Polydore met once at Mr. Bulkley's farm at which meeting Gullah Jack was—he agreed with the rest to rise against the whites—on Sunday early in the morning when the people were to rise Polydore brought to the farm three pike poles and told me to let them stay—that Robert was coming—he belongs to the African congregation

Harry Haig examined and said Polydore was in Jack's company—I met him at the meeting at Bulkley's farm where they were talking about rising against the whites and Polydore agreed to join in it.

---

92. Known formally as the Second Presbyterian Church, this place of worship was colloquially known as Flinn's Church, after its founder and first minister, Andrew Flinn.

Cross examined—Jack was there and when he made the proposition to join and ride against the whites all present gave him an answer to join.

⟪The Court *unanimously* found Polydore GUILTY, and passed upon him sentence of DEATH.⟫

⟪The trial of ROBERT, a Negro Man, the property of John Robertson—His owner attending.⟫
Charles Drayton examined and said I met him at Tom Russell's when he went for the pikes and Tom said the pikes are at your house—Tom Russell asked him if he was not to go into the country for the people—he said he had sent word.

Cross examined—I saw him at Tom's about dark—it seemed to me, from the conversation that he was going to fix the pikes—

Billy Bulkley—Robert belongs to Gullah Jack's Company—he was at the meeting of Gullah Jack's party at Bulkley's farm—he was at 2 meetings & he tried to fire the pistol off but could not—same day the Pike Poles were brought he told me not to stir, that the white people had heard of this business—Robert told me that Gullah Jack was the head man in this business—he said Gullah Jack went to Father Morris Brown about this business, and that Father Morris said he was going to the north[93]—but if you can get men, you can try this business, but don't call my name—any thing that Jack wanted, he sent Robert for—if any thing happened to Jack, Robert would be the next man—when Polydore brought the poles, he said, Robert would know what to do with the poles, and when Robert came he said let the poles lay there—the whites have found out this business—

Cross examined—There was no dispute between me and the Rope walk people—

⟪The Court *unanimously* found Robert GUILTY, and passed upon him sentence of DEATH.⟫

John Enslow
Charles Shubrick
Seymour Kunhardt
Dick Simms
Scipio Sims
} Arraigned, plea not guilty except Bacchus Hammet who acknowledges his guilt, see his confession

---

93. AME minister Morris Brown may have been traveling to Philadelphia, the headquarters of the AME church, on church business.

John Taylor
Pierre Louis Chappeau } Arraigned and plea not guilty
Mingo Lowndes

Lot Forrester
Isaac Harth } Arraigned and plea not guilty

Adjourned to 11 o'clock

WEDNESDAY, 17 JULY 1822

Present the same Court and Col. Drayton
《THE TRIAL of JACK, a Negro Man belonging to Mr. J. S. Glenn.》
Arraigned plea not guilty on his trial.
Charles Drayton—Examined and said—He is engaged in this business—we have spoken together and he told me, he belonged to the horse company—I have met him once at Vesey's, at a meeting about this business—Glenn there quoted Scripture to prove he would not be condemned for raising against the whites—he read a Chapter out of the Bible—I have often met him at Mondays where he was talking of this business—I have often conversed with him when he always said he was one and he would rather be a horseman—he belongs to the African Church.

Monday Gell—Examined and said—He was engaged in it, he and I often talked about it, and he was making every preparation as well as himself about it—I once saw him at Vesey's when we were talking of the plans—He said as he had lame feet, he would rather be a horseman. Vesey looked on him as one of his followers or men—I met him on the evening of the 15th. June in the street with Benjamin Cammer—he said that Ben. belonged to the horse, after they had parted—he said he was preparing to rise on Sunday the 16th. June—he was often at my Shop—Charles Drayton was sometimes present.

Perault Examined and said—He was concerned as much as myself—I met him at Monday's first, where he said he was one, and the 3rd. time I met him at Vesey's when we met purposely on this affair—Ned Bennett and Peter Poyas were there—Jack agreed to go into the Country to bring down the people to fight against the Whites before the 16th. June, he sent his wife to me to say he wanted to get my horse to go into the Country—at this meeting Jack carried about a hat to get money to pay a man to make pikes, I gave 12½ cents—Jack put in the same—2nd. time I met him at the Battery,[94] he said he

---

94. The Battery consisted of a sea wall that ran around the tip of the peninsula on which Charleston stood. It quickly became a popular place to meet and walk and from which to fish.

was going into the Country to bring the blacks down, he said he had joined as a horseman—at the meeting at Vesey's besides Ned and Peter, Monday, Charles, Bacchus and Smart Anderson were present—John Mitchell and several others whose names I know not.

Bacchus examined and said—I saw him at Vesey's the first time I met there—he was the man who reads the Bible—he passed a hat around that night for the contribution—Monday, Charles, Pharo and Smart and others whom I know not were present.
《The Court *unanimously* found Jack GUILTY, and passed upon him the sentence of DEATH.
[*Note*: On the trial of Charles Billings, it was proved, that Jack Glenn intended to sleep at Mr. Billing's Livery Stables on the night of the 16th June, for the purpose of assisting in saddling horses for the colored people.]》

《The trial of LOT, a Negro Man, the property of Mr. Forrester—His owner attending.》
Monday examined and said—He and I have been talking about this business, and he said he was one engaged in this insurrection, and was making ready—this was at my Shop where he frequently was, and always talking on this business—he was one of the African Church—but I believe he has been turned out—

Cross examined—not material.

Frank Ferguson Examined and Said—I heard him tell Vesey that he had gone up to Santee, but before he got there, he met some black persons who told him that the driver had heard it, and told the overseer—and that he in consequence had to make his escape—

Jack Purcell Examined and Said—He was to have gone up to Stono to a large meeting when they made great preparations for him—but he did not come—I was then up there—I afterwards met him at Mondays, and taxed him about not fulfilling his promise—he said his business prevented him—

Ned Walker—belonging to Mr. Peigne[95] on behalf of the prisoner—I was at work with Lot when Vesey came there & Lot told him not to come in, that his master would not allow it—this was about the first of June—

---

95. J. L. Peigne, a grocer, who ran a store at 55 Market Street.

Jesse [Blackwood], in his confession before sentence was passed on him and in the presence of the prisoner, stated that I am guilty, and so is that man, he is as deep in it as I am, if I am hung, he ought to be hung, and if he is passed over, no man ought to be condemned by the Court—Lot was the man who said nothing could be done without fire; and he had the combustibles for it. Note: This he said on Gibbs and Harpers Wharf where a quantity of slow match was found.

《Lot denied Jesse's accusations, and as no one at that time but Jesse acccused him, against whom Lot volunteered his evidence and was principally instrumental in his conviction, the Court dismissed Lot. After Monday, Jack (Purcell) and Frank had been arrested, however, Lot (fearing that would inculpate him) absconded, and was arrested through the vigilance and activity of several gentlemen, who plant in St. James' Santee, as he was attempting to effect his escape across Hibben's Ferry, for the purposes (it is supposed) of getting beyond the limits of the State.

A quantity of slow match which was found on Gibbs' and Harper's Wharf, and then in court, was shewn to Captain C. L. Black, Arsenal Keeper,[96] who testified that the slow match produced to him resembled that in the Arsenal precisely, and he believed it to be part of the same. [Note: Lot was proved by the next witness to have been in the employment of Mr. Peigne, who is often engaged in the Arsenal, and sometimes has servants with him there.]

The Court *unanimously* found Lot GUILTY, and passed upon him the sentence of DEATH.》

《The trial of ADAM, a Negro Man belonging to Mr. John Robertson—His owner attending.》

Harry Haig Examined and said—I met him at Bulkley's farm at a meeting there for rising against the Whites—I know that he belongs to Gullah Jack's Company and that the meetings were for considering on this subject—he did not tell me that he was one, but I heard him agree to be one in this purpose—I heard him acknowledge that he was in Gullah Jack's company—he was one of the African Church—

Billy Bulkley Examined & said—He was twice at Bulkley's farm and once at Thayer's to attend the meeting there—he belonged to the Gullah Company to rise against the Whites—he told me so—I heard him say so more than once.

---

96. Christopher Black also worked as an attorney at 13 Guignard Street.

Cross examined—This business was after I left the ropewalk.

《The Court *unanimously* found Adam GUILTY, and passed upon him sentence of DEATH.》

《The trial of JOHN, a Negro Man, the property of John Robertson—His owner attending.》
Harry Haig Examined and said—he was engaged in this business—belonged to Gullah Jack's Company and was at the same meeting with Adam—he acknowledged that he belonged to the same Company that I did—I met him but once at Bulkley's farm—he belongs to the African Church.

Billy Bulkley Examined & said—He belongs to the Gullah Company—I heard him say so once—he was twice at the farm—

《The Court *unanimously* found John GUILTY, and passed upon him the sentence of DEATH.》

《The trial of BUTCHER, a Negro Man, the Slave of Mr. Gibbs.》
Charles Drayton Examined & said—He belongs to the Company, and is engaged in this business—I met him at Bulkley's farm—he is one who acknowledged in my presence that he was to raise against the whites—the object of the meeting at Bulkley's was to consider about this business—he belongs to the African Church.

Billy Bulkley—Butcher Gibbes belongs to Peter Ward's religious class.
《Charles being the only witness against Butcher without any corroborating circumstances; THE COURT found him NOT GUILTY, but suggested to his owner the propriety of sending him away.》

PETER WARD on his trial—arraigned—plea not guilty—

The Court decided on the cases of the following persons and found:

Thomas Russell	guilty	Paris Ball	guilty
Louis Remoussin Cromwell	guilty	Polydore Faber	guilty
Joe Jore	guilty	Robert Robertson	guilty
Mingo Harth	guilty	Jack Glenn	guilty
Jack Purcell	guilty	Lot Forrester	guilty
Smart Anderson	guilty	Adam Robertson	guilty
Pharo Thompson	guilty	John Robertson	guilty
Sandy Vesey	guilty		

Adjourned 11 o'clock

THURSDAY, 18 JULY 1822

Present the same Court

Sentence of death was pronounced against the following Slaves, to be carried into execution on Friday the 26th. Instant 'twixt 6 and 9 o'clock in the morning on the Lines.

Julius Forrest	Paris Ball	Louis Remoussin
Tom Russell	Polydore Faber	Pharo Thompson
Joe Jore	Robert Robertson	Sandy Vesey
Mingo Harth	John Robertson	Jack Glenn
Smart Anderson	Adam Robertson	Jack Purcell
	Lot Forrester	

《The Trial of SCIPIO SIMS, a Negro Man, belonging to Mr. William Sims—His owner attending.》

Perault a witness examined and said—Scipio belongs to those who are to rise against the whites—he hired a horse from me on Saturday the 8th. to go into the Country to get the negroes to come down at the time the rising was to commence—I examined him myself to see if he was one of my friends to fight against the whites, I met him at Mr. Aikens Lot[97] after the 8th. when they walked down together as far as St. Philips and Wentworth Streets—we talked about this business—the 3rd time I met him near Mr. Murphey's[98] in King Street on Sunday previous to the execution of Peter Poyas—I then said to Scipio this thing was all up and now dead—Scipio replied that all the people he had engaged were cowards, and had drawn back, but that he was willing to go on as much as I myself could be.

Cross examined by his master—Scipio hired the horse, but another man took the horse who paid me $2 in part, and Adam, a free man, the remaining $1—the hire being $3—I don't know the man who took the horse, but I'd know him if I saw him again.

Re: Cross-examined—Scipio hired the horse and said he would send for it and when the man came for the horse, he said Scipio had sent for the horse—when my horse was brought back, the man was on my horse—and Scipio in company with him on another horse—my Stable was near Flinn's Church, and that came toward the lines—this was on Sunday evening 9th. June—he belongs to the African Church.

97. William Aikens was a merchant.
98. Peter Murphey ran a grocery store on the corner of King and Beaufain Streets.

Monday Gell Examined—Jack Purcell told me that Scipio had gone into the Country to collect people to come down.

Charles Drayton Examined—Monday told me pretty much what he has himself stated to the Court.

Mr. Sims—sworn on behalf of the prisoner—Scipio is an orderly, sober and industrious Servant, I raised him and we have worked together.
[Sims' trial continued on 19 July]

《The trial of DICK, a Negro Man, the Slave of Mr. William Sims—his owner attending.》

Perault Examined—Dick and I met on a Saturday evening in the Cabinet Makers Lot next to Monday's—when we met on this business, Gullah Jack, George Vanderhorst, Charles Drayton—Jack said he was going in his canoe into the Country to get people. Dick said he belonged to Gullah Jack's band, and said he was willing and ready like me—2nd. time we met at the corner of Market Street we walked up King Street & he told me he was ready at anytime—the 3rd time I met him 'twixt Crafts and Smiths Wharf and we set down and conversed on this business. I again asked him and he again said he was ready at any time we were ready—never met him any where else—

Cross examined—When I went to the meeting on the Lot, Dick was there before me—

Harry Haig examined—Dick belonged to Gullah Jack's company. I met him at Bulkley's farm & he confessed he was ready and willing to join—the meeting was about this business—he joined before I did—

Cross examined—we all consulted together at the meeting, and all agreed—this was a little before this business broke out.

Charles Drayton—I saw Dick in the Lot of the Mahogany shop, near Monday's attending one of the meetings—he was one of Jack's company—this he said out of his own mouth & that he was ready (the prisoner confessed he was at this house, but went there to see some one).

Billy Bulkley—Dick was at 3 of the meetings on this business—one at Thayer's and twice at Bulkley's farm—he was there when they tried to fire off the pistol, and it went off in his hands—(the prisoner confessed he was sometimes at Bulkley's farm to see Billy).

Cross examined—If I had not been there I would not have known of this business.

Re-examined—When ever he came, he came in company with Gullah Jack, they met at the farm to talk on this business.

⟪The Court *unanimously* found Dick GUILTY, and passed upon him sentence of DEATH.⟫

⟪The trial of BACCHUS, a Negro Man, belonging to Mr. Benjamin Hammet—Francis S. Belzer, Esq., his owner's Counsel.⟫
Perault—I engaged Bacchus myself to join in this business—he was one of my recruits—I carried him to Vesey's myself—he was willing to join—Bacchus gave one keg of powder and gave it to Vesey who carried it to Mondays—he promised to give me a Sword, but did not do so—

Cross examined—Bacchus told me that he carried the powder to Veseys.

Monday Gell examined—Bacchus told me he was one in this business—he had often been at my Shop and I there had a keg of powder got by him—I saw him one night at Vesey's.

Cross examined—Bacchus and Perault brought the powder to my Shop—

Charles Drayton—Examined—I met him at Monday's and at Vesey's, I was present when he brought the powder to Vesey's—he told me he had got 3 swords—one for himself, one for Perault, and one for Ned Bennett—add his confession.

Further Confession of Bacchus, taken July 17, 1822.
Bacchus states that at the first commencement of the African church when the City Guard took up many negroes on a Sunday (which was when Bacchus's former master, Mr. Feraud, was a City Warden)[99] that the meeting of negroes was for the purpose of insurrection or to use his own words, Monday said to him before Perault "that the time we had the uproar about the African Church[100] we been after the same thing, but had to put it off, that now they begin to raise all about it" that when Perault took him to

99. Thomas Feraud lived on Tradd Street.
100. Presumably Bacchus is here referring to the demonstration outside the AME church in the summer of 1818, when the authorities arrested a large number of black worshipers.

Denmarks, he told him it was to go to a Class meeting—and he thought so when he first went into Denmark's and saw the big book on the table—that after they called him one side and told him what it was about, he was mistaken—Perault told him that they had 3 or 400 men—Monday Gell told him they had 2,000 men, so did Denmark—that they had a letter which was placed in the big book, which letter he believes was got from some free Country of black people—may be St. Domingo (he is positive it must be some free country)—that those people who are at the head of it will try and get themselves clear—and those who are not, won't be able—that the wise ones are at the root of it, know all about it. If he can see the man he describes as Vesey's son, he can identify him (Polydore Vesey, old Denmark's son, is said to be of the description given) Bennett's fellow he thinks is a blacksmith and appeared to have more to say at the meetings—spoke quite high flown—he is a Country born negro he believes—that the ring leaders and all who joined were to go up to the farm at the forks, and wait for the Country negroes—that Gullah Jack went up and came down, and told him at Monday Gell's house that they must not go up, that the patrol was very strong up there that Perault was very busy and Jack too, giving them all notice that Sunday, be ready to join at the farm—that Denmark charged them to be very particular who they got to join—that Perault prevented him from divulging it by coming after him often, by telling him not to tell, not to tell—That he has not been in it long (according to his description about 2d or 4th May)—that Perault tried to get some others to join, but that he never asked anyone.

《The Court *unanimously* found Bacchus GUILTY, and passed upon him the sentence of DEATH.》

《The Trial of JOHN, a Negro Man, the Slave of Mr. J. L. Enslow, pleaded guilty.
His owner, who was present, stated to the Court, that John was willing to make the only reparation in his power for his conduct, and would reveal all the information he was in possession of relative to the insurrection. The Court informed John that he might state whatever he had to say, but as they would not make him any promise, he must not make confessions in hopes of pardon—John said he would state all he knew of the intended insurrection and proceeded to make the following CONFESSION:》
Monday Gell led me in it and took me to Vesey's there was a large meeting—Vesey told the people the meeting was to rise up and fight the white people for their liberty—We always went to Monday's house afterwards—Monday

did all the writing—I heard that they were trying all round the Country to George Town, Santee, and round to Combahee &c. to get people.[101] Peter was also there he was one—Peter named Poyas' plantation where he went to meet Bellisle Yates, I have seen at the meetings, and Adam Yates, Naphur Yates—Dean Mitchell, Caesar Smith, George, a Stevedore—At Vesey's they wanted to make a collection to make pikes for the Country people, but the men had then no money—Monday Gell said Perault was one to get horses to send men into the Country—I heard a Blacksmith was to make pikes—Jack McNeil is engaged—I have seen them all at Mondays—Jack said he was one and would try to get men—The plan was to take the Arsenals and Guard houses for Arms, and not fire the town unless they failed—Monday was writing a letter to St. Domingo to go by a Vessel lying at Gibbes and Harpers Wharf—the letter was about the sufferings of the Blacks, and to know if the people of St. Domingo would help them if they made an effort to free themselves—he was writing this letter in March—I am not certain of the time—Perault was present when Monday wrote the letter, and also a painter named Prince Righton—I have seen Pompey Haig at Mondays but he neither assented or dissented—Jerry Cohen was at Vesey's and said to me he was one—I heard from Vesey and Monday, that they had engaged men from the Country—Peter Poyas said, he had sent into the Country to his brother to engage men, who would send him an answer—a party was to attack the Guard House and Arsenal—another the Arsenal on the neck—another to attack the Naval Store on Mays Wharf—another to attack the Magazine—another to meet at Lightwoods Alley and then try to cut off the companies from meeting at the places of rendezvous—I belong to the African congregation—On Saturday 15th. June a man was to be sent into the Country to bring down the people, and Rolla was to command (the Country people from Ashley River) at the Bridge—Ned Bennett and John Horry to meet at Mr. Horry's corner and Batteau to come down with Vesey's party—

《The Court, having used John as a witness in the subsequent trials, passed on him the following sentence—"That he be imprisoned in the Work House of Charleston, until his master, under the direction of the City Council of Charleston shall send him out of the limits of the United States, into which he is not to return under penalty of DEATH."》

---

101. Georgetown is a small coastal settlement about sixty miles north of Charleston; the Santee River, along which there were numerous plantations and farms, marks the northern boundary of the Charleston District; and the Combahee River runs into Saint Helena Sound in the Sea Islands, which lie about sixty miles south of Charleston.

FRIDAY, 19 JULY 1822

Present the same Court

《The trial of SCIPIO, a Negro Man, belonging to Mr. Wm. Sims—His owner attending.》 Mrs. Fick on behalf of the prisoner—
Examined by the Master—He never gave to me any arms to keep for him or anything else I have always thought him a steady, sober negro and never heard anything amiss of him.

Cross examined—Never said that Scipio had left a Sword or pistol with me.
《It was reported that Mrs. Fick said that Scipio had left a sword and pistol with her to keep for him.》

Agrippa, belonging to Mr. Perry—A witness for the prisoner—I requested Scipio to hire a horse for me to go into the Country with, about the last day of the first week of June, mine being sick—Scipio carried me to the man from whom the horse was hired, I don't know the man (from whom the horse was hired) he and I went up on horse back to my Mrs. plantation on Horse Savannah, where we went for my tools, and returned the next day, Sunday—this was all we went for—we did not go.

Cross examined—The man's name was Perault who lives on the green—I paid him $2 and when I returned paid him the other $1—when I received the horse Scipio was not with me—I had a pass—Scipio's name was not on the pass—I brought down my mallet, chisel and axe—I left town on Saturday about 10 o'clock about 2 weeks before this I was in the Country—
《As soon as Agrippa's examination ceased, Perault was brought into Court, and immediately recognized him to be the man who had hired his horse, though he did not know his name—The Intendant then committed Agrippa for trial. In consequence of this charge against Agrippa, whose testimony was so important to Scipio, Mr. Sims requested the court not decide on Scipio's case until Agrippa was tried, to which request the court acceded. Agrippa was not tried until five days after, as his owner asked time to send into the country and bring down some Negroes as witnesses who were on the plantation when Agrippa and Scipio arrived there—Agrippa's trial therefore was not the next after Scipio's; but in forming their decision on Scipio's case, the testimony given in Agrippa's was considered by the Court, it is thought adviseable, that, in this publication, the report of one trial should immediately succeed the other.
The Court *unanimously* found Scipio GUILTY, and passed upon him the following sentence: "That he be imprisoned in the Work-House of

Charleston, until his master, under the direction of the City Council of Charleston, shall send him out of the limits of the United States, into which he is not to return under penalty of death."⟫

⟪THE TRIAL of WILLIAM, a Negro Man, the property of Job Palmer—His owner attending.⟫ Arraigned—plea not guilty.
Monday Gell a witness examined—William belongs to the association to rise against the Whites—he and Vesey and Jack Glenn have been at my Shop together—they were talking on this business, and said he would do as much as any other man, & confessed that he had joined—Vesey seemed to regard him as one of his men and to feel confidence in him—he and I were to be in the same band under Vesey—he was often in my shop talking on this business—and never shewed any disposition to be off—this was before the first execution.

Cross examined by his master—The time that Vesey, Glen and William was at my shop 'twas when Vesey said there was but one minister who preached the Gospel—Sometimes he came to my Shop alone—the first time he came in, he asked for the newspaper—the first conversation he had was about the rising—

Charles Drayton a Witness examined—William is engaged in the insurrection—he said to Vesey in Monday's Shop that Vesey must not think that he would not fight—that he would fight as well as any other—I met him opposite the Circular Church on Dr. Simon's step—that it was a shame they should allow the men to be hanged, that he was ready to join in rescuing them from the gallows—this was the Sunday previous to Vesey's being hung—about 2 o'clock (p.m.).

Cross examined—I knew him long before—I met him just after William Paul was taken up at Vesey's—
⟪See Monday Gell's confession, in which he says that William promised Vesey to enlist as many men as he could. THE COURT *unanimously* found upon him the sentence of DEATH. [*Note:* His Excellency the Governor has pardoned William, upon condition that his Master transports him beyond the limits of the United States.]⟫

⟪The Trial of SEYMOUR, a Negro Man, belonging to Mr. William F. Kunhardt—His owner attending.⟫
Perault a witness—I met him once at Mondays with Smart Anderson where

he acknowledged he was one to rise that he belonged to Monday's company—I met him afterwards by the Exchange, where we talked of this business—& he was as much one as myself.
Cross-examined by his master.

Monday Gell—Seymour is one in this business—he brought to my shop about 2 months ago a racoon Skin to make a Cap of—and he then agreed to join us—he and Joe Jore are particular friends, I met him afterwards in Meeting Street where he again said he was willing.

《THE COURT *unanimously* passed upon him the sentence of DEATH; but recommended to the Governor that he should be pardoned *upon the condition that he be transported out of the limits of the United States.*》

《The trial of NAPHUR, ADAM, AND BELLISLE, three Negro Men, belonging to the Estate of Joseph Yates deceased—Jacob Axson, Esq. attending as their Counsel.》 Plea not guilty & put on their Trial.
Perault—Bellisle or Blarney was engaged in this business. I met him at Craft's north wharf—this was the first meeting—the 2nd. meeting at the corner of the Scale house on Smiths Wharf—he told me, that the night that the blacks were to rise, he would engage the people at Mr. Yates & myself will sleep at Mr. Mitchells, when his people slept on Smiths wharf, where they would commence the fight—Adam and Naphur met at Bulkley's farm, where we met on this business, where were Vesey, Monday, Charles, and Smart—I there told them they had done the worst thing they could to engage these people that all Charleston would know next day—the rope walk people will get them to join—Adam and Naphur, there acknowledged they had joined—on the 16th. I saw Adam on the Street when he said he was going up the road to meet the Country and Neck people, where he intended to remain that night and come down with those people—Bellisle belongs to the African Church—they are all Africans.

Cross examined by Mr. Axson—Naphur and Adam came up to the farm about 12 o'clock in the day on Sunday, and stayed there 'till 4 O'Clock—this was a Sunday in May—every man in the house agreed to join to rise against the whites—the meeting was for this express purpose—after Peter Poyas and the others were convicted—Bellisle and I came out of the Shop together to talk on this business—and I said we must rise and not let these people be hanged, and he said yes, we must do so; this was after he said to me, he would get the people to sleep at Mr. Mitchell's Shop on 16th. June when they were to rise—Adam told me that Charles Drayton had told him to go up the road on the 16th June and stay there 'till the alarm was given, and then come down with the neck and Country people—Adam and Naphur came up to the farm together—the Sunday was about the middle of May—

Charles Drayton—They are all in this business, I met Adam and Naphur at Bulkley's farm, where we met on this business and where they acknowledged that their hearts were in this business—Bellisle I met in the streets where he told me he belonged to it—I have also met him often at Monday's where he talked of it, said he was one of the army and ready and willing to go out—

Cross examined—Naphur & Adam at the farm said when the rising commenced they were ready—Vesey was there and spoke to the whole, and all who agreed to rise against the Whites were to hold up their hands—and Naphur and Adam held up their hands with the others.

John Enslow—I know the prisoners they are as much in the plot as I am, and I am in the plot—I have met them all at Monday's—Adam gave to Monday a knife to make a Scabbard for him, which he intended to use as a dagger—the knife was such a one as Rifle men wear[102]—I have heard Naphur at Mondays agree to join—I belong to Monday's company, Bellisle said he was in it—Adam and I have often spoken on the same subject—we all agreed to rise against the Whites and fight for our freedom.

Cross examined—I saw Adam deliver the knife to Monday, and say make a scabbard if this will do—We all agreed at Mondays to join.

Monday Gell—They all were in the habit of coming into my Shop to talk on this business—I first met Naphur and Adam at Bulkley's farm—Adam brought to me a long knife to make a scabbard for it, which he intended to use in the business—they belonged to my side which was Vesey's division—I delivered him afterwards the knife—

Cross examined—Naphur was but once in my shop—Bellisle and Adam often—At the farm, Den. Vesey explained his plan to all present and on the proposition to agree all assented, Naphur I met once at Bulkley's farm where as well as at my shop he expressly agreed to join—
Two other witnesses were ready to be produced, but twasn't thought necessary.

102. Enslow is referring to a bayonet.

《THE COURT *unanimously* found Naphur, Adam, and Bellisle GUILTY, and passed upon them the sentence of DEATH.》

《THE TRIAL of DUBLIN, a Negro Man, the property of Mr. Thomas Morris—Mr. C. G. Morris attending.》 Arraigned—plea not guilty.
Perault—Dublin said to me that Wm. Garner had engaged him to join against the Whites—he belongs to the African Church—

Charles Drayton—Dublin told me one day he had heard it, but that was all—
《THE COURT *unanimously* found Dublin guilty, and passed upon him sentence of DEATH, but recommended to the Governor to pardon him upon condition that he be transported out of the limits of the United States.》

《The trial of CHARLES, a Negro Man, belonging to Mr. Samuel Billings—His owner attending.》 Arraigned—plea not guilty.
John Enslow examined—Charles belongs to this business, we spoke on it at Mondays and he said that when we were ready, he would come out and join us—I met him twice at Mondays and both times said so—after Peter was taken, I met him on Edmonston's Wharf and he said the people were beginning to be frightened and we had better say as little as possible about it—

Perault—I met him at Mondays when I heard him say he was a horseman—I heard him say he was ready & willing.

Monday Gell—He told me once that Wm. Garner had spoke to him about a horse, but I don't know that he was one of us—he was frequently at my shop to get harness mended and he there conversed on this subject and he appeared willing to join & said he had joined

Cross examined—not material.

Charles Drayton—I have met him often, and he acknowledged he was one—Jack Glenn he said was to have slept at the Stable that night of the rising to assist and Saddle the horses for the Company. (Other witnesses were ready to depose to the same effect, but 'twas thought unnecessary to do so).

His master testifies to his general good character.
《THE COURT *unanimously* found Charles GUILTY, and passed upon him the sentence of DEATH.》

SATURDAY, 20 JULY 1822

Present the same court

《The trial of PRINCE, a Negro Man, the property of Miss Righton, Mr. Joseph Righton, attending.》 Arraigned—plea not guilty, put on his trial.
Jack Enslow—Witness examined—I have seen Prince in Monday's Shop, when Monday was reading the letter to St. Domingo he must have heard Monday—The brother of the Steward[103] who was to take the letter to St. Domingo was a General as I understand in St. Domingo

Cross examined by Mr. Righton—not material.

Monday Gell—I can't say that Prince was engaged—he came once to my Shop and then agreed to join, but I have not seen him since, and did not come back to say whether he would continue or not—I therefore did not put his name down on the list—this was long before 16th. June—I then read the list of names to him, but not the letter to St. Domingo—there were three other persons there.

Cross examined—he came there without any appointment.

Charles Drayton—I saw him in Monday's shop once, but I don't know anything against him.

Harry Haig—knows nothing against him.

No. 2 Captain Hubell attends
《The Court *unanimously* found Prince NOT GUILTY—but suggested to his owner to send him away.》

《The trial of PETER, an elderly Negro Man, belonging to Mrs. Cooper—Captain Sears Hubbell, attending.》 Arraigned plea not guilty put on his trial.
Jack Enslow—I have met him at Monday's, where he signified his consent and said he was willing to join—this was about 2 months ago.

---

103. Vesey gave his letter written to Haitian president Jean-Pierre Boyer to an enslaved mariner named Williams to deliver. This letter presumably requested military assistance from the Haitian president as well as telling him that the rebels intended to sail to his island after the rebellion.

Monday Gell—Peter said he would join and I met him once at Vesey's—he there said by word of mouth that he was willing to join—this was previous to 16th June—(prisoner says he is a Guinea negro)—he had passed my Shop driving his Cart but did not come in.

Perault Examined—Vesey told me to tell Peter he wanted to see him—I told him and he said he would go and did go, but I do not know what passed there—I don't know that he agreed—I came out of Vesey's and left him there—Vesey sent me to him on this business—I only delivered my message

Cross examined—At Vesey's I met Monday there too—

Charles Drayton—Do not know him.

Harry Haig—Do not know him.

Mr. Hubbell—Peter bears a good character—an inoffensive man.
《The Court *unanimously* found Peter GUILTY, and passed upon him the sentence of death; but *in consideration of age*, recommended to the Governor to pardon him *upon condition that he be transported out of the limits of the United States.* [*Note*: His Excellency the Governor has pardoned Peter on condition of his receiving twenty lashes.]》

《THE TRIAL of GEORGE, a Negro Man, the property of Mr. Bampfield—His owner attending.》 Arraigned—plea not guilty on Trial.
John Enslow—I met him at Mondays, where he said that if all the men in the room was of one mind he would make a remark—they said we are—he then said I have spoken to two men who agreed, and mentioned their names—when Monday said for God's sake, let them alone or they will betray us—(I did belong to the African church, but they turned me out for keeping a girl).

Monday—He was once in my Shop—the conversation related by John Enslow did not take place—every day there were numbers in my Shop on this business—he was often in my Shop.

Cross examined by Mr. Bampfield—not material.

Perault—I met him once at Monday's—George did agree to join as much as I did—I did not hear him say anything about engaging two men to join—This meeting was expressly on this business—I met him afterwards in the market, when he said the Guards were too strong, let the business lay still—I have not talked to him since anyone was taken up on this business.

Charles Drayton—Monday told me that Geo. Bampfield was one.
⟪The Court *unanimously* found George GUILTY, and passed on him the sentence of DEATH; but recommended to the Governor to pardon him upon condition that he be sent out of the limits of the United States.⟫

⟪The Trial of JEMMY, a Negro Man, belonging to Mr. Clement—His 2 young Masters present.⟫ Arraigned—plea not guilty.
Monday Gell—Jemmy is engaged in this business, belongs to my company—and he agreed in my Shop—he said he would like to know when this business would begin, as he had engaged some people in the Country where his wife lived, and he would have to bring them down—he has often come to my Shop and held conversations on this subject and confessed he was willing and had joined.

Perault—I saw Jemmy at Mondays—and he knew of it before me, for at the time he was talking on this business and it was the first time I had heard of it—he was one—he was willing—He belongs to the African Church.

Charles Drayton—He told me himself in Monday's shop that he was one—he one day brought to me on the Market Wharf two or three men who he said had agreed to join and belonged to the Country—these men said they had joined and were to carry the news into the Country (Jemmy has a wife at Wm. Moores in St. Thomas Parish), this was after Peter was taken up, but before his execution.[104]
⟪The Court *unanimously* found Jemmy GUILTY, and passed upon him the sentence of DEATH.⟫

⟪The Trial of JERRY, a Negro Man, the Slave of Mr. M. Cohen.⟫
John Enslow—Jerry I met at Vesey's & Monday's he agreed & said he was one & joined in the object of the meeting—which was to plan measures against the Whites—We have often spoken on this business—At Vesey's were met, were present, Monday, Charles, Rolla, Ned, Perault, Batteau, Smart, & Jack Glenn & near 30 men in all—they then handed round the hat to make collections to purchase pikes they were to be provided with dark lanterns to

---

104. A rural parish, Saint Thomas's lies between the Wando and Cooper Rivers to the east of Charleston.

enter stores for arms—Vesey said 100 pikes were made by a black man who worked by himself—they also wanted money to pay that black man's wages to his mistress—after Vesey was taken he was afraid to speak on this business.

Monday—He was often in my Shop & confessed he was one—his name was on my list with his consent—I did not meet him at Veseys—he said when we were consulting who should take a lead, he said he would be a leader—he was not there when money was collected to procure lanterns—I did not go to the meeting that night 'till 8 O'clock.

Cross examined—not material

Perault—He was at Vesey's when they made a Collection—I am not certain, but think that Monday was present—He (Monday) was there—John Enslow was also there—the collection was for purchasing Spears—He did say we had better stop this business—but still he was willing to go on, if we went on. Charles Drayton—nothing, Harry Haig, nothing, Billy, nothing—
《THE COURT *unanimously* found Jerry GUILTY, and passed upon him the sentence of DEATH.》

《The Trial of DEAN, a Negro Man belonging to Mr. Jas. Mitchell—His owner attending.》
Perault—I have seen Dean at Vesey's where he agreed as much as myself—We met purposely to make a collection for Spears—I heard him say he had joined & no one would be allowed to enter that house if he was not one—he belongs to the African Church—

Cross examined. John Enslow summoned him to attend the meeting (prisoner admits he was there).

John Enslow—I first told him of it—he told me afterwards he saw the thing was going on well, & he was glad of it—I asked him if he would like to go to Vesey's meetings, he said yes & went with me, he put in money at Vesey's. I saw him do it—Jack Glenn handed the hat around—We afterwards conversed & he was always of the same mind—he was on the night of the rising to meet at Vesey's and march down with his party.

Monday Gell confirms in part John Enslow testimony.
《THE COURT *unanimously* found Dean GUILTY, and passed upon him sentence of DEATH.》

⟪The trial of ISAAC, a Negro Man, the property of Mr. Wm. Harth—His owner attending.⟫

Monday Gell—He was engaged in this business he told me so himself—after Mingo was taken up, he told me that Mingo would get clear if Ed. Paul[105] did not testify against him—he said he also belonged to the horse company—Mingo told me that his brother was one too—

Cross examined. I conversed with him directly after Mingo was taken up.

William Paul—Edwin did positively say that all Mr. Harth's people were engaged in it.

Charles Drayton—Mingo told me that Isaac was engaged.

⟪THE COURT *unanimously* found Isaac GUILTY, and passed upon him the sentence of Death; but recommended to the Governor to pardon him *upon condition* that he be sent out of the limits of the United States.⟫

JOHN TAYLOR on his trial ⟪A Negro Man belonging to Mrs. Taylor—Mr. James Drummond attending.⟫

Charles Drayton—The prisoner told me one Monday morning before 16th. ult. he told me that all the horses were ready, but the patrol was so vigilant, they could not come out.

Cross examined.—I understood the horses to be intended for the insurrection—this conversation took place at my master's gate—the prisoner was as willing as myself and he did not refuse—I only conversed with the prisoner but once—and then he told me the horses were ready for the insurrection—William Garner told me that the prisoner was engaged in this affair—

Perault examined—The prisoner knows nothing of this transaction to my knowledge.

Monday Gell—I do not know that he is engaged.

Harry Haig—says the same thing.

John Enslow—says the same.

Billy Bulkley—says the same.

---

105. Edwin Paul was a slave owned by John Paul, who also owned William Paul.

Mr. Drummond gives the prisoner an excellent character.

《THE COURT *unanimously* found John NOT GUILTY, but suggested to his owner to send him away.》

《The Trial of PIERRE LEWIS, a Negro Man, the Slave of Mr. Chappeau—His owner attending.》

Charles Drayton—On Sunday when the Guard were out—the prisoner told me that something serious would happen, but that I was a Country born, and he was afraid to trust me—This conversation occurred on the 16th of June—(all the other witnesses were called and declared that they know nothing against the prisoner).

《THE COURT *unanimously* found Pierre Lewis NOT GUILTY, and discharged him.》

John Gates—James Happoldt and Charles Hazel were severally arraigned and pleaded not guilty

MONDAY, 22 JULY 1822

Present the same Court

Dick Sims	Guilty	Death
Bacchus Hammet	"	"
William Palmer	"	"
Seymour Kunhardt	"	Transportation
Naphur	"	Death
Adam Yates	"	"
Bellisle	"	"
Dublin Morris	"	Transportation
Charles Billings	"	Death
Prince Righton	Not guilty	suggest to his owner to ship him
Peter Cooper	Guilty	Transportation
George Bampfield	"	"
Jemmy Clement	"	Death
Jerry Cohen	"	"
Dean Mitchell	"	"
Isaac Harth	"	Transportation
John Taylor	Not guilty	suggest to his owner to send him out of the State
Pierre Lewis Chappeau		Not guilty
Butcher Gibbes	Not guilty	suggest to his owner to send him away
Saby Gaillard	Guilty	Transportation

Friday 26 'twixt 6 and 9 a.m. to be hung on the Lines and their bodies to be buried near the gallows or delivered to surgeons for dissection if required.
Lewis Remoussin
Sandy Vesey   } Recommended to transportation
Paris Ball

TUESDAY, 23 JULY 1822

Examination and confession of Monday Gell
The first time I heard of the intended Insurrection was about last Christmas from Denmark Vesey, who called at my Shop and informed me of it—Vesey said he was satisfied with his own condition, being free—but as all his children were slaves, he wished to see what could be done for them—he asked me to join, but I then positively refused to do so—I enquired of him, how many he had enlisted, and he mentioned the name of Peter Poyas, Ned Bennett, Rolla Bennett and Jack Purcell—I inquired if those were all, and he replied yes—he then departed and had no further correspondence with him, until about three months ago—I was then walking in Wentworth Street on my way to a man named Peet Smith up King Street, and was accosted by Frank Ferguson who told me, he had just returned from the Country and had collected four plantations of negroes—he requested me to inform Vesey that he would call on him that evening, and give him an account of his operations in the Country—I went to Jack Purcell's and requested him to carry the message for me being busy—on my return home in the evening I met Vesey's son-in-law at my door, who said that Vesey wished to see me—I accompanied him to Vesey's and there found Peter Poyas, Ned Bennett, Gullah Jack, Frank and his fellow servant Adam Ferguson—Frank then informed Vesey he had collected four plantations of Negroes, and said he would start on Saturday the 15th June to bring them to Town on the 16th—he said he would conduct them through the woods, and place them about three miles from town, until Sunday night—Vesey again urged me to join and I consented—This was about three months prior to the 16th. of June—Vesey from that time continued to visit the Shop in which I worked—Peter, Ned, Vesey, Frank, Rolla, Adam, Gullah Jack, Jack Purcell and myself, the party at Vesey's, then agreed to enlist as many men as we possibly could—Vesey even then ceased working himself at his Trade and employed himself exclusively in enlisting men, and continued to do so until he was apprehended—Shortly afterwards Vesey said he would endeavor to open a correspondence with Port au Prince in St. Domingo to ascertain whether the inhabitants there would assist us[106]—he said he would send letters there, and I advised him to

106. Port-au-Prince is the capital of Haiti.

do so if he could—Some time after this he brought a letter to me which was directed to President Boyer and was enclosed in a cover which was directed to the Uncle of the Cook of the Vessel by which it was sent—the name of this Cook was Williams—his Uncle was to open the envelope and present the letter to Boyer—this Vessel, a Schooner, had been repaired at the Ship yard at Gadsdens Wharf—and was afterwards brought to Vanderhorst's Wharf where she was then lying—I walked with Vesey to the Wharf—Perault was in company with us at the time—Vesey asked Williams the Cook, if he would carry the letter for him, and he consented to do so—we then returned each of us to his respective home—Nothing extraordinary took place after this, and I met no other band or association after this time but Vesey's particular company—Bacchus Hammet brought a keg of powder to my Shop, and said he would procure five hundred (500) muskets from his master's store on the night of the 16th. of June—Bacchus also told me that he could procure more powder, but did not say where—The plan was to break open all the stores where arms were deposited and seize them—after they had procured the five hundred muskets above mentioned, Vesey said he would appoint his leaders, and places of meeting about one week before the 16th of June, but the meeting for this purpose was prevented by the Captain of some of the principals before that period—Vesey determined to kill both women and Children—but I opposed it, and offended him in doing so—Peter and all the rest agreed to the opinion of Vesey in the murder of all—Some time before any discussions or apprehensions were made myself and Perault wished to drop the business—but thought we had gone too far to retreat—I know personally of no arms, except six pikes shewn to me by Gullah Jack, which were made by Tom Russell—I know of no lists except the one which I kept, containing about 40 names and which I destroyed after the first interruption and alarm—It was said that William Paul had a list, but I never saw it— William Garner told me that he was to command the Draymen and that he had procured twelve or thirteen horses—Jack Purcell told me that Scipio Sims had been at the Savannahs in the neighborhood of Bacons Bridge to obtain men[107]—Denbo Martin belonged to the party and informed me that Stephen Smith acknowledged that he was one—Charles Drayton and Perault have both seen Denbo at my Shop—Vesey originally proposed the second Sunday or the 14th of July as the day of the rising, but afterwards changed it to the 16th of June[108]—after the plot was discovered, Vesey said it was

---

107. Bacon's Bridge traversed the Ashley River just north of the small rural settlement of Dorchester.

108. July 14 commemorates the storming of the Bastille in Paris in 1789, an event that

all over—unless an attempt was made to rescue those who might be condemned, by rushing on the people and saving the prisoners, or all dying together—Vesey said that as Peter and Ned were accustomed to go into the Country, they must go there & recruit men—Vesey was in the habit of going to Bulkley's farm—William Palmer and Vesey were very intimate—Jack Purcell knew of this conspiracy before myself—I do not recollect any person who refused when I applied to him—Some took time to consider, but they all finally agreed—Vesey was considered by the whole party as a man of great capacity and was also thought to possess a bloody disposition—He had, I am told in the course of his life, seven wives—and had travelled through almost every part of the world, with his former master Captain Vesey—and spoke french with fluency—Morris Brown, Harry Drayton and Charles Corr are other influential leaders of the African Church were never consulted on this subject for fear they would betray us to the whites—Vesey had many years ago a pamphlet on the slave trade[109]—Vesey said that his eldest step-son was engaged in this affair—

《The Court had, previously to this confession, twice applied for and obtained from the Governor a respite for Monday, Charles Drayton, and Harry Haig, with a view to obtain from them the testimony and information they appeared willing to give. On the 24th day of July, after Monday had made his last confession, they addressed the following letter to the Governor.》

[See letter to Governor Bennett on 24 July]

《THE TRIAL of JACK, a Negro Man, belonging to Mr. Neil McNeill—Mr MacKenzie, the partner of Mr. McNeill attended.》

---

signaled the start of the French Revolution. In both colonial and early national periods, Charleston played a small role in French history. A large number of Huguenot (French Protestants) settled in the lowcountry after Louis XIV revoked the Edict of Nantes in 1685, becoming important members of the colony's planting and merchant communities. In April 1793, Citizen Edmond Genêt, the French minister to the United States, landed in Charleston to considerable fanfare. The establishment of several clubs dedicated to the support of the French Revolution as well as the arrival of French planters and their retinues of slaves escaping the revolution on Saint Domingue further added to the French presence in the city at the turn of the century. Joseph Vesey, then Denmark Vesey's owner, served on several committees that provided assistance to these refugees. The symbolic value of starting a rebellion on the anniversary of the French Revolution aside, it should be noted that July 14 not only fell on a Sunday in 1822, making it an ideal day on which to catch the city off guard, but also during the last quarter of the moon, thus enabling rebel leaders to assemble their forces under the cover of near-total darkness.

109. Such materials entered Charleston with some regularity. In 1809, for example, the city intendant confiscated several hundred antislavery pamphlets from the steward, a free black from New York City, of the *Minerva*. See Kennedy and Parker, *Official Report*, 159–60.

Monday Gell examined—The prisoner belongs to the conspiracy, and in consequence of his consent, I placed him on my list—he has been frequently at my shop, and Denmark Vesey frequently saw him at my Shop—he was never at my Shop at any appointed meetings—he is an African and came here about seven years of age—he belongs to the African church and he belongs to my Company.

Charles Drayton examined—I have met the person at Monday's several times—and I heard him in his presence acknowledge that he belonged to the conspiracy—after the executions of the first 6—he appeared to regret he had joined, and appeared alarmed—We had several conversations and he always appeared to exhibit the same feelings.

Perault Strohecker examined—I know the prisoner, but do not know that he is engaged in this affair.

John Enslow Examined—I have seen him often at Monday's shop and he has acknowledged his presence and mine that he had joined—he has spoke to me often on the subject in the streets and was always willing.

《THE COURT *unanimously* found Jack GUILTY, and passed upon him sentence of DEATH.》

BEN, the slave of Mrs. Cammer arraigned and plea not guilty—David Ramsey Esq. attended as his Counsel.[110]
This trial was postponed until tomorrow—

《The Trial of CAESAR, a Negro Man belonging to Mrs. Smith》 arraigned and plea not guilty—Mr. McDow attended for his mistress.
John Enslow Examined—The prisoner is engaged and confessed it to me—I have seen him often at Mondays—he belongs to the African Church, and is a native of Africa, and came here a boy (own: Mr. McDow)—he told me sometimes in the street he was engaged—After the execution of Vesey appeared fearful of the consequences—

Cross examined—I saw him twice at Mondays before 16th. of June and once after—

Monday Gell Examined—The prisoner is one of the party, and I placed him name on my list—he was always willing to join, there is no one more so.

110. Cammer's trial does not appear in Kennedy and Parker.

Cross examined—he was engaged some time before the affair was discussed—He was as zealous as myself—He was at my Shop often—

Charles Drayton Examined—The prisoner acknowledged to me at Mondays that he was engaged, and also several times in the street.
Cross examined—I saw him after the execution of Vesey, and he appeared in the same mind.

Monday Gell was called in at the request of Mr. McDow—he answered none of the questions.

Perault Called—He knows nothing against the prisoner, but knows him—The prisoner admitted in his defence that he had frequent conversations with the witness but denied that he had joined—
《THE COURT *unanimously* found Caesar GUILTY, and passed upon him the sentence of DEATH.》

《The Trial of AGRIPPA, a Negro Man belonging to Mrs. Perry, Mr. Edward Perry, the Son of his owner, his Counsel Benjamin F. Dunkin, Esq., Mr. Bartholemew Carrol, the friend of his owner, and Mr. William Sims attending.》 Arraigned and plea not Guilty.
Perault Examined—On 8 June at 10 O'Clock (a.m.) he met the prisoner, who said he was going into the Country on some business which would be good to me and him—On his return I went to him, when after some conversation, he had informed me, that he had gone into the Country to get men to join in this insurrection, and that he had procured some men—he hired a horse from me, for which he paid two dollars in my hand and got security for a third, which he afterwards paid through Adam Creighton—the price of the horse was three dollars.

Cross examined—I never saw the prisoner before he came for the horse—I saw him the second time after his return from the Country when I examined him particularly and he confessed that he had got some men to join in the insurrection—Scipio Sims made the contract about the horse—and not the prisoner.

Mr. Perry examined on behalf of the prisoner—My mother allows the prisoner to keep a horse in the Country where he usually resides—my mother informed me yesterday that his horse is lame, and has been so for some time—The general Ticket to work out in town or Country from his Mistress was produced in evidence[111]—the mother and father of the prisoner reside on my plantation where the prisoner is in the habit of going about once a fortnight—there are not more than 4 or 5 able-bodied negroes at my plantation where the prisoner went for his tools—I have some near neighbours in the Country at whose plantations there are many negroes.

Kit—the slave of Mr. Perry examined—The witness was not present when Agrippa and Scipio arrived on my return home, in the evening I met them, his horse so lame that he once returned home on foot—he returned next day to town—I do not know Scipio—There were only 4 or 5 old persons on the plantation, the prime hands had come to town
[Perry's trial continued on 24 July]

PRINCE GRAHAM, a free coloured person on his trial—arraigned and plea not guilty ⟨⟨Mr. Jones attending as his friend.⟩⟩
Monday Gell—The prisoner is engaged in this conspiracy and belonged to the Company of William Garner—he acknowledged he belonged to it, but did not wish to have his name down as he was a free man, but confessed that he belonged to William Garner's Company—he was not often at the Shop.

Cross examined—Said he had a sword a long one, a horseman's Sword—provided for this purpose—he belonged to the Cavalry—belongs to the African Church—Never was with Denmark Vesey or attended any meetings—He told me he was to be an Officer—William Garner had made him an Officer.

Charles Drayton Examined—I met the prisoner one night with Monday Gell in company, coming out of Dr. Ramsey's with Quash Harleston—he said that he was willing as any body—after Morris Brown had returned from the north, he said he did not wish much to do with it as he was a free man, and had denied it to Morris Brown, who enquired if he was one—This was after Peter was taken up—Morris Brown returned before the 16th. June.

Frank Ferguson examined—Vesey called at the house of the prisoner in my company one day, and was informed by his wife he was not at home—I afterwards met the prisoner—and he asked me why Vesey had called on him, I said

---

111. If any slave traveled beyond the limits of the city or plantation, the law required that one carry a ticket issued by his or her owner. Signed and dated by the owner, the ticket (usually a slip of paper) gave the slave permission to fulfill the errand upon which he or she had been sent.

to get him to go into the Country, and he replied that I cannot go, as I have nothing to do with this conspiracy—This was I think before the 16th. June.

Prince, on his statement—I met William Garner who told me, he held a Commission on the horse, and if I would join the horse, he would resign in my favor, which I refused—I heard in New York that Denmark Vesey and others were to be hung, and understood that it was for an attempt to raise an insurrection—This was the first time I understood it.

Perault examined—I only conversed with him once in company with Quash Harleston—He said if Monday Gell had told him of it a little sooner, he would have joined it—but that now he had not time to prepare himself for it—This was at Prioleau's Wharf.

《 *Prince Graham's Statement and Defence.*
As I had been spoken to and asked to join in this before I left Charleston, I considered well whether I had ever said or done anything which could bring me into trouble if I returned; but as I could not reproach myself with having done so, I thought I need not fear to come on. As I was a free man, and could have stayed in New York if I pleased, I certainly would not have be such a fool as to run myself into such danger if I was in any way engaged in the plot.

THE COURT found Prince Graham GUILTY, and passed upon him the following sentence:—That he be imprisoned in the Work House of Charleston for one month, and then be transported by sea out of the State of South Carolina, by the first opportunity, into which he is not to return under penalty of death.

The prisoner at his own request, was transported to Africa on board of a vessel which sailed from Charleston. 》

24 JULY 1822

Present the same Court

Edwin Paul	Suggest to his master to send him out of the state reasons believed to be deeply implicated, but evidence not sufficient to convict
John Enslow	Postponed until after the execution Friday next
Perault Strohecker	ditto
Prince Righton	See Edwin's case
Butcher Gibbes	ditto
George Vanderhorst	See case of John Enslow

| William Paul | Suggest to be shipped out of the U.S. as his guilt is fully established |
| Frank Ferguson | ditto |

Resolved that an application be made to the Governor for the pardon of Gell on condition that he be sent out of the United States—also for Charles Drayton—also Harry Haig—

《 Charleston, 24 July, 1822
SIR,
"We recommend that Monday Gell, Charles Drayton, and Harry Haig should be pardoned upon condition that they be sent out of the limits of the United States. We feel it our duty to state to your Excellency the reasons which have influenced us in this measure. These men are unquestionably guilty of the offences with which they have been charged; but under the impression that they would ultimately have their lives spared, they have made to us disclosures not only important in the detection of the general plan of the conspiracy, but enabling the Court to convict a number of the principal offenders. Having used these individuals as witnesses and obtained from them the knowledge they could communicate, we deemed it unnecessarily harsh and amounting almost to treachery, afterwards to sacrifice their lives. In addition to this inducement, we regard it to be politic that the Negroes should know that even their principal advisers and ring-leaders cannot be confided in, and that under the temptation of exemption from capital punishment they will betray the common cause."

On the next day they received an answer, in which the Governor declines pardoning conditionally, Monday, Charles, and Harry, and says, "the cases of Monday Gell, Charles Drayton, and Harry Haig, would produce me considerable embarrassment, were you not clothed with authority to carry your recommendation into full effect."

THE COURT then resolved to *reconsider the sentence* they had passed on Monday, Charles, and Harry, *unanimously altered* their sentence, and passed upon them the following:—"That they be imprisoned in the Work House of Charleston, until their masters, under the direction of the City Council of Charleston, shall send them out of the limits of the United States, into which they are not to return under penalty of death." 》

The Trial of Agrippa Continued.
Robin Perry a witness on behalf of the Prisoner—I went into the Country with Scipio and Agrippa on Saturday morning—we arrived 'twixt 3 & 4 at

Mr. Perry's plantation—we stopped on no plantation, nor stopt to talk with any negro on the way up. When on the plantation Agrippa went to his house, and I to my mothers—about 8 O'clock Agrippa and Scipio were in bed— Agrippa answered me when I came to the door that he had gone to bed—I saw Agrippa about 7 O'clock next day preparing to start—We started for town directly after breakfast and did not speak to any one, or at any plantation and arrived in town about 3 O'clock—when we got down I carried my horse from where I got it and then went to carry theirs to that place they got theirs from—when on the plantation no strange negroes were there—and I don't believe Agrippa or Scipio went off the plantation—they were working together in Town, and as one could not go on without the other—as one had to go into the Country for his tools the other accompanied him—there were only about 5 men on the plantation—I was not all the time with Agrippa and Scipio that they were on the plantation.

Cross examined—as soon as we arrived on the place, which was about 3 or 4 O'clock we separated, and I did not see the other 'till about 8 O'clock, when I called at their house and found them in bed—from then till 7 next morning I did not see them-

Re-examined—I saw their horses frequently together with mine on the place before 8 O'Clock—I saw them together first about an hour after we arrived; and before 8 O'Clock they were put up—the nearest neighbor is about 1¾ miles.

Doll Perry—On behalf of the Prisoner—I was on the plantation when Scipio and Agrippa came up—they got up about an hour before sundown—I stayed at the big house—Robin stop't at the big house and Agrippa & Scipio went on to Agrippa's mother's house—I did not see them again 'till next morning—by about dark they sent to me for some clabber[112]—I saw them turn out their horses on the plantation directly after they arrived—and I saw their horses about sundown—they could not have gone out of the place without passing the big house—unless they rode or walked through the field, and I did not see them pass—Mr. Singleton's is about a quarter of a mile distant (Mr. Carroll says about a mile and a half) the Driver don't allow a horse to go through the field—I saw them the next day after breakfast—there are no prime men on the plantation—all old or boys—

112. Clabber is sour or curdled milk.

Cross examined—There are about 4 taskable negro men on the plantation—Mr. Lee's plantation is not half as far as Mr. Singleton's.[113]

Lydia—Agrippa's mother—I was at home when Agrippa and Scipio came to the plantation not long before sundown—they turned their horses loose, then came in and sat down—they did not leave the house that night—Robin came there after they went to bed and called them, but no answer was given to him—I got up before either of them next morning—and then I saw them laying as I left them at night—I don't think they could have gone out of the house and I not know it—they had no talk with the people on the plantation they never left the house further than the door.

Cross examined—I slept but little that night—my grand child kept me awake—they carried away Agrippa's tools next day—Robin called 3 times but no answer was given—they slept in the hall and in my room—the tools were some chisels and planes—

Mr. Perry for Prisoner—The nearest place is about ¾ of a mile, but there is but one negro man—the next nearest better than a mile.

Jack Purcell against the prisoner—Scipio spoke to me once about the insurrection.
《THE COURT *unanimously* found Agrippa GUILTY, and passed upon him the following sentence: That he be imprisoned in the Work House of Charleston until his owner, under the direction of the City Council of Charleston shall send him out of the limits of the United States, into which he is not to return under the penalty of death.》

《THE TRIAL OF BILLY, a Negro Man, the property of Mr. Robinson—William Crafts, Esq., attending as his Counsel.》
Perault examined—Billy was engaged in this business—on the 16th. June, he and I went to Vesey's in the afternoon—this day he said we must raise today, nothing must put it back—We there met Gullah Jack and Tom Russell—Smart Anderson got him to join I met him afterwards on a Sunday at his own house—Billy agreed as much as myself—he at his house which was after

---

113. The term "taskable" refers to the organization of labor that prevailed in the plantation lowcountry. Under this particular work regime, slaves would perform a predetermined task, such as hoeing a set acreage or splitting a certain number of logs, before being allowed to pursue their own economic activities, which frequently entailed cultivating their own vegetable gardens, fishing, or hunting. See Morgan, "Task and Gang Systems," 189–220.

Vesey and the others were taken—he said Jack would get more men, and then we would rise—we then spoke of rescuing Vesey etc. and Billy agreed, he is an African—

Cross examined—We stopped first at Monday's and then went to Vesey's—the day of the execution on the bay, Billy asked me what I was doing here, why I was not on the green to get men to rescue those being hung.

Monday Gell—I don't know Billy.

Charles Drayton—I don't know Billy is engaged.

The prisoner's defence—Mr. Davenport gives to Billy the best character and also does Mr. Crafts—great mildness he possesses.
Mr. Tyler Sworn—Billy is a good Character—before my store I heard a conversation before my door about the Methodist Church—something about damaged Corn.

Mr. Davis—Gives Billy a good character—very mild.
[Robinson's trial continued on 25 July]

《THE TRIAL OF JOHN VINCENT, a Negro Man belonging to Mr. Cruckshanks—Mr. Cornhill, one of the firm of D. Parish & Co. which had for some time hired him—attending.》
Monday Gell—John told me himself that he had joined in this business—this was in my Shop—I frequently conversed with him on the subject—He once belonged to the African Church—before the 16th. June, he told me he had a mould and that he was making balls—this was about 3 weeks before the 16th. June after the 16th. he was ready still.

Cross examined—He said he would give me some bullets—he said his master that he was staying with was going to the North on Monday 18th. & if he would go on Saturday before 'twould be better.

Charles Drayton—I have often talked with John in Monday's Shop on this subject, where he said he was willing—he was one and belonged to the horse Company—I have seen him at Mondays 3 or 4 times—he said the gentleman he was staying with wanted him to go to the North, but he said he wanted to stay and see the frolic out first.

Cross examined—I think 'twas in his own room in an Alley on Church Street next Elliott Street that he told me about his master—this was Sunday afternoon before Vesey was executed (30 June).

Mr. Cornhill states that the prisoner did live in Elliott Street.

Mr. Cornhill for the prisoner—gives him a good Character.
[Vincent's trial continued on 25 July]

THURSDAY, 25 JULY 1822

Present the same Court
A communication from Mr. Job Palmer, relative to the situation of William Palmer, under sentence of death, was read to the court—
A communication from Mr. John Robertson relative to his three negroes under sentence of death was also presented and read.

The Court altered the sentence passed on Monday Gell, Charles Drayton and Harry Haig—and passed on them the following sentence:
That they be imprisoned in the workhouse of Charleston until their masters under the direction of the City Council of Charleston shall send them out of the limits of the United States—unto which they are not to return under penalty of death.
Defence of Billy Robinson continued
Mr. Tyler testified—I believe that Perault was one of those who were speaking with Billy before my door—at another time within a few days Perault took away in his dray before my store some damaged corn sold him by Billy—I have powder in Cannisters in my store which Billy might have stolen if he chose so to do, but I have not missed any—

Mrs. Miller sworn for the prisoner—I live in a house in Elliot Street—there are two rooms on a floor the front occupied by Mr. Howe—the back by me—Billy occupies a room above the Kitchen and no one can go into his room without passing through my Kitchen—I never saw Perault go into Billy's room or into my Yard—Billy has lived in that room for 3 years—

Mr. Miller, Mr J. W. Howe, J. Dexter, and Mr. Mitchell say says Mr. Crafts that neither of them ever saw Perault in Billy's house—

Perault was called in by the Prisoner's Counsel & described Billy's residence exactly as Mr. Miller had done—

Smart Anderson Examined—Billy was engaged in this business—Caesar Smith said to me in Billy's presence that Billy had joined—he told me that he was willing to take a part 3 or 4 days after this—he told me after that, that he was one—

Cross examined—I did not tell Perault that I have got Billy to join, but that Caesar had.

Re-examined—I have never been at Billy's house.
《THE COURT *unanimously* found Billy GUILTY, and passed upon him a sentence of DEATH. [*Note*: His Excellency the Governor has pardoned Billy, upon condition, that his master transport him beyond the limits of the United States.》

John Vincent's Trial continued—
Mr. Ker Boyce[114] sworn—I went to D. Parish & Co. on Saturday 15th. June who was going north on Monday[115]—Mr. Parish asked John what was the matter, that he looked as if he had lost his mother—his looks then were such that after I heard of this affair next day, I could not but think that John was concerned and advised Mr. Parrish to question him about it—
《THE COURT *unanimously* found John Vincent GUILTY, and passed upon him the sentence of DEATH. [*Note*: His Excellency the Governor has pardoned John Vincent, upon condition that his master transport him beyond the limits of the United States.]》

FRIDAY, 26 JULY 1822

Present the Same Court

Jack McKenzie	Guilty	Death
Ben Cammer		
Caesar Smith	Guilty	Death
Agrippa Perry	Guilty	Transportation and imprisonment as in Gell &c. case
Scipio Sims	Guilty	Transportation & imprisonment as in Ditto
Prince Graham	A free man	Imprisoned for 1 mo. and then transportation out of the state by sea on the first opportunity and death for a return

114. Ker Boyce was a Charleston Neck merchant.
115. D. Parish was a wholesale dry goods merchant on Broad Street.

Billy Robinson   Guilty   Death
John Vincent   Guilty   Death

《THE TRIAL of JACOB STAGG, a Mulatto Man, the slave of J. Lancaster—His owner and Joseph Clark, Esq., his Counsel attending.》 Arraigned—plea not guilty.

Perault examined—Jacob and I talked together about April in Monday's Shop on this business—and I found that he knew of it before me—where were Smart Anderson, George Walker—On 15th. June we talked together near Flinn's Church, where I told him that Vesey said tomorrow the people would come from the country and we would rise and he agreed to do so—I have met him frequently at Mondays.

Cross examined—At Monday's Shop on a rainy day he said he was engaged in the business and belonged to the foot Company—Near Flinns Church, he said he was ready—It was agreed to rise in July at first as at that time the white people go to the North and to Sullivan's Island[116]—and the city would be thin of men—but in consequence of the first arrest of Peter Poyas 'twas altered and fixed for the 16th. June—Monday told me in his shop in Jacob's presence that he Jacob had joined.

Monday Gell—Jacob agreed to join with my Company in my Shop—he asked me for a Sword—and when I said I had none to give him, he said that he would get a Scythe and make a sword out of it—Vesey has met him at my Shop, and talked with him on this business—he some times came to my Shop and always said he was ready and willing—the first came to my Shop about 4 months ago—'twas cold weather—one rainy day he was a long time in my Shop talking on this business, when he said he was engaged in painting the house—there were there several persons—he said he would be ready when they rose.

Cross examined—I don't remember that I told any one that he had joined—Vesey mentioned his plans and arrangements and what he was going to do &c. in Jacob's presence—Jacob frequented my shop and I have known him for 4 or 5 years.

---

116. A barrier island that lies a few miles to the southeast of Charleston harbor, Sullivan's Island was the point of disembarkation for the thousands of slaves imported into South Carolina during the eighteenth and early nineteenth centuries. Here, newly arrived slaves would be quarantined prior to making the short trip to Charleston's slave market. In the antebellum period, the island became a popular vacation destination for planters seeking to escape the heat and dust of the city.

Charles Drayton Examined—I have seen him at Monday's when Vesey was there, but don't know that he had joined—I went out of the Shop and left them talking—he said he was tired of paying wages.

Cross examined—I have known of this about 2 months.

Mr. Lankester—Mr. Whitney gives a good Character and so does Mr. Stagg—he has a wife at Dr. Ramsey's and is always home at night—he is a good Character.

The prisoner states that Monday read daily the papers and told him that Congress was going to set them free—alluding to the Missouri question.

⟪THE COURT *unanimously* found Jacob Stagg GUILTY, and passed upon him the sentence of DEATH.⟫

⟪The Trial of SAM, a Negro Man, belonging to Mr. Henry Barnstile—William Wadsworth attends for him and put on his trial.⟫ Arraigned, plea not guilty.
Perault—Sam agreed to join, and we often talked together about it—he often said he was one and he was ready.

⟪The Court, as they placed great reliance on Perault's veracity, *unanimously* found Sam GUILTY, and passed on him the following sentence, "That he be imprisoned in the work house of Charleston, until his master, under the direction of the Council of Charleston, shall send him out of the limits of the United States, into which he is not to return under the penalty of Death."⟫

⟪The trial of TOM, a Negro Man, the property of Mr. William M. Scott—His owner attending.⟫ Arraigned—plea not guilty.
Monday Gell Examined—I told Tom of the business and he joined—he was often at my Shop talking on this business—he was willing, had joined, and said he was making ready—he was of the same mind after the 16th. June—he belongs to the African Church.

Cross examined by Mr. Scott—'tis about 3 months since I spoke to him about it—the first time it was fixed to commence on 2nd. Sunday in July and Vesey afterwards altered it to 16th. June.

Perault—Tom told me he was engaged in this business with his own mouth, and was willing—he told me the day that Monday was taken of the circumstance and said the more we stand still the more of us will be taken—he belonged to Monday's company.

Charles Drayton—I have heard him and Monday often in his Shop talking on this business and heard him assent to this business; he spoke boldly.

Mr. Harth gives the prisoner a good Character—

I have examined his Trunk and found no arms.
《THE COURT *unanimously* found Tom guilty, and passed upon him the sentence of DEATH.》

《THE TRIAL of DENBOW, a Negro Man, the slave of J[ohn] N[icholas] Martin—his owner and William Crafts, Esq., as his Counsel attending.》 Arraigned plea not guilty.
Monday Gell Examined—His name was on my list—he agreed to join about 3 months ago—Vesey has met him, and spoke to him in my Shop as one of his men—he was often at my Shop—after Peter Poyas was taken up, he said he was just as much for it as ever—he told me that Stephen Smith told him, he belonged to one of the party—none ever told me, to put their names down on my list, but those who positively agreed—I put their names down myself—prisoner did belong to the African Church, but now to the Lutheran.

Perault examined—I met him at Mondays speaking about this business about 2 or 3 months ago—when he said that so many persons were knowing of this business, we had better let it alone—

Charles Drayton examined—I have met him at Mondays—but don't know anything against him in reference to this business

Mr. Martin gives him a good character.
《THE COURT *unanimously* found Denbow GUILTY, and passed upon him the following sentence:—"That he be imprisoned in the Work House of Charleston until his master, under direction of the City Council of Charleston, shall send him *out of the limits of the United States*, into which he is not to return under the penalty of death."》

Jacob Stagg	guilty	death
Sam Barnstile	guilty	transportation
Tom Scott	guilty	death
Denbow Martin	guilty	transportation

Tuesday next the 30th. July 'twixt 6 and 9 o'clock on the lines

George Vanderhorst   imprisonment and transportation
Billy Bulkley   ditto
Perault   ditto
John Enslow   ditto
Frank Ferguson   ditto

《On Friday the 25th July the Court ADJOURNED, *sine die*, having disposed of every case before them after a session of nearly six weeks.》

3 AUGUST 1822

At a Court of Magistrates and Free Holders held at the Work House in Charleston for the trial of WILLIAM, the slave of Mrs. Ann Garner, upon a charge of attempting to excite an Insurrection in the State and for aiding and abetting this in a like attempt
This Court was organized and composed of the following persons—

Jacob Axson Jr. Q.U. } magistrates
Charles M. Furman J.P.

Thomas Rhett Smith
Joel R. Poinsett
Robt. Y. Hayne   } Freeholders
Thomas Roper
John Gordon[117]

The Prisoner was arraigned—plea not guilty—put on his trial—
Monday Gell examined states—
He knows the prisoner and that he was engaged on the attempt to raise an Insurrection—ascertained by conversation with himself that he was engaged—did not know he was engaged until the prisoner called at his shop—he then said, they should be continuing their preparation unless they were attacked before they were quite ready—he said that he commanded the horse—that he had 12 or 13—that he spoke to them separately and not together—said he was preparing—he first spoke to him in his Shop—does not recollect how the conversation commenced—this was before any person was taken up—Prince Graham told witness that the Prisoner was to give him

---

117. Robert Hayne held the post of attorney general of South Carolina; Joel Poinsett served as a representative in the U.S. Congress from 1821 until 1825; Thomas Rhett Smith and Thomas Roper were both planters.

the command of the horse and to do something also himself—knew the prisoner several years and had worked for him—this conversation took place about 2 months before Peter and Ned were taken up. Prisoner never attended a meeting at his shop—One evening Charles Drayton directed the witness to meet the Prisoner at the gate of Dr. Johnson on Broad Street—witness went there and met him with Peter Poyas and they went together to the house of an old Blind man named Philip in Elliott Street[118]—This was a week before Peter was taken up—This man attempted to dissuade them from the attempt—This old man asked William why he looked frightened—

Charles Drayton—knows the prisoner and that he was engaged in this attempt—prisoner told him he was engaged shortly after Peter and the others were first taken up—he said he had a few men and he was to command the horsemen—Saw him once at Monday Gell's heard nothing then said about this business—saw at his own house the Sunday before he left Charleston prisoner said then he was sorry he had anything to do with this business—heard him say he had spoken with Peter Poyas—saw the Prisoner once at the house of an old man named Philip in Elliott Street—had made no appointment with prisoner to go there—does not recollect that Monday Gell was ever there—they spoke upon this subject—he said he was willing to join and act with the Horsemen—

---

118. The identity of the blind Philip remains a mystery. Kennedy and Parker write: "The name of the blind man had never before been mentioned in the course of these trials, and when he was brought before the Court he exhibited great perturbation. The question put to him by the Court seemed to imply a fear that he was actually on trial for his life, and it is probable if it had been deemed advisable to investigate his character and conduct, that he would have been found deeply concerned in this conspiracy. It appeared that some of the conspirators were in the habit of resorting to his house, that he was a preacher, said to have been born *caul*, and was supposed to foresee events. His influence over the minds of his followers was no doubt therefore very considerable. It is probable that the timid and wavering were brought to this High Priest of sedition, to be confirmed in good resolutions. This would account for the address to [William] Garner about his 'looking frightened,' and would then show how applicable the text was 'let not thy heart be troubled, neither be afraid.' Peter Poyas perhaps had intimated to the Seer that Garner was timid, and hence the remark and quotation. His own account of the affair, however, was somewhat different. He said he possessed a Gift—a species of second sight—which came to him after prayer or in dreams. That the insurrection had never been mentioned to him, but that he had foreseen something of the sort, and therefore had advised his visitors, on one occasion (as he was proved to have done) 'to give up the business,' and had told them as a dissuasive 'that the white people could fire five times while they fired once.' Thus seeing Garner's timid looks—he resolved (to use his own words) to comfort him with some Scriptures" (*Official Report*, 165).

Perault Strohecker—knows the prisoner and that he was engaged—conversed with him on the subject—he asked the prisoner whether he knew about this business—he said yes—that he had a heap of people and a sword—Saw him a second time—Witness told him to get confidential people lest they should be betrayed—prisoner told him those he engaged were such—These conversations took place some time before any person was taken up—Monday Gell first told witness that William was engaged in this business—said his were horse.

Prince Graham cross examined—knows the prisoner—Monday Gell told witnesses that the Prisoner had agreed to give him 12 or 13 horses—One day upon the Bay he met William at the time of the disturbance—Wm. told him he had an office of the horse but would give up the command to the Witness and to do something also if Witness were engaged—he never saw him after—

The Prisoner and his Counsel Mr. Gantt were here called upon for the defence—Mr. Gantt stated that he had no evidence and had no remarks to make—

The Prisoner, Wm. Garner, then stated to the Court that he was acquainted with the plot for some time before it was discovered—that the proposal to join was made to him by Peter Poyas and that he also had conversation on the subject with Monday Gell, Charles Drayton, Perault Strohecker and Prince Graham—that he did not expressly agree to join them but always enquired what arms and ammunition they had possessed and told them he would give them an answer when he saw what arms they had—that he was afraid to make a discovery of the plot—as Peter Poyas had threatened him on that subject—the prisoner further admitted that he had met three of the witnesses at the house of Philip the Blind Man and that the Blind man did ask him why he was so timorous—which alarmed him much as Philip was blind—he also admitted that he held out to the witness the idea that he was concerned in the Plot and had engaged horsemen (*and also that after the discovery he told Prisoner that he would give up the command of the horsemen to him). But the prisoner that he did not engage in the conspiracy and that it was his contention to make a discovery when the arms should be shown to him—At the commencement of the business Peter Poyas came and told him the whites were about killing every one of the Black People—called again and repeated this conversation and urged him to join—said he wished him to command the Cavalry—said he had abundance of ammunition—Prisoner required to see his arms &c—he promised to permit him to do so, but constantly evaded it—Monday Gell and others also spoke to him

(*The Prisoner rather evaded than assented to the enquiry made on this subject—so that the words in brackets are doubtful evidence.)

The Court after serious deliberation unanimously found the prisoner guilty of the charge and sentenced him to be executed on the Public Lines on Charleston Neck on Friday 9th. Inst. between the hours of 6 & 9 A.M.

The Court being convened on the Sixth of August 1822.
The first person put upon trial was POMPEY, the slave of Mr. Lord, who being arraigned pleaded not guilty—
Perault Strohecker was produced as a witness against him—
He stated that he knew the prisoner and had seen him twice at Gell's shop. The first time he saw him there they were conversing upon the subject of the insurrection. His second Meeting at this place was when Billy Purse carried a Book to Monday Gell which he stated came from Africa.[119] In the course of the conversations which they had at this shop the Witness understood that Pompey had joined tho' he did not hear him say so "with his own mouth." He further stated that no person attended these meetings who was not engaged in the attempt. The witness had another meeting with Pompey at his (the witness's) Stable in the beginning of June, Pompey there asked when they would rise, and said they had better wait until Mr. Brown (meaning Morris Brown who was then absent from the City) should return.[120] The Witness thought from the circumstance of meeting Pompey at Gell's shop the first time he attended, that he was *then* engaged. At the first meeting at Gell's shop Paris Ball, James Clement, Smart Anderson, Monday Gell, the prisoner and the Witness were present.

The Witness never heard the prisoner say he had engaged others and never looked upon him as a leader. He further mentioned that those engaged never spoke upon the subject before those persons who were not concerned. Monday Gell was then produced he stated that he knew the prisoner and that he was occasionally at his shop. That when the business was first mentioned to him he appeared unwilling to join with them, and said that "they should not take it out of the eight mans hands" meaning "the Lords." After this he appeared disposed to become a party; he said to the Witness that he was sorry Peter Poyas had been taken up and rather than be treated in that manner "they should do at once what was to be done." When the prisoner was first spoken to at Witness' shop, he was there alone, he was then afterwards with Paris Ball but did not recollect that Peter Poyas, James Clement

119. This book might possibly be a copy of the Koran.
120. In the wake of the plot, Morris Brown escaped north to Philadelphia.

and Perault Strohecker were ever at the Shop with him. The Witness however here stated that Persons came so frequently to his Shop that he cannot recollect who were there at any particular day or on any particular occasion unless something remarkable had then occurred. The Prisoner spoke favorably to this business but once in a while at his Shop. He never said positively he would join but Witnesses understood from his conduct and manner, that he was one of the parties to the plot. The Witness considered Perault engaged before he understood that Pompey was concerned with them.

The Prisoner in his defence denies every thing—he was found Guilty.

PHILANDER MICHAU (a freeman of color) was then arraigned and he pleaded not Guilty.
Perault was produced as a Witness against him—He knew the prisoner. He never saw him at a Meeting of the conspirators. But one evening in May last, while walking with Smart Anderson, he met with the Prisoner at De Villers' corner, Smart spoke to him and asked what he thought "about the affair" they then conversed together about the proposed attempt. The Prisoner asked when it would be made—It was replied about July—The Prisoner said he was ready and had a sword. Never saw him again upon this subject. When they met the Prisoner, Smart said that he was one of his men.

Monday Gell was then produced. He knew the prisoner and stated that he had once carried a bridle to his shop to have it mended. Vesey was then there and was conversing upon this subject with the Witness. The Prisoner overheard the conversation and observed that he would have no part in such business as he was already free. The Witness further stated that the conversation was of a general nature and did not allude to the particular attempt then in contemplation.

Mr. W. M. Miller stated that the character of the Prisoner was very good and particularly that he had been carried by his master to England and there offered his freedom which he declined accepting and preferred to return to Charleston, & that he has since *purchased* his freedom. This statement was confirmed by Mr. Milliken. Mr. Miller further stated that the prisoner had on his being taken up voluntarily stated to him the circumstances of his going to Gell's to have a bridle mended, the conversation of Vesey and their prisoners' remark precisely as above stated by Monday Gell.

It also appeared to the Court that there had been no communication between the Prisoner and Monday and this coincidence was regarded as giving as much weight to Monday's statement. The Court here thought it advisable to enquire into Perault Strohecker's character in order to know what weight ought to be given to his evidence.

His master, John Strohecker, one of the wardens of the city, was called and stated that Perault was a very honest negro, remarkable for his strict adherence to the truth on all occasions. That he had owned him many years—that he was sober—latterly he had worked out and paid his wages with extreme punctuality—He would give full credit to his statements—The only fault he ever had to find with him was his bluntness he was so free spoken as to be occasionally rude—The Intendant was also called on and stated that in the whole course of examination before the former Court Perault's statements had been wonderfully supported and that he considered him as a Witness fully entitled to credit. The Intendant further stated that the Witnesses was kept apart and not allowed to be in the same room except in the presence of an officer who permitted no communication between them and that they never knew the persons against whom they were to testify until they were before the Court. Smart Anderson had been executed before this trial and therefore could not be examined—

He was acquitted.

NERO, the slave of Mr. David Haig, was then arraigned and he pleaded not guilty.
The testimony in the case of NERO, the slave of Mr. Haig.
Charles Drayton said he met the Prisoner once at Tom Russell's shop—he then talked to the Witness about the Plot of the black People rising up against the Whites. The Prisoner told the Witness he was one and said he would join in rescuing the negroes who were sentenced to be hanged for their offence. Some time before this the Witness met the prisoner at a Lot in Meeting Street (here the Prisoner described the place) where Gullah Jack's men always met. Witness did not see Gullah Jack there at that time, but he saw several of his party, among them George Vanderhorst, Tom Russel and a fellow of Sims. The Prisoner did not then speak to the Witness and the Witness did not hear the prisoner say any thing, the Witness did not stay there—not meeting with Gullah Jack as he expected. The Witness did not see, or speak to, the prisoner afterward, on this business except when he met him at Tom Russell's as above mentioned. Then the Prisoner said he was one of the party, and said he would join in making a rescue of Peter Poyas, Vesey and the others, who had been condemned to death. He agreed to make one in business—He is an officer. Had known him for three years.

Perault Strohecker said the Prisoner was engaged in this conspiracy against the Whites. The Witness met him twice at Mr. Haig's coopers shop. The first time he was in company with Gullah Jack, and before Peter Poyas was taken up the prisoner said he was one in the affair. Nero and Jack spoke some time together in the Gullah language, after they had finished the conversation Nero informed Witness, that Jack had said he was going to the country to get people (This was in May)—The Second meeting at Mr. Haig's shop was on Saturday 29th. June, the Saturday before Peter Poyas was hung.[121] All the people in the Shop then agreed to raise and make a rescue Jack was there, with him again, Nero was present they consulted about attempting the rescue. Pompey Haig proposed that they should attempt the rescue on Monday in preference to Tuesday as some other people had suggested, as the Guard of Monday night would probably remain under arms on Tuesday Morning. It was then agreed by all to meet at Wharton's on Monday Morning early and it was intended to seize the arms kept there. The Witness did go there at daylight, but no one else came. The Prisoner expressly agreed to meet there and join in the rescue—

Mr. James Haig here stated that he had a fortnight ago attended the Examination of Perault before the Intendant and Council of Safety that he had taken notes of his evidence and referring to notes then in his hands stated to the Court, that, on that Examination Perault stated that the Second meeting at Mr. Haig's shop was on the Monday previous to the Executions and that Nero observed it was too late to attempt a rescue. Mr. H[aig] further stated that the notes produced were not those taken at the Examination those were destroyed and these were taken from recollections a day or two after to submit to Mr. Haig but the witness's memory enabled him to speak positively. The Intendant Mr. Condy and Mr. Wesner said they were present at the examination spoken of[122]—They took no notes and cannot speak to what was said. The Examination was brief and cursory—

Mr. David Haig said Nero was timid and Hypochondriacal and had been long sickly but admitted he was now better and had for the last twelve months been at his work.

---

121. Peter Poyas along with Batteau, Ned, and Rolla Bennett, Jesse Blackwood, and Vesey were hanged on Tuesday, 2 July.

122. A former city intendant, Thomas Condy was an attorney who lived on Meeting Street. Frederick Wesner worked as a carpenter with a shop on Queen Street.

The Prisoner in his defence stated he *was* at Tom Russell's but it was only to get something he had left to be mended. He admitted also that Perault was at his Master's shop, but denied the conversation stated by the witness—

The Court unanimously found the prisoner Guilty and sentenced him to Transportation—

POMPEY, the slave of Mr. David Haig upon his arraignment pleaded not guilty.
Perault was produced. He knew the prisoner met him at Monday Gell's with Pompey Lord and several others. Monday had there a Book which he read to them encouraging them to rebel against the Whites and which stated that the Blacks no more belonged to the Whites than the Whites to the Blacks. He saw him again at Mr. Haig's Coopers shop on the twenty ninth of June, they were consulting about an attempt to rescue those persons who had been condemned and who were executed on the following Tuesday.
—Some are then prepared to make the attempt in the morning of Execution, but the Prisoner objected and persisted that it should be made the day before, & right on that day, giving for a reason that the guard on duty during the night would not be dismissed until the execution was over. At another time at Gell's shop Pompey told the witness that a Gullah man would give them a charm and that he would parch ground nuts so that those who eat of them would join and could not betray them.

John Enslow knows the prisoner, had seen him at Monday Gell's shop at different times—while there he has been in conversation about the subject. Has seen him there with Denmark Vesey and Peter Poyas. Witness never heard the prisoner say anything upon this subject tho' he was present while others were conversing upon it.

Monday Gell was then produced, he knows the prisoner, he was, at different times at his shop, but was never present but once when the subject of the insurrection was spoken of. At that time there were several others speaking with him about the business when Pompey caused the Witness to withdraw from the conversation, but then the others continued and Witness supposes that Pompey might have heard what they were saying, but Witness did not hear Pompey say anything. He went out after a few minutes.

John Enslow was not then in his shop—Enslow was seen often at his Shop, does not recollect that he was ever there with Pompey at this time. Perault and James Clement were there and Pompey and Harry—Ned came in together—the Witness also mentioned that Denmark Vesey had expressly cautioned them not to speak to any of the head leaders of the African Church, Pompey being one, he had not spoken to him, he also stated that Pompey was his class leader once that he (the witness) acted as a secretary or collector and that Pompey came to his Shop to examine the contributions which had been made by his class—

> He was acquitted.

EDWARD JOHNSON, a free black man, was then arraigned and he pleaded not Guilty.
John Vincent was produced against him, he knew the prisoner and stated that one day while he was riding with Pharo Thompson and two others in a cart, they met the prisoner who made a signal to them, a significant sign as if going to strike with his arm—Meeting the prisoner, he asked him what he meant by it—the prisoner replied that he would want but twenty men to take the Guard House. Prince Graham, who had been riding in the Cart at the time the signal was made as above stated, was called and denied the Statement, indeed it was manifest that he was resolved not to give evidence

> He was acquitted.

HARRY, the slave of Mr. Biddle was then arraigned and pleaded not guilty. Monday Gell was then presented as a witness against him. He was acquainted with the prisoner and knew that he was engaged in the conspiracy, he has spoken with the witness at his shop concerning it. Did not recollect whether any persons were present during the considerations, but they had conversed together several times on the subject, the Witness did not know when the prisoner became engaged, but thought that he had spoken [to him on the subject] both with Denmark Vesey and Peter Poyas at his shop. The prisoner was one of his men. Perault Strohecker was then produced, he knew the prisoner and had met with him twice over at Monday Gell's shop but no conversation occurred there from which he could know that he was engaged. At another time he met him upon the Bay, when he told the Witness that he belonged to Monday Gell's party—the Prisoner mentioned also there that he had just been to Haig's Cooper shop to enquire whether Gullah Jack had left a message for him and that Jack had said that when his people came from the Country they would attempt the rescue of those persons under detention. This conversation took place, he thinks, a week before the first execution. The Prisoner in his defence admitted that he had gone one evening to Mr. Haig's shop to see Pompey upon some business, but nothing upon the subject of insurrection was mentioned there. That on his return from the shop he met Perault who spoke to him concerning it and mentioned Gullah Jack's intention to attempt a rescue but he refused to join with them. He also stated that Monday Gell had told him that the white people intended to raise an alarm of fire and then destroy all the Blacks.

Wm. Butler purchased the prisoner when he was twelve years of age, he has been sober and honest and has maintained a very good character—Mr. Bacot mentioned that he has stayed in his yard for some years and has been very orderly and quiet.

He was found guilty.

STEPHEN and JAMES, the slaves of Mr. Walker, were then arraigned and pleaded not guilty. Charles Drayton was produced as a witness against them. He knew the prisoner—he stated that when Paul's negroes were taken up, he met the prisoner who told him that he was engaged that Major Hamilton had spoken to him upon the subject and enquired whether he knew any thing respecting it, and that he had denied all knowledge of the affair, but he assured the witness that he was engaged (it was in evidence that the prisoner had a wife who stayed in Mr. Hammet's yard) the witness further stated that after Vesey was taken up he again met with the Prisoner who informed him that his fellow servant Stephen was engaged in making bullets and again admitted that he was engaged, the first conversation took place at the market, and was introduced by speaking about the arrest of Paul's fellows. The second took place one afternoon when the prisoner called him out of Gell's shop. He never saw the prisoner at the meeting.

He further stated that he one day met Stephen in Monday Gell's shop and they conversed upon the subject of the Insurrection, the Prisoner mentioned that he was engaged in making Bullets. Never saw him at a meeting, said that George Evans told him that Stephen was making bullets and had them ready. The conversation took place after Vesey and Peter were arrested—

Monday Gell was then produced—he knew the prisoner, but was not aware that they were engaged in the conspiracy. George Evans told him that Stephen was engaged—one day George came to his shop with Stephen and witness spoke to George upon the business in the presence of Stephen, but the latter took no part in the conversation. He did not recollect that Charles Drayton was ever in his shop with either of the prisoners.

Perault was then produced, he knew both the Prisoners, but knew nothing of their being concerned in the attempt at Insurrection.

George Evans, a prisoner was then examined, knew both the prisoners, but denied all knowledge of this attempt.

James in his defence admitted having met with Charles Drayton in the market, but stated that they had a dispute upon another subject and that nothing was said about this business and that he was innocent.

Stephen denied all knowledge of any thing relating to this attempt.
They were acquitted.

HARRY, the slave of Mr. Nell was then arraigned and pleaded not guilty—Perault was produced as a Witness against him.
He knew the prisoner—Met with him once at Gell's shop. Pompey Haig, Smart Anderson, James Clement, Pompey Lord, Peter Poyas, Monday Gell and the Witness were there—Smart Anderson spoke to the Prisoner of the necessity of readying themselves in order to accomplish their purpose and told him that he must keep all the old tools he could get to be made use of upon the occasion.
Prisoner said he went to do so and mentioned that he could not trust his fellow servant. Never had any other meeting with the Prisoner upon this subject—this took place in April about 8 O'Clock in the evening—Some Scriptures were read to comfort them.

Mr. Righton here mentioned that Perault had stated yesterday that it was about the first of May, Monday Gell knew the prisoner slightly. He stated that one evening while James Clement and Perault were with him in his Shop, Pompey Haig and the Prisoner came in while they were speaking about this business—Upon seeing them come in the Witness said he drew back, but the others continued the conversation. We did not hear the Prisoner say anything—That this was about dusk there was no light on in his Shop—He thought also that it was after Perault was first taken up—

Upon being cross questioned he said that if the Prisoner had joined in the conversation he must have heard it & *that he did not consider him attached to his Band*. The Prisoner admitted that he went one Evening with Pompey Haig to the Shop of Monday Gell. He there saw two persons conversing suspiciously together, and perceiving Monday standing alone in a reserved manner he touched his companion and they went away. He denied ever hearing any thing upon this subject.

Mr. Haig mentioned that the Prisoner had stayed eighteen years in his yard and was always orderly and quiet and was always at home at night—He was acquitted—

GEORGE, the Slave of Mr. Evans was then arraigned and he pleaded not Guilty—
Monday Gell was produced against him. He knew the prisoner and that he was engaged in this Scheme. The Prisoner in company with the Witness has spoken with Vesey upon the subject. He then agreed to become a Party to the attempt and he was attached to the Band under the direction of the Witness—Has spoken with *him* at different times at his Shop always considered him engaged.
Charles Drayton was also produced. He knew the Prisoner but did not know anything respecting his being engaged in this attempt, but the circumstance of his informing him that Stephen was engaged in making bullets to be used on the occasion—Has seen the Prisoner once at Monday Gell's but nothing was then said respecting the insurrection—Monday Gell was the only other Person there at the time. The Prisoner was a class leader of the African Church.

Upon being cross examined at the suggestion of the Prisoner who stated that the Bullets were for a Casting net—the Witness stated that the bullets were not for a casting net, but for the purpose above mentioned—the Prisoner offered witness the loan of the mould that he might make some for himself—

The Prisoner in his defence stated that one Evening he saw Denmark Vesey at Monday Gell's shop while he was passing and that he afterwards asked Gell what Denmark was doing there who replied that he was examining the Newspaper for Lottery Reports as he had tickets in one[123]—The Prisoner intimated that this was the only occasion on which had seen Vesey and Gell together. He also stated that Monday Gell at this time mentioned that he had something to say to him but that he had once seen him intoxicated & on that account Vesey had forbid him to do so and therefore could not tell it to him—

Mr. Evans the Master of the Prisoner stated that Vesey, seven years ago had a wife in his yard but that he had parted from her and taken another—
He was found guilty.

---

123. Having won a lottery in 1799 that enabled Vesey to purchase his freedom, he apparently purchased tickets in other lotteries. The contest to which George Evans refers may be the lottery held by the South Carolina Academy of Arts.

GEORGE, the slave of Mr. Sam Parker was then produced and arraigned and he pleaded so use his own words "Not Guilty of *Joining* them."

He then voluntarily proceeded to state that in the beginning of the year he was walking with Charles Drayton, that the fellow then told him that the White people were about to excite an alarm of fire and then to kill all the blacks, but he said that on that day in the night there would be a "Gentleman's Battle." Prisoner said that he replied he hoped he would be sixteen Feet under Ground when it occurred. He further stated that he met Perault twice upon the Bay who told him that he had something to say to him and that he the Prisoner should go to his house and he would explain to him. He also saw Perault on Saturday the 16th of June near Flinn's Church, he was on horseback and asked the prisoner if he had a horse upon his replying that he had not Perault told him to go to his stable *and he would get one for him from Adam Bellamy.*

Charles Drayton a Witness against him was then produced.

He stated that the Sunday before Peter was taken up, he met the Prisoner who said to him "how is it." Witness hesitated to reply when the Prisoner observed "you need not be afraid of me for I am as willing as any other man." Prisoner was walking with a man belonging to Cross and then went into Monday Gell's house. Monday Gell had cautioned Witness not to speak with the Prisoner—and that it was the reason of his not replying to him when he addressed him in the manner above stated. The Prisoner belonged to Geo. Evans' Class.[124] He never had any conversation with him about the Whites killing the blacks—Perault was produced and stated that he never knew the Prisoner to be engaged until he came to the Witness before Mr. J. K. Rogers[125] and said to Witness "there is going to be war," the witness replied "No?" he said "Yes there is *you need not hide the thing from me, I have a hand in this affair*" On the 16th. June he met the Prisoner in Queen Street he said to the Witness "How will we raise tonight?" Witness replied that if the people come down we will & if they do not come we will not make the attempt. Does not recollect telling the Prisoner to come to his stable for a Horse. The reason why he did not speak to George at first was that several persons had cautioned them not to do as he did not associate with his countrymen and they did not think they could trust him—

He was found guilty.

---

124. A class leader in the AME church, George Evans, a slave, worked as a stone cutter and marble polisher.

125. A ship's chandler, Rogers ran a store on East Bay Street.

Monday Gell was produced as a Witness in the case but he stated that he did not know the Prisoner to be engaged—he was cautioned against speaking to him. He did one Sunday go to his house with a man of Cross but heard nothing there said about this affair—

ADAM BELLAMY, the Slave of Mr. J. H. Merritt was then arraigned and he pleaded not guilty—
Charles Drayton the first Witness introduced was acquainted with him, but did not know that he was engaged in the conspiracy—

Monday Gell was then produced—He stated that he knew the prisoner and that he was a party to the conspiracy. This man upon going to his Shop upon one occasion said to the Witness "I am your friend" he replied "How" the prisoner answered "In this good cause you have in view," he was asked "What cause." He then explained himself by saying "the rising against the Whites." (It is here to be remarked that the Prisoner was one of the Leaders of the African Church and therefore one of those to whom Monday had been forbidden to communicate the design, the Witness stated this to be the Witness' caution in replying). The Prisoner was not again at his Shop until Peter and Ned were taken up. He then went there and mentioned "*that he was ready whenever they should turn out for it.*" The Witness was under the impression that there was no one in his Shop when these visits took place.

The Prisoner also stated that he had two Horses, that one of them was a good one and he would use it himself but the other was worth but little.

The Witness did not know who first spoke to this man—He was a Carter and worked on Williams' Wharf when Paris Ball, Pompey Lord, James Clement and Nero worked all of whom were engaged in the conspiracy. The Witness supposed that Adam had been spoken to by some of these persons. He never was at a Meeting. John Vincent was then produced. He knew the Prisoner and stated that while in Company with Pharaoh Thompson and several others in a stable—It was mentioned that the Prisoner had horses ready—

Perault was then brought forward against him. He stated that he had been informed by Monday Gell that this man had been to his Shop and had spoken with him about this business and that he was willing to join. He afterwards met the Prisoner who spoke to him about the Black people rising against the Whites; he said it was too late for him to do any thing but when it did take place he would have to take care of himself as he could not then get arms; that they wanted only two parties as the whites would kill without hesitation and so would the Blacks. He saw the Prisoner again on Sunday the 30th of June, who then said to him, "For God's sake, get the People to be done with this business" the witness said "We, the people *will* rise to *prevent* the Execution for if those under sentence were executed they would give up all the names" he replied "No hanging was as good a death as any and he did not think they would tell the names." No man saw him at a meeting—

Mr. Blackwood stated to the Court that the character of the Prisoner was remarkably good

He was found guilty.

JACK, the Slave of Col. Catell was then arraigned and he pleaded not guilty—
Monday Gell the first Witness produced stated that he knew the Prisoner that Vesey had told him that he had spoken to the man about the insurrection—Witness afterwards went upon the Bay to see him they conversed together upon the subject the Prisoner was doubting he appeared to be of two minds. In the course of the conversation the Prisoner said it would be well if they could obtain the assistance of Country People and of the runaways of which they were many between this and Savannah. The Prisoner said positively that he would join them. But he asked will there not be a meeting. He agreed to attend a Meeting at Vesey's, but did not as the Witness afterwards informed him that it had been put off. While he was conversing with the Prisoner, Perault was sitting near upon a dray. This man was a drayman.

Perault was then produced. He was acquainted with the Prisoner, the first time he spoke to him was upon the Bay opposite Mr. Mitchell's office door, he then said that he had heard of the affair. The Prisoner asked if they were going to carry on such a business without having meetings. The witness replied that they did meet and informed him of a meeting at Vesey's, but he did not attend. The Witness does not know why he did not. He said that he would come out on horse back. The second time he saw him at his own house sick and in bed, the Prisoner then requested the Witness to tell Monday Gell that he should "take care of himself as many people were talking about it." The Witness recollected seeing this man speaking with Gell near the Exchange upon the Bay. The Prisoner then denied all knowledge of the business he stated that Monday Gell was speaking with him one day upon the Bay, but their conversation did not relate to the subject, he came to ask for money due him and he staid but a moment.

Perault was here again called on for the purpose of making some explanation. Some altercation had taken place between him and the prisoner during the former examination and was now renewed—Perault then said addressing the Prisoner "Why don't you remember that one day Col. Catell came down upon the Bay near the place where we were standing and you pointing to him said " 'Do you see that fellow he is my master and is the first man I shall kill.' " The witness further stated that the first conversation he had with this man was before he saw him speaking with Gell on the Bay

He was found Guilty.
The examination of testimony was here closed.

The Court in every case cautioned each Witness as he was introduced, to be careful to testify nothing but the truth and seriously warned them of the awful responsibility they would be subjected to by bearing false witness against the prisoners. While the Court were examining one Witness the others were always kept out of hearing.

The Court also as soon as they were organized resolved that no questions should be asked of the Prisoners with the view to occasion them to criminate themselves—

《There was a number of other persons charged with the same offence and arraigned by the Court, but the evidence against them being thought so insufficient they were discharged without being put on their trials.

On Friday the 25th July the Court adjourned, *sine die*, having disposed of every case before them after a session of nearly six weeks.》

《 The following account of the Trials before the second Court was politely furnished by one of its members:—
IN CONSEQUENCE *of the* DISSOLUTION of the Court over which Lionel H. Kennedy and Thomas Parker, Esqs., presided, A NEW COURT WAS ORGANIZED for the trial of William Garner, who had recently been apprehended in Columbia, and brought to Charleston, and of such other slaves as might be brought before them.[126]
THE COURT met accordingly, and consisted of the following Gentlemen, viz:

JACOB AXSON, Q.U.
CHARLES M. FURMAN, J.P. } magistrates

---

126. Garner was captured in Granby, a small village just outside Columbia.

THOS. RHETT SMITH,
JOEL R. POINSETT,
ROBERT Y. HAYNE, } freeholders
THOMAS ROPER,
JOHN GORDON.

After a free interchange of sentiments, the members of this Court were unanimously of the opinion, that with respect to capital punishments, enough had been done by way of example, in relation to this conspiracy, and that where the Court might feel themselves compelled by the weight of the evidence to convict, they would punish the offenders by banishment, and that they would only inflict capital punishment where the criminal should appear to have been a leader, or where his case was distinguished by very peculiar circumstances—Fourteen persons were tried by this Court—of these six were acquitted, and eight found Guilty—of the latter, seven were sentenced to transportation beyond the limits of the United States, and one (William Garner) was sentenced to death and suffered accordingly. The case of William Garner was one which, in the unanimous opinion of the Court came within the rule established by them. It was fully proved that he *was a leader*, on whom much reliance was placed; he was to have headed a party of the horse, and agreed to enlist men for that service among the Draymen— He stated to the witness that he had made some progress in that service, and when his fears were excited on account of the detection of the conspiracy, he did not seem disposed to abandon the enterprize, though he offered to give up to another his command in the horse. It was fully proved that Garner had entered heartily into the scheme, and was very earnest in his enquiries about the extent of the preparations. The Court having resolved to put no questions to any of the prisoners which might induce them to criminate themselves, of course did not question Garner, but on the evidence against him being closed, and on his counsel declaring that he had nothing to urge in his defence, the prisoner requested that he might be permitted to speak for himself. This being granted, he spoke with great fluency for nearly half an hour, and made a defence, which for ingenuity, would have done honor to an educated man. Finding that *four witnesses, separately examined*, had concurred in establishing facts which must lead irresistibly to his conviction, he boldly admitted the whole of the facts stated in evidence, and alledged that his intention from the beginning had been to possess himself of full information concerning the details of the plot—to discover the deposit of arms and ammunition, and then to betray the Conspirators to the white people. He stated that the premature discovery of the plot had alone prevented him from executing this purpose, and finally made an appeal to the Court, and asked "whether a man situated as he was—master of his own time, as good as free (and as he emphatically expressed it) 'as happy as the days were long,' could have any motive to engage in such a scheme"—The Court could not give credit to these *secret intentions* of the prisoner, contradicted as they were by his acts; especially as it would have been so easy for him to have given *private information* to some white person, and thus have put his intentions beyond a doubt. The circumstance of his having fled from Charleston also weighed against him; and though he had a ticket from his indulgent mistress, the Court were not on that account the less convinced, that Garner's journey to Columbia was undertaken by him as the means of escaping from punishment. His being detected and brought back to Charleston, was certainly calculated to make a deep impression on the minds of the Slaves. In every view of the subject, therefore Garner's case seemed to demand the utmost penalty of the law, and it was inflicted accordingly.

In the progress of the trials before this Court one or two circumstances occurred worthy of being noticed. The Court at the commencement of their investigations determined thoroughly to examine into the degree of credit to be attached to the witnesses and were very particular in their inquiries in respect to the two principal witnesses, *Monday Gell* and *Perault*. It appeared that the character of these men for veracity and honesty, had been unexceptional through life. Monday indeed seemed to have been distinguished for the candor, sobriety, and integrity of his life, and of Perault, his master declared that his only fault was "that he was sometimes so blunt and free spoken, as to approach to rudeness." The Court were finally of the opinion that entire reliance could be placed on these two witnesses, and that every word which came from Monday could be implicitly relied on. Several circumstances occurred during the trials to confirm the favorable impressions of the Court with respect to these witnesses—one or two of them will be here stated. The witnesses were not permitted to have any communications with each other, and they were never informed of the particular prisoner against whom they were to appear. They were brought forth separately and examined. Their *concurrence*, under such circumstances, certainly afforded strong evidence of their truth—On Monday Gell's detailed conversation he had with *Michaw* (and which was favorable to the prisoner,) Mr. Miller, who was present, stated promptly to the Court that Michaw himself had stated to him the same conversation, in all particulars, as soon as he was arrested; and it appeared that no communication had since taken place between the parties. Of several similar circumstances: only one other will be here noticed. It appeared that Garner, Monday, Peter Poyas, and others, had held a meeting at the house of a blind man named Philip—Monday stated in his evidence before the Court, concerning that meeting, that this man addressed Garner, and asked him, "*why he looked so timerous*," and quoted a text of Scripture, "*Why should thy heart be troubled?*" It appeared so extraordinary, that a blind man should speak of another's *looks*, that some suspicion rested on Monday's statement. The blind man was sent for, and on being brought forward (though totally ignorant of the statements made by Monday) stated the remark he had made to Garner about "his *timerous looks &c.*" Garner, in his defence, admitted that this remark had been made and said it had greatly alarmed him at the time, knowing that the old man was blind.

Two cases were brought before this Court, which furnished incidents worthy of remark. In one of them it was proved that Vesey had forbidden his followers to trust the prisoner, "*because on one occasion he had been seen in a state of intoxication.*" In the other case, that of George (slave of Samuel Parker), it appeared that Vesey, Monday Gell, and the other leaders of the conspiracy came to a resolution that the prisoner should not be trusted. He was an African, but they alledged against him, that he did not associate with his countrymen, and was a babbling fellow, on whom no dependence could be placed. George had heard something about an insurrection, and resolved to have his hand in it. He went about among the conspirators, declared himself one of them, and both by actions and words, manifested a determination to take his part in the contest. He was (notwithstanding his unquestionable good will to the cause) uniformly rejected as a Marplot[127] who could not be trusted. When brought before the Court the levity of manner which distinguished this Negro, convinced the Court of the wisdom and circumspection displayed by the leaders of the conspiracy *in excluding* him from their ranks.

The three following sentences were pronounced by LIONEL H. KENNEDY, Esquire, the presiding Magistrate of the first Court, organized for the trial of slaves and other persons of color, charged with attempting to raise an insurrection in this State. Several other sentences were delivered, but were not reduced into writing.

SENTENCE ON DENMARK VESEY, a free black man—Denmark Vesey: the Court, on mature consideration, have pronounced you GUILTY. You have enjoyed the advantage of able Counsel, and were also heard in your own defence, in which you endeavored, with great art and plausibility, to impress a belief of your innocence. After the most patient deliberation,

---

127. A term derived from a character in an English comedy entitled *The Busybody* (1609), it refers to a stupid and officious meddler whose interference compromises the success of any undertaking.

however, the Court were not only satisfied of your guilt, but that you were the author and original instigator of this diabolical plot. Your professed design was to trample on all laws, human and divine; to riot in blood, outrage, rapine, and conflagration, and to introduce anarchy and confusion in their most horrid forms. Your life has become, therefore, a just and necessary sacrifice, at the shrine of indignant Justice. It is difficult to imagine what *infatuation* could have prompted you to attempt an enterprize so wild and visionary. You were a free man; were comparatively wealthy; and enjoyed every comfort compatible with your situation. You had, therefore, much to risk, and little to gain. From your age and experience, you *ought* to have known, that success was impracticable.

A moment's reflection must have convinced you, that the ruin of *your race*, would have been the probable result, and that years' would have rolled away, before they could have recovered that confidence which they once enjoyed in this community. The only reparation in your power is a full disclosure of the truth. In addition to treason, you have committed the grossest impiety, in attempting to pervert the sacred words of God into a sanction for crimes of the blackest hue. It is evident, that you are totally insensible of the divine influence of that Gospel, "all whose paths are peace." It was to reconcile us to our destinies on earth, and to enable us to discharge with fidelity, all the duties of life, that those holy precepts were imparted by Heaven to fallen man.

If you had searched them with sincerity, you would have discovered instructions, immediately applicable to the deluded victims of your artful wiles—"*Servants (says St. Paul) obey in all things your masters, according to the flesh, not with eye service, as men pleasers, but in singleness of heart, fearing God.*" And again "*Servants (St. Peter) be subject to your masters with all fear, not only to the good and gentle, but also to the forward.*"[128]

On such texts comment is unnecessary. Your "lamp of life" is nearly extinguished; your race is run, and you must shortly pass "from time to eternity." Let me then conjure you to devote the remnant of your existence in solemn preparation for the awful doom that awaits you. Your situation is deplorable, but not destitute of spiritual consolation. To that Almighty Being alone, whose Holy Ordinances you have trampled in the dust, can you now look for mercy, and although "your sins be as scarlet," the tears of sincere penitence may obtain forgiveness at the "Throne of Grace." You cannot have forgotten the history of the malefactor on the Cross, who, like yourself, was

---

128. This verse along with similar texts from the Bible became an integral part of the scriptural defense of slavery in the antebellum South.

the wretched and deluded victim of offended justice. His conscience was awakened in the pangs of dissolution, and yet there is reason to believe, that his spirit was received into the realms of bliss. May *you* imitate his example, and may *your* last moments prove like his!

SENTENCE ON JACK, a slave belonging to Paul Pritchard, commonly called Gullah Jack, and sometimes Cooter Jack—
Gullah Jack: the Court after deliberately considering all the circumstances of your case, are perfectly satisfied of your guilt. In the prosecution of your wicked designs, you were not satisfied with resorting to natural and ordinary means, but endeavored to enlist on your behalf, all the powers of darkness, and employed for that purpose, the most disgusting mummery and superstition. You represented yourself as invulnerable; that you could neither be taken nor destroyed, and that all who fought under your banners would be invincible. While such wretched expedients are calculated to excite the confidence, or to alarm the fears of the ignorant and credulous, they produce no other emotion in the minds of the intelligent and enlightened, but contempt and disgust. Your boasted charms have not preserved yourself, and of course could not protect others—
"Your Altars and your Gods have sunk together in the dust. The airy spectres, conjured by you, have been chased away by the superior light of Truth, and you stand exposed, the miserable and deluded victim of offended Justice. Your days are literally numbered. You will shortly be consigned to the cold and silent grave; and all the Powers of Darkness cannot rescue you from your approaching Fate!—Let me then conjure you to devote the remnant of your miserable existence, in fleeing from the "*wrath to come.*" This can only be done by a full disclosure of the truth. The Court are willing to afford you all the aid in their power, and to permit any Minister of the Gospel, whom you may select to have free access to you. To him you may unburthen your guilty conscience. Neglect not the opportunity, for there is "no device nor art in the grave," to which you must shortly be consigned.

SENTENCE OF TEN OF THE CRIMINALS—
The Court, on mature deliberation, have pronounced you guilty; the punishment of that guilt is DEATH. Your conduct, on the present occasion, exhibits a degree of depravity and extravagance, rarely paralleled. Your professed objects were to trample not only on the laws of this state, but on those of humanity; to commit murder, outrage, and plunder, and to substitute for the blessings we enjoy, anarchy and confusion in their most odious forms. The beauties of nature and of art, would have fallen victims to your relentless

fury; and even the decrepitude of age and the innocence of childhood, would have found no other refuge than the grave!

Surely nothing but infatuation could have prompted you to enter into a plot so wild and diabolical. A moment's reflection would have convinced you, that disgrace and ruin must have been its consequence, and that it would have probably resulted in the destruction and extermination of *your race*. But if, even complete success had crowned your efforts, what were the golden visions which you anticipated? Such men as you, are in general as ignorant as you are vicious, without any settled principles, and possessing but few of the virtues of civilized life; you would soon, therefore, have degenerated into a horde of barbarians, incapable of any government. But admitting that a different result might have taken place, it is natural to inquire, what are the miseries of which you complain? That we should all earn our bread by the sweat of our brow, is the decree which God pronounced at the fall of man. It extended alike to the master and the slave; to the cottage and the throne. Every one is more or less subject to controul; and the most exalted, as well as the humblest individual, must bow with deference to the laws of that community, in which he is placed by Providence. Your situation, therefore, was neither extraordinary nor unnatural. Servitude has existed under various forms, from the deluge to the present time, and in no age or country has the condition of slaves been milder or more humane than your own. You are, with few exceptions, treated with kindness, and enjoy every comfort compatible with your situation. You are exempt from many of the miseries, to which *the poor* are subject throughout the world. In many countries the life of the slave is at the disposal of his master; here you have always been under the protection of the law.

The tribunal, which now imposes this sentence through its humble organ, affords a strong examplification of the truth of these remarks. In the discharge of the painful duties which have devolved on them—the members of this Court have been as anxious to acquit the innocent as determined to condemn the guilty.

In addition to the crime of treason, you have on the present occasion, displayed the vilest ingratitude. It is a melancholy truth, that those servants in whom was reposed the most unlimited confidence, have been the principal actors in this wicked scheme. Reared by the hand of kindness, and fostered by a master who assumed many of the duties of a parent—you have realized the fable of the Frozen Serpent, and attempted to destroy the bosom that sheltered and protected you.

You have moreover committed the grossest impiety; you have perverted the sacred words of God, and attempted to torture them into a sanction for

crimes, at the bare imagination of which, humanity shudders. Are you incapable of the Heavenly influence of that Gospel, all whose "paths are peace?" It was to reconcile us to our destiny on earth, and to enable us to discharge with fidelity all our duties, whether as master or servant, that those inspired precepts were imparted by Heaven to fallen man—There is no condition of life which is not embraced by them; and if you had searched them, *in the spirit of truth*, you would have discovered instructions peculiarly applicable to yourselves—*Servants (says St. Paul) be obedient to them that are your masters according to the flesh, with fear and trembling, in singleness of your heart, as unto Christ; not with eye-service as men pleasers of Christ, doing the will of God from the heart.*
Had you listened with sincerity to such doctrines, you would not have been arrested by an ignominious death.

Your days on earth are near their close and now you stand upon the confines of eternity. While you linger on this side of the grave, permit me to exhort you, in the name of the everliving God, whose holy ordinances you have violated; to devote most earnestly the remnant of your days, in penitence and preparation for that tribunal, whose sentence, whether pronounced in anger or in mercy is eternal.

The following were the Negroes on whom the above sentence was pronounced: Dick, Bacchus, William, Naphur, Adam, Bellisle, Charles, Jemmy, Jerry, and Dean.⟫

APPENDIX 1
A Conspiratorial Chronology

1739
9–10 September: Rebellion of enslaved plantation workers along the Stono River in lowcountry South Carolina. Local planters and militia quickly crush this revolt.

1741
A series of unexplained fires in New York City, lasting from February to December, result in suspicions of a slave conspiracy and several executions.

ca. 1744
Toussaint Breda, future leader of the revolution on Saint Domingue (Haiti) in the 1790s born at Breda, a sugar plantation near Cap Français on the island. He is more widely known as Toussaint L'Ouverture.

1757
Organized by Makandal, a maroon leader, the plot to poison white inhabitants in Saint Domingue is uncovered by French authorities.

1758
Makandal captured and publicly burned.

1766
Olaudah Equiano witnesses celebrations in Charleston to mark the repeal of the Stamp Act. Later in the year, he purchases his freedom.

ca. 1767
Telemaque [Denmark Vesey] born, either on the island of St. Thomas, then part of Denmark's Caribbean empire, or in western Africa.

1775
14 April: Pennsylvania Society for the Abolition of Slavery, the first antislavery society in America, founded in Philadelphia.
7 November: Lord Dunmore, royal governor of Virginia, issues his proclamation that promises freedom to any slaves who desert their owners and serve in the British army.

1776
4 July: Declaration of Independence.

1777
Vermont outlaws slavery.

1779
British forces invade the coastal lowlands of Georgia and South Carolina, disrupting the region's plantation economy and prompting large numbers of enslaved workers to head for British lines.

1780
May: Charleston falls to British commander Sir Henry Clinton.
Pennsylvania adopts a gradual emancipation law.

1781

Denmark Vesey sold as part of a cargo of some three hundred slaves purchased by Bermuda slave-trader Joseph Vesey in St. Thomas and sold to a Saint Domingue planter. Denmark Vesey returned to Joseph Vesey after his purchaser in Saint Domingue finds him unsuitable for plantation labor. There is no record of the precise period of time that Denmark Vesey spent on the island, but sources indicate that his owner returned Telemaque to Captain Vesey on his next journey. Vesey may have spent as much as a year on Saint Domingue before he reverted to Captain Vesey's ownership.

1782

14 December: British forces evacuate Charleston, leaving with several thousand slaves from Charleston and lowcountry plantations for Nova Scotia.

1783

Joseph Vesey adopts Charleston as his base of operation for trading slaves throughout the Atlantic basin. He also runs a ropewalk and ships' chandlery.
New Hampshire and Massachusetts prohibit slavery.

1784

Baltimore Conference of Methodist Episcopal Church adopts rules requiring members to manumit slaves or face excommunication. They suspend the rule requiring gradual manumission the following year.
Connecticut and Rhode Island enact gradual emancipation laws.

1787

28 March: The South Carolina Assembly ends the foreign slave trade for three years. As it continually renews this legislation (in 1788, 1792, 1794, 1796, 1800, and 1802), South Carolina prohibits any slaves from overseas to enter the state until December 1803.
The Constitutional Convention in Philadelphia agrees to count three-fifths of a state's slave population when calculating representation; delegates also forbid Congress to close the slave trade until 1 January 1808, and they require that fugitive slaves who cross state lines be returned to their owners. Congress enacts the Northwest Ordinance, which outlaws slavery in the territories north of the Ohio River and east of the Mississippi River.
The Free African Society is founded by Richard Allen and Absalom Jones in Philadelphia as a political organization, mutual-aid society, and church. It would be the forerunner of the Bethel African Methodist Episcopal Church, founded by Allen in 1794.

1788

23 May: South Carolina ratifies the federal Constitution.
Société des Amis des Noirs, an antislavery society, founded in France.

1789

14 July: The Bastille stormed, marking the beginning of the French Revolution.
26 August: Declaration of the Rights of Man and Citizens adopted by the National Assembly in Paris.
Publication of *The Interesting Narrative of Olaudah Equiano, or Gustavus Vassa, the African, Written by Himself* in London.
Rebellion by several hundred slaves on Martinique.

1790

March: Widespread slave restiveness on Saint Domingue (Haiti).
News of unrest on Saint Domingue reaches Charleston.
Minor outbreaks of slave unrest in Cuba, Guadeloupe, Martinique, Tortola, and Venezuela.
Elite members of Charleston's free brown community establish the Brown Fellowship Society.
The Federal Census of 1790 records that 8,089 whites (49 percent), 7,684 slaves (47 percent), and 586 free blacks (4 percent) live in Charleston. Of the U.S. population of 3.9 million people, 757,208 were of African descent (19 percent).

1791

27 April: George Washington visits Charleston on a southern tour, staying in the city for nearly a month.
August–November: Massive revolts, involving thousands of slaves, break out in the northern provinces of Saint Domingue.
Le Cap Français attacked and destroyed by rebellious slaves.
Slave conspiracies and minor outbreaks of violence break on a number of the Caribbean's islands, including Guadeloupe, Jamaica, and St. Lucia.

1792

Supporters of the French Revolution establish the French Patriotic Society in Charleston.
Refugee planters with their retinues of slaves from Saint Domingue begin arriving in Charleston as war and rebellion engulf the island.
Denmark decrees that it will abolish slave trade to its overseas possessions by 1803.

1793

April: Citizen Genêt, the French minister to the United States, lands in Charleston to considerable acclaim.
June: Le Cap again attacked by rebel slaves, leading to the mass evacuations by white inhabitants. More than 10,000 refugees sail to the United States, landing in cities including Charleston, New Orleans, Philadelphia, and Norfolk.
September: Searching for weapons, a mob storms the house of a prominent member of Charleston's free black community.
To protect their economic interests against slave craft workers, white barrel makers in Charleston form the Society of Master Coopers.
Eli Whitney designs a cheap and functional cotton gin, thus enabling slaves to clean considerable quantities of the fiber. This small device greatly accelerates the expansion of cotton cultivation throughout the Southeast.
France declares war with England and Spain, both of which invade Saint Domingue.

1794

4 February: The French National Assembly officially abolishes slavery in France as well as its overseas possessions, including Saint Domingue, and extends the rights of citizenship to all men regardless of color.
The South Carolina legislature prohibits the entry of either slaves or free blacks into the state.
Richard Allen establishes the Bethel Methodist Episcopal Church, the forerunner of the African Methodist Episcopal Church, in Philadelphia.

1795
April: Plans for a rebellion by slaves at Pointe Coupée, Louisiana, uncovered.
June: A series of fires break out in Charleston. Suspicion falls on the growing number of French slaves, refugees from Saint Domingue, who are living and working in the city.

1797
November: Charleston authorities uncover a plot organized by slaves recently arrived from Saint Domingue to burn the city. After a brief trial, the authorities execute three slaves.

1799
October: Announcements for the sale of lottery tickets in the East Bay lottery. Vesey purchased a winning ticket (number 1884) that enabled him to purchase his freedom.
December: Denmark becomes a free man.
New York adopts a gradual emancipation law.

1800
30 August: Authorities in Richmond, Virginia, uncover a slave conspiracy led by enslaved blacksmith Gabriel, owned by Thomas Prosser.
South Carolina's legislature passes new laws that forbid slave imports and tightens requirements for manumission. Justices would grant slaves their freedom only after a court had investigated their ability to obtain work.
An enraged mob attacks a Methodist abolitionist in Charleston. They ceremonially destroy his pamphlets.
Nat Turner born in Southampton County, Virginia.
The Federal Census enumerates Charleston's population to be 9,630 whites (47 percent), 9,819 slaves (48 percent), and 1,024 free blacks (5 percent).

1802
France invades Saint Domingue and captures Toussaint L'Ouverture.

1803
April: Toussaint L'Ouverture dies a prisoner in the Fort de Joux in the Jura region of France.
November: French troops evacuate Saint Domingue.
After debate, the South Carolina Assembly decides to reopen its ports to the Atlantic slave trade at the end of the year.
Restoration of slavery and the color line in France's Caribbean colonies.

1804
January: Dessalines proclaims Haiti independent after forcing the French army, ravaged by disease and guerrilla war, to withdraw.
February–April: Dessalines orders the slaughter of French colonists remaining on the island, resulting in the death of several thousand people. He proclaims himself Emperor Jacques the First.
4 July: Charleston printer and recently arrived Swiss immigrant Jean Negrin charged with spreading subversive literature after publishing Dessalines's *The Declaration of Independence of Hayti.*
5,386 slaves imported into Charleston.

A hurricane hits the city, flooding large areas and causing outbreaks of cholera and dysentery.
New Jersey adopts a gradual emancipation law.

1805
6,790 slaves imported into Charleston.

1806
October: City ordinances restrict the movement of free blacks.
11,458 slaves imported into Charleston.
City council inaugurates the City Guard, which comprises about seventy members.

1807
December: The Embargo Act goes into effect, prohibiting American or foreign vessels from leaving the United States for overseas ports. This has a major impact on Charleston's commercial economy.
15,676 slaves imported into Charleston. Between the reopening of the slave trade at the end of 1803 until its closing on 1 January 1808, some 39,310 slaves entered Charleston for sale in South Carolina and elsewhere in the South.

1808
1 January: Importation of slaves banned by U.S. Congress.
The General Conference of the Methodist Episcopal Church decides to delete rules on slavery from copies of its *Discipline* sent to southern states.

1809
Antislavery pamphlets brought into Charleston aboard the *Minerva*, a ship from New York.

1810
Federal census figures for Charleston: 11,568 whites (47 percent), 11,671 slaves (47 percent), and 1,472 free blacks (6 percent).

1811
January: Slaves rebel in St. Charles and St. John the Baptist Parishes in Louisiana, about thirty-five miles from New Orleans. Sixty-six slaves die as federal troops put down the insurrection.

1812
October: A devastating fire sweeps through Broad, Queen and Church Streets in the heart of Charleston, destroying more than 200 houses.
War of 1812 between Britain and the United States breaks out.

1813
August: A powerful hurricane hits the lowcountry, inflicting considerable damage on the city.
British raiding parties attack Beaufort and Hilton Head, taking slaves and other property from local plantations.

1814
December: Treaty of Ghent signed, formally ending hostilities between Great Britain and the United States.

1815

8 January: Andrew Jackson beats the British at the Battle of New Orleans, losing just 100 men to 2,000 British soldiers. Standing in Jackson's ranks were two battalions of free black soldiers.

Black Methodists in Charleston organize their own Quarterly Conference. Investigations by church authorities uncover financial irregularities by black leaders who have been using funds to purchase freedom for slaves.

1816

April: Richard Allen establishes the African Methodist Episcopal Church (AME) in Philadelphia. It bans any slaveowner from membership.

4 July: Authorities uncover a slave conspiracy in Camden, a small market town in the midsection of the state.

December: American Colonization Society founded in Washington, D.C. John Calhoun, the most prominent political figure in South Carolina, was among the sponsors of this organization dedicated to settling free blacks in Africa.

George Bourne, a Presbyterian minister in Virginia, publishes radical antislavery tract *The Book and Slavery Irreconcilable*.

1817

Yellow fever epidemic hits Charleston. Some 272 people die.

Bishop Theodore Dehon establishes Sunday school training in Charleston's Episcopal churches for the children of slaves and free blacks.

Black Methodists purchase two lots of land on Judith Street in the Wraggsborough District as a burial ground. Under Morris Brown's leadership, the AME churches petition the assembly to conduct services.

Free black radical James Forten leads a meeting of several thousand black Philadelphians in the city's AME church to protest the repatriation schemes of the ACS.

Steam mills open in Charleston.

1818

February: Frederick Bailey [later known as Frederick Douglass] born in Talbot County, Maryland.

March: Jean-Pierre Boyer elected president in Haiti.

June: 150 slaves and free blacks arrested in the Hampstead neighborhood over protests about the existence of the AME church.

The AME church opens its doors early in the year at the corner of Read and Hanover Streets in the Hampstead district for worship. Members of the AME church also open places of worship on Cow Alley and on Anson Street.

Short-staple cotton sells at thirty cents per pound, Sea Island cotton at fifty cents, and rice at six cents. This represents the highest price that cotton will fetch in the antebellum period.

1819

February: Congressman James Tallmadge (New York) proposes to amend the bill admitting Missouri into the Union by prohibiting slavery in the new state. This signals the opening of a long and acrimonious debate between northern and southern politicians over the future of slavery in the western lands.

April: President James Monroe visits Charleston.

July: Fire destroys a large number of houses and workshops on Meeting Street. Arson does not appear to have been suspected.
December: Speech by Rufus King, senator from New York, on the Missouri Compromise question published in *Niles Register*.
Mismanaged and overextended banks collapse, generating financial panic and a large number of bankruptcies. The Panic of 1819 results in a rise in unemployment and a depression that severely hurts Charleston's commercial economy.

1820

January: Maine admitted to the Union as a free state.
February/March: Missouri Compromise outlaws slavery in Louisiana Purchase territory north of 36°30′. Missouri admitted to the Union as a slave state the following year.
April: Haiti's president, Jean-Pierre Boyer, offers blacks emigrating from the United States land for establishing homesteads.
December: Thomas Bennett elected governor of South Carolina.
The population of Charleston stands at 11,229 whites (44 percent), 12,652 slaves (50 percent), and 1,475 free blacks (6 percent). Of the nation's 9.6 million people, 1.5 million are enslaved, of which 258,475 lived in South Carolina.
Yellow fever strikes the city.
The assembly further tightens manumission laws by requiring that an act of manumission has to be passed by the legislature before a slave can be freed. In addition, the law prohibits free blacks from entering the state. The assembly also imposes fines of $1,000 and a year imprisonment for importing "incendiary pamphlets."
The American Colonization Society purchases a site in West Africa to establish a colony for free blacks from the United States. A year later the Republic of Liberia is founded.

1821

January: Quaker abolitionist Benjamin Lundy prints the first edition of his antislavery newspaper, *Genius of Universal Emancipation*.
February: The Pendleton Messenger (an upcountry newspaper) reports a conspiracy among the black inhabitants of Cape Hayti to kill all white and interracial people in that region of Haiti.
15 May: Sarah Grimké, who would later become a leading figure in the abolition and woman's rights movements, sails from Charleston to Philadelphia, never to return to South Carolina. In 1829, Angelina, her sister, would join her in these endeavors.
October: George Creighton, a prosperous free black, along with his family and several other free black families, sails from Charleston for Cape Mesurado on the Liberian coast. Creighton had invited Vesey to join him.
Newspapers report the capture of an American merchant ship off the Florida coast that is carrying about 250 African slaves.
December: According to testimony given at the following summer's trials, Monday Gell and several other conspirators join Vesey around this time.
William Wilberforce establishes the Anti-Slavery Society in Great Britain to campaign for the abolition of slavery in the British Empire.

1822

January: Charleston Mercury reports on the American Society for Colonizing Free People of Colour surveying along the West African coast and their selection of land near Cape Mesurado for purchase.

February: Charleston Mercury reports that Haitian forces under Boyer have driven Spanish forces from the eastern half of the island, known as Santo Domingo (today called the Dominican Republic), and incorporate this new territory into the Republic of Haiti.

May: Newspapers announce the departure of Charleston's wealthy inhabitants to their summer sojourns in the north.

Saturday, 25 May: William Paul discusses the plot with Peter Desverneys in the Charleston market. Prioleau informs his master about this conversation a few days later.

Thursday, 30 May: City authorities learn of an imminent slave insurrection from John Prioleau, the master of Peter Desverneys. The authorities arrest William Paul, questioning him about the planned rising.

Friday, 31 May: Peter Poyas and Mingo Harth interrogated, but are soon released. They are placed under surveillance by the authorities.

Saturday, 8 June: William Paul confesses to the plot and gives the names of several conspirators to the authorities.

Thursday, 14 June: Working as a spy for his master, George Wilson discovers additional information about the plot and those implicated in it, informing Intendant James Hamilton about plans for a rebellion to commence on 16 June in the middle of the night.

Saturday, 16 June: Meeting at Vesey's house on Bull Street to organize the movement of slaves in the rural areas into Charleston.

The governor orders Captain Catell's Corps of Hussars, Captain Miller's Light Infantry, Captain Martindale's Neck Rangers, Charleston Riflemen as well as the city guard to muster.

A local slave patrol stops Jesse Blackwood, en route to ready rural insurgents for the attack, and escorts him back to the city.

Having met with his closest confederates, Vesey decides to cancel the revolt and prepares to escape from Charleston.

Monday, 17 June: Richard and John (both owned by Jonathan Lucas) arrested.

The city council convenes to discuss the situation.

Tuesday, 18 June: City authorities arrest the first group of suspects, incarcerating them in the workhouse. Among those taken into custody are Thomas Bennett's four slaves (Batteau, Mathias, Ned, and Rolla), Peter Poyas, Mungo Poyas, Stephen Smith, and Amherst Lining.

The council forms a Committee of Vigilance and Safety.

Wednesday, 19 June: Magistrates Lionel Kennedy and Thomas Parker preside over the first trial in the Vesey conspiracy case. Freeholders who also sat on the court were Colonel William Drayton (city recorder), Nathaniel Heyward (planter), James Legare (planter), J. R. Pringle (customs collector), and R. J. Turnbull (lawyer and planter).

William Paul examined.

Thursday, 20 June: Samuel Guifford, Jeffry Grant, Robert Hadden (free blacks), Hercules Clark, and Bram Lucas arrested.

Joe La Roche, Richard Lucas, and George Wilson examined.

Friday, 21 June: Mingo Harth arrested.

A lengthy article, entitled "Melancholy Effect of Popular Excitement," appears in *Charleston Courier*. Written by U.S. Supreme Court justice and native Charlestonian William Johnson, it offered veiled criticism of the arbitrary conduct of city officials in

the Vesey case and suggested that the authorities proceed cautiously. It prompts an immediate reaction from angry Charlestonians.
Robert Harth examined.
Saturday, 22 June: Denmark Vesey arrested by Captain Dove during a storm. Jim Ancrum and Abraham Poyas also taken into custody.
Peter Bennett, Sampson Bennett, Isaac La Roche, and Polydore Bennett examined.
Sunday, 23 June: Jesse Blackwood, Pompey Haig, Lemon Houston, and Friday Rout arrested.
Denmark Vesey put on trial.
Monday, 24 June: Lot Forrester arrested.
Sambo La Roche, John Woodworth (a white artisan), and Robert Herron (a white artisan) examined.
Tuesday, 25 June: Sandy Holmes arrested.
Rolla Bennett, Sally Howard, Lot Forrester, and Syke Waring examined.
Wednesday, 26 June: Benjamin Ford (a white apprentice) examined.
Thursday, 27 June: Adam Ferguson, Frank Ferguson, and Monday Gell arrested.
Frank Ferguson, Adam Ferguson, Jesse Blackwood, and Peter Poyas examined.
Friday, 28 June: Pompey Bryan and Harry Harleston arrested.
Denmark Vesey sentenced to death.
Monday, 1 July: Louis Cromwell and Seymour Kunhardt arrested.
William Garner escapes from Charleston and heads toward Columbia, where authorities arrest him a month later.
Tuesday, 2 July: Charles Drayton arrested.
Ned Bennett, Rolla Bennett, Batteau Bennett, Jesse Blackwood, Peter Poyas, and Denmark Vesey hanged at Blake's Lands just outside the city.
Wednesday, 3 July: Harry Haig and Robert Nesbitt (a free black) arrested.
Thursday, 4 July: Patrick Datty arrested.
Charleston celebrates Independence Day with parades, banquets, and fireworks provided by the city's Ancient Battalion of Artillery.
Friday, 5 July: John Horry, Thomas Magwood, and "Gullah" Jack Pritchard arrested.
Saturday, 6 July: Joe Jore and George Vanderhorst arrested.
Monday, 8 July: Charles Deliesseline and Julius Forrest arrested.
Tuesday, 9 July: Charles Drayton confesses to his involvement in the plot.
Charles Drayton, Monday Gell, Harry Haig, John Horry, and "Gullah" Jack Pritchard are condemned to death.
Wednesday, 10 July: Acting on information given by Charles Drayton, the authorities round up more suspects and arrest Smart Anderson, William Adger, Billy Bulkley, Tom Russel, Perault Strohecker, Peter Ward, and Smart Ward.
Trial of Julius Forrest. Prudence Bussaker and Harry Haig examined.
Thursday, 11 July: Sandy Curtis, Polydore Faber, Butcher Gibbs, Cuffy Graves, Bacchus Hammet, Thomas Lord, Mungo Lowndes, Buonaparte Mulligan, Adam, John, and Robert Robertson, Charles Shubrick, and Isaac Trapier arrested.
Billy Bulkley examined.
Friday, 12 July: William Colcock and Jack Purcell arrested.
Julius Forrest sentenced to death.
Bacchus Hammet confesses.
Charles Drayton, William Palmer, and Billy Bulkley examined.

Executions of John Horry and "Gullah Jack" Pritchard.
Saturday, 13 July: Bob Hibben, John Enslow, Isaac Harth, Saby Gaillard, Dick Sims, Scipio Sims, John Taylor, and Pharo Thompson arrested.
Monday Gell confesses to his role in the conspiracy.
Bacchus Hammet confesses again.
Due to illness, James Legare replaced by Henry Deas as a member of the court.
Sunday, 14 July: The anniversary of the storming of the Bastille in France and the day initially chosen by Vesey to start the rebellion.
Monday, 15 July: John Gates, Jim Happoldt, Charles Hasell, and Albert Inglis (a slave, belonging to free person of color Thomas Inglis) arrested.
Trials of Tom Russell, Louis Cromwell, Mingo Harth, Joe Jore, and Jack Purcell.
Perault Strohecker, Charles Drayton, and Monday Gell examined.
Tuesday, 16 July: Paris Ball, Peter Cooper, and John (Jack) Glenn arrested.
Trials of Smart Anderson, Sandy Vesey, Saby Gaillard, William Colcock, and Robert Bounaparte.
Frank Ferguson, George Wilson, Peter Parker, Monday Gell, Perault Strohecker, Charles Drayton, Billy Bulkley examined.
Wednesday, 17 July: James Dowling and Prince Dowling arrested.
Trials of Jack Glenn, Lot Forrester, Adam Robertson, John Robertson, and Butcher Gibbes.
Charles Drayton, Monday Gell, Perault Strohecker, Bacchus Hammet, Frank Ferguson, Jack Purcell, Ned Walker, Harry Haig, and Billy Bulkley examined.
Bacchus Hammet confesses for a third time.
William Colcock confesses.
Thursday, 18 July: George Bampfield, Charles Billings, Pierre Louis (owned by Monsieur Chappeau), Jemmy Clement, Louis Gell, Dublin Morris, William Palmer, Adam Yates, Bellisle Yates, and Naphur Yates arrested.
Court passes the sentence of death on Julius Forrest, Tom Russell, Joe Jore, Paris Ball, Polydore Faber, Robert Robertson, Louis Remoussin, Pharo Thompson, Sandy Vesey, Mingo Harth, Smart Anderson, John Robertson, Adam Robertson, Lot Forrester, Jack Glen, and Jack Purcell.
Trials of Scipio Sims, Dick Simms, and Bacchus Hammet.
Perault Strohecker, Monday Gell, Charles Drayton, Harry Haig, and Billy Bulkley examined.
John Enslow confesses.
Friday, 19 July: Jerry Cohen, Dean Mitchell, Caesar Parker, Agrippa Perry, Prince Righton, and Sandy Schnell, the enslaved son of Vesey, arrested.
Trials of Scipio Sims, William Palmer, Seymour Kunhardt, Naphur Yates, Adam Yates, Bellisle Yates, Dublin Morris, and Charles Billings.
Agrippa Perry, Monday Gell, Charles Drayton, John Enslow, and Monday Gell examined.
Saturday, 20 July: Billy Fordham arrested.
Trials of Prince Righton, Jemmy Clement, Jerry Cohen, Dean Mitchell, Isaac Harth, John Taylor, and Pierre Lewis.
John Enslow, Monday Gell, Charles Drayton, Harry Haig, Perault Strohecker, William Paul, and Billy Bulkley examined.
Sunday, 21 July: Prince Graham arrested.
Monday, 22 July: Ben Cammer, William Cromwell, Jack McNeil, and Caesar Smith arrested.

Court passes death sentences on Dick Sims, Bacchus Hammet, William Palmer, Naphur Yates, Adam Yates, Bellisle Yates, Jimmy Clement, Jerry Cohen, and Dean Mitchell. Seymour Kunhardt, Dublin Morris, Peter Cooper, Isaac Harth, Lewis Remoussin, Sandy Vesey, Paris Ball, and Saby Gaillard ordered to be transported out of the United States. The court finds Prince Righton, John Taylor, and Butcher Gibbes not guilty, but recommends that they be transported nonetheless. Pierre Chappeau found not guilty.
Tuesday, 23 July: Billy Robinson, Jacob Stagg, and John Vincent arrested.
Trial of Jack McNeill, Caesar Smith, and Agrippa Perry.
Monday Gell, Charles Drayton, Perault Strohecker, John Enslow, Kit Perry, Frank Ferguson, and Prince Righton examined.
Confession of Monday Gell.
Wednesday, 24 July: Edwin Paul and Tom Scott arrested.
Trial of Agrippa Perry, Billy Robinson, and John Vincent.
Robin Perry, Doll Perry, Lydia Perry, Perault Strohecker, and Monday Gell examined.
Application made to commute Monday Gell's death sentence to transportation.
Thursday, 25 July: Denbow Martin arrested.
Trials of Billy Robinson and John Vincent.
Perault Strohecker and Smart Anderson examined.
Sentences passed on Monday Gell, Charles Drayton, and Harry Haig commuted to transportation.
Friday, 26 July: Stephen Harper arrested.
Court passes sentences of death on Jack McKenzie, Ben Cammer, and Caesar Smith. Agrippa Perry, Scipio Sims, Prince Graham, Denbow Martin, Billy Robinson, John Vincent, Billy Bulkley, Perault Strohecker, John Enslow and Frank Ferguson are to be transported.
Smart Anderson, Charles Billings, Jemmy Clement, Jerry Cohen, Polydore Faber, Julius Forrest, Lot Forrester, Jack Glen, Bacchus Hammet, William Harth, Joe Jore, Dean Mitchell, Jack Purcell, John Robertson, Robert Robertson, Adam Robertson, Tom Russell, Dick Sims, Pharo Thompson, Bellisle Yates, Naphur Yates, and Adam Yates all executed on the Lines.
Trials of Jacob Stagg, Sam Barnstile, and Tom Scott, all of whom are sentenced to death.
Perault Strohecker, Monday Gell, Charles Drayton examined.
Monday, 29 July: Quash Harleston arrested.
The court organized for the trials of the Vesey conspirators is dissolved.
Tuesday, 30 July: Hangings of Jacob Lancaster, Jack McNeil, Tom Scott, and Caesar Smith.
Friday, 2 August: William Garner returned to Charleston after being caught in Granby, a small settlement outside Columbia, the state capital.
Saturday, 3 August: Adam Bellamy and Nero Haig arrested.
A new court is constituted to try additional conspirators.
Trial of William Garner. Monday Gell, Charles Drayton, Perault Strohecker, and Prince Graham examined.
Court passes sentence of death on William Garner.
Monday, 5 August: Sam Barnstile, Pompey Bryan, Jack Catell, Pompey Lord, Stephen Walker, and James Walker arrested.
Tuesday, 6 August: Harry Butler, George Evans, Harry Nell, and George Parker arrested.
Trials of Pompey Lord, Philander Michau, Nero Haig, Pompey Haig, Edward Johnson, Harry Biddle, Stephen Walker, James Walker, Harry Nell, George Evans, George Parker, Adam Bellamy, and Jack Catell.

Charles Drayton, Perault Strohecker, Monday Gell, and John Vincent examined.
Thursday, 8 August: Edward Johnson and Philander Michau (both free blacks) arrested.
Friday, 9 August: William Garner put to death.
Tuesday, 13 August: In an incident unrelated to the plot, eight escaped slaves attack a mail coach at Saltketcher Swamp in the rural lowcountry.
Monday, 19 August: Kennedy and Parker adjourn the court.
Free black drayman Prince Graham, whom the court found guilty, sails from Charleston to the settlement established by the American Colonization Society in Liberia in West Africa.
3 September: James Hamilton Jr. reelected to the post of city intendant.
30 September: A powerful hurricane hits Charleston, destroying large areas of the town.
7 October: William Allen, Jacob Danders, John Igneshias, and Andrew Rhodes (all white men) tried by Judge Elihu Bay for inciting slaves to insurrection and convicted of misdemeanors.
October: Kennedy and Parker publish *An Official Report of the Trials of Sundry Negroes Charged with an Attempt to Raise an Insurrection in the State of South Carolina.*
6 December: Thomas Bennett gives his last address as governor; John L. Wilson, owner of enslaved blacksmith George Wilson, who provided City Intendant Hamilton with invaluable information about the plot, inaugurated as South Carolina's chief executive.
19 December: Harry Haig dies in the Charleston workhouse.
December: Passage of the Negro Seaman Act by the South Carolina Assembly, which required that all slave or free black sailors be imprisoned for the duration of their vessel's stay in any port in the state. This legislation aimed to prevent the spread of subversive ideas and literature from entering the state.
Charleston Neck incorporated into Charleston.
Short staple cotton trades at 13 cents per pound, Sea Island cotton at 26 cents, and rice at 3 cents.

1823
7 January: John Enslow dies in the city workhouse.
20 January: Charles Drayton dies in the city workhouse.
July: A number of leading lowcountry planters meet in Charleston to establish the South Carolina Association.
Arrest of Henry Elkison, a British subject and free Afro-Jamaican mariner, under the Negro Seaman Act.
7 August: William Johnson, chief judge of the U.S. Circuit Court for the District of South Carolina, declares the Negro Seaman Act unconstitutional. A public outcry against this opinion follows.

1829
May: Morris Brown, former minister of the AME in Charleston, consecrated in Philadelphia as bishop of the AME Church, succeeding Richard Allen.
July: Three slaves are executed after a plot is uncovered in the small lowcountry settlement of Georgetown.
David Walker, a militant free black living in Boston, publishes *An Appeal to the Coloured Citizens of the World*, in which he calls upon slaves to rise against their subjugation.

1830
James Hamilton, Charleston's former intendant, becomes governor of South Carolina.

1831
January: William Lloyd Garrison prints the first editions of *The Liberator* in Boston.
21–23 August: Nat Turner and fellow slaves rebel in Southampton County, Virginia. The rising is quickly crushed.
11 November: Turner executed in Jerusalem, Virginia.

1833
December: American Anti-Slavery Society founded in Philadelphia.

1834
August: Slavery abolished throughout the British colonies, emancipating more than 700,000 people.

1835
29 July: A mob raids the Charleston post office, burning abolition literature.
The assembly passes a law prohibiting slaves from being taught to read and write.

1836
Former Charleston resident Angelina Grimké publishes abolitionist tract entitled *Appeal to the Christian Women of the South*.

1838
September: Frederick Douglass escapes from Baltimore, ultimately ending his journey in New Bedford, Massachusetts, where he becomes a waterfront worker.

1839
Mutiny mounted by enslaved Africans aboard the *Amistad*, a slave ship bound from Havana to plantations along the Cuban coast. The ship and its rebellious crew eventually sail into the small port of Montauk on Long Island.

1841
After a long trial during which former president John Quincy Adams defends the *Amistad* rebels, they are released and return to their homes in Africa.

1843
At the National Convention of Colored Men in Buffalo, New York, Henry Highland Garnet announces that Vesey died a martyr to the cause of freedom.
Douglass begins his career as an abolitionist speaker following an address to an audience in Nantucket, Massachusetts.

1859
October: Hoping to incite insurrection of slaves in the South, John Brown mounts an attack against the arsenal at Harpers Ferry, Virginia. Both Brown and his small band are quickly captured, tried, and executed.

1860
20 December: South Carolina secedes from the Union.

1861
12 April: Confederate artillery batteries open fire on Fort Sumter. On 14 April, Union commander Robert Anderson surrenders. The American Civil War begins.

1863
1 January: Abraham Lincoln issues the Emancipation Proclamation.
18 July: The Fifty-Fourth Massachusetts, a regiment of black soldiers, unsuccessfully attacks Fort Wagner at the entrance to Charleston Harbor.

1865
17 February: Charleston falls to Union troops. The Fifty-Fifth Massachusetts Colored Infantry marches into the city to the cheers of black Charlestonians.
9 April: General Robert E. Lee surrenders to General Ulysses S. Grant at Appomattox Courthouse in Virginia, thus bringing the war to an end.
Thirteen Amendment to the Constitution abolishing slavery ratified.

1976
Denmark Vesey's house on Bull Street listed as a National Historic Landmark.

APPENDIX 2

The Conspirators and Witnesses

The biographical data on these slaves has been drawn from various sources, including General Assembly petitions, *The Stranger's Guide and Directory for the City of Charleston*, James Hamilton's *Account of the Late Intended Insurrection among a Portion of the Blacks of This City*, and the transcript. Information on slaves who served as witnesses appears in italics.

SLAVES (ORGANIZED ALPHABETICALLY)

William Adger
   Owner: James Adger (merchant), King Street Road
   Court: Not guilty—discharged

Jim Ancrum
   Owner: J. H. Ancrum, Ancrum and Chiffelle's Steam, Saw, and Grist Mill, 94 East Bay Street
   Court: Not guilty—discharged

Smart Anderson (drayman)
   Owner: Robert Anderson (dry-goods store owner), 294 King Street
   Court: Guilty—executed 12 July
   Comments: A member of the AME church and recruited into Perault Strohecker's company of cavalry for the rebellion. Smart was also a close friend of Monday Gell.

Paris Ball
   Owner: Miss Ann Ball (seamstress), 67 Church Street
   Court: Guilty—confined to workhouse
   Comments: A member of the AME church.

George Bampfield (butcher)
   Owner: Thomas Bampfield (accountant), 16 George Street
   Court: Guilty—sentence of death commuted to transportation
   Comments: A former member of the AME church, George was expelled for "keeping a girl." By 1822, he was a member of the Lutheran church. He lived on Alexander Street in Mazyckboro.

Sam Barnstile
   Owner: Henry Barnstile
   Court: Guilty—Confined to workhouse and recommended to be sent out of the United States

Adam Bellamy (carter)
   Owner: James H. Merritt (factor, Kunhardt's Wharf), 87 Bull Street
   Court: Guilty—sentenced to transportation out of the United States
   Comments: Adam was a class leader in the AME church.

Batteau Bennett (domestic slave)
   Owner: Thomas Bennett (governor of South Carolina), 19 Lynch Street
   Court: Guilty—executed 2 July

March Bennett
   Owner: Thomas Bennett
   Court: Witness

Matthias Bennett
>   Owner: Thomas Bennett
>   Court: Not guilty—discharged

Ned Bennett (domestic slave)
>   Owner: Thomas Bennett
>   Court: Guilty—executed 2 July
>   Comments: A class leader in the AME church.

Peter Bennett
>   *Owner: Thomas Bennett*
>   *Court: Witness*

Rolla Bennett (domestic slave)
>   Owner: Thomas Bennett
>   Court: Guilty—executed 2 July
>   Comments: A member of the AME church, Rolla told George Wilson (his class leader) about the planned rising. This information further convinced the authorities that rebellion was imminent. Rolla traveled to Johns Island, where he had a wife, to recruit followers. Rolla and Joe La Roche were very good friends. Although Rolla's wife, an enslaved woman named Amaretta, once had a long-term relationship with Joe, they remained "good friends," regularly eating together.

Sampson Bennett
>   *Owner: Thomas Bennett*
>   *Court: Witness*

Charles Billings (coach maker)
>   Owner: John Billings (public stables), 122 Church Street
>   Court: Guilty—executed 26 July
>   Age: 24 [b. 1798]

Jesse Blackwood
>   Owner: Thomas Blackwood (president, Planters and Mechanics Bank), 18 Pitt Street
>   Court: Guilty—executed 2 July
>   Comments: An important figure in the plot, whom Vesey delegated to bring down slaves from the countryside to the city on the eve of the rising. On the appointed day, he evaded two patrols, but a third ordered him back to Charleston.

Pompey Bryan
>   Owner: Jonathan Bryan (merchant), 326 King Street
>   Court: Not guilty—discharged

Billy Bulkley (rope-walk worker).
>   Owner: Stephen Bulkley, 261 King Street
>   Court: Guilty—confined to workhouse
>   Comments: According to the transcript, Billy spoke very poor English, suggesting that he might have been either African-born or from the rural lowcountry, where Gullah was widely spoken.

Prudence Bussaker
>   *Owner: Charles Bussaker (dry-goods store owner), 107 King Street*
>   *Court: Witness*

Harry Butler
>   Owner: William Butler
>   Court: Guilty—confined to workhouse

Ben Cammer
    Owner: William Cammer (carpenter), 24 St. Philip Street
    Court: Not guilty—discharged

Jack Cattell
    Owner: Colonel William Cattell (planter), Ashley Hill Plantation, St. Andrews and Boundary Street
    Court: Guilty—confined to workhouse prior to transportation

Pierre Chappeau (also known as Pierre Lewis)
    Owner: Monsieur Chappeau
    Court: Not guilty—discharged

Hercules Clark
    Owner: Mr. Clark
    Court: Not guilty—discharged

Jemmy Clement
    Owner: Sarah Clement, 101 Queen Street
    Court: Guilty—executed 26 July
    Comments: A member of the AME church, Jemmy enjoyed a close friendship with Monday Gell and was a frequent visitor to his shop. He had a wife on William Moore's plantation in St. Thomas Parish. He was, according to the trial record, jointly owned by "two young masters."

Jerry Cohen
    Owner: Mordecai Cohen, 103 Broad Street
    Court: Guilty—executed 26 July

William Colcock (house painter)
    Owner: Mrs. Colcock (widow), 11 Lamboll Street
    Court: Not guilty—discharged
    Comments: A frequent visitor to Gell's Meeting Street shop, Colcock confessed what he knew about the plot to the authorities.

Peter Cooper (cart driver)
    Owner: Mrs. Cooper, 306 East Bay Street
    Court: Guilty. Although Governor Bennett commuted Peter's death sentence on 25 October 1822, due to his advanced age, he ordered that Cooper receive twenty lashes.
    Comments: African-born

Louis Cromwell
    Owner: Samuel Cromwell (bricklayer), 7 Back Street
    Court: Guilty—confined to workhouse
    Comments: Cromwell spoke Creole French, perhaps suggesting that he came from either Saint Domingue or another island in the French Caribbean.

William Cromwell (bricklayer)
    Owner: Samuel Cromwell, 7 Back Street
    Court: Not guilty—discharged

Sandy Curtis
    Owner: Francis Curtis, 13 Mazyck Street
    Court: Not guilty—discharged

Patrick Datty (cook)
    Owner: Julia Datty (school principal), 94 Wentworth Street

Court: Not guilty—discharged
 Comments: Patrick was a French slave, possibly from Saint Domingue or another island in the French Caribbean.

Charles Deliesseline (boat builder)
 Owner: F. G. Deliesseline (sheriff, Charleston District), 240 East Bay Street
 Court: Not guilty—discharged

James Dowling
 Owner: Mr. Dowling
 Court: Not guilty—discharged

Prince Dowling
 Owner: Mr. Dowling
 Court: Not guilty—discharged

Charles Drayton (cook)
 Owner: John Drayton (district judge), 24 Friend Street
 Court: Guilty—banished from the United States

John Enslow (cooper)
 Owner: Joseph Enslow (cooper), 89 East Bay Street
 Court: Guilty—confined in workhouse, where he died in late 1822
 Comments: After his arrest, Enslow confessed his role in the plot. Born in Africa, he was also a member of the AME church.

George Evans (stonecutter and marble polisher)
 Owner: James Evans, 37 Wentworth Street
 Court: Guilty—confined in workhouse prior to transportation
 Age: 35 [b. 1787]
 Comments: George Evans was a class leader in the AME church.

Polydore Faber (sawyer and ropemaker at W. Faber's Lumber yard, Gadsden's Wharf)
 Owner: Catherine Faber, 25 Montague Street
 Court: Guilty—executed 26 July
 Age: 30 [b. 1792]
 Comments: Polydore was one of the insurgents who made the pikes that were hidden at Bulkley's farm. He was also a member of the AME church.

Adam Ferguson (domestic slave)
 Owner: Ann Ferguson (widow), 5 Liberty Street
 Court: Not guilty—discharged

Frank Ferguson
 Owner: Ann Ferguson
 Court: Guilty—confined in workhouse prior to transportation
 Comments: Although Frank appears to have been a rural slave in St. John's Parish, he spent much time in Charleston. Vesey intended to use Frank to guide slave rebels from the rural lowcountry to the city on the eve of the rising.

Billy Fordham
 Owner: Richard Fordham (cooper), Chisholm's Wharf
 Court: Not guilty—discharged

Julius Forrest
 Owner: Thomas Forrest (cooper), Chisholm's Wharf
 Court: Guilty—executed 8 July
 Age: 27 [b. 1795]

Comments: A close friend of Harry Haig, they became involved in the plot together at "Gullah" Jack's urging.

Lot Forrester
  Owner: Mr. Forrester
  Court: Guilty—executed 24 July
  Comments: A member of the AME church, Lot was a close friend of Monday Gell, spending many hours at his shop.

William Garner (drayman)
  Owner: Martha Garner (widow), 76 Wentworth Street
  Court: Guilty—executed 9 August
  Age: 30 [b. 1792]
  Comments: An important figure in the plot, Garner managed to leave Charleston soon after the crisis broke. He remained at large for nearly a month until he was arrested in Granby, a small settlement outside Columbia.

John Gates
  Owner: Mr. Gates
  Court: Not guilty—discharged

Monday Gell (harness maker, Meeting Street)
  Owner: John Gell (livery stables), 127 Church Street
  Court: Guilty—death sentence commuted to banishment from the United States
  Comments: A leading figure in the conspiracy, Gell's Meeting Street shop was an important place for the plotters to meet and hide weapons and other supplies. Monday was African-born, arriving in the city in the early nineteenth century. He was to lead the Igbo band during the rising itself. The evidence suggests that he was married to a woman named Ma.

Louis Gell
  Owner: John Gell
  Court: Not guilty—discharged

Butcher Gibbs
  Owner: James L. Gibbs (baker), 44 Elliott Street
  Court: Not guilty—discharged, but the court advised his master to transport him
  Comments: He was a member of Peter Ward's class in the AME church.

Jack [Jacob] Glen (carpenter)
  Owner: John Glen (lumberyard owner and planter), 97 Tradd Street
  Court: Guilty—executed 26 July
  Age: 23 [b. 1799]
  Comments: A member of the AME church, Jack was in the horse company (the small cavalry unit that Vesey assembled for the attack on the city) and was to help in bringing slaves from the countryside to Charleston on the eve of the rising.

Cuffy Graves
  Owner: Charles Graves (factor, Chisholm's Wharf), 103 Meeting Street
  Court: Not guilty—discharged

Harry Haig (carpenter)
  Owner: David Haig (cooper), 204 Meeting Street
  Court: Guilty—death sentence commuted to banishment from the United States (died in prison in December 1822)
  Age: 35 [b. 1787]

Nero Haig (cooper)
    Owner: David Haig
    Court: Guilty—banished from the United States
    Age: 35 [b. 1787]
Pompey Haig (cooper)
    Owner: David Haig
    Court: Not guilty—discharged
    Comments: A class leader of the African church.
Bacchus Hammet
    Owner: Benjamin Hammet (merchant), Kings Road Street
    Court: Guilty—executed 26 July
    Comments: After his arrest, Bacchus confessed on several occasions, giving officials valuable information about the plot. Bacchus also acquired powder for the rebellion and was a member of Perault Strohecker's company.
Jim Happoldt
    Owner: Christopher Happoldt (butcher), Bridge Street
    Court: Not guilty—discharged
Harry Harleston
    Owner: Mr. Harleston
    Court: Not guilty—discharged
Stephen Harper
    Owner: James Harper (baker, 70 King Street), 48 State Street
    Court: Not guilty—discharged
Isaac Harth (coachman)
    Owner: William Harth (lumber merchant), 1 Gibbes Street
    Court: Guilty—death sentence commuted to transportation out of the United States
    Age: 30 [b. 1792]
Mingo Harth (cook and house servant)
    Owner: William Harth
    Court: Guilty—executed 21 July
    Age: 22 [b. 1800]
    Comments: A member of George Wilson's class at the African church.
Robert Harth
    Owner: William Harth
    Court: Witness
Charles Hasell
    Owner: Mr. Hasell
    Court: Not guilty—discharged
Robert Hibben
    Owner: Mr. Hibben
    Court: Not guilty—discharged
Sandy Holmes
    Owner: Harriet Holmes (widow), 8 Lynch's Lane
    Court: Not guilty—discharged
John Horry (coachman)
    Owner: Elias Horry (planter), Meeting Street
    Court: Guilty—executed July 12

Lemon Houston
    Owner: James Houston (carpenter), 20 Wall Street
    Court: Not guilty—discharged

Sally Howard
    Owner: Alexander Howard (city assessor), 236 Meeting Street
    Court: Witness

Liverpool Hunt
    Owner: Mrs. Hunt
    Court: Questioned but not arrested—court nevertheless recommended transportation out of the United States

Albert Inglis
    Owner: Thomas Inglis (free black, hair dresser), 75 Meeting Street
    Court: Not guilty—discharged
    Comments: The only slave implicated in the plot owned by a free black.

Joe Jore (cook)
    Owner: P. L. Jore (shoemaker), King Street
    Court: Guilty—executed 6 July

Seymour Kunhardt
    Owner: William Kunhardt (factor, Kunhardt's Wharf), 34 George Street
    Court: Guilty—transported out of United States
    Comments: A member of Monday's company, Seymour was a close friend of Joe Jore.

Joe La Roche
    Owner: Mr. La Roche
    Court: Witness

Sambo La Roche
    Owner: Mrs. La Roche (planter), Johns Island
    Court: Witness

Amherst Lining
    Owner: Mrs. Lining (widow), 17 Legare Street
    Court: Not guilty—discharged
    Comments: A member of the AME church.

Pompey Lord
    Owner: Richard Lord, 54 Beaufain Street
    Court: Guilty—transported out of United States

Thomas Lord
    Owner: Archibald Lord (porter, Discount and Deposit Office), 2 State Street
    Court: Not guilty—discharged

Mingo Lowndes
    Owner: William Lowndes
    Court: Not guilty—discharged

Bram Lucas
    Owner: Jonathan Lucas (mill wright and lumber merchant), Cannonsborough
    Court: Not guilty—discharged

John Lucas
    Owner: Jonathan Lucas
    Court: Not guilty—discharged

Richard Lucas
    Owner: Jonathan Lucas
    Court: Not guilty—discharged
Jack McNeil
    Owner: Neil McNeil (grocer), 46 Broad Street
    Court: Guilty—executed 30 July
    Comments: A close friend of both Monday Gell and Denmark Vesey, Jack was a member of the AME church. According to Gell, he was African-born, arriving in Charleston sometime around 1815 or 1816.
Thomas Magwood
    Owner: Simon Magwood (merchant, Magwood's Wharf), 122 Queen Street
    Court: Not guilty—discharged
Denbow Martin
    Owner: John Martin (bricklayer), 15 Hasell Street
    Court: Guilty—sentenced to transportation out of the United States
    Comments: A former member of the AME church, Denbow had become a Lutheran by the summer of 1822 when he was arrested.
Dean Mitchell (cooper)
    Owner: James Mitchell (cooper, Smith's Wharf, 27 East Bay), 87 East Bay
    Court: Guilty—executed 26 July
Panza Mitchel (cooper)
    Owner: James Mitchel
    Court: Questioned but not arrested—court nevertheless recommended transportation out of the United Sates.
Dublin Morris (porter)
    Owner: Christopher Morris (merchant, 80 East Bay Street), 2 Wentworth Street
    Court: Guilty—sentence of death commuted to transportation out of the United States
    Age: 39 [b. 1783]
    Comments: A member of the AME church.
Bounaparte Mulligan
    Owner: Francis Mulligan (saddler), 33 Broad Street
    Court: Not guilty—court recommended transportation out of the United States
Harry Nell
    Owner: Jesse Nell (ropemaker, Charleston Lines)
    Court: Not guilty—discharged
William (Bill) Palmer
    Owner: Job Palmer (carpenter), 64 Wentworth Street
    Court: Guilty—Sentence of death commuted to transportation
Caesar Parker
    Owner: Mrs. Martha Parker (widow), John Street, Mazyckboro
    Court: Not guilty—discharged
George Parker
    Owner: Samuel Parker (planter), 6 George Street
    Court: Guilty—sentenced to transportation out of the United States
Edwin Paul
    Owner: John Paul (grocer), 47 Broad Street
    Court: Not guilty—court recommended that his master transport him out of the United States

William Paul
    Owner: John Paul
    Court: Guilty—sentenced to transportation out of the United States
    Comments: William told Peter Desverneys about the plot, ultimately leading to its discovery.

Agrippa Perry (wheelwright and house carpenter)
    Owner: Ann Drayton Perry (planter), Horse Savannah
    Court: Guilty—sentenced to transportation
    Age: 27 [b. 1795]

Doll Perry
    Owner: Edward Perry
    Court: Witness

Kit Perry
    Owner: Edward Perry
    Court: Witness

Lydia Perry
    Owner: Edward Perry
    Court: Witness
    Comments: Lydia was the mother of Agrippa Perry.

Abraham Poyas
    Owner: Dr. John E. Poyas (physician), 49 Meeting Street
    Court: Not guilty—court recommended transportation out of the United States
    Comments: The court accused Abraham of writing a letter, found in a trunk belonging to Peter Poyas, that could have been interpreted to allude to the plot.

Peter Poyas (ship carpenter)
    Owner: James Poyas (shipwright, 35 South Bay Street), 49 King Street
    Comments: A leading figure in the rebellion, Poyas appears to have been largely responsible for planning the acquisition of weapons and organizing the assault on the city. Poyas was a class leader in the African church.

Mungo Poyas
    Owner: James Poyas
    Court: Not guilty—discharged

"Gullah" Jack Pritchard (ship caulker)
    Owner: Paul Pritchard (shipwright, Gadsden's Wharf), 6 Hasell Street
    Court: Guilty—executed 12 July
    Comments: Evidence suggests that Jack was enslaved in Africa and brought to Charleston from the Indian Ocean port of Zanzibar. Jack was a major figure in the conspiracy, using his magical practices to great effect. Vesey assigned him to lead a company of Gullah rebels during the rising.

Jack Purcell
    Owner: Mrs. Purcell (planter), Bull Street
    Court: Guilty—executed 26 July

Harry Purse (cabinetmaker)
    Owner: William Purse (clockmaker), 241 King Street
    Court: Questioned, but not arrested—court nevertheless recommended transportation out of the United States.

Louis Remoussin
    Owner: Mr. Cromwell
    Court: Guilty—Sentence of death commuted to transportation out of the United States
    Comments: A French-speaking slave, Louis arrived in Charleston from Saint Domingue in the 1790s.

Prince Righton (painter)
    Owner: Elizabeth Righton, 66 Church Street
    Court: Not guilty—court recommended transportation out of the United States.

Adam Robertson (foreman at ropewalk)
    Owner: John Robertson (merchant and navy agent, Craft's South Wharf; Robertson's Rope Walk, Meeting Street), 31 Meeting Street
    Court: Guilty—executed 26 July
    Age: 35 [b. 1787]
    Comments: A member of the AME church, he was in "Gullah" Jack's company.

John Robertson (rope maker)
    Owner: John Robertson
    Court: Guilty—executed 26 July
    Age: 35 [b. 1787]
    Comments: Like Adam, John was a member of the AME church and was in "Gullah" Jack's company.

Robert Robertson (rope maker)
    Owner: John Robertson
    Court: Guilty—executed 26 July
    Age: 35 [b. 1787]
    Comments: A member of the AME church, Robert was also part of "Gullah" Jack's company.

Billy Robinson (porter and house servant)
    Owner: P. Robinson (merchant), Tradd Street
    Court: Guilty—sentence of death commuted to transportation out of the United States
    Age: 30 [b. 1792]
    Comments: An African-born slave, Billy lived in a room on Elliott Street.

Friday Rout
    Owner: William Rout (clerk), 14 Friend Street
    Court: Not guilty—discharged

Tom Russel (blacksmith)
    Owner: Mrs. Russel
    Court: Guilty—executed 26 July
    Comments: A member of "Gullah" Jack's band, Russel was a close friend of Jack and made weapons for the rebellion.

Sandy Schnell
    Owner: Jacob Schnell (grocer), 175 Church Street
    Court: Guilty—sentence of death commuted to transportation out of the United States.

Tom Scott (day laborer and mariner)
    Owner: William M. Scott (Q.U., 183 East Bay Street), 7 Pinckney Street
    Court: Guilty—executed 30 July

Age: 28 [b. 1794]

Comments: A member of the AME church, he was in Monday's company.

Charles Shubrick

Owner: Mrs. Shubrick

Court: Not guilty—discharged

Comments: Charles was a class leader in the AME church.

Dick Sims (wheelwright, carpenter, and cotton packer)

Owner: William Sims

Court: Guilty—executed 26 July

Age: 24 [b. 1798]

Comments: A member of "Gullah" Jack's company.

Scipio Sims (house carpenter and cart builder)

Owner: William Sims

Court: Guilty—sentenced to transportation out of the United States

Comments: Part of the company that was to bring rural slaves into Charleston before the rising. He was also a member of the AME church.

Caesar Smith (drayman)

Owner: Naomi Smith

Court: Guilty—executed 30 July

Age: 25 [b. 1797]

Comments: A member of the AME church, Caesar was African-born, arriving in Charleston as a young boy.

Stephen Smith

Owner: Thomas Rhett Smith (planter), 1 Meeting Street

Court: Not guilty—discharged

Jacob Stagg (painter)

Owner: Jacob Lankester (grocer), 113 East Bay Street

Court: Guilty—executed 30 July

Age: 28 [b. 1794]

Perault Strohecker (blacksmith)

Owner: John Strohecker (blacksmith, 163 Meeting Street), 18 Cumberland Street

Court: Guilty—sentenced to transportation out of the United States

Comments: An African-born slave, Perault originated from the town of Jumba, a settlement in Upper Guinea. Following a clash with the Dar'a people, Perault was captured and sold into slavery. He arrived in Charleston sometime between 1804 and 1807, being purchased by John Strohecker in 1814. He spoke Creole French.

John Taylor

Owner: Mrs. Taylor

Court: Not guilty—court recommended transportation out of the United States

Pharo Thompson

Owner: Jane Thompson, 160 Mazyck Street

Court: Guilty—executed 26 July

Isaac Trapier

Owner: Paul Trapier (factor) D'Oyley's Wharf

Court: Not guilty—discharged

Comments: "An elderly slave."

George Vanderhorst
> Owner: R. W. Vanderhorst (planter), Judith and Alexander Streets, Mazyckborough
> Court: Guilty—sentenced to transportation out of the United States

Sandy Vesey
> Owner: John J. Schnell (grocer), 175 Church Street
> Court: Guilty—sentence of death commuted to transportation out of the United States
> Comments: Although there is no direct evidence, it is very likely that Sandy was Vesey's son.

John Vincent (laborer)
> Owner: D. Cruckshanks (tanyard operator and shoemaker), Hanover Street, Hampstead
> Court: Guilty—sentence of death commuted to transportation out of the United States
> Comments: A lapsed member of the AME church, Vincent was working on hire during the summer of 1822. He lived on Elliott Street and was hired out to D. Parish and Company, a merchant house.

James Walker
> Owner: Mr. Walker
> Court: Not guilty—discharged

Stephen Walker
> Owner: Mr. Walker
> Court: Not guilty—discharged

Peter Ward
> Owner: Mrs. Susan Ward (widow)
> Court: Not guilty—discharged
> Comments: A class leader in the African church.

Smart Ward
> Owner: Mrs. Susan Ward
> Court: Not guilty—discharged

Syke Waring
> Owner: Mr. Waring
> Court: Witness

George Wilson (blacksmith)
> Owner: Major John Wilson (state engineer), 106 Broad Street
> Court: Witness
> Comments: Wilson learned from Rolla Bennett about the planned uprising. He informed his owner about the plot and then worked as a spy to learn more about the rebels' plans. For services rendered, the state purchased his freedom. He was also a class leader in the AME church. He later committed suicide.

Adam Yates
> Owner: Estate of Joseph Yates (cooper, 83 East Bay Street and Smith's Wharf), 23 Meeting Street
> Court: Guilty—executed 26 July
> Age: 30 [b. 1792]
> Comments: Born in Africa, Adam was a member of the AME church.

Bellisle Yates
> Owner: Estate of Joseph Yates
> Court: Guilty—executed 26 July
> Age: 30 [b. 1792]
> Comments: Like Adam, Bellisle was African and a member of the AME church.

Naphur Yates
> Owner: Estate of Joseph Yates
> Court: Guilty—executed 26 July
> Age: 30 [b. 1792]
> Comments: Naphur was also African and a member of the AME church.

FREE BLACKS (ORGANIZED ALPHABETICALLY)

Saby Gaillard
> Carpenter, 5 Wentworth Street
> Court: Guilty—confined in workhouse and transported out of the United States

Prince Graham
> Drayman, 11 Cumming Street
> Court: Guilty—banished from South Carolina
> Comments: A member of the African church, Prince was an officer in William Garner's company. After the trials, he sailed aboard *The Dolphin* from Charleston for Liberia.

Jeffry Grant
> Court: Not guilty—discharged

Samuel Guifford
> Court: Not guilty—discharged after being held and whipped in the workhouse

Robert Hadden
> Court: Not guilty—discharged after being held and whipped at the workhouse
> Comments: Hadden was a mulatto.

Quash Harleston
> Court: Not guilty. By arrangement with his counsel, he left the United States.

Edward Johnson (chairmaker), 176 Church Street
> Court: Not guilty—discharged

Philander Michau
> Court: Not guilty—discharged
> Comments: Prior to 1822, Michau had spent time in England. Returned to Charleston with his owner, Michau later purchased his freedom.

Robert Nesbitt
> Court: Not guilty—discharged
> Comments: Israel Nesbitt, his great-grandson, was interviewed by the WPA during the 1930s. From the details offered in this interview, it is clear that the story about Vesey's plot had been transmitted from one generation to the next with some accuracy.

Denmark Vesey
> Carpenter, 20 Bull Street
> Court: Guilty—executed 2 July
> Age: 55 [b. ca. 1767]
> Comments: The leader of the conspiracy and a class leader in the AME church.

SENTENCES PASSED (IN CHRONOLOGICAL ORDER)

1. Prisoners found guilty and executed. Thirty-four enslaved men and one free black man were hanged. The executions on Tuesday, 2 July, took place on Blake's Lands, while the remaining slaves went to the gallows at the Lines.

Name	Owner	Comments
Batteau Bennett	Gov. Thomas Bennett	Hanged 2 July
Ned Bennett	"	"
Rolla Bennett	"	"
Jesse Blackwood	Thomas Blackwood	"
Peter Poyas	James Poyas	"
Denmark Vesey	Free black	"
John Horry	Elias Horry	Hanged 12 July
"Gullah" Jack Pritchard	Paul Pritchard	"
Smart Anderson	Robert Anderson	Hanged 26 July
Charles Billings	John Billings	"
Jemmy Clement	Sarah Clement	"
Jerry Cohen	Mordecai Cohen	"
Polydore Faber	Catherine Faber	"
Julius Forrest	Thomas Forrest	"
Lot Forrester	Mr. Forrester	"
Jack Glenn	John S. Glenn	"
Bacchus Hammet	Benjamin Hammet	"
Mingo Harth	William Harth	"
Joe Jore	P. L. Jore	"
Dean Mitchell	James Mitchell	"
Jack Purcell	Mrs. Purcell	"
Tom Russel	Mrs. Russel	"
Adam Robertson	John Robertson	"
John Robertson	"	"
Robert Robertson	"	"
Dick Sims	William Sims	"
Pharo Thompson	Mrs. Thompson	"
Adam Yates	Estate of Joseph Yates	"
Bellisle Yates	"	"
Naphur Yates	"	"
Jack McNeil	Neil McNeil	Hanged 30 July
Tom Scott	William M. Scott	"
Jacob Stagg	Jacob Lancaster	"
Caesar Smith	Naomi Smith	"
William Garner	Martha Garner	Hanged 9 August

2. Prisoners who were found guilty, but received pardons on the understanding that they would be banished beyond the borders of the United States. They remained confined in the workhouse until the authorities could arrange their exile.

Name	Owner	Comments
Paris Ball	Ann Ball	Confined in the workhouse
George Bampfield	Thomas Bampfield	"
Peter Cooper	Mrs. Cooper	Whipped and released
Louis Cromwell	Samuel Cromwell	Confined in workhouse
Saby Gaillard	Free black	"
Isaac Harth	William Harth	"
Seymour Kunhardt	William Kunhardt	"
Dublin Morris	Christopher Morris	Confined in the workhouse
William Palmer	Job Palmer	Death sentence commuted and now confined in the workhouse
Billy Robinson	P. Robinson	Confined in workhouse
Sandy Schnell	Jacob Schnell	"
John Vincent	D. Cruckshanks	"

3. Prisoners who were found guilty and sentenced to transportation beyond the limits of the United States by their masters.

Name	Owner	Comments
Sam Barnstile	Henry Barnstile	"
Adam Bellamy	James Merritt	"
Billy Bulkley	Stephen Bulkley	"
Harry Butler	William Butler	"
Jack Catell	William Catell	"
Charles Drayton	John Drayton	"
John Enslow	Joseph Enslow	"
George Evans	James Evans	"
Frank Ferguson	Ann Ferguson	Confined in the workhouse
Monday Gell	John Gell	Death sentence commuted and now confined in the workhouse
Prince Graham	Free black	Sentenced to one month imprisonment and then banished from the United States
Harry Haig	David Haig	"
Nero Haig	David Haig	"
Pompey Lord	Richard Lord	"
Denbow Martin	John N. Martin	"
George Parker	Samuel Parker	"
Agrippa Perry	Mrs. Perry	"
Scipio Sims	William Sims	"
Perault Strohecker	John Strohecker	"
George Vanderhorst	R. W. Vanderhorst	"

4. Prisoners acquitted by the court, although they recommended that their owners transport them beyond the limits of the United States.

Name	Owner	Comments
Buonaparte Mulligan	Francis Mulligan	Confined in the workhouse
Abraham Poyas	Dr. John Poyas	"

Name	Owner	Comments
Butcher Gibbs	James Gibbs	"
John Taylor	Mrs. Taylor	"
Prince Righton	Elizabeth Righton	"
Edwin Paul	John Paul	"
William Paul	"	"
Quash Harleston	Free black	Transported from the country

5. Slaves not arrested, yet arranged to be transported.

Name	Owner
Harry Purse	William Purse
Panza Mitchell	Mr. Mitchell
Liverpool Hunt	Mrs. Hunt

6. Prisoners acquitted by the court and discharged.

Name	Owner
Stephen Smith	Thomas Rhett Smith
Amherst Lining	Mrs. Lining
Samuel Guifford	Free black
Robert Hadden	Free person of color
Friday Rout	Catherine Rout
Jeffry Grant	Free black
Jim Ancrum	J. H. Ancrum
William Colcock	Mrs. Colcock
Pierre Chappeau	Monsieur Chappeau
Pompey Haig	David Haig
Philander Michau	Free person of color
Edward Johnson	Free black
Stephen Walker	Mr. Walker
James Walker	"
Harry Nell	Jesse Nell

7. Prisoners arrested, but never brought to trial due to lack of evidence and discharged.

Name	Owner
Mathias Bennett	Thomas Bennett
Mungo Poyas	James Poyas
Bram Lucas	Jonathan Lucas
Richard Lucas	"
John Lucas	"
Hercules Clark	Mr. Clark
Sandy Holmes	Harriet P. Holmes
Lemon Houston	Mr. Houston
Adam Ferguson	Ann Ferguson
Pompey Bryan	John Bryan
Harry Harleston	Mr. Harleston
Robert Nesbitt	Free black
Patrick Datty	Julia Datty

Name	Owner
Thomas Magwood	Simon Magwood
Charles Deliesseline	F. G. Deliesseline
William Adger	James Adger
Smart Ward	Mrs. Ward
Peter Ward	"
Sandy Curtis	Francis Curtis
Isaac Trapier	Paul Trapier
Charles Shubrick	Mrs. Shubrick
Cuffy Graves	Charles Graves
Mungo Lowndes	William Lowndes
Thomas Lord	Archibald Lord
Bob Hibben	Mr. Hibben
Albert Inglis	T. Inglis, a free person of color
Jim Happoldt	Christopher Happoldt
John Gates	Mr. Gates
Charles Hasell	Mr. Hasell
James Dowling	Mr. Dowling
Prince Dowling	"
Caesar Parker	Mrs. Parker
Billy Fordham	Mr. Fordham
Ben Cammer	James Cammer
William Cromwell	Samuel Cromwell
Stephen Harper	James Harper
Louis Gell	John Gell
Pompey Bryan	John Bryan

APPENDIX 3

Additional Documents

Drawn from various sources, including newspapers, personal letters, pamphlets, and official correspondence, these miscellaneous documents further contextualize the life and times of Vesey and his followers. Rather than catalog these materials by subject or author, they have been organized chronologically. Readers should also consult the bibliography for a comprehensive list of primary materials relating to the plot.

* * *

South Carolina Weekly Gazette, 28 November 1783
An Ordinance

For the better ordering and governing of Negroes and other Slaves, and of free Negroes, Mulattoes and Mustizoes, within the City of Charleston.

BE it ordained by the Honorable the Intendant and Wardens of Charleston in City Council assembled, and it is hereby ordained by the authority of the same. That after one month from the publication of this Ordinance, no owner or other person having the care and government of negroes or other slaves, shall permit any such slave to be employed on hire out of their respective houses or families, without a ticket or badge first obtained from the Corporation of this City, under the penalty of three pounds for every such offence; and every person employing a slave on hire without such a ticket or badge, shall forfeit twenty shillings for each day he, she, or they shall employ such a slave, over and above the wages agreed to be paid to such a slave for his or her work. And for each ticket or badge so obtained from the Corporation, the several sums following shall be respectively paid, (viz).—For a butcher, 40 shillings; for a carpenter, bricklayer, fisherman, blacksmith, wheelwright, pump or blockmaker, cabinet-maker, painter or glazier, and gold or silver smith, 20 shillings; for a taylor, tinman, tanner or currier, 15 shillings, for a mariner, cooper, shoemaker, barber, hatter, ropemaker, turner, or any other handicraft tradesman, 10 shillings.

* * *

Memorial Respecting the Insurrection in St. Domingo, 12 December 1791

The French division of the island of Santo Domingo was on 22 August last thrown into the utmost confusion and horror by an event to which the history of America affords no comparison of misery. Upwards of 160,000 slaves founding upon the late decree of the National Assembly of France, their claims to equal liberty, set up the standard of revolt, and spreading around them at the same moment and with most undisguised fury, with the horrors of fire and sword, they have reduced to ashes and rendered the richest and most valuable part of that once happy country to a scene of blood and desolation.

I have already received information that no less than 600 of our citizens have fallen defenceless victims to the ferocity of murderers and still a greater number have sunk under the fatigue of incessant duty.... and three hundred of our finest plantations present at this moment no other vestiges than those of fire, ravage, and desolation.

General Assembly Petitions, SCDAH

* * *

City Gazette and Daily Advertiser, 1 October 1799

Commissioners of the East Bay Lottery will, on 7th October, commence drawing. In the mean time, the holders of tickets of $6 will call at Mr. Reach of the City Exchange.

* * *

State of South Carolina

I, Mary Clodner, Send Greetings. Know ye that I, the said Mary Clodner, for and in consideration of the sum of Six Hundred Dollars and for divers good causes ... have manumitted, released and freed from the Yoke of Servitude, set free and discharged a certain Negro man named Telemaque with all his goods and chattels by him already acquired or to be hereafter acquired, and know ye also that I, the said Mary Clodner, have forever quitted claim for me and my Heirs, Executors, and Administrators, and by this present writing do relinquish, release and quit claim unto the said Telemaque and from all manner of actions, real and personal. In Witness whereof I have set my seal at Charleston, this seventh day of December, the year of our Lord one thousand and seven hundred and ninety-nine—and of the Independence of America, the twenty fourth. As Witnesses, Charles G. Core, J. Vesey of Charleston so personally appeared. Mr Charles Core, being duly sworn made oath he was present and saw Mary Clodner sign, seal and deliver the written Manumission to and for the uses and purposes for the above-mentioned, and that he together with Joseph Vesey, signed their names. Sworn before me this 31st. December 1799. Jas. Ravenel. Recorded 31st. December.

Miscellaneous Records, vol. MMM, SCDAH

* * *

City Gazette and Daily Advertiser, 2 October 1800

Caution

ALL persons are forbid employing my ship Carpenters, FRANK and CHARLES, without their being engaged of me; and are also forbid paying any money to either of them; and the first of whom has, in direct contradiction to my orders, employing himself to work in the country. The person now employing him, will therefore be sued for the money.

John Champneys

* * *

Charleston Courier, 20 April 1803

The jacobins preach, propagate, and encourage the settling of political differences by the shedding of blood. . . . They are in league with the Deists and Atheists to overthrow the Christian religion. They are equally enemies to all morality and moral and civic order.

Virtue withers under its approach, right is trampled under its bloody hoofs, and morality is extinguished in every heart that sucks in its ears to its counsels. The jacobins, malcontents, sedition leaders and traitors . . . are taken under the wing of protection, honoured, favored and encouraged under the quaint, pedantic appellation of *oppressed humanity.*

* * *

Charleston Courier, 11 October 1803

On the 9th. inst., by the Reverend Mr. Brazier, Capt. Joseph Vesey to the amiable Mrs. Blair, both of this city.

* * *

City Gazette and Daily Advertiser, 25 June 1807
Ten Dollars Reward.

Absented herself on Wednesday last, my Negro Wench, Charlotte, about 18 years of age, slender made, her complexion of a yellow cast; is well known in the city as a day-worker, particularly in Beresford's Alley—has lately addicted herself to drinking spirituous liquors; is a great street walker, and can be met with, no doubt, on the wharf, or in Queen Street, being a haunt of hers every evening, till drum-beat. The above reward will be paid on delivering her to the master of the work house, or to the subscriber. A. Huff, 141 King-street.
    N.B. All persons are cautioned against harboring or carrying her off.

* * *

City Gazette and Commercial Daily Advertiser, 27 August 1812
EIGHT DOLLARS REWARD

Ran away from the subscriber, some time in June last, his Negro fellow POMPEY, formerly belonging to Mr. Gardner Haddon, and purchased by his present owner at Sheriff's Sales. He is a painter by trade, and has constantly been employed working out, being furnished with a badge. He is so well known in and about the city, that a further description is unnecessary. The above reward will be paid to any person delivering him to the Master of the Work House. All persons are cautioned against employing or harboring said Negro, as the law will be strictly enforced against them.   George Cross.

* * *

City Gazette and Commercial Daily Advertiser, 30 July 1816
TEN DOLLARS REWARD

Ran away from subscriber on Wednesday the 24th. Inst. a Fellow by the name of JOE, a ship carpenter by trade. He is a stout, thick made fellow, an African, speaks very thick when spoken to. He is supposed to be about the city as he is very fond of liquor. John Hamilton
    N.B. All masters of vessels are cautioned not to take the above fellow away, as the law will be strictly enforced against them.

* * *

City Gazette and Commercial Daily Advertiser, 9 June 1818

Upwards of 150 negroes and persons of color were on Sunday apprehended and committed to the Guard House for violation of one of the City Ordinances. The principal characters were yesterday morning sentenced to one month's imprisonment and the others to pay a fine of $5 or receive ten lashes.

* * *

Charleston Patriot, 10 June 1818

It is well known that in every church in Charleston and throughout the state, accommodations are provided for such of the negroes and free people of colour as choose to attend divine service. . . . A few weeks ago, some black bishops and preachers from one of the northern cities came here and endeavored to hold meetings of the black congregation exclusively; and one of the congregations was taken up and confined, and the next day dismissed personally by the city magistrates who explained the law to them.

* * *

Free Persons of Colour to House of Representatives, n.d., 1818

The free persons of colour attached to the African Methodist Episcopal Church in Charleston called Zion, have erected a house of worship at Hampstead on Charleston Neck at the corner of Hanover and Reid Streets. Petitioners request to open said building for the purpose of Divine worship from the rising of the sun until the going down of the sun. . . . the doors will always remain open and that white ministers of the Gospel of every denomination shall be repeatedly invited to officiate.

General Assembly Petitions, SCDAH

* * *

City Gazette and Commercial Daily Advertiser, 7 July 1819
ANNIVERSARY OF AMERICAN INDEPENDENCE

The birthday of American Liberty having this year fallen on Sunday, the Citizens of Charleston celebrated the same on Monday, the 5th, with the accustomed demonstrations of joy, gratitude, and thankfulness. The dawn of morning was hailed with a federal salute from the Artillery, which was repeated at 1 o'clock and at sun-set, accompanied by the pealing of the chime of the bells from St. Michael's Church.

About 7 o'clock, the 7th. Brigade, commanded by Colonel SIMONS, were reviewed by His Excellency GOVERNOR GEDDES and Suite; after which they were marched to East-Bay-Street, where a federal salute from the artillery, and a *feu-de-joie* from the infantry, were fired. The troops then returned into the city, and were discharged. Most of the uniformed corps dined together, and spent the day in the utmost harmony and hilarity.

At the usual time, the '76 Association assembled, and moved in procession to St. Philip's Church, accompanied by a Band of Music. After the performance of Divine Service by Rev. Dr. GADSDEN, the Declaration of Independence was read by JAMES S. JOHNSON, Esq., and a suitable Oration pronounced by THOMAS D. CONDY, Esq.,—after which they returned to the Hotel, and dined together.

The Cincinnati and Revolution Societies also assembled at the usual hour, at the Carolina Coffee House, from whence they proceeded, also accompanied by a Band of Music, to St. Michael's Church, where, after the performance of Divine Service by the Right Reverend Bishop BOWEN, an Oration was delivered by C.C. PINCKNEY, Jun, Esq., after which they returned to the Coffee House to dine.

After the morning parade, the *Charleston Riflemen* and *Northern Volunteers* rendezvoused at Vauxhall Gardens, from whence they marched in procession, accompanied by the Rifle Band, to the French Protestant Church. After prayers by the Rev. Mr. BACHMAN, an oration was delivered by J. J. MAUGER, Esq., a member of the Rifle Corps.

The day closed in the usual festive and harmonious manner, without the occurrence of any mishap to mar its pleasure—and in the evening, a handsome display of Fire Works was exhibited.

* * *

Argus of Western America (Frankfort, Kentucky), 6 August 1819
From the *Charleston Courier*, July 6
FIRE

The festivities in honor of our great national anniversary were succeeded Monday night by a most distressing event which, together with an immense destruction of property, has rendered homeless a number of industrious citizens. About 1 o'clock, a fire was discovered in the front shop of Mr. Brodie, baker, in Meeting Street, next door to the corner of Meeting Street, which soon communicated [to] . . . all the buildings on Meeting Street up to that occupied by Mr. Pierce—in all about 200 buildings.

* * *

John Calhoun (Secretary of War) to Virgil Maxcy (Annapolis), 12 August 1820

I regret that any pretext should have been given by the Missouri Convention, by which an objection might be raised to her admission; but I do hope, that all that is virtuous or considerate in the non-slaveholding States, will in every shape discountenance the renewal of so dangerous a question. I can scarcely conceive of a cause of sufficient power to divide this Union, unless a belief in the slave holding States, that it is the intention of the other States gradually to undermine their property in slaves and that a disunion is the only means to avert the evil. Should so dangerous a mode of believing once take root, no one can calculate the consequences; and it will be found, that a reagitation of the Missouri question will tend strongly to excite such a belief.

W. Edwin Hemphill, *The Papers of John C. Calhoun*, 5:327

* * *

To the House of Representatives, 16 October 1820

Petitioners have seen with anxious concern another existing evil . . . that a spacious Building has lately been erected on the immediate Neighbourhood of Charleston for the *exclusive* worship of Negroes and coloured people from means supplied to them by abolition societies in the Eastern and Northern States. . . . this Establishment is as unnecessary as it is impolitick. . . . ample accommodation has always been provided and afforded to the Negroes and coloured People in the numerous Churches and places of Publick worship in the city.

Another evil is in permitting our free Negroes and coloured people to visit the Eastern States for *ordination* and other religious practices and again returning. . . . another evil is that of suffering schools and assemblages of negro slaves to be taught reading and writing organized and conducted not only by Negroes and coloured people, but, in some instances, by white persons of this State. . . . [It is] well known that during last winter several Masters or teachers arrived in Charleston from Philadelphia amply furnished with pecuniary means by abolitionists for the avowed purpose of educating our negroes.

Jas. Lowndes, Peter Gaillard, Thomas Wigfall, R. Vanderhorst, Benj. Seabrook, Thomas Napier, Charles Graves, Edwin Holland, Alex. Gillon, John Horlbeck, John Pringle.

General Assembly Petitions, SCDAH

* * *

Pendleton Messenger, 31 October 1820 [Charleston by-line]

The Schooner *Calypso* which sailed from this port yesterday for Sierra Leone, was fitted out by an aged and respectable black man by the name of Creighton, who had accumulated considerable property in the city by following the trade of a barber. . . . His family and several other free people of color have gone to spend the rest of their days on the coast of Africa. It is worthy of remark, that although Creighton was the owner of several slaves, to all of whom he offered the choice either to accompany him in his expedition and have their freedom, or to be sold and remain in this country, only one could be prevailed upon to proceed with him.

* * *

Charleston Mercury, 1 January 1822

We now enter upon another and new career of time. The clock of St. Michael's Church that struck twelve last night, shut out for ever from us, the year that is rounded with eternity.

* * *

Charleston Mercury, 7 January 1822

An attempt was made early yesterday to set fire to a wooden house in King Street. Some boards were ripped off and fire and combustibles forced into the opening. The fire was discovered by a gentleman smelling smoke.

* * *

Carolina Gazette, 23 March 1822

The Revolutionary Movement in the Spanish Provinces in this hemisphere attracted the attention and excited the sympathy of our fellow citizens from its commencement. . . . The

Spirit of the Age is everywhere felt in countries oppressed by despotism, in regions benighted with bigotry.

* * *

James Hamilton Jr. to William Lowndes, 16 June 1822

For the last week, I have been indulging myself with the hope that I should find time to ride to the Grove . . . but for several days I have been increasingly occupied both night and day in relation to a subject on which public anxiety has been acutely awakened. . . . I have taken it, of course, for granted that you must have heard of the rumour of a contemplated commotion among a certain part of our population.

James Hamilton Jr. Papers, SHC

* * *

The Georgian, 17 June 1822

An attempt has been made by the blacks on the island of Guadeloupe to rise upon their owners which was, however, frustrated. A large quantity of arms and ammunition was found in the houses of the black population of St. Bartholomew, intended for the use of their brethren in Guadeloupe.

* * *

John Potter (Charleston) to Langdon Cheves (Philadelphia), 24 June 1822

We have had some unpleasant anticipations here in regards to our *slaves* lately—James will inform you more particularly—at all times is it an unpleasant view and a Subject to dwell on I fear, much of the poison that flows in this way comes from your City!!!

Langdon Cheves Papers, SCHS

* * *

Anna Johnson (Charleston) to Elizabeth Haywood (Raleigh), 28 June 1822

And now my dear Betsy "I will a tale unfold" whose lightest word—Would harrow up thy soul; freeze thy young blood
   Make thy two eyes like stars start from their spheres
   Thy knotted and combined locks to part
   Like quills upon the fretful porcupine—list list oh list
   In a sober phrase, our city is now in the most fearful state.
   Gracious Heavens[,] when I think what I have escaped & what I may yet suffer my blood curdles—Alas! Sterne too truly said that "Slavery was a bitter draught"—Our slaves have revolted and the plot was only found out by the noble interposition of a Negro whom they wanted to join them—he instantly with the subtlety of his class drew from his acquaintance the design plan time & carried them with trembling anxiety informed his master who instantly informed the Intendant and my uncle who is fortunately Governor and by them every means was taken to protect the city—for the information was given only a few days before the insurrection was to have taken place—since which a court of inquiry has been

instituted of the most important and honourable men of our city who have been sitting now more than a week and the number implicated is incredible—and I blush to own that it has been traced to the Whites for this day one or two white men have been taken up and the proofs are so strong as to hang them—for some intelligent negro who acts as a spy for the court found when & where nightly meetings were held and carried our Intendant and one or two others there who saw and heard scenes of rapine and murder talked of with the coolness of demons—Their plans were simply these—they were to have set fire to the town, and while the whites were endeavoring to out it, they were to have commenced their horrid depredations—it seems that the Governor, Intendant and my poor self were to be the three first victims—The Men and Black Women were to have been indiscriminately murdered—& we poor devils were to have been reserved to fill their Harams—horrible—I have a very beautiful cousin who was set apart for the wife or more properly the "light of the Haram" of one of their chiefs—and the old and infirm women were to have shared the fate of our fathers—It is true that in our city the White & Black Population are equal 16,000—each but about Georgetown the odds is fearful—16,000 to 150 whites—I do not know the estimate of the black population thro' the state but I know that it is very great—I am told that the number in the plot is computed to be about 3000—The children were to have been spiked & murdered and I am told that the observation taken from the man taken up to day was this— I feel a little sorry for the children, but they must go, as to those already condemned, it is no matter that some must die for the cause—you have still many brave spirits among you—go on—*booty Beauty & Glory*—this from a free born American—I thought not to hearing such a villain breathing the pure air of free born America—Six of the Chiefst are to be hung the 2nd. July.

Ernest Haywood Papers, SHC

* * *

Charleston Courier, 1 July 1822

In the Inferior Court, Joseph Lawrence, a free black man from New York, who arrived on the schooner *Fair Play* was tried upon a charge of endeavoring to inveigle a negro man named Macklin, belonging to Maj. Jas. Dunwoody. He so far effected his purpose as to get the slave on board the schooner, when about to return to New York, the design was detected. He was found guilty and imprisoned for one year and is to be sold as a slave.

* * *

Charleston Mercury, 4 July 1822

Forty six years have rolled away since the intrepidity of our fathers dared to dash to earth the specter of foreign sway and to claim an independent rank among the nations of the world. What was gained in the spirit of liberty must be spread abroad in that same spirit.

* * *

Southern Patriot and Commercial Gazette (Charleston), 5 July 1822

The Anniversary of American Independence was celebrated yesterday with the usual manifestations of public joy and gratitude. . . . The Cincinnati and American Revolution Societies processed to St. Philip's Church to hear an address by Alexander Moultrie. The 76

Association processed to St. Michael's Church where Robert Elfe gave a reading of the Declaration of Independence. . . . John Legare Berwick addressed the congregation.

* * *

John Potter (Charleston) to Langdon Cheves (Philadelphia), 5 July 1822

Since I wrote you our situation here—and investigation made by the Court which has again been constituted by the same gentlemen and are still proceeding with their enquiries—altho' many are implicated in the Crime, for which six have already suffered. I do not whether more lives will atone for their plans of deep laid treachery and murder.

I fear it will have a sad effect, on this kind of property, much depends on what is now adopted for our future safety, and laws that maybe adopted at the coming meeting of our legislature. I do not recollect whether I mentioned the Circumstances of *Vesey* (the chief who was hanged) and others, had wigs and whiskers made, to wear on the business—the wretch denied the fact, never had seen the french man who made them, when confronted together, until this man took one of the wigs from his pocket, and asked him if he knew that[?] when the villain was abashed—I believe for the first time—as he had denied it totally before.—I had Major Wilson's servant (Gibb's son-in-law) was the person who first discovered and divulged the plot of murder which his mind could not submit to—

I must confess that if one of these fellows, had made his way into my bed room in the dead of night, dressed out in his *wig, whiskers, and whitened face*—that I might have been appaled, not being aware of the circumstance—but probably these precious few would have been enough to do out of doors—and that trifling business of *taking care* of *the males* would have fallen to other agents, with the Servants of the family, many of whom, are not yet known I fear, would have turned traitors on the Occasion—Certainly this discovery has awkward unpleasant feelings, tho' I firmly believe that all such dangers is over for the present—this however my friend is more than I durst own before my family who have been more alarmed than I have ever been before—nor can I deem it surprising from the horrid aspect of the transaction and consequences which might have followed in the event taking place—attended with the smallest success—tho' in the end they could not have succeeded at all—

I have already mentioned how Judge Johnson was implicated in foolish, ill-timed publications—the minds of the people were exceedingly irritated against him—Inclosed is his justifications which came out Saturday, but which somehow has not given much relief or satisfaction to the public mind—and his pushing it on Willington, the printer will only involve, I fear, more recriminations.

For a man so well informed, it is surprising he does, so may I say, many weak and imprudent acts—Certainly the anecdote he first gave the public (as he calls it) was at any time improper and a libel on his Country—but particularly at such a moment, doubly improper and unfounded—

Langdon Cheves Papers, SCHS

* * *

Mary L. Beach to Elizabeth L. Gilchrist (Germantown, Pennsylvania), 5 July 1822

My heart has been the abode of but a small share of peace or comfort if any at all for some days past; owing to the mournful state of things in our guilty City, I believe *all* danger for the *present* season is over—but to any one at all disposed to reflect, or feel for *others* as well as their *own* interests the events of this week were calculated to excite *much painful & bitter reflection*. The execution is over as to us at least for the present and has not been attended with tumult, or assistance as was feared by some of weak nerves. The Military Force out that day was so overpowering as to have rendered rescue a *desperate* attempt. Miss Ramsey told me that the Negroes were under the impression that Denmark Vesey, the free black *won't* be delivered and if in *no* other way the jail doors opened by a Supernatural Power. You will doubtless feel as I did desirous of knowing how the accused behaved at the execution for I greatly feared that they would have made some address to excite further rebellion; but they did not attempt it. Vesey was in a very hardened state in the jail say *our* people in other places they will say perhaps he behaved with Magnanimity. Mr. T. Legare says he heard from a white person a gentleman I believe but one who was near enough almost to have touched him that he did not make a single remark but appeared like *one* to use his expression "collecting his thoughts for the scene before him." You can't think what a feeling came for a moment over me when I heard this although he deserved to die for the undertaking he had embarked on. He was said to be a man of superior powers of mind & the more dangerous for it. He asserted in jail that he had not had a *fair* trial, that his accusers had not been brought before him; the last charge is a fact; but for motives of Prudence and Policy in our present state of affairs it *could* not be allowed, or *was* not at least—but they say his guilt was clearly marked from the testimony of several witnesses examined separately; but whose testimony fully agreed as to his agency etc. Poyas' Peter all I have heard speak of, as a very hardened villain died in a dreadful "state of mind." I am told two of them even laughed when first brought out of jail and preserved this state of mind to the last. Bennett's fellow Rolla was quite a young man, but had been a member for two years of our Church he evinced much feeling & penitence even to tears—his Master would not believe I have heard tell he heard it from his *own* lips that he had been engaged in it. I do pity Bennett sincerely for he has gained, if enemies can be called "gained" by it—But to a man who has studied his people I know for as he has it must be very wounding—I heard he said there was his neighbour Mrs. Townsend who keeps hens (with her bread baking you know & she a women in easy circumstance & her woman near lying in carrying a load too heavy for a man I should say to some quite here with a great clothes basket of bread) he said working day and night so *they* had not *time* for *one* even of them to be engaged in it. . . . he had three. And I am afraid this very instance of Bennett's will induce in others to be harder with them than they were previous to it; saying it is better to keep them handy.

Ah! Slavery it is a *hard* business and I am afraid we shall in this country know it to our bitter cost some day or other. Rolla confessed his being engaged in the business; but said he had felt so much about it that he resolved to leave the city before the awful event took place as he could not have to commit murder and laid the blame on Vesey—Dr. Palmer said he appeared to be more cut down when he spoke to him of his sin as a professor than on any other ground—this I thought in his favour poor deluded creature. I hear that Vesey impressed or tried to do it the [illegible] that they ought to engage in the business on account of the abridgement of their religious privileges and that he said to them that Dr. Palmer even had joined with some of the gentlemen of our Church and made a Catechism *different* for the negroes—this was the fact, but the good man did it to accommodate it to their understanding. Good man he gets it from all quarters to think of some person in an office before persons the other day calling him a Rascal with an Oath; for the part he had taken in trying to give them religious instruction; you may recollect the affair when Codgell and Turnbull had some difficulty with him or rather it was that letter when Dr. P had given some black man a ticket as a class leader or something of that sort. And now the bitterness that is poured out on the dear good missionaries is enough to make, I was going to say, Satan triumph. But God can overcome it for good as dark as the cloud now is about the increased spread of the gospel in our state. It seems this business has been of 4 years standing and ever since the affair of their being foiled about the African Church.

There are several still in confinement and it is expected I believe will be transported. They convict none on *a single testimony*. It is said that 500 had given their names in the City to join them; but this I do not vouch for, for never were more falsehoods perhaps told—it is also said that Vesey and the other ring leaders were to have the pillage of the Banks and of which they were immediately to go off to Santo Domingo & leave the fools behind to pay the reckoning. Mary Jones, I believe (caught with the Earthquakes) never went through such a night of Terror as that of the 16th. June—and can you think it *possible* I could have smiled that night or rather it was near day, yet I did—When she said, in a most solemn tone. Oh! I shall never be able to bear the sight of a Negroe again and if I go (or live to go) to the Northward I *never will* have *one* about me and at present she has almost I may say a *hatred* of them *all*. I have heard it remarked by several that all confidence in them now is forever at an end! After the treachery of *several* in this business—Poor Susan McCall is in considerable trouble about her Clarissa her children's nurse her husband if he is not hanged will be shipped off—She is I think without *any exception* the most superior black female I know— we had an opportunity of seeing her at James Island and the Ramsey's say her husband is just as fine a looking black he belongs to Harth—before belonging to Blackwood was a young creature only about 22 I hear he had a most prepossessing countenance and I have heard that James Legare wishes him pardoned—it seems there was a great openness and candour in his manner and he shewed a very tender and penitent spirit. Dr. Furman, Palmer and Mr. Bois visited them in jail, but Vesey and Poyas' fellow would hear *nothing* they had to say; they said they were condemned already and it was of no use to say anything more. They were executed near the Lines I understand, but few blacks attended. The companies on duty were out from 9 at night until 9 the next morning and the City will I understand be strongly guarded for some time to come by the different companies. Whether they think the City Guard are not to be trusted, I cannot say; but are kept at the Guard House & Arsenal. But this won't I expect sent *them* long to be out of the way of picking up Dollars in addition to their wages. It is said in the voluminous papers found it is astonishing the gain in their knowledge &c & they speak of their cause as one they expect the Lord will assist them in as he did the Israelites from their Battles; & speak of their deliverance from the hand of the Philistines. I heard Vesey said in the Jail that it was a Glorious Cause he was to die in & the singing of Psalms &c. in there the night before were carried on to a great extent—he said also that his *Spiritual* enjoyment never had been as great or greater than that night or the one before it. What do you think of *Wigs* made to order of the ringleaders being produced by the City Guard which they were to wear with their faces painted white when they first were to attack the City Guard.

Mary Lamboll Thomas Beach Papers, SCHS

* * *

Martha Proctor Richardson (Savannah) to Dr. James Screven (Liverpool), 6 July 1822

My Dear James:

The people of Charleston have been for some time past in aweful commotion, they had received information that an insurrection was in contemplation, the 16th July the day fixed on for its commencement—the city was to have been set fire to in forty different places—the whites murdered as they left their dwellings—the arsenal to be seized on—the negroes from the Country were then to join them—and the shipping in the harbour was to be also taken possession of—This information it is said was given by the coachman of Dr. Simons—The city council were called together and sat in judgement on those suspected—Six were condemned and executed on 2nd. July—it is said that the leaders in this conspiracy were class leaders of religious societies—you will recollect that in Carolina the blacks are not allowed to preach in congregations of their own—they *must* associate with the white people in the different churches—God knows how all this will end—but I fear such an attempt will one day be made—and of what consequence will it be to those who are killed by them whether they succeed or not—Mr. Harris has just called and he brought a letter from Major Hamilton the Intendant of Charleston I will copy the part relating to this unfortunate business as it will enable you to understand better than I related it—"you may feel some solicitate to learn something of the late threaten'd insurrection in this city—a few of the prominent particulars of which I will relate to you—This plot had its origin among the Black Class leaders of some of the different religious associations of this city—and altho' its causes may be in some degree referable to temporal inconveniences and suffering unavoidable incident to the state of slavery there are mainly to be attributed to religious Fanaticism—The ring leaders of the conspiracy were all of them class leaders or Deacons—six of whom were yesterday executed, and who met their fate with the heroic fortitude of Martyrs—They have been for sometime engaged in their preparations for the explosion, which was to have been consummated on the night of the 16th July. Their plan denoted a fine Military *Tact* and admirable combination. Their forces were to have been divided into Three columns—The first and the most important was to carry the main Guard House and Arsenal—This was to have been concentrated at South Bay & to have been composed of the Male Negroes from James Island, led by a determined fellow, full of carnage & sagacity—This body were to have been supplied with arms sufficient to effect their purpose and were to have formed in the centre of the city a junction with the two other divisions from the West & the North—on which the Town was to have been fired in Forty different Places and the householders murdered at their doors on coming out—This conflagration was to be a signal to the Negroes from the country to flock in & join their associates in arms in the city—The discovery of their designs was made by the fidelity of a favourite slave to his Master—We have been thus far very successful in our developments & have proceeded with great activity and perseverance—I am happy amidst all this excitement to say to you that no excess of popular feelings & prejudices have disgraced the character of our city—& that a remarkably respectable court has conducted its deliberations with humanity to the accused but with great energy as it regards the public safety—I am sorry to say that our friend judge Johnson has involved himself in an unpleasant controversy with the public authorities & court, by volunteering a very unreasonable & unnecessary admonition by which a great ferment has been excited against him"—In this place every suspicion appears at rest—and I trust there is no cause for alarm—but I am of the opinion that the Blacks knew of this business long before it was known by us—

Arnold-Screven Papers, SHC

* * *

The Georgian, 6 July 1822

Execution—Denmark Vesey (a free black man), Rolla, Batteau, Ned, Peter and Jesse (slaves), convicted of an attempt to raise an insurrection in the state of South Carolina, were executed pursuant to sentence on Tuesday morning last, between the hours of six and eight o'clock.

* * *

J. Richardson (Charleston) to Langdon Cheves (Philadelphia), 9 July 1822

You must feel anxious about your situation here. Sir, it is simply this, a well-digested conspiracy of Slaves has been discovered upon proof of [illegible] gave it, six have already been hung and some more will be, no doubt, convicted.

The owners & their counsel have been satisfied with the inquest. The court you know. The members are firm, yet considerate. They must from the number of conspirators such to lessen the incident. The attempt would have been [illegible] tho' much [illegible] to a free person.

P.S. And arguments calculated to exercise hatred had been much used, the accounts so far so complicated a conspiracy. The Slaves were assured that Congress had set them free and of course their bondage illegal while their [illegible] abroad.

Langdon Cheves Papers, SCHS

* * *

John Potter (Charleston) to Langdon Cheves (Philadelphia), 10 July 1822

Since I last wrote you about this most diabolical plot which the mercy of God prevented on the very eve & very day of destruction—the public mind has been much agitated—the first court resumed its labors—and every step they advanced, it was found that the Conspiracy had spread wider and wider—Confessions were made more fully and a vast number of slaves were taken up; on Saturday 5 more wretches were Condemned to death, to be hung on Friday next—1 belonged to Gell, who kept the Stables, 1 to Paul Pritchard (who was the "wizzard") one to John Drayton his cook who had hitherto behaved well—1 to David Haig and a favourite servant of Elias Horry—I believe his coachman!!

Indeed it is now well ascertained that most of the Coachmen and favourite servants in the City knew of it, were if they had not participated, with intentions and plans prepared.

Mr. Bryan's coachman—as well as Mrs. Fergusons—knew all—but when it came to the murder of their masters (young Bryan & Ferguson) the minds revolted they say—but as Rolla who is hung told his master the governor—tho' he would not have done the deed—another had undertaken the Office—it seems as a reported fire—that Peter Smiths house [on] South Bay a large house opposite Judge Johnson's, R. Cunningham's, and several others most conspicuous, at the opposite corner—were to be fired on the night of the 16th. ult.

when as the white males would appear—before they could leave their own doors, the indiscriminate massacre was to take place—the females were to be meant for *worse than death*—It is believed that Vesey's plans when this had been completed [were] to have forced the bank and carried off as much Plunder as he could to St. Domingo—and leave the blind agents behind (as all could not follow) and perish for their crimes—*When your kind and tenderhearted Philadelphians, as well as Quakers* preach up emancipation, let them *ponder* on the deeds of darkness and misery that well could have taken place—had this plot here even in part succeeded—but such evils are disregarded, if their favorite plan of *philanthropy* had been successful—God in his mercy reward them for it!!!! This is the part from whence our evils spring!!! We will throw back on them all these black free incendiaries—when the wretches who are implicated in consenting to the deed will go, I cannot yet say, but here they cannot remain—a high and hearty hand will go forth where the laws cannot reach—*Your Branch here* would no doubt have held their *first preference of plunder*—this is a risk you had not I suppose contemplated!!

Langdon Cheves Papers, SCHS

* * *

Confession of Bacchus Hammet, the Slave of Mr. Hammet (ca. 12 July)

Bacchus stated that *Perault* (Strohecker man) on or about the 2nd. May whilst hauling Cotton to the Wharf persuaded him to go to a Society; that he enquired of Perault what society it was, and was told to never mind but prepare earnestly to go that Perault would call for him that night which he did* [*About this time Perault was discovered by Bacchus's master as wishing to get into his gate; on enquiry found that Perault wanted to see B and when he asked *what for*. after much hesitancy stated "he wanted to give Bacchus a little bit of religion, that Bacchus was a very wicked boy, and he wanted to get him to try and serve God, and try and save his soul and be a better servant to his master." Mr. H. questioned him as to the liberty he took in attempting such a thing with his servant and enquired of Perault *if he did not belong to the African church*, he said "*Yes*" and when warned about leading his boy in to such Society as Mr. H. thought them great rascals, Perault replied "*He was sorry but he thought them as good as other people.*" Bacchus no doubt went with him as he was absent at 12 o'clock at night] That they went together to Denmark Vesey's house near Bennetts Mills, that they were rec'd by Denmark when they went into his house door and the gate locked upon them. That Denmark after ascertaining it was Perault & another man (as Perault said to D) he went with them into the house. In a large room I seen ten or a dozen men, a table in the midst of the room and a large Book upon it, probably the Bible—Denmark asked me who I belonged to and my name, Perault immediately answered "Bacchus, belonging to Mr. Hammet." Denmark asked me which Hammet, I said Mr. Benjamin Hammet, the gentleman who put old Lorenzo Dow in jail, and is an officer in Captain Martindale's company— Perault and Denmark then took me in a side room, and Perault says to me, "Bacchus I have some particular thing to say to you." I asked what it was, he said "that they was going to have a war and fight the white people" and that I must join them. I said, "Perault, I am sorry that you brought me into this business and you better let it alone" and I considered some time; at last Perault said, "Bacchus, you need not fret, you may as well join us," Denmark then said, "*any person who didn't join us must be treated as an enemy, and put to death*" and I said "if that is the case, well I will join you." We all then went into the large room, and there I seen Rolla Bennett, Monday Gell, Charles Drayton and Smart Anderson and another who I believe is Denmark Vesey's son—They had a large book open and something like a letter in it, which *believe come from some free country, may be St. Domingo* and Denmark's son says to Monday shewing him something in the letter, "look here Monday see how they are making fun of we "meaning the people off in the free country." That Denmark said "Friends, we have a friend who is to go into the country to raise the country negroes to come down, all who can, *must* put in money to raise a sum *to pay his master, wages while he is gone.*" that they all put in, and I and Perault put in seven pence. Denmark then said they must all swear, that *they all held up their right hand and swore*, and said after Denmark, "*We will not tell if taken by the whites, nor will we tell if we are to be put to death.*" That under the Sanctity of this Oath he never told his master. This was the first meeting. Denmark told me and the rest that night the next week we were to meet again at his House, I believe it was Thursday. At the next meeting, I was asked by Denmark *if I could get arms*, I told him maybe *an old sword*; and he said no matter *any arms* I can get to bring them to him, Perault told me to try to get arms and powder, I said *my master has pistols, but I am afraid to take them*, and Perault said never mind, We will *satisfy your master** [*no doubt by a murdering argument as a small hatchet with a long handle is in possession of the master; a very useful and deadly weapon it is—The horseman's sword was considered of little value and lay in the Back Store] on that subject. *That I did at the middle of the day steal out of the back store of my master when the Clerks were busy and the store open one keg of powder and the horseman's sword*—that when busy in the house, *I did steal my master's pistol out of the closet of one afternoon.* That (Ned Bennett) one of Bennett's men came and waited in the street that night until I came out to assist me in carrying the powder to Denmark's. We carried it in a bag and I gave the sword and pistol to him. He afterwards told me he gave the sword to Perault, and Perault gave it to Caesar Smith. The powder was carried to Monday Gells house by Perault, when Gullah Jack came and got it. Denmark told me on Sunday 16th. June we must not go home, that every one must stay out, and go up the road to a farm on meeting street road, as soon as we heard the noise, and then meet the country negroes under him, and another that *I must not join the people where my master lived, but join another gang and he would send a gang to take my Master, and take Capt. Martindale** [*Capt. M & Mr. H were to be tortured] every one who could was to come out. That morning I went to Monday Gell's (the 9th. June) and there I met Charles Drayton who was going with Monday to the farm; but Monday seeing me said, "Charles here is a friend he will go with you I have a hog to kill and can't go he will go" I went up to a farm on Meeting Street road to a house having a Balcony at the top is on it— here Charles Drayton called for the Old daddy and some two women came to the gate—and went back and called him. He came and Charles and myself went into the Stable with him, and Charles told him, that he must be in readiness as the Country Negroes would be down next Sunday, and he must receive them—we then went away—

On the next Sunday the 16th. June, Gullah Jack came to Monday Gell where I was and Charles Drayton and said you can't go up to the farm, I have been up the road and just came down, and the negroes can't go up as *the Patrol is out quite strong—That I was to help to get the arms of the Neck Company** [*The Charleston Neck patrol no doubt prevented an assemblage that day and consequently much alarm. Yet council arrogates all the whole and sole praise]—That Monday Gell told me when the Negroes was taken up (for holding a meeting in Anson Street) in 1820, *that the African Church was the people, and that they met for this very purpose but that business put them back, and now they had began again to try it*— After Denmark was taken, Perault came and told me, and said Denmark said nobody must tell anything—That Perault said never mind keep yourself in readiness and when you hear the noise in the street you must come out and help us *to get the arms of the Neck Company* (6th July) that Gullah Jack was to head this party and then to fight the white people with them. The General plan was to fight the white people and them that wasn't killed to be driven out of the City (That when in prison *Perault told me not to tell as I was in the same room with him** [*Perault never began to confess until the day he found Bacchus told something]—he told me *where the powder keg was—that it was buried by Gullah Jack*) That Perault told me "*we have a Blacksmith who is making bayonets or something to stick with*, we have already 2 or 300 Bayonets and 3 or 400 (hundred) men." Monday said "We are 2,000 (thousand) Strong."

When I asked Denmark about how they would be able to do this thing without arms—he said that every one must look out for the different stores that had arms such as guns &c. and take notice of them—He told me also that all the Ministers were to be killed* [*corroborated by the testimony of Jesse Blackwood] except a few who were to be saved and showed different passages in the Bible from which Denmark preached (& the rest) and they were to be asked Why they did not preach up this thing (meaning the passages on liberty &c.) to them before and that they would be made to tell.

[The passages alluded to were Exodus 1st Chpt. & 21st Chpt., 16th verse also 19th Chpt. Isaiah and 14th. Zachariah 1 & 3rd. verses etc].

Notwithstanding the evidence of guilt against this fellow and from his own confession; yet he went to the gallows, *laughing and bidding his acquaintances in the streets "goodbye,"* on being hung, owing to some mismanagement in the fall of the trap, he was not thrown off, but as the board canted he slipped; yet he was so hardened, that he *threw himself forward and as he swung back he lifted his feet so that his knees might not touch the board!*—In prison he was considered very hardened, He told a clergyman the evening before his execution that "*He never had any goodness in him and that hell was his portion*"—He was well used and had many privileges allowed him—So Hardened was he in fact, that he was seen to laugh a moment or two before the cap was drawn over his eyes.

The following is furnished by a friend of the owner who obtained it from the Rev. Mr. Backman.

That Rev. Gentleman was in the habit of visiting the prisoners; and on a visit of this kind he happened to step into the room where Bacchus was and found him very dejected, apparently in a deep study, he enquired how it was with him, meaning his future state and hopes, Bacchus replied "had enough" and said "he would go to hell." Indeed that was bad enough said the clergyman. Bacchus replied "*he was thinking if he ever did a good action*" and found he never had. He told the clergyman "*that he was the devil amongst the women*" that he believed he would go to hell "that his master thought he was a good servant and he had been a very bad boy." He also stated how he was carried to Veseys by Perault, how Vesey sat him alongside of him, and when he found he [missing] to join him He asked him queries such as "*Did his master treat him well—Yes he believes so Did he eat the same as his master*, Yes sometimes, but not always as well as his master—*Did his master sleep on a soft bed*, Yes *did he Bacchus sleep on as soft a bed as his master* No—*Who made his master*—God *Who made you*—God—*And then aren't you as good as your master if God made him and you, aren't you as free*—Yes, *then why don't you join and fight your master. Does your master* [illegible] *you well* Yes, I believe so, *Does he whip you when you do wrong*—Yes, sometimes, *Then why don't you* [missing] *as you are as free as your master turn about and fight for yourself*" Upon this delusive reasoning he joined, and then stated how his name was put down and the mode of swearing &c. &c. &c. after joining (with such delusions) he said he would have went as far as any of them in this business.

Benjamin Hammet Papers, DUL

* * *

Niles Register, 13 July 1822

The design appears to have been a pretty formidable one. Three of them (the blacks) were slaves of the governor of the state, and one of these was to have had his daughter, a beautiful young lady, as part of his share of the spoils on the destruction of her father and the whites.

* * *

Thomas Bennett (Governor of South Carolina) to John C. Calhoun, 15 July 1822

The State of Alarm which has for some time pervaded this community consequent on the discovery of insurrectionary movements has elicited anxious inquiry and awakened the most extraordinary vigilance. . . . The peculiar character of a Large proportion of our population, and the evidence of a temper hostile to peace and welfare of society which has so recently been manifested, will continue for some time to excite vigilance and elicit anxiety.

W. Edwin Hemphill, *Papers of John C. Calhoun*, 7:210

* * *

John Potter (Charleston) to Langdon Cheves (Philadelphia), 15 July 1822

Since I last wrote you, there has been [missing] of those intended conspiracies—3 of the 5 convicts, who were to have suffered on Friday last were respited a week and who have since made ample confession which has implicated many who were before above any suspicion—indeed the most confidential servants were first applied to and many either assisted or else engaged in the plot who hitherto had irreproachable characters. The Court is [missing] in session and doing its painful but no less necessary duty on Friday. 3 of Rope Walk Negroes, now belonging to the Robertsons and for many years held as our joint property (about 5 years ago he bought my half) were taken up—and I fear an evidence that will convict them or at least some of [missing], your farms would have been Capital Place of Mutiny, it seems they met at Bulkely's farm on the Meeting Street Road near the fork and always chose their conferences of blood and I believed poison by prayer and psalm singing.

Had it not been for the discovery of the plot by Maj. Wilson's servant and that only 3 days primary to the intended execution of the plot we might have been involved in a dreadful time of carnage particularly if their well laid plans had been brought to bear and put in execution in the dead of night on our unprepared unprovided sleeping people.

We have been in such a state of apathy that few people could believe such an intention could have been thought of. I hope it will lead to measures that such attempts may not be dreaded in future.

Langdon Cheves Papers, SCHS

* * *

Mary L. Beach to Elizabeth Gilchrist, 15 July 1822

Yesterday our Dear Minister preached two most excellent sermons well worth appearing in print from these words in Mark. "It must needs be that Offences come, but Woe to the world because of Offences." He endeavored to prove from various places in the Old Testament and in later days how God had overruled the actions of man even while they were under a free agency in the business to bring about his intentions both of Judgement and Mercy & particularly in the Redemption of the world—& cited some cases where even good men had done wrong & very wickedly even. . . . I suppose that these words may have had some allusion to the case of the poor blacks who I fear are in the Community at large all branded hypocrites for the wicked conduct of some—& some of these guilty ones were perhaps misled by more artful ones—for that wretched Vesey it is said applied his art to all classes of his tools. I suppose long before this reaches you, you will have seen that 5 more were to have been executed on the 12th. and that 3 were respited. One that was executed named Gullah Jack was an African a most superstitious creature and apparently one whose figure and whole deportment was of no importance—he gave some of those concerned an idea that he possessed the power of repelling any danger by mixtures he prepared and said that in his own country it had been proved that common bullets could not kill him. It is said so much [illegible] had Vesey over his superstitious mind that he was filled with dread at the thought of meeting Vesey's spirit at the Gallows. Poor wretched creature he and several others was confined in different cells in the Poor House for want of places in the Jail as I understand that they have none in the workhouse—Dr. Prioleau (I don't know what was his errand at the Poor House) saw Jack there a day or two before the execution and the creature knowing him said "Do Massa Doctor, do beg for me" and wept bitterly. Oh! my heart is often I was going to say torn with distress about these people it does appear for the general good they ought to die for there is little or no doubt of their guilt but when we look back on their sufferings what are we to say. The other man executed belonged to Elias Horry—a remarkable pleasant easy going servant previously, but very enterprising—his master before he was arrested said to Mrs. H. that he hoped he was not concerned in the business for if he was from his expressive temper he would be then to be deeply so and it has appeared so. Where or when the arrests will stop it is difficult or I should have said impossible to conjecture for on the 13th. fresh ones were arrested. I understand there were a meeting of a number of the Citizens, either on that day or the day before to consult on measures [illegible] on the present state of things. Arthur Hayne told Mary on Saturday when she was at Susan's that there has been a meeting also last week of Militia men and they had made such arrangements for the present safety that there was no cause for alarm now. Some persons I hear speak of the intention or advisability of making this a Garrison Town in future but all these precautions are yet only in compensation. Oh! that our God would grant us a spirit of humiliation under this rod and to ourselves Wisdom, forbearance, justice, mercy as well as firmness in their decisions. Though the country in general I believe remains very quiet. There have been some two or three persons it is said a few days ago rather a spirit of dissatisfaction shown but I hear nothing of it more—I was greatly disturbed however at hearing it was in more cases but this was *utterly false*. Poor old Mr. Jones has had some difficulty at his place which perhaps gave rise to the report—A very young fellow—a mere lad joined with 2 or 3 more of Mr. Martin's negroes and with fire arms attacked the stage; but providentially although they fired twice as there were no passengers in it no hurt was done of course; at the 2nd firing the ball or buck shot passed by the stage drivers hat only the last arrests we heard were that Mr. J's lad was in Jacksonborough Jail—but the Negroes in the neighbourhood from various accounts so far from having a *daring* spirit were apparently *afraid* to go off their own plantations & this solely appears to have been only a [illegible] which business they have been carrying on for some time it seems at the old gentleman's place.

Mary Lamboll Thomas Beach Papers, SCHS

* * *

Letter scrap (Charleston), 16 July 1822

... to occupy their whole attention on the Negroes—I don't believe that they would bring any price at present—I have not heard of the proceedings of the Court yesterday, but they are proceeding with a firm step and I apprehend many now will forfeit their lives, new incidents are appearing everyday—Some pike handles were found at Bulkley's farm and the pike maker is safely housed—but the pikes are not found yet, I believe, as well as powder and arms are known, to have been in their possession—the Charleston Neck Company had always left their arms and instruments. . . .

Benjamin Hammet Papers, DUL

* * *

Charleston Mercury, 17 July 1822

Three Negroes, Nashaw and Jim, the property of Mrs. Jacob Martin, and Jupiter, property of T. Jones Esq., convicted of having fired at the mail driver on the Parker's Ferry Road to be hanged at Jacksonborough.

* * *

Anna Johnson (Charleston) to Elizabeth Haywood (Charleston), 18 July 1822

I have been too selfish in my correspondence of late; but my mind has been too much agitated about the late occurrences that I could think of nothing else, and not even the dangers that have beset me have had power to make me feel but I am not always so [illegible] as I have been lately and in future I will try to be more entertaining. . . .

This time you are anxious to hear more about the unhappy business which has filled with consternation all our city and nothing but the merciful interposition of our own God has saved us from horrors equal if not superior to the scenes acted in St. Domingo—the catalogue is not filled up for our thought that it was ended and that the execution of the six of the chiefest would suffice. The court had been dismissed and the town was again sinking into its wanted security when information was given that another attempt would be made at such a time, and the State's witness gave information of such a nature as to induce the City Council to recall the court and since that period the alarm has spread most widely, and there are now between 50 & 60 of the leaders in our jail. It is said that twenty of them have been convicted & sentenced, and in all probability the executions will not end under 100, but I was told yesterday that the prisoners had been heard to say that even should there be 500 executed there would be still enough to carry the work into execution Denmark Vesey one of those already executed and who was the instigator of the whole plot acknowledged that he had been nine years endeavouring to effect the diabolical scheme, how far the mischief has extended, heaven only knows—I never heard in my life more deeply laid plots or plots more likely to succeed, indeed "'twas a plot, a good plot—an excellent plot." But 'twas a plot that had it succeeded would have told to after ages a most fearful tale—It would be absurd in me to attempt a detail of all the circumstances real or imaginary which I have heard—this much is all that I know of that bears the stamp of truth; That their intention was to take the city and keep it as long as possible and then carry *us* and the common negroes to St. D. there to be sold as slaves with as much plunder as they could find, it seems that this Vesey had been at St. D and made an agreement that at such a time so many Vessels should be hired to assist—It would have been a complete scene of desolation—as yet thank God, none of our slaves have been found in the plot, tho there are 20 of them here in the yard.

Ernest Haywood Papers, SCHS

* * *

John Potter [?] to Langdon Cheves (Philadelphia), ca. 20 July 1822

I sent you newspapers, detailing the Sentence of the Court, of the day preceeding—and from numerous arrests daily, there is no knowing how many will suffer. Robertson has three condemned, as you would see—whilst those slaves belonged to us jointly, I never had a Complaint against them for 10 years—one had *then*, a wife in my yard, and when I left the City, I always directed him to sleep in the yard—which I thought safe under his charge.

Bennett did the same with Rolla, who had indeed the Safety of his family entrusted to him, whilst absent at Columbia—This cunning and deeply devised plot was much more extensive than you had any idea of, when I wrote on the 11th. nothing could be better arranged and would have done credit to a better cause & other means.

All the arms on the Neck were deposited in one place—to which a negro had access, and was to relinquish the keys—700 stand of muskets would also bring [illegible] in their power—& there was enough powder ready at hand [missing] and when the Guard was overpowered—and Arsenal taken, the Torch was to give the signal of murder and blood—all those who were to go out on the cry of fire, which was to be multiplied, would meet their fate, the draymen, Carters and Coachmen to act as Cavalry and secure the Streets while the Cooks and Servants with the plot indoors were to murder every white man—many I hope were not implicated, I have no reason to suppose that any of my house Servants were Guilty, but there were enough to commence with, and but anyway successfull even for a moment all, or nearly all, would have joined!

It is said by a fellow in his confession that when *Vesey* was inducing him to murder his master, he hesitated—but at length agreed—then, what says he, will happen to the children? What, says this *Arch Villain*, kill the *Lice* and let the *Nit* remain no—no—never!!! Dr. Haig's Harry was ordered by Gullah Jack to poison his master's well—but he says he refused to do that deed, but assented to all the rest—had it taken place two weeks since—as the Condemned wretch *Peter Poyas* wished the result probably would have been dreadful—we were then all unprepared—Completely so—this is all private & confidential. . . .

Langdon Cheves Papers, SCHS

* * *

John Calhoun to Maj. James Bankhead (Commanding Officer, Charleston), 22 July 1822

Upon the representation of the Governor of South Carolina requiring an additional military force to be stationed at Charleston, the enclosed order has been given to Lt. Col. Abram Eustis for the removal of one Company from St. Augustine to that place with orders on its arrival to report to you.

You will consult with the Governor of South Carolina upon the distribution to be made of the Company on its arrival and co-operate with him upon such measures as may be deemed advisable in quelling the disturbances at Charleston.

W. Edwin Hemphill, *Papers of John C. Calhoun*, 7:219

* * *

John Calhoun to Thomas Bennett, 22 July 1822

. . . in relation to the state of the Garrisons in Charleston Harbour, and have ordered without delay a reinforcement of one Company from St. Augustine, which I hope will be sufficient to remove the uneasiness in the publick mind on account of the inadequacy of the garrisons. I would add another company but the Military Establishment is so reduced in proportion to the number of posts which we are compelled to occupy that it cannot be done without propriety.

W. Edwin Hemphill, *Papers of John C. Calhoun*, 7:220

* * *

John Calhoun to Lieutenant Colonel Eustis, 22 July 1822

Orders: Lt. Col. Eustis will cause to embark immediately from that place one effective Company of Artillery under the command of a suitable subaltern Officer to proceed to Charleston. . . . the Company on its arrival at Charleston will be turned over to the command of Capt. Matthew Payne who is now at that place.

W. Edwin Hemphill, *Papers of John C. Calhoun*, 7:220–21

* * *

S[tephen] Elliott to William Elliott (Beaufort), 22 July 1822

I am very glad to find that the machinations of this city did not extend to Beaufort. The leaders boasted of having secured all the negroes between Santee and Combahee and calculated or pretended to calculate on a very general cooperation. It is certain that some of their leaders were traversing the country very industriously last winter and Spring in the garb of preachers offering to all who were willing to receive the pure and unsophisticated doctrines of the Gospel which they said whites only garbles to suit their own purposes. This signal notwithstanding how quiet the country has remained and still more remarkable that no country negro has directly been implicated in this plot. If this should be the case at the end of the examinations, I think it will auger favorably for the tranquility of the country for some time to come. The City can and will be very much reformed before our Citizens are permitted again to slumber. I regret that your prospects at the next election are to unfavorable. I shall regret it much to my own account, as it will make my visits to Columbia less pleasant. . . . At the next Session many questions of great importance connected with our black population will probably arise, and think it will be desirable that the country parishes should be well represented. The Lawyers of Charleston, though frequently men of talent and generally of integrity, are not exactly the persons adapted to legislate on this subject.

Elliott and Gonzales Papers, SHC

* * *

The Georgian, 23 July 1822

The Governor of the State of South Carolina offers a reward of two hundred Dollars for the apprehension of a negro fellow named William Gardner, who is implicated in some of the late transactions in Charleston.

* * *

Mary Beach to Elizabeth Gilchrist, 23 July 1822

Oh! God has a controversy with us. Oh! for his spirit to accompany it. I often think of Mr. Newton's lines as applied to our situation: "every day new straits attend and wonders where the scene will end"—The unravelling of this awful business is like the Chambers of Ezyekiel vision of *greater* and *greater* abominations. On Friday next 26th 29 more people are to be hung and among them Mr. Palmer's *Billy*. I don't feel the surprise that *many* do about *him*; for although we often sin in two ways breaking the command of the Savior in *judging* and often in *misjudging* others; yet there was *something* about him that made me fear it was only *a profession*; but still seeing him so constantly at the Church (and it was only last Wednesday night he was at the lectern snuffing out the candles and next day arrested) that people feel it sensibly in our Church—his old and young Masters at first I believe doubted, but are now I understand fully convinced of his guilt and he will be a great loss in point of property to that poor old saint [Job Palmer]. Besides the distress of his dying in that way and two other of the communicants besides Billy are to be hanged on Friday. Mrs. Purcell's (N. Smith) man Jack who she used to appear to think [illegible] and she was so ridiculous as to say (for she was I may say half a mad woman from what I have heard when he was first arrested) "that they might as well have hung Ben Palmer as him is now convinced of his guilt"—Susan McCall's Clarissa husband is also another of *our* members and the Ramsey's Sarah's husband (He is a Methodist professor) are of those to die on Friday. . . . Ours as yet have not been implicated as I have heard in the slightest manner; but this is no security as it seems that some of them may not finish on the Gallows in ten days; if it should be the case I fear I should be a wretched being to the end of my days for having held them in a state of savagery to prove a temptation—But Oh! I fear this business is akin to the French Revolution to think that many of these people growing up like children as is the case of many of the *condemned* could be brought to such a fiend like temper that they would consent to immerse their hands in the blood of their master and their little sons who never could have shed theirs and [illegible] whether it was love of Dominion or want of revenge; But it is not to hard Masters or the case would be altered widely in its complexion; though I dare say abroad before it is *correctly* known it will be said they could *bear* their oppression *no* longer—And the bitterness of the men of the world against our poor Church and Dr. Palmer is awful; indeed I may say against religion—I told Mary after hearing of a very bitter speech of Robert Hayne about missionaries the other day that I don't know but this business may yet end in religious persecution. . . .

These wretched creatures having carried on their seditions at Meetings up out of Town under the pretense of their being religious ones has left a stain & bitterness on the minds of the men of the world that the power of God alone will be applied to the removing of it; an *age* I believe must pass before it *can* be effaced—& the hatred to them so great that I expect and I was going to say *eternal* one will exist reciprocally. The country remains as far as I know perfectly quiet—they only in the City had engaged I suspect a little help from the Islands—Old Mr. Jones's man or youth Jupiter I suppose was hung agreeable to his sentence on Friday last & two others belonging to Martin, a blacksmith in that neighbourhood. . . . Negroe men a few days ago when a few were offered could not bring $150.

Mary Lamboll Thomas Beach Papers, SCHS

* * *

A confession of Mr. Enslow's boy John (ca. 23 July)

The Plan was that every Black Man who was attached to them was to come out and assemble where the Beat Companies meet and they had their positions assigned them to push for the different magazines and guard Houses. The House servants were to kill their Masters with whatever instruments they had or could obtain, it was thought that the house servants would do the most mischief at the commencement. There was to be no signal because Denmark and the principal leaders said it would excite alarm, but at 12 O'Clock at Night, they must take their Stations & act their part. The People up the road to take the Magazine then push for the Town, and spare nothing that obstructed them the Country People was to push for the Hays Wharf and take the U. States Navy on Hays Wharf (to be commanded by Gullah Jack), Rolla Bennett to command the country People who cross the Bridge on Ashley River, Ned Bennett to meet in Mrs. Elias Horry's house and collect a number (assisted by John Horry) & push for the Guard House the Corner of Meeting and Broad Streets, and join those from the road. Negroes would be supplied with arms from their source (who had not been provided) if successful—Monday and Denmark to have the strongest force, and come to town, when they had succeeded up town and Peter Poyas was to have command along East and South Bay and try to capture the shipping. This was considered the most active station, as he would prevent the escape of the whites if they conquered. The resolve was if they did not succeed in town they would fire and retreat to the Lines and there fight man for man and if defeated go to the woods and do all the harm they could. I have spoken myself to Denmark and Peter about the people in the country and know they went into the Country often and told me, they had communications in all the Islands, also in Columbia and Santee and different places, in that direction. I also heard them say they were well informed in Georgetown. That they would let the principal men know the time of the attack, being a short distance from Charleston would communicate a day or two before. Kill all the whites between there and Charleston, make their way through the woods and be in time to assist their people in town. It is also said by them that the Population in Georgetown could be killed in half an hour. They would capture all the boats and get a great many arms from that place. I can tell you candidly that the thing was general and known.

Denmark read at the meeting (different chapters from the Old Testament, but most generally read the whole of 21st Chap. Exodus) and spoke and exhorted from 16th verse the words "and He that stealeth a man." He read frequently in a book about the complexion of people and he said the climate of Africa made them black but were not inferior to Whites on that account.

Monday Gell also wrote letters to St. Domingo by the steward of a brig lying at Gibbes and Harpers Wharf. It was understood that they would obtain assistance from St. Domingo and the North—because Monday Gell read several speeches and pamphlets and said that the *Northern Brothers* would assist them and if they failed 'twould be no disgrace. Monday Gell is the first person who spoke to me, and told me he expected a number of that time (Feb. 7) to join him for he had spoken to considerable number. Denmark, Peter Poyas, Rolla, Ned, Garner, John Vincent and others have spoken to many, particularly the first six who were hung; but in consequence of their deaths the names of a number remain secret as they spoke to them individually. Billy Palmer was also considered an active man. I was not at the last meeting but understood that they had determined to kill Men, Women and Children. I believe the report true for at the Meeting before the last Denmark & Peter Poyas said if you kill the lice, you must kill the Nits.

Master having read this over to me I do swear it true and some of the facts left out, of which I will remind him because I was at all their meetings, and was considered an active man, there was a quantity of arms of different kinds furnished, for Denmark told me in March, he was getting arms fast, about 150 to 200 pikes made, and then there was a great deal of money placed in his hands for the purpose they must have been sent in the Country by Rolla, Ned, Peter, Denmark and Batteau.

Henry Ravenel Papers, SCHS

* * *

Mary Beach to Elizabeth Gilchrist, 25 July 1822

Doctor Palmer prayed a few sabbaths ago so particularly for those under temptation that I am sure he had some particular case (though I have not heard so) in view & I told Mary I believed that Satan had a *more* than *common* manner I believed was at work in our community at this time in setting these incendiaries the Negroes to work & in the *hearts* of other people with sinful thoughts [illegible] must shudder at for that I had been in a peculiarly tempted state respecting the Magnitude of the suffering for sin in Eternity & not from my old difficulty about the doctrine of Election that I so often have groaned under. . . . Whether the country is clean of the business or only [illegible] by the stress taking in the City it is a great mercy it remains tranquil. In answer to several questions in today's letter, I will answer them in order. Denmark Vesey *was* a slave to old Mr. Vesey, but whether he was left or he purchased his freedom I can't say—he was gray-headed, he told his judges or the Council when interrogated to what church he belonged with a very firm decisive tone "None" and I asked Betsy a few weeks ago the same question and she answered with a contemptuous tone of *him* to the same effect—But I believe he was considered the Champion in the African church business & I believe it is the generally received opinion that *this* church commenced this awful business or at any rate they took this for their rallying point I understand their papers contain allusions to it—But it carries suspicion how many have got out when it is said the Court were under Oath to secrecy. *I* can only account for it in this way; that when different Negroes were trying; their white representatives or friends (I know it was the case with several & I suppose with all) heard the testimony given by the evidence & also the deceased as well as those now under the sentence have made disclosures so that I believe the whole *if any* consequence is now out & in possession of the public—I think the *attempt* of keeping their arrangements *secret* was judicious could it have been practicable, & yet perhaps it is more satisfactory to the Public to know it, as our minds must be more satisfied of the awful necessity of such *sanguinary* steps as are now taking place in our city. The Pirates, I make no doubt are in safe confinement, but I hear nothing of them; there are two—Wilson McFail's man & great many more are to be transported beyond the United States, some say to Africa, & others say to South America. I *hope* not the latter as it is said they had better be put to death & if they are less guilty surely they ought not to have the heaviest punishment as it will at any rate be in the world's eye so. . . .

[Postscript dated 27 July]

You heard before this will reach you that 29 poor miserable culprits were to have been executed yesterday but some were respited till 9th. of August & 3 had their sentences commuted for transportation so that 22 were executed—the day before I felt strangely firm about it thinking it necessary but by evening my distress about the business returned & if giving it up every one I own could have made a different state of things that is that they would be freeman with safety to us & themselves I would have done, but this can never be in my day—the night was such as you may picture from a large number of Cavalry passing back and forth the whole of it—in the middle of it the whole of the criminals for execution in the morning were brought together to the vault under the City Hall where a part of them were before; the others were divided some in the Jail & others in the Cells allotted for the Maniacs in the Poor House & about 6 o'clock the procession moved off up Meeting Street—attending with an immense crowd I understand; & a great one of white as well as black were at the awful scene & several Carriages, such as the Council, Willington and even Doct. Palmer in his; who went not in his Official capacity; but by the desire of Doct. Leland who accompanied him. With some of the poor sufferers the business was managed very badly indeed (no doubt owing to the *great* number) as it respected one of them for he was shot at last, but in order I suppose to end his suffering. I understand they behaved with great firmness—they all died on one or rather a continuation of 3 gallows in one—A deathlike silence reigned in the City at the time. Oh! that God in his mercy may have enabled them as the thief on the Cross by faith to look to that blood which alone can save any of us. Both Doct. Palmer & Mr. Jones had a very favorable opinion of the state of mind that both Mrs. Purcell man & [illegible] husband's were in. I don't wonder that with such an inflammable temper as Mrs. Purcell has that she should have gone on as she done on as the first surprise, although she had told several people that her Jack had been seen in suspicious company—Yet he was one of those unassuming evil diligent servants & had a most prepossessing countenance—he sent for Mrs. John Holmes as the intimate friend of his Mistress & told her how the business had been—& observed he could not stand the sight of his Mistress who it seems brought him up from a child & had been so kind to him; but to go on he said when Vesey first proposed it he objected for he said his wife & children were free & he lived as well as he could wish himself—however Vesey again came to him & with the Bible to quote different passages to prove the lawfulness of it; & told him that if he did not do it from himself or had no reason; he ought to do it for the sake of others—he told Mr. Jones he wished he could confess his guilt before the *whole* world. A melancholy accident happened on the ground at the Execution some say some alarm was given; others that a Horse started; but let it have come from what course it did, a sudden impulse was given & it was then by some called out "a fire in the Town" the troops immediately made a dash or move to clear the ground & of course you may have some idea of such a crowd falling back—Mr. German's carriage either in turning too short; or somehow by the pole of another striking it—but his boy behind it was knocked off from behind and literally trampled to death for his skull was fractured by the Horses that passed over him—& several persons were hurt. . . . Oh! what sort of business shall I call this sorest judgement perhaps it will prove that ever our country saw.

Mary Lamboll Thomas Beach Papers, SCHS

* * *

Anna Johnson (Charleston) to Elizabeth Haywood (Raleigh), 27 July 1822

We had yesterday the most aweful tragedy acted in this city—22 unfortunate wretches were at one fatal moment sent to render up their dread account—29 had been sentenced but 7 had their sentence commuted to perpetual banishment—but on Tuesday 6 more men are to be executed—Gracious heavens to what will all this had—certainly it will throw our city back at least ten years—30 have already been executed, and I am told that there are an aweful number yet to be tried, I wish I could act for myself I would not stay in this city another day—for my feelings have been so lacerated of late that I can hardly think speak there is a look of horror on every countenance—I wish I was with you, at least I should experience comparative happiness tho' even there what I have seen would pursue me—Do not think I saw them hung myself—tho' it was within sight of our house—But I can imagine and feel.

Ernest Haywood Papers, SHC

* * *

Charleston Mercury, 29 July 1822

The Court adjourned, *sine die*, on Friday, having no further business before them.—They have deserved and they receive the grateful thanks of their fellow citizens of their fellow creatures for their labors. Their humanity has equaled their justice, and their perseverance was not exceeded by their wisdom. Patient, inquiring and firm in the fulfillment of the duties that have devolved upon them, they have discharged their high trust in the spirit of enlightened Gentlemen and conscientious Christians. The stream of justice would never be polluted if it always flowed in the channel to which it would be directed by such a tribunal.

The public spirit and well directed zeal of the Intendant and Council, during the late agitation, call likewise for the thanks of the community. After a whole month's incessant vigilance, they at length have reached a period of comparative repose. May the sweets of their labours be found in the satisfaction that exertions like theirs, happily but seldom required, have secured the safety of the city, and the lasting gratitude of its inhabitants!

* * *

Thomas Bennett to John Calhoun, 30 July 1822

Prompt attention given to my request has proved highly gratifying to the Citizens of this place, and the arrival of the forces will no doubt contribute greatly to alay public excitement.

W. Edwin Hemphill, *Papers of John C. Calhoun*, 7:227

* * *

New York Daily Advertiser, 31 July 1822

It ought to excite no astonishment with those who boast of freedom themselves, if they should occasionally hear of plots and desertion among those who are held in perpetual bondage. Human beings, who once breathed the air of freedom on their own mountains and in their own valleys, but who have been kidnaped by white men and dragged into endless slavery, cannot be expected to be contented with their situation. White men, too, would engender plots and escape from their imprisonment were they situated as are these miserable children of Africa.

* * *

The Georgian, 6 August 1822

William Garner, the fellow recently apprehended at Granby, was on Saturday found guilty before the Court of Magistrates and Freeholders in Charleston of participating in the attempt to raise an Insurrection in South Carolina. He is to be executed to-morrow.

* * *

M. Richardson (Savannah) to Dr. James Screven, 7 August 1822

Charleston has undergone a dreadful state of things—in my last I gave you an account of what had come to our knowledge of this intended insurrection—it proves to be much more extensive than was at first suspected—Six of the insurgents had suffered when I wrote last—since then, 26 have been hung—and many ordered for transportation out of the limits of the United States—not to return on pain of death—the first court which sat five weeks, had retired from the painful duty—& a new one instituted—they are still going on with the trials—The Mail carrier had been fired on in the neighbourhood at Parkers Ferry by 4 Negroes—Three of them were executed—we are now fearful some accident has occurred—as it is stated in the papers that the Mail Carrier was persued by twelve armed negroes on Tuesday last, near Saltcatcher—since Wednesday we have had no mail from Charleston, this is Sunday—there may be other reasons—such as bad roads—sickness etc., but I always dread the worst that may happen—One white man was found aiding and abetting the negroes—he has been a pirate—Judge Johnson has published his vindication but it is very lame—in my poor opinion I should pronounce the writer humbled—at any rate it was too serious a business for jesting—and at his age evinced a degree of levity which takes from the character of a person in his dignified station—We cannot put any other motive on his conduct than a vanity to appear more wise & resolute than his neighbours—but he should have reflected that strong nerves do not belong to everyone—any more than rectitude & dignity of conduct—the Negroes too who were first convicted belonged to his Brother in law Bennett—therefore delicacy should have kept him silent—It is impossible for me to give a correct account of the proceedings in Charleston—everything has been kept a profound secret—for reasons which will occur to everyone—still enough transpired to convince us that they had too much cause for alarm—for four years has this business been in agitation—still so secret were they—and prudent also—that no suspicion from their conduct could be entertained—You may judge of their secrecy by what I am going to relate—two Negroes belonging to the same Master—both working in the same mill—were ignorant that either was engaged in the plot until they met in jail—When the constables went into Mr. Horry's yard to take up his waiting man—he assured them they were mistaken, he could answer for his innocence—he would as soon suspect himself—he accompanied him on his trial convinced still he could not be guilty—on hearing the evidence—he turned to his Man—tell me, are you guilty? for I cannot believe unless I hear you say so—Yes, replied the Negro—what were your intentions?—to kill you, rip open your belly & throw your guts in your face—It is said they were true warriors—Not a single Woman knew a word of their plans—In the course of time the whole proceeding will be published—never told—our journals are preferred for an account of the wildest plans engendered by religious enthusiasm and a wrong conception of the Bible—so true it is, "a little learning is a dangerous thing"—I am very fearful this business will not rest there, however we may hope it—and dreadful must be the state of the city when all confidence is lost in our servants—it is to be regretted that almost in every instance, the condemned slaves belonged to the most humane and indulgent owners—some plan must be adopted to subdue them—however repugnant to the feelings—their situation when compared with the poor of other countries was certainly happy—they are clothed, fed & taken care of when sick—and I may venture to say the house servants are not half-worked—had they been more employed they would have wanted time to plan mischief—I hope the laws will now force every family to keep but a certain number about them—and oblige all useless ones to be sent to the country—Huxters, day labourers, dray men all that useless class of Servants who are only a tax on their owners & a nuisance to the City—I intended to have spent the Summer in the upper country, but circumstances combined with this Charleston business has induced me to remain where I am.

Arnold-Screven Papers, SHC

* * *

Mary Beach to Elizabeth Gilchrist, 8 August 1822

I hope, my dear Sister, you have got in a more comfortable state of mind about the state of our affairs here as bad as they *have been*; I trust and believe they are not now in that state to warrant your fears and anxieties awakened by them & your tenderness for us to destroy your peace. Oh! do not indulge such apprehensions; I assure you it is far from being *our* state or experience—& I do not, believe me, say so merely to quiet you or to put the best gloss on it. With regard to the *present* danger I trust by the blessing of God the plans of these deluded creatures are frustrated for a while; some say for 20 others say for 50 years, no one can say, nor do I believe it will be in this age of revolutions. . . . Wm. Garner for whom $200 reward was offered by the Govr. was apprehended near Columbia and is to be hanged tomorrow—a new Court had to be organized for his trial, as the others declined but not in displeasure to serve any longer. . . . I understood 3 or 4 days ago that it was hoped or expected no more after Garner would be hung if others were taken up & found guilty they would be transported as it was thought the *ring leaders* were already hung & the less of death & the punishment the better. And indeed such is the wretched constitution of our vile fallen bodies that both black and white are getting familiarized for the Tuesday after the 22 were hung (3 or 4 more were) & actually [illegible] less among the immediate friends of them, it excited no more sensation in the city than any other common event that is in public expression.

Mary Lamboll Thomas Beach Papers, SCHS

* * *

Charleston Courier, 12 August 1822

We are happy to state that the tranquility of the city is now restored. The legal investigations of crime have ceased. The melancholy requisitions of Justice, as painful to those who inflicted, as to those who suffered them, have been complied with; and an awful but a necessary, and it is hoped an effectual example has been afforded to deter from further occasions of offence and punishment.

We have not been inattentive, in this distressing period, to the notice which might be taken of our situation by the journals in our sister states. It is grateful in the extreme to mark the tenderness and sympathy which, with the exception of one solitary print in New-York, have been universally manifested towards us. We are not in a state of mind to use language of acrimonious asperity. We regard with pity the individual who could deliberately sneer at our misfortunes—we leave him to the consolations of his conscience—his nightly dreams on his pillow—and hope he may always enjoy that security, which he so much rejoices that our city has been deprived of.

Yet, as an historical fact, worthy to be remembered, particularly at this time, and which Mr. STONE, of the N. York *Commercial Advertiser*, appears to have forgotten, we would remind him, as we had occasion once before to remind another editor of New-York, that in the year 1741, in the city of New-York, *thirteen Negroes were* BURNT ALIVE *for insurrectionary efforts*.

During the whole of this momentous inquiry, the utmost confidence has been felt in the State and City authorities, and in the two successive Courts organized to award justice, and acting under the most painful responsibilities. The Militia have with alacrity performed the unusual and laborious duties assigned them;—and now let us hope that the God of goodness and of mercy, who has guarded and protected us in the hour of peril, will continue to us his benevolent care, and frustrate always the evil designs of our enemies, and of those who conspire alike against our happiness and their own.

* * *

Charleston Mercury, 13 August 1822

Eight runaway Negroes made an attack last Saturday week on the mail driver in Saltketcher Swamp. Parties are still in pursuit.

* * *

Charleston City Gazette, 14 August 1822

In the opinion of the community of Charleston . . . the *Bluelight* editor of the *New York Daily Advertiser* might invent some other way of edifying his readers than in groaning over the execution of a Score of Culprits upon whose fate Justice and Humanity alike pronounced the sentence. The "bloody sacrifice" of which he so insolently speaks might have been prevented by a few peace offerings of such lambs as he and his faction can produce.

They talk of philanthropy, but the Missouri poison is still garnered in their bosoms; and although they may never have dreamed of the awful consequences of the wild and foolish doctrines which have gone abroad—they begin already to feel in New York, Philadelphia, and Boston, how very agreeable is the extension of the rights of Citizenship to those whom they pretend to regard as equals. We say pretend, for the Blacks in those cities are neither citizens nor aliens. There are few or no places where they are admitted to amusements or instruction; little or no moral education by which they can be rendered virtuous members of society; little or no interest in their spiritual happiness; no master or patron by whom they are protected, as was the case of the Freedman in ancient Rome, and as is frequently exhibited in South Carolina.

* * *

Mary Beach to Elizabeth Gilchrist, 5 September 1822

Things did appear to me about two months ago to wear the darkest and most mysterious aspect as to the moral results of the late unhappy business & viewed now only by the eye of reason it can appear in no other, but when we view the wonder of the Lord's hand in thousands of other ways, defecting the Prince of darkness & view the operation of his Hand in this day we may yet hope that this may be our experience. I recoil at times when I think of the poor Greeks at this time & also think that this country has a great deal to answer for on the score of slavery as well as the Greeks for their departure from *real* Christianity—I have no doubt that a spirit of prayer has been in more usual degree *here* excited by the late events; for Christians could not but see that awfully hostile temper showed by men of the world against religion for actually (as far at least as I have had an opportunity of hearing & observing) there seemed more showed [illegible] against it because some of these miserable men who were among the insurgents were professors than because they wished to murder them—for instance where I have heard one remorse against the St. Domingo people there have been innumerable against the Northward ones who they look upon in general I believe as the secret instigators of the Plot, unfortunately you may see their quitting King's speech in Congress. Now in the case of Vesey until I saw the Pamphlet I was under the belief that the report that was afloat & believed generally I think that he had travelled all over the New England States & also the Western ones within 2 or 3 years but from this Pamphlet it does not appear that he was absent for 20 years.

Mary Lamboll Thomas Beach Papers, SCHS

* * *

Southern Patriot and Commercial Gazette, 19 August 1822

Alexander Harleston, a free black man, with his family and 2 or 3 other free persons of color were passengers on the schooner *Dolphin* which sailed yesterday for the coast of Africa; their intention is to join the settlement of the American Colonization Society at Cape Mesurado. Prince Graham, a free black man, one of those implicated in the late plot and sentenced to be transported beyond the limits of the United States was sent off on this vessel. A slave belonging to Mr. McNellage had clandestinely produced himself on board the night previous with the intention of escaping his owner, but was discovered and brought on shore. He had secreted himself in a large pleasure boat which was upon the deck of the schooner.

* * *

Charleston Mercury, 19 August 1822

The Civil Authorities of the City have at length announced that their labours as connected with the late conspiracy among our coloured population have nearly or entirely closed.

* * *

Copy of a letter from the governor of the State of South Carolina in *Niles Register*, 7 September 1822

Sir:

After a prolonged and almost uninterrupted session of six weeks, the first court organized for the trial of slaves charged with an attempt to raise an insurrection in this city, was dissolved on the 20th. ult. Another court was subsequently convened, and after a session of three days, closed the unpleasant investigation with which it was charged, and adjourned on the 8th. instant, *sine die*.

During the interesting period, occupied by the court first organized, the public mind was agitated by a variety of rumors, calculated to produce great excitement and alarm. These had their origin in the nature of the transaction, and the secrecy and seclusion observed in the incipient stages of the inquiry; as but few of the circumstances were known to the community, and the number apprehended, and sentenced to the severest punishment, beyond any former example. Certainty gave place to exaggeration, and the general impression sustained the rumor of a very extensive conspiracy.

The effects resulting from these reports, if uncontrolled by an exhibition of facts, are too obvious to require comment. The reputation of the state must suffer abroad, and a rapid deterioration of property occur within; while suspicion and anxiety will continue long to mar the public tranquility. It becomes, therefore, a duty imperiously obligatory on me, to represent the occurrences as they have transpired, and thus evidence that to you that the attempt has not only been greatly magnified, but as soon as discovered, it ceased to be dangerous.

A servant, prompted by attachment to his master, communicated to him that he had requested to give his assent and subscribe his name to a list of persons already engaged in the conspiracy. The intendant immediately received the information, and caused the arrest of three slaves of Mr. Paul—one of whom was subsequently identified by the servant making the communication. The city council was convened, and after a very close and attentive examination, a general impression was produced that but little credence could attach to the statement. A prudent caution was nevertheless exercised, and the fellow charged committed to solitary imprisonment. A few days after his confinement, he made many disclosures to a member of council, but so amplified the circumstances that the utmost credulity was requisite to the belief of his tale.

Some consternation was obviously produced amongst a few of the conspirators by the arrest of these slaves, and I cannot doubt led to a detail more plausible and deserving of attention. Another servant, whose name is also concealed, from prudential motives, stated generally, that such a combination generally existed, and mentioned the names of several who were most conspicuous in their exertions, adding, with great confidence, that the explosion of their schemes would occur on the ensuing Sunday night. This confession was given on Thursday, the 13th June, and contained the recital of several occurrences which would precede the attempt, and evidence the intention. This suggested the propriety, while it sanctioned the effort, to conceal from the community the intelligence thus received, for the intervening time—during which extensive and efficient preparations were made for the safety and protection of the city. Saturday night and Sunday morning passed without the predicted demonstrations; doubts again were excited, and counter orders issued for diminishing the guard. The facts communicated were generally known to our fellow citizens on Sunday, producing a night of sleepless anxiety. But no one of the predicted (or any other) occurrences presented itself to disturb the general tranquility.

On the 18th June ten slaves were arrested, and on the 19th the court was organized for their trial. Investigation was retarded by the difficulty of procuring authentic evidence, and it was not until the 28th that the sentence of death was pronounced against six of the persons charged with the offence. Denmark Vesey, a free negro, was arrested on the 21st, and on the 22nd put on his trial. Although he was unquestionably the instigator and chief of this plot, no positive proof of his guilt appeared until the 25th. This grew out of the confession of one of the convicts, and on the 27th his guilt was further established by a servant of Mr. Ferguson.

The progress made, and the expectations of immunity from punishment by confession, gradually developed the plot, and produced the arrest of several others, fortunately two who were principals, Monday Gell and Gullah Jack. These, with three others, John Horry, Charles Drayton, and Harry Haig were convicted, and sentenced to die on Friday, the 12th of July last; but, at the suggestion of the court, important communications were expected from them, Monday Gell, Charles Drayton, and Harry Haig were respited.

The arrest of Perault, a servant of Mr. Strohecker, which took place the day previous to the respite, and the general and very important discoveries made by him, enabled the committee of vigilance, not only to elicit the confirmation of his statement from three convicts, but to apprehend a great number of persons engaged in the plot. Among others, William Garner, reputed to be one of the principals, the only one not then apprehended.

The number of persons at this period under arrest, evinced the necessity of such arrangements of testimony as would enable the court to progress with more rapidity. This duty devolved on the committee of vigilance: and principally from the general information of Perault, and of the convicts Monday Gell and Charles Drayton, facility was given to the further proceedings of the court. In the short space of seven days thirty-two negroes were convicted; twenty-two of whom were executed on Friday, the 20th of July: and within four days after, eleven others were convicted, four of whom have also been executed.

Having established the existence of a plot, and the places of rendezvous, all that was deemed requisite for conviction was to prove as association with the ringleaders, and an expression of their assent to the measure. On such, generally, the sentence of death has been executed. Others who, without actually combining, were proved to have known of the conspiracy, and to have given their sanction by any act, have been sentenced to die, and their punishment commuted to banishment from the United States; or sentenced, in the first instance to banishment from this state or the United States. In this manner, the whole number, seventy-two have been disposed of; thirty-five executed, and thirty-seven sentenced to banishment. With these, we may reasonably conclude that we have reached the extremities of this conspiracy, and this opinion, if not conclusive, is entitled to great weight, when we advert to the extraordinary measures pursued to effect the object and the motives which influenced the accused.

No means which experience or ingenuity could devise were left unessayed to eviscerate the plot. In the labors of investigation, the court was preceded by a committee formed by the city council, whose activity, intelligence, activity, and zeal, were well adapted to the arduous duties of their appointment. Their assiduity, aided by various sentiments which influenced the prisoners, produced a rapid development of the plot. Several of the conspirators had entered into solemn pledges to partake of a common destiny, and one, at least, was found, who, after his arrest, felt no repugnance to enforce the obligation, by surrendering the names of his associates. A spirit of retaliation and revenge produced a similar effect with others, who suspected that they were victims of treachery; and this principle operated with full effect, as the hope or expectation of pardon predominated. To the last hour of the existence of several, who appeared to be conspicuous actors in this drama, they were pressingly importuned to make further confession.

Among the conspirators, the most daring and active was Monday, the slave of Mr. Gell. He could read and write with facility, and thus attained an extraordinary and dangerous influence over his fellows. Permitted by his owner to occupy a house in the central part of the city, hourly opportunities were afforded for the exercise of his skill on those, who were attracted to his shop by business or favor. It was there that his artful and insidious delusions were kept in perpetual exercise. Materials were abundantly furnished in the seditious pamphlets brought into this state, by equally culpable incendiaries; while the speeches of the oppositionists in Congress to the admission of Missouri, gave a serious and imposing effect to his machinations. This man wrote to Boyer (by his own confession), requesting his aid, and addressed the envelope of his letter to a relative of the person who became the bearer of it, a negro from one of the northern states. He was the only person proved to have kept a list of those engaged; and the court considered his confession full and ample.—

From such means and such sources of information, it cannot be doubted that all who were actually concerned, have been brought to justice. There is no exception within my knowledge; it has, however, been stated that a plantation in St. John's was infected, but I do not know on what authority.

This plain detail of the principal incidents in this transaction, will satisfy you that the scheme has not been general or alarmingly extensive. And it furnishes much cause for satisfaction, that, although religion, superstition, fear, and almost every passion that sways the human mind, have been artfully used by the wicked instigators of this design, so few have been seduced from a course of propriety and obedience. Those who associated were unprovided with the means of attack or resistance. No weapons (if we except the thirteen hoop-poles) have been discovered, nor any testimony received but of six pikes, that such preparations were actually made. The witnesses generally agree in one fact, that the attempt was to have taken place on Sunday night the 16th June, differing a little as to the precise time; 12 o'clock appears to have been the hour.

From the various conflicting statements made during the trials, it is difficult to form a plausible conjecture of their ultimate plans of operation; no two agreeing on general definite principles. That the first essay would be made with clubs against the state arsenal in, from their being unprovided with arms, and the concurrence of several witnesses. But whether the attack would be made simultaneously by various detachments, or whether the whole, embodied at a particular spot, would proceed to the accomplishment of their object is very uncertain. Upon the whole, it is manifest that if any plan had been organized, it was never communicated by the principal conspirator to the leaders or the men as they were wholly ignorant even of the places of rendezvous, although within two days of the time appointed, and but one man arrested prior to the day fixed on the attempt.

When we contrast the numbers engaged with the magnitude of the enterprize, the imputation of egregious folly or madness is irresistible; and supposing the attempt to have been predicated on the probability that partial success would augment their numbers, the utmost presumption would scarcely have hazarded the result. Servility long continued debases the mind and abstracts it from that energy of character, which is fitted to great exploits. It cannot be supposed, therefore, without a violation of the immutable laws of nature, that a transition from slavery and degradation to authority and power, could instantly occur. Great and general excitement may produce extensive and alarming effects;

but the various passions which operate with powerful effect on this class of persons impart a confident assurance of detection and defeat to every similar design. While the event is remote, they may listen with credulity to the artful tale of the instigator, and concur in its plausibility; but the approach of danger will invariably produce treachery, the concomitant of dastardly dispositions. In the fidelity and attachment of a numerous class of these persons, we have other sources of security and early information; from both of which, it is reasonable to conclude, that, in proportion to the numbers engaged, will be the certainty of detection; and that an extensive conspiracy cannot be matured in this state.

I have entered with much reluctance on this detail, nor would it have been considered requisite, but to counteract the number of gross and idle reports, actively and extensively circulated, and producing a general anxiety and alarm. And, although their authors may have no evil design, and may really be under the delusion, it is easy to perceive what pernicious consequences may ensue from not applying the proper corrective. Every individual in the state is interested, whether in relation to his own property, or the reputation of the state, in giving no more importance to the transaction than it justly merits. The legislature has wisely provided the means of efficient protection. If the citizens will faithfully perform the duty enjoined on them by the patrol laws, I fear not that we shall continue in the enjoyment of much tranquility and safety as any state in the union.

I have the honor to be, very respectfully, sir, your obedient servant, THO. BENNETT

* * *

Martha Richardson (Savannah) to James Screven, 16 September 1822

The insurrection in Charleston (the intended one I should have said) has been happily terminated—I will give you an extract from a letter I received last week from Mr. DeSaussure. "I receive Dear Madam your kind congratulations at the successful termination of the recent disturbances in Charleston with much sensibility—The hand of Providence was singularly visible in the discovery and development of the plot & our gratitude should be commensurate with it—I do not think that the object could have been accomplished to any save a very limited extent, but probably many valuable lives would have been sacrificed before order was re-established—our examples have been written in Blood, but policy and perhaps humanity rendered them indispensable—& will perhaps deter similar efforts for 20 or 30 years"—32 of the poor wretches were hung & some shipt for Africa—The trials have been published in a small pamphlet which I have read—it is a history of the wildest plans— engendered by superstition and ignorance—Most of the ring leaders were of the Gullah tribe, mechanics and draymen—of the Methodist religion—You may hear that an attempt has been in agitation here—but it is without foundation—some few have been tried for an attempt to poison their Master—Flourinoy—but they have not as yet been sentenced or is it supposed the evidence will be sufficient to criminate them—

Arnold-Screven Papers, SHC

* * *

Charleston City Gazette, 20 September 1822

When we think of the murder and violence and destruction which those deluded wretches might have committed, we cannot but be grateful to the Negro who gave the information. We do not doubt but his reward will be commensurated to the services he rendered, while we shudder at the scenes which might have been acted, and contemplate its origin and progress in a society, we cannot but hope that our Southern fellow citizens will hereafter be permitted to manage their own concerns in their own way. They have as much humanity and intellect, and more experience on this subject, than the people of the non-slave holding states can be supposed to have.

* * *

Carolina Gazette, 28 September 1822

To our Northern Brethren

I would suppose that you were not aware of the deep atrocity of the late machinations in our city, or you would declare that we have felt as you would have felt and in our proceedings have but obeyed the dictates of nature and wisdom. We would therefore invite you temperately to survey the various circumstances of the event.

The designing leaders in the scheme of villainy availed themselves of these occasions to instil sentiments of ferocity by *falsifying the Bible*. All the several penal laws of the Israelites were quoted to mislead them, and the denunciations in the prophecies, which were intended to deter men from evil, were declared to be divine commands that they were meant to execute. To confirm this doctrine, they were told that Heshbon, that Bash with its 60 cities, had been destroyed men, women and children; that in the destruction of Midian, only the males were destroyed, at which Moses was displeased and deliberately ordered the death of the boys and their mothers. That Joshua levelled the walls of Jericho and regarded neither age or sex; that David vanquished empires and left not man, woman or infant alive. Not content with this execrable perversion—with exhibiting the God of Mercy as another Juggernaut, they were informed of what their colour had perpetrated abroad. Such was their religion, such the examples to be imitated. After having rendered them fiends in principle, they were prepared to be fiends in action. A regular plan was formed to annihilate us and our abodes; the arsenals and strong holds were to have been seized and the leaders nominated for each attack.

Besides the instruments which many of them possessed as mechanics, villains were engaged in manufacturing arms; several pike handles were discovered; Pharaoh and Peter had swords; Ned Bennett had a sword to kill wolves, but which he designed first to try on his master, of whom he had only received indulgence. The place of rendezvous, the night, the hour were determined—and the imps of rebellion were to have made Charleston one scene of flames and carnage; had they been able. It is no diminution of their crime to say that they were not able;-guilt is in the intention and not in the act.

Under such circumstances of exasperation, what did the citizens of Charleston? Did they yield to their passions and commit indiscriminate massacre, as would have been done in many places under less excitement? Nothing like it. A court was organized of distinguished integrity, respectability and intelligence. . . . The causes of the criminals were conducted with that liberality, justice and impartiality that characterize American jurisprudence.

Another impediment to the progress of conspiracy will be found in the *fidelity* of some of our negroes. The servant who is false to his master, will be false to his God. . . . But it is a reputable TRUTH that on every such occasion, servants have been found who were worthy of the kindness and confidence of their masters.

Besides when the moment of trial comes, among large bodies of men, some will tremble, some will be shocked at what they are about to perpetrate, and others will remember that by disclosure may be obtained more than they seek through perils.

A South-Carolinian

* * *

Charleston Mercury, 17 October 1822
GRAND JURY PRESENTMENTS, CHARLESTON DISTRICT

We present as a grievance the number of slaves working out and bringing wages to their owners; and recommend the number to be limited which each owner may thus employ in the city . . . to take into consideration the number of licenses issued by the City Council to individuals to open small dram shops, which we consider injurious in the extreme to our slaves, enticing them to plunder their owners.

We present as a dangerous and growing evil the frequent introduction of slaves from other states in this state.

* * *

Richard Furman to Governor Thomas Bennett, October 1822

Before we close this Address, we feel it incumbent on us, to invite your Attention, Sir, to another Subject; a Subject which though related to this, is not included in it; and in which we, as Agents of the Bible Society, are particularly concerned. This is the Apprehension we have from Intimations, that in consequence of the late projected Insurrection & the Claims laid to a religious Character by the several of those who ranked as leaders in the nefarious scheme. Ideas have been produced in the Minds of many Citizens unfavorable to the Use of the Bible among the Negroes and that Attempts will probably be made to obtain legislative Interference to prevent their learning to read it, or to use it freely—Though we are sensible that the Power of Direction and Control in this important Concern does not rest with the Chief Magistrate of our State, yet we are also sensible that his Sentiments and Recommendations have a powerful Influence in giving Tone to Public Opinion and Feeling; and think, that in Cases of Delicacy, where the Cause of Truth, Righteousness, Humanity, and Religion are to be advocated, they may be advantageously and laudably employed.

The Sentiment, Sir, that the Doctrines of Holy Writ are incompatible with the holding of slaves, has, we grant, been a Sentiment which many and some worthy Men have advanced, and which some still advocate; but, as we conceive, without just Foundation. Its lawfulness is positively stated in the Old Testament and is clearly recognized in the New. In the latter, a luminous exhibition is given of Slaves and their Masters, enjoying membership together in the Christian Church; where under the immediate Care & Government of the Inspired Apostles. Their respective Duties are also taught explicitly, and enforced by external Sanctions. By these Rules, the former are not directed to claim a Right to Liberation, nor encouraged to use Fraud or Force to effect it; but to be faithful, good and obedient. The latter are required not to emancipate [?] their Slaves, but to give them the Things which are just and equal; forbearing, Threatening and remembering, that they also have a master in Heaven.

The Bible, sir, as well as all other Things, good and sacred, which have come into the Hands of Men, may be, and has been abused. But to argue against its use from the Abuse it has suffered is to adopt a Mode of Reasoning which is not so genial, just, nor pious.

The Scriptures are given to Man (without Respect of Persons) to make him wise unto Salvation; and all are required by Divine Authority to read them; because they contain the Words of Eternal Life. To prohibit the Use of them, therefore, is to contradict & oppose the Divine Authority; and to suppose that the regular Use of them will naturally lead to Conspiracy, Rebellion & Blood, is a Reflection on the Divine Wisdom and Goodness, bordering on Blasphemy. But we have seen that, instead of encouraging Slaves to engage in Schemes of this Nature, they establish Rules of a directly contrary Character, and enforce them by Considerations which far transcend all that Human Munificence can afford as Reward; or that the Punishment of Human Laws can inflict—Were we only reasoning from the Cause to its Effect, on this Subject, we should naturally arrive at this Conclusion; that whenever the Truths of the Bible are received in an honest Mind, even by Persons in a State of Servitude, they must & will produce happy Effects in favour, not only of Piety & Devotion; but of willing Subordination to lawful Authority & Conformity to the Principles of Truth, Justice, Good-order, Peace & Benevolence. But in adverting to Matter of Fact, many can & do testify, that they have seen these Effects produced among the Class of People in Question, really.

Though it is true that a considerable Number of Persons who were concerned with the late Conspiracy professed to be of a Religious Character, yet it is also true, that the most leading Character among them and the Chief of the rebels, were members of an independent Association, which called itself the African Church and was intimately connected with a similar body in Philadelphia, from which their Sentiments & Directions in Matters of Religion were chiefly derived: whose Principles are formed on the Scheme of General Emancipation, for which they are zealous Advocates & they endeavor to support, by a Misconstruction or Perversion of the Scriptures. Very few, indeed, of the religious Negroes, in regular Churches among us, were drawn to the plot; & in some Churches, there were not any on whom a Charge of Criminality has been proved. The individuals composing the great body of the well-known, regular & esteemed Members of Churches have not been impeached. It would seem that the Conspirators were afraid to trust them; For since the plot had been discovered, voluntary information has been given that Attempts, not then understood, were made to feel the Pulse of some of them, by artful, distant approaches, which not being countenanced, were laid aside.

Vesey, the prime mover in this Plot, was, as we are informed notorious for his libidinous & petulant Conduct. Glen, though a preacher among them, & for one of his Opportunities, of extraordinary Talents, was generally considered as a Sharper & one commonly chargeable with Falsehoods.

Nothing, that we can discover, has transpired to make it appear that the Meetings of the religious Negroes, approved by the Churches to which they belong, for reading the Scripture, learning their Catechism & the general Purposes of Devotion & religious Improvements have been in anywise instrumental in directing or advancing the late horrid Design to which we refer, but on the contrary, we believe they have had a good Influence on the general State of Society by the promotion of good morals as well as piety among that Class of People.

This Circumstance corroborates a Sentiment which has been long entertained by some who have been careful in making Observations, as well as in reasoning on this Subject, with the True Interests of Society in view: It is this, that one of the best Securities we have to the domestic Peace & Safety of the State, is found in the Sentiments & correspondent Dispositions of the religious Negroes; which they derive from the Bible—If this Sentiment is just, it would seem that instead of taking the Bible away from them, & abridging the truly religious Privileges they have been used to enjoy, to avoid Danger; the better Way would be, to take

Measures for bringing them to a more full & just acquaintance with the former; & to secure to them the latter, under Regulations the least liable to abuse. That strict care should be taken to prevent abuses, & the Influence of designing Wicked Men among them is unquestionable, & highly important: And should be seriously regarded by Churches & Ministers, as well as by Civil Government. . . .

Richard Furman Papers, SCL

* * *

Charleston Mercury, 9 November 1822

A gang of armed runaways are presently infesting the New Bridge Road in St. Andrews parish and robbing passengers. On Wed. last several Negroes were stopped and money and clothes taken from them and their persons kept in custody 'till after night. The clothes were of white plains with blue collars. The robbers immediately dressed themselves in their spoils which circumstance will probably lead to their discovery. . . . their depredations are conducted in open day. They sent insulting and menacing messages to the masters of those they had robbed as to what they would do in the case of being pursued.

* * *

William Johnson to Thomas Jefferson, 10 December 1822

My dear Sir:

I have now passed my half-century, and begin to feel lonely among the men of the present day. And I am sorry to tell you, particularly so in this place. This last summer but too much cause for shame and anguish. I have lived to see what I really never believed it possible I should see,—courts held with closed doors, and men dying by scores who had never seen the faces nor heard the voices of their accusers. I see that your governors has noticed the alarm of insurrection which prevailed in this place some months since. But be assured it was nothing in comparison with what it was magnified to. But you know the best way in the world to make them tractable is to frighten them to death; and to magnify the danger is to magnify the claims of those who arrest it. Incalculable are the evils which have resulted from the exaggerated amounts circulated respecting that affair. Our property is reduced to nothing—strangers are alarmed at coming near us; our slaves rendered uneasy; the confidence between us and our domestics destroyed—and all this because of a trifling cabal of a few ignorant pennyless unarmed uncombined fanatics, and which certainly would have blown over without an explosion had it never come to light.

When the Court of Magistrates and Freeholders who tried the slaves implicated, were pursuing the course of sitting in conclave and convicting them upon the secret ex parte examination of slaves without oath, whose names were not I believe revealed even to the owners of the accused, the governor, whose feeling revolted at this unprecedented & I say, illegal mode of trial, consulted the attorney general . . . on the legality of their proceedings, and you will be astonished to hear that he gave a direct opinion in favour of it. If such be the law of this country, this shall not long be my country. But I will first endeavor to correct the evil.

William Johnson

Donald G. Morgan, *Justice William Johnson, the First Dissenter*, 138

* * *

Charleston Mercury, 16 December 1822

There is little doubt that the legislature will pass an act for the emancipation of Prioleau and Wilson's slaves with a $100 annuity exempt from tax.

* * *

An Act for the Better Regulation and Government of Free Negroes and Persons of Color; And for Other Purposes [excerpt]

III. *And be it further enacted* by the authority aforesaid, That if any vessel shall come into any part or harbour of this State, from any other State or foreign port, having on board any free negroes or persons of colour, as cooks, stewards, mariners, or in any other employment on board of said vessel, such free negroes or persons of color shall be liable to be seized and confined in jail until said vessel shall clear out and depart from this State; and that when said vessel is ready to sail, the captain of said vessel shall be bound to carry away the said free negro or free person of color, and to pay the expenses of his detention; and in the case of his neglect or refusal to do so, he shall be liable to be indicted, and, on conviction thereof, shall be fined in a sum not less than one thousand dollars, and imprisoned not less than two months; and such free negroes or persons of color shall deemed and taken as absolute slaves, and sold in conformity to the provisions of the Act passed on the twentieth day of December, one thousand eight hundred and twenty aforesaid.

IV. *And it be further enacted* by the authority aforesaid, That the sheriff of Charleston District, and each and every other sheriff of this State, shall be empowered and specially enjoined to carry the provisions of this Act into effect; each of whom shall be entitled to one moiety of the proceeds of the sale of all free negroes and free persons of color that may happen to be sold under the provisions of the foregoing clause; *provided* the prosecution be had at his information.

VIII. *And be it further enacted* by the authority aforesaid, That if any person or persons shall counsel, aid, or hire any slave or slaves, free negroes or persons of color, to raise a rebellion or insurrection within this State, whether any rebellion or insurrection do actually take place or not, every such person or persons, on conviction thereof, shall be adjudged felons, and suffer death without benefit of clergy.

South Carolina Assembly, 21 December 1822

* * *

Charleston Mercury, 21 December 1822

Major James Hamilton, junior Member of Congress for the District of Beaufort and Colleton arrived in Charleston last evening from Columbia and will shortly depart for Washington.

* * *

Petition of William Sims and others, praying recompense for slaves executed in the late Conspiracy

To the Honorable the President and Members of the Senate.

The Petition of we, the Subscribers, Humbly Sheweth, that some time in July last, a Plot of an intended Insurrection amongst part of the Negroes in the Parishes of Saint Philip and

Saint Michael, Charleston, was discovered, and thirty-five were tried by a Court and executed; that among this number your Petitioners were in part owners of the Negroes executed, and have sustained a very great loss, for most of them were valuable Mechanics.

And whereas all civil governments from time immemorial, have adopted, as fixed rule, founded on the principles of justice, that all private property, taken for public uses, or public benefits, should be paid for by the public. But in no country has the wisdom and justice of the governments been more fully displayed than in Legislative Councils of South Carolina; for in the year one thousand seven hundred and forty, the Legislature of South Carolina passed an Act for the better government of Slaves, and other persons of color, in which the intention of the Legislature at that time is most fully expressed—See 2d. Brevard, p. 233, sect.23, which reads as follows: "And to the end that owners of Slaves may not be tempted to conceal the crimes of their Slaves to the prejudices of the public, be it enacted, that in case any Slave shall be put to death, in pursuance of the sentence of the Justice and Freeholders, aforesaid, (except Slaves guilty of Murder, and Slaves taken in actual Rebellion) the said Justices or one of them, with the advice and consent of any two of the Freeholders, shall before they award and order their to be executed, appraise and value said Negroes, so to be put to death, at any sum, not exceeding two hundred pounds current money."

And here your memorialists beg leave to remark, that at the time of passing the aforesaid Negro Act, the provision made for the remuneration of the owners of slaves executed by the sentence of the Court, was ample and full compensation; but from the great lapse of time from the year 1740, to the present day, money has so depreciated, that two hundred pounds sterling money is worth but little more now, than two hundred pounds currency was in the year of 1740. We, therefore, pray your honorable body to take our case in to consideration and grant us such relief as you in your wisdom shall think best calculated to promote the happiness and growing importance of South-Carolina, and your Memorialists in duty bound will ever pray.

William Sims, B. Hammet, Peter Louis Jore, Robert Anderson, James Mitchell

General Assembly Petitions, n.d., 1822

* * *

The Petition of Ann Drayton Perry

To the Honorable President and the Other Members of the Senate

THAT your petitioner is the mistress and owner of a Negro Man Slave, called *Agrippa*, condemned to Transportation, by the Court, organised for the Trial of Slaves and others, charged with attempting to raise an Insurrection. She wishes not to screen her Negro from just punishment; but, conceives his case a singular one. Amongst the many trials reported, (to which she calls the attention of your Honorable House.) His name was never mentioned nor given in, in any of the lists made out by the Conspirators that gave evidence in behalf of the State; he was required by Capt. SIMS to appear as a witness in favor of his Fellow *Scipio*; at whose trial *Perault* was the accuser; and with which respect (*conscious of his innocence*) he willingly compiled. Here, and not before, *Perault* becomes his accusor, and he is hurried from the Court into confinement. The attention of your Honorable House is craved to examine the nature of the charge, made by *Perault*, (a fellow possessing intelligence and understanding above the generality of Negroes, glorying in the part he was to act, and boasting he would do it again, if an opportunity offered,) he charges *Agrippa* with this conversation—that, on his going to get the Horse, he asked him what he wanted the Horse for; *Agrippa* said, "*to do a thing good for you and good for me*;" which, he said, he understood to go raise men for the Insurrection. He asked the price of the hire of the Horse; Perault said three dollars; Agrippa replied that was too much, as he wanted him only a part of two days; Perault replied *that is my price, if you dont pay it you leave the Horse*. Agrippa then replied, I have but two dollars, will you let me have the Horse on paying that? I will pay you the other dollar when I come down. Perault said, "*No, the Horse dont move without the money.*" Will you take Sims as security? *Perault* answered *no!* Then *Adam* (a free man) was offered, and accepted for the dollar.

When we recur to the declaration made by *Agrippa*, to such a conspirator, as *Perault* avows himself to be, either his *truth* suffers or the *conspiracy* falls below contempt. Yet, on this single inconsistent evidence of a desperado swearing for his lief, (although disproved by the clearest testimony of five witness—to which the attention of your Honorable Body is referred in either of the reports) an unfortunate fellow creature is torn from his children and family; and your petitioner from a Negro invaluable to her, but, in estimation, of freeholders, worth $1,000. Your petitioner craves the interposition of your Honorable Body in this hard case; and that you will be pleased to restore her the Negro; or if, in your justice and wisdom, you should deem the sacrifice necessary, that you will grant her the value of the slave.

And your Petitioner, as in duty bound, will ever pray.   Ann Drayton Perry

General Assembly Petitions, n.d., 1822

* * *

Charleston Mercury, 1 January 1823

If distress and many troubles to which man is heir, have fallen upon individuals and communities during the annual period that is gone, yet we may find a general consolation in the general happiness and prosperity of our country.

* * *

Petition of the Edisto Island Auxiliary Association for Incorporation, 18 November 1823

. . . petitioners shew that a sacred regard for the safety of their property and the welfare of their state have forcibly induced them to establish a Society, in aid of the constituted authorities, with respect to the regulation of the Colored Population. Altho' it is their peculiar boast and pride that they do live under a government of laws, yet it must be conceded that in the execution . . . the midnight incendiary has escaped with impunity, and the assassin perfected his schemes of horror.

The history of the times warrant the conclusion that the period is rapidly approaching when the sober dictates of reason, on the subject of slavery, must yield to the hypocritical feelings of misguided philanthropy. To avert a serious calamity—to remove the misty veil which obscures the light of truth and justice, and forever crush the spirit of insubordination and revolt, it is not necessary only that the civil authorities should display their customary alertness and devotion to the public weal, but the zealous aid of every patriotic citizen should be freely offered. . . . The crisis is indeed assuming a critical and imposing aspect.

The ties of consanguinity and interest are insufficient to prevent even our neighbors from publically thundering their anathema against the holders of slaves.

Your humble petitioners,
William Seabrook, Senator Benjamin Bailey, John R. Matthews, William Edings, and Whitemarsh Seabrook

* * *

Address Read before the Agricultural Society of St. John's Colleton, 14 September 1825

From the general aspect of the times, a momentous crisis in the history of our country, is rapidly approaching. In the absence of political excitements, sectional jealousies have arisen, which are destined to continue, so long as the southern states shall cling to the charter of their rights, so as they shall refuse to sacrifice their constitutional immunities on the altar of sanguine philosophy. It is now susceptible of the clearest demonstration, that the tenure by which we hold our slaves, is daily becoming less secure, and more the object of acrimonious animadversion. The skeptic need no longer doubt of the proximity of danger. . . . it has been asserted that slavery contradicts the primary principles of our government; that our slaves are wretched, and their wretchedness ought to be alleviated; that they are dangerous to the community, and this danger ought to be removed; and that if the evils are not eradicated, God will raise up a Toussaint, or a Spartacus, or an African Tecumseh, to demand by what authority we hold them in subjection [3–4].

Whoever has watched the progress of our political events for the last 20 years, whoever remembers the inflammatory speeches on the Missouri Bill, must be aware, that no subject, in which the question of slavery may be directly or incidentally introduced, can be canvassed, without the most malevolent and serious excitement [11–12].

Our history has verified the melancholy truth, that one educated slave, or coloured freeman, with an insinuating address, is capable of infusing the poison of insubordination into the whole body of the black population. Possessing our means of information, it cannot be supposed, that he will be unacquainted with our domestic and political transactions. Is it not likely too, that he will draw with deeper colouring the lineaments of those baneful pictures, with which he may be furnished? Was not this really done by the leaders of what is termed the Gullah war in this state—of the insurrection at Stono in 1740, and of the contemplated risings of the negroes at Camden in 1816, and in Charleston in 1822? Did not the unreflecting zeal of the North and the East and the injudicious speeches on the Missouri question animate Vesey in his hellish efforts? . . . This manifestly indiscreet conduct of the abolitionists constitutes an evil, against which, from its essential nature, we cannot guard [13–14].

The period then has arrived, for a more powerful and systematic attack on personal and state rights, than it would be easy to find in the records of any nation. Religious and political phrenzy has lighted the torch of political desolation in many an unhappy country. . . . In the newspapers of the North and East, the question of emancipation is as calmly and soberly discussed, as if it were the subject, in the decision of which, the interests of a few individuals alone were concerned [16].

Whitemarsh Seabrook,[1] *A Concise View of the Critical Situation and Future Prospects of the Slave Holding States in Relation to Their Colored Population*

* * *

New York Herald, 24 May 1861

OUR SOUTHERN REBELLION—THE SOUND POLICY OF THE ADMINISTRATION EMBARRASSED BY OUR ABOLITION ORGANS

Our existing Southern rebellion is without a precedent or a parallel in the history of mankind. In its causes, in the materials of its organization, in the means and instrumentalities employed to bring it about, and in the grand objects of the conspirators, this revolutionary enterprise stands entirely alone.... Entered into on the plea of security to the great Southern institution of slavery, the experiment is hailed by the enemies of that institution as the harbinger of a swift, bloody, and sweeping emancipation.

... [A]gainst such impudent, dictatorial, slave insurrection preaching republican organs as the New York Tribune, Courier and Enquirer, Evening Post and Times, we are free to denounce them as dead weights to the cause of the government, and as giving "aid and comfort to the enemy" in strengthening the hands of the rebels, and in weakening the Union cause in the doubtful border States.... our abolition malignants of the Tribune, still darkening the counsels of the government with their bloody instructions, publish in their last daily issue an elaborate historical account of the "Denmark Vesey's Insurrection in South Carolina," from that venomous abolition periodical, the Boston Atlantic Monthly; and thus our old white coated philanthropist, Greely, gloats over it.

* * *

The New York Herald, 15 December 1861

BURNING OF CHARLESTON—REPORTED NEGRO INSURRECTION

We publish this morning details by telegraph of the almost total destruction by fire of the business portion of the city of Charleston—one of the most extensive conflagrations which ever took place on the American continent.... As it is, the heart of the city is burned out, and property to the amount of ten million dollars consumed.

... What was the precise origin of the fire is not yet satisfactorily settled. But there is a general belief that it was the work of the incendiary. Among the poor whites there is ample cause for discontent—oppression of the direct kind. Whether any of these have taken the present opportunity to avenge themselves, or whether they have acted in concert with the negroes, we are unable to determine. It is stated that a quantity of arms was found under the floor of a negro's cabin, "all new and in good order" ... other negroes were found to have knives and hatchets secreted. It is stated, indeed, that a negro who has been arrested is the incendiary, and that his act was but the carrying out of a plot revealed by some of the negroes to their masters.

... Should the news of the insurrection prove true, it will spread terror and consternation all over the South, as did Nat Turner's negro insurrection in Virginia in 1831, and the negro insurrection of Denmark Vesey in Charleston itself in 1822, which was fomented by abolition emissaries for St. Domingo and New York. At that time six thousand negroes were enrolled in the conspiracy, and a great number were arrested and hanged.

BIBLIOGRAPHY

MANUSCRIPTS

Chapel Hill, North Carolina
Southern Historical Collection, Wilson Library, University of North Carolina
  Arnold-Screven Papers
  Charleston Fire Masters Record Book, 1821
  Elliott and Gonzales Papers
  James Hamilton Jr. Papers
  Ernest Haywood Papers

Charleston, South Carolina
Charleston Library Society
  Robert Wilson Papers
City of Charleston Archives
  City Council Minutes, 1822
  City Ordinances, 1783–1825
Robert Scott Smalls Library, College of Charleston
  Brown Fellowship Society Papers
South Carolina Historical Society
  Mary Lamboll Thomas Beach Papers
  Langdon Cheves Papers
  Alexander Garden Papers
  Charles Graves Militia Book
  Independent Congregational (Circular) Church Accounts
  Letters of an American Traveller
  Henry Ravenel Papers
  South Carolina Militia Order Book, 1793–1814
  Denmark Vesey File
  Elizabeth Yates Papers

Columbia, South Carolina
South Carolina Department of Archives and History
  Bureau of the Census, Federal Census for the Charleston District, 1820 (microfilm)
  Executive Letterbooks, 1800–1822
  General Assembly Petitions, 1805–1822
  Governors' Messages, 1800–1822
  Grand Jury Presentments, 1822
  Letters of Administration, 1797–1803
  Miscellaneous Records, vols. CCC, KKK, MMM, RR, TT
  Senate Journals, 1800–1822
  Treasury Records, Journal C, 1814–1824
South Caroliniana Library, University of South Carolina
  Christopher Fitzsimmons Letterbook
  Jane Bruce Jones Papers

Kershaw County Papers
Napier, Rapelye, and Bennett Papers
Zalmon Wildman Papers

Durham, North Carolina
William Perkins Library, Duke University
William and Benjamin Hammet Papers
"Memoirs of Samuel Wragg Ferguson," typescript in Samuel Wragg Ferguson Papers
Rapelye Papers
Jacob Read Papers

London, United Kingdom
Public Record Office
Colonial Office. America and West Indies.
Correspondence, Original, Secretary of State: South Carolina, CO5/396

Madison, Wisconsin
Department of History, University of Wisconsin
Documentary History of the Ratification of the Constitution, South Carolina Files

Nashville, Tennessee
Southern Baptist Historical Collection
Richard Furman Correspondence

Winston-Salem, North Carolina
Museum of Early Southern Decorative Arts
Charleston County Land Records, 1810
Charleston County Wills, 1807–1818

NEWSPAPERS
Bermuda Gazette, 1783–91
Camden Gazette, 1816
Carolina Gazette, 1822
Charleston Courier, 1793–1834
Charleston Mercury, 1819–22
Charleston Patriot and Commercial Advertiser, 1817–18
Charleston Post and Courier, 1976, 1996
Charleston Times, 1806–18
City Gazette and Daily Advertiser (Charleston), 1783–1817
City Gazette and Commercial Daily Advertiser (Charleston), 1816–24
Columbian Herald (Charleston), 1789–94
Columbian Museum and Savannah Advertiser (Charleston), 1814
De Bow's Review, 1850
Evening Gazette (Boston), 1822
Evening Gazette (Charleston), 1785–1822
General Advertiser (Philadelphia), 1789
Genius of Universal Emancipation, 1821–22
The Georgian (Savannah), 1822
Hartford Courant, 1822
New York Daily Advertiser, 1822

New York Post, 1816
Niles Register, 1818–22
Pendleton Messenger (Pendleton, South Carolina), 1820–22
South Carolina Gazette (Charleston), 1772–75
South Carolina Weekly Museum (Charleston), 1797
Southern Patriot and Commercial Advertiser (Charleston), 1822
State Gazette of South Carolina, 1793
Worcester Gazette (Worcester, Massachusetts), 1797

PUBLISHED PRIMARY MATERIALS

Achates [Thomas Pinckney]. *Reflections Occasioned by the Late Disturbances in Charleston*. Charleston, 1822.
Adger, John B. *My Life and Times, 1810–1899*. Richmond, 1899.
Allen, Richard. *The Doctrines and Discipline of the African Methodist Church*. Philadelphia, 1817.
Alphabetical Digest of the Ordinances of the City Council of Charleston, 1783–1818. Charleston, 1818.
"American Freedmen's Inquiry Commission Interviews." In *Slave Testimony: Two Centuries of Letters, Speeches, Interviews, and Autobiographies*, edited by John Blassingame, 373–79. Baton Rouge, 1977.
Ball, Charles. *Slavery in the United States: A Narrative of the Life and Adventures of Charles Ball*. New York, 1837. Reprint, New York, 1969.
Bay, Elihu Hall. *Reports of the Cases Argued and Determined in Superior Courts of Law in South Carolina*. Charleston, 1798.
Boney, F. N., Richard Hulme, and Rafia Zafar, eds. *God Made Man, Man Made the Slave: The Autobiography of George Teamoh*. Macon, Ga., 1990.
Brevard, Joseph. *An Alphabetical Digest of the Public Statute Law of South Carolina*. 3 vols. Charleston, 1814.
Brown, Edward. *Notes on the Origins and Necessity of Slavery*. Charleston, 1826.
Brown, William Wells. *The Black Man: His Antecedents, His Genius, and His Achievements*. New York, 1863.
Butterfield, L. H., ed. *Diary and Autobiography of John Adams*. 4 vols. Cambridge, Mass., 1961.
Caroliniensis [Isaac Holmes and Robert Turnbull]. *On the Arrest of a British Seaman in Answer to Judge Johnson's Opinion*. Charleston, 1823.
Carteau, F. *Soirées Bermudiennes*. Bordeaux, France, 1802.
Castiglioni, Luigi. *Luigi Castiglioni's Viaggio: Travels in the United States of North America, 1785–1787*. Edited by Antonio Pace. Syracuse, 1983.
Charleston, City of. *Centennial of the Incorporation of Charleston*. Charleston, 1884.
Charleston Library Society. *A Catalogue of Books*. Charleston, 1811.
Collection of the Ordinances of the City Council of Charleston, 1818–1823. Charleston, 1823.
A Colored American. *The Late Intended Insurrection in Charleston*. New York, 1850.
A Columbian [Henry DeSaussure]. *A Series of Numbers Addressed to the Public on the Subject of Slaves and the Free People of Colour*. Columbia, 1822.
Cooper, Thomas, and David McCord, comps. *The Statutes at Large of South Carolina*. 10 vols. Columbia, 1836–41.

Coulon, J. Garron. *Rapport sur les Troubles de Santo Domingo*. 4 vols. Paris, 1798.
Davis, K. G., ed. *Documents of the American Revolution*. 21 vols. Shannon, Ireland, 1972.
Dessalines, Jean-Jacques. "Proclamation . . . in the Name of the Black People and Men of Colour of St. Domingo." In *The Life and Military Achievements of Tousant Loverture*, 74–78. Philadelphia, 1804.
De Vaissière, Pierre, *St. Domingue: La Société et la vie créoles sous l'Ancien Régime (1629–1789)*. Paris, 1909.
Directory and Stranger's Guide to the City of Charleston. Charleston, 1822.
Douglass, Frederick. *My Bondage and My Freedom*. Edited by William L. Andrews. Urbana, 1987.
———. *Narrative of the Life of Frederick Douglass, an American Slave, Written by Himself*. Edited by David W. Blight. New York, 1993.
Dow, Lorenzo. *The Stranger in Charleston! Or the Trial and Confession of Lorenzo Dow*. Boston, 1821.
Drayton, John. *A View of South Carolina as Respects Her Natural and Civil Concerns*. Charleston, 1803. Reprint, Spartanburg, 1972.
Dudley, William S., ed. *The Naval War of 1812: A Documentary History*. 3 vols. Washington, 1992.
Elliott, Benjamin, and Martin Stroebel. *The Militia System of South Carolina, Being a Digest of the Acts of Congress Concerning the Militia, Likewise the Militia Laws of This State*. Charleston, 1835.
Elliot, Jonathan, ed. *The Debates in the Several State Conventions on the Adoption of the Federal Constitution*. 5 vols. New York, 1888.
Equiano, Olaudah. *The Interesting Narrative of the Life of Olaudah Equiano, Written by Himself*. Edited by Robert Allison. New York, 1995.
Faust, Drew Gilpin, ed. *The Ideology of Slavery: Proslavery Thought in the Antebellum South, 1830–1860*. Baton Rouge, 1981.
Faux, W. *Memorable Days in America: Being a Journal of a Tour of the United States (1823)*. Vol. 12 of *Early Western Travels*, edited by Reuben Thwaites. New York, 1966.
Foner, Philip, ed. *The Life and Writings of Frederick Douglass*. 5 vols. New York, 1950.
Fraser, Charles. *Reminiscences of Charleston*. Charleston, 1854.
Freneau, Philip. "The Beauties of Santa Cruz (1776)." In Lorenzo Dow Turner, "Anti-Slavery Sentiment in American Literature." *Journal of Negro History* 14 (October 1929): 371–492.
Furman, Richard. *America's Deliverance and Duty: A Sermon on the Anniversary of American Independence*. Charleston, 1820.
———. *Exposition of the Views of the Baptists, Relative to the Coloured Population of the United States*. Charleston, 1822. Reprinted in James Rogers, *Richard Furman: Life and Legacy*, 274–86. Macon, 1985.
Gadsden, C. E. *An Essay on the Life of the Right Reverend Theodore Dehon*. Charleston, 1833.
Girod-Chantrans, Justin. *Voyage d'un Suisse dans différentes colonies*. Neuchâtel, Switzerland, 1785.
Grant, Joanne, ed. *Black Protest: History, Documents, and Analyses*. New York, 1968.
Grimké, Archibald. "Right on the Scaffold, or the Martyrs of 1822." Vol. 7 of *Occasional Papers of the American Negro Academy* (pamphlet series). Washington, 1901.
Hall, Basil. "An Illustrator's View." In *South Carolina: The Grand Tour, 1780–1865*, edited by Thomas D. Clark, 113–34. Columbia, 1973.

Hamer, Philip, George C. Rogers Jr., and David R. Chesnutt, eds. *The Papers of Henry Laurens*. Vol. 5. Columbia, 1968.
Hamilton, James, Jr. *An Account of the Late Intended Insurrection among a Portion of the Blacks in This City*. Charleston, 1822.
Hammond, James Henry. "Progress of Southern Industry." *De Bow's Review* 8 (June 1850): 508–27.
Hemphill, W. Edwin, ed. *The Papers of John C. Calhoun*. 20 vols. Columbia, 1973.
Herbemont, N. *The Life of Toussaint Louverture*. Charleston, 1802.
Higginson, Thomas. *Army Life in a Black Regiment*. New York, 1869.
———. *Black Rebellion: Selections from Travellers and Outlaws*. Boston, 1889. Reprint, New York, 1969.
———. "Denmark Vesey." *Atlantic Monthly* 7 (June 1861): 728–44.
Hodgson, Adam. *Letters from North America*. 2 vols. London, 1824.
Holland, Edwin C. *A Refutation of the Calumnies Circulated against Southern and Western States Respecting the Institution of Slavery*. Charleston, 1822.
Hunt, Benjamin Faneuil. *The Argument of Benj. Faneuil Hunt, in the Case of the Arrest of the Person Claiming to a British Seaman*. Charleston, 1823.
Hurd, Johm C. *The Law of Freedom and Bondage in the United States*. 2 vols. Boston, 1868. Reprint, New York, 1968.
Ingraham, Joseph. *The South-West by a Yankee*. 2 vols. New York, 1835.
Jameson, J. Franklin, ed. "Autobiography of Omar Ibn Said in North Carolina, 1831." *American Historical Review* 30 (July 1925): 787–95.
Johns, J. *A Memoir of the Life of the Right Reverend William Meade*. Baltimore, 1867.
Johnson, William. *To the Public of Charleston*. Charleston, 1822.
———. *Nugae Georgicae: An Essay Delivered to the Literary and Philosophical Society of South Carolina, October 1815*. Charleston, 1815.
———. "Opinion of the Hon. William Johnson, Delivered 7 August 1823 in the Case of the Arrest of the British Seaman, ex parte, Henry Elkison v. Francis Deliesseline, Sheriff of Charleston." In *Free Blacks, Slaves, and Slaveholders in Civil and Criminal Courts: The Pamphlet Literature*, edited by Paul Finkelman, 285–99. Ser. 4, vol. 1. New York, 1988.
Kaminski, John P., ed. *A Necessary Evil? Slavery and the Debate over the Constitution*. Madison, 1995.
Kelsey, R. W., ed. "Swiss Settlers in South Carolina." *South Carolina Historical Magazine* 23 (July 1922): 87–93.
Kennedy, Lionel H., and Thomas Parker. *An Official Report of the Trials of Sundry Negroes Charged with an Attempt to Raise an Insurrection in the State of South Carolina*. Charleston, 1822. Reprinted as *The Trial Record of Denmark Vesey*, edited by John Killens. Boston, 1970.
Kingsley, Zaphaniah. *A Treatise on the Patriarchal, or Co-operative System of Society as It Exists in Some Governments, amd Colonies in America, and in the United States, under the Name of Slavery*. 1829. Reprint, Freeport, N.Y., 1970.
Lambert, John. *Travels through Lower Canada and the United States of North America, in the Years 1806, 1807, and 1808*. 3 vols. London, 1810.
La Rochefoucauld-Liancourt, François Alexandre Frédéric, Duc de. *Travels through the United States of North America*. 2 vols. London, 1799.
Legare, John Berwick. *An Oration on 4th. July 1822, Delivered at St. Michael's Church*. Charleston, 1822.

MacCalman, Iain, ed. *The Horrors of Slavery and Other Writings by Robert Wedderburn.* New York, 1991.
Martin, Sidney Walter, ed. "Ebenezer Kellogg's Visit to Charleston, 1817." *South Carolina Magazine of History* 49 (January 1948): 1–14.
Martineau, Harriet. *Retrospect of Western Travel.* 2 vols. London, 1838.
Mathews, John. *A Voyage to the River Sierra Leone.* London, 1788.
"Memorial of the Citizens of Charleston to the Senate and House of Representatives of the State of South Carolina." In *A Documentary History of American Industrial Society: Plantation and Frontier, Volume Two,* edited by U. B. Phillips, 103–16. New York, 1958.
Meredith, Henry. *An Account of the Gold Coast.* London, 1812.
Mills, Robert. *Atlas of South Carolina.* Charleston, 1826.
——. *Statistics of South Carolina.* Charleston, 1826.
Moffatt, Lucius Gaston, and Joseph Médard Carrière, eds. "A Frenchman Visits Charleston." *South Carolina Historical Magazine* 49 (January 1948): 131–54.
Mohl, Raymond A. "'The Grand Fabric of Republicanism': A Scotsman Describes South Carolina, 1810–1811." *South Carolina Historical Magazine* 71 (July 1970): 170–88.
Mood, F. A. *Methodism in Charleston: A Narrative of the Chief Events Relating to the Rise and Progress of the Methodist Episcopal Church in Charleston.* Nashville, 1856.
Moore, John Hammond, ed. "A Hymn of Freedom—South Carolina." *Journal of Negro History* 50 (January 1965): 50–53.
——. "The Abiel Abbott Journals: A Yankee Preacher in Charleston Society, 1818–1827." *South Carolina Historical Magazine* 68 (April 1967): 51–73.
Murdoch, Richard K., ed. "Correspondence of French Consuls in Charleston, South Carolina, 1793–1794." *South Carolina Historical Magazine* 74 (January 1973): 1–79.
Neilson, Peter. *The Life and Adventures of Zamba, An African Negro King and His Experiences of Slavery in South Carolina.* London, 1847.
——. *Six Years' Residence in America.* Glasgow, Scotland, 1830.
Nell, William C. *Colored Patriots of the American Revolution.* Boston, 1855.
Neuffer, Claude Henry. *The Christopher Happoldt Journal: His European Tour with the Reverend John Backman, 1838.* Charleston, 1960.
Oldendorp, Christian Georg Andreas. *History of the Mission of the Evangelical Brethren on the Caribbean Islands of St. Thomas, St. Croix, and St. John* [1777]. Edited by Arnold R. Highfield and Vladimir Barac. Ann Arbor, 1987.
Ordinances of Charleston. Charleston, 1802.
Ordinances of the City Council. Charleston, 1784.
Paiewonsky, Isidor, ed. *Eyewitness Accounts of Slavery in the Danish West Indies.* New York, 1989.
Parham, Althea de Puech, ed. *My Odyssey: Experiences of a Young Refugee from Two Revolutions, By a Creole of Saint Domingue.* Baton Rouge, 1959.
Payne, Daniel. *History of the African Methodist Episcopal Church.* Nashville, 1891.
Perkins, Samuel. *Reminiscences of the Insurrection in St. Domingo.* Cambridge, Mass., 1886.
Rainsford, Marcus. *Historical Account of Black Hayti.* London, 1805.
Rawick, George P., ed. *South Carolina Narratives.* Vol. 2 of *The American Slave: A Composite Autobiography.* Westport, Conn., 1972.
Ripley, C. Peter, Roy E. Finkenbine, Michael Hembree, and Donald Yacovone, eds. *Witness for Freedom: African-American Voices on Race, Slavery, and Emancipation.* Chapel Hill, 1993.

Rules and Regulations of the Brown Fellowship Society. Charleston, 1844.

Saint-Méry, Médéric Louis Elie Moreau de. *A Civilization That Perished: The Last Years of Colonial Rule in Haiti.* Edited by Ivor D. Spence. Philadelphia, 1787–89. Reprint, Lanham, Md., 1985.

Schaw, Janet. *Journal of a Lady of Quality (Being the Narrative of a Journey from Scotland to the West Indies, North Carolina, and Portugal, 1774–1776).* Edited by Evangeline W. Andrews. New Haven, 1923.

Schoepf, Johann David. *Travels in the Confederation, 1783–1784.* Edited and translated by Alfred J. Morrison. Vol. 2. Philadelphia, 1911.

Seabrook, Whitemarsh. *A Concise View of the Critical Situation and the Future Prospects of the Slave-Holding States in Their Relation to Their Coloured Population.* Charleston, 1825.

Shecut, J. L. E. W. *Shecut's Medical and Philosophical Essays.* Charleston, 1819.

A South Carolina Federalist [Henry DeSaussure]. *Answer to a Dialogue between a Federalist and a Republican.* Charleston, 1797.

A South Carolinian [attributed to Frederick Dalcho]. *Practical Considerations Founded on the Scriptures, Relative to the Slave Population of South Carolina.* Charleston, 1823.

Starobin, Robert, ed. *Denmark Vesey: The Slave Conspiracy of 1822.* Englewood Cliffs, Calif., 1970.

Staudenraus, Philip J., ed. "Letters from South Carolina." *South Carolina Historical Magazine* 58 (October 1957): 209–17.

Washington, H. A., ed. *The Writings of Thomas Jefferson.* Vol. 4. Washington, 1854.

Weld, Theodore. *American Slavery as It Is: Testimony of a Thousand Witnesses.* New York, 1839. Reprint, New York, 1968.

Whittaker, Daniel R. "The Necessity of a Southern Literature." *Southern Quarterly Review* 1 (January 1842). Reprinted in *The Charleston Book: A Miscellany in Prose and Verse,* edited by William Gilmore Simms, 312–17. Charleston, 1845. Reprint, edited by David Moltke-Hansen, Spartanburg, 1983.

Winsnes, Selena Axelrod, ed. *Letters on West Africa and the Slave Trade: Paul Erdmann Isert's Journey to Guinea and the Caribbean Islands in Columbia* [1788]. New York, 1992.

BOOKS, ARTICLES, AND THESES

Adas, Michael. *Prophets of Rebellion: Millenarian Protest Movements against the European Colonial Order.* New York, 1979.

Alpers, Edward. *Ivory and Slaves: Changing Patterns of International Trade in East Central Africa to the Later Nineteenth Century.* Berkeley and Los Angeles, 1975.

———. *The East African Slave Trade.* Nairobi, 1967.

Aptheker, Herbert. *American Negro Slave Revolts.* New York, 1943. Reprint, New York, 1987.

Austin, Allan D. *African Muslims in Antebellum America: Transatlantic Stories and Spiritual Struggles.* New York, 1997.

Ayers, Edward. *Vengeance and Justice: Crime and Punishment in the Nineteenth-Century American South.* New York, 1984.

Bailey, N. Louise, and Walter Edgar, eds. *Biographical Directory of the South Carolina House of Representatives, 1791–1815.* 5 vols. Columbia, 1984.

Bastide, Roger. *African Civilizations in the New World.* New York, 1971.

Baur, John E. "Mulatto Machiavelli: Jean Pierre Boyer and the Haiti of His Day." *Journal of Negro History* 32 (July 1947): 307–53.
Beckles, Hilary McD. *Natural Rebels: A Social History of Enslaved Women in Barbados.* London, 1989.
Bell, R. C. *Board and Table Games from Many Civilizations.* New York, 1960.
Bellows, Barbara. *Benevolence among Slaveholders: Assisting the Poor in Charleston, 1670–1860.* Baton Rouge, 1993.
Berlin, Ira. *Slaves without Masters: The Free Negro in the Antebellum South.* New York, 1974.
Berlin, Ira, and Philip D. Morgan. "Labor and the Shaping of Slave Life in the Americas." In *Cultivation and Culture and the Shaping of Slave Life in the Americas*, edited by Ira Berlin and Philip D. Morgan, 1–45. Charlottesville, 1993.
Blackburn, Robin. *The Overthrow of Colonial Slavery, 1776–1848.* London, 1988.
Blassingame, John. *The Slave Community: Plantation Life in the Antebellum South.* New York, 1972.
Bolster, W. Jeffrey. *Black Jacks: African American Seamen in the Age of Sail.* Cambridge, Mass., 1997.
———. "'To Feel Like a Man': Black Seamen in the Northern States, 1800–1865." *Journal of American History* 76 (March 1990): 1173–99.
Bond, Oliver J. *The Story of the Citadel.* Richmond, 1936.
Brady, Patrick S. "The Slave Trade and Sectionalism in South Carolina, 1787–1808." *Journal of Southern History* 38 (November 1972): 601–20.
Brathwaite, Edward. *The Development of Creole Society in Jamaica, 1770–1820.* Oxford, England, 1971.
Brennan, Thomas. *Public Drinking and Popular Culture in Eighteenth-Century Paris.* Princeton, 1988.
Bridenbaugh, Carl. *The Colonial Craftsman.* New York, 1950.
Brown, Kathleen. *Good Wives, Nasty Wenches, and Anxious Patriarchs: Gender, Race, and Power in Colonial Virginia.* Chapel Hill, 1996.
Browning, Joseph B. "The Beginnings of Insurance Enterprise among Negroes." *Journal of Negro History* 22 (October 1937): 417–32.
Carrion, Arturo Morales. *Puerto Rico and the Non-Hispanic Caribbean: A Study in the Decline of Spanish Exclusivism.* Barcelona, 1952.
Carroll, Joseph C. *Slave Insurrections in the United States, 1800–1865.* New York, 1938.
Cassidy, Frederic, ed. *Dictionary of American Regional English.* Cambridge, Mass., 1985.
Channing, Stephen. *Crisis of Fear: Secession in South Carolina.* New York, 1970.
Clark, Peter. *The English Alehouse, 1200–1830.* London, 1983.
Clarke, Erskine. *Wrestlin' Jacob: A Portrait of Religion in the Old South.* Atlanta, 1979.
Clowse, Converse D. "Ship Owning and Shipbuilding in Colonial South Carolina: An Overview." *American Neptune* 44 (Fall 1988): 221–44.
Coclanis, Peter. *The Shadow of a Dream: Economic Life and Death in the South Carolina Low Country, 1670–1920.* New York, 1989.
Cole, Arthur. *Wholesale Commodity Prices in the United States, 1700–1861.* 2 vols. Cambridge, 1938.
Comaroff, Jean. *Body of Power, Spirit of Resistance: The Culture and History of a South African People.* Chicago, 1985.
Crapanzano, Vincent. "Introduction: Case Studies in Spirit Possession." In *Case Studies*

in *Spirit Possession*, edited by Vincent Crapanzano and Vivian Garrison. New York, 1977.
Craton, Michael, and Gail Saunders. *Islanders in the Stream: A History of the Bahamanian People*. 2 vols. Athens, Ga., 1992.
Creel, Margaret Washington. *"A Peculiar People": Slave Religion and Community-Culture among the Gullahs*. New York, 1988.
———. "Gullah Attitudes toward Life and Death." In *Africanisms in American Culture*, edited by Joseph Holloway, 69–97. Bloomington, 1990.
Creighton, Margaret. "American Mariners and the Rites of Manhood, 1830–1870." In *Jack Tar in History: Essays in the History of Maritime Life and Labour*, edited by Colin Howell and Richard J. Twomey, 143–63. Fredericton, New Brunswick, 1991.
———. "Women and Men in American Whaling, 1830–1870." *International Journal of Maritime History* 4 (June 1992): 195–218.
Curry, Leonard P. *The Free Black in Urban America: The Shadow of a Dream*. New York, 1976.
Curtin, Philip D. "The Declaration of the Rights of Man in Saint-Domingue, 1788–1791." *Hispanic American Historical Review* 30 (May 1950): 157–75.
———. *The Rise and Fall of the Plantation Complex: Essays in Atlantic History*. New York, 1990.
Da Costa, Emilio Viotti. *Crowns of Glory, Tears of Blood: The Demerara Slave Rebellion of 1823*. New York, 1994.
Darnton, Robert. "First Steps in the History of Reading." In *The Kiss of Lamourette: Reflections in Cultural History*, by Robert Darnton, 154–90. New York, 1990.
Davis, David Brion. *The Problem of Slavery in the Age of Revolution*. Ithaca, 1975.
———. *Revolutions: Reflections on American Equality and Foreign Liberations*. Cambridge, 1990.
Davis, Natalie Zemon. *Fiction in the Archives: Pardon Tales and Their Tellers in Sixteenth-Century France*. Stanford, 1987.
———. "The Reasons of Misrule." Chapter 4 in *Society and Culture in Early Modern France*, 97–123. Stanford, 1975.
Davis, Thomas J. *A Rumor of Revolt: The "Great Negro Plot" in Colonial New York*. New York, 1985.
Davis, Wade. *One River: Explorations and Discoveries in the Amazon Rain Forest*. New York, 1996.
———. *The Serpent and the Rainbow*. New York, 1985.
Dayan, Joan. *Haiti, History, and the Gods*. Berkeley and Los Angeles, 1995.
Dillon, Merton L. *Benjamin Lundy and the Struggle for Negro Freedom*. Urbana, 1966.
———. *Slavery Attacked: Southern Slaves and Their Allies, 1619–1865*. Baton Rouge, 1990.
Dirks, Nicholas, Geoff Eley, and Sherry B. Ortner. Introduction to *Culture/Power/History: A Reader in Contemporary Social History*, 3–46. Princeton, 1994.
Douglas, Mary. *In the Active Voice*. Boston, 1982.
Dowd, Gregory E. *A Spirited Resistance: The North American Indian Struggle for Unity, 1745–1815*. Baltimore, 1992.
Du Bois, W. E. B. *The Suppression of the Atlantic Slave Trade to the United States of America, 1638–1870*. Cambridge, Mass., 1896.
Durden, Robert. "The Establishment of the Calvary Protestant Episcopal Church for Negroes in Charleston." *South Carolina Historical Magazine* 65 (April 1964): 63–84.

Edward, Lillie J. *Denmark Vesey*. New York, 1990.
Egerton, Douglas R. *Gabriel's Rebellion: The Virginia Slave Conspiracies of 1800 and 1802*. Chapel Hill, 1993.
——. *"He Shall Go Free": The Lives of Denmark Vesey*. Forthcoming, 1998.
Ernst, Robert. *Rufus King: American Federalist*. Chapel Hill, 1968.
Faust, Drew Gilpin. *James Henry Hammond and the Old South: A Design for Mastery*. Baton Rouge, 1982.
Feierman, Steven. *Peasant Intellectuals: Anthropology and History in Tanzania*. Madison, 1990.
Fick, Carolyn. *The Making of Haiti: The Saint Domingue Revolution from Below*. Knoxville, 1990.
Finkelman, Paul. *Slavery and the Founders: Race and the Liberty in the Age of Jefferson*. Armonk, N.Y., 1996.
——, ed. *Slavery in the Courtroom: An Annotated Bibliography of American Cases*. Washington, 1985.
Fitchett, E. Horace. "The Origins and Growth of the Free Negro Population in Charleston, South Carolina." *Journal of Negro History* 26 (October 1941): 421–37.
——. "The Traditions of the Free Negro in Charleston, South Carolina." *Journal of Negro History* 25 (April 1940): 139–52.
Ford, Lacy K. *Origins of Southern Radicalism: The South Carolina Upcountry, 1800–1860*. New York, 1988.
Foucault, Michel. *Discipline and Punish: The Birth of the Prison*. New York, 1977.
——. "Space, Knowledge, and Power." In *The Foucault Reader*, edited by Paul Rabinow, 239–56. New York, 1984.
Fox-Genovese, Elizabeth. *Within the Plantation Household: Black and White Women in the Old South*. Chapel Hill, 1988.
Fraser, Walter J. *Charleston! Charleston!: The History of a Southern City*. Columbia, 1989.
Frederickson, George. *The Black Image in the White Mind: The Debate on Afro-American Character and Destiny, 1817–1914*. New York, 1971.
Freehling, William. "Denmark Vesey's Peculiar Reality." In *New Perspectives on Race and Slavery: Essays in Honor of Kenneth Stampp*, edited by Robert Abzug and Stephen Maizlish, 25–47. Lexington, 1986.
——. "History and Television." *Southern Studies* 22 (Spring 1983): 76–81.
——. *Prelude to Civil War: The Nullification Controversy in South Carolina, 1816–1832*. New York, 1965.
——. *The Reintegration of American History: Slavery and the Civil War*. New York, 1994.
——. *The Road to Disunion: Secessionists at Bay*. New York, 1990.
Frey, Sylvia R. *Water from the Rock: Black Resistance in a Revolutionary Age*. Princeton, 1991.
Geggus, David P. "The Enigma of Jamaica in the 1790s: New Light on the Causes of Slave Rebellions." *William and Mary Quarterly*, 3d ser., 64 (April 1987): 274–300.
——. "On the Eve of the Haitian Revolution: Slave Runaways in Saint Domingue in 1790." In *Out of the House of Bondage: Runaways, Resistance, and Marronage in Africa and the New World*, edited by Gad Heumann and James Walvin, 112–28. London, 1986.
——. *Slavery, War, and Revolution: The British Occupation of Saint Domingue, 1793–1798*. New York, 1982.

——. "Slavery, War, and Revolution in the Greater Caribbean." In *A Turbulent Time: The French Revolution and the Greater Caribbean*, edited by David P. Geggus and David Barry Gaspar, 1–50. Bloomington, 1997.

——. "Sugar and Coffee Cultivation in Saint Domingue and the Shaping of the Slave Labor Force." In *Cultivation and Culture and the Shaping of Slave Life in the Americas*, edited by Ira Berlin and Philip Morgan, 73–100. Charlottesville, 1993.

Genovese, Eugene D. "Black Plantation Preachers in the Slave South." *Southern Studies* 2 (Fall/Winter 1991), 204–29.

——. *From Rebellion to Revolution: Afro-American Slave Revolts in the Making of the Modern World*. Baton Rouge, 1979.

——. *Roll, Jordan, Roll: The World the Slaves Made*. New York, 1972.

George, Carol V. R. *Segregated Sabbaths: Richard Allen and the Emergence of Independent Black Churches, 1760–1840*. New York, 1973.

Gilroy, Paul. *The Black Atlantic: Modernity and Double Consciousness*. London, 1993.

Ginzburg, Carlo. *The Cheese and the Worms: The Cosmos of a Sixteenth-Century Miller*. Baltimore, 1980.

Gobel, Erik. "Volume and Structure of Danish Shipping to the Caribbean and Guinea, 1671–1838." *International Journal of Maritime History* 2 (December 1990): 103–31.

Goldfield, David. "Black Life in Old South Cities." In *Before Freedom Came: African-American Life in the Antebellum South*, edited by Edward D. C. Campbell and Kym S. Rice, 123–54. Charlottesville, 1991.

Goldin, Claudia Dale. *Urban Slavery in the American South, 1820–1860*. Chicago, 1976.

Gorn, Elliott. "Black Magic: Folk Beliefs of the Slave Community." In *Science and Medicine in the Old South*, edited by Ronald L. Numbers and Todd L. Savitt, 295–326. Baton Rouge, 1989.

——. "Seafaring Engendered: A Comment on Gender and Seafaring." *International Journal of Maritime History* 4 (June 1992): 219–25.

Gramsci, Antonio. *Selections from the Prison Notebooks of Antonio Gramsci*. Edited and translated by Quintin Hoare and Geoffrey Smith. London, 1973.

Gravely, William B. "The Rise of African Churches in America (1786–1822): Re-Examining the Contexts." *Journal of Religious Thought* 4 (Spring–Summer 1984): 59–73.

Greenberg, Kenneth S. *Masters and Statesmen: The Political Culture of American Slavery*. Baltimore, 1985.

——, ed. *The Confessions of Nat Turner*. New York, 1996.

Green-Pederson, Svend D. "Slave Demography in the Danish West Indies and the Abolition of the Danish Slave Trade." In *The Abolition of the Atlantic Slave Trade: Origins and Effects in Europe, Africa, and the Americas*, edited by David Eltis and James Walvin, 231–57. Madison, 1981.

Grimes, Kimberly, Dale Rosengarten, Martha Zierden, and Elizabeth Alston. *Between the Tracks: The Heritage of Charleston's East Side Community*. Charleston, 1987.

Guha, Ranajit. "The Prose of Counter-Insurgency." In *Culture/Power/History*, edited by Nicholas Dirks et al., 336–71. Princeton, 1994.

Hall, Gwendolyn Midlo. *Africans in Colonial Louisiana: The Development of Afro-Creole Culture in the Eighteenth Century*. Baton Rouge, 1992.

Hall, Neville A. T. "Maritime Maroons: *Grand Marronage* from the Danish West Indies." In *Caribbean Slave Society and Economy*, edited by Hilary Beckles and Verene Shepherd, 387–400. New York, 1991.

———. "Slavery in Three West Indian Towns: Christiansted, Fredericksted, and Charlotte Amalie in the Late Eighteenth Century and Early Nineteenth Century." In *Trade, Government, and Society in Caribbean History, 1700–1920*, edited by B. W. Higman, 17–38. Kingston, Jamaica, 1983.

———. *Slave Society in the Danish West Indies: St. Thomas, St. John, and St. Croix*. Edited by B. W. Higman. Baltimore, 1982.

———. "Slaves Use of Their 'Free Time' in the Danish Virgin Islands in the later Eighteenth and Early Nineteenth Centuries." In *Caribbean Slave Society and Economy*, edited by Hilary Beckles and Verene Shepherd, 335–44.

Hamer, Philip. "Great Britain, the United States, and the Negro Seaman Acts, 1822–1848." *Journal of Southern History* 1 (February 1935): 3–28.

Harding, Vincent. *There Is a River: The Black Struggle for Freedom in America*. New York, 1981.

Harland, John. *Seamanship in the Age of Sail: An Account of Shiphandling and Sailing Men-of-War, 1600–1860*. London, 1984.

Harris, Robert. "Charleston's Free Afro-American Elite: The Brown Fellowship Society and Humane Brotherhood." *South Carolina Historical Magazine* 82 (October 1981): 289–310.

Harvey, David. *Consciousness and the Urban Experience: Studies in the History and Theory of Capitalist Urbanization*. Baltimore, 1985.

Hatch, Nathan. *The Democratization of American Christianity*. New Haven, 1989.

Hay, Douglas. "Property, Authority, and the Criminal Law." In *Albion's Fatal Tree: Crime and Society in Eighteenth-Century England*, edited by Douglas Hay, Peter Linebaugh, John G. Rule, E. P. Thompson, and Cal Winslow, 17–64. New York, 1975.

Haynes, Douglas, and Gyan Prakesh. "The Entanglement of Power and Resistance." Introduction to *Contesting Power: Resistance and Everyday Social Relations in South Asia*. Berkeley and Los Angeles, 1991.

Hazen, Charles D. *Contemporary American Opinion of the French Revolution*. Baltimore, 1897. Reprint, Gloucester, Mass., 1964.

Henry, H. M. *The Police Control of the Slave in South Carolina*. Emory, Va., 1914.

Hickey, Donald R. *The War of 1812: A Forgotten Conflict*. Urbana, 1989.

Higgins, W. Robert. "Charleston: Terminus and Entrepôt of the Colonial Slave Trade." In *The African Diaspora: Interpretive Essays*, edited by Martin L. Kilson and Robert I. Rotberg, 114–31. Cambridge, Mass., 1976.

Highfield, Arnold R. "The Danish Atlantic and West Indian Slave Trade." In *The Danish West Indies Slave Trade: Virgin Island Perspectives*, edited by George F. Tyson and Arnold R. Highfield, 11–32. St. Croix, 1994.

Hindus, Michael. *Prison and Plantation: Crime, Justice, and Authority in Massachusetts and South Carolina*. Chapel Hill, 1980.

Hinks, Peter P. *To Awaken My Afflicted Brethren: David Walker and the Problem of Antebellum Slave Resistance*. University Park, Pa., 1997.

Hobsbawm, E. J. "From Social History to the History of Society." In *Essays in Social History*, edited by M. W. Flinn and T. C. Smout, 1–22. Oxford, England, 1974.

Holloway, Joseph. "The Origins of African-American Culture." In *Africanisms in American Culture*, edited by Joseph Holloway, 1–18. Bloomington, 1990.

Horton, James O. "Freedom's Yoke: Gender Conventions among Free Blacks." In *Free People of Color: Inside the African-American Community*, by James Horton, 98–121. Washington, 1993.

Hudgins, Carter, Carl L. Lounsbury, Louis P. Nelson, and Jonathan Poston, eds. *The Vernacular Architecture of Charleston and the Lowcountry, 1670–1900.* Charleston, 1994.

Huff, Archie Vernon, Jr. *Langdon Cheves of South Carolina.* Columbia, 1977.

———. "The Eagle and the Vulture: Changing Attitudes toward Nationalism in Fourth of July Orations Delivered in Charleston, 1778–1860." *South Atlantic Quarterly* 73 (Winter 1974): 10–22.

Hünefeldt, Christine. *Paying the Price of Freedom: Family and Labor among Lima's Slaves, 1800–1854.* Berkeley and Los Angeles, 1994.

Hunt, Alfred N. *Haiti's Influence on Antebellum America: Slumbering Volcano in the Caribbean.* Baton Rouge, 1988.

Iliffe, John. *Africans: The History of a Continent.* New York, 1995.

Jackson, Melvin H. *Privateers in Charleston, 1793–1796: An Account of a French Palatinate in South Carolina.* Washington, 1969.

James, C. L. R. *The Black Jacobins: Toussaint L'Ouverture and the San Domingo Revolution.* New York, 1938.

———. *Mariners, Renegades, and Castaways: The Story of Herman Melville and the World We Live In.* Detroit, 1953. Reprint, New York, 1985.

January, Alan. "The South Carolina Association: An Agency for Race Control in Antebellum Charleston." *South Carolina Historical Magazine* 78 (July 1977): 191–201.

Jervey, Louis P. "Thomas Hall Jervey: Man of God and the Sea." *South Carolina Historical Magazine* 96 (April 1995): 135–52.

Jervey, Theodore. *Robert Y. Hayne and His Times.* New York, 1909.

Johansen, Hans Christian. "The Reality behind the Demographic Arguments to Abolish the Danish Slave Trade." In *The Abolition of the Atlantic Slave Trade: Origins and Effects in Europe, Africa, and the Americas,* edited by David Eltis and James Walvin, 221–30. Madison, 1981.

Johnson, Michael. "Planters and Patriarchy: Charleston, 1800–1860." *Journal of Southern History* 46 (February 1980): 45–72.

———. "Runaway Slaves and Slave Communities in South Carolina, 1799 to 1830." *William and Mary Quaterly,* 3d ser., 38 (July 1981): 418–41.

Johnson, Michael P., and James L. Roark. *Black Masters: A Free Family of Color in the Old South.* New York, 1984.

———. "'A Middle Ground': Free Mulattoes and the Friendly Moralist Society of Antebellum Charleston." *Southern Studies* 21 (Fall 1982): 246–65.

Joll, James. *Gramsci.* London, 1977.

Jones, Howard. *Mutiny on the Amistad.* New York, 1986.

Jones, Norrece. *Born a Child of Freedom, Yet a Slave: Mechanisms of Control and Strategies of Resistance in Antebellum South Carolina.* Hanover, N.H., 1990.

Jordan, Winthrop D. *Tumult and Silence at Second Creek: An Inquiry into a Civil War Slave Conspiracy.* Baton Rouge, 1993.

———. *White Over Black: American Attitudes toward the Negro, 1550–1812.* Chapel Hill, 1968.

Joyner, Charles. *Down by the Riverside: A South Carolina Slave Community.* Urbana, 1984.

———. "'If You Ain't Got No Education': Slave Language and Slave Thought in Antebellum Charleston." In *Intellectual Life in Antebellum Charleston,* edited by Michael O'Brien and David Moltke-Hansen, 255–78. Knoxville, 1986.

Junger, Sebastian. *The Perfect Storm: A True Story of Men Against the Sea.* New York, 1997.

Kaplan, Sidney, and Emma Nogrady Kaplan. *The Black Presence in the Era of the American Revolution.* Amherst, 1989.

Kennedy, Michael L. "A French Jacobin Club in Charleston, South Carolina, 1792–1795." *South Carolina Historical Magazine* 91 (January 1990): 4–21.

Killens, John. *Great Gittin' Up in the Morning: The Story of Denmark Vesey.* New York, 1972.

Kirkland, Thomas, and Robert Kennedy. *Historic Camden: The Nineteenth Century.* 2 vols. Columbia, 1926.

Klebaner, Benjamin J. "Public Poor Relief in Charleston, 1800–1860." *South Carolina Historical Magazine* 55 (October 1954): 220–21.

Klein, Herbert. *African Slavery in Latin America and the Caribbean.* New York, 1986.

Klein, Rachel N. *Unification of a Slave State: The Rise of the Planter Class in the South Carolina Backcountry, 1760–1808.* Chapel Hill, 1990.

Koger, Larry. *Black Slaveowners: Free Black Slave Masters in South Carolina, 1790–1860.* Jefferson, N.C., 1985.

Kolchin, Peter. *American Slavery, 1619–1877.* New York, 1993.

Kramer, Aaron. *Denmark Vesey and Other Poems.* New York, 1952.

Lander, Ernest M. "Ante-Bellum Milling in South Carolina." *South Carolina Historical Magazine* 52 (July 1951): 125–32.

———. "Charleston: Manufacturing Center of the Old South." *Journal of Southern History* 26 (August 1960): 330–51.

Langley, Lester D. *The Americas in the Age of Revolution, 1750–1850.* New Haven, 1996.

Lerner, Gerda. *The Grimké Sisters from South Carolina: Pioneers for Woman's Rights and Abolition.* New York, 1967.

Levine, Lawrence W. *Black Culture and Black Consciousness: Afro-American Folk Thought from Slavery to Freedom.* New York, 1977.

Lindstrom, Lamont. *Knowledge and Power in a South Pacific Society.* Washington, 1990.

Linebaugh, Peter. "All the Atlantic Mountains Shook." *Labour* 10 (Autumn 1982): 87–121.

———. *The London Hanged: Crime and Civil Society in the Eighteenth Century.* New York, 1992.

Linebaugh, Peter, and Marcus Rediker. "The Many-Headed Hydra: Sailors, Slaves, and the Atlantic Working Class in the Eighteenth Century." In *Jack Tar in History: Essays in Maritime History*, edited by Colin Howell and Richard J. Twomey, 11–36. Fredricton, New Brunswick, 1991. Originally published in *Journal of Historical Sociology* 3 (September 1990): 225–52.

Link, Eugene P. *Democratic-Republican Societies, 1790–1800.* New York, 1942.

Littlefield, Daniel. "'Abundance of Negroes of That Nation': The Significance of African Ethnicity in Colonial South Carolina." In *The Meaning of South Carolina History: Essays in Honor of George C. Rogers, Jr.*, edited by David R. Chesnutt and Cylde N. Wilson, 19–38. Columbia, 1991.

———. *Rice and Slaves: Ethnicity and the Slave Trade in Colonial South Carolina.* Baton Rouge, 1981.

———. "The Slave Trade to Colonial South Carolina: A Profile." *South Carolina Historical Magazine* 91 (April 1990): 68–98.

Litwack, Leon. *Been in the Storm So Long: The Aftermath of Slavery.* New York, 1979.

Lofton, John. "Denmark Vesey's Call to Arms." *Journal of Negro History* 33 (October 1948): 395–417.

———. *Insurrection in South Carolina: The Turbulent World of Denmark Vesey*. Antioch, 1964. Reprinted as *Denmark Vesey's Revolt: The Slave Plot That Lit the Fuse to Fort Sumter*. Kent, 1983.

Logan, Rayford. *Haiti and the Dominican Republic*. New York, 1968.

MacLeod, Duncan. *Slavery, Race and the American Revolution*. New York, 1974.

Maier, Pauline. "The Charleston Mob and the Evolution of Popular Politics in Revolutionary South Carolina." *Perspectives in American History* 4 (1970), 173–196.

Masur, Louis P. *Rites of Execution: Capital Punishment and the Transformation of American Culture, 1776–1865*. New York, 1989.

Mathews, Donald. *Religion in the Old South*. Chicago, 1977.

———. *Slavery and Methodism: A Chapter in American Morality, 1780–1845*. Princeton, 1965.

Matthewson, Tim. "Abraham Bishop, 'The Rights of Black Men,' and the American Reaction to the Haitian Revolution." *Journal of Negro History* 67 (Summer 1982): 148–54.

Mays, James. *Harper's Bible Commentary*. New York, 1988.

McCalman, Iain. *Radical Underworld: Prophets, Revolutionaries, and Pornographers in London, 1795–1840*. New York, 1988.

McCandless, Peter. *Moonlight, Magnolias, and Madness: Insanity in South Carolina from the Colonial Period to the Progressive Era*. Chapel Hill, 1996.

McDonnell, Lawrence T. "Money Knows No Master: Market Relations and the American Slave Community." In *Developing Dixie: Modernization in a Traditional Society*, edited by Winifred B. Moore, Jr., Joseph F. Tripp, and Lyon G. Tyler, 31–44. Westport, Conn., 1988.

McFeely, William S. *Frederick Douglass*. New York, 1991.

McPherson, James. *Battle Cry of Freedom: The Civil War Era*. New York, 1988.

Mbiti, John. *African Religions and Philosophy*. New York, 1970.

Meinig, D. W. *The Shaping of America: Atlantic America, 1492–1800*. New Haven, 1986.

Metraux, Alfred. *Voodoo in Haiti*. New York, 1959.

Middlekauf, Robert. *The Glorious Cause: The American Revolution, 1763–1789*. New York, 1982.

Miller, Floyd J. *The Search for Black Nationality: Black Emigration and Colonization, 1787–1863*. Urbana, 1975.

Minchinton, Walter E., and David J. Starkey. "Characteristics of Privateers Operating from the British Isles against America." In *Ships, Seafaring, and Society: Essays in Maritime History*, edited by Timothy J. Runyon, 250–59. Detroit, 1987.

Mintz, Sidney, and Richard Price. *The Birth of African-American Culture: An Anthropological Perspective*. Philadelphia, 1976. Reprint, Boston, 1992.

Moitt, Bernard. "Slave Resistance in Guadeloupe and Martinique, 1791–1848." *Journal of Caribbean History* 25 (1991): 136–59.

Moltke-Hansen, David. "The Expansion of Intellectual Life: A Prospectus." In *Intellectual Life in Antebellum Charleston*, edited by Michael O'Brien and David Moltke-Hansen, 3–44. Knoxville, 1986.

Moore, Cary A. *Tobit*. New York, 1966.

Morgan, Donald G. *Justice William Johnson, the First Dissenter: The Career and Constitutional Philosophy of a Jeffersonian Judge*. Columbia, 1954.

Morgan, Philip D. "Black Life in Eighteenth-Century Charleston." *Perspectives in American History*, n.s., 1 (1984): 187–232.

———. "Black Society in the Lowcountry, 1760–1810." In *Slavery and Freedom in the Age of the American Revolution*, edited by Ira Berlin and Ronald Hoffman, 83–142. Charlottesville, 1983.

———. "British Encounters with Africans and African-Americans, circa 1600–1780." In *Strangers within the Realm: Cultural Margins of the First British Empire*, edited by Bernard Bailyn and Philip Morgan, 157–219. Chapel Hill, 1991.

———. "Task and Gang Systems: The Organization of Labor on New World Plantations." In *Work and Labor in Early America*, edited by Stephen Innes, 189–220. Chapel Hill, 1988.

———. "Three Planters and Their Slaves: Perspectives on Slavery in Virginia, South Carolina, and Jamaica, 1750–1790." In *Race and Family in the Colonial South*, edited by Winthrop D. Jordan and Sheila L. Skemp, 37–79. Jackson, 1987.

———. "Work and Culture: The Task System and the World of Lowcountry Blacks, 1700 to 1880." *William and Mary Quarterly*, 3d ser., 39 (October 1982): 563–99.

Moore, Glover. *The Missouri Compromise, 1819–1821*. Lexington, 1953.

Morris, Thomas. *Southern Slavery and the Law, 1619–1860*. Chapel Hill, 1996.

Mullin, Gerald W. *Flight and Rebellion: Slave Resistance in Eighteenth-Century Virginia*. New York, 1972.

Mullin, Michael. *Africa in America: Slave Acculturation and Resistance in the American South and the British Caribbean, 1736–1831*. Urbana, 1992.

———. "British Caribbean and North American Slaves in an Era of War and Revolution, 1775–1807." In *The Southern Experience in the American Revolution*, edited by Jeffrey J. Crow and Larry E. Tise, 235–67. Chapel Hill, 1978.

Muir, Edward, and Guido Ruggiero, "The Crime of History." Introduction to *Crime from History*. Baltimore, 1994.

Myscofski, Carole. "Ritual Trance in Brazilian *Umbanda*." In *Social History and Issues in Human Consciousness: Some Interdisciplinary Connections*, edited by Andrew E. Barnes and Peter N. Stearns, 85–107. New York, 1989.

Nadelhaft, Jerome. *The Disorders of War: The Revolution of South Carolina*. Orono, Me., 1981.

Nash, Gary. *Forging Freedom: The Formation of Philadelphia's Black Community, 1720–1840*. Cambridge, Mass., 1988.

———. *The Urban Crucible: Social Change, Political Consciousness, and the Origins of the American Revolution*. Cambridge, Mass., 1979.

Newman, Simon. *Parades and the Politics of the Street: Festive Culture in the Early American Republic*. Philadelphia, 1997.

Oates, Stephen B. *The Fires of Jubilee: Nat Turner's Fierce Rebellion*. New York, 1975.

Olwell, Robert. "'Domestick Enemies': Slavery and Political Independence in South Carolina, May 1775–March 1776." *Journal of Southern History* 55 (February 1989): 21–48.

———. "'Loose, Idle, and Disorderly': Slave Women in the Eighteenth-Century Charleston Marketplace." In *More Than Chattel: Black Women and Slavery in the Americas*, edited by David Barry Gaspar and Darlene Clark Hine, 97–110. Bloomington, 1996.

Olwig, Karen Fog. *Cultural Adaptation and Resistance on St. John: Three Centuries of Afro-Caribbean Life*. Gainesville, 1985.

Ott, Thomas. *The Haitian Revolution, 1789–1804*. Knoxville, 1973.

Packwood, Cyril. *Chained on the Rock: Slavery in Bermuda*. New York, 1975.

Palmer, R. R. *The Age of Democratic Revolutions*. 2 vols. Princeton, 1959–64.
Pancake, John. *This Destructive War: The British Campaign in the Carolinas, 1780–1782*. University, Ala., 1985.
Parrinder, Geoffrey. *West African Religion: A Study of the Beliefs and Practices of Akan, Ewe, Ibo, and Kindred Peoples*. London, 1949.
Parrish, Peter. "The Edges of Slavery in the Old South: Or, Do Exceptions Prove Rules?" *Slavery and Abolition* 4 (September 1983): 106–25.
Pearson, Edward A. "'A Countryside Full of Flames': A Reconsideration of the Stono Rebellion and Slave Rebelliousness in the Early Eighteenth-Century South Carolina Lowcountry." *Slavery and Abolition* 17 (August 1996): 22–50.
———. "From Stono to Vesey: Slavery, Resistance, and Ideology in South Carolina, 1739–1822." Ph.D. diss., University of Wisconsin, 1992.
Pease, William H., and Jane H. Pease. "Walker's *Appeal* Comes to Charleston: A Note and Document." *Journal of Negro History* 59 (July 1974): 287–92.
———. *The Web of Progress: Private Values and Public Style in Boston and Charleston, 1828–1843*. New York, 1985.
Phillips, U. B. "The Slave Labor Problem in the Charleston District." In *Plantation, Town, and Country: Essays on the Local History of American Slave Society*, edited by Eugene D. Genovese and Elinor Miller, 7–28. Urbana, 1974.
———. "The South Carolina Federalists II." *American Historical Review* 14 (July 1909): 731–44.
Pierson, William D. *From Africa to America: African American History from the Colonial Era to the Early Republic, 1526–1790*. New York, 1996.
Plotkin, Mark J. *Tales of a Shaman's Apprentice: An Ethnobotanist Searches for New Medicines in the Amazon Rain Forest*. New York, 1993.
Potkay, Adam, and Sandra Burr, eds. *Black Atlantic Writers of the Eighteenth Century: Selections from the Writings of Ukawsaw Gronniosaw, John Marrant, Quobna Ottabah Cuango, and Olaudah Equiano*. New York, 1995.
Powers, Bernard. *Black Charlestonians: A Social History, 1822–1885*. Fayetteville, 1994.
Preston, Dickson J. *Young Frederick Douglass: The Maryland Years*. Baltimore, 1980.
Price, Richard, ed. *Maroon Societies: Rebel Slave Communities in the Americas*. Baltimore, 1973.
Quarles, Benjamin. *Black Abolitionists*. New York, 1969.
———. *The Negro in the American Revolution*. Chapel Hill, 1961. Reprint, Chapel Hill, 1996.
Raboteau, Albert J. *A Fire in the Bones: Reflections on African-American Religious History*. Boston, 1995.
———. *Slave Religion: The "Invisible Institution" in the Antebellum South*. New York, 1978.
Radford, John. "Race, Residence, and Ideology: Charleston, South Carolina, in the Mid-Nineteenth Century." *Journal of Historical Geography* 2 (Fall 1976): 329–46.
Ravenel, Harriot Horry. *Charleston: The Place and the People*. Charleston, 1912.
Rawick, George. *From Sundown to Sunup: The Making of a Slave Community*. Westport, Conn., 1972.
Rediker, Marcus. "'A Motley Crew of Rebels': Sailors, Slaves, and the Coming of the American Revolution." In *The Transforming Hand of Revolution: Reconsidering the American Revolution as a Social Movement*, edited by Ronald Hoffman and Peter J. Albert, 155–98. Charlottesville, 1995.
———. *Between the Devil and the Deep Blue Sea: Merchant Seamen, Pirates, and the Anglo-American Maritime World, 1700–1750*. New York, 1987.

Reis, João José. *Slave Rebellion in Brazil: The Muslim Uprising of 1835 in Bahia.* Baltimore, 1993.

Remini, Robert V. *Andrew Jackson and the Course of American Empire, 1767–1821.* New York, 1977.

Rodger, N. A. M. *The Wooden World: An Anatomy of the Georgian Navy.* Annapolis, 1986.

Rogers, George C., Jr. *Charleston in the Age of the Pinckneys.* Norman, 1969.

———. *Evolution of a Federalist: William Loughton Smith of Charleston.* Columbia, 1962.

———. *The History of Georgetown County, South Carolina.* Columbia, 1970.

Rogers, James. *Richard Furman: Life and Legacy.* Macon, 1985.

Rogozinski, Jan. *A Brief History of the Caribbean: From the Arawak and the Carib to the Present.* New York, 1994.

Rorabaugh, W. J. *The Craft Apprentice: From Franklin to the Machine Age in America.* New York, 1986.

Rose, Willie Lee. "The Domestication of Domestic Slavery." Chapter 2 in *Slavery and Freedom*, by Willie Lee Rose, edited by William W. Freehling, 18–36. New York, 1976.

———. *Rehearsal for Reconstruction: The Port Royal Experiment.* New York, 1964.

Rotberg, Robert. *Haiti: The Politics of Squalor.* Boston, 1971.

Rule, John. "The Property of Skill in an Age of Manufacture." In *The Historical Meanings of Work*, edited by Patrick Joyce, 99–188. New York, 1987.

Said, Edward W. *Representations of the Intellectual.* New York, 1994.

Schafer, Daniel L. "Shades of Freedom: Anna Kingsley in Senegal, Florida, and Haiti." *Slavery and Abolition* 17 (April 1996): 130–54.

Schwartz, Philip. *Twice Condemned: Slaves and the Criminal Laws of Virginia, 1705–1865.* Baton Rouge, 1988.

Schweninger, Loren. *Black Property Owners in the South, 1790–1915.* Urbana, 1990.

———. "Free Blacks." In *Dictionary of Afro-American History*, edited by Randall Miller and John David Smith, 258–67. Westport, 1988.

———. "Slave Independence and Enterprise in South Carolina, 1780–1865." *South Carolina Historical Magazine* 93 (April 1993): 101–25.

Scott, James C. *Domination and the Arts of Resistance: Hidden Transcripts.* New Haven, 1990.

———. *Weapons of the Weak: Everyday Forms of Peasant Resistance.* New Haven, 1985.

Scott, Julius S. "Afro-American Sailors and the International Communication Network: The Case of Newport Bowers." In *Jack Tar in History: Essays in Maritime History*, edited by Colin Howell and Richard Twomey, 11–36. Fredericton, New Brunswick, 1991.

———. "The Common Wind: Currents of Afro-American Communication in the Era of the Haitian Revolution." Ph.D. diss., Duke University, 1986.

Scott, Kenneth. "The Slave Insurrection in New York in 1712." *New York Historical Society Quarterly* 45 (January 1961): 43–74.

Senese, Donald. "The Free Negro and the South Carolina Courts." *South Carolina Historical Magazine* 68 (1967): 140–53.

Severens, Kenneth. *Charleston: Antebellum Architecture and Civic Destiny.* Knoxville, 1988.

Sharif, Abdul. *Slaves, Spices, and Ivory in Zanzibar: Integration of an East African Commercial Economy into the World Economy, 1770–1873.* London, 1987.

Sharp, James Roger. *American Politics in the Early Republic: The New Nation in Crisis.* New Haven, 1993.

Sidbury, James. *Ploughshares into Swords: Race, Rebellion, and Identity in Gabriel's Virginia, 1730–1810*. New York, 1997.
Simon, Roger. *Gramsci's Political Thought: An Introduction*. London, 1982.
Singleton, Teresa. "Badges of Urban Slavery." *Carologue* (May/June 1985): 4–5.
———. "The Archaeology of Slavery." In *Before Freedom Came: African-American Life in the Antebellum South*, edited by Edward D. C. Rice and Kym S. Rice, 155–75. Charlottesville, 1991.
Smith, Charles Spencer. *A History of the African Methodist Episcopal Church*. Philadelphia, 1922.
Smith, Edward D. *Climbing Jacob's Ladder: The Rise of Black Churches in Eastern American Cities, 1740–1877*. Washington, D.C., 1988.
Smith, Julia Floyd. *Slavery and Rice Culture in Low Country Georgia, 1750–1860*. Knoxville, 1985.
Stallybrass, Peter, and Allon White. *The Politics and Poetics of Transgression*. Ithaca, 1986.
Stanton, William. *The Leopard's Spots: Scientific Attitudes toward Race in America, 1815–59*. Chicago, 1960.
Starobin, Robert. "Denmark Vesey's Slave Conspiracy of 1822: A Study in Rebellion and Repression." In *American Slavery: The Question of Resistance*, edited by John Bracey, August Meier, and Elliott Rudwick, 142–57. Belmont, Calif., 1971.
———. *Industrial Slavery in the Old South*. New York, 1970.
Staudenraus, Philip J. *The African Colonization Movement, 1816–1865*. New York, 1961.
Stewart, James Brewer. *Holy Warriors: The Abolitionists and American Slavery*. New York, 1976.
Stoddard, T. Lothrop. *The French Revolution in San Domingo*. Boston, 1914.
Stuckey, Sterling. "Remember Denmark Vesey—Agitator or Insurrectionist?" *Negro Digest* 15 (February 1966): 29–41. Reprinted in Sterling Stuckey, *Going Through the Storm: The Influence of African American Art in History*, 19–31. New York, 1994.
———. *Slave Culture: Nationalist Theory and the Foundations of Black America*. New York, 1987.
Sundquist, Eric J. *To Wake the Nations: Race in the Making of American Literature*. Cambridge, 1993.
Tadman, Michael. *Speculators and Slaves: Masters, Traders, and Slaves in the Old South*. Madison, 1989.
Taylor, Joe Gray. *Negro Slavery in Louisiana*. Baton Rouge, 1963.
Terborg-Penn, Rosalyn. "Black Women in Resistance: A Cross-Cultural Perspective." In *In Resistance: Studies in African, Caribbean, and Afro-American History*, edited by Gary Okihiro, 188–209. Amherst, 1986.
Terry, George. "South Carolina's First Negro Seaman Acts, 1793–1803." *Proceedings of the South Carolina Historical Association* (1980), 78–93.
———. "A Study of the Impact of the French Revolution and the Insurrection on Saint Domingue upon South Carolina." M.A. thesis, University of South Carolina, 1975.
Thomas, John. *The History of the South Carolina Military Academy*. Charleston, 1898.
Thomas, Keith. *Religion and the Decline of Magic: Studies in the Popular Beliefs in Sixteenth- and Seventeenth-Century England*. London, 1971.
Thompson, E. P. "Custom and Culture." Chapter 1 in *Customs in Common: Studies in Traditional Popular Culture*. New York, 1991.
———. *The Making of the English Working Class*. New York, 1964.

———. "The Moral Economy of the English Crowd in the Eighteenth Century." *Past and Present* 50 (February 1971): 185–258.
Thompson, Robert Farris. *Flash of the Spirit: African and Afro-American Art and Philosophy*. New York, 1983.
Thornton, John. *Africa and Africans in the Making of the Atlantic World, 1400–1680*. New York, 1992.
———. "African Dimensions of the Stono Rebellion." *American Historical Review* 96 (October 1991): 1101–13.
———. "The Development of an African Catholic Church in the Kingdom of Kongo, 1491–1750." *Journal of African History* 25 (1984): 147–67.
Tise, Larry. *Proslavery: A History of the Defense of Slavery in America, 1701–1840*. Athens, 1987.
Tragle, Henry Irving. *The Southampton Slave Revolt of 1831: A Compilation of Source Material*. New York, 1981.
Travers, Len. *Celebrating the Fourth: Independence Day and the Rites of Nationalism in the Early Republic*. Amherst, 1997.
Trouillot, Michel-Rolph. *Silencing the Past: Power and the Production of History*. Boston, 1995.
Turner, Lorenzo Dow. "Anti-Slavery Sentiment in American Literature." *Journal of Negro History* 14 (October 1929): 371–492.
Turner, Victor. *The Ritual Process: Structure and Anti-Structure*. New York, 1969.
Tyson, George F., and Arnold Highfield, eds. *The Kamina Folk: Slavery and Slave Life in the Danish West Indies*. U.S. Virgin Islands, 1994.
Unsworth, Barry. *Sacred Hunger*. London, 1992.
Vansina, Jan. *Paths in the Rainforest: Toward a History of Political Tradition in Equatorial Africa*. Madison, 1990.
Vlach, John Michael. *By the Work of Their Own Hands: Studies in Afro-American Folklife*. Charlottesville, 1991.
Wade, Richard. *Slavery in the Cities: The South, 1820–1860*. New York, 1964.
———. "The Vesey Plot: A Reconsideration." *Journal of Southern History* 30 (May 1964): 143–61.
Walker, Clarence E. *A Rock in a Weary Land: The African Methodist Episcopal Church during the Civil War and Reconstruction*. Baton Rouge, 1982.
Wallace, Anthony F. C. "Revitalization Movements." *American Anthropologist* 58 (1956): 149–65.
———. *The Death and Rebirth of the Seneca*. New York, 1969.
Wallace, Michael. "Paternalism and Violence." In *Violence and Aggression in the History of Ideas*, edited by Philip Weiner and John Fisher. New Brunswick, 1974.
Walzer, Michael. *Exodus and Revolution*. New York, 1985.
Wax, Darrold. "'The Great Risque We Run': The Aftermath of the Rebellion at Stono, South Carolina." *Journal of Negro History* 67 (Summer 1982): 136–47.
Weir, Robert M. *Colonial South Carolina: A History*. Millwood, 1983.
White, Deborah G. *Ar'n't I a Woman?: Female Slaves in the Plantation South*. New York, 1985.
White, Hayden. *The Content of the Form: Narrative Discourse and Historical Representation*. Baltimore, 1987.
Wiecek, William. *The Sources of Antislavery Constitutionalism in America, 1760–1848*. Ithaca, 1977.

Wikramanayake, Marina. *A World in Shadow: The Free Black in Antebellum South Carolina.* Columbia, 1973.
Wilentz, Sean. *Chants Democratic: New York City and the Rise of the American Working Class, 1788–1850.* New York, 1984.
Williams, Jack K. *Vogues in Villainy: Crime and Retribution in Antebellum South Carolina.* Columbia, 1959.
Wood, Peter. *Black Majority: Negroes in South Carolina from 1670 through the Stono Rebellion.* New York, 1974.
——. " 'The Dream Deferred': Black Freedom Struggles on the Eve of Independence." In *In Resistance: Studies in African, Caribbean, and Afro-American History*, edited by Gary Okihiro, 166–87. Amherst, 1986.
——. " 'Liberty Is Sweet': African-American Freedom Struggles in the Years before White Independence." In *Beyond the American Revolution: Explorations in the History of American Radicalism*, edited by Alfred F. Young, 149–85. De Kalb, 1993.
——. " 'Taking Care of Business' in Revolutionary South Carolina: Republicanism and the Slave Society." In *The Southern Experience in the American Revolution*, edited by Jeffrey J. Crow and Larry E. Tise, 268–94. Chapel Hill, 1978.
Zaslavsky, Claudia. *Africa Counts: Number and Pattern in African Culture.* Boston, 1973.
Zilversmit, Arthur. *The First Emancipation: The Abolition of Slavery in the North.* Chicago, 1967.
Zuckerman, Michael. "The Power of Blackness: Thomas Jefferson and the Revolution in St. Domingue." In *Almost Chosen People: Oblique Biographies in the American Grain.* Berkeley and Los Angeles, 1993.
——. "Thermidor in America: The Aftermath of Independence in the South." In *Prospects: The Annual of American Cultural Studies, Volume Eight*, 349–68. New York, 1983.

FILMS, MUSIC, AND RADIO

CBS Radio Workshop. *Destination Freedom: Denmark Vesey.* Radio production. New York, 1948.
——. *Sweet Cherries in Charleston.* Radio production. Chicago, 1987.
——. *The Heart of a Man.* Radio production. Chicago, 1987.
The Gift of Black Folk. Videotape. Santa Monica, 1978).
Kramer, Aaron. *"On Freedom's Side": The Songs and Poems of Aaron Kramer.* Sound recording. New York, 1973.
McDonald, Fred. *Denmark Vesey: Dark Explorers.* Radio production. Chicago, 1980.
Morse, Wayne. *Brother Future: A Wonderworks Video Recording.* Videotape. New York, 1991.
PBS Television. *Denmark Vesey's Rebellion.*
Plush, Vincent. *Denmark Vesey Takes the Stand.* Sound recording. Charleston, 1996.

INDEX

Abolitionists, 18, 96–97, 102, 119, 153, 156. *See also* Antislavery
Adger, William: biographical note, 297; sentence, 313
African Methodist Episcopal Church, 18, 63, 109, 129, 317–18; establishment of, 49–51; rules governing, 120–22; role in plot, 105, 108–10; worship in, 122. *See also* Allen, Richard; Brown, Morris; Hampstead
Akan, 21
Allen, Richard, 49, 51, 110. *See also* African Methodist Episcopal Church
Allen, William, 146–47
American Colonization Society, 133, 135; and George Creighton, 109–10; and debate among African Americans, 110–11
American Revolution, 10, 20, 82, 94, 96; and Joseph Vesey, 25; and slaves, 60, 101
Ancrum, Jim: biographical note, 297; sentence, 312
Anderson, Smart, 13, 126, 131; trial, 216; confession, 217–18; examination, 256; biographical note, 297; sentence, 310
Antislavery, 18, 96–97, 102, 119, 153, 156. *See also* Abolitionists
Asante, 21
Ashley River, 34, 43, 46, 50, 57, 134
Atlantic world, 36; commercial life, 28–30; cities, 33; radical underworld, 14, 30, 34, 53; revolutions in, 19, 82–83, 87–93, 103, 163; sailors in, 28–38. *See also* New World plantations

Bakongo, 126
Ball, Charles, 68, 62; on slave trade, 46; on master-slave relations, 101
Ball, Paris: trial, 220; biographical note, 297; sentence, 311
Bampfield, George, 121; trial, 239–40; biographical note, 297; sentence, 311

Baptists, 97. *See also* Furman, Richard
Barnstile, Sam: trial, 258; biographical note, 297; sentence, 311
Bastille Day (July 14), 84, 88. *See also* French Revolution
Beach, Mary, 16, 70, 107–8, 137, 143, 153; on executions, 145; letters from, 322–24, 331–32, 335–36, 337–39, 341, 343
Beaufort, S.C., 43
Bellamy, Adam: trial, 273; biographical note, 297, sentence, 311
Bennett, Batteau, 67, 115, 137; biographical note, 297; sentence, 310
Bennett, March: examination, 183; biographical note, 297
Bennett, Mathias: biographical note, 298; sentence, 312
Bennett, Ned, 55, 67, 121, 137; biographical note, 298; sentence, 310
Bennett, Peter: examination, 183
Bennett, Polydore: examination, 183–84
Bennett, Rolla, 42, 60, 81, 106, 112–13, 126, 134, 137; trial, 168–72; examination, 185; confession, 186–87; biographical note, 298; sentence, 310
Bennett, Sampson: examination, 183; biographical note, 298
Bennett, Thomas (governor), 47, 137, 344–47; as slaveholder, 42, 67, 108; activities during trials, 107, 139, 330, 334, 339; opinions on plot, 139–40, 143
Benin (kingdom of), 22, 61
Bermuda, 34–35. *See also* Vesey, Joseph
Biddle, Harry: trial, 268
Billings, Charles: trial, 237; biographical note, 298; sentence, 310
Bishop, Abraham, 91
Black Swamp Association, 152. *See also* South Carolina Association
Blackwood, Jesse, 71, 107–8; trial, 187; con-

fession, 188–90; biographical note, 298; sentence, 310
Bolívar, Simón, 94
Books, 91–92; classical tales, 79; on slavery, 79, 119; of Bible, 80–81, 121, 127–28. *See also* Charleston Library Society
Boston, Mass., 5, 34, 43
Boundary Street, 46–47
Boyer, Jean-Pierre (president of Haiti), 94, 117–18. *See also* Haiti
Brown, Edward, 159
Brown, Morris, 47, 50, 110; and Denmark Vesey, 78. *See also* African Methodist Episcopal Church
Brown Fellowship Society, 51, 132. *See also* Free people of color
Bryan, Pompey, 19
Bulkley, Billy, 113; examination, 196–97, 206–7, 222, 223, 226, 229; biographical note, 298; sentence, 311
Bull Street, 77
Bussaker, Prudence, 120; examination, 195; biographical note, 298
Butler, Harry: biographical note, 298; sentence, 311
Bryant, Pompey: examination, 192; biographical note, 298; sentence, 312

Calhoun, John, 107, 141, 318, 334, 339
Camden, S.C., 8, 9; 1816 plot, 94–95
Cammer, Ben: trial, 247; biographical note, 299; sentence, 313
Cap Français (Cap Haïtien, Le Cap), 23, 82, 86, 136
Cape Mesurado, 110, 133. *See also* American Colonization Society; Creighton, George
Catell, Jack: trial, 274; biographical note, 299; sentence, 311
Chappeau, Pierre (Lewis): trial, 243; biographical note, 299; sentence, 312
Charleston, S.C., 39–49; and Joseph Vesey, 35–36; population, 40, 47; government, 40, 47, 57; spatial organization, 42, 112; working population, 66–67; and French Revolution, 83–90; conspiracy against, 133–35

Charleston Library Society, 92
Charleston Neck, 38, 42, 48, 106; population of, 47. *See also* Free people of color; Grogshops
Charlotte Amalie, St. Thomas, 21–22
Churches: African Methodist Episcopal, 18, 49–51, 63, 129, 317–18; evangelical, 51, 97; reactions to plot, 157–58
Christian stewardship: articulations of, 16, 99–101. *See also* Furman, Richard
Citadel, The, 152
Clark, Hercules: biographical note, 299; sentence, 312
Clarkson, Thomas, 92
Clement, Jemmy: trial, 240; biographical note, 299; sentence, 310
Cohen, Jerry: biographical note, 299; trial, 299; sentence, 310
Colcock, William, 113, 115; trial, 221; confession, 221–22; biographical note, 299; sentence, 312
Combahee River, 117
Commemorations, 7–8
Compensation, for slaves executed, 69–70, 153; petitions for, 352–54
Conspiracy (1822), 8–9; white reaction to, 3; record of, 11–12; narratives on, 12, 99; political consequences of, 15, 147, 149–52; historiography on, 15–16; origins of, 108–12; recruiting, 111, 116, 126; numbers, 117; rituals, 123–26; tactics of, 133–35; legal definition of, 138
Conspirators, 44, 55; plans of, 3–4, 19, 133–35; and ethnicity, 62; and rituals, 124–27; mental world of, 126–28; and gender, 131; trials of, 165–282; biographies of, 297–309. *See also* Vesey, Denmark
Constitutional Convention: and slavery, 98
Cooper, Peter: trial, 238; biographical note, 299; sentence, 311
Cooper River, 28, 57, 103; commercial activities along, 42–43, 66
Courts, 1; establishment of, 107–8; procedures in, 138–39; activities in, 142–43
Creighton, George, 110, 319. *See also* American Colonization Society

Cromwell, Louis: biographical note, 299; sentence, 311
Cromwell, William: biographical note, 299; sentence, 313
Cross, Y[orrick]: examination, 175–79
Cuba, 43, 88
Cugoano, Quobna Ottobah, 14. See also Atlantic world: radical underworld
Curtis, Sandy: biographical note, 299; sentence, 313

Dalcho, Frederick (reverend), 158
Danders, Jacob, 146–47
Datty, Patrick: examination, 195; biographical note, 299–300; sentence, 312
Dehon, Theodore, 50, 158
Deliesseline, Charles: biographical note, 300; sentence, 313
Deliesseline, Francis (sheriff), 149. See also South Carolina Association
Demerara, 88
Democratic-Republican Society, 84. See also French Revolution: in Charleston
Dessalines, Jean-Jacques, 90, 117. See also Haiti; Saint Domingue
Desverneys, Peter, 103–4, 132, 137; reward, 153
DeSaussure, Henry, 5, 92, 152, 155–56
Dorchester, S.C., 117
Douglass, Frederick, 6, 67, 121, 164; on work, 70–73; on Fourth of July, 95–96
Dowling, James: biographical note, 300; sentence, 313
Dowling, Prince: biographical note, 300, sentence, 313
Drayton, Charles, 121, 126, 142, 146; trial, 195; examination, 205, 208, 209, 212, 213, 214, 219, 223, 224, 227, 229, 230, 234, 236, 237, 240, 242, 243, 247, 248, 249, 254, 258, 261–62, 265–66, 269, 271, 272, 273; biographical note, 300; sentence, 311
Drayton, John (governor), 40, 93
Dunmore's Proclamation, 83. See also American Revolution
Dutty, Boukman, 34. See also Saint Domingue

Edisto Island Auxiliary, 152, 354–55. See also South Carolina Association
Elkison, Henry, 149. See also Negro Seaman Act
Enslow, John, 79, 115, 135, 142; trial, 231–32; examination, 236, 237, 238, 240, 241, 247, 267; biographical note, 300; sentence, 311; confession, 336–37
Ethnicity, 22, 28, 30, 43–44; role in plot, 61–62
Equiano, Olaudah, 14, 29–34, 82
Evans, George, 112–13; trial, 271; biographical note, 300; sentence, 311
Executions, 144–45
Exodus, Book of, 80–81. See also Old Testament

Faber, Polydore, 44, 69, 113; trial, 222–23; biographical note, 300; sentence, 310
Faux, William, 102
Ferguson, Adam: examination, 192; biographical note, 300; sentence, 312
Ferguson, Frank, 110, 120, 137; examination, 188, 191–92, 210–11, 214, 216, 225, 249–50; biographical note, 300; sentence, 311
Fire companies, 48, 68
Ford, Benjamin: examination, 191
Fordham, Billy: biographical note, 300; sentence, 313
Forrest, Julius, 127, 137; trial, 195; biographical note, 300, sentence, 310
Forrest, Thomas, 45
Forrester, Lot, 108, 137; examination, 187–88; trial, 225–26; biographical note, 301; sentence, 310
Fort Sumter, 6
Foucault, Michel, 12
Fourth of July, 82, 94, 317–18, 321. See also American Revolution; Douglass, Frederick
Freehling, William, 15–16, 151. See also Historiography
Free people of color, 37–38, 110, 156; population of, 39, 40–41, 47; institutional life of, 51; role in plot, 131–33; laws govern-

ing, 151. *See also* American Colonization Society; Creighton, George; Manumission; Society of Free Dark Men
French Patriotic Society, 84. *See also* French Revolution: in Charleston
French Revolution, 30, 150; in Caribbean, 20, 26; in Charleston, 83–86, 92. *See also* Bastille Day; Saint Domingue
Furman, Richard, 100, 157–58, 349–51. *See also* Baptists; Slavery: and ideology

Gabriel's conspiracy (1800), 8, 93
Gaillard, Saby: examination, 220–21; biographical note, 309; sentence, 311
Games, 44, 53–54. *See also* Grogshops; Taverns
Garden, Alexander, 86, 91, 96. *See also* French Revolution: in Charleston
Garner, William, 70, 74, 108, 134, 137; trial, 260–63; biographical note, 301; sentence, 310
Garnet, Henry Highland, 5
Gates, John: biographical note, 301; sentence, 313
Gell, Louis: biographical note, 301; sentence, 313
Gell, Monday, 42, 61–62, 65, 111–13, 126, 132, 137, 142, 146; confession, 202–5, 244–46; examination, 208, 213; trial, 210–12, 216, 218, 219, 220, 224, 230, 234, 235, 236, 237, 238, 239, 240, 241, 247, 249, 254, 257, 258, 259, 260–61, 264, 267, 268, 269, 271, 273, 274; biographical note, 301; sentence, 311
Georgetown, S.C., 43, 117, 148
Genêt, Edmond, 84. *See also* French Revolution: in Charleston
Genius of Universal Emancipation, 79, 118, 120. *See also* Antislavery
Gibbs, Butcher: trial, 227; biographical note, 301; sentence, 312
Glenn, Jack, 121; trial, 224–25; biographical note, 301; sentence, 310
Gold Coast, 21, 61. *See also* Slave trade
Goose Creek, S.C., 40, 50, 117
Goree Island, 61. *See also* Strohecker, Perault

Graham, Prince, 133; trial, 249–50; examination, 262; biographical note, 309; sentence, 311
Gramsci, Antonio, 18
Grant, Jeffry: biographical note, 309; sentence, 312
Graves, Cuffy; biographical note, 301; sentence, 313
Grimké, Archibald, 6
Grimké family, 97
Grogshops, 40, 53–54; activities in, 44, 53; laws governing, 53. *See also* Games; Taverns
Guadeloupe, 88. *See also* French Revolution: in Caribbean
Guifford, Samuel: trial, 184; biographical note on, 309; sentence, 312

Hadden, Robert: biographical note, 309; sentence, 312
Haig, David: examined, 266
Haig, Harry, 67, 115, 125, 129, 136, 137, 142; examination, 196, 222, 226, 227, 229; biographical note on, 301; sentence, 311
Haig, James: examined, 266
Haig, Nero, 67; trial, 265; biographical note, 302; sentence, 311
Haig, Pompey, 115; trial, 267; biographical note, 302; sentence, 312
Haiti, 8, 19–20, 23–26, 34, 85–88, 93, 104, 119, 134, 157, 163; symbolic role of, 19–20, 117–18. *See also* Boyer, Jean-Pierre; Dessalines, Jean-Jacques; Saint Domingue
Hamilton, James, Jr., 4, 118, 123, 135, 154, 320; biography, 47; role of, 104–5, 110, 116, 137–39. *See also* Charleston: government
Hammet, Bacchus, 17, 109, 113, 143–45; confession, 198–202, 205–6, 230–31, 327–30; trial, 230–31; biographical note, 302; sentence, 310
Hammond, James Henry, 73
Hampstead (Charleston), 38, 49
Happoldt, Jim: biographical note, 302; sentence, 313

382 INDEX

Harleston, Harry: biographical note, 302; sentence, 312
Harleston, Quash: biographical note, 309; sentence, 312
Harleston (Charleston), 46
Harper, Stephen: biographical note, 302; sentence, 313
Harth, Isaac: trial, 242; biographical note, 302; sentence, 311
Harth, Mingo, 104–5, 117; trial, 213, 215; biographical note, 302; sentence, 310
Harth, Robert, 55, 95, 111, 115; examination, 179–82; biographical note, 302
Hasell, Charles: biographical note, 302; sentence, 313
Hayne, Robert, 76, 141
Hercules, 79, 120
Herron, Robert: examination, 184
Hibben, Robert: biographical note, 302; sentence, 313
Hidden transcript, 11. See also Slavery: resistance against
Higginson, Thomas Wentworth, 6, 114, 162
Hiring out, 67–74; and Denmark Vesey, 38; laws governing, 56, 68, 70–71, 73–74, 151; payment for services, 68, 70–73. See also Douglass, Frederick
Historiography, 14–16. See also Freehling, William; Wade, Richard
Holland, Edwin, 5, 50, 156–57. See also *Refutation of the Calumnies*
Holmes, Isaac, 149. See also Negro Seaman Act
Holmes, Sandy: biographical note, 302; sentence, 312
Horry, John, 3; biographical note, 302; sentence, 310
Houston, Lemon: biographical note, 303; sentence, 312
Howard, Prudence, 129
Howard, Sally, 129; examination, 185–86; biographical note, 303
Hunt, Benjamin, 149–50. See also Negro Seaman Act
Hunt, Liverpool: biographical note, 303; sentence, 312

Igneshias, John, 146
Iliad, The (Homer), 23, 92. See also Vesey, Denmark: biographical note
Inglis, Albert: biographical note, 303; sentence, 313
Islam, 62

James Island, S.C., 50, 106, 117, 134
Jefferson, Thomas, 87, 128, 140, 351
Jerry's plot (1775), 10, 83
Johnson, Anna, 109, 136, 143–44; letters from, 154, 320, 332–33, 339
Johnson, Edward, 133: trial, 268; biographical note, 309; sentence, 312
Johnson, William (judge): on master-slave relations, 100; reactions to plot, 139–40, 143, 351; on Negro Seaman Act (1822), 150–51
Jones, Charles Colcock, 73
Jore, Joe: examination, 212–13; biographical note, 303; sentence, 310
Joshua, Book of, 81

Kennedy, Lionel (judge), 2, 12, 102, 116, 120, 154, 159; court procedures, 107, 138–41
King, Rufus (senator), 120. See also Missouri Compromise
Kingsley, Zaphaniah: on master-slave relations, 100; on "Gullah" Jack Pritchard, 123–24. See also Zanzibar
Kongo (kingdom of), 21, 25, 59, 123, 127
Kunhardt, Seymour: trial, 234–35; biographical note, 303; sentence, 311

Language: Gullah, 29; creole, 29–30
La Roche, Isaac: examination, 183
La Roche, Joe, 42, 60, 117, 162; examination, 168–72, 183; biographical note, 303
La Roche, Sambo: examination, 184; biographical note, 303
Laurens, Henry, 82. See also Slave trade
Laws: and manumission, 39, 78, 98–99; and hiring out, 56, 68, 70–71, 73–74, 151; and free people of color, 151. See also Courts
Le Cap, 23, 82, 86, 136. See also Cap Français; Haiti; Sailors; Saint Domingue

Legare, John, 95–96
Liberia, 155
Lining, Amherst: trial, 174; biographical note, 303; sentence, 312
Literacy, 121–22. See also African Methodist Episcopal Church; Books
Loango (kingdom of Kongo), 21
Lord, Pompey, 62; trial, 263; biographical note, 303; sentence, 311
Lord, Thomas: biographical note, 303; sentence, 313
Lottery, 38
Louisiana, 92
L'Ouverture, Toussaint, 86, 90, 92. See also Haiti; Saint Domingue
Lowndes, Mingo: biographical note, 303; sentence, 313
Lowndes, William, 47, 98. See also Constitutional Convention
Lucas, Bram, 115; examination, 172; biographical note, 303; sentence, 312
Lucas, John: biographical note, 303; sentence, 312
Lucas, Richard: examination, 172; biographical note, 304; sentence, 312

McNeill, Jack: trial, 246; biographical note, 304; sentence, 310
Magic: voodoo, 25–26; role in plot, 125–27. See also Haiti; Pritchard, "Gullah" Jack; Saint Domingue
Magwood, Thomas: biographical note, 304; sentence, 313
Mall, James, 129; examination, 209
Mangourit, Michel Ange Bernard de, 84, 88, 92. See also French Revolution: in Charleston
Manumission, 96, 74–75; and Denmark Vesey, 39; laws governing, 39, 78, 98–99. See also Free people of color
Maroons: on Saint Domingue, 26–27; maritime maroons, 34. See also Resistance
Martin, Denbow: trial, 259; biographical note, 304; sentence, 311
Martinique, 88. See also French Revolution: in Caribbean

Masculinity: among sailors, 33, 131; among conspirators, 131
Meeting Street, 40, 46, 114, 144
Methodists, 97
Michau, Philander, 74, 132; trial, 264; biographical note, 309; sentence, 312
Militia, 47, 106, 114–15, 127, 133
Mills, Robert, 46, 66
Missouri Compromise (1820), 102, 121, 128, 156; role in plot, 113, 119–20
Mitchell, Dean: trial, 241; biographical note, 304; sentence, 310
Mitchell, Panza: biographical note, 304; sentence, 312
Mississippi, 9
Money, 41, 65, 68; and hiring out, 70–73
Monroe, James, 4, 87, 93
Morris, Dublin: trial, 237; biographical note, 304; sentence, 311
Moultrie, William, 89
Mulligan, Bounaparte: biographical note, 304; sentence, 311

Negrin, Jean, 90. See also French Revolution: in Charleston
Negro Seaman Act (1822), 140, 148–51, 352. See also Elkison, Henry; Hunt, Benjamin; Johnson, William; South Carolina Association
Nell, Harry: trial, 270; biographical note, 304; sentence, 312
Nell, William, 5
Nesbitt, Robert: biographical note, 309; sentence, 312
New Orleans, 9, 93
New World plantations, 14, 20, 24–25, 57–60; work regimes on, 24–25, 59, 64. See also Atlantic world; Saint Domingue; Slavery; Slave trade
New York, 5, 9, 10, 43
Niles Register, 101, 118, 120, 344–47
Nkisi, 123, 126. See also Pritchard, "Gullah" Jack

Oldendorp, Christian Georg, 21. See also Saint Thomas

Old Testament, 17, 19–20, 79–80, 122, 128. *See also* Exodus, Book of; Religion; Tobit, Book of

Palmer, William (Billy), 137; examination, 211–12; trial, 234; biographical note, 304; sentence, 311
Pamphlet literature, 12, 18, 90–91, 154–62; on conspiracy, 5, 12, 147, 154–62. *See also* Abolitionist; Antislavery
Panic of 1819, 75–76, 128
Parker, Caesar: biographical note, 304; sentence, 313
Parker, George: trial, 272; biographical note, 304; sentence, 311
Parker, Thomas (judge), 2, 12, 60, 102, 116, 120, 154, 159; court, 107, 138–41
Paul, Edwin: examination, 192–93; biographical note, 304; sentence, 312
Paul, William, 103–5, 129, 137, 146; trial, 165–68; examination, 182, 242; biographical note, 305; sentence, 312
Penceel, William, 104, 132, 153. *See also* Free people of color
Perry, Agrippa, 116, 130, 353; examination, 233; trial, 248–49, 251–53; biographical note, 305, sentence, 311
Perry, Doll: examination, 252; biographical note, 305
Perry, Kit: examination, 249; biographical note, 305
Perry Lydia, 116, 130; examination, 253; biographical note, 305
Perry, Robin: examination, 251–52
Philadelphia, Pa., 29, 33, 34, 50, 84; AME church in, 49; antislavery attitudes in, 154. *See also* Allen, Richard; Brown, Morris
Pinckney, Charles Cotesworth, 98, 101, 110. *See also* Constitutional Convention
Pinckney, Thomas, 5, 155
Plaine du Nord, 24–26, 86. *See also* Haiti; Saint Domingue; Seaport towns
Poinsett, Joel, 4, 110, 146, 152
Poison, 13, 135–36, 148, 159. *See also* Pritchard, "Gullah" Jack

Population figures: Charleston, 40, 47; South Carolina, 47; rural lowcountry, 59
Poro, 63, 131
Port-au-Prince, Haiti, 117. *See also* Haiti; Saint Domingue
Potter, John, 4, 106, 135, 154; letters from, 320, 322, 326–27, 330, 333
Poyas, Abraham, 122; trial, 193–94; biographical note, 305; sentence, 311
Poyas, Mungo: biographical note, 305; sentence, 312
Poyas, Peter, 2, 95, 104–6, 111, 114–15, 117, 122, 126, 134, 137, 143–44; trial, 175–79; biographical note, 305; sentence, 310
Presbyterians, 80, 97
Prison, 139, 141–43
Pritchard, "Gullah" Jack, 13, 61–62, 114, 117, 123–28, 135–36; trial, 196–98; sentence, 280, 310; biographical note, 305. *See also* Kingsley, Zaphaniah; *Nkisi*; Poison; Zanzibar
Pritchard, Paul, 109, 124; deposition of, 197
Prospect, 23, 28, 32. *See also* Vesey, Joseph
Purcell, Jack, 119; trial, 213–14; confession, 214–15; examination, 225; biographical note, 305; sentence, 310
Purse, Harry: biographical note, 305; sentence, 312

Ramsey, David, 82
Reading, 18, 121–22
Rebellions, 9, 10–12, 91, 83; on Saint Domingue, 26, 85; on slave ships, 31–32. *See also* Resistance; Slavery: resistance against; Stono Rebellion
Refugees, 37, 82, 84–86, 88–89. *See also* French Revolution: in Charleston
Refutation of the Calumnies, A (Holland), 156–57
Religion: churches, 49–51, 120–21; African Methodist Episcopal, 18, 49–51, 63, 109, 120–22, 129, 317–18; voodoo, 25–26; Exodus, Book of, 80–81; evangelical, 97; Old Testament, 121; Daniel, Book of, 122; Tobit, Book of, 81, 127–28

Remoussin, Louis: trial, 209–10; biographical note, 306
Resistance, 10–12, 15, 34, 43, 54, 64, 93, 121–22, 147–48; on Saint Domingue, 26; *marronage*, 34–35; and American Revolution, 93; and women, 131
Revitalization movements, 128
Rhodes, Andrew, 146–47
Richardson, Martha: letters from, 325–26, 340–41, 347
Richmond, Va., 8, 93
Righton, John (doctor), 139, 142. *See also* Prison
Righton, Prince: trial, 238; biographical note, 306; sentence, 312
Rio de Janeiro, 43, 93
Rituals: on Saint Domingue, 25–26; and "Gullah" Jack Pritchard, 113–14, 123–26. *See also* Magic
Robertson, Adam, 45; trial, 226; biograhical note, 306; sentence, 310
Robertson, John, 45; trial, 227; biographical note, 306; sentence, 310
Robertson, Robert, 45; trial, 223; biographical note, 306; sentence, 310
Robinson, Billy: trial, 253–55; biographical note, 306; sentence, 311
Rout, Friday: biographical note, 306; sentence, 312
Royal Danish African Company, 21. *See also* Slave trade
Russel, Tom, 113, 114, 124; trial, 208–9; biographical note, 306; sentence, 310

Sailors, 30–32, 40–43, 80, 88, 143–51. *See also* Atlantic world; Seaport towns
Saint Croix, 20, 31
Saint Domingue, 19–20, 23–26, 85, 93, 134; revolution on, 8, 19, 34, 85–88, 157, 163; refugees from, 37, 82, 84–86. *See also* Haiti
Saint Eustatius, 33. *See also* French Revolution: in Caribbean
Saint James Santee, S.C., 52, 117, 137
Saint John, 20
Saint Marc (Saint Domingue), 82

Saint-Méry, Médéric Louis Elie Moreau de, 25–26. *See also* Voodoo
Saint Michael's Church, 41, 48, 95, 106, 134, 158
Saint Thomas, 20–23, 29–30, 80. *See also* Vesey, Denmark: biographical note; Vesey, Joseph
San Martin, José de, 94
Savannah, Ga., 34, 43, 94
Scott, James, 11, 54
Scott, Tom: trial, 258–59; biographical note, 306; sentence, 310
Seabrook, Whitemarsh, 157, 355
Seaport towns, 28, 32–34, 40–44, 66–67. *See also* Atlantic world; Sailors
Senegal River, 22
Sentences, 3, 102, 141, 276–82
Ships, 28, 43; work on, 30–32. *See also* Sailors
Shubrick, Charles: biographical note, 307; sentence, 313
Sims, Dick, 45, 70; trial, 229–30; biographical note, 307; sentence, 310
Sims, Scipio, 65, 70; trial, 228–29, 233–34; biographical note, 307; sentence, 311
Slave patrols, 57, 152
Slavery, 19, 22–27, 64–75, 98; resistance against, 8–10; slave population in South Carolina, 40–47, 59; rural, 57–61, 116; and ethnicity, 61–62, 123–25; and work, 64–75; and American Revolution, 82; and ideology, 99–102; urban, 116
Slave trade, 23, 98, 123; transatlantic, 31–32, 61, 98, 123; internal, 45–46, 70
Society of Free Dark Men, 52, 132. *See also* Brown Fellowship Society; Free people of color
South Carolina Association, 149. *See also* Negro Seaman Act
Smalls, Robert, 16, 62
Smith, Caesar, 45; trial, 247; biographical note, 307; sentence, 310
Smith, Stephen: biographical note, 307; sentence, 312
Smith, William Loughton, 98

Stagg, Jacob: trial, 257–58; biographical note, 307; sentence, 310
Stamp Act, 29, 82
Stedman, John, 92
Stono Rebellion (1739), 9
Streets, 55–57. *See also* Charleston: spatial organization; Slavery, urban
Strohecker, John: examined, 265
Strohecker, Perault, 61, 66, 111, 113, 134; examination, 208, 216, 219, 220, 221, 224, 228, 229, 230, 234, 235, 237, 238, 239, 240, 241, 248, 250, 253, 257, 258, 259, 263–64, 269, 270, 273, 274, 275; biographical note, 307; sentence, 311
Sullivan's Island, 45, 133. *See also* Slave trade

Taverns, 40; activities in, 44, 53–55. *See also* Grogshops; Seaport towns
Taylor, John: trial, 242; biographical note, 307; sentence, 312
Thompson, Pharo, 69, 114–15; examination, 211; trial, 218–19; biographical note, 307, sentence, 310
Tobit, Book of, 81, 127–28. *See also* Old Testament; Revitalization movements
Tortola, 88
Trapier, Isaac: biographical note, 307; sentence, 313
Trial transcript, 108; literary aspects, 12–13; illustration of, 160–61
Turner, Nat, 6, 7, 9, 95. *See also* Resistance
Turner, Victor, 127. *See also* Pritchard, "Gullah" Jack

Vanderhorst, George, 125; examination, 197–98; biographical note, 308; sentence, 311
Vesey, Denmark, 2, 5–7, 17–39, 77–80, 108, 143, 148, 315; ideology, 11, 17, 80–83, 85–86, 103, 162; relationship with free people of color, 53, 131–32; trial, 191–93; sentence, 278–80, 310; biographical note, 309
Vesey, Joseph, 20–21, 28, 35–38, 89, 315
Vesey, Mary Clodner (May), 38–39, 315

Vesey, Sandy (Sandy Schnell), 78, 126; trial, 219–20; biographical note, 308; sentence, 311
Vincent, John: trial, 254, 256; examination, 268; biographical note, 308; sentence, w311
Voodoo, 25–26. *See also* Haiti; Saint Domingue

Wade, Richard, 15. *See also* Historiography
Walker, David, 78; reaction to *Appeal* in Charleston, 152
Walker, James: trial, 269–70; biographical note, 308; sentence, 312
Walker, Ned: examination, 225–26
Walker, Stephen: trial, 269–70; biographical note, 308; sentence, 312
Ward, Peter: biographical note, 308; sentence, 313
Ward, Smart: biographical note, 308; sentence, 313
Waring, Syke: examination, 188; biographical note, 308
War of 1812, 108–9
Weapons, 113–15, 133
Wedderburn, Robert, 14
Wilson, George, 105, 153; examination, 173–74; biographical note, 308
Wollstonecraft, Mary, 92
Woodworth, John: examination, 184
Women, 65, 78; enslaved, 57–59; slaveholders, 69–70; role in plot, 129–32
Work, 42, 56, 64–76, 130–31, 162; workshops, 20, 65, 112–13; laws governing, 56, 68; in rural lowcountry, 58–61; in Charleston, 66–72; hiring out, 67–72

Yates, Adam, 45; trial, 235–37; biographical note, 308; sentence, 310
Yates, Bellisle, 45; trial, 235–37; biographical note, 309; sentence, 310
Yates, Naphur, 45; trial, 235–37; biographical note, 308; sentence, 310

Zanzibar, 100, 123. *See also* Pritchard, "Gullah" Jack